CONTEMPORARY CRIMINOLOGY

CONTEMPORARY CRIMINOLOGY

WALTER S. DEKESEREDY
Carleton University

MARTIN D. SCHWARTZ
Ohio University

Wadsworth Publishing Company

I⊤P® An International Thomson Publishing Company

Belmont • Albany • Bonn • Boston • Cincinnati • Detroit • London • Madrid
Melbourne • Mexico City • New York • Paris • San Francisco • Singapore • Tokyo
Toronto • Washington

Criminology Editor: Eve Howard
Editorial Assistants: Carrie Kahn, Julie McDonald
Production Editor: Jerilyn Emori
Managing Designer: Andrew Ogus
Interior and Cover Designer: Gary Head
Print Buyer: Karen Hunt
Permissions Editor: Jeanne Bosschart
Copy Editor: Thomas Briggs
Compositor: Thompson Type
Printer: R. R. Donnelley & Sons

I(T)P The ITP logo is a registered trademark under license.

Printed in the United States of America
1 2 3 4 5 6 7 8 9 10

For more information, contact Wadsworth Publishing Company:

Wadsworth Publishing Company
10 Davis Drive
Belmont, California 94002, USA

International Thomson Publishing Europe
Berkshire House 168-173
High Holborn
London, WC1V 7AA, England

Thomas Nelson Australia
102 Dodds Street
South Melbourne 3205
Victoria, Australia

Nelson Canada
1120 Birchmount Road
Scarborough, Ontario
Canada M1K 5G4

International Thomson Editores
Campos Eliseos 385, Piso 7
Col. Polanco
11560 México D.F. México

International Thomson Publishing GmbH
Königswinterer Strasse 418
53227 Bonn, Germany

International Thomson Publishing Asia
221 Henderson Road
#05-10 Henderson Building
Singapore 0315

International Thomson Publishing Japan
Hirakawacho Kyowa Building, 3F
2-2-1 Hirakawacho
Chiyoda-ku, Tokyo 102, Japan

Library of Congress Cataloging-in-Publication Data
DeKeseredy, Walter S.
   Contemporary criminology / Walter S. DeKeseredy, Martin D. Schwartz.
      p.   cm.
   Includes bibliographical references and index.
   ISBN 0-534-19764-7
   1. Criminology.   I. Schwartz, Martin D.   II. Title.
HV6025.D35   1995
364—dc20   95-39257

CONTENTS

PART I

WHAT IS CRIME AND HOW MUCH OF IT IS THERE? 1

CHAPTER 1

IMAGES OF CRIME AND ITS CONTROL 3

Personal Knowledge of Crime 5

Media Knowledge of Crime 8

Mass Media Exposure and Fear of Crime 10

Moral Panics About Crime 11

The Media as a Cause of Crime 14

The Strengths of Media Knowledge 20

Official Knowledge of Crime 21

Sociological Knowledge of Crime 24

Summary 27

Suggested Readings 27

CHAPTER 2

DEFINITIONS OF CRIME 31

The Legalistic Definition 32
The Consensus Model 32
The Change in Laws over Time 33
What Is and What Should Be 39
Challenges to Legalistic Definitions 41

Societal Reaction/Labeling Definitions 43
Crime as a Social Construct 45
Class and Race in Criminology 48
Critique of the Labeling Approach 50

The Critical Approach 52

Different Groups' Views of Criminality 56
Women and the Law 57
Minorities and the Law 60

Summary 62

Suggested Readings 63

CHAPTER 3

CRIMINAL LAW AND POLITICAL CRIME 67

Definition and Brief History of Criminal Law 68

Consensus Perspectives 71
Critique of the Consensus Perspective 72

Conflict Perspectives 76
Weberian Conflict Theories 77
Critique of Weberian Conflict Theory 80
Marxist Perspectives on Law 81

Beyond Class: Feminist Perspectives 90
Patriarchy and Social Relations 91
Critique of the Radical Feminist Perspective 92

Political Crimes 94

Definitions of Political Crime 94

Crimes Against the State 96

Crimes by the State 100

Crimes Against Other Groups 102

Summary 104

Suggested Readings 105

CHAPTER 4

METHODS OF GATHERING CRIME DATA 109

Official Police Statistics 110

The *Uniform Crime Reports* 111

Origins and Characteristics of the UCR 112

General Limitations of the UCR 117

The Effects of Citizen Nonreporting 117

Additional Limitations of the UCR 122

Victimization Surveys 125

A New Focus on Victims 126

The National Crime Victimization Survey 130

The Limitations of Victimization Surveys 131

Self-Report Surveys 134

The Limitations of Self-Report Surveys 134

The Validity of Self-Report Surveys 136

Observational Procedures 139

Types of Observation Procedures 139

The Limitations of Observational Research 143

Summary 148

Suggested Readings 149

PART II
WHO COMMITS CRIME AND WHY? 151

CHAPTER 5

INDIVIDUALISTIC THEORIES 153

The Devil Made Him Do It 155

The Classical School of Criminology 159
Human Rationality and Cost/Benefit Analysis 161
The Characteristics and Purpose of Punishment 162
Classical Ideas in Modern Times 164

Neoclassical Criminology 166

Critique of Classical and Neoclassical Thought 169
Cost/Reward Analysis and Deterrence 169
Punishment and Deterrence 171

Biological and Psychological Theories of Crime 176
Biological Theories: The Born Criminal 177
Psychological and Personality Theories 182
Popular Culture Support for Psychological Explanations 186
A Sociological Critique of Biological and Psychological Theories 188

Summary 191

Suggested Readings 193

CHAPTER 6

SOCIOLOGICAL PERSPECTIVES ON CRIME 195

Explaining Crime: The Need for a Sociological Imagination 196

Strain Theories 198
Durkheim's Sociological Ideas 199
Merton's Anomie Theory 202
Cohen's Theory of Delinquent Boys 210
Cloward and Ohlin's Differential Opportunity of Delinquency 213

The Gender-Blind Nature of Strain Theories 215
The Emancipation Theory of Female Crime 217

Social Control Theories 218
Hirschi's Social Bond Theory 219
Power-Control Theory 221

Interactionist Theories 223
Primary and Secondary Deviance 224
Differential Association Theory 225

Ecological Models 227
Routine Activities Theory 227
Rational Choice Theory 230

Summary 232

Suggested Readings 233

CHAPTER 7

NEW DIRECTIONS IN CRITICAL CRIMINOLOGY 237

Definition of Critical Criminology 238

Critical Criminology: A "Peripheral Core" Area 240
Academic Criminology in the United States 240
Critical Criminology in Canada 243

Left Realism 245
Basic Principles of Left Realism 247
Left-Realist Attacks on Left Idealists 249
The Left-Realist Response to Right Realism 255
Critique of Left Realism 256

Feminism 258
What Is Feminism? 258
Liberal Feminism 261
Marxist Feminism 263
Radical Feminism 264
Socialist Feminism 266

Peacemaking Criminology 268
Principles of Peacemaking Criminology 269
Practical Applications of Peacemaking Criminology 270

Postmodern Criminology 273

Summary 276

Suggested Readings 276

PART III

WHAT CRIMES SHOULD WE BE MOST CONCERNED ABOUT? 279

CHAPTER 8

MURDER AND MANSLAUGHTER 281

Definitions of Homicide 282

Trends in Murder in the United States 286

Risk Markers of Homicide in the United States 287
Sex 288
Intimate Relationships 289
Age 291
Race/Ethnicity 294
Geographic Variations 296

Homicide in the United States: The Contribution of Firearms 297

Serial and Mass Murder 300

Theories of Homicide 306
Routine Activities Theory 306
Feminist Theories 309
The Subculture of Violence 310
Inequality and Homicide 312

Summary 314

Suggested Readings 315

CHAPTER 9

VIOLENCE AGAINST WOMEN IN INTIMATE RELATIONSHIPS 317

Definition of Violence Against Women 320

Why Don't Battered Women Leave Home? 322

How Much Male Violence Against Women Is There? 327

Risk Markers of Male-to-Female Violence in Intimate Relationships 337

The Distribution of Wife Abuse 338

Violence Against Women in Dating 341

Theories of Male Violence Against Women in Intimate Relationships 341
Psychological Approaches 342
Social Support and Male Peer Support Theories 344
Feminist Theories 350

Summary 352

Suggested Readings 353

CHAPTER 10

CORPORATE AND ORGANIZED CRIME 355

Definition of Corporate Crime 356

Types and Prevalence of Corporate Crime 358
Data Collection Problems 359
Corporate Violence 364
Economic Corporate Crimes 372

The Distribution of Corporate Crime 375

Theories of Corporate Crime 376
Subcultural Theory 377
Structured Action Theory 379
Anomie Theory 381

Organized Crime: Crime Syndicates and Corporate Crime 383

Historical Overview 384

Syndicated and Corporate Crime 385

Infiltration of Legitimate Businesses 389

Summary 393

Suggested Readings 395

CHAPTER 11

DRUG USE AND ABUSE 397

Why Are Only Certain Drugs Criminalized? 399

Some Types of Illegal Drugs 404

Cocaine 404

Heroin 408

Angel Dust, Acid, and Ecstasy: The Initials Drugs 412

Marijuana 413

Health Risks and Problems 415

Pregnancy and Female Drug Users 416

Needles, Cramps, and Victimization 419

How Many People Use Cocaine and Heroin? 422

The Distribution of Cocaine and Heroin Use 424

Sex 425

Age 426

Socioeconomic Status 427

Race/Ethnicity and Location 427

Theories of Drug Use 428

Strain Theory 429

Social Learning Theory 430

Social Bond Theory 433

Inequality and Drugs 433

Summary 436

Suggested Readings 437

PART IV

WHAT CAN WE DO ABOUT CRIME? 439

CHAPTER 12

POLICY RECOMMENDATIONS 441

What About the Victim? 443

"Target Hardening": Crime Prevention Through Opportunity Reduction 445

"Lock 'Em Up and Throw Away the Key": The Failure of Prisons 449

African-Americans and Prison 451

Prisons and Drugs 453

Prisons and Crime Reduction 454

Individual Treatment 457

Drawbacks to Individual Treatment 458

Reasons for the Popularity of Individual Treatment 461

Rethinking the Prevention and Control of Crime: Some Progressive Policy Proposals 463

Job Creation and Training Programs 465

Adequate Social Services 467

Corporate Crime 474

Family Violence and Street Crime 477

Growing Up in a Violent Home 478

Confronting Woman Abuse:
The Contribution of Pro-Feminist Men 480

Summary 484

Suggested Readings 485

References 487

Name Index 534

Subject Index 541

PREFACE

Elizabeth MacPherson, the lead character in a series of mysteries by Sharyn McCrumb, complains in *Highland Laddie Gone* that she took an undergraduate course in criminology because it sounded exciting. "Actually, it's deadly dull," she reports. "Mostly statistics" (1991, p. 170).

We'd like to see this changed. Many of us became criminologists because we *knew* it would be exciting, not just in the classroom but as a career. When we stand in front of a class, however, we devote so much attention to the *facts* that we forget the *story*. Why is criminology interesting? Why is it exciting?

There is even a sense of urgency about the entire discipline. For example, anthropological archaeology is also interesting and exciting, but those seeds and pottery shards can remain buried for another year or twenty if need be. In the United States, however, we now lock up more than one million men and women in prisons—more than the entire population of some countries—and no rational person can believe that we are locking up more than a small percentage of those who violate the criminal law. The questions we will ask in this book are immediate and important.

Of course, there is a great deal of rhetoric throughout North America on crime. For politicians, nothing is easier than making stern pronouncements about working-class criminals and crime. After all, what is going to happen if they are wrong? Will they lose the campaign contributions of the criminals' political action committee? The more difficult task is to form a reasoned and rational opinion on the causes of and solutions to crime. These are the questions that most students bring to a criminology course. Why do people commit crime? What can be done to prevent crime?

We wish we could tell you that we have discovered the answers to these questions and that we will give them to you in this book. The problem is that there are many conflicting answers to criminological questions, in terms of both facts and theory. As you will see in this book, policymakers don't really even have a good idea of how much crime there is, let alone what to do about it.

We propose to avoid the tendency of too many criminology textbooks to provide an overload of information on every possible criminological topic. Rather, our goal is to provide you with a comprehensive and critical sociological understanding of a relatively smaller number of important and timely issues in criminology. Yet, one should not get the impression that this is a cut-down primer in criminology. All of the major issues and theories are covered here, and certain topics are covered in more detail than in most criminology textbooks. Our intent is to provide more depth than usual, but on a smaller number of topics.

One of our major goals was to write *about* criminology. Years ago, historians used to teach their students to "tell a story." This phrase is now out of fashion because it doesn't convey the years historians spend accumulating the facts behind the story. Yet, the heritage remains, and many historians tell vivid and interesting "stories" about their subjects. Sociologists, on the other hand, are all too often attacked for being pedantic and boring, concerned more about impressing each other with their footnotes and citations than with their research topics. We have tried, at least, to tell the story of criminology here, without ever losing sight of the content that we need to cover in a textbook.

For example, whenever possible, we provide real-life anecdotes to illuminate complex issues. Sometimes, these anecdotes are about our own lives. This goes against the grain of how most of us were trained—to remove ourselves as much as possible from the subject matter and to talk as if we were a disembodied voice on a TV special. Yet, it is how many of us learn. Burglary isn't something that happens only to other people; it is the time someone broke into Martin Schwartz's apartment and stole the penny jar from his dresser. Middle-class kids are vandals, too, and Walter DeKeseredy's experiences as a drunken teenage vandal are very telling.

Still, we have tried to present and to critique a wide range of theoretical positions within criminology. While being as fair as possible, this is not a "value-free" book. For one thing, with its decidedly sociological orientation, it sees a smaller role for biological and psychological theories of crime. For another, it gives room to theorists, topics, and policy proposals that are often ignored or poorly treated in other texts. In particular, the critical criminology perspective, in all of its many and varied forms, is given some attention here. Still, the strengths and the weaknesses of all of the various sociological and critical theories are noted.

In a somewhat unusual approach, there is no chapter in this book on "women and crime" and no chapter on "minorities and crime." Thus, women are not completely ignored for eleven chapters, only to have their own "ghettoized" chapter. Instead, materials on women are integrated into every single chapter at relevant points. It isn't only gender issues that are fully integrated; race, class, *and* gender issues are brought up whenever they are relevant.

These considerations all come together in the topical chapters. Certainly, our basic goal was to examine a smaller number of topics in depth. However, just as we wanted to develop an appreciation for the many ways criminologists look at crime (theoretical diversity), we wanted to avoid what we have called the "immunization factor of crime theory." That is, you read about theory in, say, Chapters 5 and 6 and are now immunized and never have to hear about it again. In this book, we try to return to some relevant theories when covering substantive topics like murder and manslaughter, violence against women in intimate relationships, corporate and organized crime, and drug use and abuse. Rather than just describing the extent, distribution, and correlates of these crimes, we also attempt to show how different theorists explain them. In our opinion, this is a valuable way of showing students that there is more than one way to explain any type of crime. In short, this approach helps make theories "come alive."

In perhaps the greatest break from tradition, in Chapter 12, we suggest progressive, short-term alternative strategies to what we and many others view as ineffective crime control techniques (for example, imprisonment and capital punishment). As we state throughout this book, the fact these and other "get-tough" initiatives are doomed to failure does not mean that other strategies do not have a better chance of success. Interestingly, although virtually all sociologists would agree that criminological problems cannot be solved within the criminal justice system, criminology textbooks have not devoted much attention to the implications of this finding. If sociologists are going to argue that crime is caused by poverty, inequality, and a lack of economic opportunity, then it seems obvious to us that solutions to crime must operate within that framework.

KEY FEATURES OF THIS BOOK

To summarize, what sets this book apart from others is the following:

- Clear and interesting writing, designed to tell the *story* of criminology.
- A critical sociological understanding of a smaller number of key issues in criminology.
- Fair but not value-free coverage of all of the major perspectives in criminological theory.
- Special coverage of newer, critical theories.
- Race, class, and gender issues integrated throughout the book, rather than "ghettoized" into single chapters.
- Material on short-term, progressive solutions to some of the problems addressed in the book. The discussion ranges far outside the criminal justice system to speak to the direct concerns raised by criminological theorists.

PEDAGOGICAL FEATURES

Each chapter begins with an introduction that briefly states the main objectives of the discussion to follow. At the end of each chapter is a summary of the key issues that have been discussed and a brief list of suggested readings for students who want to acquire in-depth understanding of these issues or wish additional readings in order to write assigned papers.

APPROPRIATE COURSES

This book is appropriate for courses in a wide variety of departments, although it is perhaps most useful in sociology, criminology, criminal justice, and social work departments. The course is taught by these various departments at very different levels, and this book is particularly appropriate for standard criminology courses in a quarter or semester school. For upper-division courses, it is particularly amenable to being used with a reader.

SUPPLEMENTS

Contemporary Criminology is accompanied by an instructors' manual and a computerized test bank. These materials were developed by Carol Gregory and Martin Schwartz.

ACKNOWLEDGMENTS

Contemporary Criminology would not have been written without the encouragement of Serina Beauparlant, our former editor. When she recruited us in the fall of 1991, we had major concerns about the hard work and stress associated with completing this text. As it turned out, our fears were warranted. Nevertheless, Serina managed to convince us to accept the challenge of writing this book, and we are glad that she did. Our new editor, Eve Howard, was instrumental in figuring out ways to get us to finish the book.

Even more central to the completion of this book was the support provided by our families. We are especially indebted to Carol Blum, Patricia and Andrea DeKeseredy, and Marie Barger. Their inexhaustible emotional support helped us maintain our energy and focus, although it may have drained theirs.

We have also benefited from the comments, criticisms, lessons, and influences provided by the following friends and colleagues: Leon Anderson, Henry Brownstein, Dawn Currie, Kathleen Daly, Desmond Ellis, David Friedrichs, Colin Goff, Keith Haley, Suzanne Hatty, Ronald Hinch, Michael Lynch, Molly Leggett, Brian MacLean, James Messerschmidt, Jody Miller, Dragan Milovanovic, the late Michael D. Smith, Elizabeth Stanko, and Barry Wright. Because many of these people disagree with one another, it is obvious that we are fully responsible for what we took from each of them. In any case, we appreciate all of their input, as well as that of many others we have not named. And we wish to apologize to a kind friend, Larry Siegel, for writing this book.

Special thanks go to Lisa Leduc, Amy Phillips-Gary, and Carol Gregory, who devoted a considerable amount of time and effort to collecting materials summarized in this text. Their contributions to the completion of *Contemporary Criminology* are too numerous to mention.

David Friedrichs was helpful beyond any call of duty in giving us permission to rework and use some material on organized crime from his own brilliant Wadsworth book on white-collar crime, *Trusted Criminals: White Collar Crime in Contemporary Society.*

Other reviewers we wish to thank include those who read chapters of this book in progress and provided valuable advice on how to proceed. They include: Yoko Baba, San Jose State University; William D. Cole, University of Kentucky; James DeFronzo, University of Connecticut; Patrick Donnelly, University of Dayton; Karen Heimer, University of Iowa; Dennis E. Hoffman, University of Nebraska at Omaha; John W. King, Baldwin-Wallace College; Peter Kraska, Eastern Kentucky University; Ineke Haen Marshall, University of Nebraska at Omaha; M. Joan McDermott, Southern Illinois University at Carbondale; Eleanor M. Miller, University of Wisconsin at Milwaukee; Patricia Murphy, State University of New York at Geneseo; R. K. Prine, Valdosta State University; Polly F. Radosh, Western Illinois University; Gordon M. Robinson, Michigan State University; A. Javier Trevino, Marquette University; N. Prabha Unnithan, Colorado State University; and Robbyn R. Wacker, University of Northern Colorado.

The support of Carleton University and Ohio University is also greatly appreciated. Financial assistance provided at Carleton by the office of the Dean of Social Science and by the Faculty of Graduate Studies and Research helped us collect information on various topics addressed in this book. A sabbatical leave provided by Ohio University helped us get some of the chapters written.

Last, we want to thank the staff at Wadsworth for their patience, cooperation, and editorial assistance, especially Eve Howard, Julie McDonald, Susan Shook, Jerilyn Emori, Jeanne Bosschart, Tom Briggs, and Andrew Ogus.

ABOUT THE AUTHORS

WALTER S. DEKESEREDY completed his doctorate in sociology at York University on the subject of violence against women. He has published numerous journal articles and book chapters on woman abuse and left realism. He is author of *Woman Abuse in Dating Relationships: The Role of Male Peer Support;* with Ronald Hinch coauthor of *Woman Abuse: Sociological Perspectives;* with Desmond Ellis coauthor of the second edition of *Wrong Stuff: An Introduction to the Sociological Study of Deviance;* and with Martin D. Schwartz coauthor of *Sexual Assault on the College Campus: The Role of Male Peer Pressure* (forthcoming with Sage Publications). DeKeseredy was associate editor of *Justice Quarterly* and coeditor of *The Critical Criminologist,* and he is now a member of *Woman and Criminal Justice*'s Editorial Board. Currently, he is associate professor of sociology at Carleton University in Ottawa, Ontario, Canada.

MARTIN D. SCHWARTZ has twice been named arts and sciences outstanding professor at Ohio University, where he is professor of sociology and former department chair. The author or editor of more than fifty journal articles and several books, he currently serves as deputy editor of *Justice Quarterly* and on the editorial boards of such journals as *Violence Against Women; Race, Class and Gender;* and *Teaching Sociology.* In 1994 he received the Division on Critical Criminology Award of the American Society of Criminology for his scholarship and teaching. Most recently he has coedited a book on race, class, and gender in criminology with Dragan Milovanovic and published in such journals as *Criminology, Justice Quarterly,* and *Deviant Behavior.*

PART I

What Is Crime and How Much of It Is There?

CHAPTER 1

IMAGES OF CRIME AND ITS CONTROL

*Man's fascination with news of crime is insatiable. The sensational crimes and
their trials ... engage public interest to a degree matched by little else.*

FRIENDLY AND GOLDFARB, 1968, P. 3

Why do you suppose North Americans are so preoccupied with
crime? Of course, for some people the reason is fairly obvious.
Those who *are* at high risk of victimization *should* be concerned
about crime. For some reason, however, people at low risk of victimization
seem to be just as concerned or even more concerned with crime. In any
public opinion poll of what North Americans think are significant social
problems, crime tends to rank at or near the top (Elias, 1986; Livingston,
1992; Sacco, Glackman, & Roesch, 1984; Skogan & Klecka, 1977).

People don't just worry; they also take action. Some of these actions are
well thought out and do indeed reduce the chances of becoming a crime
victim. However, entire industries have emerged that service or exploit
people's fears about their vulnerability to criminal acts. You can see this
in the rapid increase in rates of gun ownership and sales of home alarms
and protection devices, cans of tear gas and pepper spray, and automobile
alarms and steering wheel locks. Some people have made themselves virtual
prisoners in their own homes or apartments by installing window bars,
metal doors, extraordinary locking devices, and amazingly expensive alarm
systems. Although some of these devices may provide protection from
strangers, all too often people find that they are useful only in limited
circumstances. They certainly do not protect from crimes committed by
nonstrangers or from a variety of other victimizations. To cite just one
example, they certainly won't help much in cases of wife or child abuse
(DeKeseredy, Burshtyn, & Gordon, 1992; Stanko, 1990; Walklate, 1989).
For another, they won't protect from unsafe products, cancer-causing agents

dumped into the water supply, or rip-off telephone solicitors. To some degree, many of these worried people are economically victimized by others who whip up and exploit their fears to sell them useless or unneeded safety devices.

Perhaps the most important action that people take, however, is a change in their lifestyle. What is it, after all, that brings individuals together and creates a sense of community? Is it seeing the same familiar and friendly faces every day on the street corner or park benches? Is it knowing all of your neighbors and having them know you? Certainly, one thing that undermines this sense of community is residents huddled fearfully behind their own locked doors. Women and the elderly particularly alter their daily routines because they are terrified of being mugged, robbed, or raped (Livingston, 1992; Stanko, 1990). The problem, unfortunately, is that these strategies only tend to increase rather than reduce fear of crime (DeKeseredy, Burshtyn, & Gordon, 1992; Walklate, 1989).

Not everyone is at equal risk of being victimized by crime. Later in this book, it will become obvious that, not unreasonably, people with relatively less power are more likely to be targeted than are members of more powerful groups. Thus, individuals with less ability to defend themselves, such as the poor, women, and members of some ethnic minority groups, are more likely to be victimized. Individuals with more ability to defend themselves, including upper- and middle-class white men, are less likely (Messerschmidt, 1986).

This does not tell us, however, why people who are relatively immune from street crime are so afraid of it. Worse, it does not tell us why people are so afraid of some crimes, such as assault, burglary, and robbery, but not others. Nor are the reasons for such attitudes completely logical. Deviant acts committed by large corporations are significantly more economically, socially, physically, and environmentally harmful than street crimes (Reiman, 1995), but "crime in the suites" is not what generates the most fear. Why aren't people more worried that a bank officer will steal their life savings than they are afraid that a teenager will hold them up for $5? Why aren't most people worried that the rate of corporate violence (which results in their exposure to toxic elements, in hazardous working conditions, and so on) is at least thirty times greater than the rate of interpersonal violence (Ellis & DeKeseredy, 1996)?

These are important questions. Before we can answer them, we must first look at where the general public obtains its information about crime.

There are four major influences that tend to shape images of crime in people's minds: (1) personal knowledge, (2) the mass media, (3) official state knowledge, and (4) sociological knowledge (West, 1984).

PERSONAL KNOWLEDGE OF CRIME

A considerable amount of our knowledge of crime is based on our personal experiences, either as victims or perpetrators. Although most of us would like to believe that we were, and still are, law-abiding citizens, almost all of us can remember taking part in at least relatively minor types of crimes, such as underage drinking, speeding, shoplifting, and vandalism. Undoubtedly, many readers of this book are still engaging in these activities regularly. Others may have engaged in them once but no longer do so. For example, despite firm lectures from his parents about the physical and legal consequences of drinking alcohol, one of the authors of this text routinely drank vast quantities of beer every weekend with his high school pals. Occasionally, these "parties" resulted in the destruction of both public and private property and periodic acts of interpersonal violence. Nevertheless, he was never caught and he simply regarded these actions as "good fun" instead of crimes.

What would he have thought about his "good fun" if he had been caught by either informal (for example, parents) or formal authority figures (for example, teachers, police officers, park officials)? Given that it is not uncommon for teenagers to break rules, different cultures have different methods of dealing with rebellious youths. To cite just one example, the Old Order Amish recently have had some serious problems with teenagers drinking, driving cars, listening to rock music, dressing in contemporary teenage garb, and engaging in other behaviors that deviate from the core values of the Old Order Amish communities in the United States. However, their culture does not allow for the harshest penalties to be given to boys who have not yet been baptized, which happens in the late teens. Rather, there is some allowance for teenaged rule breaking, and after baptism virtually all youths obey the group's rules (Kephart & Zellner, 1994).

In the dominant North American culture, however, being arrested and labeled a criminal can have serious consequences for many years. Perhaps the "good fun" author's middle-class status kept him from being officially designated as a delinquent. After all, as criminological research repeatedly reveals, working-class youths and members of ethnic minority groups are much more likely to be both stigmatized and punished for such activities as underage drinking, use of drugs, vandalism, and even interpersonal violence than their more affluent and white counterparts (Chambliss, 1973; Reiman, 1995; Thornberry, 1973).[1] What may be very interesting is, given this author's reinterpretation of his teenage "hijinks" as crimes, is he correct in thinking that he will be able to closely monitor and successfully control his daughter's drinking behavior when she becomes a teenager?

In addition to committing minor crimes, some of us (whatever our class background) belonged to violent youth groups or gangs, broke into houses, went on joyrides in stolen cars, and routinely vandalized both private and public property. Like the activities described previously, these represent some of our early direct crime experiences, and whether or not we were caught, they contribute to the development of a personal knowledge base on crime.

We may be not only the perpetrators of crime but the victims, which can also play a key role in shaping our personal knowledge of crime. Moreover, being victimized seems to make people more fearful of crime (Fattah & Sacco, 1989; Garofalo, 1979; Livingston, 1992). For example, before he was 14 years old, Walter DeKeseredy's exposure to crime was restricted to what he saw on television shows such as "Kojak," "Policewoman," "Hawaii Five-O," and "Columbo" and movies such as *Dirty Harry.* Perhaps the primary reason for his lack of experience was the fact that he was closely monitored by his parents and he lived in a relatively homogeneous, white, middle-class community. This district, in sharp contrast to cities such as East St. Louis, Los Angeles, and Chicago, was characterized by very low rates of predatory street crime, mainly because it did not have high levels of both economic and racial inequality—two major correlates of predatory street crime (Blau & Blau, 1982; Braithwaite, 1979; Currie, 1985).

Until one hot summer evening in 1973, one of your authors, Walter DeKeseredy, always thought that crime was limited to large U.S. cities and that both his house and town—Oakville, Ontario—were, as Christopher Lasch (1977) termed it, "havens in a heartless world." Arriving home from a lacrosse game, he realized that his parents were out and that he had forgotten to leave a few lights on in the house. Still, a burglary was the last thing

---

[1] See MacLean and Milovanovic (1990) for an excellent collection of articles on the relationship between race and the administration of criminal justice in the United States.

on his mind. Unfortunately, when he reached the front door, he discovered that it was wide open. Although extremely scared, he walked toward his bedroom and found a man searching through his dresser drawers. De-Keseredy responded to this intrusion by screaming and running out of the house toward the safety of his neighbor's home. Needless to say, he no longer trivialized the possibility of being a crime victim. Furthermore, he became considerably more fearful of crime and stereotyped all people who looked like the burglar as potential criminals. To make matters worse, his house was broken into again six months later.

These two burglaries significantly affected not only DeKeseredy but also his mother, now an elderly woman who is extremely fearful of crime. Based solely on empirical research, one might suggest that her fear level is too high. First, elderly people are less likely than younger persons to be victimized (Fattah & Sacco, 1989). Second, his mother now lives in a relatively rural community, and rural areas have significantly lower rates of burglary than do urban areas. Nevertheless, no matter what criminologists have to say, DeKeseredy's mother is terrified of burglary, and in order to minimize her risk of further victimization, she has purchased a sophisticated $4,000-security system.

Interestingly, as a youth, Martin Schwartz lived and worked in areas with significantly higher crime rates but had little experience with or fear of crime victimization. Long walks in bad neighborhoods did not bother him unduly, for example. The one time he was burglarized, he was somewhat traumatized for a while. However, he was able to recover all of his property and to discover on his own that the burglar was a neighborhood youth who was neither particularly threatening nor intelligent. In fact, the amateurish nature of the burglary was the source of many jokes and stories for Schwartz afterwards.

Thus, one source of our knowledge about crime is personal experience. People's personal knowledge of crime should not be trivialized, especially if the experiences harmed their (or others') economic, social, psychological, and physical well-being. This knowledge is a useful resource for interpreting crime. However, as we have seen, knowing one person's crime experience does not tell us very much about the experiences and interpretations of other individuals. Just because you committed a particular crime or were victimized in some way does not mean that other members of your community have had, or will have, similar experiences.

To further complicate the issue, there is a form of personal knowledge that might be termed *common knowledge*. One of the earliest lessons taught in an introduction to sociology course is that all social groups share certain things, including worldviews. The more similar the members of the group, the more likely they are to have similar views. Thus, to grow up and live among people who look and think in a fairly similar manner means that there will be some things—such as crime—that everyone will "just know." The problem is, different groups "just know" different things. You may "just know" that members of a different racial or ethnic group are danger-ous, that long-haired youths take drugs, that the police harass teenagers, that welfare mothers have babies to get more money, or whatever. Of course, another group may "just know" something very different.

To complicate matters yet again, even within a fairly tight community, different people may believe different things. If you doubt this, just read three magazines: one aimed at men, one aimed at women, and one aimed at teenagers. Although everyone may share ethnic, racial, religious, and social class characteristics, the worldview of teenagers may still be very different from that of men or women. Most communities are not that tight—resi-dents have different political and social beliefs, so there are even more vari-ations of common knowledge. In all of these cases, however, these people "know" the arguments as to why we need more or less police and prisons, whether it is safe to walk outdoors at night, whether date rape is a serious problem in society, and so on.

The solution to this "information gap" is obvious: turn to sources of information about crime that are less subjective than just personal experi-ences or beliefs. Unfortunately, when we do this we find limitations that may be just as serious.

MEDIA KNOWLEDGE OF CRIME

How is it that most people are never victimized by crime (Fattah & Sacco, 1989) and have little direct experience with it but still manage to have very strong opinions about crime, viewing it as one of the most pressing problems facing society today? Why do people worry about criminal victimization if it never happened to them or their family or friends?

The answer, of course, is that we have more information at our disposal than our personal and direct experiences. We make use of information not only passed on to us by others directly but also obtained from sources such as newspapers, television, magazines, movies, and books. These sources, collectively called the mass media, undoubtedly have some influence on our perceptions and opinions. In fact, for many people, the mass media are their major source of information on crime and its control (Ericson, Baranek, & Chan, 1987; Graber, 1980). For example, in 1987, the average U.S. citizen watched more than four hours of TV each day (Klain, 1989), and at least 33 percent of broadcast content featured stories about crime or law enforcement (Graber, 1980). Furthermore, roughly 25 percent of the total newspaper content addresses these issues (Ericson, Baranek, & Chan, 1987). These estimates were made before the popularity of many new shows such as "COPS," "Rescue-911," "Hard Copy," and "A Current Affair," all of which focus on crime and law enforcement.

As touched on previously, a key question becomes, Are all types of crime equally covered by the mass media? As you can answer for yourself, of course not. Crimes such as murder, sexual abuse, assault, gang-related incidents, and drug abuse receive the most attention (Beirne & Messerschmidt, 1991; Ericson, Baranek, & Chan, 1987, 1989; Humphries, 1981; Livingston, 1992; Sheley and Ashkins, 1981). Up to a point, we can even develop a formula: the less common a crime event (for example, kidnapping or murder), the more space it gets in the media; the more common the crime event (for example, burglary or theft), the less space it gets. Further, there is some selection as to which crimes receive attention in the press. For example, a shooting is fairly sure to make the 11 o'clock news in virtually all markets. In contrast, it is relatively uncommon to receive as much information on corporate crimes such as price-fixing, the illegal dumping of toxic waste, and unsafe work conditions. This is one of the main reasons there is so much "collective ignorance" about these pressing issues (Box, 1983). As will be shown in Chapter 10, corporate crime is more socially, physically, environmentally, and economically costly than street crime. Given the lack of media attention devoted to this problem, many North Americans do not appreciate its threat to their well-being. There are many reasons for this lack of attention, not the least of which is that local police departments often hold press conferences just before news deadlines to give very inexpensive news to the media. However, as we will see, other reasons must be considered as well.

Many people are concerned that the various media primarily cover acts of interpersonal violence and drug-related crimes and the criminal justice system's response to these crimes. Whether this is in fact a problem is a complex issue that requires extensive discussion. Some excellent criminology books are available on the media's relationship to crime and its control.[2] Because we can cover only a part of this subject, we have chosen to focus here on the relationship between mass media exposure and fear of crime, on "moral panics" fueled by the media, and on the media as a cause of crime.

Mass Media Exposure and Fear of Crime

A common contention is that mass media exposure is closely related to fear of crime; the more people listen to or read the mass media, the more fearful they become (Fattah & Sacco, 1989; Friedberg, 1983). At first glance, this reasoning seems logical. It is based primarily on three arguments. First, crime, especially violent acts committed by both poor and African-American males, is a central feature of both fictional and nonfictional mass media presentations (Box, 1983; Reiman, 1995). Second, as we've mentioned before, most people have not knowingly been victimized. Thus, their knowledge of crime presumably is obtained from other sources. When they obtain their knowledge from television, what they are more likely to see (according to the first point above) are African-American and poor male offenders. Third, social groups characterized by high levels of fear (for example, the elderly) have higher levels of media consumption than those who are less fearful of crime.

Although these arguments may be logical, criminologists have not been able to support them in research studies. For example, in their critique of the argument that media exposure is a key in determining the amount of fear of crime, Ezzat Fattah and Vincent Sacco (1989, p. 221) contend that:

- Most studies do not find a direct relationship between exposure to the media and fear of crime.[3]

- Although some studies do show a relationship between media exposure and fear of crime, they have not been able to show that media exposure causes fear of crime, rather than the opposite—that fear of crime causes media exposure. For example, maybe fearful people stay at home all day and watch television.

---

[2] See, for example, Cohen and Young (1981), Ericson, Baranek, and Chan (1987, 1989), and Surette (1992).

[3] See Fattah and Sacco (1989, p. 221) for a list of studies on this issue.

- Most people are exposed to a variety of knowledge sources, such as friends, family members, and so on. Thus, people do not base their fear solely on media portrayals.

- Simply measuring something like the number of hours a person spends watching TV or reading newspapers (as many researchers do) may not be the best way to find out how much people know about the crime reported in the mass media. Some people with high media exposure may be watching ballgames and MTV and reading *Sports Illustrated*. Some people who do not watch much TV may be told by friends or relatives what they see, hear, and read in the media and therefore know about many crimes from media sources. So, the level of exposure to the media may not be an adequate guide.

Based on these arguments, we can conclude that the media has, at best, some influence on fear of crime. Fear may be more an outcome of listening to both the victims' and neighborhood networks' stories, rumors, and gossip about crime. This information usually is immediately relevant to both problems people are exposed to and the individuals they know, live near, or share social characteristics with (Clarke, 1984; Clarke & Lewis, 1982; Goodstein & Shotland, 1980; Miethe & Lee, 1984; Sacco, 1982; Skogan & Maxfield, 1981; Surette, 1992).

Having said all of this, keep in mind that a great deal of research does show that the media can influence people's concern about crime as a social issue. For example, media exposure may convince people that crime in general or drug use or teenage gangs are major social problems. Further, media exposure can shape public discussions on crime-related issues and influence policies for both crime's prevention and control. For example, whether the public clamors for more prisons (to lock up the dangerous) or less prisons (to stop wasting taxpayers' money by locking up too many people) may be fed in part by media reporting (Fattah & Sacco, 1989; Gordon & Heath, 1981; Skogan & Maxfield, 1981; Smith, 1986; Surette, 1992; Tyler, 1984). Worst of all, the media can contribute to moral panics about crime.

Moral Panics About Crime

Stanley Cohen (1980) has developed the highly useful concept of the *moral panic* to describe a situation in which a condition, episode, person, or group of persons comes to be defined as a threat to society. At that point, the mass media describe the "threat" in detail, although not necessarily accurately, and various editors and politicians jump on the bandwagon with their own claims to be defending the "moral barricades." Sociologists, lawyers, psychologists, and other "experts" quickly join the fray with diagnoses and solutions.

Most typically, the object of moral panics has been people. They could be hippies, anti-war protestors, drug users, criminals, neo-Nazis, motorcycle club members, militia groups, or any other group likely to provoke the moral indignation of some members of the community. However, the target of a moral panic also can be an object, such as—silly as it might sound—a rather big water pistol like the Super Soaker. For example, in May 1992, an Ottawa, Ontario, resident filled his Super Soaker with bleach and sprayed an innocent bystander in the tourist-oriented Ottawa Market. Shortly before this incident, in Boston, a water gun fight escalated into a handgun shooting incident. While the pain and suffering of the victims should not be trivialized, it is the media response that is of greater interest here.

Ottawa's leading newspaper, the *Citizen,* devoted considerable space to the alleged criminal use of the Super Soaker, even though only a tiny handful of such incidents ever took place in both Canada and the United States. Similarly, an Ottawa radio news reporter expressed great alarm over the potential dangers associated with the popular toy. The media created a social problem suddenly and dramatically: the water gun changed from a popular but harmless toy to a tool of criminal victimization. Perhaps it is overstating the case to say that the mass media *created* public fears about the amount and seriousness of violent water gun use, but we can certainly state that the mass media *amplified* such fears.

What difference does it make that fears about water guns were amplified? Cohen argues that the public concern, anxiety, indignation, or panic caused by media reporting can result in the creation of new rules. For example, U.S. politicians called for a ban on the Super Soaker, while in some communities, stores refused to sell it. Are these rational responses? Are these reactions based on a careful examination of the true risk of criminal victimization? Obviously, although this is a relatively minor example, it highlights the role of the media in creating moral panics.

More often, however, the objects of media-related moral panics are people. For example, prior to the Second World War, the public was not as concerned with the behavior of young people (Tanner, 1992). Since then, youth subcultures have generated a considerable amount of moral disapproval in England, Canada, and the United States (Brake, 1985; Ellis, 1987; Hall & Jefferson, 1977). The distinctive appearance and conduct of youth groups, and especially their participation in vandalism and gang fights, was regarded by various adults, including news reporters, as "deliberately directed against adult notions of propriety" (Tanner, 1992, p. 207). Various subcultures, such as the Mods and Rockers, hippies, Skinheads, soccer hooligans, and Punks, were, and still are, "targets of one moral panic after another" (Ellis, 1987, p. 199).

Previously, we talked about how the media can amplify the public fear of an alleged threat to the social fabric. The media also can *amplify the behavior* of targeted groups. Cohen's (1980) analysis of the highly exaggerated mid-1960s conflicts between British Mods and Rockers, for example, demonstrates that the mass media's coverage of these two groups created a moral panic that transformed "loose stylistic associations" into well-organized gangs (Downes & Rock, 1988), or folk devils. A *folk devil* is, according to Desmond Ellis (1987, p. 199), "a socially constructed, stereotypical carrier or source of significant social harm." The creation of this deviant category resulted in far more unconventional behavior than otherwise might have occurred had there been more modest news coverage. A large number of British teenagers who initially existed only on the fringe of the Mod and Rocker subcultures came to identify more strongly with these groups and behave in a similar fashion (Downes & Rock, 1988).

The mass media also escalated the tensions between the Mods and Rockers, as well as between the two groups and the overall adult community. Prior to the sensationalistic news reports, Cohen (1980, p. 165) states that

> although . . . the Mods and Rockers represent two different consumer styles—the Mods the more glossy fashion-conscious teenager, the Rockers the tougher, reactionary tradition—the antagonism between the two groups was not initially very marked. Despite their real differences in life styles—visible in symbols such as the Mods' scooters and the Rockers' motor-bikes—the groups had a great deal in common, particularly their working-class membership. There was, initially at least, nothing like the gang rivalry that is supposed to characterize the type of violent conflict gang enshrined in folklore by the "Sharks" and "Jets" of *West Side Story.* Indeed, one could not

justifiably talk of "gangs" at all in any meaningful sociological sense. The only structured grouping one could find in the early crowds was based on slight territorial loyalty and it was tenuous enough to be broken up in the crowd situation.

In sum, the moral panic about the Mods and Rockers amplified and entrenched the behavior it was intended to regulate. Based partially on media reports, these youths began to act the way they felt they were supposed to act, and the gang problem escalated far beyond what it might have been without the media coverage.

As we have seen, the media may be able to take crime that already exists and amplify it. But what about situations in which no crime exists—can the media be held responsible for sometimes directly causing unlawful behavior?

The Media as a Cause of Crime

This may seem strange, but the effect of the media on violent behavior has been studied more than any other topic related to human aggression (Goldstein, 1986). At the same time, there is very little research on the media as a direct cause of a wide range of crimes.[4] How can these *both* be true?

Before we tackle this provocative topic, we should first point out the obvious: the media, and television in particular, do report or portray quite a bit of violence. Anyone who believes that the media causes crime certainly will have no problem finding a sufficient number of examples of violent media. This concern is nothing new. After all, the first congressional panels studying violence on television were convened in the early 1950s, before most American families even owned televisions. Based on the increasingly frequent and sophisticated studies of violent acts on television, we can draw several conclusions: (1) there is a very high frequency of violent acts shown on all networks; (2) there is much more violence on Saturday morning and daytime TV than on prime-time TV; and (3) this level of TV violence has been stable over the past two decades (Gerbner & Signorielli, 1990).

---

[4]According to Surette (1992, p. 107), "There is no evidence of and little concern about a potential print media effect on social aggression." Yet, see Sparks (1992) for an analysis of the arguments on the effects of television violence.

Media Violence and "Copycat" Crime   But what is the effect of all of this media violence? Most studies have been conducted in laboratories by psychologists and social psychologists who focused mainly on the question of whether violence and aggression in TV shows and movies causes viewers to become more aggressive (Surette, 1992). Citizens and policymakers are greatly concerned about the effects of TV and movies on violent behavior (Smith, 1983), so the vast majority of research on the media as a cause of crime is devoted to this problem. Before summarizing some academic research on the media as a cause of violent crime, perhaps we should provide some anecdotal examples of events that generate considerable fear about violent media images for both the public and politicians. The following are a few "copycat" crimes found in a much longer list produced by Ray Surette (1992, p. 130):

- In Boston, a woman was doused with gasoline and set on fire following a movie on TV in which teenage boys roam Boston burning tramps for fun and amusement.
- An 11-year-old boy murdered a postman in imitation of an adventure show.
- Another 11-year-old boy, who became fascinated by strangulation scenes on TV, acted out his fascination by strangling a 4-year-old girl.
- In John Hinckley's assassination attempt on President Reagan, Hinckley was emulating the main character in the movie *Taxi Driver.*

Events such as these are shocking, and not surprisingly, many people respond to them by calling for a ban on violent TV shows and movies. Their fear of copycat violence is based mainly on two arguments:

First, the media coverage both triggers the occurrence of crime and shapes its form, creating crime that otherwise would not exist and turning formerly law-abiding individuals into criminals. The result is an immediate increase in both the number of crimes and the number of criminals within society. Second, the media coverage shapes the criminal behavior of already active criminals, molding the characteristics of crime without actually triggering it. (Surette, 1992, pp. 129–130)

One area of debate among researchers is whether television teaches children to become violent as they grow up.

However, research findings do not support the first of these assertions (Comstock, 1980; Milgram & Shotland, 1973). The so-called copycat effect is clearly not as widespread as people think, and there is no compelling evidence of a media influence that affects law-abiding people. Moreover, even though the media provide sensationalistic coverage of violent copycat incidents, most copycat criminals are not violent. Media images do seem to have some influence on the behavior of already active criminals—specifically, on the choice of criminal techniques—but this mainly affects career criminals who primarily commit property offenses.

In one realm, however, there is strong research support for copycat incidents: highly publicized nonfictional and fictional suicide stories can generate imitating behavior, especially among teenagers (Bollen & Phillips, 1982; Gould & Shaffer, 1986; Ostroff & Boyd, 1987; Ostroff et al., 1985; Phillips & Bollen, 1985; Phillips & Carstensen, 1986; Phillips & Paight,

1987; Surette, 1992). For example, David Phillips (1974) found that one month after the death of the famous movie star Marilyn Monroe, suicides increased by 12 percent in the United States and by 10 percent in England and Wales. In total, Monroe's death triggered 363 "excess" suicides in two countries.

Problems with Laboratory Studies   Even though the relationship between media exposure and interpersonal violent copycat crime is weak, a large number of studies (most of which were conducted in laboratories by psychologists) report a strong correlation between viewing media violence and committing other forms of aggression, such as sports violence (Smith, 1983). One problem with these studies is the difficulty in *measuring* violence in the laboratory. If the criterion was "punching out the research associate," the turnover rate for employees would be rather high! Rather, these studies might give the participants opportunities to punch out plastic dolls—acts that, while aggressive, are hardly criminal.[5]

Another problem is that, according to the research literature, the media contribute more to increases in property crime than violent crime (Surette, 1992). Because most crime-oriented TV shows and movies contain more violence than property crimes, this doesn't seem logical. Nevertheless, as most scientists realize, logic is often not the best predictor of empirical research findings.

Finally, as we said earlier, most of the research on the media as a source of aggression was done in laboratories, artificial environments that differ sharply from the contexts of peoples' everyday lives. What people do in the lab does not necessarily reflect their actions in less controlled social settings (Goldstein, 1986). For example, Edward Donnerstein and Daniel Linz (1984, 1986) found that after watching "aggressive pornography" in a lab, some men said that they would rape a woman if they could get away with it, and they increased their aggressive behavior toward female participants in the experiment. Are these findings valid indicators of what the subjects would do in the outside community (Brannigan & Goldenberg, 1987)? Keep in mind that, in laboratory studies, researchers attempt to strip away dozens of influences on human behavior and isolate exactly what they want

---

[5]See Bandura (1965) for data on this type of aggression.

to study. However, in the real world, we live and operate under the influence of all these confusing factors. What happens when we step out of the laboratory and return to real life? To the best of our knowledge, no studies have been conducted showing that peoples' laboratory behavior is consistent with their conduct in the community. Daniel Linz and Neil Malamuth (1993) point out that we may still want to base public policy on these studies if we feel that such media exposure makes people more tolerant of violence. They suggest that much of the debate over whether various studies have proven that media representations cause violence is really a debate over what evidence we are willing to accept. If our ultimate goal is to avoid censorship, then we may require proof beyond a reasonable doubt. If our goal is to protect potential victims, we may have a much lower burden of proof.

Pornography and Sexual Violence It should be noted, meanwhile, that a few studies done outside of the laboratory demonstrate a relationship between one form of media representation—pornography—and violent behavior such as woman abuse. For example, Diana Russell (1990) asked 930 female residents of San Francisco if they have "ever been upset by anyone trying to get you to do what they'd seen in pornographic pictures, movies, or books." Ten percent of her survey respondents answered yes to this question. Of those women who reported being raped by their husbands, 24 percent answered yes.

These findings have been replicated. Patricia Harman and James Check (1989) found that 6 percent of their 604 Toronto subjects reported that they were "upset" by a partner who asked them to do what he had seen in pornographic media. Martin Schwartz and Walter DeKeseredy (1994), using a national Canadian sample of 1,638 college and university women, found in a similar question that 8.4 percent said that they had been made "upset." In each case, the victims of physical violence by intimate partners were about three times as likely to report being disturbed by being asked to act out pornographic behavior as were women who were not physically assaulted. Schwartz and DeKeseredy found that the victims of sexual assault by intimate partners were four times as likely to report being made upset in this manner.

While these studies suggest some relationship between male use of pornography and violence against women, the findings should be read with some caution. First, as Harman and Check point out, the data do not reveal the "direction of causality." In other words, we do not know whether pornography causes men to abuse women or whether woman abusers later become more interested in pornography. Second, these researchers did not specifically ask women if their abusers were exposed to *violent* pornography. Undoubtedly, some women were asked to imitate violent pornographic scenarios, but many of them could have also been offended by being asked to emulate nonviolent scenes.

Larry Baron and Murray Straus (1984) wanted to know if laboratory findings on the violent effects of pornography were consistent with survey data collected from the wider U.S. society. They compared state-by-state differences in rape rates with state-by-state differences in sales of eight mass market soft-core pornographic magazines such as *Penthouse, Playboy,* and *Hustler.* They found a very strong relationship between rape rates and magazine sales: the higher the rate of magazine sales, the higher the rape rate. However, as all social scientists know, it's one thing to show a *relationship* and quite another to show *causality.* When Baron and Straus introduced a new variable, "violence approval," there was no longer a relationship between sales and rape. In other words, men who approve highly of violence (what the researchers call *hypermasculinity*) may both read a great deal of pornography and create a climate in which more men commit rape.

Baron (1990) later returned to this issue by looking at the overall social climate for women, as best that can be measured. Of course, we don't own a thermometer that measures "social climate" in the same way we can check the data in a weather report. Nevertheless, Baron measured such things as the percentage of elected female officials in a state, the presence or absence of such laws as equal pay statutes, and the percentage of all small business loans given out to women. In comparing his twenty-four-item index to the amount of soft-core pornography sold, he discovered a *positive* relationship between the two; in other words, the more gender equality, the higher the rate of circulation of the magazines. Baron theorizes that political tolerance seems to be the operative factor—that the more we embrace ideas such as full female equality, the more some people will move in other directions such as buying previously forbidden magazines.

The most appropriate conclusion to draw here is that the complexity of human behavior makes it difficult to draw absolutely firm and positive conclusions. Despite the large amount of empirical knowledge accumulated so far, there is still great uncertainty about whether the relationship between violent media images and behavior is causal. Still, the critics appropriately argue, what would make you think that there was a simple relationship to be found? Do most of us really believe that watching an episode of "NYPD Blue" or "Walker, Texas Ranger" would induce us to acts of violence? What people who worry about media violence are concerned about is the cumulative effect. They worry that these shows glorify violence as a means of solving problems, suggest that violence is much more common and acceptable than it really is, and reduce our sensitivity to the effects of this violence. When combined with many other factors, these media effects may make it easier for some of us to commit violent acts ourselves. Thus, at the very least, we can conclude that the media have some effect on violent crime, and we can worry that the effect is actually much stronger than that.

The Strengths of Media Knowledge

It should be noted that, compared to personal knowledge, media knowledge of crime has major advantages, at least for people who are not part of the criminology research community. These advantages include the following:

- The media provide more extensive information than most people ever directly experience.
- The media offer different types of knowledge than a person would likely encounter directly, such as information on gang violence and racketeering.
- As a public institution, the media facilitate the exchange and sharing of personal knowledge. Consequently, the media could transform various individual beliefs and opinions into a "general will" of consensual public opinion, based on which collective action might be taken.
- Media knowledge holds out the promise of allowing us to move beyond our own limited experiences by applying our knowledge to a wider base.
- Media knowledge is so central in policy debates that it becomes important in its own right, whether or not it accurately reflects people's experiences (West, 1984).

OFFICIAL KNOWLEDGE OF CRIME

Since the crime knowledge we gain from both the media and our personal experiences is riddled with shortcomings, many people believe data produced by the government are much more accurate.

Government agencies that generate data on crime can be divided into two broad categories: criminal justice institutions and special commissions. The most widely known crime data are produced by a key player in the criminal justice system—the police. Certainly, these data are more accurate than information generated by personal knowledge or the mass media. Unfortunately, police data may not tell us very much about the real extent, distribution, and nature of crime. Except for a select group of crimes, such as homicide,[6] police data are perhaps more useful for evaluating how criminal justice officials deal with behaviors that they officially designate as criminal (Hagan, 1985).

For example, the most widely used and reported national police statistics, such as the U.S. and Canadian *Uniform Crime Reports* (UCR), exclude a wide range of events. This may seem a bit obvious, but police statistics reflect only crimes that come to the attention of the police. For the most part, that means crimes reported to the police by private citizens. Yet, for a variety of reasons, many incidents are not reported to the police. Some crimes go unnoticed, or the victims are not aware that they have been harmed by criminal activities. For example, you may be illegally overcharged on your electric bill, or someone may be stealing things from you that you don't notice are missing. Sometimes, people don't think that it is worth the bother of calling the police, feeling that they can do nothing to help. Actually, they may be right. If you come back from vacation and find your TV set stolen, and you know it was a nineteen-inch color set but don't have the serial number, can't remember if it was a Hitachi or an RCA, and don't really

---

[6]Unlike other types of police-generated crime data, homicide statistics are generally reliable because "dead bodies are almost always reported" (Boyd, 1988, p. 54). Furthermore, most murderers reveal their crimes to the police and do not avoid detection. Thus, there is no significant "dark figure" of murder (Taylor, 1983). Police statistics, however, do not include both missing persons who were murdered and homicides disguised as accidental deaths or suicides (DeKeseredy & Hinch, 1991; Koenig, 1987).

know the week in which it was stolen, chances are the police really can't do anything at all for you.

Other times, people may not call the police because they are embarrassed and don't want to admit how they came to be victimized. For instance, they may not want it widely known that they truly believed that the out-of-town bikers who knocked at the door were selling Girl Scout cookies and they let them into the house voluntarily, hoping for a box or two of Thin Mints. Or people may feel they were at fault themselves for being drunk and unable to resist, for bragging about how much money they were carrying, for leaving their doors unlocked, and so on. Some people may even believe that they have been victimized but not want to "get involved" with the police (De-Keseredy & MacLean, 1991; Solicitor General of Canada, 1986). What all of this means is that what comes to the attention of the police may not be all, or even most, crimes.

Perhaps worst of all, it is not unheard of for local officials to report data to the UCR that have been inflated or deflated by police officials "intent on proving some point through the manipulation of statistics" (Karmen, 1990, p. 52). Sometimes, data can be manipulated in ways that tell us just as much about policing activities as they do about criminals. If, for example, most patrol officers in a precinct are patrolling low-income neighborhoods looking for street corner drug dealers, this area presumably will have an extremely high number of drug offenses and arrests. If the police decide to completely ignore street drug sales and devote all of their resources to preventing youth crime, crime data certainly will reflect this shift in focus.

A final problem with police data is that, except for homicide cases, they provide little information on crime victims (Akman & Normandeau, 1980). The key point here is that, while some criminologists derive valuable information from police data, especially homicide statistics,[7] these data are not produced to answer the kinds of questions we often have as ordinary citizens or as students of criminology. Rather, as W. Gordon West (1984, p. 7) points out, the data

> serve the administrative needs of state agencies, justifying programs, budgets, personnel complement, and the like. This not only suggests

---

[7]See Ellis and DeKeseredy (1996) for a detailed analysis of both U.S. and Canadian homicide data produced by police.

that some of the statistics may be self-serving, but that many research questions are not directly addressed (such as how delinquency develops).

We will return to these issues in Chapter 4, where we will look at other problems with crime data, such as the class bias reflected in the focus on street crimes at the expense of crimes of the powerful, such as corporate violence.

However, official crime data are not limited to police statistics. In response to the preceding and other criticisms, criminal justice institutions such as the U.S. Bureau of Justice Statistics, the Solicitor General of Canada, and the British Home Office have conducted *victimization surveys*. In these studies, people in households mathematically computed to be representative of all households might be asked to report on crimes committed against them; on the economic, physical, and psychological impact of these events; and on their perceptions of both crime and the criminal justice system (Silverman, 1992). While victimization surveys have several objectives, their primary purpose has been to uncover the extent and distribution of crimes that are not reported to the police.

Official victimization surveys, such as the U.S. National Crime Victimization Survey (NCVS), the British Crime Survey, and the Canadian Urban Victimization Survey, provide a more realistic image of crime than police data. Even so, like all modes of collecting data, they have several pitfalls, which will be discussed in Chapter 4. Examples of these problems include the lack of attention given to corporate and white-collar crimes; the lack of attention to "victimless crimes" (for example, drug use and prostitution); and several gender, class, and ethnic dimensions of victimization.

Another major source of official knowledge are the *special commissions* established by governments to examine various issues of concern to policy-makers, the general public, and researchers. Recent examples of such commissions include the U.S. Attorney General's Commission on Pornography and the Canadian Panel on Violence Against Women. Special commissions generally consist of various experts on the particular subject of inquiry; they obtain data from several sources, such as police and court statistics and oral testimony by individual citizens, members of community groups, and state agents. Information is also gathered in special research studies (Currie, DeKeseredy, & MacLean, 1990; West, 1984). After the data collected from all of these sources are analyzed, a report containing policy proposals is made available to the general public.

Like police data and victimization surveys, special commissions have limitations. First, they rely on state-sanctioned definitions of topics, issues, and concerns. Thus, they are generally biased against alternative positions. Second, despite the availability of a wide range of empirical data, they tend to rely on methodologically problematic official statistics and information provided by spokespersons for the criminal justice system and special interest groups (West, 1984). Third, the commissions' recommendations are rarely put into operation, and if they are, such suggestions often take years to implement.

Dawn Currie, Walter DeKeseredy, and Brian MacLean (1990) list a few other problems with the knowledge produced by special commissions. For example, they contend that these panels are usually commissioned only after a crisis has emerged, such as a popular uproar over an incident of police brutality or racism. Hence, they are at best reactive and often more concerned with political damage control than progressive social change, especially if they happen to be operating around election time. Moreover, even when commissions attempt to interview a broad cross-section of the community, they generally obtain far too few briefs and testimonies to truly represent the population at large (Currie, DeKeseredy, & MacLean, 1990).

SOCIOLOGICAL KNOWLEDGE OF CRIME

Many sociologists attempt to obtain crime data that is, in their opinion, more accurate than the information obtained through direct and indirect personal experiences, media reports, and official sources. These include smaller victimization and self-report surveys, observational procedures, comparative techniques, and historical methods. It is beyond the scope of this chapter to critically evaluate these techniques of gathering data. Instead, we want to stress that each method has its strengths and limitations and that no technique has a "monopoly on the truth." The value of a given data collection procedure depends on the problem being studied.

One method of gathering data that has been very valuable is the self-report study. Whereas victimization surveys ask persons if they have been the victim of a crime, self-report studies ask persons if they have committed any crimes. Quite a few possible problems with this data source may leap immediately to mind. Perhaps the most important is that no one has ever asked a truly representative group of the population of all potential criminals to fill out such surveys—which means that any results may not be true of all criminals. Who, then, tends to fill out these surveys? For the most part, it has been high school students. This is true for several reasons: where else can you get a reasonable cross-section of the population of a town sitting in one place, who are used to taking tests and following directions?

Self-report studies are widely quoted because they show something very different than official statistics. They show that most people have committed at least some serious crimes (although many have successfully evaded getting caught, like one of the authors of this book, as discussed earlier) and that some people have committed an astounding number of crimes. The opportunity to compare who does and does not get caught to all of those who admit to doing the crimes simply does not exist using official statistics.

There are other reasons to use such instruments as victimization and self-report surveys. We discussed previously the flaws in police data. If a crime victim does not pick up the phone and call the police, then the police usually do not know about the crime. Further, if the police do not take the behavior seriously and fail to file formal reports, as they are commonly accused of doing in cases of family violence, petty theft, or bar fights, then no official data exist. Thus, if a researcher wanted to know the extent and distribution of nonfatal male violence against female intimates (wives, co-habitators, dating partners) but was working in a jurisdiction where the police routinely did not file formal reports on these events, then official statistics would be very misleading. In this case, victimization and self-report surveys would be much more reliable than police statistics.

However, every method contains its own limits and flaws. For example, a survey asking women in the community about their experiences of being victimized by male intimates would provide extensive information on the patterns and distributions of these events, such as whether younger or older women, or members of one racial or ethnic group, or married women or cohabitators, are more at risk. However, unofficial, sociological "number-crunching" techniques would not provide information on the subtle communications between members of all-male alliances that often result in the psychological, sexual, and physical victimization of women (Berg, 1995). To do this one must study a smaller number of people in great depth, through a variety of techniques known as *ethnography.* For example, sexist jokes are a core part of everyday male student life and are frequently used as mechanisms of male "dominance bonding" (Farr, 1988) that might lead to woman abuse (Whitehead, 1976). Researchers rarely can obtain such insights without ethnographic field strategies, such as participant observation, where the researcher actually participates in the male group's activities (DeKeseredy & Schwartz, 1993a).

While any one of the methods discussed here and in Chapter 4 can provide a rich vein of information on criminal behavior and the criminal justice system's response to it, the tendency has been to rely only on one research technique, even though this fosters "methodological parochialness" (Sugarman & Hotaling, 1989). Of course, research designs often are determined by time and funding limitations. Ideally, however, sociologists who study crime and other issues should be open-minded and attempt to use a variety of methods, in what has been called "data triangulation" (Denzin, 1978). As Bruce Berg (1995, p. 4) correctly points out:

> By combining several lines of sight, researchers obtain a better, more substantive picture of reality; a richer more complete array of symbols and theoretical concepts; and a means of verifying many of these elements.

R. Emerson Dobash and Russell Dobash's (1979, 1983) context-specific study of wife abuse is an excellent example of methodological triangulation. They conducted in-depth interviews with 109 battered Scottish women, analyzed 34,724 police and court records, examined historical documents, studied media coverage, and arranged informal interviews with members of social agencies. By combining quantitative methods with historical, institutional, and interaction research strategies, Dobash and Dobash's methodology brought researchers closer to bridging the gap between micro- and macrolevels of analysis of wife abuse. We can only hope that other sociological criminologists will adopt the context-specific model to help provide a true "image of crime."

SUMMARY

The main objective of this chapter was to answer the question, Where do we get our knowledge of crime? Consistent with the argument that humans are social animals who accumulate crime information from a variety of social interactions and institutions, we have shown that people's knowledge of crime is derived from four major sources: personal experience, media exposure, official data banks and actors, and sociological research. Each of these sources has strengths and limitations, and the value of each is contingent on the type of criminological problem being investigated.

Thus, the question becomes, Is one of the four basic kinds of data better than the others? One can argue, as do Piers Beirne and James Messerschmidt (1991), that, in principal, one data source is not necessarily better than another. However, this assertion is aimed primarily at scientific methods of accumulating knowledge. Not surprisingly, as sociologists who are grounded in research on various types of crime and their control, we believe that empirical sociological methods provide a much more accurate understanding of the extent, distribution, nature, and causes of crime and of methods of control than do personal experiences, media reports, and official agents and agencies.

SUGGESTED READINGS

Cohen, S. (1980). *Folk Devils and Moral Panics,* 2nd ed. New York: St. Martin's Press.

> In this widely cited book, the author offers empirical findings on, and a theoretical explanation of, the societal reaction to the mid-1960s conflicts between the British Mods and Rockers.

Fattah, E., and Sacco, V. (1989). *Crime and Victimization of the Elderly.* New York: Springer-Verlag.

> Although this book focuses mainly on the elderly as victims and perpetrators of crime, Chapter 10 includes an excellent review of a large body of empirical research on fear of crime.

Livingston, J. (1992). *Crime and Criminology.* Englewood Cliffs, NJ: Prentice-Hall.

> Similar to Chapter 10 in Fattah and Sacco's book, Chapter 2 in this text provides a highly intelligible summary of some of the major findings on fear of crime.

Surette, R. (1992). *Media Crime and Justice: Images and Realities.* Pacific Grove, CA: Brooks/Cole.

This book is one of the most comprehensive analyses of the various issues in the media's relationship to crime and criminal justice.

West, W. G. (1984). *Young Offenders and the State: A Canadian Perspective on Delinquency.* Toronto: Butterworths.

The book is an excellent analysis of Canadian research on youth crime. Chapter 1 includes a detailed critique of the various ways in which we acquire information on juvenile delinquency.

DEFINITIONS OF CRIME

Think of a crime, any crime. Picture the first "crime" that comes into your mind. What do you see? The odds are you are not imagining a mining company executive sitting at his desk, calculating the cost of proper safety precautions and deciding not to invest in them. Probably what you do see with your mind's eye is one person physically attacking another or robbing something from another via the threat of physical attack.

REIMAN, 1995, PP. 59–60

Each year, at the start of introductory criminology courses, hundreds, perhaps even thousands, of instructors ask their students, "What is crime?" Of course, most students have never been exposed to the definitional debates in criminology. Further, as we saw in Chapter 1, most student knowledge about crime is derived from direct and indirect experiences with crime, media images, and community gossip. Thus, not surprisingly, Reiman's quote does accurately describe most responses. Most people would give a *legalistic* definition—one suggesting that crimes are acts that violate the criminal law. The process of definition is simple: just open the law book and see what laws are there. Certainly, the legalistic response is the most common response, but it still is just one of many possible answers to the question, "What is crime?"

The primary objective of this chapter is to make you sensitive to the fact that there are other answers: that there is substantial disagreement within the criminological community and among policymakers and the general public over what behaviors should and should not be designated as criminal. In the discussion that follows, we critically review the legalistic approach and two of several major sociological definitions offered by criminologists: (1) the societal reaction/labeling approach and (2) the critical approach. We turn first to the legal definition.

THE LEGALISTIC DEFINITION

For many criminologists, state officials, and members of the general public, the word *crime* for the most part refers to behaviors that are officially designated as criminal by law. In other words, to decide what is a crime, we don't refer to our personal list of rights and wrongs. We simply open up the state, federal, or local criminal law book and see what the appropriate legislature has placed there.

The Consensus Model

Although he wrote close to fifty years ago, Paul Tappan is probably still the most prominently quoted advocate of a legalistic approach to defining crime. He asserted that "crime is an intentional action in violation of criminal law . . . committed without defense or justification, and sanctioned by the state as a felony or misdemeanor" (1947, p. 100).[1] Tappan's definition encompasses many behaviors that most, if not all, of us strongly disapprove of, such as murder, armed robbery, rape, and automobile theft. Often, this method of discussing the roots of the criminal law is termed the *consensus model.* The basic idea is that the people generally agree that a behavior is bad and should be criminalized, and the legislators react by passing a law. Here, the process of passing new legislation can be seen as consensus building: an individual or group may start out in the minority but slowly acquire more and more friends and partners until it has enough popular support that the legislature is forced to act.

As we shall see later in this chapter, this is not the only way to define crime or to describe how laws come into being. However, we can easily understand what a crime is to Tappan and other proponents of the legalistic approach. If it is against the criminal law, it is a crime. Behaviors that are not officially outlawed cannot be labeled crimes.

---

[1] Each state, province, or country will define these technical terms in its own way, but generally a person can break laws with a *very* narrowly defined "justification," such as trespassing to call an ambulance for a dying person. A police officer can carry a gun and can use it under specific circumstances that may not apply to other citizens. How crimes are defined as "felonies" or "misdemeanors" is also decided by each state. Generally, felonies are more serious crimes for which one *could* get one year or more in prison, while misdemeanors have a *maximum* sentence of less than one year.

Legalists should not be considered naive people who are unaware that there is a great deal of behavior that is very dangerous but not officially criminally outlawed. They may well know that crooked real estate agents are cheating people out of their life's savings, that the local factory is dumping deadly chemicals into the area's drinking water, or that telephone solicitors are targeting gullible consumers and selling them inferior or even dangerous merchandise. Nevertheless, they would argue, if your particular state or country has not gotten around to putting these actions into the criminal code, then they are *not* criminal acts. Of course, these actions may be violations of various administrative codes. The unethical real estate agent, for example, may be subject to an administrative hearing with a possible penalty of a loss of license. Certainly, to a professional real estate broker who may have spent thousands of dollars in tuition to take the courses necessary to get the license in the first place, losing such a license is serious. But it is not criminal, because it is not stated as such in the criminal law books.

Susan Shapiro, for example, disapproves of scholars who expand the meaning of terms such as *white-collar crime.* There are a tremendous number of harms (often noncriminal) that corporations intentionally do as part of their quest to make money. The actions of these scholars, she feels,

> derives from their outrage that powerful corporations are able to manipulate the law to spare their delicts from criminal penalties, but, by definitionally stipulating all illicit acts as crimes, their moral outrage has clouded their sociological good sense. (1983, p. 306)

Shapiro feels that it is none of our business what the legislature wants to criminalize, that scholars should not be advocates for change. Rather, we should study the law as it exists.

The Change in Laws over Time

Shapiro's views are difficult to understand, given that few legalistic theorists would argue that the criminal law is cast in stone and can never be changed. They are aware that our beliefs about crime evolve and change, and that behaviors may at one point be legal and at another point illegal, depending on the consensus of the majority of society. For example, opiates such as morphine are considered among the most serious drugs abused in North America today. We spend billions of dollars on law enforcement, trying to stop people from using opiates. Yet in the late 1800s, there were few important laws on the use of drugs. Drugs were sold over the counter in pharmacies without a prescription. They were even used as ingredients in over-the-counter remedies. People who took quite a bit of certain cough syrups probably had more addictive drugs in their system than many street addicts today! Some people have speculated that as much as 2 percent of the U.S. population was addicted to drugs. Perhaps many people were not happy about this state of affairs. But it wasn't illegal.

For a number of reasons that are unique to North America in general and to the United States in particular, the situation has changed over the past one hundred years. Where previously an enormous number of people were addicted to drugs and society didn't much care, we now devote enormous resources to a criminal justice system that punishes people who take the same drugs our great-grandmothers did. See Box 2.1 for one person's idea of how to change the law yet again.

Another excellent example of how our view of the definition of what is a crime changes is the early twentieth-century prohibition against the sale of alcohol. Anyone who grew up watching Elliot Ness in the "Untouchables" on TV certainly knows that the sale and importing of beer, wine, and liquor was made illegal in the United States in 1919. If you were a beer distributor in 1925, perhaps Ness and his G-men would burst in, machine guns blazing, and destroy your business before hauling you off to prison. If you were a beer distributor in 1935, after the repeal of Prohibition, you might have been a solid businessperson, counted on by local charities and the Chamber of Commerce to show up to accept your awards for good citizenship.

Later in this book, we will go into more detail on why the drug commonly cited as the number-one contributor to health problems in the United States (alcohol) was changed from illegal to legal while a drug with considerably fewer health risks (marijuana) was criminalized at roughly the same time. What's important here is to recognize that most people have a legalistic view of crime. If you break the law (sell beer in 1925, sell marijuana in 1945) you are a criminal. If you do not break the law (sell beer in 1945, sell marijuana in 1925) then you are not.

And this is a key point: How do we decide what behavior is criminal? In the case of drugs, since many of us think that it is very important to protect ourselves by making drug sales and use illegal, perhaps we should look at how we go about deciding *which* drugs we need to protect ourselves against. After all, if the only reason to criminalize drugs is to protect ourselves as a society, we need to think about what harm is involved. This is essential to helping us define what is a crime and what is not.

One would think that, if the reason we make some drugs illegal is to protect people, then we would be making the *most dangerous* drugs illegal. Yet we seem to do this only selectively. After his office completed a review of two thousand scientific studies on the subject, former U.S. Surgeon General C. Everett Koop argued that tobacco is every bit as addictive as heroin or cocaine. Given the direct link between nicotine addiction and various cancers, lung diseases, and heart failure, researchers have estimated the number of *annual* deaths from this drug at between 350,000 and 500,000 in the United States alone. No other drug can come even close to matching this horror story. As James Henslin (1994) points out, the kind of deaths that tobacco causes tend to be slow, lingering, and particularly painful, which means tremendous psychological, physical, and financial (health care) costs for victims and their families. He estimates the health-care expenses and lost production and wages from smoking-related sickness to be roughly $28 billion annually. These mind-boggling numbers make it plain that if your measure for making a drug illegal is the harm it does to the individual, our absolute number-one priority should be to outlaw cigarette smoking immediately. What has been the U.S. government's reaction? Has there been a massive move to criminalize smoking and a federal "War on Tobacco"? Actually, the U.S. Department of Agriculture has an active program to subsidize and support tobacco farmers. Some of the government's most powerful figures, such as Senator Jesse Helms of North Carolina, come from tobacco-growing states and provide strong support for the tobacco industry.

Another drug that we know is very dangerous is alcohol. One effect of alcohol is particularly hard to measure, because we don't know exactly how many people die in alcohol-related fights, household accidents, or falls each year. We do know that alcohol abuse can make many diseases much worse and that more than 25,000 people die each year from cirrhosis of the liver, which is directly caused by alcohol abuse. Certainly, we know that tens of thousands of lives are taken each year in alcohol-related automobile accidents. Of course, you may quickly interject, that is only when the drug (alcohol) is abused—it isn't dangerous at all when used in responsible

BOX 2.1

WANT A REAL CRIME-FIGHTING PLAN? ASK A STREET COP

They're all over television and the papers talking about crime: the president, his aides, members of Congress, lawyers, professors. They are promising this and that and vowing to do such and such.

But I've noticed the absence of one group that might be expected to have some opinion on crime and what, if anything, can be done to reduce it.

Cops.

Oh, once in a while you might get a high-ranking police official, a chief of some big-city department. But police brass sound like the politicians, since they deal with budgets, manpower charts and other administrative matters.

By cops, I mean the men and women who go out on the street every day and try to solve crimes and arrest criminals.

In all the blather coming out of Washington about crime, and what the big spenders will do about it, the invisible man is the street cop.

So the morning after President Clinton blew hot air at the nation, I called a friend who has been a cop for many years. He's worked on homicides, robberies, rapes—just about every form of foul behavior.

Because he aspires to higher rank, and clout still means something in the Chicago Police Department, it wouldn't help his career to be known as my friend. So his name can't be used.

But he's real. And when I asked him what his reaction was to the current anti-crime frenzy in the White House and Congress, he said, "It's a lot of bull——."

He elaborated. "There's nothing we haven't heard before. 'Three strikes and you're out.' We already send up three-time losers in Illinois. Hasn't done anything to the crime rate. 'Build more prisons.' We can't build enough prisons to hold all the bad guys. 'Tougher gun laws.' Look, the only people the gun laws affect are honest people. Frankly, I wish every decent family in America had a gun and knew how to use it.

"Besides, federal crime laws don't mean a thing to me, because about 95 percent of the crimes in this country are local, not federal. The feds aren't dealing with shootings in saloons or guys going nuts and killing their wives and kids or the neighbors. Most of their busts are white-collar.

"Now, I'm in a minority, but a lot of cops agree with me on this. And that's the drug laws. We're wasting our time trying to control that crap.

We're wasting billions of dollars and throwing people in jail who are just self-destructive goofs.

"We'd be better off doing what we do with liquor and cigarettes: tax them and license the sale. Sure, people abuse booze, and they smoke. But smoking is way down, because most people know it's bad for them. The same thing with booze: more white wine and light beer and fewer boilermakers.

"It's the same thing with drugs. Right now, most people don't use drugs. If you legalize it, most people still won't use drugs.

"But if you take away the illegal profit motive, there go the drug peddlers, the gangs and the other serious crime. And most of the police and political corruption.

"Then you wouldn't have thousands of cops wasting their time trying to bust some small-time dealer. You wouldn't have them clogging up the courts and filling up cells that somebody dangerous should be in.

"But you don't hear the politicians say that, because they're afraid of the people who say: 'I don't want my kids buying drugs.' Hey, lady, if your kid wants to buy drugs right now, he can do it. And maybe he already is.

"Look back 20 years. Anybody who said we ought to legalize gambling in Illinois was treated like a nut. Now we got gambling boats all over Illinois. We're going to have them in Chicago and the suburbs. And it's no big deal. The sky isn't falling.

"Same thing with drugs. What, somebody is going to smoke some marijuana at home, listen to music, then go out and shoot everybody he sees? No, he's going to fall asleep and get up the next morning with less of a hangover than if he drank three boilermakers.

"Now, if you legalize the stuff and tax it, you save billions of dollars that we're wasting now, and you bring in a lot of extra money from the taxes.

"Then you take that money and use some of it for rehabbing the junkies.

"But you also find ways to invest it in places like the West Side, in public works projects or to help start private businesses that will create jobs. Because that's where it all started, the craziness and the higher crime rate. When the low-skill jobs disappeared, the husbands were out of work and they disappeared. And that's why we have all these one-parent or no-parent families that turn out the street criminals.

"Hey, but what do I know? I only go out there and arrest them, fill out the paperwork and go to court. It's not like I'm some expert in Washington and get on C-Span."

SOURCE: Mike Royko, *Chicago Tribune*. Reprinted by permission of Tribune Media Services.

moderation. This is absolutely true, and if you find either of the authors of this book at a criminology conference, they likely will have a beer in hand. Yet, this statement is just as true for many illegal drugs—that, used in responsible moderation, they are not particularly dangerous.

Many scholars have suggested that our definition of various crimes depends on who is engaging in the behaviors. For example, David Musto (1987) has argued that most illegal drugs in the United States have become illegal as we have come to associate their use with certain minority groups. When whites began to believe that cocaine made African-Americans wild, immune to small-caliber bullets, and prone to commit sexual assault, that drug was criminalized. Likewise, marijuana was made illegal only when it became connected with Mexican-Americans; the same is true for heroin and youth gangs. Other scholars have been even stronger in their analyses: such anti-drug laws were designed, John Helmer (1975) argues, to give the police powers to drive Chinese-Americans and Mexican-Americans out of the country, or at least to exclude them from American society (Mann, 1993).

We could cite dozens of other situations in which the definition of what is or is not a criminal act has changed over the years. For example, the United States has had many laws enforcing racial segregation and discrimination, most of which have been repealed or declared unconstitutional. So, if you are African-American and choose to sit in the front of a bus in Montgomery, Alabama, as Rosa Parks did in 1955, are you a criminal? She was arrested and charged, but the law was later found unconstitutional and overturned. Still, according to Tappan's definition, she was a criminal.

So, the legalistic definition can put us into a difficult position. If you use a dangerous drug that has been officially labeled illegal, you can be arrested and imprisoned, and you can lose your license to practice your profession. It is hard to keep a marriage and family together when one member is branded a criminal and sent to prison. But, if you choose to use an equally dangerous drug that has not been officially labeled illegal, all that you need to do is to avoid being intoxicated in public, driving under the influence, or smoking in a no-smoking zone. As we shall see later in this chapter and again in Chapter 10, the same issues arise in many contexts: we often need to decide that some things are against the law and some things are not. How do we make these decisions? Who makes these decisions? Why is it murder to kill a woman with a handgun but not to kill her by purposely providing an unsafe working environment in order to increase profits?

What Is and What Should Be

The problem with this discussion is how easily it moves from a descriptive level to a proscriptive level. In other words, most criminologists would at least partially agree with the basic descriptive premise that what is illegal is what is against the criminal law. The debate in criminology centers on whether this *should* be the case. For example, some critics contend that just because some actions are prohibited by law does not mean that they are harmful to society and should be criminalized. Legal theorists, who love to use Latin whenever possible, refer to such crimes as *mala prohibita.* Since *mala* means "bad," the phrase should be easy to interpret: crimes that are *mala prohibita* are bad because they are prohibited. They may not be harmful, but they are illegal (bad) because we said so. An easy example of this is traffic lights: by law, we go on the green and stop on the red. There is nothing in the Bible or the Koran suggesting which light to stop on (except, perhaps, suggestions that we should obey the secular law). Society established this law because it is a convenient way to safely and efficiently move automobile traffic. We could have gone on the red and stopped on the green. The alternative to this, *mala in se,* supposedly refers to crimes that are bad in and of themselves, such as murder or rape. Again, later in the book, we will discuss whether this distinction is particularly sound.

In any case, many criminologists feel that some *mala prohibita* crimes need not be part of the criminal law. Edwin Schur (1974) referred to acts such as gambling, prostitution, narcotic use, and abortion as "victimless crimes" that do not involve a clear-cut victim or offender. Instead, drug deals, high-stakes poker games, and sex with prostitutes constitute

> the exchange between willing partners of strongly desired goods and services. The "offense" in such a situation, then, consists of a consensual transaction—one person gives or sells another person something he or she wants. (Schur, 1974, p. 6)

Another way of looking at the same issue, some criminologists argue, is that these social exchanges are issues of private morality rather than major threats to the conventional social order (Hagan, 1985). Therefore, they should be exempt from criminal prosecution.

Others who want victimless crimes excluded from the criminal law warn us about the dangers of "overcriminalization." Norval Morris and Gordon Hawkins (1969), Gary Marx (1988), and Robert Elias (1986), for example, argue that applying criminal "labels" to drug abuse, prostitution, public drunkenness, gambling, and similar behaviors can create trouble for society. First, it gives a criminal record to the people who engage in them. People with criminal records are less likely to succeed in school, get good jobs, or find paths to conventional careers. Worse yet, it can actually create new crimes, or new opportunities for crime, such as the following:

- Drug laws often result in "golden" economic opportunities for organized crime groups. Groups that are unable to penetrate deeply into crime circles can suddenly make extraordinary amounts of money and gain tremendous influence by taking advantage of the fact that many popular drugs are illegal. When the United States made alcohol sale illegal in the 1920s, many illegal entrepreneurs made enormous fortunes by selling people what they wanted—alcohol. Names like Al Capone became household words.

- To the extent that criminal laws are actually successful in reducing the amount of drugs on the streets, the main result will be higher drug prices, which in turn will influence some people to steal or to commit violent crimes in order to purchase the more expensive drugs to support their habits (Inciardi, 1992).

- Where prostitution is illegal, both female and male prostitutes are discouraged from seeking the help of the police to deal with violent clients. Anti-prostitution legislation forces some "hookers" to purchase protection from "pimps," who often beat and rape them. Other prostitutes who do not have such "protection" suffer from extreme and repeated violence at the hands of their clients (Miller, 1993).

- To control victimless crimes, which typically take place behind closed doors, the police often use illegal forms of law enforcement such as entrapment, illegal wiretaps, and illegal searches (Marx, 1988). Some officers may even accept bribes from drug dealers and owners of illegal gambling establishments because they may not be personally in favor of the legal prohibition of their activities or because the officers themselves use drugs or turn to prostitutes for sexual pleasure.

Criminologists refer to this process of overcriminalization as *amplifying crime* because it increases crime. Laws against "victimless crime" do not create crime where none ever existed before. Rather, they create a situation in which laws and enforcement create more crime than would exist without the laws and enforcement. All of this occurs in an atmosphere in which already strained criminal justice resources are spread thin. Police and other law enforcement authorities have to make daily decisions about what to make top priorities. No police department has the staff to pay equal attention to all laws. If a large percentage of policing time, energy, money, and personnel is devoted to drugs and other "victimless crimes," then these resources are not available for the control and prevention of far more serious criminal activities, such as wife-beating, homicide, kidnapping, and child abuse. For these and other reasons, some criminologists argue that many "victimless crimes" should be decriminalized.

No doubt, many of you have noticed a rather large problem with these arguments. The whole discussion has been based on the presumption that these crimes are *mala prohibita*. What if, in your personal moral code, they are *mala in se*? What if you feel that it is inherently evil to take drugs, get an abortion, visit a prostitute (whether male or female), gamble, or be intoxicated in public? In the next section, we will deal with this problem: my criminal acts are your fun and games, and vice versa.

Challenges to Legalistic Definitions

Meanwhile, however, let's address an issue that bridges the discussions in these two sections. Some people have tried to define crime as including those acts that are harmful to society at large. Perhaps the most common complaint about legalistic definitions is that in most jurisdictions they exclude or minimize the very events that are *most* harmful to us. Many criminologists have pointed out that, in addition to behaviors prohibited by criminal law, another broad group of behaviors cause extensive social, economic, physical, and environmental harm. These include corporate crimes and the wrongdoings of government agencies. If these misdeeds are more harmful to us than street crimes, why are they exempt from criminal prosecution? We will deal with this issue in depth both in the next section and in later chapters; for now, we will limit ourselves to two points.

When most people think of crime as a danger to their children, they think of street crime only.

First, legalistic definitions can divert our attention from the "crimes at the top" just mentioned. As Jeffrey Reiman (1995, p. 61) points out, a narrow legal definition acts

> like a set of blinders. It keeps us from calling a mine disaster a mass murder even if ten men are killed, even if someone is responsible for the unsafe working conditions in which they worked and died. I contend that this particular piece of mental furniture so blocks our view that it keeps us from using the criminal justice system to protect ourselves from the greatest threats to our persons and possessions.

Interestingly, threats from powerful members of our society are generally dealt with by civil or administrative law and are not punishable by criminal penalties such as prison (Schwartz & Ellison, 1984).

Second, although some criminologists have focused on the crimes of large corporations (Hills, 1987), others point out that the normal behavior of society's elite may be very dangerous to the rest of us. The most influential of these latter theorists are Herman and Julia Schwendinger (1975), who argued that the concept of crime should be expanded to include such things as economic violence. Therefore, crime would consist not only of stealing a purse but also of providing a society in which a few individuals live in the world's greatest wealth while many others are homeless, have no health care, and are unable to provide reasonable food, clothing, and shelter for themselves even with full-time work at minimum wages. In short, the Schwendingers are concerned about racism, sexism, and poverty, which they feel should be criminalized as human rights violations. They note that we provide long prison sentences for purse snatchers but none for persons who can manipulate prices to drive millions into poverty.

To summarize, the point of legalistic definitions is to define crime simply as those activities that are against the law. Criminals, then, are the people who commit crimes. To be a criminologist, to study criminals, one need only look to see who has been arrested or convicted of crimes and treat them as legitimate objects of criminological research.

In response to all of the criticisms of legalistic definitions of crime,[2] some criminologists have developed alternative approaches, such as societal reaction/labeling definitions.

SOCIETAL REACTION/LABELING DEFINITIONS

A number of theoretical traditions are included in this definition, some of which are rather radical in their approach. The basic approach, however, is the same: they are all primarily concerned with how we label people as criminal. In the previous section on legalistic definitions, we discussed the fact that legalistic theorists rarely have a problem about whom to study in criminology: one studies the people who are criminals. Sometimes, however, this is a bit difficult. If you are talking about anyone who has ever broken a

---

[2]See Beirne and Messerschmidt (1991), Hagan (1985), Lynch and Groves (1989), Quinney and Wildeman (1991), and Schwendinger and Schwendinger (1975).

law, you no longer are dealing with criminology but rather with *sociology*—the study of society. Not to get religious on you ("Let he or she who is without sin cast the first stone . . ."), but how many of you have *never* broken one of your state laws? Have you gone a few miles over the speed limit? Perhaps driven after having a couple of beers? Shoplifted a candy bar? Smoked a joint? In many U.S. states, having consensual sexual relations when unmarried is a crime. In fact, in about half the states, engaging in anal or oral sex is a serious crime, even between married people. Those of you (and there are some) who have done *none* of the above are in a distinct minority when compared to the other readers of this book.

So then, do criminologists really study all of those people who break the law? No, that isn't what we *really* want. We know that there is something else out there that we want to study: "them"—"the criminals." The problem is how to come up with a definition of "them" that separates out "us," the people who commit dozens of crimes but aren't "them." To handle this problem, most criminologists limit their study group to people who have been arrested or who have been convicted. In many ways, everyone agrees, the best group to study are those who have been convicted. Although innocent people are convicted of crimes, most of us believe that there are fewer of these people than there are innocent people arrested, and much fewer than innocent people accused. So, we get the most guilty people and the fewest innocent people by studying those convicted in a court of law.

Still, many criminologists are hesitant to use only groups of convicted people in their study groups. The group itself is fairly small when compared to all people who are arrested or all people who commit crimes. If you believe that there are biases in the criminal justice system, then you will be especially leery of focusing solely on convicted persons. If you believe that courts are racially or sexually or class biased (meaning, for example, that young, poor black men are more likely to be convicted than similarly accused rich white men), then this bias should show up in your study group if you only study convicted people. For this reason, many criminologists who do this type of research compromise by studying people who have been arrested. It may not be a very good compromise, but it is the compromise most widely used nevertheless. Thus, criminology faced the interesting problem of being unable to concretely decide even who the criminals might be.

Crime as a Social Construct

The labeling theorists, in some ways, stood criminology on its very head. Until the 1960s, virtually all criminologists had one question to ask: Now that we have this group of criminals to study (arrested people), what can we find out about them that sets them apart from the rest of the population? In other words, what makes Johnny a criminal? Is he crazy, angry, deprived, bad, mad, sad, or just a cad? Why is he doing these things that got him arrested? The labeling theorists asked instead: What made you decide that Johnny is a criminal? This is a very powerful question when explored in all of its implications. *Who* decided that what Johnny did was to be considered a criminal act? *Who* decided that what other people like Johnny did *wasn't* a criminal act? *Who* decided that Johnny should be arrested? Didn't we just say that almost every one of us has committed crimes? In Chapter 1, we pointed out that one of your authors did some serious stuff as a teenager. Why is Johnny being studied as a criminal instead of him?

In the most extreme (and most controversial) formulation, the societal reaction/labeling definitions do not view *any* act as inherently deviant or criminal. Think about that for a minute. Perhaps you can understand why this perspective was seen as such a major attack on criminology when it was introduced thirty years ago. There is *nothing* inherently criminal? Not murder? Rape? Aggravated assault? Whatever could these people be thinking?

They were thinking that "crime" is a social construct or a "label" attached to a behavior during the course of social interaction between lawbreakers and law enforcers (West, 1984). Perhaps the most well-known proponent of this viewpoint is Howard Becker.[3] He contends that

> *social groups create deviance by making the rules whose infraction constitutes deviance,* and by applying those rules to particular people and labelling them as outsiders. From this point of view, deviance is *not* a quality of the act the person commits, but rather a consequence of the application by others of rules and sanctions to an "offender." The deviant is one to whom that label has successfully been applied; deviant behavior is behavior that people so label. (1973, p. 9)

---

[3]Other well-known formulators of societal reaction/labeling definitions are Erikson (1962), Kitsuse (1962), Lemert (1951), and Tannenbaum (1938).

The rationale for Becker's argument can be found in both criminological research and perhaps your own personal experiences. Let's try to illustrate this with a simple formula. We said earlier that most people would define a criminal as a person who breaks the law. Certainly, our best definition of a criminal is a person who has been convicted of a major crime. Thus, our formula takes into account both whether you did the crime and whether you are convicted in a court of law:

criminal act + conviction = criminal

This should be relatively unproblematic, particularly if we assure you that we have a direct line of access to God and we know that you are in fact guilty of this crime. However, what if our "direct line" shows us that you are innocent but, through some unfortunate miscarriage of justice, you are convicted anyway? Thus, the formula becomes:

no criminal act + conviction = ___?___

Well, are you a criminal or not? Unfortunately, even if you didn't commit the crime, you can fill in the blank with the word "criminal." You have been convicted in a competent court of law, and you are officially the holder of the label "criminal." There's an old joke about the guy who interviewed the prisoners in a jail and became confused about the purpose of the institution because everyone in it told him that he was innocent! The reality is, if you are convicted in a court of law, you are guilty. Whatever happens to convicts will happen to you: execution, prison, lost licenses, a permanent record, destroyed families, a ruined career, or whatever.

Let's try this again:

criminal act + no conviction = ___?___

Perhaps you have caught on by now. There may be evidence that you are guilty, but who cares? You were not convicted. You are innocent for all earthly purposes. An obvious example of this is Oliver North, who in 1994 ran for the U.S. Senate from Virginia and just barely lost. He had previously been convicted of felony crimes, but the convictions were overturned on a legal technicality. It did not make any difference whether he committed the crime or not or whether the original trial court found him guilty. Since his conviction was overturned, he was considered innocent for all legal purposes and thus was legally able to run for the Senate. This was not particularly controversial; if he had won the election, he would have been seated as a senator, not refused a seat as a convicted felon.

What was the point of all of this? Simply to emphasize that the one element that didn't make the slightest bit of difference as to whether you were to be a "criminal" or not was *whether or not you committed the crime!* What counted was whether you were convicted in a court of law. Refer back to Becker's quote about deviance as a social construct. He was speaking much more broadly about how you could commit some behavior that you might consider to be perfectly normal but that those around you might successfully label as deviant. If they react poorly to you, you are a deviant. If they react well or don't react, then you are not a deviant. For example, in the 1990s, many male editors in big publishing houses wear long hair and even ponytails. If no one minds, then there is no problem. In the 1950s, however, these same men would have successfully been labeled as deviant and no doubt fired. Same behavior, different reaction. Becker's conclusion: that there is nothing about the behavior of wearing a ponytail that determines whether or not you are a deviant. All that counts is what reaction you get from the people around you.

Becker's argument relates to some of the discussion in Chapter 1. Although both affluent and disenfranchised people commit violent crimes (sometimes in different contexts and for different reasons), there are significant differences in the social and legal responses to their actions. Although we know that few robbers actually plan to kill their victims (Reasons, Ross, & Paterson, 1991), poor people who accidentally kill bank tellers while attempting to rob them are labeled as murderers and are subject to harsh punishment. On the other hand, corporate executives who create unsafe work conditions are often exempt from both formal censure and prosecution, despite the fact that their decisions result in injuries and even death for thousands of people each year (Hills, 1987).

A Canadian provincial head of the government agency responsible for occupational health and safety inspection explains the rationale behind such practices. To justify the lenient treatment of corporate executives who violate safety standards, he argues:

> We are not dealing with criminals when we take people to court. A guy who breaks into your house knows what he is doing and knows the consequences and probably has been through the process before.

To be dragged before a judge and be sentenced to twelve months in jail is not pleasant to him, but it is not unexpected, and it isn't demeaning to him; he will stand there with a smile on his face and be defiant. When we are talking about individuals or entities being prosecuted for infractions of Occupational Health and Safety legislation, we are talking about an entirely different animal. We are talking about a person who basically is honest and an upright citizen. We are talking basically of a person who finds this process of being prosecuted and having this process publicized extremely distasteful. (quoted in Reschenthaler, 1979, pp. 82–83)

This is just what Jeffrey Reiman (1995) was talking about when he chose the title for one of his books: *The Rich Get Richer and the Poor Get Prison.*

Class and Race in Criminology

If you are trying to figure out how to compare burglary with occupational safety law violations, this example may be a bit difficult to understand. This subjective process of labeling occurs, however, even when affluent and poorer people commit the same crimes. We briefly mentioned in Chapter 1 what a self-report survey could do. One frequently used technique is to ask younger people to report anonymously on a survey form what offenses they have committed. A common finding is that, except for the most serious crimes, there are few variations in the proportion of offenses committed by middle- and lower-class young offenders (Currie, 1985; Elliott & Huizinga, 1983; Reiman, 1995; West, 1984). In other words, for the most part, middle-class youths are committing the same crimes as lower-class youths. However, as we explained in Chapter 1, if members of both social classes commit the same crime, the lower-class youth is more likely to be arrested, charged, and convicted than the middle- or upper-class youth (Liska & Chamlin, 1984; Sampson, 1986; Thornberry, 1973). Similar biases are found in the criminal justice system's response to white and black youths (Beirne & Messerschmidt, 1995; Reiman, 1995). Again, except for serious forms of delinquency, research indicates that black and white offense rates are similar (Elliott & Ageton, 1980; Hindelang, Hirschi, & Weis, 1979; Huizinga & Elliott, 1987). Even so, blacks are much more likely to be arrested, charged, and punished.

In later chapters, we will take up in more detail the arguments that economic and racial bias are important elements in the process of applying "labels" in the criminal justice system. Note that these are not unrelated issues. In fact, it is very hard to discuss one without the other. In the United States, Reiman (1995) argues, African-Americans are disproportionately poor, and African-Americans who are locked up in prisons have the same class background as imprisoned whites. Regardless of whether one is poor or black or both, in Reiman's opinion, the U.S. criminal justice system is more likely to label these people as criminal because it functions to "weed out the wealthy." In other words, it protects upper- and middle-class interests.

As the saying goes, "You don't have to have a Ph.D. to know that." You may recall from Chapter 1 Walter DeKeseredy's observation that, even though he engaged in delinquent activities, he escaped punishment while others who did similar things did not. To further illustrate this phenomenon, consider this experience: DeKeseredy was forced to take what was in his opinion a "very boring" high school history class. To break the monotony of lectures, he would periodically throw textbooks out of the classroom window. He was never caught until one day when a book landed on a geography teacher's head. Unfortunately, DeKeseredy was looking out the window and the "victim" saw him. The geography teacher dashed upstairs to the classroom and informed the history teacher. Not surprisingly, De-Keseredy expected to be sent immediately to the principal's office, but he was not. Instead, the history teacher simply told him to calm down and to never throw any more books out of windows. Keep in mind that De-Keseredy was, and still is, a member of the middle-class.

Some working-class students in the same history class were not so lucky. Two or three of them would occasionally throw chalk or erasers at each other, and when they were caught they were sent promptly to the principal's office for punishment. Were they more deviant than DeKeseredy? Hardly! In fact, DeKeseredy frequently engaged in criminal "extracurricular activities" (for example, drinking and vandalism) with these people on the weekends. Why, then, were they punished instead of DeKeseredy? William Chambliss (1973) is probably correct when he says that the answer lies in the class structure of society and its formal institutions, such as the school. As Albert Cohen (1955) points out, teachers are generally middle-class people who use middle-class measuring rods to evaluate students, and they often view working-class dress and demeanor negatively. DeKeseredy was probably exempt from punishment because of his middle-class characteristics. According to W. Gordon West (1984), by labeling DeKeseredy's working-class friends as delinquent, the history teacher was maintaining the traditional social structure whereby those already at the bottom of the economic and social heap are kept there.

In summary, societal reaction/labeling approaches can make us sensitive to the subjective nature of defining crime. In the extreme formulations of this approach, nothing and no one is inherently criminal. If you are not labeled as a criminal, then you are not a criminal. This insight has had an enormous impact on several important areas of criminology. In Chapter 4, when we begin to discuss the various indicators of the extent and distribution of crime in North America, we will present research suggesting that police and court statistics may not be accurate indicators of the amount of crime. After all, the more we accept the arguments of the labeling approach, the less we can rely on court and police statistics to tell us much about crime.

This brings us to an essential point about what the labeling approach theorists argue about the proper role of criminological research. Recall that, according to the legalistic theorists, our primary purpose is to ask what it is about the criminals that make them different from the rest of us. Labeling theorists suggest that any differences we find may be the result of whom we decided to put in group I (criminal) and whom we decided to put into group II (not criminal). After all, if most of us have committed at least some criminal acts, why aren't we in group I? While no doubt some of us may have criminal convictions, most of us do not. Why then are we in group II?

The study of crime statistics and criminal justice agencies, labeling theorists argue, may tell us something about the behavior of police and court personnel, but not necessarily about the behavior of criminals. What we should be studying is how and why we decide who gets group I status.

Critique of the Labeling Approach

Still, societal reaction/labeling definitions have been roundly criticized by criminologists ranging from the political right to the political left. The conservative attacks will be discussed in detail in Chapter 6. Primarily, these critics question the empirical validity of the various assertions of this school of thought. They feel that in a great many ways these theorists are quite simply wrong and unable to support their arguments with facts.

The attack from the left is sometimes difficult for students to understand. With every standard textbook saying that the labeling approach "stands mainstream criminology on its head" and attacks seemingly everything that mainstream criminology studies and believes in, most students assume that the labeling approach is a leftist approach that would be automatically embraced by critical scholars. Of course, some of the basic arguments of the labeling approach were in fact adopted by many critical theorists. However, as we shall see, the key formulation of the critical theorists was that criminal justice decisions do not happen in a vacuum. Rather, they are influenced by the type of society we have—an advanced capitalist society based on the maximization of profit, too often at the expense of basic human rights. The critical theorists argue that scholars such as Becker did not explicitly describe the broader structural and cultural forces that influence the criminal justice system's and various other social control agencies' labeling processes. Ian Taylor, Paul Walton, and Jock Young (1973, pp. 168–169), for example, contend that labelists do not "lay bare the structured inequalities in power and interest which underpin processes whereby laws are created and enforced."

Another strong attack from the left is related to this argument. Because labeling researchers often were uninterested in political and economic factors, all too often they seemed to lean toward studying people who were deemed deviant because they had moral beliefs or acted in ways that offended other segments of the population. Labeling theorists were less interested in studying daily street crimes or the behavior of elites. Thus, critics claim that the labeling perspective focuses too much on responses to so-called exotic people (for example, homosexuals, drug users, prostitutes, and so on). To this day, some textbooks on deviant behavior center on what are known, according to student slang on many campuses, as "nuts, sluts, and preverts." Alex Liazos (1973) was one of the first to point out that many labeling theorists were more interested in wife-swapping (no one ever mentioned husband-swapping in those days), massage parlors, and prostitutes than they were in "the everyday oppression that affects a large number of persons" (Davis & Stasz, 1990, p. 46). Examples of this oppression are poverty, unemployment, and racism—topics that critical criminologists obviously are more interested in.

THE CRITICAL APPROACH

In the section on legalistic definitions of crime, we said that another way of approaching that perspective is to call it the *consensus model.* The basic premise is that people agree on what should be against the law; the way to get a new law is to slowly build coalitions until a majority of the people want the law.

There is, as you might expect, an alternative way of viewing the process of how we get laws, usually termed the *conflict model.* Here, as the term implies, society is in a state of conflict, and laws arise from that conflict. This does not mean that the purpose of laws is to mediate conflicts; some people from all theoretical positions can agree with that statement. Rather, it means that in a society where there is a struggle for power, the ability to influence the law is one of the prizes. There is a little joke that perfectly sets out the conflict approach: "Our society follows the Golden Rule—those who have the gold get to make the rules."

The key to this joke is the presumption that we are not all equal partners in this thing called "society." Rather, different groups (usually, but not necessarily, defined in terms of economic classes) are in a constant struggle to impose their will on the other groups. The power to control the legislature and to pass laws, then, is the power to decide who is "right" and who should be a criminal for holding the wrong beliefs and acting in the wrong way. Your opponents become the nasty criminals, not the loyal and honorable opposition.

An example of this is provided by Joseph Gusfield (1986), who argues that the process of passing new laws often reflects something other than the majority putting its beliefs into law. Gusfield cites Prohibition, whereby the U.S. Constitution was amended in 1919 to prohibit the sale of alcohol. In the 1800s, he argues, middle-class morality against drunkenness was very powerful. Laws were not particularly needed, because such a broad variety of citizens shared these values—probably a majority. However, after the arrival of millions of immigrants, mostly from countries where the use of alcohol was not frowned upon, no doubt the majority of people in the United States were in favor of the sale of alcohol. Prohibition, to Gusfield, was a "symbolic crusade" whereby the anti-alcohol middle class wanted to have its particular brand of morality embedded in the criminal law. Those who disagreed with the white, Anglo-Saxon, Protestant middle-class were "officially" branded as evil by the U.S. government. In other words, Gusfield argues, it wasn't a rising consensus that led to Prohibition. It was exactly the opposite: when the middle class could no longer enforce its morality through informal social controls and when it found itself in the minority, it was forced to exercise its control over the legislatures to make the political statement that its morality was superior.

There is, at least superficially, some truth to the arguments of the conflict theorists. Just look at any state or provincial legislature and see who is sitting there. No doubt you will spot lawyers by the dozens; some doctors, dentists, and engineers; at least one college professor; and, depending on where you are, some wealthy farmers, businesspeople, or professional politicians. Occasionally, you get someone who insists on describing him- or herself as an "ordinary guy" or "just a concerned housewife," although you might check out the annual income of these "ordinary" people and compare it to the average income in your area. Do you see many welfare mothers? People who work thirty hours a week at the local department store for the minimum wage (the store keeps them from working enough hours to qualify for medical insurance)? Skilled workers such as mechanics, plumbers, carpenters, coal miners, or bricklayers? Of course, you will find an occasional coal miner or police officer, but not very many. From this point of view, the laws of the land that we must all follow are in fact passed by the relatively elite.

These insights were fueled in the 1960s throughout North America and Europe by a variety of events that focused attention on how governmental power can be used to benefit some groups over others. The Vietnam War alone was extremely powerful in taking a generation of youths raised on scouting, sock hops, and conformity and showing them that their government was capable of doing wrong, which many of them had never before considered. Once that door was opened, conflict theorists began to discover a wide range of ways in which governmental and legal power could be—and was being—abused. Certainly, in the 1960s, seeing anti-war protestors and civil rights activists being clubbed and hosed by law enforcement authorities on TV, and reading about how government agents broke laws, planted evidence, and lied to try to discredit their opponents, caused many conflict theorists to look for other examples of governmental excess.

A powerful part of criminology in the 1970s was the approach termed *radical criminology.* This approach was never particularly unified into one set of principles, although it certainly focused heavily on class conflict and the manner in which the law benefits the small number of people in the elite (Lynch & Groves, 1989). By the late 1980s, radical criminology was succeeded by *critical criminology,* which itself is really an umbrella term for a variety of perspectives that share in some broad principles but that often are at very strong odds with one another on specifics.

Critical criminologists may attack labeling theorists for ignoring major structural and cultural questions, but they share with them the belief that definitions of crime are both the result of a process of social negotiations and a reflection of political interests. Obviously, both critical criminologists and labeling theorists are sharply opposed to legalistic definitions of crime. However, whereas labelists have emphasized the state's negative reaction to "underdogs," critical theorists tend to concentrate on the lack of interest by the criminal justice system in violations of human rights and crimes of the powerful. As mentioned earlier, various criminologists want to broaden the definition of crime to include such socially injurious behaviors as racism, poverty, unemployment, sexism, imperialism, inadequate social services (such as housing, day care, education, and medical care), corporate wrong-doings, and state terrorism (Barak, 1991a, 1991b; Elias, 1986; Friedrichs, 1980; Lynch & Groves, 1989; Michalowski, 1985; Quinney, 1980; Reiman, 1995; Schwendinger & Schwendinger, 1975).

In Chapter 7, we will examine how critical criminology has become so multifaceted that it is not something that can be easily discussed. For example, feminist criminologists have raised important questions about both the treatment of women in the criminal justice system and our very way of thinking about how and why people commit crimes (Messerschmidt, 1993). Peacemaking criminologists have been most vocal in their argument that all of our current criminal justice efforts are doomed to failure (Quinney & Pepinsky, 1991) and that, as their name suggests, we need to abandon "wars on crime" in favor of campaigns for peace. Left realists have tried to take on the issues of crime not only against the working class but within the working class (Matthews & Young, 1992; Young & Matthews, 1992).

Given that critical criminology embraces such a broad spectrum of theorists, it is not surprising that some critical theorists find such sweeping definitions of crime to be problematic. Robert Bohm (1982), for example, suggests that they may be too broad and vague, while Michael Lynch and W. Byron Groves (1989), speaking more about the radical strain of critical criminology, admit that radicals have occasionally included too much in their "laundry list of crimes."

As one might expect, conservative criminologists have rejected much of the critical approach. Mainstream criminology has emphasized examining the extent, distribution, causes, and control of predatory street crime. Thus, some of these criminologists regard problems such as poverty and homelessness as moral rather than criminal issues (Hagan, 1985). Others maintain that radical definitions are subjective political agendas rather than legitimate social scientific contributions. To illustrate this position, we return your attention to Tappan, who argued that

> the rebel may enjoy a veritable orgy of delight in damning as criminal anyone he pleases; one imagines that some expert would thus consign to the criminal classes any successful capitalistic businessman. . . . The result may be fine indoctrination or catharsis achieved through blustering broadsides against the existing system. It is not criminology. It is not social science. (1947, pp. 44–45)

Tappan would like us to limit our definition of criminals to only those officially convicted in a court of law, something to which labeling and critical criminologists would never agree.

At any rate, there are many fewer advocates today within critical criminology of what Austin Turk (1975), in the earlier days of radical criminology, described as the tendency toward "everything-but-the-kitchen-sink" definitions. Still, critical formulations continue to encourage us to take note of various behaviors that are much more economically, socially, environmentally, and physically injurious than predatory street crimes. Simply put, why is it that the criminal justice system only rarely criminalizes these behaviors if they are such major threats? Raymond Michalowski (1985, p. 317) makes it plain that we cannot adequately examine the law's bias "unless we compare those things that are illegal with similar forms of social injury that are not." We will discuss this issue further in Chapter 10.

So, who should be the object of study for the critical criminologist? Radical criminology made that plain: the ruling elite, the corporate criminal, the lawbreaking government official, and the people who make the decisions on what is to be criminalized and what is not. More recent critical criminologists have become interested once again in the so-called street criminal and have explored ways to study such crime without losing their roots in radical and critical criminology.

DIFFERENT GROUPS' VIEWS OF CRIMINALITY

As mentioned earlier, one of the biggest problems with a consensus view of crime is that, as a nation, we *don't* look at crime in the same way. Sometimes, that can be strikingly obvious. In the last days of 1994, John C. Salvi III was charged with killing two abortion clinic receptionists. A friend and neighbor, John Christo, defended Salvi in a telephone interview with the news media. He was quoted by the Associated Press as insisting that "there's nothing wrong with John whatsoever other than he killed a couple people." Meanwhile, Donald Spitz, director of Pro-Life Virginia, stood in front of the jail where Salvi was held, shouting into a megaphone, "Thank you for what you did." Spitz said that killing front desk receptionists was "a righteous deed."

For many Americans struggling to come to a definition of murder, bursting into a medical clinic and gunning people down would certainly seem to qualify as some sort of problematic behavior. Yet, obviously, the extremists of the anti-abortion movement define killing those in favor of abortion in some other way. To make the issue even more complex, columnist Ellen Goodman (1995) argues that the decision by many of the mainstream anti-abortion groups to avoid public criticism of those who commit murder makes "them allies of extremists."

The dilemma of many people in the movement (should we or should we not publicly denounce others in the same anti-abortion movement?) illustrates well a particular problem of definitions of what is and what is not crime. Criminologists have long noted that, although it is easy to get agreement on a vague and broad statement like "murder should be against the law," things get harder when very specific behaviors are involved. For example, although most people worldwide would agree that murder should be against the law and heavily punished, many people have a list of exceptions. Some men feel that if they find their wife in bed with another man, they are within their rights to kill one or both of them. In some parts of the world, the code of the vendetta means that a hostile act must under virtually any circumstances be avenged with a similarly hostile act—that the requirements of the vendetta overrule the fact that the act (such as murder) is "technically" illegal (Newman, 1976). Many people do not believe that abortion is murder. Obviously, although we can all agree in North America that "murder" should be against the law, we begin to falter when we have to decide exactly which behaviors fall into the category of "murder." Others of us have troubles when we agree that a behavior is murder but feel that we might be acting within our rights to commit murder nonetheless.

Two groups that have had much to say about the nature of crime and criminality have been women and racial minorities. Therefore, we will examine some of the views of these two groups.

Women and the Law

It is not unusual to suggest that women and men have different views on the law and the criminal justice system. Perhaps the perfect example of this comes from Susan Glaspell's wonderful play *Trifles* (1920), which was later made into a short story, "A Jury of Her Peers." Here, the men gather in the sitting room to examine the hard-core evidence of a murder while the women sit in the kitchen, seeing the evidence totally differently than the men and discussing their very different views on what murder is justifiable.

Glaspell, who deals with the death of a violent man who destroys what is most valuable to his wife, anticipates by many years some of the best contemporary analysis of the law. Today, a centerpoint of much feminist evaluation is that the law and the formal processes of the criminal justice system are out with the men in the sitting room, totally excluding the viewpoint of the women. For the most part, sociological and psychological theories on crime do not cover the experiences of women, but rather are theories of male crime masquerading as theories of crime generally (Messerschmidt, 1993). In other words, we develop theories based on how men behave and then announce that these are theories on how *people* behave. This process becomes problematic when it becomes part of the law, such as when the law presumes that all people will act the way a reasonable man would, which may not be at all the way in which a reasonable woman would act.

This is particularly true when looking at violent sexual assault. Here, one of the biggest arguments has been whether such acts are sex crimes or crimes of violence. Most scholars in North America now take for granted that rape and sexual assault are crimes of violence (Allison & Wrightsman, 1993). However, Catharine MacKinnon (1983) argues that legislatures are for the most part made up of men who interpret events and then write laws to cover these events. The problem is, legislatures generally deal with the actions of men from the point of view of men. Rape law, then, although it may for the most part be written to protect women, is written from the male perspective—and a great many men in society still see rape as a sexual act. Thus, in many places, rape law, or at least the interpretation of rape law, is based on the notion of rape as sex. The law requires women to act the way men feel they would act in similar situations and decides guilt or innocence based on the point of view of the rapist.

Maria Los (1990) offers an excellent example of how the law looks at rape from the point of view of the rapist. She points out that an essential element of rape is a lack of consent by the woman. The problem is that men and women have different views of what "consent" means. One major problem, she argues, is that too many men still think that if a woman accepts a free dinner or enters a man's house, she is agreeing to sexual intercourse. In fact, in many areas in North America, the law allows for a jury to dismiss rape charges if it finds that a reasonable man would have a belief that the woman consented to the intercourse. What happens if the rapist argues that the reasonable man in his position would be bound to believe that the woman had agreed to sexual intercourse because she had entered his house? The law places women in a difficult position. Although a reasonable woman would view the man's behavior as rape, the law may reflect the notion that a man need only prove that he was acting in accordance with traditional male beliefs.

Another problem with rape law is the issue of how a woman must show her lack of consent. For many men, brought up (depending on their class level) with street fights, contact sports, bar fights, or dueling clubs, it seems only right that "the legal system [define] resistance in *male terms,* with the standard being a fight in which one's fists, elbows, or knees were used to fight back" (Allison & Wrightsman, 1993). However, this is not the behavior of a reasonable woman, Carol Bohmer (1991) argues. The reasonable woman, then, may find the charges against the rapist dismissed because she did not act in the way that the law felt a reasonable man should act.

In other cases, scholars have argued, the law is applied differently to men and women simply by not being applied at all! Given that about 93 percent of all victims of spousal violence are women (Bureau of Justice Statistics, 1994), the lack of enforcement of laws against assault within the family becomes a situation in which the law itself "reinforces the cultural climate of acceptance of wife abuse" (Edwards, 1990, p. 154).

In other instances, the law is not so obviously biased against women, but for some reason the effect of these laws and their enforcement is just as biased. Morgan-Sharp's (1992) review of numerous studies in the field found that women, particularly minority women, were more likely to be the objects of the criminal justice system at every turn. They are more likely to be arrested, denied bail, imprisoned, put in prisons far from their family, denied access to prison programs, and denied parole. Nowhere in the law books is it written that boys should not be locked up in institutions until they are convicted of breaking an adult criminal law but that girls may be institutionalized for violating standards of behavior that are not criminal for adults (for example, getting pregnant, acting unruly and difficult, being hard to manage). Yet, it so happens that girls are indeed disproportionally imprisoned in this way (Chesney-Lind & Shelden, 1992).

Further, there are hidden costs to women involved with the criminal justice system. One is that many are mothers (Baunach, 1985; Heidensohn, 1985), and this fact of motherhood is often a major source of their identity (Weisheit & Mahan, 1988). Fathers who are arrested often have no worries at all about their children, particularly if they haven't been great fathers in the first place. They know that the mothers will take care of the children while they are in prison, no matter how long that will be. Women, on the other hand, have no such assurance and may be all too aware that their children are being emotionally neglected and starting on the path to behavioral problems. Children's fathers are unlikely to take care of the children while the mothers are in prison. The psychological harm of knowing that the children have been removed by welfare agencies, then, is a burden that women tend to carry much more than men (although, of course, some fathers will indeed carry a similar burden).

The point of this discussion is to remind you that the law does not apply equally to men and women. Although textbooks (including this one) talk about the law, elements of the crime, potential punishments, and theories of criminality, we should remember always that men and women will often be affected by these supposedly neutral factors differently.

Minorities and the Law

In a society in which racism is endemic, there is no reason to believe that the criminal justice system would be spared, and it is not. Close to one-fourth of all young African-American men in the United States are under the control of the criminal justice system in some way. African-Americans, Hispanics, and other minorities now make up the overwhelming majority of inmates in state prisons in the United States, with the white non-Hispanic percentage down to 35.4 percent of the prison population (Maguire & Pastore, 1994). It is important to note that African-Americans and Hispanics make up only about 20 percent of the U.S. population but over 62 percent of the state prison population.[4] Where other minority groups predominate, such as in Hawaii, similar numbers can be found—native Hawaiians make up about 20 percent of Hawaii's population but a majority of the state prison inmates. This racism does not occur just at the stage of imprisonment: "The condition of blacks in relation to the law and at each stage of the criminal justice system is significantly worse than it is for whites" (Sokoloff & Price, 1995, p. 17).

There is every reason to believe that this racism spirals in on itself, causing the differential treatment to continue. No doubt as a result of generations of this treatment, African-Americans are more distrustful of the criminal justice system (Wideman, 1984). Further, a common finding in criminal justice research is that police officers commonly make decisions related to arrest based on stereotypes (Mann, 1993). Earlier in this chapter we discussed how dressing, talking, and acting middle class (in fact, *being* middle class) allowed DeKeseredy to avoid punishment while working-class friends who were identically guilty were not so lucky. Youths who look like gang members or who simply conform to the police officer's stereotypes of gang members (wearing Raiders jackets, for example) are more likely to be arrested and prosecuted. Youths who are deferential, polite, and remorseful are less likely to be prosecuted. It is possible that African-American youths *look* more criminal to the police and, based on the youths' distrust of the system, *sound* more criminal to the police.

---

[4] Other minorities make up the remainder of the prison population, after the white, African-American, and Hispanic prison populations are added together to get about 97.6 percent.

We have been concerned thus far with explaining the higher arrest rates for African-American youths by discussing issues related to image. If the police believe that you are a generally good person whose parents will exert control when they find out about your misbehavior, they are more likely to let you go with a warning. If they believe (no matter what the truth is) that inner-city minority teens and, say, white teens with blue Mohawk haircuts or with imitation "gangsta" clothing are not under parental control, then they will be more likely to arrest. This discussion assumes that all of these youths (those arrested, those let go with a warning) have committed exactly the same offenses. A very different problem with the law that affects minorities is when society decides to put its resources into arresting those who engage in behavior particularly favored by minority and working-class youths. Are these youths guilty? Certainly. But why did we choose this behavior on which to focus our attention?

Traditionally, the example used was that we arrested men who played dice and card games in alleys, but under no circumstances would we think of raiding the equally illegal high-stakes poker games played in gentlemen's clubs by upper-class white men. More recently, our attention has been focused on gambling on college campuses. *Sports Illustrated* reports that major gambling rings that operate for white college students are virtually immune from police attention (Layden, 1995a, 1995b, 1995c).

However, the most serious difference of all is the decision made by both the federal government and most states to target for police action and massive penalties the drug-taking behavior of teenage African-American males. In particular, being caught with the same amount of crack cocaine (favored by African-American youths) rather than powder cocaine (favored by the white middle-class) could lead to a difference of ten or fifteen more years in prison for the offender. Further, the War on Drugs is very heavily a war on crack in minority neighborhoods. Michael Tonry (1995) claims that the government knew full well what it was doing when it decided that the focus of the $16-billion-a-year War on Drugs would be crack. It would mean that an extraordinary number of young African-American males would be locked up in prison for very long terms, swelling the ranks of the prison community drastically, at extraordinary expense, while having no effect whatsoever on either the crime rate or the white middle class's similar drug-taking activities. This is exactly what has happened over the past ten to fifteen years: prison populations have expanded far beyond the breaking point, but most of the expansion has come from lower-class minority youths convicted of drug offenses.

So, are these youths guilty? No doubt, all or most are. However, we seem to have developed laws and a law enforcement policy aimed specifically at one group in society while letting another equally guilty group off more easily. Our short coverage of the labeling approach should make you at least aware that we could have taken a different approach. For example, if we had decided to force into treatment all crack users, we might have many fewer African-Americans in prison. If we had put the $16 billion a year for the War on Drugs into subsidizing inner-city private enterprise to create jobs that would attract young men away from drug sales, we might have had far fewer problems today with gang wars, unemployment, family dysfunction, and unsafe streets. Or we might have chosen to spend much of our attention going after college students who sell LSD and middle-class white youths who sell powder cocaine. Our prison populations might look very different then. We made choices about who we want in our prisons.

In any case, whites, African-Americans, and Hispanics account for about 97.7 percent of state prison inmates. The final group, officially termed "other," refers to other minorities in the system. One of these groups consists of Native Americans. Because their numbers are so small, not as many studies have been done on Native Americans. However, the studies that have been done commonly find that Native Americans, especially youths, are at a more significant disadvantage than even African-American youths. For example, in comparing youths of similar backgrounds and legal histories, Michael Leiber (1994) found that African-American youths in juvenile court had more severe outcomes than white youths and that Native American youths had more severe outcomes than either of the other two groups.

In other words, once again we consistently talk about crime and the criminal justice system as if these terms applied to everyone equally and were perceived by everyone equally. This may not be a valid assumption.

SUMMARY

The primary objective of this chapter was to sensitize you to the various ways in which criminologists answer the question, What is crime? All three of the approaches we reviewed—legalistic, societal reaction/labeling, and critical—have limitations, although the legalistic seems to be the most problematic. But are the other two much better? We think so; however, our opinion is likely to be sharply criticized by many other criminologists who advocate alternative formulations, several of which were not discussed here. Examples of these include the cross-cultural approach (Sellin, 1938), the statistical definition (Wilkins, 1964), and Hagan's (1985) attempt to define crime as a continuous variable.

Regardless of which definition you prefer, choosing the particular one that suits your fancy constitutes what Desmond Ellis (1987, p. 210) refers to as a "primal sociological act or decision." In other words, the way in which a criminologist defines crime will determine his or her choice of research method and the theoretical perspective that is used in the gathering and analysis of research findings. If you are a legalistic theorist, you are most likely to divide people into criminals and noncriminals and to try to figure out how they differ. You might test them on intelligence, look at their family backgrounds, measure their school adjustment abilities, or see what TV shows they watch. Your objective will be to see if you can show a difference between the criminals and the noncriminals.

If you are a labeling theorist, you will be more interested in the process by which the legalistic theorist splits up the group into criminals and noncriminals. Generally, you will be looking for examples of how the government shows bias toward the weak and the poor.

Finally, if you are a critical criminologist (although there are many different types of critical criminologists), you might be more interested in the structural aspects of North American capitalist society that promote the interests of the wealthy and powerful over the interests of those lower on the racial, sexual, and economic ladder.

The final warning from this chapter was to be careful not to presume that whatever definitions of crime you decide are correct will apply to everyone. Women and men may have very different views on the law and the way it affects them, as might different racial and ethnic groups.

SUGGESTED READINGS

Hagan, J. (1985). *Modern Criminology: Crime, Criminal Behavior, and Its Control.* Toronto: McGraw-Hill.

Chapter 2 provides a comprehensive critique of various definitions of crime.

Lynch, M. J., and Groves, W. B. (1989). *A Primer in Radical Criminology.* New York: Harrow & Heston.

Lynch and Groves provide an excellent overview of the radical conception of crime.

Reiman, J. (1995). *The Rich Get Richer and the Poor Get Prison,* 4th ed. Boston: Allyn & Bacon.

In Chapter 2, Reiman provides a radical explanation for why crimes of the powerful are not officially designated as crimes.

West, W. G. (1984). *Young Offenders and the State: A Canadian Perspective on Delinquency.* Toronto: Butterworths.

Chapter 1 features critical reviews of six different definitions of delinquency.

CHAPTER 3

CRIMINAL LAW AND POLITICAL CRIME

Never in the history of human social groups have people depended so heavily on the functioning of a single institution for the preservation of security and social order as they do today on the criminal law. The criminal law and the criminal justice system are expected to solve practically every problem that occurs, from getting cats out of trees to settling domestic disputes, as well as to arrest murderers, drunks, thieves and nuisances. The law and law enforcement institutions have become indispensable in the modern world.

CHAMBLISS AND COURTLESS, 1992, P. 3

Modern North American society has become more and more dependent on laws rather than, say, private actions between individuals to resolve disputes. As a consequence, more and more laws are created each day to deal with this dependence. In the United States, for example, "There are more laws passed each year than there are cats on farms" (Chambliss & Courtless, 1992, p. 9). Similarly, Canada already has about 90,000 federal laws in addition to the many laws made at the provincial (state) or local level (Caputo et al., 1989). Given these numbers, you can understand why publishers who put out law books make quite a bit of money; no one who depends on the law can afford to slip the slightest bit behind by using last year's books.

But why are there so many laws? Who creates them? How do they create them? For whom are they created? Although these questions were briefly addressed in Chapter 2 and will be again later, the primary objective of this chapter is to review several sociological theories designed specifically to explain the origins and functions of criminal law in advanced Western societies such as ours. However, one type of crime that criminal law has always had trouble categorizing is political crime. Thus, when we complete our discussion of the creation of criminal law, we will turn our attention to political crimes.

In discussing the sociology of criminal law, it is common to categorize the various sociological contributions under two broad headings: (1) the consensus perspective[1] and (2) the conflict perspective.[2] We will follow that tradition here. However, before we turn our attention to these two competing approaches, we must first clarify what we mean by *criminal law*.

DEFINITION AND BRIEF HISTORY OF CRIMINAL LAW[3]

Criminal law is defined as "a set of rules legislated by the state in the name of society and enforced by the state through the threat or application of punishment" (Gomme, 1993, p. 20). Here, "state" refers to the government—whether federal, state, or local.

There are several key points to this definition. First, the state declares a behavior to be a "wrong" in the name of the state. If you are personally wronged by another person in a situation in which the state feels it has no interest, you generally use another set of laws: the civil code. Thus, if someone insults you, you can file a civil suit for slander. If someone hits your car, perhaps you can use the civil law to win damages. However, certain behaviors—such as burglary, arson, rape, and murder—are deemed by the state to be wrongs not just of you, but of society in general. Supposedly, crimes are those wrongs that are so dangerous that society must step in and deal with offenders.

Second, in civil cases, the courts generally can award only financial damages. Criminal law announces a specific set of potential punishments for a given banned behavior. In fact, an honored tradition of American law is that a criminal law is not valid unless the legislature also specifies the penalties or punishments for those who are found guilty. This is such a strong tradition that it even has its own Latin slogan: *nullum crimen sine*

[1]Some writers refer to this approach as order, functionalist, or liberal theories (see, for example, Caputo et al., 1989; West, 1984).

[2]Of course, squeezing the wide variety of material in the literature into these narrow categories means that much must be left out. Because this is an introductory criminology text, we have excluded several other important sociological perspectives on law creation, such as critical legal studies and postmodernism. See Boyd (1995), Burtch (1992), and Milovanovic (1994) for in-depth introductory overviews of these contributions.

[3]See Milovanovic (1994, pp. 5–8) for a detailed overview of various definitions of law. For an in-depth account of the origins of contemporary criminal law, see Michalowski (1985).

poena (no crime without punishment). Of course, the line between civil and criminal wrongs is notoriously difficult to draw. A criminal court may fine you $25 for being involved in a bar fight while a civil court may require you to pay $250,000 in compensation for the injuries you caused and the damage you did. In theory, the criminal court applies the more serious penalties for the more serious behaviors; in reality, this is not always the case.

Third, out of all of the immoral, antisocial, and just plain annoying behaviors in any culture, only selected ones are criminalized. This process of choosing which behaviors to criminalize and which to ignore can be intensely political. It reflects human choices born out of political struggle, and the "winners" are those with the most influence on the legislature, not necessarily those who are "correct" or who represent the most people. In other words, criminal law is not "an earthly expression of the will of God; it may not represent the interests of 'the people,' and it has no necessary connection with justice" (Beirne & Messerschmidt, 1991, pp. 22–23). Further, as we saw in Chapter 2, criminal law is not cast in stone. Some behaviors may at one time be legal, and at another time illegal (for example, alcohol and drug consumption).

What is the point of criminal law? Why do we need it? Some of you may be thinking, "What a stupid question." Others are likely saying, "If, under our current legal system, people are killing, beating, and robbing each other, can you imagine what society would be like without any formal means of social control?" Actually, one of our key contentions is that the provisions of the criminal law, or even the absence of criminal law, are not directly related to the amounts of crime. Although this assertion is addressed in greater detail in Chapter 12, it warrants brief discussion here.

Comparative criminological research shows that the United States takes the most punitive stance against predatory street crime, and yet it is the most violent nation in the industrialized world (Currie, 1985). Regardless of any type of criminal law reform implemented in the near future, there is no reason to believe that U.S. citizens will become safer until economic and racial inequality is eliminated. Support for this argument is found in the empirical literature reviewed in Chapter 8. This body of knowledge shows that a disproportionate number of people who are either economically disadvantaged or African-American commit violent crimes such as homicide. One of the problems of dealing with crime is that we must decide whether to deal with crime on the individual level—going after individual offenders—or on the broader level—going after the conditions that breed large amounts of crime. Traditionally, the U.S. government has dealt with crime by looking to individual-level solutions—capital punishment, long-term prison sentences, and other harsh sanctions. Over the past ten to fifteen years, the United States has been involved in a massive social experiment whereby state and federal governments have responded to crime by dramatically increasing the legal sanctions. "Three strikes and you are out" has become a popular phrase, but there are no catchy phrases to capture the huge increases in criminalization in the United States today. As Todd Clear (1994, p. 46) notes, "When it comes to the issue of harming its own citizens through the penal process, a quite unprecedented and dramatic escalation occurred during the 1970s and 1980s." After forty-five years of essentially stable rates, the number of prison inmates increased between 1973 and 1992 by 332 percent, while between 1975 and 1990, probationers increased by 203 percent and parolees by 270 percent.

Unfortunately, this conservative social experiment with extremely harsh legal measures has clearly failed (Currie, 1985, 1993; Reiman, 1995). Simply put, enacting ever-harsher penalties does not, and will not, have any important effect on crime. Raymond Michalowski (1985, p. 66) argues the alternative: "The key to social peace is not in better *control* of the criminal. It is the creation of societies where people have little reason and little opportunity to behave criminally." Solutions to crime based on this assertion will be discussed in Chapter 12.

If the argument that crime is strongly related to social inequality is correct, then a similar argument can be made about criminal law. For example, based on historical research, some scholars claim that criminal law was not designed to protect people's physical and psychological well-being (Beattie, 1986; Burtch, 1992). Rather, criminal law was created to protect private property (Hay, 1975). According to this argument, primitive hunting-and-gathering societies had no social classes because everyone was required to help with food gathering. Disputes tended to be resolved by informal mechanisms. Consequently, notes Michalowski (1985, p. 66), in these societies, offenders were "permitted to retain their personal dignity and membership in a community instead of being relegated to a class of permanently disgraced outsiders, as they are in many modern societies when they are labeled 'criminal.' "

However, as agricultural societies developed, technological improvements meant that a smaller number of people could provide enough food for everyone. Ruling and propertied classes emerged along with militaries as some people were able to make claims to ownership of the land and to enforce this ownership by force or threat of force (Ellis, 1987). The roots of criminal law, then, may be found in the need to protect this private property, and legal scholars often trace the modern law to a continued expansion of this need to the current era. Of course, in a capitalist society, there is a great deal more property at stake, and thus a great deal more dependence on the criminal law.

CONSENSUS PERSPECTIVES

Several criminologists and many socio-legal scholars devote a great deal of attention to answering two important questions that we touched on previously: Where do laws come from? and, for that matter, Why do we have laws at all? Consensus theorists' answers to these questions are heavily rooted in the writings of Thomas Hobbes (1963), a conservative seventeenth-century English philosopher who devoted a substantial amount of his intellectual energy to addressing the issues of social order and social control.

Hobbes assumed that human beings are innately egoistic. In other words, he regarded people as naturally selfish beings who are insensitive to the physical and psychological needs of others and who will do anything to satisfy their own desires. What, then, is to be done about this sad state of affairs? Hobbes's answer was that, in order to avoid a society characterized by a "war of all against all" and rampant egoism, people need to agree to band together and surrender some of their autonomy to an all-powerful sovereign or centralized authority. Generally referred to as the "state," this centralized authority punishes those who violate rules by pursuing desires in a way that may result in injurious conduct (for example, robbery, assault, rape). Without such social control, people are incapable of controlling themselves.

The central belief here is that law reflects values, norms, and customs that are widely shared in society.[4] There are, of course, many consensus theorists and many variations of the theory, but Michael Lynch

---

[4]Some of the widely cited, more contemporary consensus theorists who popularized these ideas are Emile Durkheim, Roscoe Pound, Talcott Parsons, and Jerome Hall.

and Casey Groves (1989) summarize the basic principles of the approach as follows:

- Law reflects the need for social order.
- Law is a product of value consensus; people in society generally share the same values.
- Law is an impartial system that protects public rather than private interests.
- Where differences between groups exist, law is the neutral mechanism that helps parties resolve their conflicts.

In the next section, each of these principles will be evaluated in turn.

Critique of the Consensus Perspective

Many disenfranchised people who live in impoverished inner-city areas, such as East St. Louis, South Chicago, or Watts, agree with Hobbes and others who argue that laws are necessary to instill social order. On a day-to-day basis, these people witness a wide variety of problems that symbolize a "war of all against all." As Elliott Currie (1993, p. 10) notes in his commentary on the relationship between drug use and inner-city life in the United States:

> To anyone observing the state of America's cities in the 1990s, it seems devastatingly obvious that we have failed to make much headway against the drug crisis. Americans living in the worst-hit neighborhoods still face the reality of dealers on their doorstep and shots in the night; many fear for their lives, or their children's lives, and sense that their communities have slid downward into a permanent state of terror and disintegration. Even those fortunate enough to live in better neighborhoods cannot pick up a newspaper or watch the news without confronting story after story about the toll of drugs and drug-related violence on communities and families. For most of us, the drug plague seems to have settled in, become a routine feature of an increasingly frightening and bewildering urban landscape.

Thus, many Americans believe in the need for social control. Similarly, most North Americans agree on the need for laws against homicide, rape, and other brutal acts of interpersonal violence. Still, as we saw in Chapter 2, because the United States and Canada are home to people from a wide range of ethnic, religious, and political backgrounds, it is extremely difficult, if not impossible, to develop long lists of shared norms. What, for example, do a Mennonite farmer, developer Donald Trump, the president of General Motors, actor/singer Kenny Rogers, a Florida State University sociology student, a Navaho truck driver, the rock band Soundgarden, members of the National Rifle Association, and a homeless East St. Louis mother have in common? Well, they probably all are U.S. citizens and all oppose violent crimes such as those described above. However, they are most likely sharply divided on issues such as recreational drug use, restrictive firearms legislation, abortion, capital punishment, and U.S. military involvement in Third World nations. As we discussed in Chapter 2, if different groups view crime in different ways, then the consensus implied by this model may be lacking.

Let's take a specific example. Certainly, the vast majority of U.S. citizens oppose murder and are appalled by those who murder, beat, or rape innocent people. However, in other situations, murder seems to be more acceptable. Many of these same people have applauded the killing of civilians in foreign countries at certain times and places, such as in Iraq during and after Operation Desert Storm. Similarly, although anti–Vietnam War protestors raised a huge fuss when it was revealed that U.S. troops had slaughtered innocent villagers in My Lai, the most common reaction, according to Weis and Weis (1974, p. 3), was, "It never happened—and what's more, they deserved it."

The societal reaction to the September 13, 1971, Attica Correctional Facility massacre also challenges the notion that murder is universally condemned in the United States. This incident is briefly described in Box 3.1.[5] It also challenges the consensus notion that we all operate from the same basic value set.

Previously, we noted that consensus theorists assert that the law protects public rather than private interests. This is a very difficult proposition to defend. We could cite many examples in which the overwhelming majority

---

[5]For more in-depth analyses of the Attica uprising and massacre, see *Social Justice* 18(3) (1991) or Wicker (1975). The HBO movie *Against the Wall* is a very powerful account of the Attica crisis.

BOX 3.1

THE UPRISING AND MASSACRE AT THE ATTICA CORRECTIONAL FACILITY

At 9:05 A.M. on the morning of Thursday, September 9, 1971, a group of inmates forced their way through a gate at the center of the prison, fatally injured a guard named William Quinn, and took 50 hostages. The Attica uprising had begun. It lasted almost exactly four days, until 9:43 A.M. on the morning of Monday, September 13, when corrections officers and state troopers stormed the prison and killed 29 inmates and 10 hostages. During those four days the nation saw the faces of its captives on television—the hard black faces of young men who had grown up on the streets of Harlem and other urban ghettos. Theirs were the faces of crime in America. The television viewers who saw them were not surprised. Here were the faces of dangerous men who should be locked up. Nor were people outraged when the state launched its murderous attack on the prison, killing many more inmates and guards than did the prisoners themselves. Maybe they were shocked—but not outraged. Neither were they outraged when two grand juries refused to indict any of the attackers, nor when the mastermind of the attack, Governor Nelson Rockefeller, was named to be vice president of the United States three years after the uprising and massacre.

They were not outraged because the faces they saw on the TV screens fit and confirmed their beliefs about who is a deadly threat to American society—and a deadly threat must be met with deadly force.

SOURCE: Reiman, 1990, p. 132.

of the population may not be well served by the law. Perhaps the best example is one that will be of interest especially to individuals who are concerned with preserving the environment, promoting occupational health and safety, and providing for consumer safety. Chapter 10 will document many of these claims, but as we have already noted, "crimes in the suites" are much more economically, physically, and environmentally injurious than street crimes. Unfortunately, the penalties for committing corporate crimes are extremely weak. Violations by corporate decision-makers and their executive colleagues are typically dealt with by civil or administrative laws, which lack criminal penalties such as prison (Ellis & DeKeseredy, 1996).

Similarly, as our discussion in Chapter 1 should make plain, working-class youths and members of visible minority groups are more likely to be punished for violating various laws than their wealthier and/or white counterparts. Rather than being a "justice for all" system, ours is more one that operates to "weed out the wealthy," even if they and lower-class people commit the same crimes. This should not be seen as a carefully constructed overt conspiracy, but rather a situation in which the wealthy simply have certain advantages under law. For example, wealthier people can post bail because they can use their homes as security. On the other hand, poor people typically rent and have little, if any, disposable income. Thus, they are denied the opportunity to help their attorneys gather evidence (Brannigan, 1984). Likewise, rich people, such as O. J. Simpson, have the money to hire prominent, experienced lawyers. In contrast, poor people tend to be represented by legal aid lawyers, who generally are not very successful and who, compared to private attorneys, do not devote a substantial amount of energy and attention to their clients' cases because of time and financial constraints. Consequently, compared to private attorneys, legal aid lawyers tend to "cop a plea" and to see many more of their clients ending up in jail or prison. For example, according to Amnesty International (1994), the attorney for Roosevelt Pollard, a mentally retarded man on trial for murder, said in his closing statement:

> . . . here I am before you, after about four days of trial, and I'm supposed to argue for life. And I'm not really prepared. . . . I knew that the possible punishment on this charge was death. I knew that. And yet I didn't like to think about it. I probably could have been really working up an argument at this phase of the trial, probably time I should have been working on it when I just decided not, I'd rather do something else. I didn't want to think about it too much. In that respect I'm not really prepared to talk to you about life. I'm not the right person to be talking to you about life, but I guess, you know, I'll just have to do the best I can, I reckon.

Despite this stirring oratory, Roosevelt Pollard was sentenced to death. Subsequently, appeals courts ruled that since his trial attorney had not introduced evidence of his mental retardation at the trial, it could not be brought up by other attorneys on appeals. Can you imagine O. J. Simpson suffering from this sort of defense?

In sum, given its limitations, few people today use the consensus perspective to explain the origins and functions of criminal law. In fact, the popularity of this approach substantially decreased in the 1960s because events such as civil rights protests and opposition to the Vietnam War could not be adequately addressed by consensus theorists (Comack & Brickey, 1991a). People came to realize that, rather than being in a state of harmony, North American society is in a constant state of conflict and that laws arise from that conflict. A set of explanations commonly referred to and broadly defined as conflict perspectives attempt to explain this problem; we now turn to these contributions.

CONFLICT PERSPECTIVES

Conflict theories of law are currently popular among criminologists and socio-legal scholars. Unfortunately, space limitations make it impossible to review all of the different conflict theories. Instead, we have decided to focus on Weberian, Marxist, and radical feminist contributions because of their importance in the criminological literature. Although each one is distinct, some common themes are evident:[6]

- No behavior or person is inherently criminal. Rather, "crime" and "criminal" are labels attached to certain behaviors or people by those in positions of power.
- Competing groups constantly struggle to create laws that represent their specific interests.
- Conflict, rather than consensus, best explains the nature of the social order in Canada and the United States.

---

[6]This section is informed by summaries of conflict perspectives offered by Caputo et al. (1989), Lynch and Groves (1989), and Sheley (1985).

- People, rather than supernatural beings (for example, God), create laws.
- Law is not a neutral mechanism that serves to protect the interests of society as a whole. Rather, it is an instrument of power used to protect dominant groups' interests.

With these basic principles in mind, we will begin by examining Weberian conflict theories.

Weberian Conflict Theories

Nineteenth-century German sociologist Max Weber was for many years considered by sociologists to be one of the three or four most important sociological theorists. More recently, several legal theorists have begun to carefully examine his views on law (Milovanovic, 1994).[7] Stanislav Andreski (1984, p. 86) noted the reason: Weber's legal writings are "almost superhuman: it is astonishing that anyone could know so much about so many legal systems."

Weber opposed what he regarded as "simplistic models of law" (Burtch, 1992), such as the Marxist perspectives we will cover in the next section, in which class is seen as the most significant determinant of law creation and enforcement. In fact, Weber attempted to develop an alternative to Marxist theory (Hinch, 1992). Perhaps his opposition to single-factor Marxist explanations is best summarized in the following statement:

> I would like to protest the statement . . . that some one factor, be it technology or economy, can be the "ultimate" or "true" cause of another. If we look at causal lines, we see them run, at one time, from technical to economic and political matters, at another from political to religious and economic ones, etc. . . . [T]he view . . . that the economic is in some sense the ultimate point in the chain of causes is completely finished as a scientific proposition. (cited in Bendix & Roth, 1971, pp. 242–243)

---

[7] The bulk of Weber's writings on law are found in Chapter 8 of the second volume of his widely cited *Economy and Society* (1978). Milovanovic (1994) notes that Weber also presents some of his legal ideas in Chapters 1 and 3.

This is not to say that Weber did not regard class as a major influence on legal development. For him, class was just one of several sources of power that competing groups used in their struggle to create and implement laws that reflect their interests. Status and power were also deemed to be significant factors in this struggle. Weber defined *class* as material wealth and control of the economic system, while *status* referred to prestige or esteem and *power* reflected the ability to control others' actions (Hinch, 1992, p. 272). In sum, Weber was concerned with developing a multicausal theory, one that emphasizes how several factors operate together to influence the development of law (Milovanovic, 1994).

Even though contemporary Weberian theorists view conflict as endemic to society, some of them also argue that consensus is evident in our social order.[8] According to Elizabeth Comack and Stephen Brickey (1991a, p. 19), the Weberian notion of consensus is "rooted in the idea that the system in which competition occurs is viewed as *legitimate.*" Thus, Weberian conflict theorists see the state as an "umpire" or "referee" that oversees conflicts and struggles between competing interest groups (Caputo et al., 1989). For example, diverse interest groups constantly compete with one another to use the state to fulfil their legal goals, and the state provides the "rules of the game by which this competition is played out" (Comack & Brickey, 1991a, p. 19).

Austin Turk (1969, 1977, 1979), William Chambliss and Robert Seidman (1971), and Richard Quinney (1970) are contemporary criminologists who have developed some of the most widely cited Weberian conflict theories of law. Although each of their perspectives is unique, they all contend that different social groups compete to develop and enforce legal definitions of crime. In addition, they suggest that the competition is not between groups with equal amounts of power but that some interest groups have a stronger influence on law creation and enforcement than do others (Hinch, 1992).

---

[8]Weberian conflict theorists do not reject all of the consensus arguments discussed previously in this chapter. For example, some theorists, such as Dahrendorf (1959), argue that conflict theory should supplement consensus theory and that some problems can be best explained by the former perspective while others can be best understood by the latter (Hinch, 1992).

Quinney is no longer a Weberian conflict theorist. In fact, he now defines himself as *peacemaking criminologist* (see Chapter 7). Even so, his *Social Reality of Crime* (1970) made an important contribution to a Weberian understanding of law creation and enforcement, and thus his work will be briefly described here as an example of a contemporary application of Weber's analysis of law.

Like the labeling theorists cited in Chapter 2, Quinney stood criminology on its head. When he wrote his 1970 book, most criminologists were asking questions such as, "What makes Johnny a criminal?" Quinney, on the other hand, asked questions such as, "What made you decide that Johnny is a criminal?" In other words, he was mainly concerned with understanding how and why some behaviors come to be defined as crimes because, for Quinney, nothing and no one is inherently criminal. He was also interested in explaining how legal definitions of crime are applied.

Quinney's conflict theory includes six propositions, which generally suggest that in a politically organized society, authorized agents define crime and then apply these definitions to behavior that conflicts with the interests of those who have power. Where you are in the power structure determines your chances of being defined as criminal. Thus:

> *PROPOSITION 6* (The Social Reality of Crime): The social reality of crime is constructed by the formulation and application of criminal definitions, the development of behavior patterns related to criminal definitions, and the construction of criminal conceptions. (Quinney, 1970, p. 25)

Quinney's theory is depicted in Figure 3.1 and summarized in the following statement:

> In general . . . the more power segments are concerned about crime, the greater the probability that criminal definitions will be created and that behavior patterns will develop in opposition to criminal definitions. The formulation and application of criminal definitions and the development of behavior patterns related to criminal definitions are thus joined in full circle by the construction of criminal definitions. (Quinney, 1970, p. 23)

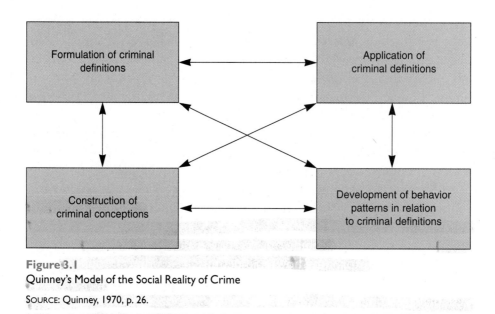

Figure 3.1
Quinney's Model of the Social Reality of Crime

SOURCE: Quinney, 1970, p. 26.

Critique of Weberian Conflict Theory

Weberian conflict theories of criminal law have some empirical support and should be commended for making the following contributions:

- Directing attention toward a historically "neglected partner in the production of crime and deviance" (Ellis, 1987, p. 62): those who make and enforce criminal laws.
- Challenging the view of law as a neutral or nonpartisan agent of social control.
- Pointing out how criminal labels can amplify and stabilize the behavior they are intended to regulate.
- Reaffirming the importance of power and privilege in debates about the creation and enforcement of criminal law (Lynch & Groves, 1989).

Nevertheless, only a handful of criminologists (for example, Austin Turk) continue to develop Weberian conflict theories of crime and law because they have several major pitfalls. For example, these accounts:

- Ignore the broader social, political, and economic factors that determine law creation (Comack & Brickey, 1991a).
- Fail to differentiate between the intended and unintended functions of law (Hinch, 1992; Sykes, 1974).
- Fail to define clearly the terms *conflict* and *power* (Liska, 1981).
- Incorrectly assume that law is always a function of conflict, that crime is always a product of conflict, and that law always represents the interests of powerful social groups (Beirne & Messerschmidt, 1991).

Weberian conflict theorists also have been attacked because they do not address the causes of crime (Akers, 1980; Lynch & Groves, 1989), but in fairness to them, they generally have not been interested in this question.

Marxist Perspectives on Law

A second theorist widely considered to be one of the most influential writers by sociologists is Karl Marx. Unfortunately, Marx had very little to say about crime, and the sociology of law was of little more than secondary interest to him (Milovanovic, 1994). Marx was more interested in studying the development of capitalism and its negative effects on social, political, and economic life (Burtch, 1992). Orthodox Marxists (for example, Hirst, 1975), then, argue that Marxist theory cannot be applied to the study of crime and law, which in some ways may be true. However, particularly during the 1970s and 1980s, many critical scholars, such as Richard Quinney, Herman and Julia Schwendinger, Ian Taylor, Jock Young, Michael Lynch, and the late W. Byron (Casey) Groves, have drawn from Marx's writings to provide both innovative and alternative explanations of crime, law, and social control.[9]

Like Weberian conflict theorists, Marxists contend that conflict is endemic to society, that law is a tool used by powerful social groups to promote and protect their interests, and that definitions of crime favor those in privileged economic and political positions. Marxists and Weberians differ, however, in several key respects. For example, Marxists see advanced capitalist

---

[9]See Lynch and Groves (1989) for an excellent overview of contemporary Marxist contributions to the study of crime, law, and the state.

society as consisting of a struggle between two major economic classes: the *bourgeoisie* and *proletariat*. The former constitutes that small segment of the population that owns and controls the means of production, such as corporations, factories, and so on. The latter consists of the working class or wage laborers, who must sell their labor power to the bourgeoisie for money in order to live. Thus, workers are no longer workers, but rather wage-labor—just one of the cost elements for owners. As Brian MacLean (1986a, p. 9) points out, this means a constant struggle between the two classes to

> obtain greater control over the means of production—labour so they can gain job security, better wages and better working conditions, and capital so they can restructure the work environment to make it more profitable, generally at labour's expense.

As you can see, Weberians fundamentally disagree with Marxist interpretations of societal conflict. For Weberians, society consists of a multitude of competing interest groups with various and changing sources of power (Gomme, 1993).

With these differences in mind, we turn next to an examination of three variations of the Marxist perspective on law: the instrumentalist, structuralist, and structural contradictions approaches.

Instrumental Marxism   The first Marxist theory of law to gain popularity, the instrumental approach, is rooted in a classic statement set out by Marx and Friedrich Engels: "The executive of the modern state is but a committee for managing the common affairs of the whole bourgeoisie" (1975, p. 82). Some contemporary Marxist theorists have interpreted this to mean that the state is but a tool or instrument used by the ruling class to promote its financial interests and maintain its control over the disenfranchised. The law, then, is seen by instrumentalists as a "weapon of class rule" (Comack & Brickey, 1991a, p. 24).

To support their arguments, instrumentalists cite evidence that members of the government and the bourgeoisie come from similar class backgrounds, attended the same schools, have the same financial goals, and share the same ideology (Miliband, 1969; Quinney, 1974). In sum, instrumentalists assert that government and business elites both belong to the ruling class, and thus, as one would expect, the law functions to promote the interests of capitalists. For example, Richard Quinney, during the period in which he was an instrumentalist Marxist, argued that

> the legal system is an apparatus that is created to secure the interests of the dominant class. Contrary to conventional belief, law is a tool of the ruling class. The legal system provides the mechanism for the forceful and violent control of the rest of the population. In the course of battle, the agents of law (police, prosecutors, judges, and so on) serve as the military force for the protection of domestic order. . . . The rates of crime in any State are an indication of the extent to which the ruling class, through its machinery or criminal law, must coerce the rest of the population, thereby preventing any threats to its ability to rule and possess. (1975, p. 193)

Further, instrumental Marxists have played an important role in sensitizing us to the class-based nature of the origins and functions of law. Theorists such as Frank Pearce (1976) and Colin Goff and Charles Reasons (1978) were among the first criminologists to show that crimes of powerful corporations, such as those described in Chapter 10, are for the most part excluded from the oversight of criminal law, while disenfranchised offenders stand a very good chance of being incarcerated even when they commit relatively minor street offenses. For example, as the American Federation of Labor and Congress of Industrial Organizations (AFL-CIO) has pointed out:

> More people have gone to jail for violations of the Wild Free Roaming Horses and Burros Act for harassing a wild burro on federal lands (seven people jailed) than have gone to jail for violating the Occupational Safety and Health Act's ban on wilfully killing workers (one person jailed). The maximum penalty for harassing a wild burro is one year; the maximum penalty under the OSH Act for wilfully killing a worker is six months. (1993, p. 45)

Critique of Instrumental Marxism   Some of you, especially if you belong to labor unions or know others who do, are likely to find instrumental Marxist arguments problematic and even rather extreme. You might be asking yourselves, "If the law and state only function to protect the interests of the ruling class, then why do many people have collective bargaining rights and why are people allowed to create and join unions? Don't unions and collective bargaining challenge the interests of bourgeois elites?" They certainly do, and thus, contrary to the instrumentalist position, the working class periodically does have considerable influence on the legal process (Lynch & Groves, 1989).

A second challenge to the instrumentalist position is that, while they are extremely lenient, there *are* regulatory laws seemingly designed to curb corporate wrongdoings. If the state were truly a puppet of the ruling class, such legislation would not exist. Moreover, in North America, laws exist to safeguard human rights, to set minimum wage standards, to protect the environment, to promote workers' safety, and so on—none of which are in the financial interests of the propertied class.

Because of these and the following criticisms,[10] instrumental Marxist theories of law are no longer popular:

- Instrumental Marxists incorrectly assume that the capitalist class always acts as a "united whole" (Comack & Brickey, 1991a). In fact, there are conflicts between members of the ruling class. As Gold, Lo, and Wright (1975, p. 37) note, instead of being a cohesive group, the ruling class is "highly fractionalized" with diverse political and economic interests.

- Instrumentalists fail to recognize that economic factors do not always influence law creation and enforcement, a point raised long ago by Max Weber. For example, as described in Chapter 9, many police officers and court officials do not punish wife beaters, regardless of the offenders' socioeconomic status. As we will demonstrate later in this chapter, some feminist legal scholars contend that the law's failure to take a punitive stance against woman abusers is a function of patriarchal rather than economic forces.

- Instrumentalists tend to dismiss the fact that the state is often the site of class struggle (Greenberg, 1981). In some parts of North America, the working class has managed to get the state and law to represent its interests (for example, forcing passage of laws granting the right to strike). Moreover, in some capitalist societies, political parties that strongly support working-class interests, such as the provincial New

---

[10]Lynch and Groves (1989) were very valuable in developing this listing.

Democratic Party in Ontario, Canada, get their candidates elected. (Of course, there is some question as to whether working-class parties ever change any relations substantially when in power or whether they are just a variation on a theme.)

- The instrumental approach cannot account for conflicts between different state agencies and between the government and the ruling class it's supposed to represent. For example, government agencies occasionally compete with one another to obtain more funds from the agency in charge of the federal or state budget. As another example, governments sometimes limit the ability of businesses to make money, such as the regulation of the cable TV industry.

- Instrumentalist Marxist theories are similar to conspiracy theories, which characterize corporate elites and politicians as gathering in secret proceedings to oppress labor and develop laws that protect their financial interests (Greenberg, 1976; Shoham & Hoffman, 1991). Although members of the financial establishment and politicians do meet, the two groups are not sufficiently organized to behave in a consistent conspiratorial manner.

Structural Marxism   In response to these criticisms of instrumentalism in the late 1970s, several theorists developed an alternative Marxist explanation of the state and law—structural Marxism. Heavily influenced by the writings of Louis Althusser (1971), Nicos Poulantzas (1973), and Isaac Balbus (1977), criminologists such as Chambliss and Seidman (1982) and Quinney (1980) argued that the state is not simply a tool or instrument of capitalists. Although they acknowledged some link between the state and the interests of business elites, they viewed the state as "relatively autonomous" from individual capitalists. In other words, in order to protect the long-term interests of capitalism, the state must occasionally act against the short-term interests of particular members of the ruling class (Gold, Lo, & Wright, 1975).

For example, in the preceding critique of instrumental Marxism, we noted that various laws work against ruling-class interests. For example, health and safety legislation and other laws designed to improve work conditions do, to a certain extent, improve laborers' material conditions. However, these laws are primarily strategies used by the capitalist state in its attempts to resolve conflicts between the ruling and working class, reproduce the existing capitalist system, and maintain social harmony (O'Connor,

1973; Poulantzas, 1973; Smandych, 1985). Moreover, legislation that obstructs the overriding goals of capitalist elites is weak. For example, in Chapter 10, we point out that while there are regulatory laws ostensibly designed to curb corporate violence against workers, thousands of people are still either killed or injured in the workplace because corporate executives continue to avoid formal sanctions. When business elites are punished, they typically receive fines, which is not an effective means of forcing them to comply with health and safety legislation. Rather, these penalties are viewed as simply the "cost of doing business" (Hinch, 1994).

In sum, structural Marxists contend that in order to preserve the capitalist political economic order, and also to generate an image of itself as an "honest broker" between the ruling and working class, the state creates weak laws that give disenfranchised people a sense or impression that their voices are being heard. However, in reality, the legal reforms noted previously offer "no significant impediment to the accumulation of capital and the continuation of the capitalist system" (Hinch, 1992, p. 279).

Critique of Structural Marxism   The structuralist Marxist approach to understanding the origins and functions of law is considered by several sociolegal scholars (for example, Comack & Brickey, 1991a) to be a more powerful and accurate account of the relationship between class and law. Some variations of this Marxist perspective also have considerable empirical support, such as Russell Smandych's (1985) analysis of the early Canadian anti-combines legislation.

Still, others have found shortcomings in the structuralist position, which may be summarized as follows:

- Although they base their claims on it, structuralists have yet to adequately document short-term neutrality and long-term bias (Sheley, 1985).

- Structural Marxists appear to pay little attention to legal discrimination against visible minority and female workers (Sheley, 1985).

- Although structural Marxists use the concept of the relative autonomy of the state from the ruling class to explain many things, they have not really explained how this is determined or what factors create it (Comack & Brickey, 1991a).

- Structuralists are said to lack a complete understanding of the ways in which people create and sustain social order because these theorists place too much emphasis on "the system" and thus lose sight of the "real people engaged in the struggle" (Hinch, 1992, p. 296).

- Structuralists often treat the state as if it were a real thing, with a life of its own, rather than as a collection of relationships (Sheley, 1985).

Structural Contradictions Theory   The third variant of Marxist legal theory to be described here is the structural contradictions theory, originally developed by William Chambliss.[11] This theory "sees law creation as a process aimed at the resolution of contradictions, conflicts and dilemmas which are inherent in the structure of a historical period" (Chambliss, 1986, p. 30). For example, in capitalist societies, a basic contradiction exists between capitalists and the working class. Both groups want to increase their share of the profits derived from the production of goods and services. This contradiction results in workers organizing and demanding better wages and working conditions and in capitalists resisting these demands. According to Chambliss and Thomas Courtless (1992), if nothing intervenes to mediate the conflict between these two classes, the capitalist system will be so riddled with conflict that it will either stop functioning or destroy itself. Consequently, the state must try to solve these conflicts.

However, the dilemma for the state is that it can only address the conflicts. It cannot resolve the basic contradiction of capitalism. According to Chambliss and Courtless:

> If the state represents only the interests of capitalists, the conflicts will increase in intensity and will pit the workers against the state (as in fact has happened in the history of capitalism). If the state sides with the workers against the capitalists, then the system will collapse and a new social order will have to be constructed. Faced with this dilemma, officials of the state attempt to resolve the conflict by passing various laws, some that represent the interests of the capitalists and some that represent the interests of the workers. (1992, p. 13)

The state's attempts to resolve conflicts, however, often generates new ones because the basic contradictions are not resolved. Further, these

---

[11] See Chambliss and Zatz (1993) for an excellent collection of recent articles on structural contradictions theory.

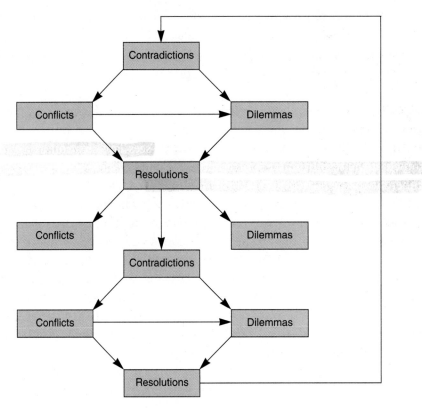

Figure 3.2
The Contradictions-Resolutions Cycle

solutions can draw attention to other contradictions that were previously not obvious (Chambliss, 1986). This structural contradictions theory is presented in Figure 3.2.[12]

Ron Hinch (1991) used Chambliss's (1986) structural contradictions theory to explain the passage of Canada's sexual assault legislation in 1983 (Bill C-127). For more than ten years, feminist critics had argued that Canada's rape laws were sexist and should be changed. The government's dilemma was to seek a method of reforming the law so that it would appear to meet feminist demands while at the same time leave the system intact.

------

[12]This is a slightly modified version of the structural contradictions model described by Chambliss and Courtless (1992, p. 13).

After all was said and done, the government achieved this goal: major change did not occur.

For example, under the new legislation, female sexual assault survivors apparently are given greater protection from having their sexual histories attacked in court, and men can be charged for sexually assaulting their wives. However, in reality, under Section 246.6, evidence related to prior sexual relations between the accused and the victim can be introduced, and the "honest-but-mistaken" defense is still permitted. These two factors reduce the value of having women's sexual histories banned as evidence. Moreover, the broader social pressures that keep women from reporting their husbands' sexually abusive behavior were not substantially affected by the bill (Hinch, 1994). In other words, men can be charged for raping their wives, but in a society that makes it almost impossible for a woman to charge her husband with rape. Thus, "specific features of the law and its enforcement remain as patriarchal today as they were before January 1983" (Hinch, 1991, pp. 246–247).

Critique of Structural Contradictions Theory   Structural contradictions theory encourages critical socio-legal theorists to move beyond either instrumental or structural Marxist accounts as a means to understanding the origins and functions of law. These earlier Marxist accounts ignore the ways in which people both influence and are influenced by wider social forces (Zatz, 1993); structural contradictions theory sensitizes us to the fact that people are not "merely atoms being bounced around by social force fields" (Reasons, 1989, p. 20). For example, according to Chambliss and Richard Seidman (1982, p. 316):

> People . . . make choices, respond to realities, and struggle against oppression. Those at the top act as a class to perpetuate their privilege; those sprinkled below do likewise. The contrary interests generate conflicts, in response to which the government becomes complex, interactive and ever-changing. In a word, it is dialectical. (Chambliss & Seidman, 1982, p. 316)

Several theorists have recently expanded and refined Chambliss's original structural contradictions theory (see Chambliss & Zatz, 1993), and we are likely to see more improvements in the near future. Nevertheless, this perspective has been criticized by Ron Hinch (1992, 1994) for its inability to specify how the cycle of "conflict, resolution, conflict" can be concluded. In other words, although it may have some explanatory value, the theory offers little to inform social policy and action. For example, we noted one of structural contradictions theory's main arguments is that, even if conflicts between capitalists and laborers are resolved, the basic contradiction between these two groups remains intact, as the ruling class will now face new problems protecting its dominant position. According to Hinch, this assertion is problematic because it suggests that there is no way to break the cycle or to address the contradictions themselves. Marxist theorists have always argued that their intellectual work should assist in practical action. However, in its present form, structural contradictions theory does not answer the question of what is to be done about generating social transformation (Hinch, 1992). The response to Hinch, of course, is that he presumes the cycle should be concluded; others see the constant struggle as valuable.

BEYOND CLASS: FEMINIST PERSPECTIVES

So far, we have examined four variants of the conflict perspective on law, all of which pay scant attention at best to the ways in which gender and patriarchy influence the creation and enforcement of law. *Gender* refers to "the sociocultural and psychological shaping, patterning, and evaluating of female and male behavior" (Schur, 1984, p. 10). *Patriarchy* is defined here as male control of women's labor and sexuality. A rapidly growing body of feminist literature reveals that both of these factors are major characteristics of the law and that they are "principal domains" of its operations (Messerschmidt, 1993). This body of theoretical and empirical work shows that the state and law play key roles in the subordination of women and the dominance of men. Moreover, feminists point out that all of the theories discussed so far in this chapter need to be "radically rethought" to account for the role of the state and law in preserving the patriarchal nature of advanced Western societies such as the United States and Canada (Knutilla, 1994). Their key contention is that most of the theories covered here have little relevance to women. As Martin Schwartz and Gerald Slatin (1984, p. 248) note:

Marxist theorists generally are concerned with the plight of an entire class, and occasionally for all men. This stance tends to preclude a concern either for individual women, or for generalized women's interests.

Further, much of the concern in feminist writings has been with women as the victims of crimes, such as rape, battering, incest, and sexual harassment. Marxist analyses generally have been extraordinarily silent in dealing with the concerns of crime victims (Friedrichs, 1983), which undermines its relevance for these writers.

Patriarchy and Social Relations

There are, as you might expect, several different contemporary feminist theories of law, but perhaps the most widely cited are radical feminist accounts, especially Catharine MacKinnon's (1989). Before we review her contributions, we should note that not all radical feminist theories of social relations are alike. However, the following themes, as noted by Walby (1990, p. 3), are evident in most of them:

- Sexual roles are socially constructed around male rather than female notions of desire.
- Sexuality is a primary site of male domination over women, through which men impose their notion of femininity on women.
- In contemporary societies such as ours, heterosexuality is institutionalized and organizes most aspects of male-female relations.
- Male-to-female physical, sexual, and psychological abuse is part of a system of controlling women.

These themes are apparent in MacKinnon's theory of law. For example, she argues that rape, abortion, obscenity, and sex discrimination laws are integral to sexual politics because the state, through law, institutionalizes male power over women through institutionalizing the male point of view in law. Its first state act is to see women from the standpoint of male dominance; its next act to treat them that way. (1989, p. 169)

MacKinnon further argues that male power is systemic, coercive, and legitimated. Male power, for her, is the "regime."

Jill Radford (1987) provides another example of a radical feminist theory of law. Hers, however, focuses on law enforcement rather than law creation. Feminist academic and activist communities know quite well that the police are reluctant to charge men who physically, psychologically, and sexually abuse their intimate female partners. On the other hand, the police typically take a punitive stance against stranger-to-stranger assault on the street. What accounts for this differential response?

According to Radford (1987), historically, the police have generally avoided supervising or changing women's behavior. Instead, these tasks were left to either individual men or all-male peer groups. The most important sources of the social control of women are heterosexual, monogamous relationships. In these domestic contexts, men often assault women to maintain their patriarchal power. Strongly supportive of the patriarchal "status quo," the police do not protect abused women because they define these women as "legitimate targets" that men have the right to control.

In sum, instead of acting as "value-free" institutions of social control, to radical feminists police departments are "bastions of male authority and interests" that function on behalf of men to maintain female subordination in dating, marriage, and cohabitation (Edwards, 1989, p. 31). As noted previously, one way in which the police achieve this goal is by taking a nonpunitive approach to male perpetrators of intimate violence.

Critique of the Radical Feminist Perspective

Radical feminist theories such as MacKinnon's are supported by "overwhelming" empirical evidence showing that the state and law play a significant role in perpetuating and legitimating oppressive gender relations and politics (Connell, 1990; Knutilla, 1994). Moreover, in the history of social theory, radical feminism was the first school of thought to emphasize the powerful influence of three factors previously ignored by many socio-legal scholars—namely, gender, patriarchy, and sexuality (Messerschmidt, 1993).

As pointed out in Chapters 7 and 9, radical feminists have also played a vital role in "breaking the silence" on male-to-female violence (Kelly, 1988), and they have successfully shown that this crime is pervasive in advanced Western nations (Liddle, 1989).

Despite these important contributions, radical feminist theories are criticized for suffering from pitfalls similar to those associated with instrumental Marxism. For example, in viewing the law as an "instrument" used by men and the state to subordinate women, radical feminists ignore the fact that law often responds to a variety of different pressures—not just those created by men (Walby, 1990). While biased toward protecting male interests, the state is also an institution in which many competing social groups struggle to impose their will on others (Messerschmidt, 1993).[13]

Moreover, theories such as MacKinnon's fail to account for the idea that the state is relatively autonomous and occasionally acts against the short-term interests of men. For example, the state gives economic support to shelters and treatment programs for battered women and has, due largely to feminist lobbying and education initiatives, influenced many police departments to take a more aggressive stance against men who abuse their female partners (Jones, 1994; Ursel, 1991). Indeed, a growing body of feminist empirical research reveals that women can "use the full force of the state, its money, its legal apparatus and its political legitimacy to provide more support and more options to battered women and women at risk to escape such violence" (Ursel, 1991, p. 268).[14]

Another common criticism of radical feminist theory is that it incorrectly assumes universal female subordination and male domination. As extensive anthropological literature reveals, some societies are characterized by somewhat equal gender relations (Messerschmidt, 1986). In other words, not all governments and legal systems function to oppress women.

Radial feminist theories of law also tend to ignore the oppressive experiences of working-class women and female members of visible minority groups (Walby, 1990). For example, black women's experiences with the law and other institutions of social control differ considerably from those of

---

[13] See Currie (1991) for a more in-depth critique of instrumental feminist theories of the state.

[14] Arguments such as this have generated considerable debate within feminist academic and activist communities. See Edwards (1989), Snider (1991), and Ursel (1991) for more in-depth discussions of the controversy surrounding the role of the state in advancing feminist concerns.

white women (Ahluwalia, 1991). As Dawn Currie and colleagues (1990), Claire Lewis and colleagues (1989), and Amina Mama (1990) have shown, arrest policies designed to curb male-to-female violence are not implemented evenly across Western societies because many black women are exempt from police protection. These researchers found that in responding to battered women, many officers gave lesser assistance to women of color than to their white counterparts.

POLITICAL CRIMES

Perhaps the area in which the criminal law has proved most problematic is in political crime, which may be why it is often ignored by criminologists. As a group, criminologists have not yet come to a firm agreement on exactly what political crime is and how it should be conceived. For this reason, probably every book you consult will have a different definition of "political crime."

Definitions of Political Crime

One problem is that, as the somewhat bloody old English expression goes, "One's point of view depends on whose ox is being gored." If you are upholding the state and constitution and preserving the American way of life, then how can you be committing a political crime? If you are fighting for your people against a racist oppressive government, how can that be a crime? What if you are caught up in a vendetta of several generations' duration?

As a concrete example, some German officers were horrified at Adolf Hitler's actions in World War II. They became convinced of the madness of a man who ordered the extermination of entire groups of people, including Jews, the mentally ill, homosexuals, Gypsies, and anyone else he felt were not proper Aryans. They even plotted to assassinate Hitler. Had they succeeded, perhaps the war would have ended earlier, and *literally* millions of lives would have been saved. Similarly, no one outside Iraq is exactly sure just how many Iraqis have been executed over the years for plotting to kill their leader, Saddam Hussein, although the number is rumored to be at least several hundred. In a single day (January 7, 1995), Air Force General Mo-hammed Mathlum al-Deleimi and nineteen other senior Army and Air Force officers were executed two days after the official Islamic Republic News Agency reported that an assassination plot had been foiled.

If you look at a criminal law book, you will find that the cold-blooded murder of a man you do not agree with is fairly clearly listed as murder, not a righteous act. Further, since these were Germans acting against the legiti-mate German government and Iraqis acting against the legitimate Iraqi government, they were involved in an act of treason—certainly the most easily understood political crime. So, are we dealing with cold-blooded mur-derers? With true patriots? With potential saviors of millions of lives? This point was often made by the comedian Lenny Bruce in the late 1950s, when he suggested that because we *won* the Second World War, the official line on why we dropped atomic bombs on the civilian populations of Nagasaki and Hiroshima was to *save* lives—that by ending the war earlier, we did not have to fight a series of bloody Pacific battles that would have cost many American lives. Bruce pointed out that if we had *lost* the war, the Japanese would have had the power to decide what acts were "war crimes," just as we did after the war in the Nuremburg Trials, in which some leaders of the other side were sentenced to death. Surely dropping atomic bombs on civil-ian populations would have put President Harry Truman in some very *deep* trouble with the Japanese courts!

Another example, closer to home, involves the murder of people who work in medical clinics that, among many other treatments, perform abor-tions. Few Americans, including those who are antichoice, regard fetuses to be the same as people who have been born. For example, rarely are funeral services held after a miscarriage. Some extremists, however, believe that in-duced abortion is murder and that they may legitimately kill those who help women get abortions. In the United States, after more than two hundred fire-bombings, shootings, and acts of arson, and many more death threats, some members of the antichoice movement have begun to carry out assassi-nations. From Massachusetts to Florida, leaders and members of political groups have engaged in cold-blooded murders.

How about if we change the words? Are these people terrorists who engage in cold-blooded assassinations and bombings? Or are they people who answer to a higher power, committing a righteous act, somewhat like the German officers who tried to kill their leader? Are they the vanguard of a movement to save the lives of the unborn? Just as in the other examples, the ideological component makes it more difficult to classify these crimes. If you stole money to buy drugs or committed burglaries in order to purchase better clothes, you would seem to fit the model for which the criminal law was written. When you claim to answer to a higher power, however, the issue becomes more muddled. In the same way, criminologists who try to explain the causes of crime have had a lot of trouble dealing with political crime. None of their standard theories or wisdom are relevant in explaining these crimes.

Although many authors will define political crime in terms of only one or two of the categories below, we think that there is merit to seeing some behavior in each category as politically motivated.

- *Crimes against the state.* These include treason (spying on one's own country for a foreign government, say), participation in riots and insurrections, assassination of political leaders, physical attacks on government officials, and the like.
- *Crimes by the state.* These encompass a wide variety of acts ranging from denying some citizens their rights (such as keeping minorities from voting) to murdering political opponents or other "troublesome" individuals. Some call this "state crime."
- *Crimes against other groups.* These include a wide variety of hate crimes (such as bombing abortion clinics). Many Americans think it is acceptable behavior to beat up anyone they do not like, such as gays, for example. White Americans also murdered (lynched) thousands of African-Americans, mostly for not being properly subservient.

Examples of political crimes are provided in Table 3.1.[15]

Crimes Against the State

Americans should never forget that political violence was at the heart of the origin of their country. "The British soldiers killed by the shots heard round the world were real people—young men serving their country" (Kirkham,

---

[15]This is a slightly modified version of Table 13.1 constructed by Michalowski (1985, p. 380).

Table 3. Varieties of Political Crime

BENEFICIARY	BY PEOPLE HOLDING POLITICAL OFFICE OR POSITIONS OF DELEGATED POLITICAL POWER		BY PEOPLE OUTSIDE OF GOVERNMENT	
	For Economic Gain	For Political Gain	For Economic Gain	For Political Gain
Individuals	Accepting bribes or favors Theft of government property or funds Illegal use of campaign funds for personal expenditures Influence peddling	Using power of political office to harass or discredit political opponents or critics Seeking or accepting illegal campaign contributions Making deals or doing "favors" in return for campaign contributions "Dirty tricks" political campaigns	Bribing law enforcement personnel Offering bribes or favors in return for legislation or regulatory practices favorable to personal businesses	Making campaign contribution deals in return for appointed political positions
Private organizations or government	Lax or nonenforcement of laws regulating businesses or other organizations Legislative favoritism Imperialist policies and actions to protect control over foreign resources, markets, or labor forces	Repression of opposition to governmental actions or policy through violations of civil rights False representation of governmental actions in order to preserve legitimacy Agent provocateurism	Offering bribes, favors, or illegal campaign contributions in return for directly advantageous legislation, domestic or foreign policy, or avoidance of law enforcement	Making campaign contribution deals to have business representatives placed in regulatory or other governmental positions Illegal contributions or other tactics to ensure election of candidates who are allies

Levy, & Crotty, 1970, p. 213). Following a series of violent political crimes, Americans fought a violent revolution against the state. There cannot be crimes against the state much more serious than declaring war against it! And, to be sure, this was a guerilla war characterized by "slash and burn" tactics, which caused great suffering in many places, such as South Carolina.

> The operational philosophy that the end justifies the means became the keynote of Revolutionary violence. Thus given sanctification by the Revolution, Americans have never been loathe to employ the most unremitting violence in the interest of any cause deemed to be a good one. (Brown, 1969, pp. 63–64)

Americans fought against more than England at the end of the eighteenth century. After the war, several states experienced rebellions as farmers fought against governments that attempted to uphold debtor laws against men economically wiped out by bad conditions, taxes, and high interest rates. Another example of such political crimes is Native American rebellions, the most famous of which is popularly known by whites as "Custer's Last Stand." Here, at the Battle of Little Big Horn, Native Americans who had been victimized repeatedly by the U.S. government, including General Custer (who provided protection for miners on treaty-guaranteed sacred ground), banded together in 1876 to attack and kill Custer and his men. As Piers Bierne and James Messerschmidt (1991) point out, however, events such as these often can only be understood as responses to other crimes. In other words, the Native Americans unquestionably engaged in violence and crimes against the state, but then they were forced and goaded into such actions by repeated and regular crimes *by* the state against them.

For many crimes against the state, the "criminal" claims allegiance to a greater right or to a higher power or cites the need to oppose a state that is wrong. Certainly, the Civil War was a rather extreme example of armed insurrection. As a more contemporary—and nonviolent—example, the entire civil rights movement in the United States, as exemplified by Dr. Martin Luther King Jr., found its most effective device in *civil disobedience.* When Rosa Parks refused to sit in the "colored" section at the back of the bus in Montgomery, Alabama, in the 1950s, she was violating a law and committing a crime against the state. Sit-in demonstrations, parades without a permit, and other violations of laws requiring segregation of the races were all crimes. Those who took part in them actively described their acts as crimes against the state, or political crimes, but claimed that all were justified on the grounds that the laws themselves were unjust. It is important to note, however, that Dr. King did not recommend breaking the law in order to "get away" with something. His idea was that the purpose of breaking the law was to be punished—to go to jail and become a thorn in the consciousness of the people and a constant reminder of the ways in which the state was unjust. Still, the main point was to purposefully commit a crime for political reasons, which can be defined as a crime against the state.

On the other hand, when people engage in assassination as a way of achieving their political ends, the act can just as well be considered political crime (Kirkham, Levy, & Crotty, 1970). The problem in the United States has been that most assassinations and assassination attempts over the past generation have been committed not by well-organized political groups, but by isolated individuals or splinter groups, leaving many to wonder if the crimes were truly political or simply random acts by deranged individuals (Manchester, 1975). For example, Sirhan Sirhan killed Bobby Kennedy in 1968 to keep a pro-Israel candidate from running for president, no doubt a political act. The strangeness of the circumstances and personages of Lee Harvey Oswald, who killed President John F. Kennedy, and of James Earl Ray, who killed Dr. Martin Luther King Jr., to this day lead many people to believe that they could not have acted alone, which suggests that these were political acts. However, John Hinckley most certainly was not committing a political crime when he tried to assassinate President Ronald Reagan; he may have chosen a major political figure, but he was acting for intensely personal reasons: a warped attempt to gain the attention of an actress. A well-documented set of crimes against a legitimate government were the actions of the *Contras* in Nicaragua, the group that Reagan administration officials such as Oliver North were accused of breaking the law to help to the tune of many millions of dollars. The *Contras* engaged in a fairly open campaign of violence and mass intimidation against people who supported the government in power, which was opposed by the Reagan administration and the right-wing *Contras* (Brody, 1985).

Crimes by the State

In many ways, crimes by the state are the most difficult to classify and discuss.[16] Generally, the power to define what is against the law is held by the state. Few governments are going to come to the public conclusion that they broke laws and committed crimes against their own citizens. As suggested previously, only by winning World War II were we able to justify the bombing of Hiroshima. No doubt, if the Japanese had won, your standard American history books would give a rather different version of that event.

Sometimes, we can make these judgments by comparing a nation's behavior with "higher" laws, such as international accords or treaties that the country has agreed to follow. For example, Article 6 of the International Covenant on Civil and Political Rights, ratified by the United States in 1992, forbids executions that violate the customary norms of international law. Further, as an example of what is "customary," the United Nations passed a resolution in 1989 whereby members pledged to work to eliminate any laws that allowed the execution of mentally retarded or mentally ill criminals. Yet, on January 17, 1995, Texas executed Mario Marquez, whose functional IQ was 65, which means that he was capable of reasoning at about the level of a 5-year-old child. By applying the provisions of international law, can we suggest that Texas itself committed an international crime?

Within the United States, we could cite dozens of examples of crimes by the state. One of the best known is the work of the Federal Bureau of Investigation under long-term director J. Edgar Hoover. Scholars given access to FBI files after Hoover's death have discovered that the FBI kept intensive investigatory files on anyone Hoover did not like, including top political and civil rights leaders, and devoted enormous energy to trying to undermine their leadership (Theoharis & Cox, 1988). These efforts were achieved through what we would now call "dirty tricks," including forged letters claiming secret love affairs, forged letters to political contributors, illegal wiretaps, the "leaking" of outright lies to the press, and fabricated, unsigned hate letters demanding that the leader commit suicide.

One of the best-known groups keeping track of political crimes committed by the state is Amnesty International, which claims that each year

---

[16]See Barak (1991a) and Tunnell (1993) for in-depth accounts of various political crimes committed by the U.S. government and ruling parties in other nations.

It is not easy to discuss crimes by the state using definitions from standard criminology. This cemetery monument from Manzanar, California, marks the spot where the U.S. government operated one of its internment camps for American citizens of Japanese heritage. There were no such camps for German Americans, Italian Americans, or Spanish Americans. Is it a crime to round up second- and third-generation citizens and imprison them for years, based on their skin color?

many hundreds of people are executed in dozens of countries around the world, generally for opposing the government in power. Further, torture is still used as a political tool by at least a third of the world's governments.

Perhaps the best known of these state murder situations is in contemporary Latin America, where several governments maintain death squads designed to kill anyone they target as a threat to the government. An example is the death squads maintained in the 1990s by the police and business owners in parts of Latin America. During the day, these squads sweep the streets of abandoned children who might annoy shoppers by begging; at night, the squads go out looking for homeless children without families. Often, the children are shot or simply "disappear," never to be seen again.

Between 1988 and 1991, for example, over seven thousand street children were killed in Brazil, and several thousand are killed each year in Colombia (Hatty, Davis, & Burke, 1994). Nor are these the only countries in which such death squads have existed. Haiti's Tonton Macoutes were the most famous of several in Latin America, and such "official" forces as Stalin's KGB and Hitler's Gestapo operated openly to ruthlessly suppress opposition, through murder if necessary. Likewise, the South African government, before the end of apartheid, maintained a police murder unit to kill black nationalist leaders.

Without a doubt, the worst type of state crime is genocide—the mass destruction of an entire population of people. Of course, the world has a long history of such attempts, such as regular pogroms—campaigns of massacre against European and Russian Jews from the Middle Ages through the nineteenth century. Yet modern civilization seems to have sped up, rather than slowed down, such attacks. The most recent case of genocide was by the Pol Pot regime in Cambodia in the 1970s. In an attempt to create a new society, this government may have killed as much as one-third of the population and terrorized or tortured many others.

By the mid-1990s, the most hotly debated purported crime by the state in the United States involved the multiple deaths in Waco, Texas, over an issue that seemed to revolve around whether cult leader David Koresh had paid a $200 tax to make his arsenal of weapons legal. Across the country, right-wing militia members have found this a very powerful organizing tool, arguing that if the government can storm in and kill David Koresh's innocent children, why can't they just do it at any time to anyone?

Crimes Against Other Groups

Although there is some literature on crimes committed by larger organized groups against minorities, the criminology literature is still weak on what are now called "hate crimes"—crimes motivated by the race, ethnicity, sexual orientation, or religion of the victim (Berk, 1990). With the tremendous explosion of membership in such avowed violent hate groups as the neo-Nazi Skinheads in America (Hamm, 1993), there likely will be more hate crimes, and thus more literature on them, in the future.

Still, there is hardly a minority group in America that has not been the victim of violence. If there is a thread that ties together American history, it is one of hate crimes, often authorized and sometimes urged on by society at large. The worst example was the killing by hanging or burning of African-American men by white mobs in the South. Although lynchings took place both earlier and later, and vigilante mobs frequently killed white criminals in the North and West, one horrifying statistic is that, from 1882 to 1903, 1,985 African-American men were killed by white mobs, often for very little overt reason. Overall, there were more than five thousand lynchings and uncounted numbers of beatings, whippings, and brandings of African-Americans for nearly a hundred years after the official end of slavery (Hofstadter, 1970). As noted historian Richard Maxwell Brown stated, "Lynch mob violence became an integral part of the post-Reconstruction system of white supremacy" (1969, p. 50). Nor were these the only forms of such violence. From 1900 to 1950, there were thirty-three major urban riots in America, and with the exception of two in Harlem, all of these riots consisted of white aggressors attacking African-American people and property.

By far the longest war fought by Americans was the one against Native Americans. Tragically, most of these battles did not need to be fought at all; virtually all historians agree that the small number of natives allowed plenty of room for white expansion. Further, more than a few American historians believe that the constant attacks on Native Americans, always justified by the rationalization that they were inferior and could therefore be slaughtered, have gone a long way to developing the uniquely American proviolence ethic. "It is possible," Richard Maxwell Brown says, "that no other factor has exercised a more brutalizing influence on the American character than the Indian wars" (1969, p. 67).

Other groups have scarcely been immune to such crimes. There was extensive violence against Catholics in the nineteenth century, marked by convent burnings and riots. From the executions and mutilations of Quakers in colonial times for their audacity in questioning the Puritan faith to the violence perpetrated against Mormons, America has a rich history of approved violence for religious reasons (Commager, 1971; Sloan, 1970). Anti-Chinese violence was rampant on the West Coast in the nineteenth and early twentieth centuries. In World War II, although there had not been and never was a documented case of spying, all persons of Japanese heritage, including second- and third-generation American citizens, living on America's West Coast were locked up in prison camps for the duration of the war.

Short of a loss of life, one can hardly find a political act more damaging than forced removal from (and often the loss of) homes and businesses for years. This drastic wartime move, approved personally by President Roosevelt, was never seriously suggested for, say, German Americans, some of whom were closely affiliated with pro-Nazi groups. Finally, on another front, Philip Taft and Philip Ross summarize management/labor strife simply: "The United States has had the bloodiest and most violent labor history of any industrial nation in the world" (1969, p. 281).

One hate crime that has rarely been reported, but that recently has been studied sufficiently to warrant the conclusion that it is rampant and increasing in incidence, is violence against gay men and lesbians. Most of the studies conducted so far have shown that more than 20 percent of gay men and a smaller number of gay women have been the objects of physical attacks (Berrill, 1990). A much larger number, of course, have been subjected to verbal attacks and other types of threats and intimidation. Still, the most common reported form of antigay violence is when young men harass, beat, and even kill gay men simply because they either do not like them or find their sexual orientation threatening. The crime has become so common that it has picked up its own slang name, "gay-bashing."

SUMMARY

The main objective of this chapter was to introduce you to several sociological theories of law and to discuss the idea of political crime, which criminology seems incapable of discussing. We reviewed six major perspectives on criminal law: the consensus approach, Weberian conflict theories, instrumental Marxism, structural Marxism, structural contradictions theory, and radical feminism. Each has strengths and limitations. However, those that are broadly referred to as *conflict* theories are seen by most contemporary socio-legal theorists as providing more adequate accounts of the origins and functions of law than do *consensus* perspectives. In fact, as we stated previously, the popularity of the consensus approach declined significantly during the 1960s because it could not account for major societal conflicts, such as those surrounding the Vietnam War, the civil rights movement, and the women's movement.

A key theme of this chapter is that law reflects and helps maintain various types of social inequality, such as patriarchal gender relations and the unequal distribution of wealth. How does the law foster racial inequality? Unfortunately, this question has not been adequately answered here. So far, most socio-legal scholars, regardless of their theoretical orientation, have devoted little theoretical and empirical attention to the ways in which the state promotes racism within the legal system. As Elizabeth Comack and Stephen Brickey (1991b, p. 321) correctly point out in their commentary on future directions in the sociology of law ("aboriginal" is the word Canadians often prefer to "native" and certainly prefer to "Indian"):

> Indeed, it is easier for sociologists teaching in the area to find material on the emergence of vagrancy statutes in 14th century England than on the Canadian state policy of sending aboriginal children to residential schools in the 20th century—a policy that aboriginal people have labelled "cultural genocide."

Thus, perhaps the next important step to be taken by those involved in the "sociological movement in law" (Hunt, 1978) is to develop a theory of law that includes race/ethnicity as well as class and gender. This issue and others raised by the socio-legal community (for example, the need for comparative historical studies) are likely to be addressed in the near future.

In discussing political crime, we noted that criminal law and criminologists have had enormous difficulty in categorizing these crimes. We argued that all three of the major types of political crime should be included in any definition: crimes against the state, crimes by the state, and crimes against other groups. Although there is no reason to see crimes against the state as increasing in North America, crimes by the state certainly are at a very high level around the world. Hate crimes, or crimes against other groups, do seem to be increasing in frequency in North America.

SUGGESTED READINGS

Barak, G. (ed.). (1991). *Crimes by the Capitalist State: An Introduction to State Criminality.* Albany: SUNY Press.

Tunnell, K. (ed.). (1993). *Political Crime in Contemporary America.* New York: Garland.

These two books of readings provide an excellent overview of a wide variety of issues and problems in the field of political crime.

Chambliss, W. J., and Zatz, M. S. (ed.). (1993). *Making Law: The State, the Law, and Structural Contradictions.* Bloomington: Indiana University Press.

This book of readings contains several important essays, all of which expand and refine William Chambliss's original structural contradictions theory of law.

Lynch, M. J., and Groves, W. B. (1989). *A Primer in Radical Criminology*, 2nd ed. New York: Harrow & Heston.

Chapter 3 of this overview of radical or critical criminology provides students and faculty alike with a comprehensive critique of the consensus, instrumental Marxist, and structural Marxist perspectives on the state and law.

MacKinnon, C. A. (1989). *Toward a Feminist Theory of the State.* Cambridge, MA: Harvard University Press.

This book offers one of the most important and widely cited contemporary radical feminist theories of law.

Milovanovic, D. (1994). *A Primer in the Sociology of Law,* 2nd ed. New York: Harrow & Heston.

Written by one of North America's most prominent socio-legal scholars, this book provides students with an excellent introduction to the sociology of law. The theoretical perspectives reviewed in this chapter, as well as other important contributions (for example, postmodernism), are described and critiqued in a highly intelligible manner. Milovanovic's book is also an excellent resource for experienced researchers seeking up-to-date information on the key developments in the sociology of law.

CHAPTER 4

METHODS OF GATHERING CRIME DATA

The government is very keen on amassing statistics. They collect them, add to them, raise them to the nth power, take the cube root and prepare wonderful diagrams. But what you must never forget is that every one of these figures comes in the first instance from the chowty dar [village watchman], who puts down what he damn pleases.

JOSIAH CHARLES STAMP, BARON (1929, PP. 258–259)

If it is true that North Americans suffer especially from math fear, then a chapter on research methods might be just what the torture chamber operator would be calling for about now. There may even be some validity to this fear: a boring course in research methods might be worse than a boring course in some other fields. After years of dull math courses, most criminology students "approach a course in research methods with the enthusiasm of a recalcitrant patient in a dentist's office. Even if the experience is not going to be painful, it most certainly is not anticipated to be exciting or interesting" (Hagan, 1993, p. 1).

Yet, it *can* be exciting and interesting, particularly when you take the time to understand its relevance. If all criminal justice statistics were straightforward and accurate, all that you would need would be a few simple definitions. Unfortunately, as we have been telling our students for years: "All of your lives you have been hearing about how statistics lie, about how you should be very cautious around numbers. When you are in criminology, double that concern."

"So what?" we hear you cry out. What difference does it make that many people don't know how various crime statistics were generated? This is one of our problems: too many people tend to accept as true any numbers that seem to have an official stamp of approval. People just crumble up and give in when faced with a number, particularly when the word *fact* appears before it. Groups of all political leanings have learned to print brochures that consist of a number of "facts": "FACT: only 25 percent of theft victims ever report the crime to the police"; "FACT: 50 percent of all rape victims never tell anyone about their experience, including their best friends"; "FACT: Border patrolling stops only 4 percent of the drugs entering this country by ship." These "facts" seem to make sense, so we tend to accept them rather than question how we know these things. For example, if they were never reported, how do we know the thefts occurred? If rape victims never tell anyone about the assault, how do we know to count those persons as victims? Illegal drug smuggling being a fairly hidden activity, how do we know whether we are stopping 4 percent or 50 percent?

The truth is, much of the time, we don't know. In other cases, in order to decide if you are going to accept a claim as factual, it's important to check the source of the data. All criminology data sources have their flaws, but there are different advantages and disadvantages associated with each source. In this chapter, we will lay out some of these good and bad points while introducing you to some of the techniques criminologists use. There are many technical books around if you wish to understand the mathematics or go deeper into these problems. Our goal is not to make you an expert, but simply to introduce you to the basics of the field.

The major data sources we will discuss are: (1) police statistics, (2) victimization surveys, (3) self-report surveys, and (4) observational procedures. There are other sources of "official" information, such as prison inmate counts and juvenile justice records, and many other important sources of data (biographies, discourse analysis, comparative techniques, historical research). Still, the ones discussed cover the bulk of the findings that you are likely to encounter in criminology.

OFFICIAL POLICE STATISTICS

Most people do not think very deeply about crime data. We commonly hear that city X is the safest U.S. city or that city Y is the aggravated assault capital of Canada. How do we know these things? Where do these data come from? Certainly not from the hundreds of academic journal articles and books on crime produced each year, because the results of these studies are rarely reported in the mass media. Something is being reported, however; we read the crime stories all the time.

There are solid structural reasons why reporters rarely take the time to understand complex studies but love simple numbers. One of your authors

(Martin Schwartz) spent some years as a reporter on a major morning daily newspaper and remembers too often being handed a complicated three-hundred-page report late in the afternoon and facing an 11 P.M. story deadline. He might also have had an evening meeting to attend and probably wanted to take some time for dinner. Did he read the entire report, take notes, go to the library, and try to develop a cogent and coherent critique? Or did he use the press release and two-page executive summary to write his story, perhaps occasionally making a phone call to one of the authors? Take a guess. The problem is even worse for TV and radio reporters, who typically have much less of an opportunity to specialize and learn than print reporters.

Now that, as criminologists, *we* are the "experts" being called by reporters, we can see it from the other side. The criminologists called most often are those who can speak in "sound bites" or "print bites"; being brilliant might be helpful, but we suspect we are called instead because we can say something that sounds useful in ten seconds or fifty words. Of course, in the case of crime, very often police public relations officers are called. After all, police officers are the front-line agents in the "war against crime." Because they have to deal with offenders on a day-to-day basis, don't they know more about crime than anyone else? Well, police departments certainly have a substantial amount of crime knowledge. Nevertheless, their data are not accurate accounts of the extent, distribution, and sources of crime. In some areas, such as corporate crime, police data are particularly poor.

What *are* police data? How do we know that city X is the safest place to live? How do we know that burglary is down 2.77 percent since last year? The answer in the United States comes from one single national source: the FBI's *Uniform Crime Reports* (UCR). If crime data are reported in the mass media, they probably come from the UCR (Schmalleger, 1993).

THE *UNIFORM CRIME REPORTS*

Before 1930, it was impossible to make any reasonable comparisons about crime between cities, states, and regions. In a country where laws differ from state to state, simple words like *burglary* can have very different meanings just across a state line. If a large city has 13,000 reports of burglary (defined as entering an occupied dwelling for the purpose of committing *a felony*) while a smaller city has 3,000 reports of burglary (defined as entering an occupied or unoccupied dwelling for the purpose of committing *any crime*), which one has the bigger crime problem? Who knows? You are comparing apples and oranges.

Origins and Characteristics of the UCR

Based on the work of the International Association of Chiefs of Police (IACP), the U.S. Congress in 1930 began a new program whereby four hundred police departments voluntarily supplied their annual crime statistics to FBI officials, who compiled and published the *Uniform Crime Reports.* Actually, this is a pretty small number of police departments. One of the traditional problems with the UCR was that, as more and more departments began to voluntarily participate, more and more crime was obviously being reported. But was the crime rate going up, or were there simply more participating departments? Today, more than 16,000 police departments participate, although some of these departments are rather small. Many of the smallest departments in the country still do not participate, but few supporters of the UCR worry about this: the police departments that serve over 97 percent of the U.S. population now are part of the UCR program.

From the beginning, it was argued that the public and policymakers could not make sense of data on thousands of crimes. To illustrate why, think of the New York Stock Exchange. Many people choose to follow the Dow Jones Industrial Average of the stocks of just thirty major corporations, rather than trying to get the complete picture of what is happening to all stocks. With crime, too, an *index* was developed: a small number of crimes that would be extensively reported to serve as a substitute for reports on all crimes. These eight Part I crimes, or *Index crimes,* make up the bulk of UCR reports and statistical analyses. Police departments supposedly report to the FBI (usually through their state data system) every case that has come to their attention, by whatever means, of each Part I crime. Table 4.1 shows UCR data on reports of Index crimes for 1991 and 1993.

There are also twenty-one Part II offenses used by the UCR, consisting of some of the other crimes not in Part I and some catchall categories. Table 4.2 shows all Part I and Part II crimes for 1993; note that information on Part II offenses is limited to *arrests.* Thus, Table 4.1 shows all *reports* of

Index crimes to police forces, as reported to the FBI, while Table 4.2 shows all *arrests* for a much wider variety of crimes.

Originally, there were seven Index crimes. The first four were the violent crimes: criminal homicide, forcible rape and attempted rape, aggravated assault (plus attempted assault and attempted murder), and robbery (plus attempted robbery). On the property crime side, the categories were burglary, larceny, and motor vehicle theft. In 1978, reflecting congressional concern about a possible increase in arson in America, arson became the eighth Index crime. Unfortunately, this addition has been more symbolic than real: only a small amount of arson data have ever been gathered, and systematic underreporting has made what data are available of limited value (Jackson, 1990).

Interestingly, UCR instructions call for a crime to be counted only once, according to what some call the *hierarchical principle* whereby only the most serious category is counted (except in the case of arson, which theoretically is always reported). Thus, if a woman is robbed, then badly beaten, then

Table 4.1 UCR Data on Reported Index Crimes, 1991 and 1993

	1991	1993	PERCENT CHANGE
Total Crime Index	14,872,883	14,140,952	−4.9%
Total Violent Crime	1,911,767	1,924,188	+0.6
Murder and nonnegligent manslaughter	24,703	24,526	−0.7
Forcible rape (and attempts)	106,593	104,806	−1.7
Robbery	687,732	659,757	−4.1
Aggravated assault	1,092,739	1,135,099	+3.9
Total Property Crime	12,961,116	12,216,764	−5.7
Burglary	3,157,150	2,834,808	−10.2
Larceny-theft	8,142,228	7,820,909	−3.9
Motor vehicle theft	1,661,738	1,561,047	−6.1

SOURCE: Federal Bureau of Investigation, 1992, 1994.

raped, and finally murdered, with the killer stealing her car to get away, five Index crimes will have been committed, but only the one murder will show up in the UCR.

As quirky as the logic behind this practice may seem, things are further complicated by larceny, the most problematic of all Part I offenses. Historically, most state laws made theft of property worth over $50 a major crime. This made some sense in an era when $50 was equivalent two to four weeks' pay for a worker or farmer. With inflation, however, one can barely even find a textbook for under $50. Some states kept up with inflation, making the break between a minor and a major crime at $100, $250, or even more. Thus, the problem: some states were reporting to the FBI all thefts of over $250; some, all thefts over $100; and some, all thefts over $50. Because this was so unwieldy, the Index crime was changed to include all larcenies.

How much better did this make things? Now, theft of a packet of pork chops (or a bunch of carrots) goes into the UCR index of crimes as one

Table 4.2 Total Estimated Arrests, United States, 1993

Total	**14,036,300**	Stolen property (buying, receiving, possessing)	158,100
Murder and nonnegligent manslaughter	23,400	Vandalism	313,000
		Weapons (carrying, possessing, etc.)	262,300
Forcible rape	38,420	Prostitution and commercialized vice	97,800
Robbery	173,620	Sex offenses (except forcible rape and prostitution	104,100
Aggravated assault	518,670		
Burglary	402,700	Drug abuse violations	1,126,300
Larceny-theft	1,476,300	Gambling	17,300
Motor vehicle theft	195,900	Offenses against family and children	109,100
Arson	19,400		
		Driving under the influence	1,524,800
Violent crime	754,110	Liquor laws	518,500
Property crime	2,094,300	Drunkenness	726,600
Crime Index Total	**2,848,400**	Disorderly conduct	727,000
		Vagrancy	28,200
Other assaults	1,144,900	All other offenses	3,518,700
Forgery and counterfeiting	106,900	Suspicion (not included in totals)	14,100
Fraud	410,700	Curfew and loitering law violations	100,200
Embezzlement	12,900	Runaways	180,500

NOTE: Arrest totals are based on all reporting agencies and estimates for unreported areas; because of rounding, figures may not add to totals.

SOURCE: Federal Bureau of Investigation, 1994, p. 217.

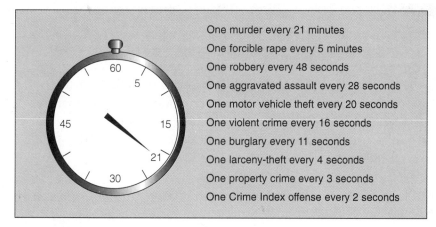

One murder every 21 minutes
One forcible rape every 5 minutes
One robbery every 48 seconds
One aggravated assault every 28 seconds
One motor vehicle theft every 20 seconds
One violent crime every 16 seconds
One burglary every 11 seconds
One larceny-theft every 4 seconds
One property crime every 3 seconds
One Crime Index offense every 2 seconds

Figure 4.1
FBI Crime Clock, 1993

crime. So does theft of a Boeing 757. When we say that theft is up this year, are we talking about shoplifted bunches of carrots or hijacked warehouse cargos? Based on UCR data, it's hard to say.

In any event, once the FBI has all of these raw numbers, what happens next? Calculations are performed on the Index crimes to produce some statistics: the number of offenses; the crime rate per 100,000 people; crime rates by year; regional, state, and municipal variations in crime; the age, sex, and race of perpetrators and victims; and numbers of "crimes cleared by arrest." In addition, the UCR provides a "crime clock" that reports the frequency of the first seven Index crimes (see Figure 4.1). Unfortunately, the crime clock is much like that character most of us remember from our high school days: the one who was both "most popular" and simultaneously "most useless." The crime clock is well loved and often reprinted, despite being at best fairly meaningless and at worst very misleading. The biggest problem is that it is based on time rather than population. Suppose you live in a small village of ten residents and one crime is committed in a year. That is a rate of one crime per ten people per year. With population increases, you later have one hundred residents and five crimes committed in a year. That is one crime per twenty people; your crime rate has dropped in half. Yet, on the crime clock you have gone from one crime a year to five crimes a year, a 500 percent increase. This isn't very useful information.

The FBI, of course, finds quite a few strengths in the UCR. It contends that its data

> have over the years become one of the leading social indicators in the country. The American public looks to the UCR for information in the level of crime, while criminologists, sociologists, legislators, municipal planners, the press, and other students of criminal justice use the statistics for varied research and planning purposes. (1988, p. 1)

The FBI has a valid point. No other source of U.S. crime data receives more popular attention than the UCR, especially from the media. The FBI has worked hard over the years to make the UCR available, sending out reams of press releases and issuing copies of the full report. Thus, accessibility itself is one of the UCR's most significant strengths, although they do not make the raw data available in an easily used format.

Criminologists have argued for two basic uses of the UCR, although virtually all agree that certain limitations, discussed in the next section, must be taken into consideration. First, some feel that the UCR can be used to evaluate how police officers deal with those behaviors that have been officially defined as criminal (DeKeseredy & MacLean, 1991). Others feel that if crime definitions and police reports are used consistently from year to year, UCR data can be of some value in charting crime trends (Gove, Hughes, & Geerken, 1985; Inciardi, 1990). This is a long way from being an indicator of the extent and distribution of crime in the United States. Rather, it suggests that if the biases in the data collection remain the same from year to year, the UCR data can be helpful in seeing whether "whatever it is we are counting" is going up or down.

This final point in support of the UCR can be stated more strongly. Walter Gove, Michael Hughes, and Michael Geerken (1985), for example, argue that the factors the public generally associates with a serious crime are fairly consistent: it involves a threat or completed bodily harm, breaking and entering, valuable property being stolen, and a stranger for an offender. When these factors are present, the crime tends to be reported and the police tend to record these reports. The argument, then, is that the UCR records some vague agreement by the citizenry and the police as to what "important" crime is and does a relatively good job at measuring those crimes.

General Limitations of the UCR

The problem with assessing the value of the UCR, however, is that its strengths are also its limitations. In the preceding quote, the FBI's major claim was that the official statistics in the UCR are widely used in the United States. True enough, but does that make them accurate or valid? Perhaps as important, Index crimes consist of eight offenses that people, acting as part of a political process, decided should be included in the index. You may agree or disagree with the choices, but you should recognize that the decision was a political one. This should help you understand why shoplifting a bunch of carrots is an Index (Part I) crime but embezzling $14 million is a Part II offense. Or why snatching a purse is an Index crime but running a fraud operation that steals the life savings from hundreds of people is not. Or why stealing a rusted-out 1963 Dodge Dart that runs on only three cylinders is an Index offense but crushing a brand new BMW 525i into a pile of scrap metal is not. Of course, if the person took a few cassette tapes from the glove box first, it would be an Index crime.

The UCR have many other limitations. We can't address them all, but the most important one is citizen nonreporting.

The Effects of Citizen Nonreporting

If you reflect on your own crime experiences, you will—perhaps reluctantly—remember periodically breaking the law. Did you get arrested? Every single time? Did someone witness your offenses and report them to the police? Every single time? For most of us, the answer is no. Similarly, you may not have reported to the proper authorities the last time you were victimized by crime, particularly if the crime was minor. For example, someone recently unhooked the garden hose from the back of Martin Schwartz's house and made off with it, while at a shopping mall someone else reached into his wife's shopping bag and stole a sack containing about $15 worth of moisturizing lotion. Neither crime was reported.

How do the police learn about crime? In most advanced Western industrialized nations, more than 90 percent of crimes known to the police come to their attention because of public reports (Kinsey, Lea, & Young, 1986). Despite some undercover work, and mass media portrayals notwithstanding, answering the phone is the main way that police learn about crime

(Brannigan, 1984). Yet, as with your crimes, thousands—maybe millions—of events never come to the attention of the police. Criminologists debate many issues among themselves, but they never challenge the assertion that most of the crimes committed in the United States are never reported to the police. This is an important point. After all, if the police don't know about crimes, they will not appear in the UCR, which means that the UCR greatly underestimates the extent of behavior defined as Part I and Part II offenses.

Of course, if the police depend on the willingness of private citizens to report offenses, then the second half of that equation is that the police should be willing to take a report. Unfortunately, many citizen reports are not recorded; estimates of the percentage recorded range from one-third (Samaha, 1994) to three-quarters (Inciardi, 1990). Worse, we know that local departments commonly do not follow the standard FBI crime definitions when making a report, although we don't know how often this happens.

What may be particularly interesting about the widespread public silence is that the United States in the past decade has been characterized by a growing public hysteria about crime, with a resulting pressure on government to strip away defendants' rights, lock up convicted offenders for longer periods, and add tremendous numbers of police officers to the nation's forces. In a 1992 Roper Poll, two-thirds of all Americans felt that one of the necessary remedies for crime was "much stricter law enforcement and severer penalties than we have now" (Maguire, Pastore, & Flanagan, 1993, p. 195). If people are extremely worried about being victimized, then why wouldn't they report their own victimization or the harms inflicted on others that come to their attention?

There are several answers to this question. First, some people are not aware that they have been victimized. Someone may have damaged your property or stolen something from your backyard without your even knowing it. Martin Schwartz, for example, knew he had scratches on his car, but he didn't know that they were the result of criminal vandalism until it was pointed out to him by an insurance adjuster looking at a windshield cracked by a stone. Neighbors may observe somebody carrying goods out of your home but just assume that a friend is borrowing something. Some people still think that all burglars dress in black and sneak over back fences in the middle of the night, so they won't see an unhurried daytime stranger as a problem.

Second, people may know that a crime is taking place but not regard the event as socially injurious. For example, despite the "war on drugs," it is not uncommon for college students to purchase and smoke marijuana, but they are rarely reported to the police, partly because many people oppose the criminalization of "soft drugs" (Currie, 1993).

Third, some witnesses suffer a range of emotions, from embarrassment to traumatization, due to their own victimization or to what they have observed happening to others. A woman or man who is forcibly raped may not wish to report the crime because she or he is embarrassed by the crime and does not want parents, friends, or neighbors to know it happened. Our society sends out powerful messages about blame, and an extraordinary number of people feel that *they* (rather than the offender!) are to blame for a crime because they forgot to lock a car door, opened their apartment door to a stranger, or were out on the streets late at night.

Although embarrassment can keep some people from reporting, others may fear that they will have to deal with insensitive or sexist law enforcement officials who will not take their suffering seriously or who will blame them for their victimization (Allison & Wrightsman, 1993; Barnett & LaViolette, 1993). A number of rape victims have said that their treatment by the criminal justice system amounted to a "second rape" (Madigan & Gamble, 1989), and there is no way of knowing just how many women are deterred from reporting because of this fear. Worse, even in the growing number of areas where the police respond sensitively, the "second rape" problem may continue to exist when hospital personnel are insensitive or when defense attorneys or trial judges are allowed to attack the victim (Fairstein, 1993; Vachhs, 1993). Consider the experience with the criminal justice system of this woman, who was regularly beaten in an intimate relationship:

> The thing that has never left my mind from that point to now is what the judge said to me. He took a few minutes and he looked at me and he said, "I don't believe anything you're saying. The reason I don't believe it is because I don't believe that anything like this could happen to me. If I was you and someone had threatened me with a gun, there is no way that I would continue to stay with them. There is no way that I would continue to stay with them. There is no way that I could take that kind of abuse from them. Therefore,

since I would not let that happen to me, I can't believe that it happened to you."

I have just never forgotten those words. . . . When I left the courtroom that day, I felt very defeated, and very powerless and very hopeless, because not only had I gone through an experience which I found to be very overwhelming, very trying and almost cost me my life, but to sit up in court and make myself open up and recount all my feelings and fear and then have it thrown back in my face as being totally untrue just because this man would not allow anyone to do this to him, placed me in a state of shock which probably hasn't left me yet. (Smith, as cited in Maryland, 1989, p. 3)

It isn't only people who fear their treatment by the criminal justice system who might not report crimes to the police. For property crimes, people may recognize that it is hardly worth the effort to file a report; only about 10 percent of all theft and burglary victims ever recover some or all of their stolen property (Zawitz et al., 1993). Take the extreme example of a college student, Sam, who returns from winter break to find his TV stolen. He thinks it was made in Japan, but he has forgotten the make and model and certainly does not know the serial number. Sam wonders what the police can do if he tells them this TV was stolen, especially since he can narrow the time of the theft only to "some time over the past three weeks." If he is uninsured, why bother reporting the crime? Indeed, the police will no doubt ask the same question: Could they put out a bulletin to be alert for a TV of *that* description? In many areas where police are understaffed, they no longer even will come to crime scenes. For example, both authors of this book have had car parts taken from autos sitting in their driveways. Walter De-Keseredy's car wheels were stolen in Ottawa, Canada, but when he called the police he was given a badge number and a complaint number to give to his insurance company. Similarly, Martin Schwartz had an auto stereo stolen in Lexington, Kentucky, and was simply told to inform his insurance company that a telephone report had been made. In each case, our insurance companies required that a report be made. If we were not carrying optional theft insurance, why would we bother to call the police the next time now that we know they do not do investigations? Lower-income people (including many college students) commonly do not have or cannot get renter's insurance or theft insurance and thus would have very little incentive to

It is very difficult for us to know just how many crimes are committed, even when we can agree on the definition of crime. If you had semiabandoned an uninsured car on the street and then found it in this condition, would you bother to call the police?

report such crimes. Worse, some people believe that filing small claims will result in increases in their premiums or cancellation of their policies. When all of these people stop calling the police, it does not mean that such thefts are not happening; it just means that these thefts stop appearing on police reports.

The police are aware that their chances of solving these crimes, or even major felonies such as burglary or armed robbery, are very slim unless they have a good lead within hours of the report. Thus, even for those cases in which people do report their victimizations, the overwhelming majority of all robbery and burglary cases are dropped by the police within a day (Inciardi, 1990). No one disputes that the TV was stolen; it's just that filing a report will take time and it will have no effect whatsoever on getting the TV back. So, why is it a problem if Sam doesn't file a report? Well, if you want to know whether Sam lives in a safe neighborhood or what the rate of residential break-ins might be in student apartments, both of which are very good criminology questions, you are not going to get a true picture because break-ins at places like Sam's apartment are not being recorded.

Of course, some victims have a special interest in avoiding reporting their victimizations to the police. Drug dealers who are the victims of armed robbery, prostitutes who are raped, and even customers of prostitutes who have a wallet lifted when their attention is diverted often feel that the police would not welcome hearing of their complaints (Miller & Schwartz, 1994). Nevertheless, an armed robbery, a rape, and a theft have been committed but not reported.

Other victims figure that being involved in the criminal justice system is another form of victimization. For example, Martin Schwartz's mother was a bookkeeper when the office she worked in was broken into and the petty cash box stolen. The police soon caught a young man who they thought had committed the burglary. However, after spending several mornings sitting in the courtroom hallway, submitting to lengthy interviews, filling out forms, and suffering lots of anxiety, Mrs. Schwartz figured that it was better to just "write off" $20 in petty cash than to lose several days of productivity by cooperating with the justice system. Worse, some people know they will not be paid if they take time off from work to go to court, while others are afraid they will be the victims of retaliation by the offender.

Overall, then, people have a great many reasons for not reporting victimizations to the police. Whatever their reasons, the result is that, in the United States, the large majority of victimizations are *not* reported.

Additional Limitations of the UCR

We have mentioned several reasons why many criminologists feel that the UCR is an unreliable source of data on the extent, distribution, and sources of crime. Actually, the effect of some of these problems has not been studied extensively by criminologists. For example, we noted that many crime reports are not recorded by police. We have always known that some departments limit the number of crimes that they are willing to record. For example, when Martin Schwartz was an undergraduate, he lived in a city that has often been praised for having one of the lowest rape rates in the country. A cynic would argue that a refusal to accept rape reports could account for this low rate. One year, in fact, Schwartz personally heard of as many women who claimed to have been raped by strangers within blocks of the campus as were reported in the police statistics for the entire city of 100,000 people! Later on, as a newspaper reporter in the same city, he interviewed homeless people who claimed that they were not "allowed" to be crime victims: if they went to police headquarters to report being the victim of an armed robbery, they were physically ejected from the police station. Needless to say, the armed robbery rate was also quite low in that city! Interestingly, years later, Schwartz told that story in a criminal justice class at a midwestern university. A student who was a police captain in a force covering a city of 400,000 angrily denied that this could happen in his department, one of the most "professional" in the region. Over the following weeks, every other police officer in the class stopped by Schwartz's office to say something like, "Well, I couldn't say anything in front of the captain, but we refuse to take rape cases all of the time! I've refused several this year already because I didn't believe her."

Sometimes, entire categories of people are not "allowed" to be crime victims. One California police department stamped all reports of violent crimes against prostitutes as NHI—"No Human Involved"—and did not follow up on them (Fairstein, 1993). Certainly, prostitutes and street people in many other cities feel that the police refuse to take their victimizations seriously (Miller & Schwartz, 1994).

On the other hand, exactly the opposite accusation has sometimes been made: that the police inflate crime statistics to make the crime problem look worse or inflate arrest statistics to make themselves look like better crime fighters. For example, a mayoral commission accused the New York City police of the widespread use of "testilying," or engaging in perjury and faked evidence to inflate arrest statistics (Sexton, 1994). This results in large increases in arrests, which can make the crime problem look much worse than it would if the police made only legitimate arrests. Another popular example is long-time FBI director J. Edgar Hoover, who was reputed throughout his career to somehow manage to uncover huge crime increases every time he wanted an increase in his budget and was finding congressional resistance.

Even if the crime figures are correct, the problem remains that the UCR is selective in what it covers. One form of selectivity is that the UCR does not cover federal offenses. This made some sense fifty years ago, when the states handled virtually all criminal prosecutions, leaving the federal government to deal with espionage and various interstate frauds. However, with the tremendous expansion in recent years of the federal jurisdiction (and the growing population in federal prisons), the logic behind this practice is less clear.

We could argue that the most important problem with the UCR, however, relates to the other form of selectivity. As we have discussed, a political decision was made to include some crimes in the UCR and not others. Even more political were the choices for the Index crimes. Simply put, most white-collar, corporate, and political crimes are omitted from the UCR crime classification schemes. Why is it that stealing a slice of pizza is an Index crime but defrauding the taxpayers out of $14 million in a savings and loan scandal or illegally overcharging the Navy $11 million for parts are not? When you hear that crime is up in the United States, would you worry more about shoplifting or multimillion-dollar schemes?

In Chapter 10, we will deal with the very specific argument that white-collar and corporate crimes are not minor events, but rather "crimes of the powerful" (Pearce, 1976) that are equally, if not more, injurious than many of the Index or Part II offenses. Suppose your brother died because some gang kids were randomly firing guns in the neighborhood, not meaning to kill anyone but being extraordinarily and criminally careless. Certainly, you would have a right to be very upset. But suppose your brother died in an industrial accident because his employer decided to save money by not following federal and state safety laws, not meaning to kill anyone but being extraordinarily and criminally careless. Would you feel any different? Why, then, is only one of these two deaths going to show up as an Index crime? Actually, you can defend or criticize the way that the UCR is set up, but you should recognize that the system is a political one, in that decisions must be made to include some things and exclude others. The way in which these decisions were made, and who benefits from these decisions, is a legitimate line of inquiry.

We should note that the U.S. Department of Justice is aware of these criticisms, and has been for many years. The problem is carrying out any change. Some of the more obvious recommendations include changing the definitions of some crimes. The definition of aggravated assault could be sharpened, and the definition of rape could be updated to match the definitions now used by many states—which include forced anal or oral sex, and therefore male victims. Rather than the current practice of merely lumping completed and attempted offenses together, these could be more clearly differentiated. More attention could be paid to getting police departments to more accurately report data.

A solution to some of these problems has been reached with the development of the *National Incident-Based Reporting Program* (NIBRS). This program is designed to upgrade the UCR from a system that merely counts the number of times something happened to one in which large amounts of data will be available. NIBRS would require a form to be filled out for every criminal incident and provide room for enormous amounts of detail (fifty-two "data elements") not currently available. The entire concept of Index crimes would be dropped, and all crimes would be reported, not just the most serious. Further, attempted crimes would be distinguished from completed crimes. With computerization, the theory goes, police would possess an enormous amount of information across jurisdictions, and researchers and policymakers would also be able to obtain this information.

Actually, this system is already in place in several states, and the FBI is accepting data in this format. The budget crises of the early and mid-1990s, however, ensure that this reform will go slower than many have hoped. A good guess as to when the entire nation will be on this system is simply not possible.

VICTIMIZATION SURVEYS

There is a perfectly horrible phrase we feel forced to tell you about, because it is so widely used in criminology. We have established in the preceding section that it is common for the law to be broken (crimes) but for the event to be missing from police statistics (the UCR). This is often termed the "dark figure of crime."

As we shall see, it is possible to develop a survey that discovers many crimes that were not reported to the police. Nearly two-thirds of the victimizations uncovered by the U.S. National Crime Victimization Survey were not reported to the police (Zawitz et al., 1993). In Canada, the equivalent figure is closer to 40 percent (Sacco & Johnson, 1990).

A New Focus on Victims

Studying victims, however, is a fairly recent phenomenon. Most of the history of criminology has been what Andrew Karmen (1990) terms "offender-ology," whereby the focus was on the person accused of committing a crime. Our new concern with victims has mirrored that of the criminal justice system. Just as the victim, like it or not, mainly existed (from the system's point of view) as a witness for the prosecution, for criminologists victims existed primarily to give researchers data on offenders (Pointing & Maguire, 1988). Since the 1960s, however, a number of political movements have focused concern on victims and spurred the emergence of a new field, victimology, within criminology. Interestingly, those responsible include not only civil rights and human rights activists and feminists but also conservative, "law-and-order" politicians, all of whom brought attention to the specific individuals victimized by at least selected criminal acts (Elias, 1986; Mayhew & Hough, 1988). Thus, two factors came together in the late 1960s and 1970s: a dissatisfaction with official crime data and a greater appreciation for victims of crime in both the academic and general communities.

The result was the victimization survey, an effort to collect information on crimes unknown to the police (Walklate, 1989). There are many different such surveys, conducted in many different ways, but all of them ask people to provide information on crimes that may have been committed against them. While the interviewers have their "feet in the door," they may also ask about fear of crime, the effects of victimization (such as injury), reasons the crime wasn't reported, and so on.

At the risk of oversimplifying things, there are two broad types of victimization surveys. Generally, government-sponsored surveys seek data on the extent, nature, and consequences of legally defined types of property and predatory street crime. These include the U.S. National Crime Victimization Survey, the Canadian Urban Victimization Survey, and the British Crime Survey. Simply put (perhaps too simply), these surveys ask an enormous number of people, scientifically chosen from across the country and representing most types of citizens, questions about the same events covered in official crime statistics such as the UCR, to see if additional information can be obtained. Of course, murder is not part of victimization surveys ("Sir, in the past six months, have you been murdered?").

A growing number of other, smaller surveys focus on more specific issues, such as victimization in intimate relationships, anti-gay violence, child physical and sexual abuse, sexual harassment, racially motivated assaults, and, to a much lesser extent, corporate crime. As you will notice in subsequent chapters of this text, different methodological procedures are used in these studies, but the one thing all victimization surveys have in common is that they ask people to describe their own experiences.

One unfortunate problem with descriptions such as the one we just gave is that some people get the impression that victimization surveys are relatively simple to do (Sykes & Cullen, 1992). Each of us has often been surprised by students who suggest on exams that conducting a survey is simply a matter of going door to door and asking people to tell you about how and when they were victimized. Having considerable experience conducting these studies ourselves, we can only respond with this careful scientific assessment: "It ain't that easy!"

Particularly in the discipline of sociology, the home of mass survey techniques, there is an extraordinarily large literature on such topics as sampling—how do you choose whom to interview? For example, if you interview only street drug dealers, you probably will get a different victimization picture than if you interview only country club members. So how do you get a representative cross-section of the entire population? It is widely known that the way you word the questions and the order in which you ask them can influence the answers. Politicians are expert at this, commonly sending out "questionnaires" to people's homes asking, "Are you in favor of taking money away from law-abiding citizens to give unneeded comforts to imprisoned rapists and murderers?" Or the same question: "Do you believe that a civilized society must maintain at least a minimal standard of decency in its prisons?" Of course, these are extreme examples, but there is a science to wording survey questions. When you combine these problems of deciding whom to ask and what to ask with time and budget limitations (who is paying the salary and expenses of the questioners?), conducting a victimization survey can be an extremely difficult and challenging task. Using sophisticated statistical procedures to analyze the data often creates even more problems (which may explain why UCR data are rarely analyzed by the government in this way).

Perhaps the world's most sophisticated, comprehensive, and frequently cited victimization survey is the U.S. Department of Justice's National

Crime Victimization Survey (NCVS), which has examined all UCR Index offenses except murder and arson by administering a survey nationally. Each year, NCVS researchers conduct about 166,000 interviews of persons over age 12 in 84,000 housing units; since 1972, more than 4.6 million such interviews have been done. There are some differences between the UCR

Table 4.3 NCVS Data on Victimization Levels and Rates for Personal and Household Crimes, 1991–1992

	NUMBER OF VICTIMIZATIONS (1,000s)			VICTIMIZATION RATES		
	1991	1992	Percent Change	1991	1992	Percent Change
All Crimes	**35,497**	**33,649**	**−5.2%**	—	—	—
Personal Crimes	**19,472**	**18,832**	**−3.3%**	**95.3**	**91.2**	**−4.3%**
Crimes of violence	6,587	6,621	.5	32.2	32.1	−.5
Completed	2,528	2,410	−4.7	12.4	11.7	−5.7
Attempted	4,059	4,212	3.8	19.9	20.4	2.7
Rape	174	141	−19.0	.9	.7	−19.8
Robbery	1,203	1,226	1.9	5.9	5.9	.8
Completed	802	806	.6	3.9	3.9	−.4
With injury	266	334	25.6	1.3	1.6	24.3
Without injury	535	472	−11.8	2.6	2.3	−12.7
Attempted	402	419	4.4	2.0	2.0	3.3
With injury	126	103	−17.8	.6	.5	−18.7
Without injury	276	316	14.5	1.4	1.5	13.3
Assault	5,210	5,255	.9	25.5	25.5	−.2
Aggravated	1,634	1,849	13.1	8.0	9.0	11.9
Completed with injury	601	658	9.5	2.9	3.2	8.4
Attempted assault with weapon	1,034	1,191	15.2	5.1	5.8	14.0
Simple	3,575	3,406	−4.7	17.5	16.5	−5.7
Completed with injury	1,056	905	−14.3	5.2	4.4	−15.2
Attempted assault without weapon	2,519	2,501	−.7	12.3	12.1	−1.7
Crimes of theft	12,885	12,211	−5.2	63.1	59.2	−6.2
Completed	12,004	11,448	−4.6	58.8	55.5	−5.6
Attempted	881	762	−13.5	4.3	3.7	−14.4
Personal larceny with contact	497	485	−2.4	2.4	2.3	−3.4
Purse snatching	142	152	7.1	.7	.7	6.0
Pocket picking	355	333	−6.2	1.7	1.6	−7.2

and the NCVS in what is recorded. Although the UCR includes all crimes that come to the attention of the police, since 1977 the NCVS has recorded only those crimes affecting individuals and their household. Thus, if your house was burglarized or your wallet taken by a thief, it could be included in both. If, however, a burglar breaks into the safe at the Fiftieth National Bank, that would be included in the UCR but not usually in the NCVS. Table 4.3 lists NCVS data for 1991–1992.

	NUMBER OF VICTIMIZATIONS (1,000s)			VICTIMIZATION RATES		
	1991	1992	Percent Change	1991	1992	Percent Change
Personal larceny without contact	12,389	11,726	−5.3	60.6	56.8	−6.3
Completed	11,537	11,006	−4.6	56.5	53.3	−5.6
Less than $50	4,491	4,391	−2.2	22.0	21.3	−3.2
$50 or more	6,460	5,942	−8.0	31.6	28.8	−9.0
Amount not available	585	673	15.0	2.9	3.3	13.8
Attempted	852	720	−15.5	4.2	3.5	−16.4
Household Crimes	**16,025**	**14,817**	**−7.5**	**166.4**	**152.2**	**−8.5**
Completed	13,592	12,586	−7.4	141.2	129.3	−8.4
Attempted	2,433	2,231	−8.3	25.3	22.9	−9.3
Household burglary	5,187	4,757	−8.3	53.9	48.9	−9.3
Completed	4,050	3,785	−6.6	42.1	38.9	−7.6
Forcible entry	1,689	1,602	−5.1	17.5	16.5	−6.1
Unlawful entry without force	2,362	2,183	−7.6	24.5	22.4	−8.6
Attempted forcible entry	1,136	972	−14.4	11.8	10.0	−15.3
Household larceny	8,702	8,101	−6.9	90.4	83.2	−7.9
Completed	8,169	7,582	−7.2	84.8	77.9	−8.2
Less than $50	3,414	2,801	−18.0	35.5	28.8	−18.8
$50 or more	4,308	4,200	−2.5	44.7	43.2	−3.6
Amount not available	447	581	30.1	4.6	6.0	28.7
Attempted	533	519	−2.5	5.5	5.3	−3.5
Motor vehicle theft	2,136	1,959	−8.3	22.2	20.1	−9.3
Completed	1,372	1,220	−11.1	14.3	12.5	−12.1
Attempted	764	739	−3.3	7.9	7.6	−4.3

SOURCE: U.S. Department of Justice, *Criminal Victimization in the United States* (Washington, DC: Bureau of Justice Statistics, 1994).

The National Crime Victimization Survey

As we have said, the NCVS asks a large number of people if they have been crime victims and summarizes the types of crimes they report, the characteristics of those crimes, the effect of the crimes on the victims, and whether the crimes were reported to the police. The survey itself has a very sophisticated design and is administered by field representatives from the U.S. Census Bureau selected to match the characteristics of each neighborhood by race and ethnic background. Translations are provided if needed. An extraordinary 95 percent or more of households invited to participate do so.

The most important crimes surveyed are rape, robbery, assault, burglary, personal and household larceny, and motor vehicle theft. Interviewers, using simple language like, "Was anything stolen from you?" ask a brief screening question to see if anyone in the household has been a crime victim within the past six months. Then, extensive questions are asked about each incident.

After twenty years of these interviews, the NCVS staff has claimed that they can draw some overall conclusions about crime victimization (Zawitz et al., 1993):

- About 23 percent of all U.S. households are victimized by one or more crimes each year, with African-American, Hispanic, and urban households the most likely to be victimized. Still, this is the lowest number in twenty years, continuing a steady downward drop, although the drop for white households is much greater than the drop for African-American households.

- About one-half of violent crimes and one-third of all crimes are reported to the police. Interestingly, the proportion of crimes reported to the police was higher in 1992 than in 1973, including a rise of 34 percent in the reporting of personal theft. How this affects the UCR statistics is very difficult to measure.

- Those most likely to be victimized are teenagers and young adults. An exception to the overall trend of decreasing crime is that violent crime rates for young people have been increasing.

- Males are much more likely to be crime victims overall, and especially to be victimized by strangers. Females are as likely to be victims of violence by intimates and family members as they are by strangers.

- When family violence is studied specifically, the overwhelming majority of victims are female, with about 20 percent of them repeatedly victimized. Victims of family violence are more likely to be injured than victims of stranger violence.

- One crime for which rates began rising again in the late 1980s is motor vehicle theft, which hits African-American and Hispanic families particularly hard. The rate for African-Americans, when you take into account how many cars are owned, is almost three times what it is for whites; the rate for Hispanics is even slightly higher.

One of the more interesting differences between the NCVS and the UCR is that the UCR has in many years shown crime on the rise in the United States and overall has shown a fairly dramatic rise over the past twenty years. At the same time, the NCVS has shown no particular rise at all, except for the violent crime victimization rates of young people. How can this happen? Is one right and the other wrong?

Part of the answer may be in differing rates of reporting crime. As noted previously, more and more people are reporting their crime victimizations to the police. This would cause a UCR crime rate with no rise at all in the "true" crime rate. Still, it is unlikely that this can account for all of the difference. A much more important conclusion, and one that we will return to later in this book, is that we truly don't know the answer to this question. We really don't know which set of data is more correct. We really don't know how much crime there is in the United States. Keep this in mind when we later ask a simple question like, "Will increasing prison sentences decrease the crime rate?" If we don't even know what the crime rate is, how can we answer such questions?

The Limitations of Victimization Surveys

As with all social scientific research methods, many problems limit the usefulness of this form of data gathering. Although a primary strength of victimization surveys is that many people do tell researchers about much more crime than has previously been revealed to the police, other people are withholding information from both the police *and* the researchers. This is called *underreporting*. Further, some people are simply not able to accurately assess the number of crimes committed. Of course, the more crime there is, and the more minor the crime, the more likely people are to have memory lapses. Often, this is considered to be a problem for those who live in areas characterized by high levels of poverty, unemployment, and subemployment. However, in many circumstances, this could be true for anyone. For example, some of you might recall living in a college dormitory where there was quite a bit of property crime. Both of your authors have that memory of mobs of students returning from the local bar or pub and smashing windows, breaking bottles, pulling fire alarms, destroying washroom facilities, and so on. Asked, even at the time, to report the precise number of these activities, we would probably have underestimated, having forgotten many specifics.

Many victimization surveys are accused of underreporting even fairly major assaults, as people in general tend to hold back information when the assailants were friends or family members (Hagan, 1993). Over the twenty-year history of the NCVS, one criticism has been that respondents were told that the survey was a measure of crime. If they do not understand, for example, that violence or rape by a husband is a crime, and if the questions are not designed to point this out to them, they may not disclose these events (Straus, 1989). The newest NCVS questionnaires partially deal with this, as interviewers now at least remind respondents to include crimes committed by family members and friends. Still, the most controversy associated with the NCVS has traditionally been over the rape question. The NCVS simultaneously is credited with uncovering twice the victimization found in the UCR and accused of underreporting tremendously. Simply put, the NCVS never has, and still does not, flat out ask people if they have been raped, although lately questions have been sharpened to eliminate some ambiguity.

Another reason for underreporting is that victimization surveys tend to reflect the experiences of those people who live relatively stable lives. If you have an apartment or home and tend to move infrequently, you are the type of person who typically gets asked to participate in the NCVS. Although some attempts have been made to include people in college dorms, prisons, and even homeless shelters in the surveys, a basic problem remains: the people *most* likely to be victimized are the ones *least* likely to be questioned. Runaway teenagers, the homeless, people living in transient hotels, individuals who pass out drunk in alleys—all are much more at risk of victimization than other North Americans (Barak, 1991b; Snow & Anderson, 1993), but they are the very ones we don't reach with surveys (Currie, 1993). As we move, to save money, from expensive face-to-face interview techniques to more random-digit-dialing (RDD) telephone interviewing, this problem will only get worse. The NCVS makes a special effort to do face-to-face interviews for households without telephones, but this is not true of all surveys. Obviously, people without households (who don't have homes to plug telephones in) are going to be less-than-adequately represented.

One of the biggest criticisms of the NCVS, however, is that it may mainly gather additional information on relatively minor crimes. Walter Gove, Michael Hughes, and Michael Geerken (1985, p. 489) argue that most serious crime is reported to the police and that "the 'dark figure' of crime uncovered in victimization surveys primarily involves rather trivial events" such as minor larcenies and assaults. They also uncover rapes for which it would be difficult to gain a conviction. As yet, however, this viewpoint has not been widely adopted in criminology.

The final limitation of victimization surveys we wish to mention (there are excellent research methods books and research monographs for anyone who would like to read more about this issue) is one way in which the NCVS does *not* improve on the UCR. The decision to define crimes similarly means that they have the same political dimension mentioned earlier. People are asked, in effect, to disclose when the local teenagers stole their garden hose. However, they are not asked if toxic chemicals were dumped in the creek behind their house, if they were cheated out of a month's rent by the local bank or rental agent, if their children were made sick by companies selling lead-based crayons, or if they lost their union retirement benefits when the local savings and loan closed down after the president left for the Cayman Islands with $100 million (Pfuhl & Henry, 1993). They are rarely asked about racial or sexual harassment in the streets, school, or workplace, although these may be criminal acts and be more psychologically harmful than having a purse snatched.

Some victimization surveys, however, have been more attentive to these problems. Feminist researchers, for example, have looked into behaviors specifically excluded from the NCVS, such as child abuse. As they become relevant, such findings will be introduced later in this book.

SELF-REPORT SURVEYS

Earlier, we noted that victimology depends on victims reporting their victimizations but that most of criminology depends on what we jokingly referred to as "offenderology." For years, many important researchers have argued that, to study offenders, the proper place to start is *with* offenders (Sellin, 1931), asking them what their behaviors have been.

The Limitations of Self-Report Surveys

While this is completely logical, one of the drawbacks is that it depends for its vitality on the idea that there are two groups of people in the world: offenders and nonoffenders. "We," the nonoffenders, will give surveys to "them," the offenders. The problem is, what if "we" sell illegal Quaaludes to our co-workers to make some extra money, cheat on our income taxes, beat up our spouse last week, and perhaps, as college students, took part in a gang rape in a fraternity house (which we called "pulling train" to avoid sounding criminal). Who, then, are the offenders? We? Or the kids we give the survey to, who admit to some vandalism, underage drinking and sex, and shoplifting?

In Chapter 2, we discussed how, according to labeling theory, if the police decide you are an offender, then you are an offender; you have a label. Nor does it make any difference whether you are guilty or innocent; if you are convicted, then you are a criminal, and if you are not convicted, then you are not a criminal. We will discuss this in more detail in a later chapter.

However, the picture gets a bit more complex here. Now, we are giving out questionnaires to large numbers of youths and asking them to self-identify whether they are offenders. We are not basing our label on who has been arrested or convicted. We are basing it on self-reports.

The first sign that this could be somewhat problematic came in 1947, when James Wallerstein and Clement Wyle asked 1,020 men and 678 women whether they had committed any of forty-nine different offenses. Virtually every single person admitted to at least one crime! For example, 89 percent of the men and 83 percent of the women admitted to committing petty theft. Fully 26 percent of the men admitted to auto theft, 49 percent to assault, and 17 percent to burglary. Of course, this was not a very sophisticated survey, but it does illustrate how self-report surveys can paint a different picture of who the criminals are than, say, looking over the wall into your local prison.

Do self-report studies simply ask people to admit which criminal acts they have committed? Not exactly. If we walked up with a pen and clipboard and asked you about crimes you have committed, you would probably refuse to answer or would at least lie. On the other hand, if we gave you a questionnaire with guarantees that your answers would be anonymous and confidential, you would probably fill out the forms. This is how researchers who use self-report surveys attempt to overcome the problems of embarrassment, deception, fear of reprisal, and the like.

So far, most North American self-report crime surveys have been given to high school students. In fact, to our knowledge, the only national self-report surveys have focused specifically on drugs (NIDA, 1991a, 1991b), spouse abuse (Lupri, 1990; Straus, Gelles, & Steinmetz, 1981; Straus & Gelles, 1986), and dating violence (DeKeseredy & Kelly, 1993a; Koss, Gidycz, & Wisniewski, 1987; Stets & Henderson, 1991). In a few cases, smaller-scale self-report surveys have been done with persons housed in community and penal institutions (for example, Scully, 1990; Wright & Rossi, 1986). Particularly since half of the studies cited here were aimed at youths, it is quite fair to say that the largest gap in our knowledge remains self-reported adult crime.

The reason for using students is fairly simple: it is easier and cheaper. Rather than spending months deciding mathematically whom to interview and then tracking these people down and convincing them to fill out the form, researchers find it much easier to convince the school administration to allow them to administer the survey to the entire student body during a single homeroom period. People are already at desks, they are used to taking tests, they have pencils, and they notice that everyone else is going along. Indeed, the number of people who go along and fill out the form—the response rate—can be extraordinarily high. Further, in many communities, by choosing the high schools correctly, one can easily get a group of students that reflects the ethnic and racial make-up of the community reasonably well. At the end of one day, all of the forms are filled out.

As an example of the cost problems, both of your authors have conducted surveys of this sort on a smaller scale to university students. Getting about 300–600 self-report surveys filled out ranged in cost between $200 and $1,200. On the other hand, when Walter DeKeseredy and Katharine Kelly (1993a) developed a national sample mathematically chosen to be representative of Canadian college and university students, the cost was nearer to $200,000. Even with this amount of money, they could not afford to mail questionnaires to individual people or to conduct face-to-face interviews; instead, they had to administer their survey in classrooms from coast to coast.

The Validity of Self-Report Surveys

A key issue with a self-report instrument is whether respondents will tell the truth. This is hardly a new concern; Lewis Yablonsky warned us over thirty years ago that "to the gang boy every researcher could be a cop" (1962, p. vii). As you might suspect, it is even easier to lie anonymously than face to face, and the reality is that some people will underreport their criminal activity. However, many researchers argue that the self-report survey has proven to be an effective method of uncovering a vast amount of hidden crime. A wide range of researchers have used a wide range of techniques to check on the accuracy of these tests, and generally they have found them to be reasonably accurate. As Michael Hindelang and colleagues (1981, p. 212) argue:

> The self-report method easily demonstrates that people will report crimes, that they will report crimes not known to officials, and that their crimes are internally consistent. These facts are rightly taken as evidence that the procedure is potentially useful as an alternative to traditional procedures, particularly for studying the etiology of delinquency.

Some researchers have checked responses against police and school records. In one imaginative study, John Clark and Larry Tifft (1966) even threatened the use of a polygraph test and then allowed youths to change their answers. Only a small number did so.

The one area in which researchers have become very worried about the validity of self-report studies is in the admitted use of illegal drugs. Some recent studies of drug offenders have shown that many of those who have the most reason to lie in fact will do just that. Elliott Currie (1993), for example, reports that the Drug Use Forecasting Program (DUF) administered questionnaires about drug use to arrestees and then followed up with urine tests. Only about half of those who tested positive to a drug had admitted earlier on the questionnaire to using it. Not surprisingly, the higher the legal penalty for possessing the drug, the lower the percentage who admitted using it. Currie's conclusion is that, "Because the validity of the responses is so uncertain, we really do not know how accurately the figures found in the self-report studies describe actual drug use" (1993, p. 24).

Of course, other problems are associated with self-report studies. In some ways, the most serious is that no central clearinghouse or agency takes responsibility for the studies. For example, the NCVS has a staff constantly discussing ways to improve survey technology, and the results of each year's survey are available to outside researchers (including students) to do their own analyses. Not only is this not true of self-reports, but no national studies exist that can give us information comparable from region to region or year to year.

Another criticism is the disproportionate focus on youths (Sheley, 1985). Of course, this attack is not really on the method, but on scholars who are interested in adult crime for not using the method more often. Still, the self-report surveys typically conducted with youths have had their share of criticisms. For example, too much attention has been paid to relatively trivial behaviors such as truancy, and not enough to more serious ones such as rape. Further, many researchers have been caught in the dilemma of how to word their questions. For example, if you ask respondents whether they skip school "often," "sometimes," or "occasionally," then you can be accused of vagueness. On the other hand, if you ask for the precise number of times the behavior was committed, few respondents would likely be able to remember well enough to give an accurate answer.

Despite all of these limitations, self-report surveys are generally credited with helping us to understand a great deal about crime that we did not know from other data sources. The first and most obvious finding relates to the tremendous number of people who break the law—many times the number that we would expect from seeing other statistics. If we include crimes that are often considered acts of juvenile delinquency but are not adult crimes (like truancy), plus the usual teenager misbehavior (alcohol abuse, shoplifting, fighting), then probably 90 percent of all youths commit delinquent and criminal acts. How can this be true? Why isn't *everybody* in jail? The answer is simple, and it explains why some researchers prefer self-report data to official or police statistics: when researchers have come up with imaginative hidden research designs to compare self-reports to police records, they typically find 2–3 percent of all admitted crime to have been officially noted (Williams & Gold, 1972). Self-report studies find out about a *lot* of crime that is not in police records.

So, big deal. There is a lot of crime. What else can these surveys do? Actually, quite a bit. Granted, their full energy has not been harnessed, and too many researchers worried about how many times teenagers cut school or abused alcohol instead of how many adults committed burglary and armed robbery. Still, we have already learned a great deal from them. Most important is that, based on official statistics, delinquents appear to be, more often than not, African-American males from lower-class backgrounds. White, female, and middle- and upper-class youths are much less likely to be officially labeled criminals or delinquents. Although there is much controversy over some of the findings in this area, one indisputable fact we have learned from self-report studies is that youths from *all* backgrounds—white and African-American, male and female, lower, middle, and upper class—commit a wide range of offenses. The reason there are major differences in the police statistics is that police are more likely to arrest African-Americans, males, and lower-class youths. In one famous study, for example, William Chambliss (1973) compared a lower-class youth gang to a middle-class youth gang and found that both groups engaged in delinquent behavior. For a number of reasons, however, the lower-class youth gang members were the ones always in trouble with the police.

Thus, we know that youths of all social classes commit both frequent and serious crimes. Harwin Voss (1966) even found that upper-class white males committed more serious and more frequent offenses than lower-class white males. However, some researchers believe that working-class youths *more frequently* commit serious crime and that this is why they are arrested more often. Perhaps the safest thing we can say is that the interpretation of the data is fairly difficult at this point (Tittle & Meier, 1991).

In any case, although there has been steady improvement in the self-report studies, but we still have a ways to go to make them completely useful. However, some researchers contend that overcoming these problems is not good enough. If we want to get the most accurate crime data, then we have to move even closer to the source—we have to conduct observational procedures.

OBSERVATIONAL PROCEDURES

Victimization and self-report studies have long been criticized by those who worry that you cannot gain insight into people's motives for committing crimes if you are sitting at a computer terminal analyzing data or reading crime surveys. This breed of researcher prefers to hit the streets and interact with people in their own environments. In other words, they go "where the action is." Of course, this practice is not new. Robert Park was telling young University of Chicago sociologists this seventy years ago:

> You have been told to go grubbing in the library, thereby accumu-lating a mass of notes and a liberal coating of grime . . . one thing more is needful: first hand observation. Go and sit in the lounges of the luxury hotels and on the doorsteps of the flophouses; sit on the Gold Coast settees and on the slum shakedowns; sit in Orchestra Hall and in the Star and Garter Burlesk. (quoted in Hagan, 1993, p. 189)

Types of Observational Procedures

This "real research," or observational research, generally takes one of two forms: (1) field observation or (2) participant observation. Of course, there are modifications and variations of each. The basic idea of both, however, is that we can learn the most about humans by seeing how they interact with one another. If your object is to learn about the social world, then you must look directly at the social world itself.

Field Observation   Doing *field observation,* in some ways, resembles using a gigantic one-way mirror to watch how people behave. The researcher heads for the site where the behavior is being practiced, watches people's activities, and listens to their conversations. Because people may alter their behavior if they know that they are being watched, one skill a researcher may need is to "become invisible" (Berg, 1995; Stoddart, 1986).

For example, a colleague of ours wanted to observe the ways in which young drug dealers in Toronto's Jane-Finch Corridor sell their products. He knew that the dealers liked to "hang around" a small shopping center located near a government-sponsored housing project, and he assumed that if he were caught watching them, they would leave, attack him, or stop selling. Thus, he hid behind several bushes. Fortunately, no one noticed him, and he managed to uncover some valuable information unlikely to be captured by self-report studies, victimization surveys, and police statistics. He discovered that buyers would drive slowly through the shopping center parking lot with their car windows rolled down, periodically nodding their heads. Three to five dealers would then quickly approach the car and compete with one another to sell "clients" small packages of hashish and marijuana. Once the transaction was completed, the dealers would run behind a nearby wall and the buyers would speed off to their destinations. Observation showed that most of the buyers were white and apparently middle-class since they drove fairly expensive cars. Unfortunately, their socioeconomic status could not be more accurately estimated by the usual methods (stopping the cars and interviewing the occupants). Certainly, the buyers would have thought the researcher was an undercover police officer.

Participant Observation   As well as being more time consuming, participant observation can be dangerous. In the traditional sense, it involves joining a group to experience the world as they do, or at least as closely as possible. This may not be a major problem if it means hanging out on a street corner or joining a bowling league. However, it does present some ethical problems when criminal activities are taking place. The most notorious case in criminology involved Laud Humphreys, who took on a role termed "watchqueen" in public restrooms in St. Louis city parks (1975). Watchqueens were allowed to observe men engaged in impersonal homosexual acts in return for acting as sentries to warn of approaching outsiders. In itself, this was a mildly deviant role. What became a more controversial act, however, was that Humphreys took down the auto license numbers of the men who engaged in these acts, looked up who they were, and later slipped their names into a sample of men being interviewed as part of an unrelated major health study. The research payoff was magnificent. Humphreys was able to study men who engaged in impersonal, illicit, and illegal homosexual sex and to discover that they were typically "normal" family men (who often voiced homophobic attitudes). Their names were never revealed. Nevertheless, the study is still heavily debated in books on research methods, as writers continue to argue over the ethics of obtaining license plate numbers without the permission of the owners and setting up a study in which someone else theoretically might have discovered who these men were and done something unfriendly.

Serving as a watchqueen is relatively mild. It is in the tradition of the many anthropological and sociological researchers who took on the roles they were studying in order to learn from the inside. Judith Rollins (1985), for example, toiled as a domestic worker as part of her study of women who worked in that field. However, even if it is the best way to obtain data, many people in society would have an ethical problem with a criminologist who decided to turn tricks in order to study prostitution (Chancer, 1994), let alone one who committed rapes or robberies to get "in" with a criminal gang.

Observer as Participant   Thus, criminologists are more likely to engage in some version of the observer-as-participant role (Gold, 1958), which mixes the two categories just discussed. The goal often is to be a participant to the extent that the researcher is accepted and allowed to gather personal accounts from members, but not to be a participant in the sense of committing the criminal or deviant acts themselves. Leon Anderson and Thomas Calhoun (1992) argue that researchers who prove themselves trustworthy and willing to accept *courtesy stigma* may find informants quite willing to share information. Courtesy stigma is somewhat like guilt by association—a sort of stigma by association. If you are willing to allow people to see you and treat you as a prostitute, a thief, a drug dealer, or a gang member, then you may be granted a courtesy status within the group making you acceptable even though you don't actually commit any crimes.

For example, two sociologists who tried to understand the social organization of male street prostitutes were Livy Visano (1987) and Calhoun (1992). Each "hung around" with young men and observed a wide range of activities, but not those involving sex acts. Calhoun spent a great deal of time on the block where these young men picked up older men cruising for sex. Once trust was established, particularly by the researcher refusing to give information to the police, some street hustlers "became so interested in the attention received that they would stop hustling and talk to the researcher. Several began taking the researcher's field schedule into consideration when planning their trips to the cruising area" (Anderson & Calhoun, 1992, p. 494). Visano, on the other hand, spent more time off the cruising area:

> I moved along with them from one activity to another, standing on street-corners, sitting on steps, making the rounds at arcades, hostels, doughnut shops, bars, and baths. By observing how they spent most of their time, I was better able to collect information relating their involvements with other hustlers, police, social workers, street connections, or the gay community. This pursuit carried me along their activities related to both work and leisure. I came into contact with their friends and acquaintances. Although most of my time was spent in coffee shops, parks and street-corners, many hours were also spent observing them in their leisure activities—playing billiards, roller skating, or video games. Interestingly, a considerable portion of the matters they discuss during their recreational pursuits deals with hustling sex. This field approach was appropriate given that many boys did not plan their movements with great regularity. They did not structure their working hours with any great precision. This observational technique of being with the boys as much as possible also helped overcome some of their suspicions. (1987, p. 70)

Studies of this type can be useful in answering questions about why people join subcultures that include lawbreaking activities. They also help us to understand how people join and why they stay.

Other attempts have been made to get around the ethical problem of possibly helping individuals to commit real crimes while at the same time attempting to get information from the very people who commit these crimes. For example, Paul Cromwell and colleagues (1991) chose to employ *staged activity analysis*. They recruited thirty active urban Texas burglars for "extensive interviews and 'ride alongs,' during which the informants were asked to discuss and evaluate residential sites they had previously burglarized and sites previously burglarized by other informants in the study" (1991,

p. 16). Based on these interviews, the researchers proposed several practical ways of decreasing the likelihood of being burglarized, such as getting a noisy dog and installing dead-bolt locks.

In sum, the strength of observational research is that it produces information that cannot be obtained by other methods. As we have seen, surveys and police statistics cannot provide the detailed information on burglars' breaking-and-entering techniques that Cromwell and colleagues' approach does. Furthermore, although giving out self-report surveys in schools is a useful research technique, and conducting household victimization surveys yields an enormous amount of information, these techniques will overlook many members of society. Young male prostitutes, for example, are often school dropouts and may be transient and homeless, so they would not be part of other data collection devices.

The Limitations of Observational Research

Practical Concerns A major drawback to observational studies is that they often are more time consuming than other methods because they take months or even years to complete. This is especially true for white, middle-class researchers who want to gain access to disenfranchised subcultures such as ethnic youth gangs who mistrust members of the "status quo." Certainly, researchers trying to gain access to a group that is greatly interested in finding a sympathetic ear may have an easier time (Anderson & Calhoun, 1992). However, "poor minority communities deeply distrust academic research. If a researcher's sole purpose is to do some quick-and-dirty interviews and publish an article, then trust will of course be difficult and the data will be suspect" (Hagedorn, 1990, p. 252). Even after gaining access, the researcher has no way of knowing how long he or she will be doing research:

> The observer is often not in a position to control the action and must often wait for the activities of interest to occur. In studying criminal groups, for instance, researchers may have to spend hours or days in what some may regard as boring activities, for example, marathon card games or drinking bouts before something noteworthy happens. (Hagan, 1993, pp. 201–202)

Even if time is no problem for observational researchers, it might be for their friends, family members, and employers. We know several people who ended up getting divorced because their partners were fed up with their spending more time in the street than at home. Observational researchers are also at risk of losing their academic jobs or of not being promoted because it can take such a long time to publish the needed scholarly articles. Further, funding may be very difficult, because few government agencies will pay for long-term participant observation studies, generally preferring statistical studies that help support law-and-order objectives (Hagedorn, 1990).

For researchers planning to study violent people, the observational work can also be extremely dangerous. When Mark Hamm studied American neo-Nazi Skinheads, he had some problems:

> Early in the research, I was assaulted by members of the American Front at the corner of Haight and Ashbury in San Francisco. . . . I was assaulted because I was seen by skinheads in the company of an Indonesian woman who was a well-known prostitute in the Haight Street area. For this, I was called a nigger lover and kicked in the shins with a pair of steel-toed Doc Martens. (1993, p. 91)

Another problem that many researchers have is that they may think that they have gained access to or been fully accepted by the group, but actually the group is only allowing them onto, to use a videogame metaphor, level one. For example, inner-city youth gang members may use various "defenses against outsiders" (Humphreys, 1975, p. 24), such as lying about their true identities, using symbolic gestures and their eyes to communicate with one another, being unwilling to expose the locations of their criminal activities, hiding the locations of their initiation rituals, being extraordinarily cautious about revealing group norms and values, and admitting observers to certain places or events only in the company of a trusted and respected person.

Camille Bacon-Smith (1992), for example, spent two years at the first phase of initiation into the national community of women who write and self-publish fan magazines (fanzines) for such defunct TV shows as "Star Trek," "Starsky and Hutch," and "Blake's 7." It took additional time to be accepted into the much smaller circle of fans who circulate sexually explicit homoerotic stories based on the genre. The people by whom she thought she had been fully accepted did not open further doors to her for some time.

Data Triangulation   You may recall that in Chapter 1 we encouraged you to be open-minded and to strive for "data triangulation" (Denzin, 1978). We also briefly discussed R. Emerson Dobash and Russell Dobash's (1979, 1983) use of several different methods to study wife abuse. The idea of triangulation, or multiple data methods, centers on the notion that any one technique might accidentally misrepresent the "real world," or empirical reality. Using a variety of "sightings" (like a civil engineer) from different angles makes it more likely that we will correctly survey the terrain (Fielding & Fielding, 1986). Perhaps some other examples of triangulation would be useful here. Mark Hamm (1993), for example, used a variety of techniques in his study of neo-Nazi Skinheads, starting with traveling to various cities to look for Skinheads in their "natural habitat" (for example, street corners, bars, record stores, survivalist outlets, and so on). After engaging in observational study, he approached some "skins" and asked them to participate in a formal structured interview. Then, using the White Aryan Resistance mailing list, he sent letters to the leaders of twenty-six Skinhead groups, inviting them to call him for an interview, and later followed up with letters to people who did not respond the first time. After using the White Aryan Resistance electronic bulletin board to solicit participants and conducting interviews with Skinheads locked up in California, South Carolina, Indiana, and Illinois prisons, he ended up with thirty-six people who either were interviewed or completed written questionnaires.

Another example of a combination of techniques was the study coordinated by Claire Renzetti (1992) on battering in lesbian relationships. She used a feminist participatory research model that is actually more complex than any we have described here thus far. Not only does it involve the investigation stage, but it also includes a design to help educate both the researcher and the participants, and it commits both to social action afterwards to apply the new knowledge to finding solutions. Here, Renzetti had identified a topic for which neither field observation nor participant observation by an academic researcher was likely to yield significant data. In this model, her first step was to establish the entire basis of the study as a collaborative effort with a battered lesbian support group. This group, who certainly had real-life experiences as observers and participants, worked as equal partners in developing the study. As Renzetti points out (1992, p. 9):

> I developed the first draft of the questionnaire, but it soon became clear that while I brought to the project technical skills in research methodology and data analysis, I knew far less about lesbian relationships than I had originally presumed. The questionnaire went through six drafts over a period of nine months.

Only then could recruitment of volunteers (victims of lesbian relationship battering) begin, so that anonymous written questionnaires could be distributed. It was much later before a recruited group of these women could be interviewed face to face to provide more information than could be gleaned from answers on a questionnaire.

Two other interesting examples of the use of multiple methods, although the studies could not be more different, are recent books by Kathleen Daly (1994) and Jeff Ferrell (1993). Daly took on the question of whether women are in fact treated more leniently than men during sentencing in criminal court. In a statistical analysis based on an examination of data contained in court records, she found that women were more likely to be incarcerated but for a shorter time than men. For most quantitative methodologists, this would be the end of the study. She would have "proven" gender bias in the court system. However, Daly then went on to what would normally be considered a qualitative methodology of case descriptions of men and women matched (by pairs) for such factors as offense, race, prior record, and age. Proving her point that standard statistical analysis cannot completely capture the decisions being made in such complex areas as criminal courts, Daly found that virtually all of the sentencing disparity can be explained by the fact that many of the women had lesser criminal backgrounds than the men and therefore deserved lesser punishments.

Ferrell has produced an extraordinary study of graffiti writers in Denver that works on so many levels that it cannot be easily described here. He begins with an ethnographic study of the graffiti writers themselves—why would someone want to write on building walls? What do they get out of it? He does not stop here, but simultaneously studies the reactions of the Denver media and politicians, showing how they demonized and dehumanized the graffiti writers and created a moral panic. His argument that graffiti writers are resisters to the cultural establishment and the propertied class has led to his work being labeled an anarchist interpretation of crime. The key point here is that staying only within a single point of entry, such as the interviews with graffiti artists, would have produced an interesting study but not the rich and multifaceted book that finally emerged.

Ethical Problems   Earlier, we noted that a strength of observational research is that you can gain access to places where the very people who commit criminal acts will act relatively naturally while you are around to observe them. Unfortunately, as we have suggested several times already, this might involve legal or ethical dilemmas. We noted the problems many people have had with Laud Humphreys's decision to facilitate illegal behavior, and we later suggested that a willingness to prove that you will not inform the police about criminal activity may be a precondition to being allowed to observe.

Let's put this into a residential campus setting. Suppose you have been given permission by the interfraternity council to attend a variety of university fraternity parties. On some campuses, common events that you might observe include aggressive attempts to "pick up" women, men watching their friends have sex with female guests, all-male circle dances designed to reinforce male bonding, the screening of pornographic films, antihomosexual discussions, sorority sisters serving drinks and acting as hostesses, and, of course, heavy drinking (Ehrhart & Sandler, 1985; Martin & Hummer, 1989; Sanday, 1990). You may even have the terrifying opportunity to observe or hear forced sex or rape committed by individuals or groups. Although too many college men seem unaware of this, you as a senior researcher and perhaps a faculty member are fully aware that it is a serious crime to have sexual intercourse with a woman who is unable to consent because she has lost consciousness from alcohol. Whether you agree with it or not, you know that it is a felony, as well as a violation of the national fraternity rules that could result in the chapter's expulsion from your campus.

If you promised the fraternity members anonymity and confidentiality in order to conduct the research, then you are obligated to protect their privacy. However, this raises a host of issues. If every person at the party has not given permission to be observed, then the commonly used "informed consent" ethical standard may be violated (McKinney, 1992). Few researchers have addressed this issue directly. There are many discussions in the literature on whether to lie to hide one's identity or to cover up the minor crimes of research subjects (see, for example, Punch, 1986), but few on what to do when faced with a major victimization. Do you ignore the men dragging an unconscious woman up the back stairs in order to save your months of hard work and data collection? Do you just record the sexual assault in your notes to be revealed in your final report, after your research is done (Neuman, 1994)? Or do you jeopardize your study by reporting the event to the police or by using physical force to stop someone from victimizing a woman? Ned Polsky (1967) has argued that the greater good of advancing scientific knowledge makes it legitimate for the researcher to take the short-run step of obstructing justice in specific cases by ignoring the crimes. Bruce Berg (1995) takes the stronger stance of arguing that it is unethical to study criminal behavior and then to give evidence of that behavior to the police. What do you think?

SUMMARY

The main objective of this chapter was to describe and evaluate four methods of collecting crime data: police statistics, victimization surveys, self-report surveys, and observational procedures. Each has strengths and limitations, and the decision to use one or more of them typically depends on a researcher's time and financial constraints, theoretical preference, and topic of interest. Unfortunately, too many researchers are "methodological narcissists" who contend that their favorite approach is the best method. This is particularly a problem when different methods yield such different results. Carl Pope (1984), for example, has shown how the different findings about the effects of race on crime rates often can be attributed to the different methods being used. We subscribe to the alternative school of thought: that there is no one correct method, but rather a method or combination of methods that will best suit your needs in a given research context. "A research method for a given problem is not like the solution to a problem in Algebra. It is more like a recipe for beef stroganoff; there is no one best recipe" (Simon, 1978, p. 4).

SUGGESTED READINGS

Pfuhl, E., and Henry, S. (1993). *The Deviance Process,* 3rd ed. New York: Aldine de Gruyter.

Chapter 2, "Counting Deviants," is an excellent representation of the social constructionist school on the problems of official data such as police reports. It outlines in detail the idea of "culture work"—how images of deviance are constructed through the use of statistics, and how organizational interests, strains, and rewards are made a part of the data-gathering process.

Reinharz, S. (1992). *Feminist Methods in Social Research.* New York: Oxford University Press.

This comprehensive book is excellent in discussing both theory and practice, generally taking the position that there is no one "correct" feminist position. It covers statistical research, field observation, multiple methods research, and much more.

Snow, D., and Anderson, L. (1993). *Down on Their Luck: A Study of Homeless Street People.* Berkeley: University of California Press.

Perhaps the best study ever done on street people, this multi-award-winning book is an excellent example of the multimethod or data triangulation approach. It involved field observation, researcher-as-observer work, and life history analysis; the authors also drew a random sample of the homeless from agency files to study institutional records.

Wesler, S. (1990). "Ethical Obligations and Social Research." In K. Kempf (ed.), *Measurement Issues in Criminology,* pp. 78–107. New York: Springer-Verlag.

This chapter is an excellent treatment of the various ethical problems in criminological research.

PART II

WHO COMMITS CRIME AND WHY?

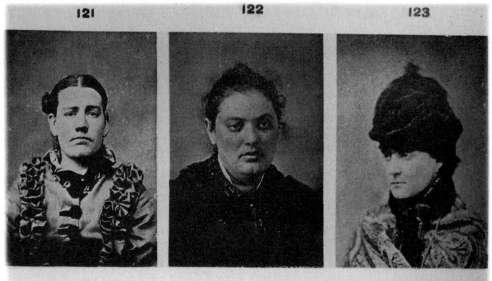

121

MARY ANN WATTS,
PICKPOCKET AND SHOP LIFTER.

122

BERTHA HEYMAN,
CONFIDENCE.

123

ELLEN DARRIGAN,
ALIAS ELLEN MATTHEWS,
PICKPOCKET.

124

ELIZABETH DILLON,
ALIAS BRIDGET COLE
PICKPOCKET.

125

TILLY MARTIN,
ALIAS PHIEFER.
SNEAK.

126

MARY BUSBY,
ALIAS JOHNSON
PICKPOCKET AND SHOP LIFTER.

CHAPTER 5

INDIVIDUALISTIC THEORIES

Wicked people exist. Nothing avails except to set them apart from innocent people. And many people, neither wicked nor innocent, but watchful, dissembling, and calculating of their chances, ponder our reaction to wickedness as a clue to what they might profitably do.

WILSON, 1985, P. 260

[T]he traits of the typical offender cannot be assumed to be caused either by how he or she was treated by society. . . . [T]he average offender is psychologically atypical in various respects, not necessarily to a pathological degree, but enough so that the normal prohibitions against crime are relatively ineffective.

HERRNSTEIN, 1995, PP. 39–40

Thus far, we have concentrated on sociological answers to four important questions: (1) Where do we get our knowledge of crime? (2) What is crime? (3) What are the origins and functions of criminal law? and (4) How are crime data collected? The next question is the one that, over the years, has concerned criminologists more than any other: Why do people commit crime?

It would be nice if, as a result of many generations of exhaustive research and deep thought, we could provide a straightforward, easily understood explanation for why people steal, kill, evade taxes, sell drugs, and do so many other things. Unfortunately, few criminologists would be so bold as to declare that we are now ready to conclusively answer that question. If anyone does claim to have the answer, most other criminologists would be quick to find fault with it! People who attend the annual meeting of the American Society of Criminology intending to discover from the most prominent women and men in the field the current thinking on the root causes of crime are likely to encounter something akin to the Tower of Babel. They will not be offered one answer but a series of competing and contradictory visions of the nature of man, deviation, and the social order. Very typically, they will be informed that their questions cannot even be discussed because they are not correctly phrased: they must first reconstruct their problem so that it can be placed with others in one of the master theories of deviance. (Downes & Rock, 1988, p. 2)

Students have a tendency to see the smorgasbord of theories presented in the typical criminology textbook as incredibly diverse, confusing, and partisan. That is simply because they *are* diverse, confusing, and partisan! Worse yet, texts commonly outline every single theory that scholars in criminology are exposed to, and perhaps a few more to show off the learning of the authors. Over the next few chapters, we will not mention every theory we know. Rather, we will try to show the broad range of theories used in criminology. We will try to give you some appreciation for the variety of ways in which people can answer the question, "Why did Johnny become a criminal?" We will further discuss those theorists who hate that question and want to know why you picked out Johnny to brand a criminal, those who want to know why there are so many North American Johnnys, and those who want to know just what you mean by "criminal" anyway. We will not be particularly shy at pointing out that many of these approaches have some substantial problems or drawbacks.

Although this book has a primarily sociological approach, criminology contains a great many nonsociological theories. In this chapter, we will center our attention on those nonsociological theories. Of course, sociology generally is a twentieth-century phenomenon, so this chapter will include a discussion of what people thought in earlier times. In Chapter 6, we will focus on sociological theories of crime, and in Chapter 7, we will look at the newer, critical theories of crime.

In this chapter, we will discuss classical and neoclassical theories, the biological perspectives, and psychological accounts. Despite the fact that each of these perspectives is completely distinct, they share a key perspective: crime is a property of the individual. What does this mean? It means that they find the main sources or causes of crime *inside* offenders. Sometimes, these are called predispositional *criminogenic traits* because they reside inside the person and predispose that person to commit crimes. That does not mean that these people *will* commit crimes. It just means that they are more likely to commit crime than other people because, in the right situation, these predispositions are already there. The rest of us will have to develop dispositions toward crime; these people already have predispositions. For example, some of the criminogenic traits that some people have identified include low intelligence, bad genes, frontal brain lobe dysfunction, a breakdown of self-control, and a "wicked" human nature (Brennan, Mednick, & Volovka, 1995; Gottfredson & Hirschi, 1990; Herrnstein, 1995; Wilson, 1985).

So, why is it that the most important idea in this chapter is that the nonsociological theories find the cause of crime within the individual? As you will see in the next chapter, the reason is that sociological theories of crime generally find the cause of crime *outside* the individual offender—in society or the way in which some aspects of society are structured. Sociologists don't often state it explicitly, but they seem to imply that anyone caught up in these circumstances could end up a criminal. You don't need to be different than other people; you just need to be in the wrong place at the wrong time, with the same life options and opportunities.

THE DEVIL MADE HIM DO IT

Prior to the late 1700s, most European legal authorities thought that crime was caused by supernatural forces. Those who were officially designated as deviant were seen as sinners who either fell from grace with God (for example, moral failure) or were possessed by the devil or other evil spirits (Vold & Bernard, 1986). At least, that was the official explanation; in reality, there were other factors at work. Weakness in the Catholic church and in the various governments led to an alliance between church and state that lasted throughout the Middle Ages. Now commonly called the Inquisition, this reign of terror was designed to root out heresy and heretics—which meant anyone who disagreed with the official beliefs. It allowed authorities to torture and execute anyone they wished in order to locate witches and others who might oppose the power of those in authority. Of course, as might be expected, the Inquisition generally persecuted those with limited power, such as women and the poor. For example, the overwhelming bulk of those executed for witchcraft were women, and virtually all were poor.

The Inquisition might be but a gruesome footnote to history, some criminologists argue, were it not for the fact that this method of questioning suspects, including the use of torture, has provided the basis for today's criminal procedure (Brown, Esbensen, & Geis, 1991). More than a few observers have noted that the witch-hunters did more than find heresy; they also served to support the power structure, mainly by finding one group of people to attack and to scapegoat (Chambliss, 1988). To "scapegoat" a group means to blame it for all of the problems everyone has, thereby diverting peoples' attention from other possible causes of their troubles. As Marvin Harris points out, "The principal result of the witch-hunt system (aside from charred bodies) was that the poor came to believe that they were being victimized by witches and devils instead of princes and popes" (1978, p. 237). Rather than confront corrupt clergy and greedy nobles with demands for a more equal distribution of wealth, people suddenly found a use for the government and church—to save them from witches. Over two centuries, more than 500,000 people were burned alive as part of this witch craze or mania. Throughout history, the number likely is closer to a million, most of whom were women (Pfohl, 1994).

The most common way of determining guilt was through torture. It was a simple system: if you confessed, you were executed; if you did not confess, the torture continued until you died. Note that this was not a system designed by a weird cult of crazed religionists. The number of deaths alone made it plain that this was the accepted method of running a criminal justice system, supported by the entire governmental, religious, and military power structure. The tortures and executions were virtually always carried out by the state. Although church officials could pass sentences of torture and slow, painful death, they felt that they could not get blood on their hands by carrying out the sentences themselves.

Slowly, although the witch mania began to die out, the state monopoly over punishment did not. Further, the same methods of inquisition and punishment continued to be applied, with the "ritual application of physical pain" remaining the standard form of punishment (Pfohl, 1994). One problem for authorities was figuring out what to do to escalate penalties. After all, if the penalty for minor crimes is torture and execution, what do you do for *major* crimes? For example, in the mid-1700s, when an admittedly mentally ill man stabbed King Louis XV, the authorities needed to come up with a punishment far worse than torture and execution! In Box 5.1, Michel Foucault describes how cruel punishment actually could be in 1757.

Foucault told this ghastly story to make the point that within a hundred years, in Europe and the United States, torture and most physical punishments began to diminish in use, and executions were drastically reduced. This change took place not only in the criminal justice system, but also in the military, public schools, and throughout society (Travis, Schwartz, & Clear, 1992). Of course, Foucault only accounted for official punishment. In the United States, more than five thousand people have been "lynched" by vigilante mobs, and untold thousands, perhaps hundreds of thousands, of people, mainly African-American, have been whipped and beaten by such groups as the Ku Klux Klan.

Foucault's argument is that we have moved official state policy, at least as publicly announced and defended, away from punishment of the body and toward punishment of the soul, such as by imprisonment. Of course, his compelling and important account is essentially true, in that few countries today have legal systems that call for torture and execution. At the same time, we must recognize that torture and execution are still widespread in the world and commonplace in some countries. For example, during the mid-1970s, Amnesty International found that, in Chile,

> the most common forms of physical torture have been prolonged beating (with truncheons, fists or bags of moist material), electricity to all parts of the body, and burning with cigarettes or acid. Such physical tortures have been accompanied by the deprivation of food, drink and sleep. More primitive and brutal methods have continued to be used. [O]ne prisoner was found dead, his testicles burned off. He had also been subjected to intensive beating and electricity. One day later another prisoner who died from torture had the marks of severe burns on the genital organs. (cited in Herman, 1982, p. 113)

In Brazil, between 1988 to 1991, over seven thousand street children and adolescents were assassinated by police officers, private security police, and death squads (Huggins, 1993). In Colombia, several thousand street children are killed by police every year (Hatty, Davis, & Burke, 1994). What is different is that these deaths are much less often official state policy in the

BOX 5.1

THE EXECUTION OF ROBERT FRANCOIS DAMIENS (1757)

There were still very extreme sentences on March 2, 1757, when Damiens was sentenced to an execution consisting of: "the flesh will be torn from his breasts, arms, thighs and calves with red-hot pincers, his right hand, holding the knife with which he committed the said parricide, burnt with sulphur, and, on those places where the flesh will be torn away, poured molten lead, boiling oil, burning resin, wax and sulphur melted together and then his body drawn and quartered by four horses and his limbs and body consumed by fire, reduced to ashes and his ashes thrown to the winds."

Unfortunately, things did not go easily. The sulphur barely burned the skin, and the instrument designed to tear flesh didn't work very well either: "Though a strong, sturdy fellow, this executioner found it so difficult to tear away at the pieces of flesh that he set about the same spot two or three times, twisting the pincers as he did so, and what he took away formed at each part a wound about the size of a six-pound crown piece.

"After these tearings with the pincers, Damiens, who cried out profusely, though without swearing, raised his head and looked at himself; the same executioner dipped an iron spoon in the pot containing the boiling potion, which he poured liberally over each wound. Then the ropes that were to be harnessed to the horses were attached with cords to the patient's body; the horses were then harnessed and placed alongside the arms and legs, one at each limb. . . .

"The horses tugged hard, each pulling straight on a limb, each horse held by an executioner. After a quarter of an hour, the same ceremony was repeated and finally, after several attempts, the direction of the horses had to be changed, thus: those at the arms were made to pull towards the head, those at the thighs towards the arms, which broke the arms at the joints. This was repeated several times without success. He raised his head and looked at himself. Two more horses had to be added to those harnessed to the thighs, which made six horses in all. Without success. . . .

"After two or three attempts, the executioner Samson and he who had used the pincers each drew out a knife from his pocket and cut the body at the thighs instead of severing the legs at the joints; the four horses gave a tug and carried off the two thighs after them, namely, that of the right side first, the other following; then the same was done to the arms, the shoulders, the armpits and the four limbs; the flesh had to be cut almost to the bone, the horses pulling hard carried off the right arm first and the other afterwards."

SOURCE: Foucault, 1979, pp. 3–5.

sense that they are written into the official laws, with sentences passed at trials attended freely by the public and the media. Still, as you will recall from Chapter 3, Amnesty International argues that torture and secret execution are practiced regularly in every part of the world.

THE CLASSICAL SCHOOL OF CRIMINOLOGY

By the 1700s, not everyone agreed that inflicting extraordinary pain and suffering was the best way for the state to deal with its daily problems. In this era, the *classical school of criminology* began to contribute to the creation of more humane ways of punishing criminals in Western society. Whatever our perspective two hundred years later, to the people who were living in an era when the proceedings described in Box 5.1 were taking place, these theorists were certainly humane reformers. Of course, the horrors described in Box 5.1 were rather extreme, but at least in Europe, almost complete power in the hands of prosecutors and judges, combined with widespread corruption, provided the arena for extensive abuse. Judges could do virtually whatever they wanted, based on whatever evidence they wished.

Although it is beyond the scope of this chapter to explain this relationship fully, the classical thoughts relevant to the study of criminology cannot be understood out of context from the rest of society. The late 1700s are commonly known as the Enlightenment, when a number of important philosophers popularized a series of optimistic ideas about the nature of humans and human society. Unlike Medieval times, when the church and the nobility simply told people what to believe, the Enlightenment theorists felt that many truths existed outside of religious revelation. Just as people had recently discovered that they could learn things about gravity, light, and color simply from carefully observing them, so they could also learn about morals and justice through rational thought. These theorists' conceptions of individual human rights were exceptionally powerful and no doubt led directly to revolutions in France and America.

One of the most important philosophical developments of this period was the *social contract*, whereby people consented to surrender certain rights to the government in exchange for individual protection and guarantees of human rights for all citizens. These concerns with human dignity meant that important thinkers and writers throughout Europe began looking at

BOX 5.2

CESARE BECCARIA (1738–1794)

Perhaps the most influential theorist in criminological history was a modest man who may have accomplished little in his lifetime—and who may not even have done what little he has been given credit for doing! Cesare Bonesara, Marchese di Beccaria, was born to a modestly wealthy aristocratic family and graduated from the University of Pavia in 1758 after studying law, evidently in an undistinguished fashion. He was shy and obese and did whatever he could to avoid being in the public eye, such as traveling (Brown, Esbensen, & Geis, 1991). He took part in several literary study groups, one of which produced writings critical of Italian society of their era.

Evidently, he was either a very slow writer or a very lazy one, because he did not produce much. At the age of 26, he produced a short anonymous essay entitled *On Crimes and Punishments*. The book was a tremendous success, and after he put his name on the second printing, it was translated into virtually all European languages. Read by the top political and governmental officials throughout Europe, Russia, and America, the essay became very influential in efforts to reform laws in many countries. The Enlightenment provided a strong incentive in many places to develop new law, and Beccaria provided the first powerful blueprint on how those new laws might look. Of course, it was seen as a major attack by those very people it attacked! The Catholic church declared Beccaria an enemy of Christianity and placed the book on its Index of banned books. It stayed there until the 1960s, when the Index was abolished (Brown, Esbensen, & Geis, 1991).

One of Beccaria's close friends and mentors, Pietro Verri, complained that the youth could only put down small ideas before losing energy and that Verri had to write them out, arrange them, and make them into a book. It is possible that Verri was just jealous of Beccaria's fame, but,

> Given the description of Beccaria's work habits, his lack of knowledge of the penal system, the speed with which he finished the essay and the fact that he produced nothing else of note in his career, the speculation about actual authorship is provided with circumstantial support. (Martin, Mutchnick, & Austin, 1990, p. 5)

On the other hand, Vold and Bernard (1986, p. 20), although agreeing that the book was completed "with help from the Verri brothers," suggest based on an entry in the *Encyclopedia of Social Sciences* that Beccaria went on to a career as a professor and government official "whose ability in mathematics led to a number of original and brilliant applications of quantitative methods to the field of social and political study."

> **BOX 5.3**
> # JEREMY BENTHAM (1748–1842)
>
> Once again, one of the greatest of the classical thinkers was a quiet, solitary man. He was a child prodigy who studied law at Oxford at the age of 12 but soon withdrew to a life of relative solitude. Evidently, his dietary habits were the opposite of Beccaria's, being mostly limited to fruit, bread, tea, and ale (Brown, Esbensen, & Geis, 1991). Although he was extremely prolific and had a major influence on English law reform, he was, to say the least, an eccentric. Allen and Simonsen don't mince words: they call him "something of a crackpot in his later years" (1995, p. 23), perhaps mainly for his extreme attention to developing the Panopticon, a prison building often kindly referred to as a monstrosity. It was never built, although a couple of American prisons actually adopted some of its design features. Much more important was Bentham's effect on criminal law through his extensive writings.

various social conditions, generally being shocked by what they found. These people took the second half of the social contract formula seriously—that the government should be forbidden to harm any citizen any more than it had to for the good of the entire community.

Human Rationality and Cost/Benefit Analysis

Of course, it is with crime that we are concerned here. The social reformers widely acknowledged as forming the core of the classical school were Cesare Beccaria (see Box 5.2) and Jeremy Bentham (see Box 5.3). Classical thinkers did not really have a theory of criminology; they already had a complete theory of human behavior. They certainly did not believe in demons and witches, but rather felt that people had free will to determine their own behavior. Human beings were regarded as rational, calculating actors whose behaviors are designed to maximize pleasure and minimize pain. Following one of their most influential thinkers, Thomas Hobbes (described in Chapter 3 as a consensus thinker), they believed that people were self-serving; they would always try to maximize their pleasure. Without some system of restraints on individuals, society would be impossible, because everyone would attend only to their own interests. Therefore, the purpose of society was to restrain those impulses. Still, society had to work for the people, rather than the reverse. Laws had to apply to all segments of society, and judges had to impartially try to determine facts: Did someone break the law? If so, then the agreed-upon sentence would be imposed. The punishment should not only fit the crime but also be applied equally to all members of society, not just to disenfranchised people.

For example, classical theorists believed that in contemplating a robbery, people calculate the probability of being caught and the penalties for committing robbery. They will not commit this crime if they believe that the costs of doing so are greater than the rewards. Thus, the best or most effective criminal justice system is one that ensures that the costs of committing crime are greater than the benefits. Of course, if everyone in society is subject to exactly the same punishment, then everyone can more easily figure out that the pain of punishment outweighs the rewards of the crime. Punishment isn't desirable in itself, but only as a way of deterring crime; it generates fears of the consequences of breaking the law.

The Characteristics and Purpose of Punishment

What, then, is the appropriate punishment for crimes? These classical scholars were humanistic philosophers, strongly opposed to the use of any punishment except when absolutely necessary. Of course, deterrence through punishment was necessary to ensure that the costs of crime outweighed the benefits. In fact, to most classical theorists, deterrence was really the only legitimate reason for carrying out a punishment. Thus, for Beccaria and Bentham, execution and torture were unjust. The offender's punishment should match the harm done to society. According to Beccaria:

> It is to the common interest not only that crimes not be committed, but also that they be less frequent in proportion to the harm they cause society. Therefore, the obstacles that deter man from committing crime should be stronger in proportion as they are contrary to the public good, and as the inducements to commit them are stronger. There must, therefore, be a proper proportion between crimes and punishments. (1963, p. 62)

Why should the punishment be proportionate to the harm done to society? Wouldn't people be less likely to, say, rob banks if society executed those who did? Stiffer penalties might deter some people from robbing banks; however, these sanctions might also make other crimes attractive. For example, an inmate serving his fourth term for armed robbery told Martin Schwartz recently that if his state adopted a mandatory life sentence or capital punishment statute for three- or four-time offenders, he would be forced to kill any witnesses to his crimes. Once the penalties for murder and robbery were roughly equal, he said, he might as well commit the murders, since doing so would give him a chance to get away. Still, even if all robbers refrained from killing witnesses, classical theorists would still object to executing or torturing these offenders because such treatment is unwarranted and cruel.

Classical theorists also thought that punishment works best if it is swift and certain:

> The more promptly and the more closely punishment follows upon the commission of a crime, the more just and useful will it be. I say more just, because the criminal is thereby spared the useless and cruel torments of uncertainty . . . [and] because privation of liberty, being itself a punishment, should not precede the sentence except when necessity requires. I have said that the promptness of punishment is more useful because when the length of time that passes between the punishment and the misdeed is less, so much the stronger and more lasting in the human mind is the association of these two ideas, crime and punishment. (Beccaria, 1963, pp. 55–56)

The certainty of punishment was also deemed necessary by Beccaria because, in his opinion,

> One of the greatest curbs on crime is not the cruelty of punishments, but their infallibility. . . . The certainty of punishment, even if it be moderate, will always make a stronger impression than the fear of another which is more terrible but combined with the hope of impunity; even the least evils, when they are certain, always terrify men's minds. . . . Let the laws, therefore, be inexorable, and inexo-

rable their executors in particular cases, but let the legislator be tender, indulgent, and humane. (1963, pp. 58–59)

Thus far, we have reviewed Beccaria as the major thinker in favor of swift, certain punishments that need not be severe. Bentham agreed with this philosophy. Because he advanced the related idea that the entire point of deterrence was to prevent crime, not to "get even" with people who commit crimes, Bentham has been associated with what has been called the *utilitarian* philosophy. According to Bentham, if people do indeed engage in a calculation of pain versus pleasure, then a goal of the legal system should be to manipulate the punishments to come up with the right formula to keep people from committing crimes. He came up with a *felicity calculus,* purporting to be a mathematical model of the amount of pain needed to overcome pleasure, although perhaps it would be kindest to term it "interesting guesswork."

In sum, the major points of the classical school are:[1]

- Supernatural forces do not drive people to commit crime.
- Human beings are innately egoistic and have free will. Moreover, people are seen as making rational, calculated choices to maximize pleasure and minimize pain.
- All people have equal rights and should be treated accordingly by the law.
- Crime is a moral offense against society.
- Punishment should be proportional to the crime.
- Punishment should be swift and certain and used only to deter people from harming others.
- Capital punishment is to be avoided because it is an evil that is worse than the evil of the crime itself.

Classical Ideas in Modern Times

The classical school has had a major impact on the criminal justice system as we know it today. This may seem somewhat the opposite of common sense. In virtually all of North America, and in many other countries, the

---

[1] This list is informed by summaries provided by Taylor, Walton, and Young (1973), Vold and Bernard (1986), and Williams and McShane (1994).

current mood among politicians and many of their constituents is to, as Texas newspaper columnist Molly Ivins puts it, "Git Tuff on Crime." The classical theorists opposed capital punishment, were against the idea of punishment for retribution, and were trying to find the least amount of punishment possible to keep people from committing crimes. Why is this perspective, and minor variations of it, still alive and well? Why would something so obviously "liberal" be the favorite theory of people who identify themselves as "conservative"? As we shall see, the major reason (as you might expect) is that it serves the political agendas of quite a number of people. Recall that the primary characteristic of nonsociological theories such as the classical is the view of crime as the property of the individual rather than a function of social forces (for example, unemployment, poverty, or poor schooling). If you want to blame crime on bad people, rather than to put money into making society a better place to live, then this is an attractive theory. Thus, it suits both the political and economic interests of conservative presidents, senators, and other legislators (Eitzen & Timmer, 1985). For example, the notion that criminals are egoistic, rational, and calculating individuals

> makes it easier to blame the offender for all aspects of crime, rather than share some of that blame with society for creating conditions that force some people into crime. If it is an individual's decision to commit crime, then he or she is morally responsible and deserves to be punished. The great advantage of this reasoning is that we do not have to do anything other than punish while the individual is in our control. Thus, rehabilitation and skill training are no longer a part of what a prison must do. In addition, we do not have to engage in expensive social programs to improve conditions that create crime, nor do we have to engage in even more expensive social reform. An assumption that individuals make fully rational decisions to engage in criminal behavior can save a lot of money. (Williams & McShane, 1994, p. 23)

As we shall see in Chapter 12, two factors that are very closely associated with predatory street crime are economic and racial inequality. Policies based on classical thinking will not curb the high rates of crime in our society. We will discuss this in more detail, but first it is important to describe contemporary versions of this perspective.

NEOCLASSICAL CRIMINOLOGY

As the label suggests, neoclassical criminology represents a return to the theories of classical criminology. Certainly, there is currently a major resurgence of appreciation for some of the major arguments of this school of thought. As we suggested previously, however, only some of the ideas of the classical theorists have been adopted by the neoclassical theorists.

James Q. Wilson has played a leading role in the revival of classical thinking, and thus his contributions deserve considerable attention here. According to Wilson, in order to adequately control crime, policymakers should develop solutions based on the "radical individualistic" writings of Beccaria and Bentham. Like these classical thinkers, Wilson does not offer a formal theory of crime. In fact, for him, the search for "root causes" is a useless endeavor because "a free society can do little about attacking these root causes so that a concern for their elimination becomes little more than an excuse for doing nothing" (1985, p. 6). Rather, Wilson asserts that we should devote all of our energy to improving the ability of the criminal justice system to deter people from committing crimes.

Still, Wilson does offer elements of a causal theory, one that views crime as a function of "inadequate control." Generally, however, he concurs with the basic beliefs of classical theorists such as Hobbes, Beccaria, and Bentham. Wilson assumes that all people are both free-willed and predisposed to committing crimes. He contends that punishment should be used to deter crime and that punishment should be proportional to the severity of the crime committed. Further, he asserts that swift and certain penalties are more effective than severe punishments. His reasoning here may be a bit different than the classical theorists. Wilson suggests that severe punishments are too often doomed: "The more draconian the sentence, the less (on the average) the chance of its being imposed; plea bargains see to that" (1995, p. 494).

Still, much of the current interest in neoclassical theory over the past thirty years has come from economists, who have continually proposed and tested theories arguing that people are rational. To the question that classical theorists ducked—why some people and not others commit crimes—Gary Becker has a neoclassical answer: "Some persons become 'criminals,' therefore, not because their basic motivation differs from that of other persons, but because their benefits and costs differ" (cited in Currie, 1985, p. 26).

Ernest van den Haag is another neoclassical theorist who assumes that crime is like "any other exchange in the marketplace" (Currie, 1985, p. 26). For him, people commit crime because it does not cost them much. Thus, to reduce the high rates of predatory street crimes discussed in this text,

> our only hope . . . lies in decreasing the expected net advantage of committing crimes (compared to lawful activities) by increasing the cost through increasing the expected severity of punishments and the probability of suffering them. (van den Haag, 1982, p. 1035)

With these arguments in mind, how would neoclassical theorists explain the rising rate of homicide (see Chapter 8) and other crimes committed in the United States? They might agree with the following *Wall Street Journal* editorial:

> The sharp increase of crime in many states has undoubtedly resulted from the absence of punishment. . . . As the certainty of punishment rises, prison populations will rise. But so will the cost of crime. If states stay on their present course, it is reasonable to expect that the present surge in prison populations will cease. There will be less crime and fewer people going to jail. If so, it will be worth the cost of correcting those years of neglect. (cited in Currie, 1985, p. 28)

How does prison increase the costs of crime? According to neoclassical theorists, prison meets this objective by functioning as a *deterrent.* There are two types of deterrence: specific and general (Zimring & Hawkins, 1973). *Specific deterrence* refers to the effects of imprisonment on those who are incarcerated. For example, if you spend two years in prison for robbing a grocery store, the assumption is that the "pains of imprisonment" (Johnson & Toch, 1982) will be sufficiently high to make you want to avoid ever returning to the prison; you will stop robbing grocery stores. To some people, the worse prison is, the better the specific deterrent. An atmosphere characterized by interpersonal violence, suicide, confinement, and sexual aggression might have some kind of serious effect on you. One of Hans Toch's respondents told him:

> They put a note in my cell and say they're going to come and kill me, they're going to hang me. So I showed the note to the police and told them I didn't know what was going on. Because I had heard they will kill you in the Tombs, people have told me that on the outside . . . and the day before that they tried to kill another guy. They stabbed him with a piece of wire. . . . So nothing couldn't tell me that they wasn't going to do the same to me. (Toch, 1992, pp. 208–209)

If you had a similar prison experience, would you risk going back? This may seem like a stupid question. However, there is one major problem with this entire argument: despite the violent and depressing nature of prison, a very high number of people are willing to take this risk. Put simply, prison, as a specific deterrent, does not seem to work. In fact, most inmates, after they are released, continue to commit serious crimes (Currie, 1985). This failure of specific deterrence suggests that after two hundred years we have not yet mastered Bentham's felicity calculus.

General deterrence refers to the effects of your punishment of individuals on the general population. For example, if people hear about your sentence for robbing a grocery store, particularly if combined with stories similar to the one provided by Toch's incarcerated respondent, general deterrence predicts that they are not likely to commit crimes for fear of going to prison themselves. One well-known example of general deterrence in the early 1990s was the decision by a Singapore Court to cane youngsters who had engaged in repeated acts of vandalism. Many people loudly proclaimed their agreement with this move and told both authors of this book that they felt that Canadian and American courts should begin this kind of bloody reprisal against vandals. "I certainly wouldn't do anything bad if there was a chance that I would be caned," was the typical refrain. Interestingly, the boys who were caned were living in Singapore, where caning was regularly used. There was a chance that they would be caned, but they vandalized anyway! As we will soon discuss, even the death penalty does little, if anything, to deter people from murdering others in the United States.

CRITIQUE OF CLASSICAL AND NEOCLASSICAL THOUGHT

To review, classical and neoclassical theory has two major suppositions: (1) criminals are rational actors who weigh the costs and rewards of breaking the law before they actually commit an offense, and (2) punishment is an effective deterrent. These assertions will be evaluated in turn.

Cost/Reward Analysis and Deterrence

The argument against the idea that criminals rationally choose to commit crime is best stated by Currie: "The idea that criminals (or anyone else) could be understood as simply atomized, rational calculators of costs and benefits, carefully weighing the gains of crime against the risks of punishment seems grossly inadequate" (1985, p. 55). This theory may explain *some* crimes in *some* contexts. However, most offenders do not evaluate the negative consequences of their actions. Some of Ken Tunnell's interviews with property offenders exemplify this point (1992, pp. 88–89):

> **Question:** Come on now. You're not saying you didn't think about getting caught, are you?
>
> **Answer:** I never really thought about getting caught until, pow, you're in jail, you're in juvenile or something. That's when you go to think about it.
>
> **Question:** As you did burglaries, what came first—the crime or thinking about getting caught for the crime?
>
> **Answer:** The crime comes first because it's enough to worry about doing the actual crime itself without worrying about what's going to happen if you get caught.

Thus, overall, "We don't have much research on what goes on in the minds of criminals before they commit crimes, but what we do have suggests that rational planning is the exception rather than the rule" (Currie, 1985, p. 55).

Further, if property offenders too rarely engage in "rational planning," chances are, even less advance planning characterizes those who murder in the heat of passion or who commit crimes while under the influence of drugs or alcohol. A more difficult problem is that some people may be rational and calculating when they plan criminal activities, but they put into the "rewards" side of the calculations things that we cannot affect through deterrence. For example, young male gang members often engage in criminal activities primarily because these acts are an excellent way to engage in what James Messerschmidt (1993) terms "doing masculinity." Often, these youths have no other resources at their disposal to do this, and it is of primary importance for young men in some cultures to earn a reputation as masculine. Even worse, some gang members and other youths who commit violent acts on the street don't care about the possible negative consequences because "doing time" enhances their status as "badass" men (Katz, 1988). Such an image may be very useful in their futures, since it reduces competition for criminal opportunities, makes for fewer challenges to authority, and may result in greater wealth. In other words, in compiling a list of pleasures and pains, for some people in some places, being punished has to be put on the *pleasure* side of the ledger, not the *pain* side!

Even when some offenders weigh the costs and benefits of committing crime and then elect to break the law, they often don't make their choices in conditions of their own choosing. In other words, their criminal career paths are not determined solely by free will. For example, a large sociological literature shows that many girls are physically and sexually abused by their parents (see, for example, Russell, 1986). Many girls are also raised in homes characterized by high levels of husband-to-wife violence (see Chapter 9). To escape these traumatic and even terrifying circumstances, some girls run away from home and end up trying to survive on the streets.

Why don't they turn to government agencies for help? John Lowman's answer is that they left home seeking *autonomy* and that group or foster homes are just variations of the oppressive forms of social control they experienced at home. After a while, these *lumpen* or *defamilied* girls realize that while they cannot find a job or obtain welfare, they can sell their bodies to men willing to pay for sex. Thus, prostitution is a solution to the problem of situational poverty, and "as a person becomes more and more ensconced in the subculture of the street, so it becomes more and more difficult to escape it" (Lowman, 1992, p. 62). Indeed, the overwhelming majority of youths engaged in sex work in the United States are homeless girls (Yates et al., 1991). Both boys and girls, however, are more likely to commit crimes the longer they are on the streets and homeless. As Bill McCarthy and John Hagan (1991) point out, the problem is the need to provide some basic necessities in order to survive. There are, to be sure, conservative neoclassical theorists who argue that teenaged prostitutes are impulsive sexual delinquents who are driven completely by the "rational expectation of benefit" (Brannigan & Fleischman, 1989, p. 79). However, John Lowman (1992) counters that circumstances can be seen as more to blame.

Punishment and Deterrence

A central claim of classical and neoclassical theorists is that punishment, and especially imprisonment, can deter crime. Unfortunately, there is also a large body of research that suggests that it does not. For example, the United States unquestionably is the most violent country in the advanced industrial world. Can this problem be attributed to what the *Wall Street Journal* calls an "absence of punishment"? Is our government making it too easy for people to commit crimes by handing out weak sanctions? The answer to both of these questions is no, for the following reasons.

The Use of Prisons   First, while the United States is an extremely violent country, it is also the most punitive industrialized democracy (Selke, 1993). For many years, the only countries that locked up a greater proportion of their citizenry were the former Soviet Union and South Africa, and in both cases the comparison was problematic because of the large numbers of overtly political prisoners held by those two countries. In any case, by the 1990s, the United States had shot far ahead. In 1991, the Sentencing Project in Washington, DC, reported that the U.S. rate of incarceration was 426 people per 100,000 population, as compared with 333 per 100,000 for South Africa and 268 per 100,000 for the Soviet Union. No other country had a rate of more than 200, and most were below 100. For black males alone, the project found that the U.S. rate of 3,109 incarcerated per 100,000 African-American males was extraordinarily higher than South Africa's rate of 729 per 100,000 black men—and that latter rate was under the white apartheid government (Mauer, 1991). Since these 1991 data, there have been some changes. It is impossible to make comparisons today to the full former Soviet Union. The Russian republic seems to be escalating its imprisonment rate dramatically in the face of an enormous and violent crime wave. What we do know is that the United States has continued and even accelerated what John Irwin and James Austin (1994) call an "imprisonment binge." Has this imprisonment helped us out? Is the United States now a safer country? As Todd Clear points out, we really can't even begin to answer that question. Although UCR data show an increase in crime since the early 1970s, the National Crime Victimization Survey data do not:

> This statistical discrepancy demonstrates starkly the grossly speculative nature of our knowledge about crime. Having embarked on this stupendous experiment in punishment, we lack even rudimentary statistical bases for concluding what changes have accompanied it, much less what changes it caused. (1994, p. 40)

We will return to a discussion of prisons in Chapter 12, but what is important here is that we really don't know what we are doing. We don't know whether imprisonment reduces crime. We don't even know how much crime there is, so it is impossible to measure whether increased imprisonment reduces crime. What should be noted, as Elliott Currie points out, is that we have managed to create an extraordinarily overcrowded and violent prison system without making our streets safer: "We have created an overstuffed and volatile penal system of overwhelming barbarity, yet we endure levels of violence significantly higher than in the more 'permissive' sixties" (1985, p. 11). Clearly, prison does not have a general deterrent effect.

The Death Penalty In the same way, one of the most difficult areas to discuss is the death penalty. This ultimate penalty is not only supported by a majority of Americans (although support is significantly lower in minority communities) but justified by most criminal justice and government officials on classical theory grounds: it acts as a general deterrent to murder. Of course, the classical theorists themselves opposed the death penalty and felt that a lengthy prison sentence was a better deterrent. Further, the scientific community, including virtually all scientists working on the subject for the government, have concluded that there is no deterrent effect from executions. Victor Kappeler, Mark Blumberg, and Gary Potter state it bluntly:

Probably no other question has received as much attention as the issue of whether the death penalty is a more effective deterrent to murder than a lengthy prison sentence. [However, the] overwhelming majority of studies report finding no deterrent effect. (1993, pp. 214–215)

In fact, William Bowers and Glenn Pierce (1980) and Brian Forst (1983) found evidence to conclude exactly the opposite: that by legitimating the notion that vengeance for past misdeeds is acceptable, executions actually *increased* the number of murders in some jurisdictions. One study, a mathematically complex econometrics design carried out by Isaac Erlich (1975), shows a deterrent effect; of course, this is the one usually chosen to quote from all of the many dozens of studies by proponents of the death penalty. Unfortunately, no one has been able to duplicate this study, and many scientists have demonstrated how to make minor changes in the mathematical model and come to opposite conclusions (Walker, 1994).

Still, the majority of the American people support the death penalty. Robert Bohm (1991, p. 114) contends that they might change their position if they only knew that the death penalty:

- Does not prevent or reduce crime more effectively than nonlethal punishments such as life imprisonment.
- Causes the executions of innocent people.
- Is administered in a capricious, arbitrary, and discriminatory manner.
- Costs much more than life imprisonment.
- Is a method of racial oppression (for example, African-Americans are more likely to be executed than whites).
- Protects the interests of the powerful white majority.
- Is a repressive response to the brutal symptoms of racial and social inequality.

However, there is no reason to expect much change in the near future. Interestingly, white Americans of all religions, regions, incomes, and occupations are strongly in favor of the death penalty. Perhaps because they are more sensitive to the arguments made by Bohm, African-Americans are significantly less in favor of the death penalty (Maguire & Pastore, 1994).

As mentioned previously, in the scientific community at least, it has become progressively difficult to argue that capital punishment deters murder. Those who favor capital punishment have begun more and more to justify it on the grounds that it somehow evens the score, or is just. For example, many criminology and criminal justice professors around the world belong to an Internet electronic discussion group called the United Nations Criminal Justice Information Network. Capital punishment is a common topic there, although few non-Americans take part in the dialogue. A common argument in favor of executions is that the government must take the side of the victims, that it must uphold the value of a life, that it is part of the social compact that the government makes that it must defend the social order. For example, in response to a notice that a man had just been executed in Texas for a crime committed almost fifteen years ago and that the inmate had long since completely reformed himself, one person said: "[He] may or may not have been 'reformed' when Texas executed him —but I would argue that Texas told its law abiding citizens that they matter and persons who murder them will pay a price. Texas demonstrated that it will defend its social order against those who would destroy it."

Although such arguments seem to be fed by a neoclassical view, support from that camp is lacking. As we have seen, classical theorists opposed capital punishment, to say nothing of cruel punishments such as death rows. They would want absolute proof that capital punishment reduced crime before they would even discuss the issue. Today, people make blind guesses as to what the effect might be and argue that we need to execute people anyway to uphold the social order.

What is most interesting about these arguments is that the people who make them rarely extend the arguments to other arenas. To illustrate, consider the fact that the United States has one of the highest infant mortality rates in the industrialized world (Henslin, 1994)—higher than virtually all of Europe and Scandinavia, plus Japan, Hong Kong, Australia, and Singapore. Further, states such as Texas, which perform the bulk of executions in America, are also the ones with terrible poverty, high unemployment, and problem schools. Why is it that we seldom hear death penalty advocates issue the call to save innocent lives and uphold the value of human life in these circumstances? The point we are making is that, unlike classical theorists, who tried to balance their views with the best available data, many of those who claim to be influenced by these thinkers are only selecting those parts of classical thought that fit their own political and social agendas.

Even worse, the U.S. zeal to "get tough on crime" seems to be affecting other countries. Consider Canada, a country that is considerably less violent than the United States. In the mid-1990s, young offenders were the objects of a major moral panic (see Chapter 1) even though they did not pose a significant threat to the social order. Contrary to "conventional wisdom" or public opinion, there was no major increase in serious violent youth crime in 1993–94. Nevertheless, by 1995, many Canadians were arguing that the Young Offenders Act should be "toughened up" (Shepard, 1995, p. A3) to provide stronger sentences for these people.

Informal Community Sanctions   If the general deterrent effects of formal punishment are at best minimal, then what does work? Actually, one form of deterrence does seem to have some effect, although it is not the type of general deterrence anticipated by the classical theorists. It is not the fear of going to jail that seems to keep people on the straight and narrow, but rather a fear of the disapproval of friends, family, and neighbors. A large body of research shows that informal community sanctions are much more effective general deterrents than prison (Currie, 1985). Many social control theorists (see Chapter 6) share the view that informal social control processes involving parents, peers, teachers, co-workers, and so on as agents of social control are primarily responsible for ensuring that most of us conform with social and legal norms most of the time (Ellis & DeKeseredy, 1996). In fact, most deterrence studies show that perceived certainty and severity of formal sanctions (such as arrest and imprisonment) are not key determinants of conformity (Miller & Simpson, 1991; Paternoster, 1987). However, the guilt, shame, and fear associated with such sanctions—what have been called the "indirect costs" of these sanctions—seem to be effective deterrents.

For example, Kirk Williams and Richard Hawkins (1989) found that men report self-stigma and social disapproval to be the most costly effects of being arrested for wife beating. Thus, a sense of "shame" is an important mechanism underlying effective deterrence (Braithwaite, 1989). Certainly, this is the theory behind the actions of many shopkeepers and police officers, who look for evidence of shame and remorse before deciding whether to press charges, especially against younger people. For example, no doubt many of you have witnessed situations in which a youth is caught shoplifting or committing a minor offense and the police decide not to make an arrest. Normally, this is because the youth expresses considerable fear of his parents' responses. If he cries hard enough, the police officers might feel that the fear of informal shaming would be enough to deter him from stealing again. Of course, as you may cynically point out, middle-class youths are much better at "faking" this shame, especially in an environment in which they will get more prestige for beating the charges than they will scorn for crying in front of the police. Still, most youths stop committing crime less because they are afraid of being caught and locked up than because the rewards of becoming valued and productive members of a community and earning the approval of family and peers begin to seem more important than the lures of delinquency (Currie, 1985, p. 57).

These issues will be addressed in more detail in Chapter 12.

BIOLOGICAL AND PSYCHOLOGICAL THEORIES OF CRIME

For the purpose of this chapter, those who medicalize crime are defined as *clinical criminologists* (Hilton, Jackson, & Webster, 1990) and characterized as advancing *predispositional* theories of crime (Eitzen & Timmer, 1985). These theorists contend that "organic anomalies" or "psychological defects" such as the following are the major sources of crime (Lilly, Cullen, & Ball, 1995):[2]

- Premenstrual syndrome (PMS)
- Attention Deficit Disorder (ADD)
- Low IQ
- Hypoglycemia
- XYY chromosomes
- Psychosis
- Schizophrenia
- Neuroses
- Weak superego

---

[2] See Andrews and Bonta (1994), Brennan, Mednick, and Volovka (1995), Herrnstein (1995), Hilton, Jackson, and Webster (1990), and Siegel (1995) for in-depth discussions on these and other individualistic determinants of crime.

BOX 5.4

DIET: TWINKIES AS A CAUSE OF CRIME

Some evidence indicates that children who are on sugar-intensive diets are more likely to engage in aggressive behavior. The problem is trying to make the next connection, which is to criminal behavior; here, the evidence is lacking. As Shoemaker (1990, p. 31) points out, however, it is entirely possible that "the true value of this approach would be in the connection between biochemical imbalances and other conditions that might be more directly related to delinquency, such as school problems and interpersonal difficulties." Of course, no sooner does a theory emerge than a lawyer introduces it into evidence. In the late 1970s, San Francisco Supervisor Dan White admitted killing his political enemies, Mayor George Moscone and Supervisor Harvey Milk. Despite the evidence, White's claim that he was suffering from a chemical imbalance brought on by junk foods won him a reduced charge and a light sentence. Ever since, this has been known as the "Twinkie defense."

- Egocentric personality
- Behavior modeling
- Antisocial personality syndrome

Of course, we will not have space in this chapter to explain all of these in detail, although we will discuss some of them. Box 5.4 discusses one suggested source of aggression.

Biological Theories: The Born Criminal

Theories suggesting that criminality is caused by some biological or genetic factor sweep over criminology about once every generation. Because we are now about due for another of these waves, and indeed have begun to see the first swells on the horizon, it might be instructive to delve into the history of such theories. As we shall see, again and again, some theorist, often after years of painstaking work, has declared that he or she has located the born criminal type. Again and again, other scientists have pointed out extreme methodological flaws in these studies. The most common flaw is the lack of a carefully worked out definition of "criminal." Another drawback is that sometimes the studies are of convicts, who may be very different than criminals. For example, if judges are more likely to send to prison men who look ugly, large, and dangerous, then it may not be much of a biological finding to study men in prison and find that they are more likely than chance to be ugly, large, and dangerous-looking!

Physical Characteristics   The earliest theory of "born criminality" in modern times was based on the so-called science of phrenology, which was popular in the first half of the 1800s in the United States. The idea here was that in certain people, distinct parts of the brain were over- or underdeveloped. Criminals, of course, were people who had overdeveloped violent or base-instinct brain "faculties." For a number of reasons, this theory fell out of favor generally, although parts of it are alive even today.

Still, the most important criminological theorist of the 1800s in Europe and the United States, Cesare Lombroso (1835–1909), was obviously heavily influenced by this emphasis on facial and biological features. Lombroso usually is discussed not as a biological theorist, but as the first *positivist* scientist in criminology. Positivists were—and in many ways still are—very influential in turning our attention away from the classical concern with the crime act to a concern with the criminal. They believe that they can study human behavior and locate the factors that cause patterns of uniformity. Of course, if crime is caused by bad genes, or a crooked nose, or poor education, then the entire free-will orientation of the classical school does not make much sense.

As the "father of positivist criminology," Lombroso was heavily influenced by Charles Darwin's studies on evolution. Based on Darwin's methodology, it seemed obvious to Lombroso that the way to study an important scientific question was to develop a research hypothesis and then go directly to the relevant subjects and take measurements or engage in observation. An Italian physician with a specialty in psychiatry, Lombroso had an "insight" one day while doing an autopsy on a violent criminal. He decided that the skull was more suited to an animal than a human. Lombroso then began to develop a theory that criminals were not as far along on the evolutionary ladder as normal people. These born criminals were *atavistic,* or a biological throwback to an earlier stage of development. Atavistic men share a number of characteristics, such as chimpanzeelike ears, shifty eyes, and large jaws.

Lombroso did very extensive tests of his theory, mainly on convicts, with Italian soldiers as a control group. He found some support for his theories, although he spent the rest of his life fending off massive criticism from detractors. As Daniel Curran and Claire Renzetti (1994) point out, his greatest contribution to criminology was that he generated enormous debate and opened up new areas of inquiry for many other scientists. Still, his work has many drawbacks, in addition to serving as a source of ridicule for today's college students. Lombroso convinced many courts to introduce into evidence the facial characteristics of the accused and may have been responsible for the conviction of many innocent people. Further, his work on women is significantly worse than his work on men. With women, he had a distinct problem—he could not find *any* differences between criminal women and noncriminal women. Thus, he concluded that *all* women were atavistic, that they were not as far up the evolutionary ladder as men. Women who were criminals had adopted male characteristics, the worst possible thing for women to do, since it made them into monsters.

As popular as Lombroso's work was, scientists dropped it fairly quickly when Charles Goring's *The English Convict* was published in 1913. Goring took many years to, in effect, try to replicate Lombroso's work using better samples and better mathematics, but he found no differences between criminals and the rest of the population. Interestingly, although Goring has always been well known for his rejection of Lombroso, he did agree with Lombroso's main point—that criminals are born with defects. He felt that a defective physique and a defective intelligence marked the difference between criminals and law-abiding citizens (Akers, 1994).

Other biological theories in criminology have had a small effect, but none has had the overwhelming influence of Lombroso's. Earnest A. Hooten attacked Goring and published his own extensive study in 1939 showing a criminal type, but he is perhaps better known today for tremendous methodological flaws and enormous assumptions. For example, he believed that physical inferiority was inherited but never presented any evidence on the subject (Brown, Esbensen, & Geis, 1991). William Sheldon gained prominence briefly in 1949 for his system of body types. A gross oversimplification might be that *endomorphs* are fatter, *mesomorphs* are more muscled, and *ectomorphs* are tall and skinny. Sheldon and Eleanor Glueck, in 1950, offered support for Sheldon's theory of body types in their finding that incarcerated delinquents were more homogeneous than the general population and more likely to be mesomorphic. Generally, North American scientists who had just witnessed the horrific consequences of Adolf Hitler's racial superiority notions in World War II were not warm toward racial arguments on criminals. Further, the finding that juvenile delinquents who were locked up were more likely to be muscular than fat or gawky did not seem to many to be much of a finding. It could simply mean that judges were more likely to lock up more muscular children or indicate that gangs were more likely to recruit youths who had athletic potential.

Genetic Abnormalities   Another theory that created a flurry of interest for a few years may have the singular disadvantage of simultaneously being correct and mostly irrelevant. Mainly in the 1960s, researchers became intrigued by a genetic abnormality that occurs in about one man in every 1,000: the XYY syndrome. Normal men have an XY configuration in the chromosome that determines sex, and an enormous number of studies were conducted on these abnormal XYY men. Based on all of these studies, we can accept that men with an extra Y chromosome are indeed overrepresented in the criminal justice system, although mainly for petty property offenses. We don't know just why or how this is so, but given the minuscule number of men with this extra chromosome, whatever answer we come up with is not going to tell us anything about the nature of crime in the United States today. After all, virtually all crime is committed by men without the XYY syndrome. Further, some criminologists argue that XYY men, who tend to be very tall and to have acne-scarred faces, may both have trouble fitting in with society (meaning an increase of likelihood of criminality) and look threatening to judges, who could send them to prison more often. In other words, perhaps their overrepresentation in prison stems partially from their looks (Voigt et al., 1994).

Premenstrual Syndrome   One of the latest biological explanations of crime—premenstrual syndrome (PMS)—has actually been recognized as a form of legal insanity in France, and has been successfully used as a defense in courts in England and the United States (Brown, Esbensen, & Geis, 1991). Essentially, the argument is that in certain women the stress just before their monthly period can cause violent rages. Given that we do not have a particularly good definition of PMS, we don't really know what symptoms are caused by it. In addition, the studies conducted thus far have been seriously flawed. Therefore, it is difficult to believe at this time that PMS will have a serious legal effect.

Family Theories   One of the most popular and influential books on criminology is Richard Dugdale's (1877/1910) *The Jukes*. Henry Goddard's (1925) study of the Kallikak family is almost as popular. In each case, the author took a single family and showed how successive generations produced an extraordinary number of criminals. The Kallikak study is the more interesting, in that it involved a man who produced an illegitimate son with a "feeble-minded" woman and later married a woman from a good Quaker family. Goddard's point was that, on the illegitimate side of the family, the infant mortality rate was extraordinarily high, many descendants became prostitutes and alcoholics, and some became criminals. On the "good" side, the family became part of some of the best families in the early 1800s. Unfortunately, neither Goddard nor Dugdale addressed the problem of life chances, whereby children born into poverty may be more likely to have problems than children born into the very best families in the country (Brown, Esbensen, & Geis, 1991).

Modern Biological Theories   As the preceding discussion suggests, many older theories are simply brought out of the closet every now and then for a new airing. Perhaps the most popular airing is James Q. Wilson and Richard J. Herrnstein's (1985) *Crime and Human Nature*. Here, they review uncritically a large number of works arguing that criminals are biologically predisposed to commit crimes, from having low IQs to mesomorphic body types. This book, which received widespread attention, particularly in the media, offered little that was new, but rather evidence long considered inadequate or obsolete (Voigt et al., 1994).

Ronald Akers has summarized both why we abandoned earlier theories, and why most criminologists are not impressed by the modern ones:

> The major reason for the rejection of these earlier biological theories . . . is simply because the theories were found to be untestable, illogical, or wrong. They seldom withstood empirical tests and often espoused simplistic, racist and sexist notions that easily crumbled under closer scrutiny. . . . Some of these modern proponents have not offered any new theories, but have simply resurrected many of

the older biological explanations of crime, relied on the same old, flawed studies, and presented little evidence that could be any more convincing. (1994, pp. 74–75)

One of the reasons Akers called these theories racist is because of their history. If you hear North Americans constantly demanding that "them" or "criminals" be locked up, you know that we are seeking easy answers to complex problems. If we can further identify "them" as "African-Americans," "people with big ears," "people with low IQs," "people from bad genetic backgrounds," or whatever theory is in vogue, it feeds that tendency. As Peter Kraska (1989, p. 5) points out:

> It provides a scientifically based justification for targeting certain individuals and/or groups of people—by virtue of their biological make-up—for the purpose of controlling or eliminating their "dysfunctional" physiology, a rationalization used for oppression against various targeted groups throughout history. (The most extreme examples are the practice of slavery in the 1800s, the holocaust/genocide of various targeted groups during WWII, and the judicial mandate and implementation of a sterilization program for certain undesirables in the United States.)

Psychological and Personality Theories

Freudian Approaches   Certainly, a great deal of attention has been paid within the criminal justice community to the various theories of Sigmund Freud and his followers. Presuming that our readers are fairly likely to have taken an intro psychology course, we will simply review briefly what Freudian psychologists offer as explanations of crime. Criminal behavior is not in itself important, these people would argue, but rather is a symptom of an inner psychic conflict between the *id* (the unconscious home of antisocial desires), the *ego* (the conscious mind), and the *superego* (roughly, the conscience). Most commonly, therapists point to an underdeveloped superego, so that the criminal does not feel any guilt, or to an underdeveloped ego, so that the criminal gives in too easily to desires for irrational or antisocial action. Rather than putting energy into punishment, advocates of psycho-analytic theory would suggest that therapy aimed at repairing or curing the underlying emotional disturbance will automatically stop the criminal behavior (Akers, 1994).

For many people, a prime benefit of Freudian theories is that they highlight the importance of childhood experiences in developing the adult mind. The more we learn about how adult criminals were battered, abused, or sexually abused as children, the more urgent it becomes for us to consider one of the most important elements of a crime prevention program to be curbing violence against women and children in the family (Schwartz, 1989).

The problem with using Freudian concepts, however, is that they are virtually untestable. An entire theory may be based on unconscious motivation, whereby offenders themselves are unaware of what is happening. Thus, we (the researchers) must try to figure out what is going on by subtle guesswork, such as using subjective techniques like interpreting dreams and interpreting people's ideas of what inkblots look like (Rorschach tests). Small wonder that different researchers so often come to different conclusions about the same patients (Shoemaker, 1990). The history of researchers interpreting patients' words to suit the therapists' biases extends all the way back to Freud's own works (Curran & Renzetti, 1994). Of course, one of these biases is that Freud regarded women as inferior to men in a number of different ways, which has influenced several generations of criminal justice officials who dealt with female offenders accordingly.

Personality Trait Theories   Other researchers have tried to deal with this problem by using standardized personality tests. These theorists have taken the position that crime is not a function of the unconscious, but rather is the direct result of some personality flaw. The trick is to find those bad personality traits, which presumably noncriminals do not have.

One of the more famous of these tests is the heavily used Minnesota Multiphasic Personality Inventory (MMPI), which consists of 550 true/false statements. In fact, when one of your authors (Schwartz) was a college student, the MMPI was administered to all in-coming students to check for problems (he was told that he was outgoing and liked going to parties, traits that had not escaped anyone's attention). Most of the many administrations of the MMPI to offenders have found differences between offenders and others, particularly in the so-called psychopathic scale, which more recently has been called Scale 4 (Waldo & Dinitz, 1967). The problem, unfortunately, is that Scale 4 asks questions about whether the testtakers have been in trouble with the law, whether relatives agreed with their behavior, and whether they are satisfied with their sex life. Not surprisingly, inmates scored differently on these questions! Thus, "It seems likely that differences in the Scale 4 scores do not reflect any personality differences, but simply reflect differences in the situations in which delinquents and criminals find themselves" (Vold & Bernard, 1986, pp. 120–121).

More evidence for a criminal personality comes from a variation of the MMPI, the California Psychological Inventory (CPI). Here, for the eighteen different scales, groups of offenders and nonoffenders differed on three: socialization, responsibility, and self-control. Some people have made much of this finding, claiming to have pinpointed how criminals differ. Others have worried about the complex and confusing overall picture one obtains from the entire 480-true/false-question test.

The biggest problem with all these tests, unfortunately, is an issue for all scientific studies of this sort. Simply put, these studies all assume that there are two types of people in the world: criminals and noncriminals. Let's give an example. Suppose that Martin Schwartz wanted to check out the difference between criminals and noncriminals. He could go into one of the local men's prisons and get permission to have fifty inmates take a standardized test like the CPI. Then, he could come back to campus and administer the same test to fifty of his male senior students and look for differences. Sound simple enough? What if he knew that several of his students had done time in state prisons for felony crimes and several others had been in juvenile detention facilities? What if still more have told him that they were found guilty as juveniles, served terms on probation, and then successfully had their records erased? What if Schwartz is almost positive that a couple of others are engaging in felony drug sales in the dorms? And what if, in an anonymous questionnaire last year, several more said that they had sold drugs, committed burglaries, stolen cars, engaged in aggravated assaults, and in general committed crimes that could have gotten them sent to prison or reform school if they had been caught, come before the wrong judge, or been represented by the wrong lawyer? In other words, out of the fifty students, many might be known criminals. Others might be criminals and have kept it a secret from Schwartz.

So, we give a test to fifty offenders and compare the criminals to the noncriminals. Or do we? Worse yet, as Daniel Curran and Claire Renzetti (1994) point out, we assume someone is *all* criminal or *all* noncriminal. Some certainly are each, but others might be kind, gentle, warm, friendly, helpful people who, when faced with economic ruin, will sell drugs for a short time. If they are caught, they are criminals. Or, as in the musical *West Side Story* about the street gangs the Sharks and the Jets, they might get pulled into a situation in which someone is killed and suddenly find themselves a murderer.

Whatever the problems, what we have found is very weak and inconsistent evidence of differences between offenders and nonoffenders. Akers (1994, p. 88) simply concludes: "The research using personality inventories and other methods of measuring personality characteristics have not been able to produce findings to support personality variables as major causes of criminal and delinquent behavior."

Mental Illness   Of course, some offenders are mentally ill. Often, the casual observer of the crime scene develops an incorrect picture of crime, since the crimes of the mentally ill often get the most attention. When one hears about an offender who was "told by God" to commit a murder, or who shoots the president of the United States in order to "impress" a film star, it is easy to get worried. These people are not, in the language of people who study psychotics, testing reality and coming to appropriate conclusions. The problem is that there are mentally ill people in every single walk of life. As one top prison official remarked to Schwartz recently, "Of *course* there are a lot of people who are mentally ill in this prison!! Even some of the inmates are mentally ill." The question is whether there are more mentally ill people among offenders than there are in the general population. In fact, because the psychiatric community tends to find a higher incidence of mental illness among working-class people, and because the criminal justice community tends to lock up mostly lower-class people, the *real* question is, How many offenders are diagnosed as mentally ill as compared to working-class individuals? The answer, simply, is that there is no difference in these rates (Sutherland, Cressey, & Luckenbill, 1992).

What about the flip side: Do the mentally ill commit more crimes? Although a number of studies have been done on this subject, most suffer dramatically from the problems involved in using the official statistics described in Chapter 5. For example, in the 1980s, Martin Schwartz had a very bright student who worked nights as an intake officer in a jail. Sort of as a hobby, she tried to predict which arrestees would be referred the next morning to the mental health authorities and which would be referred to the local prosecutors for criminal charges. Although one of the top students in the program, and someone who has gone on to some fame, she never was able to locate a pattern. How many charges, over the years, have been dropped because we knew that the person was on his way into a secure mental health lockup? How many mental health adjudications were dropped because the person was on his way to prison? After all, the people we tend to think of as the most disturbed are or were mostly in prison, not mental institutions: Jeffrey Dahmer, Ted Bundy, David Berkowitz (the "Son of Sam," who supposedly took orders to kill from his dog), Richard Speck (who murdered eight student nurses one at a time in a Chicago apartment), Albert DeSalvo (the Boston Strangler), and Richard Ramirez (the Los Angeles Night Stalker).

Some unsophisticated studies "prove" that the mentally ill commit more crimes, mainly by showing that former mental patients have higher arrest rates than the general population. However, a more careful look reveals that ex-mental patients with no history of arrest have about the same arrest rates as the general population. Ex-patients with a prior history of arrests also have a higher rate of subsequent arrests after release (Cocozza, Melick, & Steadman, 1978; Steadman, Vanderwyst, & Ribner, 1978). In a still more sophisticated study, Linda Teplin (1985) could find no differences between mentally ill and other citizens in terms of criminal activity, seriousness of crimes committed, or dangerousness.

Popular Culture Support for Psychological Explanations

Although many of us think that criminals are essentially bad people, there is no question that, to a significant part of the population, people who steal, murder, or rape are "sick" or mentally ill. Certainly, some of us come by this attitude naturally: if you think of rape as a disgusting and perverted act, it cannot be hard to think of rapists as mentally ill. Still, many of us are supported and even pushed in this direction by highly popular films. One example might be "cut-and-slash" films that portray violent criminals as

Popular culture often reflects current theories of crime. In this scene from Fritz Lang's movie *M*, made in Germany in the early 1930s, Peter Lorre is a child murderer who looks so normal that children are not frightened by him. The film shows Lorre as driven by an inner compulsion, claiming to be "mad," not "bad."

"crazy" or "deranged." Examples of these movies include *The Texas Chainsaw Massacre, Psycho Cop, Psycho,* and *Don't Go into the House.* Films of this type often

> combine a psychopathic antagonist with a supermale theme to create seemingly indestructible murderous supercriminals. . . . Psychotic supermales generally possess an evil, cunning intelligence, and superior strength, endurance, and stealth. Crime in these films is generally an act of meaningless violence. A historical trend in such films has been to present psychotic criminals as more and more violent and bloodthirsty and to show their crimes more and more graphically. (Surette, 1992, p. 36)

A similar phenomenon exists with female criminals. From watching American movies, one would have to conclude that women in conflict with the law are masculinized monsters, lesbian villains, incarcerated teenage predators, or pathological killer beauties (Faith, 1993a; Holmlund, 1994). Examples of these films include *Single White Female, Basic Instinct,* and *The Hand That Rocks the Cradle.* Or consider *Fatal Attraction,* a "women-hating-women" film that attracted millions of North Americans to theaters. In this film, actress Glenn Close

> takes the lead as the prototype of the postmodern failed-woman. Close's character is a woman whose rage at "not having it all" takes nasty turns against a family that seems idyllically happy (except for the husband's secret adultery). She is the image of the beautiful, solitary, ominous, male-identified, childless, pathologically obsessive woman, "liberated" in anti-feminist terms, who would take what she wants at any cost. In the end, she pays with her life at the hand of the injured wife. (Faith, 1993a, p. 265)

Thus, what we find is that very few violent crime films challenge the stereotype of the psychotic killer. In an earlier chapter, we dealt with the problem of whether Hollywood changes people's minds or just follows the public mood. Certainly, even in the latter case, films help to legitimate existing thoughts. If, as we suspect, films do have a major effect, this could be a part of the reason so many people see criminals as monsters who need to be locked up for long terms, rather than as community members who need to be corrected and welcomed back into the fold.

A Sociological Critique of Biological and Psychological Theories

Unquestionably, biological and psychological factors cause some people to commit some crimes. Actually, research has consistently shown that two of the most significant correlates of crime are "biological" ones: age and sex (Braithwaite, 1989; Currie, 1985; Wilson & Herrnstein, 1985). Young (age) men (sex) tend to commit a disproportionate amount of the street crime in America today. However, theories that emphasize only psychological and/or biological factors cannot answer some major questions typically posed by sociologists. If Americans who live in inner-city neighborhoods are more prone to commit street crimes than people who live elsewhere in the United States, then why don't inner-city residents in Germany, Canada, and Japan seem to have the same characteristics? Biological and psychological theories also do a poor job of explaining why the risk of being murdered in the United States today is *greater* than it was a decade ago (see Chapter 8). Has our genetic structure gotten worse? Of course, you could answer (and some people have) that Americans are more genetically predisposed to committing crimes than are people in less criminogenic countries. Unfortunately, thus far no one has been able to identify an "American" crime gene. You could further argue that the same number of people are predisposed everywhere, but in the United States the environmental and social factors needed to "trigger" this criminal activity exist to a greater extent. This very eloquent solution, first proposed by Cesare Lombroso and more recently by Wilson and Herrnstein, is less a theory than an attempt to deflect criticism. If you can't prove your theory, you can just add on a section that seems to account for the criticisms. Certainly, Lombroso made it clear this is what he was doing when he added this qualification to his biological theory.

Several other problems with predispositional theories warrant attention here. The first is that it would be much easier to accept these theories if only a handful of people harmed others. Unfortunately, the U.S. street crime rate is alarmingly high. If crime is a function of mental illness, then a rather amazingly large number of Americans are "sick" or "deranged." Of course, as we suggested previously, some offenders have medical problems. For example, who would argue that serial killer and cannibal Jeffrey Dahmer was not mentally ill, except perhaps the officials who kept him out of a mental hospital and in a prison for the sane? Even so, it is important to recognize that the vast majority of lawbreakers are not pathological.

Second, predispositional theories typically include what Elliott Currie (1985) calls the "fallacy of autonomy." The idea of autonomy is that people act on their own, without the influence of others. The implication of many of these theories is that peer groups and broader social forces have little impact on people's behaviors, attitudes, norms, and values. Those who break the law are seen as living in a "world strangely devoid of social or economic consequences, even of history" (Currie, 1985, p. 215). This is true of some offenders; however, most violent street crimes, especially those committed by youths, are committed in groups. This is why incarcerating or "treating" several gang members will do nothing to lower the rate of violent crime in the United States. You can lock people up or make them undergo therapy, but such measures do not eliminate the social, psychological, or interpersonal forces that influence people to harm others. For every gang member you take off the street, others will replace them.

If people's peers motivate them to commit violent acts, the same can be said about the U.S. social structure. It is not surprising that the U.S. crime rate is higher than that of other industrial societies. After all, the United States is a nation characterized by gross economic inequality, poverty, high infant mortality rates, homelessness, and inadequate social support services (for example, unemployment insurance and health care). The high rates of violent crime are major symptoms of these problems, and these crimes are committed mainly by groups of "underclass" people (Blau & Blau, 1982; Wilson, 1987). In fact, social and economic inequality—not personality or biological factors—are the most powerful predictors of predatory violent crime (see Chapter 8).

There is another worrisome aspect to predispositional theories. Although one would presume a flawed person would be commonly violent, much more often, violent people only victimize certain selected people. There are always a few people who randomly open fire on railroad trains, in post offices, or in restaurants. However, they are very rare. Most people kill only their wives, or members of a specific youth gang, or certain selected other people. The mesmerizing 1995 trial of O. J. Simpson brought home to many people the idea that few men are violent everywhere. Whether Simpson is guilty or innocent, the point remains that the pattern is typical—a man can beat his wife but remain a model of perfect behavior to the outside world. Data presented in Chapters 8 and 9 show that most men who engage in lethal and nonlethal forms of woman abuse typically do not hurt their friends, relatives, co-workers, and employers. They somehow manage to maintain self-control (hold in check their biological and psychological predispositions?) until they are alone with their intimate partners. Predispositional theories do a poor job of accounting for this fact.

Perhaps most importantly, we must ask why predispositional theories focus only on disenfranchised street offenders (Eitzen & Timmer, 1985). Why aren't corporate criminals considered pathological or sick given that they commit many more highly injurious crimes than lower-class people (see Chapter 10)? If the cause of crime is low IQ, bad genes, the wrong physical type, or other similar problems, how do we account for people who steal millions of dollars; pollute our rivers, air, and land; perform dangerous, unnecessary surgery to gain more fees; create unsafe working conditions that can injure or kill dozens of people at a time; or take bribes in public office? Thus far, clinical criminologists have offered only the most unsatisfactory of explanations: because crimes of the powerful are not topics of "generally recognized importance" and because corporate, political, and white-collar crimes are not "universally condemned" or "subject to criminalization," there is no great need to study or explain them (Andrews & Bonta, 1994, p. 27). More likely, the many books and thousands of articles simply remain silent on the subject. Criminals are, to most criminologists, lower-class people.

Actually, they are more than just lower-class people—they are males. Most theorists also are silent in dealing with females. If low IQ, bad genes, body type, or other biological factors cause crime, why are so few women affected? If personality disorders cause crime, why do mainly men have these disorders? Rare indeed is the theorist who tackles this question, although some theorists have tried to come up with separate theories on why girls commit crimes (see, for example, Konopka, 1966).

SUMMARY

In this chapter, we have begun our search for answers on why people commit crimes with a review of some of the more important nonsociological theories. The key to virtually all of these theories is that advocates find the cause of crime within the individual.

In the still very influential classical era of criminology, about two hundred years ago, reformers trying to end the extraordinarily harsh punishments of their time proposed a set of arguments on human rights, which also included responsibilities. They felt that people *decided* to become criminals, which made it society's job to change the odds a bit to change their thinking. Today, many criminologists claim to be neoclassical, meaning that they want to go back and reaffirm the views of the classical thinkers. Our contention is that they want to pick and choose those bits that support their already existing views and to ignore all of the classical thought that does not support them. We also argued that some of the primary points of classical thought, such as deterrence, have been shown not to work very well.

We also reviewed biological arguments that crime is related to internal flaws, ranging from low intelligence to bad genes to an improper body type. Psychological theories, on the other hand, presume that the offender is in some way mentally flawed. Biological and psychological theories have very little empirical support. However, they do have one important implication: if the problem is within the individual, then the future of criminal justice intervention also lies within the individual. This means we would need to increase deterrence by increasing the length of imprisonment and the use of capital punishment. At the same time, we would need to increase the use of rehabilitation and treatment, to "fix" the others. But why is it that these responses have been so popular if we know that they are incorrectly based and won't work?

As Jeffrey Reiman (1995) has pointed out, it is only for those at the lower levels that the system has been a failure. The title of his book, *The Rich Get Richer, and the Poor Get Prison,* summarizes his view that for those in control, the current system is a *success.* With the help of conservative academics, U.S. federal and state governments have revitalized the idea that crime is a "property" of the individual. This idea helps to justify support for a political-economic system that simultaneously benefits the rich and harms the poor (Eitzen & Timmer, 1985). In a country where the gap between the rich and the middle class has been increasing dramatically in recent years (unlike most countries, where it has been narrowing), there is little call from above to reform the basic economic and social structures. If you accept the notion that crime and poverty are caused by individual flaws or failures, then you will certainly find little reason to improve social services, let alone eliminate massive economic and social inequality.

Still, sociologists should not treat offenders simply as products of their social situation, with no individual input. Some offenders are mentally ill, and there may indeed be areas in which it is worthwhile to look at personality. Yet, "there is little empirical support" for using this model to explain human behavior (Sutherland, Cressey, & Luckenbill, 1992, p. 150). George Vold and Thomas Bernard (1986, p. 128) agree that

> there is no question that for some individuals personality is the major determinant of criminal behavior, but those individuals ap-

pear to be relatively infrequent exceptions. In order to understand the behavior of most criminals and delinquents, it is more profitable to start by analyzing their life situation rather than their personality characteristics.

It is for this reason, then, that we turn next, in Chapter 6, to those sociological theories that look at the life situations of people identified as offenders.

SUGGESTED READINGS

Andrews, D., and Bonta, J. (1994). *The Psychology of Criminal Conduct.* Cincinnati: Anderson.

This book provides students and researchers alike with a comprehensive overview of psychological perspectives on crime and its control.

Conrad, P., and Schneider, J. (1992). *Deviance and Medicalization: From Badness to Sickness.* Philadelphia: Temple University Press.

Based on the societal reaction/labeling perspective on crime and deviance, this book shows how various behaviors that were once designated as immoral, sinful, or criminal have come to be defined as medical problems.

Vold, G., and Bernard, T. (1986). *Theoretical Criminology,* 3rd ed. New York: Oxford University Press.

Chapter 2 in this classic work provides readers with a highly intelligible overview of classical and neoclassical criminology. Some readers may also find Vold and Bernard's review of biological theories (Chapter 6) to be useful.

Wilson, J. (1985). *Thinking About Crime.* New York: Vintage.

This best-selling book contributed heavily to the revitalization of classical criminology. Moreover, the conservative policy proposals presented in this text have heavily influenced the administration of North American criminal justice today.

CHAPTER 6

SOCIOLOGICAL PERSPECTIVES ON CRIME

*Every act, including every criminal act, is located somewhere in the social
system. Every kind of act is distributed somehow in a social system. Social
systems are extended and differentiated in space and time; acts are therefore
located and distributed in both dimensions. We must then ask, What is it about
a system that accounts for the kinds of crime we find in it and how these crimes
are distributed in space and time? This is, of course, the quintessentially
sociological question. What we are being asked to explain is a property or, if you
will, a product of a social system (how rape, for example, varies by age, race, or
time of year) and the answer must consist of identifying other properties of the
system (structural, cultural, demographic) and describing how they articulate and
interact to produce the product. The systems can be of any scale—families,
gangs, factories, neighborhoods, cities, countries—and what is constitutive of
one system may be environment relative to another. The relevant theory here is
a theory about how social systems work.*

COHEN, 1985, P. 230

In Chapter 5, we described our problems with "pre- and nonsociological"
theories of crime. We are well aware that among the general public and
many decision-makers in the United States, sociological criticisms are not
well received. One major reason is because the United States is "the world
capital of psychological-mindedness and therapeutic endeavor" (Zilbergeld,
1983, p. 32). R. Emerson Dobash and Russell Dobash (1992) point out
that approximately one-half of the world's clinical psychologists and one-
third of the world's registered psychiatrists currently work in the United
States. New York City alone has more psychoanalysts than any European
country, to say nothing of the enormous number of psychiatric social workers, holistic healers, therapists of dozens of schools of thought, and others
who can afford an office and a couch.

Thus, not surprisingly in a country that supports such an array of self-
help books and therapists, crime is seen as a property of the individual. As

discussed in Chapter 5, proponents of nonsociological theories argue that people kill, rape, mug, and steal because there is "something inside" that predisposes them to commit these crimes (for example, bad genes, low intelligence, mental illness, emotional disturbance, and so on).

Sociologists strongly oppose such explanations. The primary objective of this chapter is to review four widely cited and applied sociological perspectives on crime: (1) strain, (2) social control, (3) interactionist, and (4) ecological. Of course, many other theories could be covered, and the suggested readings section for this chapter will lead you to more comprehensive works. The goal here is to cover the most influential theories, in sufficient depth, to illuminate how sociologists think and how they differ from the theorists covered in Chapter 5. It is not our intention to encourage you to completely reject the "psychology of criminal conduct" (Andrews & Bonta, 1994) and biological theories. These points of view do, to a certain extent, help us make sense of criminal acts committed by *some* people. Only a fool would argue that there are not some people who have biological or psychological problems that are factors in their decision to commit crime. Further, some people have been stopped from committing future crime through the use of therapy, psychotropic drugs, and other psychologically and biologically informed treatments.

EXPLAINING CRIME: THE NEED FOR A SOCIOLOGICAL IMAGINATION

If only a handful of U.S. citizens committed crimes, it would be easy to accept nonsociological accounts of their behavior. They must be disturbed individuals. Unfortunately, crime is deeply entrenched in our society. Statistics presented throughout this text clearly show that the United States today is the most violent country in the advanced industrial world (Currie, 1985). For example, Chapter 8 shows that the U.S. homicide rate has consistently remained substantially higher than that of any other industrialized nation, and the risk at least for some Americans of being murdered today is markedly higher than it was a decade ago. Chapter 9 shows that in North America, many outwardly loving, intimate, heterosexual relationships are instead characterized by violence and abuse. As you read this chapter, an alarmingly high number of wives, female dating and cohabiting partners, and separated/ divorced women are being beaten, raped, and psychologically abused by their current or former male partners (Landsberg, 1989). This does not apply only to violent crimes; rates of property crime are also substantially higher than they were twenty years ago.

Indeed, Elliott Currie (1993) argues that we are currently experiencing an "American nightmare." Although President Clinton and House Speaker Gingrich promised that new crime legislation would make our lives safer, there is no indication that things are going to substantially improve in the near future—or ever—until we seriously consider some of the progressive policy proposals described in Chapter 12. As Currie has pointed out, a crime wave could accurately be called an *epidemic*. In the United States, however, since crime has "stubbornly resisted eradication," it instead should be considered *endemic*, that is, a constant and permanent feature of life.

Therefore, sociologists ask, given the widespread (endemic) nature of predatory, corporate, and domestic crimes, how can we maintain that these problems are acts committed by "sick" or pathological individuals? Even if this were the case, one would have to spend a great deal of time looking at the social structure of a country that produces more sick or pathological individuals than the rest of the world. Because the United States has astoundingly high rates of crime, individualist perspectives have little to offer.

Rather, we need to develop what C. Wright Mills (1959) calls the *sociological imagination*. This perspective calls for an understanding of the ways in which *personal troubles* are related to *public issues*. Personal troubles are just what you might think. If you are raped, robbed, beaten, or cheated, you have a problem and you will have to deal with it. You may need medical attention, comfort from friends or family, financial help, or any of a number of other forms of aid. Sometimes, however, many people are suffering individually from the exact same personal problem at the same time. If a hundred women are raped in one year on one campus, each one of these women has a personal problem, or personal troubles. At the same time, however, something about the broader structural and cultural forces, such as patriarchy or capitalism, Mills would argue, allows for so very many women to be victimized. To be able to look beyond the personal troubles of one or two female students who have been sexually assaulted and see the broader problem of rape on campus and its causes is to possess the sociological imagination.

Consider wife beating (see Chapter 9). At first glance, a man who beats the woman he shares an intimate relationship with apparently must be either suffering from life stress or mentally ill. Perhaps that seems an adequate explanation for the two or three cases you know well. However, when you begin to look at all of the 11 percent or so of women in North American marital/cohabiting relationships who are physically abused annually by their male partners, you begin to find "an indication of a structural issue having to do with the institutions of marriage and the family and other institutions that bear upon them" (Mills, 1959, p. 9). Further evidence of a linkage between broader social forces and wife beating is provided by Richard Gelles and Murray Straus (1988), who found that only 10 percent of all wife beaters had some mental disorder. In other words, certainly, some men with psychological problems beat their wives; it is just that psychological perspectives cannot account for 90 percent of wife beaters.

The sociological imagination, when applied to the study of crime, shows us that North American society is set up in such a way as to promote criminal activity. If we had different attitudes, customs, and economic structures, we would have a very different crime pattern. Currie (1985, p. 19) reminds us that if we set up a social system that promotes crime, we also have the power to change the system to reduce crime:

> The unusual dangerousness of American life is not simply the result
> of fate or of human nature, but of forces which, within broad limits,
> are subject to social action and control. We have the level of criminal
> violence we do because we have arranged our social and economic
> life in certain ways rather than others.

Now that we have provided you with a rationale for analyzing crime sociologically, we can go ahead with a review of four sociological perspectives that have had a major impact on modern criminology.

STRAIN THEORIES

Like Mills, strain theorists possess the sociological imagination. Rather than viewing crime as the result of some deficiency in the individual, they contend that it is a function of America's social structure. Simply put, strain theories suggest that there is something in the social forces generated by society that pushes or forces people into committing crimes. In other words, the impulse to commit a crime comes from outside rather than inside the offender. Strain is not something that everyone in society equally shares. Some people suffer more strain than others. This is why, these theorists argue, some parts of society have more crime than others—they have more strain.

Four major strain perspectives will be reviewed here: (1) Merton's anomie theory, (2) Cohen's theory of delinquent boys, (3) Cloward and Ohlin's differential opportunity theory, and (4) the emancipation theory of female crime. First, however, we will review Émile Durkheim's writings on crime, deviance, and social control because they heavily influenced the development of strain theories.

Durkheim's Sociological Ideas

In Chapter 3, we presented two of sociology's greatest thinkers: Max Weber and Karl Marx. The other sociological theorist in a class with these two is the Frenchman Émile Durkheim. Unlike Marx and Weber, however, this nineteenth-century scholar devoted a considerable amount of intellectual energy to analyzing crime, deviance, and social control. In order to understand his position on these issues, it is necessary to briefly summarize his four major sociological ideas.

First, like Thomas Hobbes (see Chapter 3), Durkheim viewed human beings as innately egoistic. Compared to animals, they are not satiated when they fulfill their biological needs. According to Durkheim, "The more one has, the more one wants, since satisfactions received only stimulate instead of filling needs" (1951, p. 248). Because people cannot control their desires by themselves, they must be held in check by external forms of social control. Society must control people's rampant egoism by acting as a "regulative force [that] must play the same role for moral needs which the organism plays for physical needs" (1951, p. 248). Without such control, many people are likely to rob, beat, and kill one another to satisfy their ever-increasing financial and psychological desires. In his interpretation of Durkheim's call for external control, Desmond Ellis asks us to imagine what society would be like if it was composed solely of "infants whose every psychological and material want must be continuously satisfied without regard to the wants of others" (1987, p. 28).

Second, Durkheim argued that social order is based on value consensus. All of us are assumed to believe that it is wrong to beat, kill, and rob others. These values are learned and preserved through interaction with others who advocate them.

Third, sports, religion, corporations, crime, schools, and so on exist in our society because they are *functional.* In other words, these phenomena and institutions exist and will continue to exist because they have a function: they benefit society as a whole.

Finally, because Durkheim was what sociologists term a "structural functionalist," he viewed society as similar to a biological organism. In a perfectly working human body, all of the parts work together to provide health. A great body with a broken-down liver is in deep trouble. In the same way, society consists of many interdependent parts that operate to give it equilibrium. In North American society, families, schools, criminal justice systems, churches, and other institutions all help to maintain a balanced social system. Although a change in one or more of these parts will change the others, the direction of change is usually toward restoring equilibrium (Stebbins, 1987).

These four ideas (and others) are evident in Durkheim's analysis of crime. For him, crime was a "social fact"—normal, inevitable, and functional. In fact, we can safely say that, for Durkheim, not only are certain behaviors innately criminal, but, to some degree, the "worst" people in any society are going to be labeled as deviants and perhaps criminals. Regardless of where you live and how kind and "respectable" the members of your community are, you will always find behaviors and people officially designated as criminal:

> Imagine a community of saints in an exemplary and perfect monastery. In it crime as such will be unknown, but faults that appear venial to the ordinary person will arouse the same scandal as does normal crime in ordinary consciousness. If therefore that community has the power to judge and punish, it will term such acts criminal and deal with them as such. (Durkheim, 1982, p. 100)

Because some crime is normal and functional, Durkheim felt that it could never be completely eliminated. But wait! If acts such as drive-by shootings, crack dealing, wife beating, and armed robbery cause so much pain and suffering, how can they be *functional?* Durkheim's answer was that only a *certain amount* of crime is functional, and certainly not the level that exists in North America today. Remember Durkheim's assumption that society is characterized by widely shared values and norms. Because we are supposed to strongly disapprove of theft and shootings, if someone commits these or other crimes, the bond between "respectable," law-abiding members of a community is strengthened. Just in case we forgot the line between good and bad behavior, we are reminded by regular crime what constitutes the "bad" behavior. Likewise, widely publicized arrests and trials remind us of the penalty for being bad and help us to remember to be good. In other words, lawbreakers provide the law abiders with a target for "their self-righteous indignation" (Ellis, 1987, p. 29). If you are worried about moral laxity, punishment also reminds you that legitimate community values—not the offender's values—are the appropriate ones. To Durkheim, "Crime brings together upright consciences and concentrates them" (1956, p. 103).

In *Suicide* (1951), Durkheim expanded his position on social control by attempting to explain why individuals from certain groups were more likely to kill themselves than others. After all, if suicide was the act of mentally deranged or biologically deficient individuals, why did the rates vary from year to year, from country to country, and among different types of people in any one society? These changes could only be explained by examining broader social forces. Durkheim identified four types of suicide: egoistic, fatalistic, altruistic, and anomic. Here, we will focus only on the fourth type because Durkheim's concept of anomie was refined by the three strain theorists discussed in this section.

For Durkheim, *anomie* refers to something we tend to call "normlessness." This lack of norms, or social values, means that a person is living in a condition in which there is no social regulation. Generally, Durkheim concentrated on situations in which a person might live in a stable atmosphere for years, but then be exposed to some major social disruption that overturned or undercut some of that person's basic beliefs or values. When there is rapid social change, society is less able to maintain control over people through traditional values, and therefore suicide increases. To explain how anomie is created, Durkheim addressed the relationship between sudden economic changes and suicide. For example, during economic disasters,

> something like a declassification occurs which suddenly casts certain individuals into a lower state than the previous one. Then they must reduce their requirements, restrain their needs, learn greater

self-control. All the advantages of social influence are lost so far as they are concerned; their moral education has to be recommenced. But society cannot adjust them instantaneously to this new life and teach them to practice the increased self-repression to which they are unaccustomed. So they are not adjusted to the condition forced on them, and its very prospect is intolerable; hence the suffering which detaches them from a reduced existence even before they have made trial of it. (1951, p. 252)

Interestingly, high suicide rates also can be caused by economic booms, when there is no restraint on people's high aspirations: "Appetites, not being controlled by public opinion become disoriented, no longer recognizing the limits proper to them" (Durkheim, 1951, p. 253). People's desires increase without control, and as Stephen Pfohl (1994, p. 260) points out, "The sky appears to be the limit. But it is not." When people do not have the opportunities to meet their high expectations, they become angry, frustrated, and disillusioned, and thus the suicide rate increases.

Of course, this work has not been uncontroversial. Some criminologists have sharply faulted Durkheim for viewing people's aspirations as egoistic, contending instead that such behavior is learned. Some critical criminologists have found his approach too biological and inherently conservative (Taylor, Walton, & Young, 1973). Yet, many criminologists have found Durkheim an important resource for developing their own work. Even some critical criminologists (see Chapter 7) have found that much of Durkheim's work can be of great value "to help specify a realistic set of socialist goals" (Pearce, 1989, p. 10). Regardless of how critical criminologists interpret his writings, Durkheim unquestionably influenced the contemporary strain theories reviewed next. Perhaps his strongest influence was on Robert Merton, to whose contribution we now turn.

Merton's Anomie Theory

To say the least, Robert K. Merton's (1938) anomie theory has strongly influenced contemporary sociological analyses of crime, deviance, and social control. Although it was one of Merton's first papers, written when he was still in his twenties, his "Social Structure and Anomie" spelled out a theory that dominated from the 1950s until the early 1970s. In fact, when Randall

Collins (1981) was writing, he found that Merton's (1938) article was still the most cited sociological paper.

Merton was fundamentally opposed to individualistic explanations of crime, such as those heavily based on the writings of Thomas Hobbes (see Chapter 3) and Sigmund Freud (see Chapter 5). These approaches prevailed in the 1930s and typically viewed crime as a function of human nature. In the following quote, in which Merton states his strong opposition to the Hobbesian-Freudian position, can you see why this is a sociological argument?

> There persists a notable tendency in sociological theory to attribute the malfunctioning of social structure primarily to those of man's imperious biological drives which are not adequately restrained by social control. In this view, the social order is solely a device for "impulse management" and the "social processing" of tensions. These impulses which break through social control, be it noted, are held to be biologically derived. Nonconformity is assumed to be rooted in original nature. Conformity is by implication the result of an utilitarian calculus or unreasoned conditioning. This point of view, whatever its other deficiencies, clearly begs one question. It provides no basis for determining the non-biological conditions which induce deviations from prescribed patterns of conduct. (1938, p. 672)

For Merton, crime and deviance can be adequately explained only by examining the structure of wider society. To support his argument, he looked no further than at his own country—the United States, the most violent country in the advanced industrial world. Many criminologists typically put Merton and Durkheim in the same scholarly camp and highlight a strong intellectual relationship between Merton's work and Durkheim's. To be sure, Merton drew from Durkheim's writings. However, it is important to note that these two theorists also differ substantially (Cullen, 1984). For example, Merton moved some distance from Durkheim's original theory by completely rejecting individualistic, Hobbesian-Freudian accounts of crime. Rather, Merton took Durkheim's idea of anomie and adapted it to suit his own theory.

Disjunction Between Goals and Means Because he did not view crime as a function of human nature, Merton reconceptualized Durkheim's original discussion of anomie accordingly. It was fine to argue that anomie came from a breakdown in social norms, but Merton pondered "[why] the frequency of deviant behavior varies within different social structures and how it happens that the deviations have different shapes and patterns in different social structures" (1957, p. 131). In other words, in the terms we used earlier, Durkheim seemed to suggest that anomie is the result of an epidemic (a sudden acute breakdown), while Merton saw anomie as endemic (a regular feature of society).

There are two important elements of social and cultural structures to Merton: (1) culturally defined *goals* that are held up as legitimate for all members of society and (2) acceptable or legitimate *institutionalized means* of achieving these goals. In an ideal world, these two would be in complete agreement. Everyone would understand and agree with the goals, such as financial security, nice clothes, decent housing, and adequate nutrition. Everyone would have access to an acceptable method of achieving these goals, such as a wide variety of jobs paying enough for people to purchase clothes, housing, and food. Merton gave Durkheim's concept of anomie "an American stamp" by using it to describe the disjunction between these two elements (Hagan, 1994). Disjunction? He simply meant that, although in the United States the goals are available to everyone, the means are not available to large numbers of people.

For example, a goal that virtually all Americans share and that is completely socially acceptable is financial success and the accompanying status. "Money," according to Merton, "has been consecrated as a value in itself over and above its expenditure for articles of consumption or its use for the enhancement of power" (1957, p. 136). From a very early age, Americans are socialized to strive for an ideal lifestyle, one that will enable them to buy expensive commodities such as a Mercedes Benz or at least a fully loaded Jeep Cherokee, a Sony Trinitron TV set, and a luxurious suburban home. Such material desires are promoted and legitimated in many contexts, such as the school, the church, and, most obviously, the media. In these and other contexts of socialization, we are constantly told to strive for the "American Dream." Pfohl asks us to think about how many times we have heard messages that, even if they didn't use these exact words, at least conveyed these messages: "Become rich! Become powerful! Become prestigious! Everybody can do it. Any child can become president. Everyone should try" (1994, p. 262).

This should be familiar stuff. Most of you are probably working toward a college degree that you hope will move you one rung up the ladder toward material success. According to Merton, you have the legitimate means of meeting your financial objectives because you are a college student with a promising future. The institutionalized means for success in the United States include getting a good education, working hard in a job to get promotions, or at least marrying into an influential family. Unfortunately, many U.S. citizens do not have even the opportunity you have to attend school. You are no doubt aware that the United States is a country with high levels of unemployment, poverty, homelessness, and other symptoms of class inequality. The people who suffer from these social problems want the same material things as you and the status associated with financial success, but their social condition means that they will not achieve these goals. This disjunction means they experience strain. America may have some particularly big problems in this regard. Although many countries have large numbers of people with a lack of opportunities, the United States may be unique in its promotion of the goals of material acquisition and success. Durkheim found it only natural that people would wish to amass enough wealth to purchase what they needed, but Merton pointed out that American culture is unusual in encouraging wealth accumulation far in excess of what any person realistically needs. Further, wealth is used to measure personal value, and a lack of money is used to degrade people even if they have other very desirable attributes, such as wisdom (Vold & Bernard, 1986).

Modes of Individual Adaptation to Anomie How do people respond to this structurally induced strain? Merton identified five "modes of adaptation," four of which he referred to as deviant types. These modes of adaptation are schematically presented in Table 6.1 and will be briefly described here.[1] Note that these five categories are not personality types. Rather, they are "role behaviors" that occur in specific kinds of social situations. Moreover, Merton (1957) asserts that people may shift from one mode of adaptation to another as they engage in different kinds of social activities. Further, every example we use here is based on the idea that the primary goal of society is material success—the example that Merton also used. However, the same adaptations

---

[1] This is a slightly modified version of the typology presented in Merton's (1957, p. 138) *Social Theory and Social Structure.*

can be used to explain behavior in other situations in which the goals that a person prizes are not well matched with institutionalized means for achieving these goals. There are those, for example, who feel that although many stranger rapists seek to humiliate their victims through force, many date rapists would prefer to have sexual relations with willing women. Because these willing women do not exist, they use deviant (innovative) means of force or alcohol to achieve their goal of sexual relations.

Merton contends that the first mode of adaptation, *conformity*, is the most common. People play by the rules, even if objectively they do not have much of a chance to achieve the goals. Although he does not explain why most Americans respond this way, Merton contends that if they didn't, "the stability and continuity of the society could not be maintained" (1957, p. 141). This category is much more important than many writers seem to think. Sometimes, reading about Merton, one might think that everyone in America having some difficulty getting rich immediately switches over to one of what Merton terms "deviant reactions." Quite the contrary is true. In the most high-crime areas of the United States, many residents are conformists (Curran & Renzetti, 1994). Still, Merton did not devote a lot of attention to conformity because he was mainly interested in accounting for deviant adaptations to anomie.

Innovation is of central concern to both Merton and the wider criminological community. Although innovation is to be found at all class levels in American society, Merton felt that it was a deviant mode of adaptation more commonly found in the working class. Innovators accept the dominant goal

Table 6.1 Merton's Typology of Modes of Individual Adaptation

MODE OF ADAPTATION	CULTURAL GOALS	INSTITUTIONALIZED MEANS
Conformity	+ (accept)	+ (accept)
Innovation	+ (accept)	− (reject)
Ritualism	− (reject)	+ (accept)
Retreatism	− (reject)	− (reject)
Rebellion	± (reject, but wants to substitute new values)	± (reject, but wants to substitute new values)

Merton argues that when a person has the same goals as conformists, such as money and material objects, but does not see conformity as a way to obtain these objects, she or he may turn to illegitimate means to obtain these same goals. Burglary is one such method of innovation.

of material success; however, they use illegitimate means of achieving it because legitimate ones are considered useless. For example, we live in a society characterized by gross economic inequality. Some people have high-paying jobs, but most do not. Consider disenfranchised inner-city residents. If they are employed, they usually have low-paying jobs that do not generate enough income to buy "nice clothes," cars, and other material status symbols. No matter how hard they work, they will probably remain at the bottom of the class hierarchy.

In a society in which someone can work full-time at a minimum-wage job but *still* be far below the "official" federal poverty line (and that arbitrary figure is awfully low), what is to be done? For some disenfranchised people, "creative" solutions are necessary. Such strategies may result in criminal activities such as burglary, theft, drug dealing, and armed robbery. Many people may find it much easier to use these illegitimate means to gain money or goods than to save whatever they can from their low wages and let it slowly accumulate interest in a bank (Williams & McShane, 1994). "For persons systematically deprived of access to avenues of success, how can the 'honest job' of dishwashing compete with the easy money obtained through dishonest behavior?" (Pfohl, 1994, p. 264).

This theory does more than just explain the crimes of the lowest class. Businesspeople may find that they are not making money through legitimate means as fast as they would like and that, by innovating through fraud or cheating on their income taxes, they can accumulate wealth faster. Skilled workers can steal valuable items regularly from their workplace, such as copper wiring. All of these, however, are crimes of individual people. Steven Box (1983) contends that Merton provides a better explanation of the crimes of entire corporations (see Chapter 10) than he does of street crimes such as burglary and armed robbery. For example, the dominant culturally prescribed goal for corporations is profit. However, "environmental uncertainties" such as unions, consumer advocate groups, and corporate competitors occasionally make it difficult for a company to achieve this goal. In an ideal capitalist marketplace, the best competitor wins while the others lose money. However, although they may favor the capitalist marketplace in theory, few corporations favor losing money or going out of business because they aren't as good as their competitors. Thus, corporations periodically experience a disjunction between their goals (profit) and the uncertainty about achieving them. Box suggests that when these and other environmental uncertainties increase, so will the strain toward corporate crime. In sum, corporate crime is an innovative response to corporate anomie, an issue to be addressed in Chapter 10.

This is another area in which we can see the connections discussed earlier between Merton and earlier classical thinkers. The earlier theorists thought that an innate inability ever to have "enough" would cause people to look for the fastest, quickest method of achieving their goals, unless restrained by punishment. Merton did not believe this would happen unless there was a breakdown in norms. Rather, when the goal of financial success was so widely emphasized and when no institutionalized means existed for reaching those goals, the kind of innovation the classical thinkers were afraid of would—and did, Merton believed—occur in the United States (Vold & Bernard, 1986).

Ritualism, the second deviant mode of adaptation, is primarily found among the lower middle class. Ritualists do not have high aspirations. Their response to anomie involves "the abandoning or scaling down of the lofty cultural goals of great pecuniary success and rapid social mobility to the point where one's aspirations can be satisfied" (Merton, 1957, pp. 149–150). In other words, ritualists reject cultural goals but accept legitimate means. Sometimes, this can mean that individuals accept the reality that they will never get rich and simply treat doing the job itself as the goal. At other times, it can mean that individuals will take the job so seriously that they become the bureaucrat we all know—the one who has no power whatsoever, except to worry about whether you made a tiny mistake in filling out a form.

Ritualism is tolerated or permitted, but it is often considered deviant because it rejects the dominant cultural goal of material success and status achievement. You may have an example of it in the school you are attending. Academic departments occasionally have senior professors who stopped doing productive scholarship years ago and who now are just going through the motions (Holman & Quinn, 1992). Young, hard-working professors often express their contempt for these ritualist senior professors.

Retreatism, the third mode of deviant adaptation, involves the rejection of both goals and means. These people, according to Merton, don't want success and don't want to work. In other words, they just give up on the entire game and drop out. Merton found "psychotics, autists, pariahs, outcasts, vagrants, vagabonds, tramps, chronic drunkards and drug addicts" the best examples of retreatists (Merton, 1957, p. 153). These are "the socially disinherited who if they have none of the rewards held out by society also have few of the frustrations attendant upon continuing to seek these rewards" (1957, p. 155). Of course, it is entirely possible that these people would be in the "game" if they had any chance of success, but since they do not, they just drop out.

Rebellion is the most difficult to explain of Merton's deviant modes of adaptation because it is fundamentally distinct from the other three. Rather than simply rejecting culturally prescribed goals and legitimate means, rebels are like revolutionaries. They respond to strain by attempting to "introduce a social structure in which the cultural standards of success would be sharply modified and provision would be made for closer correspondence between merit, effort, and reward" (1957, p. 155). Rebels want to replace the old goals and means with "something better" (Pfohl, 1994). For example, some neo-Nazi and left-wing subcultures engage in so-called terrorist activities (for example, cross burning, publication of racist magazines, vandalism, and the like) in their attempts to foster radical structural change. Unlike burglars and muggers, they don't want money. They engage in deviant activities to "hasten the birth of a new set of norms" (Pfohl, 1994). Those who seek a higher state of spiritual consciousness could also fit in here, as could virtually anyone who just plain rejects our entire culture.

In sum, Merton's anomie theory explains "how some social structures exert a definite pressure upon certain persons in the society to engage in nonconforming rather than conforming conduct" (1957, p. 132). Although his theory emphasized the relationship between anomie and lower-class crime, it is, as was stated previously, also applicable to the problem of "suite crime." Data presented in Chapter 10 show that many people who clearly have legitimate means of achieving success (for example, corporate executives) cause North Americans much more economic, physical, and environmental pain and suffering than street criminals.

Now, you may say that this theory does not explain all crime. For example, how does it account for rape, incest, aggravated assault, drive-by shootings, and many other crimes? Simply, "Merton argues that his theory and typology are not intended to explain all forms of criminal and deviant behavior, but rather to focus attention on the problem of anomie" (Curran & Renzetti, 1994, p. 179).

Cohen's Theory of Delinquent Boys

Some theorists suggest that Albert K. Cohen's (1955) critique and modification of anomie theory significantly contributed to Merton's fame, in that it focused much more attention on Merton than had ever been done before. Cohen argued that Merton's theory is useful for explaining both instrumental, adult "professional crime" and the "property delinquency" crimes of some older and semiprofessional juvenile thieves. However, he found it incapable of accounting for "the distinctive content of the delinquent subculture" (1955, p. 36).

The problem seems to be that adult "innovators" were dealing with their goal of financial success by committing crimes specifically aimed at achieving this goal. Thus, the adult crimes were financial and purposeful. When Cohen looked at juveniles, however, he found them extremely different.

Although they suffered from anomie, the problem was that their goal was to achieve respect and status, perhaps mainly from their peers. The delinquent acts of those juveniles who did not get this respect were hedonistic, nonutilitarian, malicious, and negativistic. They were *hedonistic* in that they were aimed at having fun, with no regard for longer-term gains or costs. They were *nonutilitarian* in that there was no particular "use" to what they were doing—they stole because they felt like it, not because there was any particular value in what they stole. They were *malicious* in that they destroyed property, tore down signs, taunted people, and enjoyed making other people miserable. They were *negativistic* in that they developed a set of values that were, from the point of view of the middle class, pretty negative.

Perhaps just as important, while Merton was concerned with the individual acts of adults, Cohen noted that these destructive acts of juveniles are committed primarily by gangs consisting of lower-class, male, urban youths. In short, Cohen argued that delinquency is an expressive group activity. But what accounts for the emergence of lower-class, urban delinquent subcultures?

Much as Cohen liked Merton's ideas, he could not see how a failure to achieve financial goals had an effect on these young men. Rather, he saw the problem in a similar way, but with the problem being an ability to achieve status. For young men, the primary granter of status is the school. However, lower-class young men find that any possible status from this institution is out of reach.

According to Cohen's strain-subcultural theory, the U.S. school system consists mainly of middle-class teachers who use "middle-class measuring rods" to assess their students' academic performance. They measure students according to the following middle-class standards: ambition; individual responsibility; academic or athletic achievement; the ability to defer immediate gratification; rationality; manners, courtesy, and personality; control of aggressive behavior; "wholesome" or constructive leisure; and respect for property (1955, pp. 88–91). It is, Cohen reports,

> characteristic of American culture generally—an aspect of its "democratic" ethos—that young people of different origins and backgrounds tend to be judged by the same standards so that young people of different social class, race, and ethnicity find themselves

competing with one another for status and approval under the same set of rules. (1966, p. 65)

Middle-class boys whose parents prepared them to successfully meet these standards will do very well in school. Working-class boys, who receive the same training but not as well or not as strongly, are thrown into a competitive setting in which they cannot achieve status from their middle-class peers and teachers.

As a consequence of being denied status, these youths experience *status frustration,* which generates "guilt, self-recrimination, anxiety, and self-hatred" (Cohen, 1955, p. 126). In what Randy Martin, Robert Mutchnick, and W. Timothy Austin (1990, p. 251) call the "most memorable aspect of Cohen's theoretical statements," he suggests that there are several different possible reactions to this status frustration. A youth might get better at meeting the middle-class measuring rod and strive for legitimate success, in what Cohen terms the "college boy route." Other youths may adopt the "corner boy response," which is not particularly far from Merton's ritualist. This youth simply withdraws from the middle class and hangs out with other lower-class males. Finally, some frustrated youths withdraw from the school setting, come into contact with other working-class boys with similar status problems, and form a delinquent subculture or gang as a way of dealing with their problems of adjustment. "The delinquent subculture deals with these problems by providing a criteria of status which these children *can* meet" (Cohen, 1955, p. 121). The gang's criteria for status achievement is fundamentally distinct from the middle-class criteria. To achieve status in the gang, youths resort to *reaction formation;* that is, they invert middle-class values. For example, if teachers and other authority figures value punctuality, respect for property, and nonphysical means of resolving conflict, gang members will value lateness, destruction of property, and aggressive behavior. The gang will confer high status on members who act accordingly.

In sum, the delinquent subculture solves the problem of status frustration by conferring status on those who engage in malicious, negativistic, and destructive behavior—acts that directly conflict with middle-class norms and values. In this case, the behavior is not very far from what Merton called "rebellion," although it is a specific form of rebellion aimed at middle-class values in society.

Note that this is a theory of lower-class *male* behavior. Cohen thought that girls faced similar problems, which they resolved by engaging in sexual delinquencies. To say the least, this has never been considered an important contribution.

Cloward and Ohlin's Differential Opportunity of Delinquency

There was one important perspective to add to the two strain theories just covered. Richard Cloward and Lloyd Ohlin's *Delinquency and Opportunity* (1960), one of the most referred-to criminology books ever, develops the concept of *differential opportunity theory.* Essentially, they accept Merton's proposition that youths are striving for money and Cohen's proposition that some juvenile males form delinquent gangs in their desire for status. Still, Cloward and Ohlin thought something was left out: that both of these could be true at the same time. That is, some youths could be committing crimes with a goal of financial reward (in Merton's terms, innovation), while others could be committing crimes with no regard to money (as Cohen describes). Even more youths, as Merton claimed, could be retreatists. Where Cloward and Ohlin make their unique contribution, however, was in arguing that the most important group of juvenile delinquents in the country fit none of these categories. In fact, they argued that there are three main types of delinquent subcultures, all of which emerge depending on the type of opportunities available in working-class neighborhoods. These are the criminal subculture, the conflict subculture, and the retreatist subculture.

The problem, according to Cloward and Ohlin, was that all of the attention had been paid to whether youths could enter into the legitimate opportunity structure (socially approved jobs). It was just as important, they argued, to learn whether the youths were living in an environment in which they could learn and gain access to an *illegitimate opportunity structure.* In a stable but criminal environment, these youths can learn from the local criminal subculture the skills and values necessary to become part of the subculture itself. They learn how to break into businesses, where to sell stolen property, which police officers and judges take bribes, and which lawyers can get charges dropped. In other words, the question is not only whether these youths will adopt Merton's conformity role. There is also a similar criminal conformity role that socially integrates some youths into criminal apprenticeship roles. According to Cloward and Ohlin: "Just as the middle-class youth, as a consequence of intimate relationships with say, a banker or a businessman, may aspire to *become* a banker or a businessman, so the lower-class youth may be associated with and aspire to become a 'policy king' " (1960, p. 162). Movie fans can find examples of the criminal subculture in popular films such as *Good Fellas, A Bronx Tale,* and *Once upon a Time in America.* Youths who join established criminal networks are known as a *criminal subculture.*

What happens when there are neither legitimate means to success nor a stable criminal subculture in the neighborhood? Conflict subcultures exist in communities characterized by the absence of both legitimate and illegitimate means of achieving financial success. Further, successful adult offenders who can teach youths strategies of committing crime for material gain are absent from these neighborhoods. Most likely, such neighborhoods are characterized by large housing projects or run-down slums; most people do not know their neighbors and move to different apartments often. The basic frustration expressed by Cohen still exists: these youths are suffering from status frustration and are concerned with gaining status from their peers and in the neighborhood. The one method available to them is through the use of violence, such as gang wars over "turf." One doesn't have to be a skilled fighter to acquire status from his peers; however, he should have "guts," be able to endure pain, and be willing to risk injury or death in his search for "rep" (1960, p. 175).

Still, some youths cannot find success in the illegitimate opportunity structure and are similarly unsuccessful in the gang context. They do poorly in school, have no career ambitions, and are both incompetent street fighters and "innovators." Some of them may turn to drugs and alcohol for solutions to their problems, thereby withdrawing from the broader community. Of course, not all "double failures" become drunks or drug addicts, but they are more likely to end up this way than other lower-class youths. Becoming an addict depends heavily on the presence of older drug users who can teach youths how to use and acquire drugs.

In sum, for Cloward and Ohlin, it is important to identify the factors that motivate people to engage in deviant and criminal activities. However, it is also necessary to explain how people's motivations to commit crime are influenced by their opportunities to learn and use illegitimate means of achieving status. After all, young people may feel pressured to commit white-collar crimes, but their ability to do so is governed by the availability of opportunities and older role models or "teachers." Although little evidence exists that gangs are actually organized along the lines of Cloward and Ohlin's three types, the overall theory is not harmed if this particular element turns out to be wrong (Vold & Bernard, 1986).

Cloward and Ohlin were extremely important in the history of criminological theory, in that perhaps no other theory was responsible for generating so much government funding. The logic was simple: money was better spent on prevention than on cure, and if the problem was a lack of legitimate opportunity structures, then the solution was to increase these opportunities. Under President Kennedy, and especially President Johnson with his "War on Poverty" in the 1960s, a wide variety of programs were instituted to deal with educational deficiencies and job training. Under what Curran and Renzetti (1994) call President Reagan's "War on the Poor" in the 1980s, those programs not earlier killed off by President Nixon were eliminated. As George Vold and Thomas Bernard (1986, p. 201) point out: "Although billions of dollars were spent on these programs, the only clear result seems to have been the massive political resistance that was generated against this attempt to extend opportunities to people without them."

The Gender-Blind Nature of Strain Theories

There is a very large literature on the strengths and limitations of strain theory, although much of the criticism seems to revolve around the fact that strain theory is extraordinarily difficult to test empirically. Where the empirical evidence is limited to looking at seriously delinquent urban male gang members, the supporting evidence is rather strong (Vold & Bernard, 1986). Rather than provide a (boring) "shopping list" of "pros" and "cons" here, we will instead narrow our focus to how the strain theorists address gender, an issue of major importance to feminist theorists and researchers (see Chapter 7). What do strain theories have to say about female delinquents and adult offenders? So far, the answer to this question is, not much: "A long-standing deficiency of most strain theories is their neglect of the gender issue" (Hackler, 1994, p. 1987).

Consider Merton's anomie theory. In the United States, women's aspirations appear to be the same as men's (Morris, 1987). Men and women are socialized to desire things such as nice clothes, a suburban home, luxurious vacations, and perhaps an expensive car. Nevertheless, many women are excluded from the paid work force, and those who do find jobs are "concentrated overwhelmingly at the lower levels of the occupational hierarchy in terms of wages and salary, status, and authority" (Messerschmidt, 1993, p. 125). Furthermore, although there is a growing number of female executives, managers, and administrators, further examination shows that they tend to hold low-status positions (for example, personnel, research, affirmative action) within these occupations (Blau & Winkler, 1989).

Because of gender discrimination, a large number of women do not have the same legitimate opportunities as men to achieve their material goals. According to Merton's theory, these women should experience more strain than men and therefore commit more crimes than men. A large body of mainstream and feminist research reveals that this is not the case.[2] Women are clearly not more criminal than men, a fact that seriously challenges anomie theory (Chesney-Lind & Sheldon, 1992). Anomie theory still may be of some value here, however. Although economic marginalization has not made women more criminal than men, it very well may explain the kind of crimes that women *do* commit. The bulk of women's crimes tend to be petty property offenses such as shoplifting, passing bad checks, fraud, and whatever else people who cannot earn enough money to make ends meet might be tempted to try in order to pick up a few extra dollars (Naffine, 1987). In other words, women *innovate* to make ends meet.

Like Merton's strain account, the strain-subcultural theories developed by Cohen and Cloward and Ohlin do not address the situation of disenfranchised young girls who live in impoverished inner-city neighborhoods (Chesney-Lind & Sheldon, 1992). What little Cohen did have to say about girls has been strongly attacked,[3] since it suggests that "natural" sex differences account for women's lack of participation in crime.

---

[2]See Chesney-Lind and Sheldon (1992) and Faith (1993a) for in-depth reviews of research on the extent, nature, and distribution of female crime.

[3]See Messerschmidt (1993) for an in-depth analysis of Cohen's (1955) treatment of gender and delinquency.

The Emancipation Theory of Female Crime

Perhaps the theory of female crime that has gained the most attention in both criminological circles and the popular media has been the emancipation theory. This theory is a direct outgrowth of strain and opportunity theories.

Unlike earlier works claiming that women were naturally inhibited from committing crime by their passive and sexual female natures, in the mid-1970s two books based on opportunity structures began to challenge this notion. Rather than female "nature" inhibiting crime, it was just plain lack of opportunity. Given the opportunity to commit crime, women would act, and actually are acting, just like men.

Freda Adler (1975) received the most attention for her claims that women's crime rates were increasing much faster than men's crime rates; in fact, she argued that the United States was in the midst of an increasingly violent female crime wave. At about the same time, Rita Simon (1975) was making a more sophisticated, but similar, argument. In both cases, the key argument is one of opportunity structure: that as the women's liberation movement began to open up new roles for women in the military, education, business, and politics, it was simultaneously opening up new roles for women in crime. In the area of property crime, both Adler and Simon felt that as women were liberated from the home, they were beginning to act like men: stealing, robbing, and embezzling.

Although there have indeed been some changes in female criminality, the many studies of what Adler called "the new female criminal" have not supported Adler's and Simon's claims. The best criticism has come from Darrell Steffensmeier (1980), who noted that much of Adler's and Simon's errors come from misleading uses of official data such as the UCR (see Chapter 4). Certainly, the percentage of women's crime has increased, but women started so far behind men that this might not mean much. For example, if one group's number of crimes increases from 10 to 20, that is a 100 percent increase. If the other group's number increases from 100 to 175, that is "only" a 75 percent increase. Looking only at percentages can be misleading. Further, Darrell Steffensmeier found, women are still primarily involved in the lowest property crimes; their crimes are still the petty crimes of the economically deprived and have nothing to do with work or occupations. They are still much less likely to have the sort of jobs that allow crime (dock worker, truck driver), and they are still almost completely excluded from crime rings, mobs, drug operations, and certainly corporate and "upperworld" crimes (Steffensmeier & Allen, 1995).

The better conclusion reached by virtually all researchers has been that comparative crime *rates* of men and women are relatively stable. Both may be going up, but women are not "catching up." The one exception seems to be in petty property crimes, long considered traditional female crimes in a society where women are given the role as "shoppers." Why there is an increase in this area has not been adequately addressed by any of these theorists (Curran & Renzetti, 1994).

SOCIAL CONTROL THEORIES

In Chapter 3, we introduced you to Thomas Hobbes, and earlier in this chapter, we discussed the legacy of Émile Durkheim. One of the reasons for this was to trace the intellectual underpinnings of social control theories of crime. To review, then, social control perspectives assume that: (1) there is a widespread consensus in society about inappropriate and appropriate behavior, (2) behaviors labeled criminal or deviant are those that violate this consensus, (3) human beings are naturally inclined to commit crimes, and (4) social control is necessary to curb violations of the law and other deviant activities. More modern social control theorists questioned the idea that people are "naturally" motivated to commit crimes when most people obviously do not! Therefore, they began to organize their research around this question: Why do people *obey* the law?

Of course, they argue that *social control* causes this conformity. Although there are many different definitions of social control, we suggest it refers to "any reaction or communication to wrong doers (norm violators or alleged norm violators) that is invoked with the intention of reducing the occurrence of wrongdoing" (Ellis & DeKeseredy, 1996). Exactly how does social control regulate crime and deviance? As you might expect, a wide variety of social control theorists offer slightly different answers to this question. Rather than attempt to cover them all, we will focus on two of the most widely known and cited perspectives: (1) Hirschi's (1969) social bond theory and (2) Hagan, Gillis, and Simpson's (1987) power-control perspective.

Hirschi's Social Bond Theory

Travis Hirschi's answer to why most people obey the rules is that an individual's strong *social bond* to conventional society stops him or her from breaking the law. Stated in reverse, "delinquent acts result when an individual's bond to society is weak or broken" (1969, p. 16). Hirschi argued that the social bond has four elements: attachment, commitment, involvement, and belief.

The first element, *attachment,* is considered the most important and refers to the degree to which people have close emotional ties to conventional members of society such as parents, friends, teachers, and so on. The more attached young people are to these significant others, especially to parents, the more likely they are to take their concerns, feelings, wishes, and expectations into account, which, in turn, inhibits delinquent behavior. However, youths who are isolated or detached from conforming members of society are less likely to respect the norms, values, and wishes of these people. Thus, there is a greater chance that they will engage in delinquent activities.

People may be detached from significant others but still conform because they have a strong *commitment* to the conventional social order or a stake in conformity. Some people think of this in terms of "What do you have to lose?" If you have nothing, you have nothing to lose, and you might not be inhibited from committing crimes. On the other hand, if you have a solid conventional reputation, a good job, relationships you might lose if you are branded a criminal, career prospects, or other commitments, you have a lot to lose. For example, in 1987–88, Walter DeKeseredy was obsessed with completing his Ph.D. thesis and getting a tenure-track university job. Thus, he spent little time with his friends and family and a great amount of time writing and interacting with prominent scholars at both conferences and at York University. Earlier in this book, DeKeseredy mentioned his high school criminal activities; now, however, the enormous amount of time and effort invested in getting his Ph.D. and a job could be jeopardized by a crime conviction. He kept his nose clean.

The third element of the social bond is *involvement.* This refers to the amount of time one spends engaging in conventional or legitimate activities such as studying, playing or watching sports, doing volunteer work, and so on. If you are busy day and night, you (by definition) won't be hanging out on the street corner, getting into trouble. Or, to continue the preceding example, DeKeseredy was so busy finishing his thesis that he didn't have time to drink vast quantities of beer with his friends, let alone go drinking and driving. As we learned trying to write a textbook on deadline while working full-time jobs, it can sometimes be hard to find enough time to get into trouble.

The fourth element of the social bond, *belief,* refers to an acceptance of conventional norms and values. Because they believe that obeying the law is "the right thing to do" and that law enforcement officials are exercising proper authority, many people do not commit crimes. On the other hand, what if you don't happen to strongly hold these beliefs? According to Hirschi, "The less a person believes he should obey the rules, the more likely he is to violate them" (1969, p. 26).

There still are some serious questions about exactly how these four elements of the social bond operate. Certainly, to Hirschi, these four elements are interrelated, yet he has never stated exactly *what* the relationship is. For example, if a person has only three of the four, will deviance result? Does weakening one element of the social bond affect the other three (Williams & McShane, 1994)? For Hirschi, these and other questions about the interrelationships between the four elements are empirical questions that can only be answered by conducting research.

Criminologists have found Hirschi's theory to be tremendously appealing, primarily because it is easy to test. Akers (1994), in fact, argues that it is the most discussed and most tested criminological theory. It has received considerable empirical support,[4] although studies have been far from unanimous in supporting this theory.[5] Overall, it seems best suited for explaining less serious (for example, nonviolent) types of delinquent behavior (Shoham & Hoffman, 1991; Wiatrowski, Griswold, & Roberts, 1981). Studies of more serious forms of delinquency and adult criminality have been less likely to support Hirschi's theory (West, 1984).

Much more problematic to many criminologists (for example, Chesney-Lind & Sheldon, 1992; Naffine, 1987) is Hirschi's dismissal of women's experiences. Although Hirschi's empirical work on social bond theory involved collecting self-report survey data from female high school students,

---

[4]See Akers (1994) for a review of studies that support Hirschi's theory.
[5]See Curran and Renzetti (1994) for a review of studies that do not support Hirschi's theory.

he excluded their responses from his statistical analysis. For example, in his book *Causes of Delinquency*, Hirschi states in a footnote that "in the analysis that follows the 'non-negro' becomes 'white,' and the girls disappear" (1969, pp. 35–36). This is just as true of those who followed in Hirschi's footsteps; virtually all studies of his theory have used all-male samples (Curran & Renzetti, 1994).

Power-Control Theory

We have been complaining that most of these theories apply only to boys and/or men. One sharp contrast to Hirschi is the power-control theory offered by John Hagan, John Simpson, and A. R. Gillis (1987) and Hagan (1989). They attempt to answer the question, "What differences do the relative class positions of husbands *and* wives in the workplace make for gender variations in parental control and in delinquent behavior of adolescents?" (1987, p. 789). They argue that there will be lower rates of female delinquency in a family where the father is controlling, and more equal male and female rates of delinquency when parental power is equalized.

According to Hagan, delinquency is defined as a form of risk-taking behavior. It is fun and liberating and gives youths the "chance to pursue publicly some of the pleasures that are symbolic of adult male status outside the family" (1989, pp. 152–153). However, compared with girls, boys are more willing to take such risks because they are supervised less closely and sanctioned less frequently and severely by their parents. In order to understand how the "taste for such risk-taking is channeled along sexually stratified lines" (Hagan, 1989, p. 154), we need to focus on the relationship between the family and the work force.

According to Hagan and colleagues, parents' positions of power in the workplace are reproduced at home and influence the likelihood of their children engaging in delinquent activities. These theorists identify two general types of family structures based on parents' power in the workplace: patriarchal and egalitarian. The *patriarchal* family consists of a husband who works outside the home in a position of authority and a wife who does not work outside the home. In such families, most typically found in the working class, the power of husbands, as derived from their occupational positions, is reflected in their power at home. They delegate responsibility to their wives for socializing and controlling their children. Male children are encouraged to take risks because this prepares them for participation in the labor force, while females are closely supervised and are expected to both grow up to be like their mothers and to avoid risk-taking behavior.

In an *egalitarian* family, both the husband and wife work outside the home in positions of authority. Such a family "socially reproduces daughters who are prepared along with sons to join the production sphere" (Hagan, Gillis, & Simpson, 1987, p. 792). Here, both sons and daughters are inclined to engage in risk-taking activities such as delinquency.

Data on relatively minor offenses gathered from 436 youths enrolled in Toronto-area high schools support Hagan and colleagues' (1987) main assertions. However, data derived from samples of U.S. youths do not support their arguments (Hill & Atkinson, 1988; Jensen & Thompson, 1990; Morash & Chesney-Lind, 1991; Singer & Levine, 1988). S. Shoham and J. Hoffman (1991) suggest that this discrepancy might be due to differences in Canada and the United States. In particular, they suggest that Canada is more racially homogeneous than the United States, making such analyses more difficult.

While some criminologists call for further evaluations of power-control theory, feminist scholars contend that it needs to be substantially revised.[6] For example, important variables such as social class, negative parental sanctions, victimization, peer group influence, and the role of the school need to be addressed (Chesney-Lind & Sheldon, 1992). The worst problem of all seems to be that in its current form, power-control theory is but a variation of the sharply criticized and outdated "women's-liberation-leads-to-crime hypothesis" discussed earlier in this chapter and again in Chapter 7 (Morash & Chesney-Lind, 1991). In this case, Hagan is not arguing that women's emancipation causes them to commit crime, but he is making the rather similar suggestion that "mothers' liberation" in joining the paid work force causes daughters to break the law. One problem with this is rather obvious: there has been a tremendous increase in the number and percentage of women in the paid work force in the past generation, with no corresponding increase in female delinquency.

Another problem is the concept of the egalitarian or equal family based simply on the fact that both husband and wife have jobs. Most working

---

[6]See Chesney-Lind and Sheldon (1992, pp. 96–99) for a more in-depth feminist critique of Hagan and colleagues' power-control theory.

wives can tell you that they are not equal in the house: they not only have jobs but still do all of the cooking, cleaning, and child care and lack an equal voice in many decisions. Even though more men today "help" at home, most household chores in families where both partners work are still done by women (Armstrong & Armstrong, 1994). In addition, as we will see in Chapter 9, many middle-class employed women are battered and raped by their husbands and cohabiting partners. Perhaps a place in the paid marketplace is a first step toward equal status for women, but it certainly does not automatically translate into power at home.

INTERACTIONIST THEORIES

The perspectives reviewed in this section are derived from *symbolic interactionist theory,* a major sociological school of thought developed by University of Chicago scholar George Herbert Mead (1863–1931). Briefly, symbolic interactionists argue that

> human actions are best understood in terms of the *meaning* that those actions have for the actors, rather than in terms of preexisting biological, psychological, or social conditions. These meanings are to some extent created by the individual, but primarily they are derived from intimate personal interactions with people. (Vold & Bernard, 1986, p. 250)

In Chapter 2, we briefly described one type of interactionist theory that has been applied to the study of crime and deviance: the societal reaction/labeling perspective. There, we said that societal reaction/labeling theorists want to develop a sociological understanding of how people and behaviors come to be designated as criminal or deviant. This is very different from wanting to describe the causes of crime. For scholars such as Howard Becker, nothing is inherently deviant or criminal. Rather, crime is a social construct or a label attached to a behavior during the course of social interaction between rule-makers and rule-breakers. Here, we will introduce you to two variations of the interactionist perspective: (1) Lemert's theory of primary and secondary deviance and (2) Sutherland's differential association theory.

Primary and Secondary Deviance

Edwin Lemert's (1951) perspective is a variant of the societal reaction/labeling approach that emphasizes the consequences of labeling or stigmatization. According to Lemert, everyone, at one time or another, commits *primary* criminal or deviant acts. As we suggested in Chapter 2, it would be hard to find someone who has never broken the law or committed a deviant act. We all do. When you do this, you are committing an act of primary deviance. The causes of these behaviors are many and varied and have an insignificant impact on perpetrators.

For example, suppose a classmate comes to class one day under the strong influence of drugs. She could be experiencing a considerable amount of life-events stress, such as divorce or unemployment. Or perhaps she met some old friends and didn't fully realize that the recreational drugs they shared would affect her so badly. In any case, if her drug taking remains unnoticed, she will probably just see it as a one-time event, and her self-concept and relations with teachers and peers won't be affected. But suppose the students sitting next to her complain to the instructor that she is acting strange and is certainly under the influence of drugs. She is kicked out of the class and asked to report to the dean, who is under intense pressure from the Board of Trustees to deal with the drug problem on campus. He expels her. With this blemish on her record, she not only can't get her degree but is unable to get a "decent middle-class job." She is bitter, and as she dwells more and more on her bad luck, she takes more and more drugs. Soon, she is selling drugs to support her purchases. Following a few arrests, she gradually comes to see herself as "no good"—as a drug addict and a criminal. She is now a *secondary* deviant because she has come to identify with the negative labels attached to her. One does not just jump from being a primary to a secondary deviant; it is a long process. However, the process is complete when the individual accepts as accurate the deviant label for him- or herself proposed by society at large.

In sum, Lemert's interactionist theory inverts the traditional or "mainstream" notion of the deviance–social control relationship. Unlike those who contend that crime leads to social control, Lemert argues that social control leads to crime.

Compared to the other theories reviewed in this chapter, labeling theory has not been sharply attacked by the feminist academic community. In fact, some labeling theorists, such as Edwin Schur (1984), have used it to explain the stigmatization of women. Schur shows that labeling and feminist perspectives (see Chapter 7), "far from necessarily being in conflict, can be brought together in an intellectually fruitful manner" (1984, p. 19). Meda Chesney-Lind and Randall Sheldon's (1992) *Girls: Delinquency and Justice* is another example of an important piece of scholarly work that draws from both feminist and labeling theory.

Differential Association Theory

Symbolic interactionist theory heavily influenced the development of Edwin Sutherland's differential association theory of crime.[7] Sutherland, who is widely regarded as the leading criminologist of his generation, is particularly noted for bringing sociological analyses to the center of criminology. Sutherland was not impressed by the work of some other criminologists, who invented elaborate theories of how people became criminals. He argued that the exact same processes are involved in learning criminal behavior as in learning noncriminal behavior. One may *learn* to be a priest or a carpenter, or one may *learn* to be a burglar or a gambler, but in either case, the sociological and psychological processes of learning were identical. Further, you tend to learn from those people you are closest to and have the most respect for. Sutherland was not happy with theories arguing that criminals are driven by a desire for attention, money, or luxury goods. After all, those identical needs and desires drive other people to attend college, get a good job, and save their money.

Generally, symbolic interactionists feel that we construct meaning through social interaction with others. We do not just passively absorb the values and meanings we are fed by others, but play an active role in determining who is more important to believe or imitate.

Sutherland's theory is very easy to follow. It includes the following series of propositions (1947, pp. 6–7):

- Criminal behavior is learned.
- Criminal behavior is learned in interaction with other persons in a process of communication.

---

[7]See Vold and Bernard (1986, p. 211) for a description of how Sutherland drew from Mead's theory.

- The principal part of the learning of criminal behavior occurs within intimate personal groups.

- When criminal behavior is learned, the learning includes (1) techniques of committing the crime, which are sometimes very complicated and other times very simple, and (2) the specific direction of motives, drives, rationalizations, and attitudes.

- The specific direction of motives and drives is learned from definitions of the legal codes as favorable or unfavorable.

- A person becomes delinquent because of an excess of definitions favorable to the violation of law over definitions unfavorable to violation of law.

- Differential associations may vary in frequency, duration, priority, and intensity.

- The process of learning criminal behavior by association with criminal and anticriminal patterns involves all of the mechanisms that are involved in any other learning.

- Although criminal behavior is an expression of general needs and values, it is not explained by those general needs and values, because noncriminal behavior is an expression of the same needs and values.

The point, then, behind the term *differential association* is that everyone is exposed to definitions in favor of lawbreaking and law abiding, but that things are not equal. As suggested, frequent exposure to ideas, long-term exposure, early exposure, and definitions that come from people whom the person holds in high regard will all help to push a person in one direction or another.

This theory has appealed to a great many sociologists over several generations. Because it shows that different people are influenced differently, it explains why some people commit crimes and some do not, even if they come from the same neighborhood, equally lack legitimate or illegitimate opportunities, are equally devalued by a middle-class measuring rod, or whatever. It can be just as useful in explaining why some very privileged people choose to steal their company's money or to engage in stock fraud. Still, this overarching theory comes with a price: it is very difficult to test.[8]

---

[8] See Pfohl (1994) and Beirne and Messerschmidt (1995) for criticisms of Sutherland's theory.

Despite many attempts, researchers have been unable to figure out how to measure such things as "an excess of definitions."

ECOLOGICAL MODELS

Virtually all the criminology theories we have covered so far can be described as theories of motivation. They all ask, in one way or another, Why do people go out and commit crime? What is their motivation? Are they bad? Mad? Sad? Ill-clad? Taking part in a fad? Lawrence Cohen and Marcus Felson (1979) made an attempt to develop a radically apolitical theory. They wondered what a criminology theory would look like if it completely ignored the entire question of motivation. Further, they decided not to discuss the concept of crime. They could not even discuss victimology, since that would inevitably feed back, sooner or later, into a discussion of the offender's motivation (Clarke & Felson, 1993).

Routine Activities Theory

How much crime there is and where it occurs, routine activities theory suggests, is affected by three factors: (1) the presence of likely offenders, (2) the absence of capable guardians, and (3) the availability of suitable targets (Cohen & Felson, 1979). Although, to be sure, mainstream criminologists who have been the primary supporters of this theory almost immediately and without fanfare stuck motivation right back in, the entire idea of the "presence of likely offenders" means just what it says: where there are more of the kind of people who seem to commit crimes, more crimes will be committed. Usually, though, researchers in the United States have simply assumed that motivated offenders are always present. The absence of capable guardians is a more subtle concept, but it means that people are less likely to break into occupied dwellings. If there are police on the beat, or people at home, or people on the street who are trying to stop drug sales or graffiti, or an alarm system in the store, there is less likely to be crime. The reverse, of course, is true as well: the more you leave your home or apartment empty, the more likely it is to be burglarized. Generally, the availability of suitable targets is thought about in property terms. If everyone dresses in rags and has no money, crime will be lower. If lots of kids have Starter jackets and Air Jordan shoes, there are a lot of suitable targets out there for robbery. An important component of this theory is that one of the reasons crime has increased over the past two generations is that there is a lot more *stuff* out there. Whereas kids didn't even have portable radios in the 1950s, and few dressed expensively or had a lot of toys, today we all have VCRs, CD players, boom boxes, expensive clothing and shoes, boxes of tapes and CDs—just plain a lot more stuff to steal.

Essentially, this theory argues that people may or may not become involved in certain events, depending on the circumstances. If one or two elements of the equation are missing, the crime may not take place. A popular refinement of the theory is that it isn't only people and things that add up to crime. A simple look at a city map and a list of reported crimes will quickly reveal that a tremendous number of any city's crimes take place along a rather small number of streets. Lawrence Sherman, Patrick Gartin, and Michael Buerger (1989), for example, along with Dennis Roncek and Pamela Maier (1991), argue for a refinement of routine activities theory into a criminology of *places:* they wonder if places can be conceived of as a cause of crime.

Many criminologists have been intrigued by this theory, but whatever the intention of the original formulators, much of the internal debate has been over the influence of lifestyle on crime, or what Leslie Kennedy and Stephen Baron (1993) call a "victimogenic approach" to the study of crime. For example, some researchers argue that for crimes such as burglary, robbery, and assault, there is a serious lifestyle effect; that is, when large numbers of people regularly go out for leisure activities, there is a higher rate of victimization (Messner & Blau, 1987). Further, people who stay out late and drink heavily are more likely to become crime victims (Lasley, 1989; Miethe, Stafford, & Stone, 1990).

For men, then, going to risky places, or "hot spots" such as certain bars and taverns, can lead to trouble (Oliver, 1994). Young, unemployed, single men are more vulnerable to violent victimization than married men who spend most of their leisure hours at home with their families.

What about women? Marcus Felson (1994, p. 39) assumes that they are less vulnerable than men because they spend more time at home with family members and "time spent in family and household settings is less risky than time away from those settings." The data we present in Chapter 9 would suggest otherwise. For example, Table 9.1 shows that at least 11 percent of North American women are physically abused by those whom theorists consider their "capable guardians": their husbands and cohabiting partners. As Elizabeth Stanko correctly points out in her critique of routine activities theory, "For women, the home, not the street, poses the greatest threat" (1994, p. 13).

If female spouses experience high rates of intimate violence, the same can be said about female college students, especially those in dating relationships (DeKeseredy & Kelly, 1993a; Koss, Gidycz, & Wisniewski, 1987; White & Koss, 1991). Data presented in Chapter 9 also show that these women's fear of crime, especially sexual assault, is justified. Routine activities theory, in its original form, cannot account for the high rates of sexual assault on college campuses; however, Martin Schwartz and Victoria Pitts' (1995) modified version can.

Schwartz and Pitts offer a *feminist routine activities theory,* one that integrates three concepts: routine activities, place, and lifestyle. Their starting point is the disproportionately high number of sexual assaults on North American campuses. Routine activities theory partially accounts for this: there are male students motivated to assault women, there are available suitable targets, and there is an absence of capable guardians willing to intervene. However, Schwartz and Pitts argue that feminist theory is strongest exactly where routine activity theory is weakest: explaining why there are motivated offenders on college campuses. Part of the reason is the presence of male peer groups that encourage and legitimate the sexual exploitation of women, particularly intoxicated women (DeKeseredy & Schwartz, 1993; Sanday, 1990). Men who belong to these social networks are more likely to be motivated to sexually assault women than are nonmembers (DeKeseredy & Kelly, 1993b). For example, several studies show that men who report having friends who support getting women drunk so that they cannot resist sexual advances are themselves likely to report using similar strategies (Boeringer et al., 1991; Schwartz & Nogrady, 1995).

Schwartz and Pitts contend that two lifestyle factors increase women's "suitability" (in the words of the theory) as targets of sexual assault. Although no lifestyle offers protection against rape, for campus-oriented acquaintance rapes, two contexts increase vulnerability: (1) drinking to the point of being unable to resist forceful sexual advances and (2) engaging in social activities with sexually predatory men.

So far, we have motivated offenders and vulnerable victims. Their co-presence on campuses provide men with opportunities to engage in predatory sexual assault. Nevertheless, opportunities for assaulting women do not necessarily translate into action. An essential element of routine activities theory is that the presence or absence of capable guardians will help to determine whether these events take place. Unfortunately, many campuses are "effective guardian absent" contexts. For example, many campus officials do not seriously punish those who sexually abuse women, even if they engage in extremely brutal behavior, such as gang rape (Bohmer & Parrot, 1993; DeKeseredy, 1995; McMillen, 1990; Schwartz, 1991). Even criminal justice personnel often disregard acquaintance and/or date rapes (Warshaw, 1988).

Rational Choice Theory

As you might expect, the popularity of certain theories often matches the general mood of the times. Criminology is not divorced from society in general; it is a part of it. In an era when we feel sympathy for those less fortunate than ourselves, criminological theories that emphasize the role of poverty, poor education, and structural inequality seem to be popular. Today, of course, we are in the midst of an era when more and more people are convinced that the poor deserve their fate—that less fortunate people are also less intelligent, less hard working, less thrifty, and less moral. Not surprisingly, then, criminologists have been recently attracted to theories that blame the criminal for being criminal and may even blame the victim for being a victim.

In Chapter 3, we pointed out that early classical (consensus) theorists assumed that people will do whatever they please unless restrained. Of course, as a history of policing and corrections in the United States shows, the idea that people need to be punished for poor choices has always been more popular than the view that people need to be treated or helped. As we have seen in this chapter, however, criminology has always been more interested in poverty, education, family structure, job opportunities, and other factors that push people toward crime. Where the classical or consensus punishment assumptions are most alive today is in economic analyses. These analyses, which entered criminology a few years ago, have become known as *rational choice theories*. The argument here is that people are rational: they consider the effort to commit a crime and the possible rewards from it, then factor in the possible negative consequences, and finally decide whether to do it or not.

Such theories are attempts to place the attention back on the individual. Worried that rehabilitation efforts do not work with criminals and that criminological theory has not unequivocally located the cause of crime in such social conditions as broken homes or lower-class membership, many criminologists have turned to rational choice theories as an ideological statement. In an atmosphere in which politicians and many members of the general public call for increased punishment, rational choice theorists

> give permission for punishment of offenders, because offenders are responsible for their actions and make purposeful decisions to commit crime. This, then, is a politically popular approach to crime causation. Criminals can be punished because they deserve it and they should have known better. (Williams & McShane, 1994, p. 226)

These theories are not as simple-minded as this discussion might make them sound. Particularly in the hands of such popular writers as Ronald Clarke and Derek Cornish (1985), rational choice refers to a multistage process of decision making, whereby different crimes, targets, and conditions all require different decisions. Still, all of these theories suffer from several problems, the most important of which are empirical and ideological.

Ron Akers (1994) points out the empirical problem. In the pure form, it is just plain untrue that people make rational decisions. Think about it. How often are your daily decisions particularly rational? Can you imagine a kid trying to decide whether to stick his hand into a car on a dark street to steal some cassette tapes pondering the economic advantage of theft, the possible chances of being caught, the likelihood of conviction, the most likely term of sentence, and the way that sentence equates with the economic advantage of obtaining several more tapes? However, virtually no rational choice theorist suggests this sort of theory. Rather, in order to test such theories, they say that such choices are modified by other factors, such as moral beliefs about breaking the law, opportunities, ties to other persons, and informal social sanctions. If you have been paying attention in this chapter, these ideas should sound pretty familiar. Akers notes that, although there is no support for pure rational choice theory, the modified theory does have some support.

> However, when rational choice theory is modified in this way, the level of rationality it assumes is indistinguishable from that expected in other theories. . . . When the modifications reach this point, it is no longer appropriate to call the result rational choice theory. (1994, p. 60)

The ideological component is made clearer by Daniel Curran and Claire Renzetti (1994). Everyone might agree that an inner-city kid with no job prospects and few life prospects could find life as a drug dealer more interesting and financially rewarding, at least for a short time, than the alternatives. Rational choice theorists would argue for harsh punishment to beef up the other side of the equation—so that the desire to sell drugs is beaten back by the fear of a huge punishment. Such theorists, however,

> fail to recognize that one plausible solution to the crime problem may be a more equitable distribution of resources in society . . . it does not logically follow that increasing the threat and severity of punishment would successfully deter such youth from crime when few, if any, reasonable alternatives are available. (Curran & Renzetti, 1994, p. 21)

SUMMARY

In this chapter, our concern has been with sociological theories that promote the *sociological perspective,* and in particular the idea that American society is set up in such a way as to promote a large amount of crime. Specifically, sociological theories reject the idea that crime is caused by biologically or psychologically deficient individuals.

Strain theories like Robert Merton's and subcultural theories like Albert Cohen's in particular suggest that the push toward crime comes from outside the individual and that crime may be a reaction to social forces. Travis

Hirschi's social bond theory suggests that one can look at the individual's relationship with society—the social bond—to predict whether the individual will be prone to committing crime. None of these theories has been particularly effective in discussing the situation of girls and women; they are theories about boys and men. Perhaps more useful has been Sutherland's theory, which suggests that all of what we know about learning to engage in conventional behavior also applies to deviant behavior—it is learned in just the same way, for just the same reasons. However, this theory has been particularly difficult to test.

Ecological theories have become increasingly popular in recent years. Perhaps the most popular is routine activities theory, which suggests that crime is more likely to happen when there are motivated offenders, likely targets, and an absence of capable guardians. This theory has been used to study the related question of lifestyle—whether some people engage in activities that make them particularly vulnerable to victimization. Once again, many of these formulations either are irrelevant to women or else misunderstand that an extensive amount of women's victimization takes place at home; women are not automatically safe just because they stay out of dangerous bars.

The other ecological theory, rational choice, has been popularized by a conservative mood swing in North America and elsewhere. This theory suggests that, at least on some level, offenders are making some rational decisions to commit crimes. The implication is that we therefore are much more justified in punishing them than otherwise. Further, it eliminates the need to change society to stop producing criminals. It is the criminals' fault that they are criminals, not society's for producing poverty, injustice, a lack of legitimate opportunities, poor education, high disease and death rates in inner cities, and a bleak future for large numbers of youths.

SUGGESTED READINGS

Downes, D., and Rock, P. (1988). *Understanding Deviance: A Guide to the Sociology of Crime and Rule Breaking*, 2nd ed. London: Oxford University Press.

  This book is an excellent and fair guide to the major sociological theories of crime and deviance. Unlike most U.S. theory texts, this book devotes a considerable amount of attention to *both* North American and British contributions.

Lilly, J., Cullen, F., and Ball, R. (1995). *Criminological Theory: Contexts and Consequences,* 2nd ed. Thousand Oaks, CA: Sage.

This book examines the social context, content, and political consequences of major criminological theories.

Taylor, I., Walton, P., and Young, J. (1973). *The New Criminology.* London: Routledge & Kegan Paul.

Considered by many critical criminologists to be a classic, this book provides an in-depth appraisal of a wide range of mainstream and liberal theories of crime from a Marxist perspective.

Williams, F., and McShane, M. (1994). *Criminological Theory,* 2nd ed. Englewood Cliffs, NJ: Prentice-Hall.

This book provides students with a comprehensive, intelligible overview of major sociological theories of crime.

CHAPTER 7

NEW DIRECTIONS IN CRITICAL CRIMINOLOGY

Forty years of accumulated research, then, confirms that endemic drug abuse is intimately related to conditions of mass social deprivation, economic marginality, and cultural and community breakdown—in Europe as in the United States, in the eighties as in the sixties, among poor whites and Hispanics as well as inner-city blacks. The effects of those conditions on individuals, families, and communities help explain why some kinds of people, in some kinds of places, are more vulnerable to drug abuse than others.

CURRIE, 1993, P. 103

Elliott Currie's explanation for the drug crisis in the United States is also useful for understanding a wide variety of crimes that occur in North America (as you will discover after reading Chapter 8). However, note that Currie's account differs from those presented in Chapter 6. Perhaps the major difference between Currie's theory and the *traditional* sociological perspectives reviewed so far in this text is that his (and the others to be reviewed in this chapter) is a *critical* theory. Simply, Currie strongly emphasizes a causal connection between broader social and cultural forces (such as a capitalist economy), inequality, and crime.

Critical criminology has its roots in what was once called *radical* criminology or *Marxist* criminology. Many critical criminologists, especially those who produced theories of crime and its control in the 1970s and early 1980s, relied on Marxist analyses of capitalist society.[1] These early works were important for their contribution to a sociological understanding of crime and the administration of justice. This is not to suggest, of course, that critical scholars no longer apply Marxist perspectives to criminological problems; this perspective still is especially powerful among those studying the origins and functions of law (see Chapter 3). However, a number of new schools of thought have emerged within critical criminology, all making a

---

[1] See Lynch and Groves (1989) for an in-depth discussion on the ways in which some critical criminologists have applied Marxist methods and concepts to the study of crime.

partial break with the past and all operating in more or less sharp contrast to one another. These new approaches include left realism, feminist criminology, peacemaking criminology, and postmodern criminology. The primary objective of this chapter is to describe and evaluate these traditions.

It should be obvious from the following analyses where these perspectives break with one another. One thing they have in common might be, as we shall see, their opposition to mainstream proposals for more prisons, more police, and more punishment. Jeffrey Reiman (1995) has developed a theory of why we continue to keep in place a criminal justice system that not only is oppressive but actually benefits a fairly small portion of Americans. He calls this *historical inertia.* Among other things, Reiman notes that the criminal justice system gets to define what is dangerous, that it claims to fight the most important harms to society, and that it suggests there are no alternatives except more of the same. If one thing unites all critical criminologists, it is a desire to provide an alternative vision—to place on the floor of public debate the idea that there are other ways of looking at crime and other ways to work with those who offend against us.

Before we examine these new perspectives, however, we need to define *critical criminology.*

DEFINITION OF CRITICAL CRIMINOLOGY

Are you getting worried that after several paragraphs you still do not have any real idea of what critical criminology is? Join the crowd. Although the term has been around since the early 1970s, many criminologists today are not exactly sure what the words *critical criminology* mean. This applies not only to people who don't consider themselves critical criminologists but to people who actually feel that they are part of the tradition. To be a critical criminologist, do you have to be opposed to broader social forces that perpetuate and legitimate social inequality, such as patriarchy and capitalism? Or, as one of your authors pointed out once only half-jokingly, does a stance essentially based on lots of complaining and whining count (Schwartz, 1991)? Are you special if you are critical? Really, shouldn't all criminologists be critical of their own and others' definitions, research, theories, and policy proposals (Bohm, 1982; Lynch & Groves, 1989)?

After reading the first six chapters of this text, you are now probably aware that most intellectual contributions to criminology are subject to much debate. The term *critical criminology* is no exception. Although various definitions of this term have been proposed,[2] there is no widely accepted precise formulation. For the purpose of this chapter, however, *critical criminology* is defined as a perspective that views the major sources of crime as the class, ethnic, and patriarchal relations that control our society. Further, it is a perspective that rejects as solutions to crime short-term measures such as tougher laws, increased incarceration, counseling therapy, and the like. Rather, it regards major structural and cultural changes within society as essential steps to reducing criminality.[3] All four of the new directions discussed in this chapter view major social change as the most effective way both to reduce all types of crime and to eliminate the unequal administration of justice.

Now, we may have just given you the impression that critical criminology is a unified school of thought. It isn't. Not only does it not have a closed set of membership rules, but quite a variety of different types of critical criminology have developed since the late 1960s (Schwartz, 1991). The four perspectives that we will discuss are related in the sense that each draws to some extent on the others—philosophically, conceptually, theoretically, and methodologically (Currie, MacLean, & Milovanovic, 1992). Still, they likely will appear to be distinct and at odds with each other, and in some ways they are.

To give you an idea of what critical criminologists do, however, here are some of the questions that they might seek answers to (Lynch & Groves, 1989, p. viii). Certainly, some scholars outside the tradition ask some of these questions, and even more certainly, the list omits some tremendously important questions for critical criminologists. Still, the seven questions taken together should give you an idea of the general direction that critical criminologists take.

- Who has the real power in society?
- Do those who wield power and authority get away with murder (both literally and figuratively)?
- What do social class and poverty have to do with crime?

---

[2]See Hinch (1989), Lynch and Groves (1989), and Thomas and O'Maolchatha (1989) for various definitions of critical criminology.
[3]This is a modified version of Young's (1988) definition of radical criminology.

- Why do affluent people commit so many crimes?
- Is our system of criminal justice fair?
- Are people well informed or deluded about the nature of crime?
- What do racism and sexism have to do with crime?

Of course, many critical criminologists are interested in the same questions as other criminologists: Why do some people rape, commit robbery, beat up women they are intimate with, and steal cars? The most important difference is that they are not likely to look at flaws in the makeup of the individual actor, but rather at the flaws in the makeup of a society that breeds, creates, and sustains such people.

CRITICAL CRIMINOLOGY: A "PERIPHERAL CORE" AREA[4]

Even though critical criminologists have conducted path-breaking studies, developed major theories, and proposed innovative ways of curbing both street and "suite" crime, many American criminologists, universities, politicians, criminal justice officials, members of the U.S. general population, and even some textbook publishers are not receptive to their intellectual and political contributions. This is, of course, because they challenge the political, economic, and cultural status quo. In fact, many American critical criminologists experience hostility, academic isolation, and marginalization (DeKeseredy & Schwartz, 1991a).

Academic Criminology in the United States

In the United States, critical criminologists rarely have gained control over an entire university department (for example, sociology, political science, and so on). Where they did, such as at the University of California at Berkeley, the result was more likely to be the disbanding of the department than the establishment of a beachhead of critical criminological theory, re-

---

[4]Parts of this section are based on materials previously published in the *International Journal of Offender Therapy and Comparative Criminology* 35(3) (1991).

search, and policy development. Although isolated radicals are often tolerated as long as they do not cause too much trouble, critical criminologists and critical legal studies scholars have been heavily victimized by what David Friedrichs (1989) calls "academic McCarthyism." By this, he means that they are more likely to be fired for their political views, even when they are as good as or better teachers and scholars than others in their departments.

Further, the history of academic scholarship in criminology is substantially different in the United States than in most countries. Starting about twenty-five years ago, the Law Enforcement Assistance Administration of the U.S. Department of Justice devoted extraordinary funding to law enforcement education, including providing scholarships for law enforcement personnel. To meet this demand, colleges and universities nationwide decided to form departments of criminal justice. Because of the severe shortage of professors with expertise in this area and the fact that the majority of criminal justice students were either working in or training for law enforcement, schools typically hired faculty with law enforcement experience rather than a scholarly background. Of course, we do not want to give the impression that there are not excellent academically trained scholars who have work experience in policing or corrections. There are. Unfortunately, many people with very poor academic backgrounds were hired to teach college courses on the basis of their work experience.

As an obvious result, the curriculum commonly focused on conservative, "law and order" criminology and technical law enforcement. Students were primarily taught that crime is a property of the individual (the biological/psychological orientation) and that the most effective ways of dealing with criminals were to "police 'em, jail 'em, [and maybe even] kill 'em" (Barak, 1986, p. 201). In many cases, these departments in later years duplicated themselves, and continue today to duplicate themselves, by requiring work experience in law enforcement for new faculty. Of course, there were academically trained faculty in the 1970s teaching courses in criminology or the sociology of deviant behavior, but these courses often were marginalized in the discipline or taught only in sociology departments as electives for sociology majors. This is very different from the academic tradition in most other Western countries, where criminology is a subject taught primarily by academically trained scholars.

At the same time, the U.S. research funding sources in criminology were very different than in other fields. In most fields, scholars can compete for money to support their research both in applied areas and in what is called basic research, or the search to simply expand our knowledge base. Federal agencies, which provide much of the U.S. grant funds, tend to fund both. Thus, for instance, scholars in the United States compete for basic research funds from the National Science Foundation, the National Institutes of Health, the Office of Naval Research, the Air Force Office of Scientific Research, the National Aeronautics and Space Administration, and many more. In criminology and criminal justice, however, the U.S. Department of Justice has spent extraordinary amounts of money mainly for applied research, always attempting to find ways to improve efficiency in criminal justice operations. There was very little money available for scholars who did not believe that the solution to the crime problem simply lay in fine-tuning the criminal justice system.

Many textbooks also marginalize critical criminologists. For example, most of the major criminology texts published each year in the United States purport to present a balanced view of the many conflicting theories within criminology. In fact, virtually none do, and perhaps this is an impossible goal to achieve. However, one area that is consistently given poor treatment is critical criminology. Some texts simply ignore this side of the field. Others give extensive coverage, perhaps an entire chapter, but limit themselves to ancient intellectual and political battles and a detailed coverage of long discredited leftist theories.

Indeed, you would never know that critical criminology is increasingly influential from reading the current crop of U.S. textbooks. For example, the Division of Critical Criminology is one of only three divisions of the national association of teaching, government, and industry criminology scholars: the American Society of Criminology (ASC). It overlaps in both content and membership with the ASC's strongest division: the Division on Women and Crime. One of the "pioneers" of critical criminology, William Chambliss, was a recent president of both the ASC and the Society for the Study of Social Problems (SSSP), arguably the second most important organization in sociology. Stephen Pfohl, a postmodern criminologist and deviance theorist, succeeded him as president of the SSSP. Robert Bohm, another widely cited critical criminologist, recently completed a term as president of the Academy of Criminal Justice Sciences (the national association for criminal justice scholars and practitioners), and many would consider another recent president of this association, Francis Cullen, to be a critical criminologist. The Association for Humanist Sociology has had two critical criminologists in a row as presidents (Martin Schwartz and Henry Brownstein), and one a few years ago (Stuart Hills).

There are dozens of other examples of critical criminologists who have held key positions, such as annual meeting or major committee chairs (for example, Gregg Barak, Meda Chesney-Lind, David Friedrichs, Susan Caringella-MacDonald, and Drew Humphries). The key point is this: despite widespread opposition to American critical criminology and the people who work within this tradition, critical criminologists are an integral part of the broader academic criminological community.

Critical Criminology in Canada

As stated previously, U.S. criminology textbooks commonly devote little attention to critical scholarship beyond, say, a few brief statements on Ian Taylor, Paul Walton, and Jock Young's (1973) *The New Criminology*. Further, most of these texts pay little, if any, attention to critical work done in other countries such as Canada, Australia, and the United Kingdom. This cross-cultural or international approach is missing even in widely cited American texts, such as Michael Lynch and Byron Groves (1989) *A Primer in Radical Criminology*. Although American critical criminologists such as Richard Quinney, Hal Pepinsky, Elliott Currie, Dorie Klein, Susan Caringella-MacDonald, and many others unquestionably have had a major impact on our discipline, critical criminology is not solely a U.S. enterprise.

In fact, unlike in the United States, critical criminology is not a "distinctly minority phenomenon" in the United Kingdom, Australia, and Canada (Young, 1988, p. 293). For example, in Britain, deviance and criminology courses are taught by sociology departments. In the 1970s, these courses were often taught by instructors affiliated with the National Deviancy Conference, created in 1968, so that radicals established "power bases" in various polytechnics (for example, Middlesex, "home" of the left realists),[5] universities, and colleges of education (Young, 1988). Because scholars such as those belonging to the left-realist cohort were able to work in close proximity, it is not surprising that united schools of thought were able to develop in Britain. One of these major schools of thought, to be covered later, is left realism.

---

[5] Recently, in the United Kingdom, all polytechnics were transformed into universities.

In Canada, although critical criminology may not be a core component of the broader Canadian criminology curriculum, critical criminologists are much more likely to hold tenured positions at prominent universities. This is due in part to the fact that Marxist and feminist analyses of Canadian social problems, such as those published by various members of the Canadian Political Economy Network, are highly respected by many Canadian sociology departments.[6] Although influenced heavily by both U.S. and British contributions, many Canadian criminologists incorporated ideas generated by the Political Economy Network into their own writings. Books informed by this tradition include Brian MacLean's (1986b) *Political Economy of Crime,* Thomas Fleming's (1985) *New Criminologies in Canada,* Elizabeth Comack and Stephen Brickey's (1991) *Social Basis of Law,* and R. S. Ratner and John McMullan's (1987) *State Control.* These texts received critical acclaim and, until recently, were used in many Canadian criminology courses.

Although several Canadian critical criminologists still work within the political economy tradition, a newer influence on critical criminologists in Canada has been the Human Justice Collective. This has motivated many criminologists to incorporate left realism, feminism, peacemaking, and postmodernism into their analyses of crime and criminal justice.[7] Even though the Human Justice Collective consists of a wide range of Canadian scholars with diverse theoretical, methodological, substantive, and political interests, most of its members believe that a strictly criminological orientation is insufficient on its own to address the real issues of human justice. The same issues of human justice that criminologists were studying could be found in other systems of social control, such as mental health and civil law. Interestingly, some of the main elements of this analysis also could be found in mainstream criminology in the 1970s and were influential in starting such programs as the Department of Justice, Law, and Society at American University and the School of Justice Studies at Arizona State University. The original argument that one could not study the complexity of justice through the narrow lens of criminal justice did not spread very far, however.

---

[6]See DeKeseredy and MacLean (1993) for a brief history of the Canadian Political Economy Network.

[7]See DeKeseredy and MacLean (1993) and MacLean (1992a) for more detailed descriptions of the history of the Human Justice Collective.

In the 1990s, the argument remains in the hands of such groups as the Human Justice Collective.

In this chapter, we will cover the four main schools of thought within critical criminology: left realism, feminism, peacemaking, and postmodernism. Although they all have things in common, they mainly share an opposition to or disagreement with mainstream criminology, as outlined in Chapters 5 and 6. We turn our attention first to left realism. Be careful to note the important disagreements with the similar-sounding "left idealism" and "right realism."

LEFT REALISM[8]

Over the past twenty-five years, the most powerful influence among critical criminologists has been the discovery that mainstream criminologists are interested only in crimes committed by working-class, poor, or unemployed people. They have been totally uninterested in crimes that actually cause more monetary loss and physical injury but that are committed by people and corporations with money. In reaction, critical criminologists generally have gone in exactly the opposite direction. They have made important contributions to the study of crimes of the powerful, such as corporate crime (see Chapter 10), government wrongdoings, and white-collar crime. This reaction was very powerful. Most critical criminologists working during this period ignored the causes and possible control of crime committed by members of the working class against other members of the working class. It was almost as if they feared they would lose their credentials as critical criminologists if they studied "street crime." Certainly, there are exceptions to this sweeping generalization, chief among them being the critical studies on violence against women, children, and members of ethnic groups.[9] Even so, this general failure to acknowledge working-class crime has come at a great price to the left. It has allowed right-wing politicians in several countries to claim opposition to street crime as their own issue, giving them the room to generate ideological support for harsh "law and order" policies (for example,

---

[8] This section includes modified sections of articles published previously (see DeKeseredy & Schwartz, 1991a, 1991b).

[9] See DeKeseredy and Schwartz (1991b) for examples of these studies.

lengthy prison terms, capital punishment, and so on). Certainly, these policies have been detrimental to the powerless and have hardly furthered the goals of the critical criminologists (Taylor, 1982). Moreover, the left's failure to take working-class crime seriously has contributed to a situation whereby in North America politicians presume that only conservatives have expertise and knowledge about crime and policing.

In a variety of countries, a movement is underway to remedy this situation. Left realists based in the United Kingdom, the United States, Australia, and Canada have attempted to provide a response to both the left's tendency to neglect victimization among working-class people and the conservatives' extremely harsh social control strategies. *Left realism* has sometimes been called radical realism, new realism, and critical realism, but under whatever name, the response is a perspective that attempts to explain and measure street crime and propose short-term policies to control it.

Although the roots of left realism can be found in the writings of Jock Young (1975, 1979), Tony Platt (1978), and Ian Taylor (1981), this perspective was not expressed formally until the publication of John Lea and Jock Young's (1984) *What Is to Be Done About Law and Order?* Here, a tendency found in most left-realist writings (to be explained later in this chapter) takes a central role: an attack on *left idealists,* those critical criminologists who offer simplistic analyses based heavily on instrumental Marxist and feminist views of the state and law,[10] but who ignore street crime and offer no practical proposals for change. Although left realists have never provided the names of so-called left idealists, the books they have written, or really much on their theories (Michalowski, 1991; Schwartz & DeKeseredy, 1991), they have devoted considerable time and energy to attacking idealists. We understand the difficulty of understanding left realism mainly in terms of its attacks on something else that is poorly understood, but given the centrality of these attacks to the left-realist agenda, they need to be addressed. Some of the main principles of left realism will be discussed in the next section; further explanations are available elsewhere.[11]

One of the more important things to keep in mind about left realism is that it finds the leftist theory cited in most criminology textbooks to be

[10]See Chapter 3 of this text for a review of instrumental Marxist and feminist theories of the state and law.
[11]See, for example, Kinsey, Lea, and Young (1986), Lea and Young (1984), Lowman and MacLean (1992), MacLean (1991), and Young (1986, 1992).

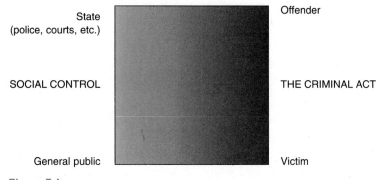

Figure 7.1
Left-Realist Square of Crime

simplistic and wrongheaded. This alone makes it particularly significant for critical criminology, in that the alternative to foolish leftist theory is not even worse right-wing theory, but rather a well-considered leftist theory.

Basic Principles of Left Realism

First, left realists see working-class crime as a serious problem for the working class. Crime is more than a function of moral panics, and working-class people are victimized from all directions in a capitalist society. According to John Lea and Jock Young (1984, pp. 23–24):

> The more vulnerable a person is economically and socially the more likely it is that both working class and white collar crime will occur against them; that one sort of crime tends to compound another, as does one social problem another. Furthermore, it notes that crime is a potent symbol of the antisocial nature of capitalism and is the most immediate way in which people experience other problems, such as unemployment or competitive individualism.

Second, realists provide a theoretical perspective on crime for which the *square of crime* is a central component (see Figure 7.1). The square consists of four interacting elements: victim, offender, state agencies (for example, the police), and the public. The social relationships between each point on the square are best described by Young (1992, p. 27):

It is the relationship between the police and the public which determines the efficacy of policing, the relationship between the victim and the offender which determines the impact of crime, the relationship between the state and the offender which is a major factor in recidivism.

If the square of crime is a major component of the left-realist perspective, then so is the concept of *relative deprivation*. As we point out in greater detail in Chapter 8, "sheer poverty" or the absence of "glittering prizes" (cars, houses, color TVs, and so on) do not motivate working-class people to commit crime (Young, 1992). Rather, it is, according to Lea and Young (1984, p. 88),

poverty experienced as unfair (relative deprivation when compared to someone else) that creates discontent; and discontent where there is no political solution leads to crime. The equation is simple: relative deprivation equals discontent; discontent plus lack of political solution equals crime.

This argument constitutes an attempt to link macro- and microlevels of analysis. Although Marxist thought plays a key role in realist thinking, after reading the previous chapter, you can see that left realists are also influenced by other criminological viewpoints. Can you locate the elements of subcultural theory and strain theory in the left-realist stance?

Third, left realists advocate the use of both quantitative and qualitative research methods. The local crime survey is, in fact, considered to be the most suitable research technique (MacLean, 1992b). Left realists believe that national surveys on the amount of crime or the amount of fear of crime that people have may be completely irrelevant in any one particular area. In contrast, a local survey can be tremendously useful to inform the police, city council, and other local agencies about both specific local problems and people's perceptions of what does and does not bother them. Thus, left realists have conducted local surveys on victimization, fear of crime, woman abuse, and perceptions of the police (Crawford et al., 1990; Jones, MacLean, & Young, 1986; Kinsey, Lea, & Young, 1986; Mooney, 1993).

Fourth, left realists propose short-term anticrime strategies that both challenge the right-wing law-and-order campaign (for example, "three strikes and you're out") and take seriously working-class communities' legitimate fear of street crime. Sometimes, they use bigger words than necessary to describe these solutions, and sometimes, their solutions are not fully worked out. However, the kinds of areas in which left realists are interested include "preemptive deterrence." This involves working in a neighborhood to try to prevent crime from happening, rather than coming in with a massive police presence after the fact. They believe in "demarginalization," or moves to eliminate the problem of large numbers of young men who feel that they are not part of society and have nothing to lose by committing crime. Further, they argue that democratic or community control of the police, as well as community participation in crime prevention and policy development, should be a goal of city councils (Lea & Young, 1984). For example, local communities should decide whether the police should intervene in bar fights.

Left-Realist Attacks on Left Idealists

As discussed previously, a primary focus in the writings of left realists has been an attack on those whom they term *left idealists*. We will address their opposition in four general areas. In addition, we will discuss left-realist opposition to so-called right realists.

Poverty and Crime   Realists contend that left idealists offer a simplistic explanation of working-class crime, one that draws heavily on the concept of *absolute deprivation* (Lea & Young, 1984). For example, the causes of crime are fairly obvious—unemployment and poverty. In some early left-idealist scenarios, working-class offenders were viewed as contemporary "Robin Hoods" or "proto-revolutionaries" trying to fight social, political, and economic inequality. Although working-class thieves may not have been aware on a conscious level that they were the first wave of the coming revolution, they were certainly reacting to the brutal class oppression of capitalism. Thus, working-class criminals should be seen as heroes fighting for their rights under an oppressive system. In this context, working-class crime was primarily *interclass* rather than *intraclass* in nature (Young, 1986). Through some intellectual sleight of hand, robbing, beating up, and raping other working-class people were transformed into acts committed against the rich.

Left realists challenge these idealist arguments by noting that nothing automatically causes people in poverty to commit street crimes. Many poor and unemployed groups, including the elderly and some ethnic and racial minorities, have low crime rates. Further, much dangerous crime is committed by people who are not impoverished: corporate executives (see Chapter 10), middle-class individuals, and the "respectable working-class" people (Lea & Young, 1984). In fact, the correct image of street crime is that it is primarily intraclass and intraracial in nature (Platt, 1978). In other words, working-class people commit crimes against working-class people, African-Americans commit crimes against African-Americans, and whites commit crimes against whites. For example, as we point out in Chapter 8, homicide is the leading cause of death for African-American males age 15–24, and the perpetrator is most often another African-American male (Mann, 1993; Reiss & Roth, 1993). Moreover, in the early 1990s, 94 percent of all African-American homicide victims were killed by other African-Americans, while 83 percent of whites were killed by whites (Sugarman & Rand, 1994).

Left realists are much more attracted to an argument that might be called *relative deprivation.* It isn't absolute and total poverty that causes crime so much as a desire to have more "stuff" than one now has. Criminologists who have worked very closely with gang members and other street criminals have come away with the feeling that they are dealing with the ultimate capitalists. These are people who watch the same TV ads as everyone else and who are hustling to obtain products and status symbols such as color TVs, fancy cars, and expensive gold jewelry—desires created almost solely by advertising (Campbell, 1984; DeKeseredy & Schwartz, 1991b). In some parts of the country, a substantial amount of armed robbery consists of stealing very expensive Starter brand jackets and extraordinarily expensive athletic shoes such as Air Jordans. These are not cold and shoeless people stealing any warm coat and any decent shoes—the specific aim is to steal Starter jackets and Nike shoes. Elizabeth Burney's study of street robbery supports this interpretation of disenfranchised criminals. She contends that

> poverty is . . . not the immediate motive for street crime, since most offenders do not lack necessities: rather, they crave luxuries. The outstanding characteristic of young street offenders is their avid adherence to a group "style," which dictates a very expensive level of brand-name dressing, financed by crime. (1990, p. 63)

Theory of the State Left realists argue that left idealists too often seem to offer an *instrumentalist* theory of the state. Here, a fairly simple theory is set up in which virtually everything can be explained in terms of how all of the institutions of the state (the military, law enforcement, local government, the judiciary, and so on) work together to promote the interests of the ruling class. In the instrumental model, criminal law is the handmaiden of the rich, serving only to protect their property and power by criminalizing the poor. The media often serve the state by generating a *moral panic* about crime that diverts the public's attention away from the crimes of the powerful (for example, white-collar and corporate crime) and the real problems of capitalism such as unemployment, poverty, and the like.[12] Crime statistics showing high crime rates in African-American neighborhoods, idealists argue, are created by statistical manipulation by the police (see, for example, Gilroy, 1987). Thus, to realists, there is a serious crime problem in inner cities; to idealists, it is mostly exaggeration designed to divert attention away from crimes of the wealthy. Left realists are more likely to argue that the creation of law in modern industrial states is a very complex phenomenon. How can the law serve only the wealthy when they often don't know what is best for themselves and fight about it all of the time? Have you ever watched the economists for each political party (both essentially representing the interests of wealth) argue over what policies to implement? Left realists also see some elements of the state working against other elements of the state; for example, some social welfare agencies may be actively working against the interests promoted by the police.

Sole Attention to Crimes of the Powerful Because idealists feel that the state attempts to divert attention away from the many injurious effects of capitalism and oppresses working-class people, they tend to call for a criminology that directs attention to ruling-class misdeeds rather than working-class crime. Crimes of the powerful, idealists argue, are more socially, economically, and physically injurious than theft and occasional episodes of interpersonal violence (Maguire, 1988; Reiman, 1995).

Unfortunately, while crimes of the powerful clearly are more injurious (see Chapter 10), the realists are just as correct in arguing that the working

---

[12]You may recall that in Chapter 1, we stated that the concept of the moral panic was developed by Cohen (1980) to describe a situation wherein a condition, episode, person, or group of persons comes to be defined as a threat to the values of society.

class are for the most part more fearful of predatory street crime. A prime target of many critical criminological attacks, conservative theorist James Q. Wilson (1985), cheerfully dismisses left idealists on this score, pointing out that people do not bar and nail shut their windows during heat waves, avoid public parks, stay in at night, harbor deep suspicions of strangers, and in general watch the social fabric of society be ripped apart because of unsafe working conditions or massive consumer fraud. The left realists generally agree that public fear of crime and working-class criminals is a serious barrier to developing a society in which people trust one another and work together toward any common goal.

We do not mean to suggest that the left realists have been completely successful in convincing the people they call idealists to abandon their earlier positions. Particularly in England, idealists argue that fear of crime is a result of government statistics showing a high crime rate among blacks. Idealists charge the government with manipulating crime statistics to show higher crime rates in black neighborhoods and then claiming that the people suffer from a very high fear of crime. This, then, justifies repressive measures. The only fear of crime, idealists claim, is among middle-class people who have purchased beautiful old houses in run-down neighborhoods. These theorists claim that official racism is the cause of this manipulation (Bridges, 1983; Gilroy, 1987; Gutzmore, 1983).

Weak Strategies for Change   Left realists also accuse idealists who emphasize crimes of the powerful of trivializing street crime. Those who trivialize street crime, of course, are hardly the most likely to provide strategies (like the bulk of the policy proposals described in Chapter 12) to prevent and control it. The crime problem might actually be exacerbated by this refusal to discuss the issue. If the only ones talking about crime are demanding massive law-and-order measures, one can easily see how this can contribute to an "undue fear of crime" among the poor. In some North American cities, it is almost impossible to watch a newscast or read a newspaper without finding virtually all of what is elsewhere considered news crowded out by lurid crime stories. For years, these citizens have been told that they live in the most dangerous environment in the world. Not surprisingly, many of them begin to identify crime as one of their greatest fears and to support repressive police practices (Gilroy, 1987). Data presented in Chapter 4 show that such support does now exist. Further, in a 1992 Roper Poll, two-thirds of respondents favored much tougher law enforcement and harsher penalties to remedy the "crime problem" (Maguire, Pastore, & Flanagan, 1993). In state after state, politicians who wanted to win voter approval pushed for sharp reductions in the government budget but big increases in government expenditures for policing and prisons. With strong voter approval, politicians in virtually every state and the federal government doubled, and then doubled again, the number of people locked up in prisons, at drastic cost to the government's ability to provide for other needs. Likewise, at a time when the Clinton administration was committed to reducing the federal deficit and few scholars believed that more police or more prisons would reduce crime, the federal government decided to use up virtually all of its political capital in passing the 1994 crime bill to provide more police and more prisons.

Unquestionably, the public attitude toward crime and punishment has changed in recent years. Although the United States already has what may be the harshest and most punitive imprisonment system in the world, many if not most Americans believe it when politicians and media figures claim that most criminals receive only a "slap on the wrist." Despite only slight increases in most areas of reported crime, the incarceration rate has about doubled since 1980, so that we now imprison roughly 350 people for every 100,000 persons in the civilian population. In some states, the rate is even higher; for example, Texas has an incarceration rate of 553 per 100,000 population (Cole, 1995).

Left realists would argue that one of the reasons for this strong support for the law enforcement approach is that there are no viable alternatives on the public agenda. For example, no political groups argue that we cannot end crime by locking up the criminals. Even if we stay within traditional state definitions of crime, as Currie (1993) points out, we could bankrupt the country merely by locking up one-third of drug offenders. Nor would this approach seriously affect the size of the drug problem in America, because new addicts would pick up much of the slack.

One of the major differences between left realists and left idealists, then, is the question of what to do in the immediate future about crime in the working class. Realists and idealists have a great deal in common. Both believe that the capitalist economic structure has much to do with our current crime problem. This system encourages people to live and work as individuals rather than work together, sets up an economy in which companies have no stake in the community or obligation to their workers but focus only on the bottom line, and promotes the racial and class differences that breed street crime. Further, in the United States, infant mortality rates are among the highest in the Western world, health care is spectacular for those with insurance and unavailable for large numbers of the population, and an ever-increasing proportion of the total wealth is concentrated in the hands of a small number of ultrawealthy people. Crime is more likely to occur in such a system than in a society where people see themselves as all working toward common goals.

Some idealists, the argument goes, believe so strongly in this equation that they feel that any reform measures are useless. Only a fundamental change from a capitalist economy to one based on more socialist principles can reduce or eliminate crime (Lynch & Groves, 1989). In its most extreme expression, the idealist argument is that implementing criminal justice re- forms could convince people that things might get better, and therefore must be opposed, since that would delay the revolution (Collins, 1982). More reasonably, some idealists oppose short-term solutions to crime be- cause they believe that virtually all community-based strategies will be taken over by the state and turned into yet another mechanism to broaden the state's social control network (Cohen, 1986).

Realists, of course, similarly believe that such an economic transforma- tion would reduce or eliminate crime. The issue the left-realist movement has taken on is what to do while living under the current capitalist system. Left realists believe that a failure to challenge conservative "law-and-order" policies with workable plans of their own plays into the hands of the right wing. People in the working class, realists argue, have a legitimate and strong fear of street crime and a strong desire to end it. This desire to end crime is much stronger than any desire to institute a new economic system, a posi- tion that should be recognized and legitimated by scholars.

Summary of Left Realists' Criticisms of Left Idealism   In sum, rather than regarding left idealism as a *different* model, left realists contend that idealists are "wrongheaded" (Michalowski, 1991). More specifically, left idealists are criticized for the following:

- Romanticizing working-class offenders who prey upon members of their own social class
- Offering a simplistic view of the state, one that ignores the fact that progressive reforms have occurred because of working-class struggle

and fights within and between state agencies (for example, occupational health and safety legislation, health care, unemployment insurance, and so on) (Young, 1986)

- Neglecting structural factors (for example, unemployment and poverty) that are among the most important causes of a wide variety of crimes and emphasizing instead cultural factors (for example, ideologies and "moral panics") that are not major causes of the singular forms of crime (for example, crimes of the powerful) they focus on

- Ignoring the devastating effects of predatory street crime and only emphasizing the injurious actions of "suite" criminals

- Failing to address the question of what is to be done about law and order under the current capitalist system

The Left-Realist Response to Right Realism

Right realists, who are often called *administrative criminologists* for their work in helping the state to administer the criminal justice system, have also been criticized by left realists. James Q. Wilson in the United States and Ron Clarke, who did most of his work in the United Kingdom, are two of the best-known right realists. Because their views tend to coincide more with the views of politicians, right realists have tended to have had a much greater impact on U.S. criminal justice policies than any other type of criminologist.

As suggested previously, left-wing criminologists historically have trivialized street crime and its control. This has enabled right-wing politicians, with the support of criminologists such as Wilson, to use the "law-and-order" issue to obtain ideological support for policies that both fail to curb a broad range of crimes and attack and bring under the control of the state a broad range of working-class people. Certainly, an important reason for the development of left-realist policy development was the need to challenge the strong influence of conservative criminologists on contemporary governments.

Some of the major arguments of right realists that are relevant here are the following:

- Crime is not determined by social forces, but rather by forces within the individual.

- Searching for the causes of crime is a "distraction and a waste of their valuable time" (Platt & Takagi, 1981, p. 45).
- Individuals *choose* to commit crime, and fewer criminal choices will be made if the government creates more effective and appropriate punishments.
- Improving social conditions will not reduce crime rates.
- Rehabilitation is an ineffective way of dealing with offenders (Wilson, 1985).

There is a reason that left realists have been upset both with those they have termed left idealists and with right realists. Generally, although these two groups operate from completely different theoretical bases and span the political spectrum from left to right, they share a number of ideas. Jock Young (1986, p. 27) identifies some similarities, or a "convergence," between these two groups. For example:

- Both disregard the value of searching for the causes of crime.
- Both agree that rehabilitation is impossible.
- Both believe that economic and social reforms will not curb crime.
- Both focus on government reactions to crime.
- Both try to explain the effectiveness of crime control without explaining crime.

Obviously, given that left realists advocate finding the causes of crime and developing social and economic reforms to eliminate them, beliefs such as those listed above will not be popular with left realists. This does not mean, of course, that left realists themselves are immune from attack, as we shall see in the next section.

Critique of Left Realism

Left realists have filled a major gap in critical criminology by attempting to explain street crime, conducting local surveys, and proposing innovative, progressive control and prevention policies. This relatively new school of thought has clearly had a major impact on criminology (MacLean, 1991).

From Martin Schwartz's (1991, pp. 119–20) vantage point, left realism's "first plus" is that it does not just acknowledge realism, it makes it a centerpiece of its agenda. It recognizes that people are victimized both from above and below and that people at the bottom are doubly victimized. Left realists are at least working to move critical criminological theory forward, synthesizing prior theories to extract what value they have and placing these ideas in new frameworks. They demand that we turn our attention to workable crime control strategies.

While left realism has much to offer, it has attracted extensive criticism. For example, realism has been attacked for doing the following:

- Not adequately including the concerns of feminists, prison abolitionists, and a variety of other critical criminologists (DeKeseredy & Schwartz, 1991b; Schwartz & DeKeseredy, 1991). The general argument is that, while much of critical criminology has been concerned with violence against women and with imprisonment, the left realists have not addressed these issues sufficiently.

- Oversimplifying definitions and perceptions of "the community." Recall that a major interest of the left realists is to provide for local control of policing, based on community desires and priorities. But who is the community? What if the community is made up of various elements that disagree? Several theorists have been concerned that left realists have not carefully addressed the worst-case scenario of communities where racist and sexist elements are in political control. Would it be proper there to implement community-based strategies that might be more socially injurious and more vindictive than the current criminal justice system (Hunt, 1982; Michalowski, 1991)?

- Not expressing sufficient support for economic crime control policies (DeKeseredy & Schwartz, 1991a).

- Having the potential to degenerate into another form of oppressive state control over the disenfranchised (Schwartz, 1991).

In sum, while "the jury may still be out when it comes to left realism" (MacLean, 1991, p. 13), this critical tradition has infused criminology with enormous energy, a new focus, and an interest in developing workable and supportable strategies. The same can be said about feminism, so we now turn to this school of thought.

FEMINISM

As we stated previously, many critical criminologists, especially those who produced theories of crime and its control in the 1970s and early 1980s, relied on Marxist analyses of capitalist society. Perhaps because they were so concerned with economic structures, these scholars for the most part took a "gender-blind" approach to criminological studies (Gelsthorpe & Morris, 1988). Some of the most widely cited of these radical works ignore gender, sexuality, and women (for example, Chambliss, 1975; Gordon, 1971; Greenberg, 1983; Spitzer, 1975). Even Ian Taylor, Paul Walton, and Jock Young's (1973) *The New Criminology,* perhaps the most important work of its generation, "contains absolutely nothing about women" (Valverde, 1991). Of course, this criticism can just as easily be leveled against the overwhelming majority of criminologists holding "mainstream" theoretical and political positions.

The one major exception to this tendency is research on woman abuse (see Chapter 9). Feminist contributions are clearly evident in the theoretical and empirical literature on the physical, sexual, and psychological victimization of women. In fact, much if not most feminist criminology today is still primarily concerned with the victimization of women (Schwartz, 1991). Even so, other topics, such as female delinquency, prostitution, and gender inequality in the law and criminal justice system, are receiving increasingly more attention from feminist scholars. Before we describe their theoretical contributions, we should define feminism.

What Is Feminism?

Historically, as well as in the current political atmosphere Susan Faludi (1991) terms the "backlash," a substantial number of people mock those who refer to themselves as "feminist." Heavily influenced by the media, religious groups, and conservative politicians, these people equate feminism with hating men, not shaving one's legs, going braless, being gay or lesbian, and being pro-choice. Of course, some feminists fit into one or more of these categories; however, many men and women are feminists. In fact, we define ourselves as pro-feminist men. We and other feminists are united by a deep desire to eliminate all forms of gender inequality, several of which are

The starting point for much feminist theory of crime is that if most of the people who are identified as criminals are male, then there must be something about learning to be male that makes one particularly prone to becoming a criminal. We can study oppression, economic opportunity, and other factors, but the number one predictor of criminality is being a man.

described in this text (for example, woman abuse). Moreover, as Claire Renzetti (1993, p. 232) correctly points out, the goal of feminist scholars is "not to push men out so as to pull women in, but rather to gender the study of crime and criminal justice."

It is misleading to paint all feminists with the same brush. In fact, many forms of feminism exist. For example, Rosemary Tong (1989) lists eight distinct brands of feminism, and there are major debates within each brand (Schwartz, 1991). For the purpose of this book, we offer Kathleen Daly and Meda Chesney-Lind's definition, which refers to *feminism* as "a set of theories about women's oppression *and* a set of strategies for change" (1988,

p. 502). Their elements of feminism make it distinct from other perspectives occasionally referred to as "male stream," because the latter theories omit and/or misrepresent both gender and women's experiences (Messerschmidt, 1993):

- Gender is not a natural fact but a complex social, historical, and cultural product; it is related to, but not simply derived from, biological sex difference and reproductive capacities.
- Gender and gender relations order social life and social institutions in fundamental ways.
- Gender relations and constructs of masculinity and femininity are not symmetrical but are based on an organizing principle of men's superiority to and social and political-economic dominance over women.
- Systems of knowledge reflect men's views of the natural and social world; the production of knowledge is gendered.
- Women should be at the center of intellectual inquiry, not peripheral, invisible, or appendages to men.

Before we review several feminist contributions to criminological thought, we should note in passing the contention of some scholars that a feminist criminology does not exist because neither feminism nor criminology is a monolithic enterprise (Daly & Chesney-Lind, 1988; Morris, 1987). In other words, scholars use different feminist perspectives to explain a variety of criminological problems, such as those discussed throughout this text.

Again, at least eight variants of feminist theory exist, each of which takes a distinct approach to understanding gender issues, asks different types of questions, and offers different theories of crime and its control (Beirne & Messerschmidt, 1995). In the sections that follow, we will limit our description of feminist contributions to four major perspectives because they are the ones most often outlined in the feminist literature on criminology. The problem is that neither reality nor scholars fit neatly into the slots needed by textbook authors to organize separate sections. Writings by most feminist authors may easily bridge two or three of these categories or may not really fit into any of them at all. Still, these are the categories most identified by the writers themselves. We begin by describing the major elements of liberal feminism.

Liberal Feminism

Of all the feminist theories developed so far, liberal feminism is the most widely recognized in North America. In the United States, it emerged in the late 1960s and significantly contributed to the development of the National Organization for Women (Danner, 1991; Messerschmidt, 1993). Liberal feminists contend that women are discriminated against on the basis of their sex, so that they are denied access to the same political, financial, career, and personal opportunities as men (Messerschmidt, 1993). Liberal feminists further argue that this problem can be eliminated by:

- Removing all obstacles to women's access to education, paid employment, political activity, and other public institutions
- Enabling women to participate equally with men in the public sphere
- Enacting legal change (Daly & Chesney-Lind, 1988, p. 537)

In sum, the problem of gender inequality can be solved by clearing the way for "women's rapid integration into what has been the world of men" (Ehrenreich & English, 1978, p. 19) and by eliminating sexist stereotypes promoted by gender-role socialization in domestic settings, educational contexts, the media, and the government (Messerschmidt, 1993).

Several criminologists have used liberal feminist theory to explain crime. Perhaps the most famous contributions are those offered by Freda Adler (1975) and Rita Simon (1981). They were among the "first wave of women" of their generation to engage in criminological research, and they helped to legitimate serious research on female crime and punishment, topics that had previously been neglected (Faith, 1993).

Adler and Simon challenged sexist assertions made by members of the "Lombrosian underground" (Downes & Rock, 1988, p. 275), a group of male criminologists who contended that biological factors influence women to commit crimes. Many men saw "criminal women" as more masculine than feminine and as physically stronger in some ways than men (Lilly, Cullen, & Ball, 1995). In sharp contrast to this position, Adler and Simon argue that sociological factors, not physiology, best explain women's criminality.

Their analyses of 1960s and early 1970s female arrest data generated slightly different conclusions; however, Adler and Simon agreed that a strong relationship exists between women's emancipation and the increase in female crime rates. For example, according to Simon:

> As women become more liberated from hearth and home and become more involved in full-time jobs, they are more likely to engage in the types of crime for which their occupations provide them with the greatest opportunities. Furthermore . . . as a function both of expanded consciousness, as well as occupational opportunities, women's participation role and involvement in crime are expected to *change* and *increase*. (1975, p. 1)

Liberal feminist arguments such as this lack empirical support. Although emancipation theorists expected that new freedoms and ideological support from the women's movement would lead to equality in the rate of crimes against strangers, Simon (1981) at least believed that they would also result in a reduction of the number of crimes committed by women against husbands and children. This did not happen. Generally, although North American female property crime rates increased in the 1970s and 1980s, contrary to the "liberation thesis," women maintained gendered patterns of crime (Faith, 1993; Messerschmidt, 1986). In other words, most of the crimes committed by women were not related to improved labor market opportunities. Even now, women primarily commit petty property crimes (for example, shoplifting, bad checks, welfare fraud, and so on), offenses caused by an increasing "feminization of poverty" (Gimenez, 1990). As Karlene Faith correctly points out, women's crimes tend to follow their traditional roles as shoppers, consumers, and health care providers within the family:

> Females primarily commit thefts of value under $1,000, and men dominate in offences exceeding that amount. Males steal electronic equipment, tools and other goods of significantly higher values than those taken by females. In other words, in the age of women's liberation, female offenders continue to commit primarily "feminine" offences; they write bad cheques and take items useful to them as homemakers and for feminine appearances. They commit fraud against the government from need and in resistance against the destitution level of welfare allotments for their children's care. (1993, p. 65)

Moreover, contrary to media-inspired public perceptions of "violent, unruly women's liberationists running amuck and signifying a new social danger" (Faith, 1993a, pp. 65–66), female violent crime rates are significantly lower than male rates. Nevertheless, even though women are not becoming more violent, societal reactions to their behaviors have become more punitive. For example, the public is now more likely to report violent females, the police are more likely to arrest them, the criminal justice system is more likely to prosecute them, and judges and juries are more likely to convict them. Apparently, women who challenge the traditional patriarchal gender-role structure are viewed as "unruly women" worthy of punishment (Faith, 1993a; Messerschmidt, 1986).

Marxist Feminism

Marxist theory argues that the economic formation of a society is the primary determinant of other social relations, such as gender relations. Marxist feminism emerged in the late 1960s and early 1970s in response to the "masculine bias" in Marxist social theory (Messerschmidt, 1993). Rather than simply ignoring women, as did traditional Marxist theory, Marxist feminist theory agreed with liberal feminism that women in North American capitalist society are dominated by men and prevented from full participation in all aspects of society. However, as Marxists, these theorists still believe that, ultimately, the key explanatory factor is the nature of the economy. Heavily informed by the work of Friedrich Engels, Marxist feminists contend that class and gender divisions of labor determine male and female positions in any society. However, the gender division of labor is viewed as the product of the class division of labor. Because women are seen as being primarily dominated by capital and secondarily by men, the main strategy for change advocated by Marxist feminists is the transformation from a capitalist to a democratic socialist society (Daly & Chesney-Lind, 1988; Messerschmidt, 1986).

Julia and Herman Schwendinger's (1983) *Rape and Inequality* is a widely cited example of a Marxist feminist analysis of crime. In this book, the Schwendingers contend that rape is not common in all societies. Rather, based on their analyses of historical, cross-cultural, and anthropological data, they conclude that capitalist societies have the highest rape rates because they produce unequal gender relations that spawn increased violence. They also conclude that in noncapitalist societies, male-female relations are egalitarian, and thus rape is almost nonexistent. According to the Schwendingers:

> The variation in violence that we have seen here and elsewhere on the face of the globe is not produced by the inherent nature of man. Clearly this variation is socially determined, and different modes of production are basic to this determination. Finally, the exploitative modes of production that have culminated in the formation of class societies have either produced or intensified sexual inequality and violence. (1983, pp. 178–179)

Sophisticated Marxist feminist analyses are rare, and the Schwendingers have been widely acclaimed for their innovative approach to understanding male-to-female sexual violence. However, this analysis has been sharply disputed by James Messerschmidt (1986), who was arguing on behalf of socialist feminist theory (also covered in this chapter). He charges that the Schwendingers base their analysis on the state or official definition of rape, omitting marital rape and rape by the use of authority. If all of these rapes were included, he contends, the picture would look very different. Further, to Messerschmidt, the findings might have been different if socialist countries had been included in the analysis. In any case, the debate between the Schwendingers and Messerschmidt[13] is highly informative in providing insight into how Marxist feminists and socialist feminists interpret criminological and gender-related problems such as rape.

Radical Feminism

As we point out in Chapter 9, radical feminism has dominated feminist perspectives on woman abuse, and it was the first "radical perspective" to criticize the assertions of liberal feminists as "simplistic" (Messerschmidt, 1986). Marxist feminists view capitalism as the primary cause of both crime and male dominance over women. In contrast, radical feminists see male power and privilege as the "root cause" of all social relations, inequality, and

---

[13] See *Social Justice* 15(1) (1988): 123–160.

crime. To radical feminists, "The most important relations in any society are found in patriarchy (masculine control of the labor power and sexuality of women); all other relations (such as class) are secondary and derive from male-female relations" (Beirne & Messerschmidt, 1991, p. 519).

The main causes of gender inequality identified by radical feminists are: (1) the needs or desires of men to control women's sexuality and reproductive potential and (2) patriarchy. Some strategies for change advanced by these scholars are:

- Overthrowing patriarchal relations.
- Developing biological reproduction techniques that enable women to have sexual autonomy.
- Creating women-centered social institutions and women-only organizations (Daly & Chesney-Lind, 1988, p. 538).

Unlike liberal feminism, which has dominated the theoretical work on female offenders, the bulk of radical feminist's criminological attention has focused on female victims/survivors of male violence (Simpson, 1989). As we point out in greater detail in Chapter 9, radical feminist theory contends that men physically, sexually, and psychologically victimize women mainly because they need or desire to control them.

Radical feminists have played a vital role in "breaking the silence" on the multidimensional nature of male-to-female victimization (Kelly, 1988), and they have successfully demonstrated that this problem is "widespread" and "omnipresent" in advanced Western societies (Liddle, 1989). Nevertheless, some radical feminists are accused of committing several of what Messerschmidt (1993, pp. 45–50) refers to as "theoretical errors." For example:

- Differences among men tend to be ignored. In other words, radical feminists describe a "typical male" rather than address the ways in which men vary across age, race, sexual preference, and class categories.
- All violent men are seen as abusing women solely for the purpose of controlling them. Although some male-to-female violence is instrumental, we know that not all men who use violence do so as a means of social control.

- Gender is seen as strictly dichotomous. For example, all men are painted as corrupt and obsessed with death, while all women are seen as inherently nurturing and life-giving (Tong, 1989). This "black-and-white distinction" ignores the fact that there are various types of masculinities and femininities that are historically, socially, culturally, and psychologically constructed.

- Patriarchal domination is seen as existing in every society; however, a large anthropological literature indicates that this form of oppression is not universal (Messerschmidt, 1986).

Socialist Feminism

Socialist feminism is informed by some elements of both Marxist and radical feminism. For example, class and patriarchy are considered key variables in socialist feminist analyses of crime and other social problems. Nevertheless, neither class nor patriarchy is presumed to be dominant. Rather, class and gender relations are viewed as equally important, "inextricably intertwined," and "inseparable," and they interact to determine the social order at any particular time in history (Jaggar, 1983; Messerschmidt, 1986). Socialist feminists, as Piers Beirne and James Messerschmidt (1991, p. 520) point out, argue that "to understand class . . . we must recognize how it is structured by gender, conversely, to understand gender requires an examination of how it is structured by class." In sum, socialist feminists argue that we are influenced by both class and gender relations.

One of the most important contributions to the development of a socialist feminist theory of crime was the publication of Messerschmidt's *Capitalism, Patriarchy, and Crime* (1986). Like other socialist feminists, Messerschmidt's perspective treated class and gender as equally important, interacting factors that shape the types and seriousness of crime. According to Messerschmidt:

It is the powerful (in both the gender and class spheres) who do most of the damage to society, not, as is commonly supposed, the disadvantaged, poor, and subordinate. The interaction of gender and class creates positions of power and powerlessness in the gender/class hierarchy, resulting in different types and degrees of criminality and varying opportunities for engaging in them. Just as the powerful have more legitimate opportunities, so they have more illegitimate opportunities. (1986, p. 42)

Messerschmidt's theory was an attempt to improve on radical and Marxist feminism by simultaneously explaining class and gender differences in crime. However, his perspective has several limitations. There are two in particular that he agrees are problematic and need to be corrected in future theoretical work. In the first place, although Messerschmidt tried to develop a perspective in which class and gender were equally important, reviewers, including Carol Smart (1987), argue that his theory did not achieve this goal because it "retained basic Marxist formulations" onto which he simply added gender. This is a difficult hurdle to overcome. Marxist formulations, as we have seen, are primarily interested in finding the "underlying cause" of current social arrangements. Although Marxism has several variations, all share a belief that in some way the ultimate causative factor is economic interests. That is, social institutions such as law, education, political structures, or our general beliefs are all put into place because they more or less serve the interests of the dominant economic class. Feminist theory, on the other hand, has been mainly interested in the fact that ours is a patriarchal society in which men have attained political and economic power over women. It "is more likely to see patriarchy as the cause of the problem being examined, and to leave aside the question of the cause of patriarchy itself" (Schwartz & Slatin, 1984, p. 246). Merging these two theories is particularly difficult.

Further, in Messerschmidt's theory, crime was mainly seen as the product of patriarchal capitalism. In other words, those who committed crime were seen as having no creativity, as perhaps being unable to exercise free will or free choice, or even as being incapable of seeing crime as a meaningful social construct in itself. Rather, their behaviors only resulted from "the system" (1993, p. 57). The difficulty, as Messerschmidt agrees, is to find the middle ground where we allow for individual creativity without losing sight of the tremendous influence that social structures have on us. After all, desert tribespeople act differently than residents of urban capitalist enclaves such as, say, Chicago.

Messerschmidt (1993) has recently used these and other criticisms to develop a new feminist theory of crime, one that emphasizes the relationship between various masculinities and crime. It is beyond the scope of this chapter to reproduce his complex *structured action* perspective here; however, it is applied to several substantive problems described later in this text, such as corporate crime (see Chapter 10).

PEACEMAKING CRIMINOLOGY

As we have already noted, the United States is both the most violent and the most punitive advanced industrial society in the world (Currie, 1985; Friedrichs, 1991). In many states over the past fifteen years, prison populations have gone up 300–400 percent. We have begun executing large numbers of people again. The entire country has been on a massive prison-building binge, at a conservative cost of about $80,000 per cell and perhaps $14,000 a year per prisoner. In many states, such as Texas and California, excellent educational systems that took many years to build up are being slowly dismantled to pay for prisons. It would be one thing if, as in World War II, we could all believe that these tremendous sacrifices were absolutely essential to preserve our way of life. Yet, capital punishment, long-term prison sentences, and other harsh sanctions obviously are not making our streets, homes, and intimate relationships safer. Jeffrey Reiman (1995), in fact, calls our past ten years of extreme harshness a conservative social experiment that clearly has failed. In response to this ongoing dilemma, many criminologists contend that maybe it is time for politicians, criminal justice officials, and members of the general public to recognize that we are going about things the wrong way. However, by now, you probably know that there are many conflicting answers to the question, What is to be done about crime and its control?

For example, some people call for a criminal justice system that is even more punitive than the current one. One nice thing about claiming that the system is not harsh enough is that, no matter how harsh it becomes, there is no way of proving that it isn't harsh "enough." If getting harsher does not seem to have any important effect on crime, there is always room for people to argue that we need to get harsher still. Other people, however, assert that radical individual, structural, and cultural changes constitute the solution to the crime problem. Among this group are the peacemaking criminologists, such as Richard Quinney, Hal Pepinsky, and the late W. Byron (Casey)

Groves. Peacemaking criminologists see crime as only one of many different types of violence, such as war, racism, and sexism, that contribute to human suffering (Thomas & O'Maolchatha, 1989).

Principles of Peacemaking Criminology

Peacemaking criminology is informed by anarchism, humanism, Christian socialism, liberation theology, Eastern meditative thought, penal abolition-ism, feminism, and Marxism.[14] In fact, this diversity of roots is both the perspective's strength and perhaps weakness. Although it can draw on a wide variety of thinkers and philosophies to develop its analyses, members of the peacemaking network have yet to come together to form a coherent and uniform philosophy. For this reason, it is rather premature to consider their contributions a "school of thought" (Friedrichs, 1991). Still, peace-making criminologists tend to agree on or generally advance a perspective that includes the following basic principles outlined by Quinney (1991, pp. 11–12):

- Crime is suffering, and crime can only be eliminated by ending suffering.
- Crime and suffering can only be ended through the achievement of peace.
- Human transformation will achieve peace and justice.
- Human transformation will occur if we change our social, economic, and political structure.

For peacemaking criminologists, the current criminal justice system is a failure because it is rooted in the very problem it is ostensibly designed to eliminate—violence. A "war on crime," a "war on drugs," and all of the other "wars" we fight are based on the presumption that we can "stamp out," "eradicate," "push back," or otherwise do something violent to crime. Thus, for example, we presume that we can stop crime by enacting ever-

---

[14]See Pepinsky and Quinney's (1991) edited book for essays giving more detailed descriptions of peacemaking criminology's intellectual, spiritual, philosophical, and political roots.

harsher sanctions. When this doesn't work, we increase penalties more. And then more again. And then still more again. Peacemaking criminologists do not believe that we can end violence through violence; such tactics can only lead to violent reactions to our own violence.

As you can see, peacemaking criminology shares some ideas with other critical criminology perspectives. Where these theorists are more likely to strike out on their own is in their suggestion that we "make peace on crime." They call for a nonviolent criminology, one that simultaneously rejects repressive measures (prison, capital punishment, and so on) and embraces humane, progressive, community-based strategies such as mediation, reconciliation, alternative dispute resolution, and other nonpenal means of making our society safer. For example, in many parts of the country, reconciliation programs work with victims and offenders. These programs often surprise victims, who discover that the vicious, horrible criminal who stole something from them is really a kid with fairly low self-esteem and a lack of achievements who turns out not to be all that scary in person. Offenders often learn from coming face-to-face with the people they have made to suffer that there are consequences to their actions—that real people suffer real damage when victimized. As most public defenders can tell you, one of their biggest problems is that many teens just can't understand why breaking into a house to steal a few minor items is such a big deal. There is, of course, a technical problem—that popping inside to grab a stack of CDs or a TV can make you eligible in many states for up to twenty-five years in prison. However, when you are dealing with offenders early in their careers (not professional thieves), forcing them to have long talks with their victims works better than dropping the proverbial "ton of bricks" of the criminal justice system on their heads.

Practical Applications of Peacemaking Criminology

Utopian as their approach may sound, several strategies advocated by peacemaking criminologists are currently being used and have proven to be successful. For example, in Canada, under the Young Offenders Act, many young first-time offenders who have committed "minor" nonviolent offenses (for example, shoplifting) are dealt with outside the formal youth court process through the use of "alternative measures." Examples of strategies that fall under this legislative framework include an apology, restitution (paying back the victim), volunteer work (paying back the community through free labor), a charitable donation, and victim-offender mediation. If young people agree to participate in the recommended alternative measures, the charges must be dropped. There are various small programs of this sort across the United States and in many other countries, sometimes even including felony offenders.

The success of such strategies and other less punitive community-based initiatives, such as those described in greater detail in Chapter 12 and by the contributors to Hal Pepinsky and Richard Quinney's (1991) *Criminology as Peacemaking,* support the following argument put forth approximately ten years ago by Stanley Cohen:

> It still makes sense to say that mutual aid, good neighbourliness and real community are preferable to the solutions of bureaucracies, professionals and the centralized state. . . . [I]t should not be impossible to imagine a way of stopping the relentless categorization of deviants. (1985, p. 131)

While it should indeed not be impossible to imagine such a system, we have not gotten very far in North America in entering such ideas into the public imagination. To date, as discussed earlier, the lack of alternative public agendas has helped develop widespread popular support for punitive "justice."

As you might expect from the fact that critical criminology is split into several camps, there is not unanimity that proposals put forward by peacemaking criminologists are the best direction in which to turn. Several critical criminologists, such as Lance Selva and Robert Bohm (1987), contend that we should be cautious about implementing crime control strategies based on mediation, mutual aid, and reconciliation. They argue that such programs could fairly easily end up serving the needs of the government more than the needs of the community. Criminologists who have seen such programs fail many times before also suggest these programs could degenerate into yet another form of punishment, with all traces of the original goals being eradicated by the bureaucratic needs of the criminal justice system. For example, judges who feel that probation is not a strong enough sanction might "sentence" a youth to restitution, community service, and charitable donations. Already, across the country, juvenile court judges are doing this mainly with the idea that such moves are more of a punishment than regular probation. The juveniles themselves figure out quickly that this is a form of punishment, and the probation officers send out that message easily enough. In such an environment, some restitution might be paid and some beer cans picked up out of the gully outside of town, but no lessons are being learned either by the offenders or by the community.

Many criminologists also worry whether such plans will widen the current net of oppressive social control. In other words, people who might get a needed second chance could instead get criminal records and punitive "restitutive" sentences. People who would not be "under the net" of the criminal justice system might be now drawn into it.

There might even be some pressure in some places to widen the definition of deviance. People might think, "Hey, if this restitution stuff is so good, why not use it for other things that bother us, even if they aren't against the law now. After all, we are doing something good, so why not expand it?"

Although these dangers need to be carefully considered, peacemaking criminologists point out that restitution programs are considerably less violent than prisons, canings, boot camps, and all of the other War on Crime "solutions." Further, there is no chance of reconciliation between the offender and the community after, say, a caning. There is only lingering resentment that might find ultimate expression in far more harmful acts. Remember, a central argument of peacemaking criminology is that violence by individuals cannot be overcome by state violence. The problem can only get worse.

Hal Pepinsky (1992), one of the leading peacemaking criminologists, clearly recognizes that harsh "law-and-order" initiatives are not going to be replaced by peacemaking strategies in the near future, but that does not mean that he and other peacemaking criminologists are going to support the current system. Every move toward peace must start with an individual working to change her- or himself and then moving out to affect the community at large. This is where peacemaking criminologists are at work.

In sum, even if peacemaking criminologists' strategies for making the world peaceful stand little chance of being implemented under the current social order, their work can constantly alert criminologists, politicians, the mass media, and the general public that there are alternatives to ceaseless wars on crime. They can take the first steps toward developing the social transformations and interconnections between people that peacemaking criminologists feel are essential to reducing crime. As Martin Schwartz (1991, p. 123) points out in his assessment of peacemaking criminology, at the very least this perspective can help us think through our "facile acceptance of violence against others."

POSTMODERN CRIMINOLOGY

If it is true that peacemaking criminology has not yet reached the stage where it can properly be termed a school of thought, then postmodern criminology perhaps can be reduced to simply a nagging question. Still, postmodern thought has had an enormous influence on many academic fields and has begun to affect a number of critical criminologists. Bluntly, postmodern theory is so hard to grasp even for those who have deeply studied the issues involved that only a very superficial introduction will be attempted here. You should not read this section and conclude that the field has been adequately explained.[15]

Part of the problem is the wide variety of postmodern perspectives. We mentioned previously that there are a number of feminist perspectives, but the spread in postmodern theory is so broad that anyone can get easily confused. Further, much of postmodernism is derived from European theorists who seem to believe that being difficult to read is a virtue. Still, this perspective would hardly have the effect that it has had if it had nothing to offer except hard-to-read texts. We will try to explain some of the key points.

The most important of all is a deep skepticism about knowledge claims. Modernists, which is to say most of us over the past couple of hundred years, tend to believe that truth is knowable. We believe that we can harness science and logic, discover truth, and then put that truth to work to solve our problems. We know what our problems are, either because they are obvious or because we have used our science to discover them. Such is the progress that will free or emancipate us.

Postmodernists tend to dispute all of this. They generally argue that "truth" is a form of domination because it represents a way of looking at

---

[15]For an introduction to the influence of postmodern thought on criminology, see Schwartz and Friedrichs (1994).

things that is imposed by those with more power. Reality is not easily know-able, but rather is very complex, hard to read, and contradictory. Now, these ideas are not totally new and original. Other (modernist) social scientists have suggested that there are difficulties in seeing knowledge as "common sense," because "common sense" depends on what we have been taught. Many (modernist) criminologists believe that we decide what should be made legal and illegal by social processes of the construction of knowledge. As we shall note again in the chapter on corporate crime, nothing in our religion and morals suggests that there are differences between some of the things that are against the law and some that are legal. For example, you might pay 25 percent interest plus massive late charges and an annual fee for loans made through your VISA card, under threat of major economic retaliation and damage if you don't pay. Or, you might pay 50 percent interest to a local loan shark, under threat of major physical retaliation if you do not repay. How do we develop the "knowledge" that one is the normal business of a legitimate banking concern while the other reflects the terrible influence of organized crime? Is it just the interest rate? The point here is that many criminologists raise questions about knowledge—how do we "know" something is bad?

What makes postmodernists different is that many of them in a sense don't believe that *any* knowledge is knowable. They think that *any* truth claims are a form of tyranny and reject any claims by anyone who purports to know what is right. Essentially, if nothing can ever be known as a "truth," then our search for knowledge must come from an understanding that everything is related to everything else. We need to be careful that we are not imposing our values (truth) on other people. This latter point is a key issue to many postmodernists. Whereas progressives have always tried to speak for oppressed peoples, postmodernists warn about trying to speak for these people, rather than allowing them to speak for themselves (Denzin, 1990).

Certainly, this is all quite abstract. Postmodernists must contend with accusations that they are irrelevant theorists who are more concerned with making petty academic points in obscure terms than they are with effecting serious change in the world (Schwartz & Friedrichs, 1994). They rarely offer practical guidance on policy (Dews, 1987). Postmodernists have argued against any broad, general theory on anything, at best suggesting that local people everywhere need to develop their own definitions of their experiences and to work out their own methods of resistance to oppression.

Of course, the problem is that there are so many versions of postmodernism in the social sciences (Rosenau, 1992) that virtually any broad claims do not encompass everyone working within the tradition. For example, two of the American criminologists who have made the most use of postmodern theory are Stuart Henry and Dragan Milovanovic, who have attempted to develop a "constitutive criminology." What is particularly interesting is that they have tried to integrate postmodernism into a more traditional criminological framework. Their goal is to work on the production of meaning in the area of crime. They argue that such meaning is "co-produced" by those who engage in crime, those who try to control it, and those who study it.

Henry and Milovanovic do not automatically reject the insights of others. They would agree with much of the left-realist and feminist analyses and strongly approve of peacemaking criminology's rejection of the use of state violence to overcome individual violence. However, they would define crime as the power to create pain or harm in any context, so that

> law is not just a definer of crime, it is also the maker of crime. This is because it conceals some people's harms by reflecting power relations, and it manifests crime through its own exercise of power over others, especially those whose own activities have not been to deny others their own expression, such as in the case of consensual "crimes," or crimes without victims. (1993, p. 12)

Thus, Henry and Milovanovic argue for a short-term response to violence of "social judo," whereby, instead of engaging in violence with the state, those who are oppressed by it must learn to bend or channel others' exercise of power over them into the exercise of power over others. The goal is

> a minimal use of energy toward redirecting the considerable power of those seeking to exercise power over us, such that they are made abundantly aware that the more energy they expend in harming us the more that energy converts into constraining them, limiting their further ability to harm us. This is the challenge of a transformative political agenda. (1993, p. 12)

This analysis is consistent with the arguments of feminist postmodernism generally, which has strongly opposed romantic theorists who have championed their identification with oppressed groups. Gathering strength by such identification is impossible, they argue. A better goal would be resisting "group identities that have been formed in hierarchical contexts [that] will only reproduce those hierarchical relationships (or, at best, create new ones)" (Grant, 1993, p. 137).

SUMMARY

In this chapter, we have tried to introduce some of the most important current trends in critical criminology. Critical criminology itself is defined as a perspective that views the major sources of crime as the class, ethnic, and patriarchal relationships that control our society. Further, all versions of critical criminology reject as solutions to crime short-term measures such as tougher laws and the increased use of prisons. Rather, all versions of critical criminology see the ultimate "solution" to the problem of criminality in North American society as major structural and cultural changes within society.

Major perspectives within critical criminology include left realism, feminism, peacemaking criminology, and postmodernism. Left realism and feminism are the perspectives with the most followers and the most worked-out analyses and suggestions about solutions. Therefore, they are the perspectives that have truly achieved the status of "schools of thought." In contrast, although peacemaking criminology and postmodern criminology both represent an important presence within criminology today, neither is as advanced in developing a set of unifying propositions or proposals for change, and neither is yet ready to be called a school of thought. All four perspectives, however, have shown themselves to be important alternatives to traditional criminological theory.

SUGGESTED READINGS

Dobash, R. E., and Dobash, R. P. (1992). *Women, Violence and Social Change*. London: Routledge.

In this book on shelter houses for battered women, the Dobashes outline how the feminist movement has and continues to successfully challenge various state institutions. It is one of the only books to focus on the difficulties of a movement attempting to work with the state.

Gelsthorpe, L., and Morris, A. (eds.). (1990). *Feminist Perspectives in Criminology.* Philadelphia: Open University Press.

This book of readings contains several extremely important essays on feminist criminology.

Milovanovic, D. (1994). *Primer in the Sociology of Law,* 2nd ed. Albany: Harrow & Heston.

Although nominally a book on the sociology of law rather than criminology, this remains the best source of information and material on postmodern views as applied to legal and criminal issues.

Pepinsky, H. E., and Quinney, R. (eds.). (1991). *Criminology as Peacemaking.* Bloomington: Indiana University Press.

This is the best place to go for an introduction to various views that loosely fall under the umbrella of peacemaking criminology. Included are religious, humanist, feminist, and critical views of peacemaking criminology.

Young, J., and Matthews, R. (eds.). (1992). *Rethinking Criminology: The Realist Debate.* Newbury Park, CA: Sage.

There are actually quite a few books that could be read on left realism, most of which are edited works by Jock Young, Roger Matthews, or both. Young's "Ten Points of Realism" in this book is one of the best theoretical statements of realism.

PART III

What Crimes Should We Be Most Concerned About?

CHAPTER 8

MURDER AND MANSLAUGHTER

"I watch what I eat, I race-walk, I read all this stuff about health and nutrition,
and here I am, a middle-aged two-hundred-pound tub of shit. This son of a bitch,
he works in a fast-food place, probably eats greasy, soggy fried shit two, three
times a day, goes out after, has three, four forty-ounce malt liquors, Ring Dings,
grape soda, all kinds of crap, probably never did a sit-up in his life. And look ..."
His hand on Touhey's, Rocco tilted the flashlight down to the body's midriff.
"See that? A washboard gut. I have yet to observe the black male victim
in this town with more than a thirty-inch waist."

"That's 'cause they all get killed when they're twenty-one."
Mazilli walked up out of the darkness.

PRICE, 1992, P. 137

The above conversation, from the best-selling novel *Clockers,* is between two fictional New York City homicide detectives, but it has some elements of truth in it. Homicide is the leading cause of death for African-American men age 15–24 (Mann, 1993; Reiss and Roth, 1993). Some researchers regard this problem as a major public health issue (O'Carroll and Mercy, 1990), while others refer to it as "a form of black genocide, since the victim of homicide is most often another black person and the incidence of this crime is so pervasive" (Mann, 1993, p. 46).

There are other everyday victims, including the very high-risk group of women who attempt to leave their abusive husbands. If you read your local newspaper closely, you may be used to seeing stories about women found shot to death in their backyards. The local police may be reported as saying: "It looks like a 'domestic,'" as if that explains why a woman is lying dead in her backyard. The amount of media coverage devoted to the victims of "everyday violence" pales in comparison to that given to famous serial and mass murderers such as Jeffrey Dahmer, Ted Bundy, Marc Lépine, John Wayne Gacy, and Charles Manson. Although the pain and suffering caused by these killers is significant, the truth is that you are extraordinarily unlikely to become the victim of a serial or mass murderer.

More to the point of most people's fears, you are unlikely to be accosted by a stranger and murdered. Josh Sugarman and Kristin Rand (1994, p. 32) point out that, "faced with the staggering facts of crime and living under a barrage of TV and movie images that reinforce the link between crime and guns," Americans not surprisingly have a stereotyped vision of gun violence that involves street gangs, robbers, or crazed loners. Unfortunately, if you need to worry about being murdered, the prime sources of your concern should be your family members, romantic partners, friends, and drinking buddies—these are the people who account for most murders (Holmes & Holmes, 1994; Jenkins, 1992). In Canada, for example, an estimated 7 percent of all homicides are committed by strangers (Silverman & Kennedy, 1993), while in the United States, the best guess seems to be about 14 percent (Sugarman & Rand, 1994). This holds true not only for adults but for juveniles (ages 10–17), where the rate of stranger homicide is also about 14 percent (Maguire, Pastore, & Flanagan, 1993).

In this chapter, we will describe the "empirical reality" of homicide in the United States and review the current state of sociological knowledge on homicide. After reading the research presented in this chapter, you may be more critical of typical media portrayals of murderers and agree with Neil Boyd that

> this evidence speaks for itself—most murderers are basically ordinary people in socially and economically desperate circumstances. They were fuelled by alcohol or other drugs, and killed family and friends, usually over money or sexual betrayal. (1988, p. 9)

DEFINITIONS OF HOMICIDE

Some people find it useful to learn the legal definition of homicide. Of course, there are many definitions used by the fifty U.S. states, the U.S. and Canadian federal governments, and a variety of other territories and countries, but the law typically distinguishes homicides based on whether the offender planned the crime in advance and whether the offender really intended to harm the victim. The more serious crime of *murder* usually reflects something like "the willful killing of one human being by another." Even then, most jurisdictions divide murder into first- and second-degree murder. *First-degree murder* requires that the action be planned and deliberate (Holmes & Holmes, 1994) and that it involve malice. Further, homicides that occur while offenders are committing crimes such as rape, robbery, burglary, kidnapping, and arson are also typically defined as first-degree murders. *Second-degree murder* involves malice but no premeditation or deliberation. A common example of such a crime is an "act of passion" in which a person may be totally overcome with anger at an insult or irrationally upset with jealousy at seeing her boyfriend dancing with another woman. Often, the person who takes out a gun and shoots someone in this frame of mind is charged with second-degree murder: the offender certainly wanted to hurt the victim but did not plan to commit a crime until just before the violent event.

Whereas a key element of murder is that it was done on purpose, *manslaughter* is usually defined as the killing of another person through gross negligence. Once again, the law typically divides this crime into two types. *Voluntary manslaughter* can be the crime of passion described above. However, it also includes a broad set of circumstances in which both the victim and the offender are engaged in a set of behaviors and actions (perhaps with a number of other people) that culminates in one person's death. Criminologists and police have long known that in some circumstances, such as certain bar fights, the difference between the murderer and the victim consists simply of who got in the luckier blow (Luckenbill, 1977). Erving Goffman (1967) called these "character contests," in which both the assailant *and* the victim agree that violence is an appropriate way to settle a dispute and both escalate their dispute to the point of death. A good example of voluntary manslaughter was highlighted on an episode of the popular television series "NYPD Blue." Two friends playing basketball had a verbal dispute over a rule interpretation. One started pushing the other. The man who was pushed responded by punching his assailant, and, unfortunately, the man who began by pushing died.

Involuntary manslaughter generally is defined as the unintentional killing of another person through grossly reckless or negligent behavior. For example, the motorist speeding through the city streets for the fun of it who accidentally hits and kills a pedestrian is guilty of involuntary manslaughter. The same would be true of the target shooter who missed the target in his backyard and struck and killed a child playing in the next yard over.

As with most criminal law, the more general we are, the easier it is to obtain agreement on what is a crime; the more specific we get, the more exceptions we find to the rule. In most societies, the taking of a human life is the most serious crime to both the general public and to the legal system. Still, for both people and the law, there are always situations in which killing humans is allowed—although we don't always agree on what these exceptions are.

Generally, police officers who follow departmental rules and procedures properly are allowed to shoot certain people under certain circumstances. To cite an easy example, if a postal employee suddenly begins shooting co-workers and customers and continues to fire his weapon, a police officer on the scene would be duty-bound to stop the killing. If the officer had no alternatives, she could shoot at the killer to prevent further killing. If she killed the killer, it would still be homicide (she *did* kill the man), but it would be *justifiable homicide* as allowed under the law. In certain circumstances, a private citizen could act in a similar fashion, but different states and countries have different rules. Generally, in a life-threatening situation in which there is no chance of escape, a person has the right to use deadly force in self-defense of their own bodily safety. Only in a few states, however, may people use deadly force to protect property.

These legal definitions are important, but they have their problems, too. In Chapter 10, we will discuss how the deaths caused by corporations, government agencies, and other powerful institutions outnumber those resulting from lethal street crimes, but how legal definitions often miss these crimes. An interesting topic for discussion is why so many members of the media (out to sell ads?) find common ground with politicians (out to win votes?). Although virtually all of them are fully aware that crime packages providing for extreme sentences won't have a deterrent effect on homicide, an amazing number of politicians have whipped voters into a frenzy of fear and anxiety over the possibility of being murdered on the streets. In the case of gun manufacturers, who began losing sales when crime rates dropped in the early 1980s, we can at least understand a simple motive for their successful strategy of convincing more Americans to purchase guns for self-protection.

Interestingly, one rarely hears a politician insist that because the corporate death rate is more than six times greater than the street death rate, a major new crime control package is needed to deal with industry (Ellis & DeKeseredy, 1996). Throughout the United States, and in many other Western democracies as well, politicians are now demanding extremely long prison sentences for people who sell drugs, commit a burglary, or hold up a gas station. Yet, these same politicians generally approve of laws that trivialize workplace deaths. Commonly, such laws remove these homicides from the criminal law, where an offender might go to prison, and place them under civil or administrative law, where the worst penalty is typically a fine.

Thus, we suggest that defining murder is difficult, because for the most part society tends to limit applying the label of murder to what are often called "street crimes" and "interpersonal crimes." Even when we limit our definitional selves in this manner, however, researchers still have major problems. There may be some value to calling any purposeful killing a "murder," such as making it easier to run a court of law. However, if your goal is to *understand* homicide, there is an additional problem: when you do this you are lumping together into one category a great many completely different events. The word *homicide* or *murder* includes a gang or drive-by killing, a death during a bitter dispute over family priorities, an event like the episode of "NYPD Blue" discussed earlier in which a shoving match ends up with someone dead, a rape-murder, the long-planned killing of Aunt Nancy to try to get her inheritance before she can change her will to leave everything to the Save the Whale Foundation, and a random killing at the grocery store by a customer who pulls out an AK-47 and begins spraying bullets. For this reason, many researchers try to separate these issues out by devoting attention in their studies to the relationship between the offender and victim, the social roles and statuses of the victim and offender, or the characteristics of lethal incidents (Gartner, 1995).

Because corporate homicides are covered in great detail in Chapter 10, and because the bulk of the criminal homicide literature focuses on deaths resulting from interpersonal acts of violence, we will focus in this chapter on lethal behaviors defined by criminal law as homicide.

TRENDS IN MURDER
IN THE UNITED STATES

Some ten years ago, Elliott Currie wrote the following:

> To live in the urban United States in the 1980s is to feel that the elementary bonds of society are badly frayed. The sense of social disintegration is so pervasive that it is easy to forget that things are not the same elsewhere. Violence on the American level comes to seem like a fact of life, an inevitable feature of modern society. It is not. Most of us are aware that we are worse off, in this respect, than other advanced industrial countries. How *much* worse, however, is truly startling. (1985, p. 5)

In the decade since, U.S. homicide rates have remained substantially higher than those of any other industrialized country. If anything has changed, it is that the risk of being murdered in the United States today is *greater* than it was a decade ago. For example, in 1987 and 1988, the annual risk of being murdered was approximately 1 in 12,000; by 1990 it had risen to 1 in 10,504 (Reiss & Roth, 1993). If you look at the differences over a longer period of time, they become even more dramatic. For example, in 1960 the annual risk of being murdered was 1 in 19,646. Compare that to the risk of 1 in 10,504 for 1990, and you can see that the risk has just about doubled.

Nor is there any reason to believe that things are going to get better in the immediate future. As Currie (1993, pp. 280–281) notes, the United States has "both the developed world's worst drug problem *and* its worst violence, poverty, and social exclusion, together with its least adequate provision of health care, income support, and social services." What is the relationship here? One thing that researchers consistently have found is that there is a relationship between economic and racial variables and homicide. Among murder victims a disproportionate number are economically disadvantaged and African-American. Given that African-Americans are disproportionately at the bottom of the U.S. economic hierarchy, there is likely to be a great deal of overlap between these two groups. In plain English, murder victims are likely to be *both* poor and African-American, although to be sure, poor whites are more likely to be murdered than other whites. If Currie (1993) is right in arguing that U.S. companies have deliberately sought to lower their overhead by hiring more and more part-time employees (who get no health care or other benefits), then we can expect an even higher proportion of our population to be caught in poverty as time goes on. If there is indeed a relationship between one's place on the economic ladder and homicide (at least in the United States), then we should worry about a continuing increase in the number of homicides.

In addition to race and economic status, several other factors might be related to murder.

RISK MARKERS OF HOMICIDE IN THE UNITED STATES

Before trying to develop a theory of crime, such as murder, it is often a good idea to try to find out as many "facts" about the behavior as possible. Those with an empirical orientation often look at the studies already published ("the literature") to see if there are any "risk markers" established with what they are trying to study. Here, we will define a *risk marker* as any attribute of the victim, the perpetrator, or social situations that is associated with an increased probability of homicide. As with most social science, it is extremely difficult to ever "prove" that a risk marker "causes" an event. It may or may not. The most that we can usually do is to point out that it is associated in some way, so that when one thing happens the other is very likely to happen. Thus, we may find that youths are disproportionately murder victims. The next step is to try to develop a theory that explains those connections.

As is so often the case, many factors are related to homicide. However, murder tends to follow the pattern Rosemary Gartner (1995, pp. 199–200) points out:

> In virtually all modern societies, the highest rates of victimization and offending occur among persons who are disadvantaged in status, power, and economic resources. . . . Often these disadvantages are associated with ascribed characteristics, such as age, race/ethnicity, and gender.

In this section, we describe how homicides that occur in the United States differently affect persons according to race, sex, economic class. Other important factors include age, marital status, and geographic variations.

Sex

It is, of course, a vast overstatement, but we are going to make it anyway: murder is a crime essentially committed by men. U.S. arrest rates have their flaws as statistics, but it is still instructive that women make up only about 10 percent of those arrested for murder (Maguire, Pastore, & Flanagan, 1993). Further, men are the ones most likely to be murdered. The lifetime risk of becoming a victim of murder is roughly three to four times higher for males than for females (Reiss & Roth, 1993). Thus, sex is the first and most important variable to look at when discussing murder.

One reason for this disparity in murder rates comes from the problem discussed at the beginning of this chapter: that a great many murders are character contests or somewhat trivial disputes or arguments that escalate into murder. Martin Daly and Margo Wilson (1988) make a powerful argument that the sex difference may be biological, or at least sociobiological. In every known society, they suggest, men constantly compete for status and respect. They argue that it is not productive to see the steady stream of murders as events resulting from minor insults or meaningless arguments. Rather, we must recognize that the participants give a great deal of meaning to maintaining status, "face," or honor by both risking their own life and taking the life of another. Men's psyche was formed, claim Daly and Wilson, "obsessed with social comparisons, with the need for achievement, and with the desire to gain control over the reproductive capacities of women" (1988, p. 136). Whatever the reason, they provide evidence that the entire concept of *intrasexual competitive homicide* is about men killing men. Citing a wide variety of studies from throughout the world and back to thirteenth-century England, they show that there are relatively few "female-killed-female" homicides. Competition that escalates into homicide is a male phenomenon.

Generally, these findings are not disputed. The controversy comes in the area of spousal homicides in the United States. Do women kill their husbands as often as men kill their wives? The contention that killings within marriage or intimate relationships are about equal, or "sexually symmetrical," is the main issue of debate.

Intimate Relationships

In Chapter 9, we will discuss how men are most likely to be the physical aggressors and women most likely to be the victims in marital and other intimate, heterosexual relationships. Most of that discussion centers on sublethal attacks, or attacks that do not lead to death. However, some researchers use homicide data to make a strong argument: that wives are as violent as husbands. The most prominent study cited was done by Marvin Wolfgang (1958), who found that 53 men murdered their wives and 47 women killed their husbands in Philadelphia between 1948 and 1952. Based on this study, Suzanne Steinmetz and Joseph Lucca contend that

> data on homicide between spouses suggest that an almost equal number of wives kill their husbands as husbands kill their wives. . . . Thus, it appears that men and women might have equal potential for violent marital interaction; initiate similar acts of violence; and when differences of physical strength are equalized by weapons, commit similar amounts of spousal homicide. (1988, p. 241)

Further support for this position came from Michael Maxfield (1989), who found that, between 1976 and 1985, 10,529 wives and 7,888 husbands were murdered by their spouses nationwide. This translates into a 57 to 43 ratio of female-to-male victims. In sum, there is no question that almost as many husbands are murdered as wives.

Still, many criminologists are uncomfortable with these numbers, suggesting that we must consider the circumstances involved in these killings. They argue that the dynamics can be very different when women kill and when men kill. They conclude that

> men often kill wives after lengthy periods of prolonged physical violence accompanied by other forms of abuse and coercion; the roles in such cases are seldom if ever reversed. Men perpetrate familial massacres, killing spouse and children together; women do not. Men commonly hunt down and kill wives who have left them; women hardly ever behave similarly. Men kill wives as part of planned murder-suicides; analogous acts by women are almost unheard of. Men kill in response to revelations of wifely infidelity;

BOX 8.1

INTIMATE FEMICIDE

The following is an example of what is often called "intimate femicide." The narrator is the mother of Ann, a woman who had endured five years of severe physical, sexual, and psychological abuse before she decided to escape to a women's shelter and terminate her marriage.

Ann had clearly decided to leave her husband. Her mind was made up and she had taken steps to secure housing and was putting furniture together, making plans for her sons' schooling, and taking legal action to finalize the separation. While determined about there being no possibility of reconciliation, Ann wanted to meet with her husband to finalize details of their separation. She wanted to try to help him understand why she was leaving him and what those years of abuse had done to her. She felt it was important that he understand these issues; and she had written him a lengthy letter outlining all of these things to him. She also did not want to refuse his requests to visit their sons, as long as the visits were supervised and controlled.

At his fourth and last visit to Ann, he was finally convinced that she was leaving him and that he no longer had power or control over her. She was determined, brave, courageous, and clear-headed when she faced him that day. He shot her twice, at very close range. She died shortly after being shot, despite extensive medical attempts to save her life. He was charged with first-degree murder, but it was plea bargained down to second-degree and he received a life sentence, with 14 years before full parole. Fourteen years for one life and the tearing apart of many others. My grandchildren will never know the loving person who was their mother or her love. This man owned his own business and never drank or used drugs, as far as I know.

SOURCE: Crawford and Gartner, 1992, pp. 132–135.

---

women almost never respond similarly, though their mates are more often adulterous. (Dobash et al., 1992, p. 81)

In sharp contrast to men, women who kill their partners typically do so only after years of enduring various forms of physical, sexual, and psychological abuse. Typically, these women have used up all available forms of social support, perceive that they cannot leave their abusive relationships, and fear for their lives (DeKeseredy, 1993; Dobash et al., 1992). Women kill men in their own homes during periods of great fear. Interestingly, although many people ask (as we will see in the next chapter) why women stay in battering relationships, such women very often correctly judge that they are less likely to die than if they try to leave (Browne, 1987). As Karlene Faith notes (1993, p. 98): "Women who are living apart from abusive husbands are most vulnerable to being stalked and killed by them. Battered women who kill do not go chasing after the abuser to kill him; it happens most commonly in the home where she is assaulted."

This notion that women who leave abusive marriages are likely to continue to be beaten, and in fact may be in more danger than women who stay in battering relationships, has been supported by a variety of studies. Some surveys show that, compared to married women, separated and divorced women are more likely to be harmed by the men they live or lived intimately with. Similarly, data gathered in Canada, New South Wales (Australia), and Chicago reveal that these women are much more likely to be killed by their husbands after separating from them than when they are still living with them. These wives are at significantly high risk within the first two months of leaving (Schwartz, 1989; Wilson & Daly, 1993). Box 8.1 describes the tragic fate of one such woman.

What are the key factors associated with estrangement homicide? Several studies indicate that two of the most significant determinants are sexual jealousy and the fear of losing one's wife (Wilson & Daly, 1993). For example, an Australian man who killed his wife one month after she left him stated that he "was in love with Margaret, and she would not live with me anymore. I knew it was all finished so I bought the rifle to shoot her and then kill myself. If I can't have her, nobody can" (quoted in Wallace, 1986, p. 120).

Age

In recent years, younger people unquestionably have been more likely to be involved in street homicide either as offenders or victims. Arrest statistics are the main data we have to count offenders, and based on this measure, we can certainly find a dramatic explosion of juvenile involvement. For example, the FBI was able to match together 7,073 police agencies that reported homicide data in the same way for the years 1982 and 1991 and compare what they reported. Adult (age 18 and above) arrests for murder and non-negligent manslaughter went up during the decade from 13,213 to 14,601, an increase of 10.5 percent. Arrests of juveniles (those under 18), however, skyrocketed a full 92.7 percent, from 1,279 to 2,465.

Another way to look at the same information can be found in Table 8.1, which covers males only and gives the rate of males arrested for murder and nonnegligent manslaughter per 100,000 males in each age group. Thus, rather than just raw numbers, this table automatically adjusts for the fact that there may be more males of one age than another. Here, after adjusting the data in this way, Glenn Pierce and James Alan Fox (1994) found that the arrest rate for each age group did not change very much from 1970 to 1985. From 1985 to 1991, however, there was an enormous increase in arrests of teenagers and men in their early twenties. At the same time, for older men there was a continuation of a decline in the arrest rate that has been going on for more than twenty-five years.

Table 8.1 Rate (per 100,000 males in each age group) of Males Arrested for Murder and Non-negligent Manslaughter, by Age, 1970–1992

	ARREST RATE							PERCENT CHANGE BETWEEN 1985 AND 1992
AGE	1970	1975	1980	1985	1990	1991	1992	
12 and younger	0.2	0.2	0.1	0.1	0.1	0.2	0.1	0%
13–14	4.2	3.6	4.4	4.0	8.8	9.6	8.1	103
15	17.2	14.9	13.5	11.8	31.0	37.4	29.8	153
16	26.8	24.9	24.6	22.4	56.5	57.7	59.3	165
17	32.9	29.2	38.2	34.5	72.4	76.1	77.7	125
18–20	44.5	43.4	46.4	41.8	73.5	89.0	91.9	120
21–24	45.6	45.4	44.3	39.0	49.4	54.7	58.7	51
25–29	36.1	36.9	34.4	30.4	31.4	31.2	30.5	0
30–34	27.7	26.5	28.0	22.3	21.2	21.5	18.0	−19
35–44	19.5	19.5	19.4	15.4	13.9	12.9	11.7	−24
45–54	11.8	9.6	9.8	8.5	7.7	7.1	7.3	−14
55–64	7.1	6.0	5.4	4.9	3.8	3.3	3.4	−31
65 and older	3.5	3.2	2.5	2.1	1.7	1.6	1.8	−14

Source: G. L. Pierce and J. A. Fox, "Recent Trends in Violent Crime: A Closer Look," Boston: National Crime Analysis Program, Northeastern University, October 14, 1992 (mimeographed) p. 9; and data provided by Fox and Pierce, National Crime Analysis Program, Northeastern University; as reprinted in Maguire and Pastore, 1994, p. 448.

When you look at murder victims, the picture does not seem very different. Those age 18 and younger made up 14 percent of arrests for murder in 1991. Although the exact equivalent number for victims is not easily available, youths age 19 and under made up 17.6 percent of victims. If the number is limited to those age 10–19 (infants are more likely to be murdered than to be arrested for murder!), youths make up about 14 percent of victims (age 10–19), which is very similar to the percentage of those arrested (age 10–18). These numbers do not change very much when looking at sex or race: both boys and girls and whites and African-Americans have similar victimization rates.

Data like these get a bit numbing after a while, but they highlight a key issue: Just who is it that should be scared about this increase in juvenile crime? Much of the fear seems to be located in the white community, particularly among older men and women. As we noted in Chapter 1, media portrayals and scare tactics by politicians have made many older U.S. residents very afraid for their lives. The National Crime Analysis Program at Northeastern University has developed rates of victimization that show that these fears may be misplaced. Fox (1994) has shown that the victimization rate has actually been dropping steadily since 1980 for those age 25 and older. There hasn't been very much change for either males or females age 10–13, despite all of the TV specials to the contrary, nor is there any change since 1980 for white females age 14–17. African-American females have a slightly higher rate.

Most of our interest should be with young men age 14–17. The victimization rate for white males increased from 5.6 per 100,000 population in 1980 to 8.5 in 1991. Of course, this is a serious problem. However, for African-American males, the increase has been from 29.1 per 100,000 population to 65.9! In other words, yes, the U.S. murder rate has increased over the past decade, but virtually all of the *increase* in victims has been African-American males age 14–17.

Thus, you can see how difficult it is to discuss one factor, such as race, or age, in isolation. Certainly, age is a factor that must be considered when talking about homicide, but not in isolation from race and sex. It is not just youths who are being murdered in the United States today, but specifically young African-American males. Unfortunately, knowing *what* is going on does not tell us much about *why* this is the case. Most homicide researchers agree that age is powerfully associated with murder, but few agree on why this is so (Gartner, in press:).[1] James Q. Wilson and Richard Hernnstein (1985, p. 145) suggest that there are a great many possible explanations for the relationship, but that, thus far, none have very much empirical support:

> Youthful criminals live fast and dangerously, and therefore tend to die young, leaving a more law-abiding population to grow old. . . . Young people are more exposed to the disinhibiting influences of the mass media; old people are more interested in religion, with its moral injunctions. And so on.

Race/Ethnicity

Table 8.2 shows that the majority of the people arrested for murder and nonnegligent manslaughter are African-American, although this is not the case for all violent crime. Further, as we just saw with juveniles, African-American males are at extremely high risk of being homicide victims. For example, in 1991, almost 50 percent of all the homicide victims known to the police and recorded in UCR statistics were African-American. However, the more instructive figure is the homicide rate, since that takes into account

---

[1] For more information on the controversy surrounding the relationship between age and violence, see Greenberg (1985) and Hirschi and Gottfredson (1983).

Table 8.2 Percentage of Persons Arrested for Violent Crime, by Race, 1993

	RACE			
CRIME	White American	African-American	American Indian or Alaskan Native	Asian or Pacific Islander
Murder and nonnegligent manslaughter	40.7%	57.6%	0.6%	1.1%
Forcible rape	56.9	41.3	1.0	0.8
Aggravated assault	58.4	39.8	0.9	1.0
Total Violent Crime	**52.6**	**45.7**	**0.8**	**1.0**

Source: Federal Bureau of Investigation, 1993, p. 235.

not only the number of victims but also the number of potential victims. Here, the 1991 estimated rates are 4.9 murder and nonnegligent manslaughter victims per 100,000 white Americans, and 34.0 per 100,000 African-Americans (Maguire, Pastore, & Flanagan, 1993). Once again, despite messages to the contrary from the media and politicians, *both* of these rates are substantially lower than they were in 1980.

It is difficult to calculate exactly the equivalent rates for Native Americans and Alaskan natives from information already collected, but the best guesses, made by the Indian Health Service, seems to be that the victimization rate for these groups substantially exceeds that of whites but is substantially lower than that of African-Americans (Reiss & Roth, 1993).

So far, we have only told you what the rates are for people who are murdered and who are arrested for homicide. How can these data be put together? Like most violent crimes, murder is mainly an *intraracial* crime— that is, whites usually kill other whites, African-Americans generally kill other African-Americans, and so on (Mann, 1993). For example, 94 percent of African-American victims were killed by other African-Americans, while 83 percent of whites were killed by whites (Sugarman & Rand, 1994). Furthermore, regardless of their ethnicity, people tend to kill someone they know. For example, from 1976 to 1984, 75,000 African-Americans were murdered, and almost 60 percent of the victims were killed by either family members (13.2 percent) or acquaintances (44.9 percent) (O'Carroll & Mercy, 1990). Similar rates are found among whites and other minority groups (Mann, 1993).

Why are African-Americans at such great risk of being either offenders or victims of homicide? The answer to this question does not lie in their biological makeup, skin color, or culture. As Coramae Mann (1993, p. 75) argues:

> There is no empirical evidence to support the idea that African Americans have a more powerful instinct to kill than whites. On the contrary, studies in Africa reveal that African blacks not only have lower homicide rates than African Americans, but also such rates are lower than those for the general American population. . . . Moreover, in our examinations of "race," we have already seen that so-called black Americans are not a pure racial type, since the majority have "white" blood.

In discussing theories of homicide later in the chapter, we will argue that an understanding of homicide among economically disadvantaged minority groups can only be obtained by looking at broad structural factors in society (Hagan, 1994; Mann, 1993; Sullivan, 1989). As Robert Sampson (1987, p. 348) explains, pointing to African-American culture is as poor an explanation as biological differences:

> There is nothing inherent in black culture that is conducive to crime. Rather, persistently high rates of black crime appear to stem from the structural linkages among unemployment, economic deprivation, and family disruption in urban black communities.

Geographic Variations

Thus far, we have been talking about homicide rates on a nationwide basis. To make the story more complex, these rates differ across regions, states, cities, and other geographic contexts. Some places are more or less "safe" than others. For example, research consistently shows that the southern United States has about 40 percent of the nation's murder (Holmes & Holmes, 1994). Although many have argued that Southerners are naturally violent or have a culture of violence (Gastil, 1971), others suggest that the explanation can be found in the socioeconomic conditions in that region. They feel, as we shall see later in this chapter, that racial and economic inequality are the most important explanations of violent crime and that the South has higher levels of inequality (Blau & Blau, 1982). This issue has been a source of much debate and controversy and is not likely to be resolved soon.[2]

As you might guess, it isn't only the Deep South that is dangerous. In general, people feel safer in small cities than larger ones—and legitimately so. Murder rates are high in many large cities, with New York, Dallas, Washington, DC, Philadelphia, New Orleans, and San Antonio leading the pack. For example, using 1991 arrest rates as a measure, the fifty-three largest U.S. cities (250,000 residents and over) had a rate of 24 murder arrests per 100,000 inhabitants. Cities with a population between 100,000 and

---

[2] See Dixon and Lizotte (1987) for a comprehensive review of several explanations for the high rate of homicide in the South.

250,000 had a rate of 12, while cities with 50,000–100,000 inhabitants had a rate of 7.4. Finally, in towns with fewer than 10,000 inhabitants, the rate was 2.9 (Federal Bureau of Investigation, 1992). There is strong empirical support for the suggestion that murder rates are fairly closely related to the size of the city,[3] although for some unknown reason, murder rates do not rise as a particular city gets bigger over time (Archer & Gartner, 1984).

Within cities, areas characterized by high levels of poverty and other forms of social inequality (regardless of their ethnic composition) report higher levels of homicide than do better-off communities (Crutchfield, 1989). In fact, African-American homicide rates are higher in those areas marked by strong racial segregation (Peterson & Krivo, 1993). These are, of course, descriptive statements. Just why are economically disadvantaged and racially segregated inner-city residents more likely to be involved in homicide than those who live in more affluent parts of the city? The truth is, we really don't completely understand the process. Those people whom William Julius Wilson (1987) has called the "truly disadvantaged" are at great risk of being involved in murder because they experience some or all of a wide variety of problems strongly associated with all kinds of violent street crime: high rates of family disruption, inadequate access to prenatal and child care, low infant birth weight, breakdown of community-based networks of informal social control, unemployment, lack of employment prospects, extreme poverty, and other major devastating economic changes (Messner & Tardiff, 1986; Sampson, 1985, 1987; Smith & Jarjoura, 1988). Still, we are not exactly sure how each of these factors operates with each of the others. The puzzle is very complex.

HOMICIDE IN THE UNITED STATES: THE CONTRIBUTION OF FIREARMS

Have you heard these lyrics from Michael Jackson's most recent album?

> I guess I will resort to gun-toting . . . I will kill a nigger, I ain't joking. I will blow him open. (Michael Jackson, "This Time Around," *HIStory*)

---

[3] See Reiss and Roth (1993) for rich data on the relationship between community size and homicide.

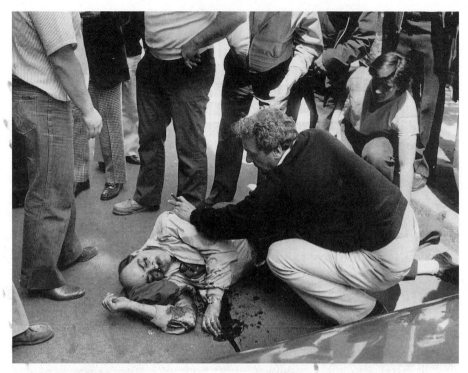

About half of all homicides are committed with guns, very often under circumstances where two men are engaged in a "character contest." If one of them turns out to have a gun, it is entirely possible that at some stage in the argument he will shoot.

It is impossible to discuss homicide in the United States without also discussing firearms. First, the simple fact is that guns are involved in two-thirds of all homicides in the United States (Federal Bureau of Investigation, 1992). That alone makes it essential that firearms be discussed. Second, in talking about murder, we are mainly talking about handguns, the American weapon of choice in committing murder. What is particularly interesting is that actual firearms usage patterns in murder differ from both the typical buying patterns in gun stores and the political arguments so often heard in the media. We've said that in two-thirds of all homicides, firearms are involved. Of these firearms murders, over 80 percent are committed with handguns. In other words, over half of all known murders in the United States are committed with handguns.

These figures do not include guns used in justifiable homicide cases. However, that data would not have much effect on the discussion because, in 1992, handguns were used only 262 times in a way that could be classified as lawful homicide (Sugarman & Rand, 1994). Further, note that our focus is on gun homicides in a criminal context, which omits from consideration the recent increase in the suicide rate (almost all due to handgun use) and the thousands of accidental deaths from firearms.

We've said that 80 percent of the gun homicides are committed with handguns. That leaves the rest to be split between rifles and shotguns, the weapons that account for about two-thirds of all gun ownership in the United States. Certainly, assault rifles scare the heck out of many of us. It is absolutely terrifying to turn on the TV and find that one man armed with an assault rifle has just killed most of the people in a restaurant, a West Bank mosque, a post office, or a railroad car. Still, FBI statistics show little use of these weapons in murder. We don't know whether to attribute this to a problem with the math or to the fact that such weapons simply are rarely used. The major problem is that the United States has very few checks on who purchases or owns guns, so there is no valid method for distinguishing which guns, including handguns, are more likely to be used in crimes than others (Reiss & Roth, 1993).

Here are some other facts about gun homicide:

- If two-thirds of all murders are committed with guns, these numbers are even higher for youths. In 1990, 81.7 percent of all murder victims age 15–19 were killed with firearms and 76 percent of victims age 20–24 were killed with guns (Maguire, Pastore, & Flanagan, 1993).

- African-American males age 15–24 are at particularly high risk of being killed with guns. For example, in 1990, over 90 percent of the murders of African-American males age 15–19 were by firearms.

- The firearm murder victimization rate for African-American males age 15–19 was 105.3 per 100,000 population in 1990. The rate was 9.7 for white males in the same age category (Maguire, Pastore, & Flanagan, 1993). In other words, approximately eleven African-American males age 15–19 were killed by gunfire in 1990 for every one white male of the same age.

- Young African-American males are much more likely to be killed with guns today than they were in 1985. For example, compared to the

1990 figure of 105.3 per 100,000 population, the 1985 firearm victimization rate for those age 15–19 was 37.4 per 100,000. For African-American males age 20–24, the rate increased from 63.1 in 1985 to 140.7 in 1990. There have been no comparable increases in victimization for females, whites, or older black males.

According to Jeffrey Roth (1994), each firearm homicide involves a specific chain of events similar to those associated with the "character contest" described in the beginning of this chapter, except that "lashing out" with a handgun is more likely to result in a fatality. For example:

> One person acquires a firearm; two or more people come within reach of the firearm; a dispute escalates into an attack, the weapon is fired; it causes an injury; and the injury is serious enough to cause death. (1994, p. 2)

Some studies support Roth's argument (for example, Felson & Steadman, 1983; Luckenbill, 1977); however, many murders do not involve this sequence of events or character contests. As some researchers point out, such an account is certainly not applicable to serial, professional (for example, "mob hits"), and mass murders (Beirne & Messerschmidt, 1995). Also, women who kill their abusive partners or fathers in self-defense typically are not engaging in character contests.

As the alarming trends suggest, society eventually will have to address the firearms issue. Many Americans oppose gun control on the grounds that "guns don't kill people, people do." Others are convinced that if the streets were not flooded with these handguns, the murder rate would be significantly lower. Although it is beyond the scope of this chapter to deal with this question, we will give it considerable attention in Chapter 12.

SERIAL AND MASS MURDER

Homicides occur every day throughout the United States, but for the most part, they are not particularly newsworthy. Lately, what with TV news teams in many cities abandoning the practice of reporting actual news in favor of providing "body counts," we are seeing more reporting than ever before on homicide. Still, what captures the public's and the media's attention for more than a few fleeting seconds of "film at 11" are people such as John Wayne Gacy, Ted Bundy, and Jeffrey Dahmer. For some reason, Americans have long been fascinated with multiple killers, even to the point of glamorizing their worst slayers and making them into heroes. Perhaps some people enjoy the thrill of being scared (somewhat like watching a good horror movie), but an amazing number of us make idols out of the most outrageous pathological murderers of innocent men, women, and children. Nor is this a recent phenomenon. One of America's worst murderers, Billy the Kid, is one of Hollywood's favorite subjects, while Jesse James, Buffalo Bill, Doc Holliday, John Dillinger, Bonnie and Clyde, and other sociopathic assassins and cold-blooded killers are also favorite characters out of American folk history. Today, rock groups like the Lemonheads and Guns N' Roses sing about Charles Manson, while top media personalities buy the paintings of John Wayne Gacy and people sent tens of thousands of "fan" letters to Gacy at his death row cell (Jackson, 1994). Large numbers of women told reporters that they viewed serial killer Richard Ramirez as a sex symbol (Kappeler, Blumberg, & Potter, 1993).

Media coverage of the bizarre nature of some serial and mass murders and our perception of vulnerability greatly contribute to our fear of these killers. However, people's fascination with such characters feeds the media and leads to ever more sensationalist coverage. While many people were afraid of Gacy, others sent him so much fan mail that he eventually set up a "900" telephone number where, for a high fee, callers could hear a recording of Gacy rambling about how he was really a victim himself rather than the boys he murdered. Box 8.2 recounts Gacy's killing spree. At conferences for criminal justice scholars, sessions that rehashed popular press treatment of Ted Bundy or John Wayne Gacy drew the big crowds (especially students) away from cutting-edge panels on other crime issues.

It is worth noting that the highly violent multiple murderers we speak of here are virtually all men, and in the United States they are for the most part white men who target women. Likewise, throughout the world, these killers are predominantly male even when they are not white, as in the *Amok* homicidal rampages that occasionally occur in Southeast Asia (Daly & Wilson, 1988). Of course, there have been female mass murderers, but they tend to have very different crime profiles than the men. Kerry Segrave (1992), who portrays eighty-two of them, suggests that women for the most

---

BOX 8.2

JOHN WAYNE GACY: CHICAGO'S "KILLER CLOWN"

One of the most written about serial killers in the past fifteen years has been John Wayne Gacy. When not dressing up in a clown outfit to entertain children, Gacy over a few years in the late 1970s murdered 33 young boys and buried 29 of them beneath his house and driveway, mainly in the crawlspace.

Some of his victims were young males who worked for Gacy; others were male prostitutes he picked up late at night at "Bughouse Square," a well-known locale in Chicago frequented at night by homosexuals and male prostitutes. Gacy would lure the victim to his home promising money or employment. When they arrived at Gacy's home, he would talk his victim into participating in his "handcuff trick." Once he had the youth in handcuffs, he would chloroform the victim and then sodomize him. Next followed the "rope trick," usually when the victim was conscious. Gacy would tie a rope around the victim's neck and, after fashioning two knots, would insert a stick and proceed to twist it slowly like a tourniquet. The terrifying deaths sometimes were accompanied by Gacy reading passages from the bible.

NOTE: For more information on the John Wayne Gacy murders, see Sullivan and Maiken (1983).
SOURCE: Hickey, 1991, p. 166.

---

part kill people from their immediate or extended family. The rest of women's victims tend to come from powerless groups such as toddlers or nursing home patients. Also, women tend to use poison rather than weapons, and none are known to use sexual violence. "Women simply don't go into the street and mass-murder total strangers" (Segrave, 1992, p. 5).

Men such as Gacy, Bundy, Ramirez, and Dahmer, along with David ("Son of Sam") Berkowitz and many others, are *serial killers,* typically defined as individuals who murder at least three people (one at a time) over more than a thirty-day time period (Hickey, 1991). By this definition, there are about 450 serial killers in prison today, while the best guess is that about 20 of them are at large at any given time (Jackson, 1994). Even if this "best guess" is completely wrong, however, and the actual number is much higher,

"Multiple murder remains an extreme fringe of American crime" (Jenkins, 1993, p. 60).

In any case, there was a serious media panic in the 1980s over serial killers. Much of this panic was caused by irresponsible politicians and media representatives misreading official data and inflating numbers to the point where it seemed that an enormous proportion of American crime was being committed by persons such as Gacy, Ramirez (the "Night Stalker" of California), and Albert De Salvo (the "Boston Strangler"). A great many people accepted as fact that there were at least 4,000 serial murders a year (see, for example, Caputi, 1987) at a time when there were less than 17,000 total homicides in the United States. As Philip Jenkins (1993) points out, a simple conspiracy theory will not work because of the many honest government officials who argued publicly for accurate statistics. Nevertheless, it certainly was convenient that many Justice Department officials were releasing wildly inflated estimates that whipped up public fears at exactly the moment they were trying (in the face of major political opposition) to get the Reagan administration to fund a new FBI National Center for the Analysis of Violent Crime.[4] It was just as convenient that funding was approved before we found out how wildly inflated our fears were. Still, some criminologists believe in the higher figures. Gennaro Vito and Ronald Holmes (1994), for example, estimate that there are 5,000 serial killing victims a year, although their only support for this is a 1983 newspaper clipping from the *Desert News.*

Events such as the one described in Box 8.2 are enough to frighten anyone. However, other factors also generate our deep-rooted fear of falling prey to serial killers. For example, as Ronald and Stephen Holmes point out:

> More "traditional" forms of homicide typically involve a personal or tangential relationship between the victim and the offender, such as when a woman kills her abusive husband, or an argument outside a bar turns violent. In serial murder, as in mass murder, becoming a victim may very well depend on nothing more than being in the wrong place at the wrong time; anyone can be a victim. There is

[4]See Ressler, Burgess, and Douglas (1988) for a description of the FBI's National Center for the Analysis of Violent Crime.

no personal confrontation in serial murder; there is no personal relationship, as exists in other forms of homicide. This makes serial murder all the more difficult to understand. The knowledge that we are all equally vulnerable leads not only to a shared sensation of controlled panic, but to a growing fascination with serial murder. (1994, p. 93)

This is why it is important to understand that the tremendous fear of the 1980s was caused by exaggerated claims about serial murderers. Some of this came from the killers themselves. Serial killers like Henry Lee Lucas got the enormous publicity they sought by claiming to have killed three or four hundred people, including most of America's missing children. However, when it comes down to facts (like a coherent story and a body), Lucas might not even qualify as a serial murderer. As one student of these crimes notes, "False confessions sometimes appear to be part of the psychological make-up of such criminals" (Jenkins, 1993, p. 58).

How real is our fear? The chances of being killed by a serial killer like John Wayne Gacy, Ted Bundy, or Jeffrey Dahmer are so slim that they are barely worth mentioning:

The odds of becoming a victim are minuscule when one considers the size of the population as a whole. Of all types of crime, homicide in general has one of the lowest victimization rates. If we were to take all of the victims in this study on serial killers between the years 1975–1988 and assumed for a moment these deaths occurred in one year instead of 14 years, the serial murder rate would still only be approximately .2 per 100,000 population. (Hickey, 1991, p. 166)

However, a belief in the myth that most murderers are crazed strangers allows people to ignore the sad fact that most homicides are committed by acquaintances and relatives. This myth is why much of the public appears to be significantly more afraid of serial murderers who typically kill strangers or "slight acquaintances" (Egger, 1990; Holmes & DeBurger, 1988).

If serial murderers are rare in the United States, then the same can be said about *mass murderers*, defined as those who kill three or more people at one time and in one location (Holmes & Holmes, 1994). Once again, these murders account only for a very small proportion of all homicides (Reiss &

Roth, 1993), but they are extremely effective at sending shock waves throughout communities or even entire countries.

Unfortunately, although there have always been mass murderers who could kill several people with a knife or gun, modern technological advances have made it possible to kill so many more people and cause that much more panic. The 1995 bombing of the Federal Building in Oklahoma City is an extremely unusual example of a mass murder in modern North America. Part of our fear is that we have no idea whether this is a random, once-in-a-generation event or the first of a wave of such mass murders. Terrorists have been blowing up Israeli buildings in Latin America, airplanes, U.S. military barracks, and so many other targets around the world that we certainly know mass murder is a possibility.

In Canada, perhaps the biggest shock wave recently was created by Marc Lépine who, on the afternoon of December 6, 1989, shot and killed fourteen female engineering students at the University of Montreal.[5] Lépine, who killed himself before he could be captured, left behind a lengthy note stating that his sole purpose was to kill feminists, whom he evidently didn't think should be studying at an engineering school. As Joanne Stato (1993, p. 132) points out, many Canadians spent a great deal of time worrying whether society itself was so antiwoman that Marc Lépine was only the worst symptom, not an exception:

> The murders vaulted the issue of violence against women into the mainstream press because the admission by Lépine that his intent was to kill feminists stymied the usual tendency of the media to portray violence against women as the isolated acts of maniacs and focused attention on the pervasive phenomenon of woman hating in our society.

Although the U.S. press has generally forgotten the case, it is still very much a part of the Canadian consciousness.

In the United States, cases like that of James Oliver Huberty, described in Box 8.3, serve as an example both of the pain and suffering caused by a mass murderer and our almost complete inability to even understand, let

---

[5] See Malette and Chalouh (1991) for a collection of essays, letters to newspapers, and poems about this shocking incident.

alone predict, who the next mass murderer will be. As Jack Levin and James Fox (1990, p. 68) point out: "Most unexpectedly, in background, in personality, and even in appearance, the mass murderer is *extraordinarily ordinary*. This may be the key to his extraordinary 'talent' for murder: After all, who would ever suspect him?"

THEORIES OF HOMICIDE

Although there are many theories of homicide, we will discuss only the most widely read and cited contemporary perspectives, especially those relevant to the data presented in previous sections. We begin our review by describing the contribution of routine activities theory.

Routine Activities Theory

In Chapter 6, we pointed out the contention of some criminologists that routine activities theory cannot explain spontaneous, conflict-related, and expressive crimes, such as murder and assault (Gomme, 1993; Miethe, Stafford, & Long, 1987). More recently, however, some researchers have conducted studies to show that, when slightly modified, routine activities theory can explain violent victimization. Here, we will apply the theory to both homicide in public places and homicide of the elderly.

The relationship between lifestyle and "deathstyle" is a major element of routine activities explanations of homicide (Ellis & DeKeseredy, 1996). According to this perspective, murders are likely to occur when suitable ("likely") victims' daily activities bring them into contact with motivated offenders in places where there is an absence of capable guardians or people who are likely to intervene. For example, young, single, minority males are at a greater risk of being murdered than are young, single women. The reason, simply, is that these males spend a considerable amount of time in high-risk settings interacting with potential murderers (for example, other single, young, minority males) (Sacco & Kennedy, 1994). In broad terms, one can look at another group, elderly and married women, and see that they are less likely to be killed in public places because they spend little time in high-risk locations such as dangerous bars late at night.

B O X   8 . 3

WHAT MAKES A MASS MURDERER?

A skilled worker for the Babcock and Wilcox Company in Massilon, Ohio, [James] Huberty was laid off from his job as a welder because of deteriorating economic conditions in Northeast Ohio at the time. Moving to California, Huberty and his wife and two daughters settled in a working-class neighborhood. Gaining employment as a security officer, a job for which he was "overqualified," he soon found himself again unemployed. . . . [T]he morning of July 18, 1984, started off quietly enough. The family went to the San Diego Zoo and later stopped for lunch at a McDonald's restaurant a half block from the Huberty apartment. After a lunch of Chicken McNuggets, fries, and a Coke, Huberty left the restaurant with his family. Mrs. Huberty stated that she was tired from the morning excursion to the zoo and had plans to go to the local grocery store for food for dinner. She decided to take an afternoon nap. While she was lying down in the bedroom, her husband came in and told her he was "going to hunt humans." He often said things to get her upset, and this time she decided that whatever he said it was not going to bother her. He kissed her good-bye, armed himself with weapons he kept in the apartment, walked out the front door, and turned right. Walking into McDonald's, he started firing, shooting 40 persons and killing 21. Huberty was eventually killed by a police sharpshooter from a building across the street.

SOURCE: Holmes and Holmes, 1994, p. 78.

Some places with large amounts of crime, like certain bars, are what routine activities theorists call "hot spots" for criminal activities (Sherman, Gartin, & Buerger, 1989). Since the major urbanization of the nineteenth century in the United States, we have known that one of the most likely spots for criminal homicide is the street outside urban bars and saloons (Daly & Wilson, 1988). We know further that in areas where large numbers of leisure activity centers are situated (bars, dance halls, bowling alleys) and where people typically go out often for leisure, there is a higher rate of all types of victimization (Messner & Blau, 1987). Thus, routine activities theory would predict that, for people of similar age, sex, and social group membership, public homicide rates would be higher in urban settings

(Hartnagel & Lee, 1990; Roncek & Maier, 1991). As we have seen in this chapter, this is exactly what we do find.

This perspective integrates Vincent Sacco and Holly Johnson's (1990) explanation for variations in nonlethal victimization and Desmond Ellis and Walter DeKeseredy's (1996) application of their account to homicide in public places. Unfortunately, it has not yet been tested using homicide data. Further, the U.S. data on the subject only deals with broad activities by masses of people. All of the available information on how often individual people go out drinking, go out alone, and use public transportation has been derived from Canadian and British victimization surveys. Thus:

> We have no way of knowing whether these are also risk factors in the United States, which differs significantly in terms of the use of private transportation, access to neighborhood bars and other sources of alcohol and drugs, and racial composition. (Reiss & Roth, 1993, p. 147)

Another problem with this perspective is that it deals only with homicide by strangers and acquaintances. It assumes that the home is a safe place even though this is not necessarily the case. As we have seen, for many women the most serious threats typically are violent acts committed in the home by male partners.

The elderly are another group more likely to be killed in their homes than in public places. Because they spend most of their time in their own homes, most routine activities theorists would argue, such people are less likely to be victimized. Further, their presence in the home would provide "guardianship" that would protect the home from crime victimization.

Two theorists, however, argue that this misses the point that inactivity is itself a routine activity. Robert Silverman and Leslie Kennedy (1993, p. 198) suggest that "the social isolation that virtually every researcher has thought lowers victimization rates is sometimes a liability." Elderly people typically live quietly alone in an area in which most of the residents are absent from their homes during the daytime. Because the elderly rarely go outside, their houses appear unoccupied and therefore easy targets. Thieves break in, not realizing that there are people at home. Finding the relatively weak and vulnerable elderly home, however, generally does not concern the thieves. If alone, elderly victims may or may not resist; however, they often are beaten anyway (Kennedy & Silverman, 1990). Whereas younger victims of such theft-related attacks are likely to recover, the elderly may die, creating what is often called theft-related homicide. In sum, "For the elderly, the safety of the home is offset by the vulnerability to attack during a crime and the recovery from beating" (Silverman & Kennedy, 1993, p. 199). Murder, in this context, is an artifact of the weak physical condition of elderly burglary victims. This is an area with which routine activities theorists will need to deal in the future.

Feminist Theories

Earlier in this chapter, we discussed mass murderer Marc Lépine, who came to the University of Montreal, isolated female students, and, while shouting obscenities about feminists, shot 23 women, killing 14.[6] He made it plain that his grievance was against women generally, but particularly women who were smart enough to get into engineering school when he was not. For some reason, many people seem to think that we should treat this as the work of a demented man who might have killed anyone. In contrast, few people seem to have a problem in categorizing the lynching of African-Americans or the targeting of gays or Jews as a race-specific hate crime. A similar form of crime is the killing of women *because* they are women. Many criminologists are now calling this crime *femicide*. To be sure, all femicides are murder, but in some cases the gender-neutral term *murder* obscures more than it illuminates. Jane Caputi and Diana Russell (1992, p. 15) define femicide as

> the most extreme form of sexual terrorism, motivated by hatred, contempt, pleasure, or a sense of ownership of women. Femicide includes mutilation murder, rape murder, battery that escalates into murder, the immolation of witches in Western Europe and of brides and widows in India, and "crimes of honor" in some Latin and Middle Eastern countries, where women believed to have lost their virginity are killed by their male relatives.

---

[6]He also wounded four men in his attack.

Theorists who write on this subject point out that femicide themes can be seen throughout society. The key consideration here is whether a woman just happens to be the person killed (which would make it murder) or whether she is being killed specifically because she is a woman (which would make it femicide).

Anyone who has watched movies over the past decade should be able to come up with dozens of femicide themes, from the genre of slasher movies in which only young, sexually active women are targets to the ample collection of sexual thrillers and even superhero comic books. The term *femicide* was invented to make it plain that in a male-dominated culture (a patriarchy), one effect is to blind many people to the seriousness of crime against the subordinate sex. Women are often told that films and novels are "just entertainment" and that they should "lighten up."

However, as we have seen, although the majority of homicide victims are male, it would take a rather sophisticated argument to suggest that they are killed because they are male. In a great many cases, however, women are killed specifically because they are women. For example, Jacquelyn Campbell (1992) has argued that a typical threat to battered women, carried out all too often, is "If I can't have you, no one can." This threat, rooted in male notions of ownership of women, is responsible for a substantial amount of the murders of women not only in the United States but worldwide. For example, because boys are valued more than girls, most infanticide in the world is of females. In India, just to pick another example, there may be as many as six hundred cases a year in the city of Delhi alone (and many more elsewhere) of "accidental burning" of women, in a set of circumstances that very few think are accidental, since virtually all take place in the context of disputes about the size of dowries (Kelkar, 1992; Pandya, 1990).

The study of femicide is very new, so there are no strong theories to test other than those we will cover in Chapter 9 in discussing violence against female intimates. Rather, at this early stage, it is more important for readers and researchers to be sensitive to these issues and concerns in their future studies.

The Subculture of Violence

In a fascinating attempt not only to bring together sociological and psychological theories but also to find the intersection between race, sex, class, and age as they affect homicide, Marvin Wolfgang and Franco Ferracuti (1967) developed an influential thesis called the *subculture of violence*. As a descriptive theory, it has many things to recommend it.

Essentially, in a very sociological argument, they suggested that within the overall broader culture, smaller subcultures emphasize different norms and values. This thesis had strong roots in criminological theory. For example, in 1955, Albert Cohen had similarly suggested that boys created their own subcultures, and Walter Miller had suggested that inner cities had their own subcultures (focal concerns). Wolfgang and Ferracuti, however, suggest that this subculture is rooted in violence, whereby members expect violence to occur under some circumstances and are willing to take part in it. These members are more than willing, actually: they receive strong positive support for doing so and strong disapproval for refusing to take part. Responding to an attack on one's manhood or an insult to one's mother with violence, then, is expected by all members within the subculture. This is, Wolfgang and Ferracuti argue, learned behavior.

Throughout the world, (and they use examples from Mexico, Albania, Colombia, Italy, and India), we find a higher violence rate among young men who are both poor and members of oppressed minority groups. The subcultural support given to young African-American men in inner-city slums, Wolfgang and Ferracuti suggest, helps to explain the high U.S. murder rate.

This theory was instrumental in spurring a national debate on the causes of the extensive violence in America's inner cities. It has fallen into disfavor, however, for a number of reasons. Perhaps most important is that it seems to have racist undertones, whether applied to inner-city African-Americans or to southern Appalachian whites. Why the high amount of violence? This theory suggests that people in these categories have poor values and that they could stop their high homicide rate by adopting better values. As we shall see in the next section, sociologists and criminologists today are more likely to see problems in the dominant culture, not the subculture, as the main causal agents.

Second, and there is no delicate way of saying this, "No one has yet been able to *find* the subculture of violence—and not for lack of trying" (Currie, 1985, p. 164). This may not bother Wolfgang and Ferracuti, who noted in their original work that "basic evidence for the existence of a subculture of violence is still missing or tautological" (1967, p. 312). They argued that its existence could be proven by theoretical arguments, but not many criminologists have agreed with this.

Still, this powerful thesis has affected many commentators on crime. Even as it loses credence in most of criminology, others are adapting some of its major features. Anne Campbell (1993), for example, endorses Wolfgang and Ferracuti's subculture of violence but develops it further by pointing out that it is a common male behavior to seek pride and identity through violence. She argues that middle-class men have the same need to show toughness but must find other methods because "their three-piece suits and credit cards have emasculated them, torn them away from the natural relationship between manliness and physical courage still retained by the working class" (1993, p. 13).

Inequality and Homicide

Earlier in this chapter, we pointed out that economically disadvantaged people who live in metropolitan areas, especially African-American males, are at much higher risk than others of committing homicide. Simply being poor or African-American, however, does not cause people to kill others. After all, most socioeconomically disadvantaged people do not commit violent crimes. What, then, accounts for the strong relationship between homicide and both racial and economic inequality? A widely cited answer to this question, one that attempts to bring us further than the subculture of violence thesis, is provided by Judith and Peter Blau (1982).

They argue that "sheer poverty" or the absence of material goods (cars, houses, color TVs, and so on) does not motivate poor people to kill others. Rather, homicide is the product of *relative deprivation.* In other words, disenfranchised people commit homicide because they harbor deep feelings of despair, frustration, hopelessness, resentment, and alienation generated by inequalities that they define as unjust. (Inequality that is not seen as unfair would not be a problem.) For example, impoverished African-Americans are told that "all men are created equal"; however, they can see the economic inequalities associated with their racial status, along with financial prosperity (or at least the opportunities for employment or advancement) of others. This can generate deep hostility and weaken support for social norms that restrain this attitude, which ultimately can lead to violence.

Actually, this classic and path-breaking study argues that economic inequality is a strong factor in generating violence such as murder. Thus, white Americans brought up in poverty and poorly educated will generally find a lack of opportunity for success, and this will increase their crime rates. However, the addition of racial inequalities to this powerful factor creates a new dynamic that is much stronger than the effect of economic inequality alone. Simply put, "High rates of criminal violence are apparently the price of racial and economic inequalities" (Blau & Blau, 1982, p. 126).

This argument, which has influenced many other formulations on inequality and crime (Mann, 1993), is very strongly rooted in sociological theory. For example, it agrees with the implications of Robert Merton's (1968) theory, which suggests that in a class society, some people will have better opportunities than others to reach society's goals. Those with fewer opportunities will be under more pressure to deviate from the approved paths. Merton does not claim that people who are poor will automatically commit crime. Rather, he suggests that the issue is relative poverty—that it is not how much you get, but whether you are getting your fair share, that puts pressure on a person to deviate. As another example, inequality is a central part of Marxist arguments about the growing class conflicts in advanced capitalist societies.

An interesting finding of Blau and Blau (1982) also ties the theory in to some other classical sociological theory. Having discovered that poverty, race, and geographic region were by themselves insufficient explanations of homicide and other violent crime, they looked at the number of divorced and separated people living in an area. They did not argue that such people commit crimes, but rather that a very high number of broken personal relationships were a sign of what has traditionally been called *social disorganization.* The Chicago school of ecological theories of crime, one of the most influential in the early days of criminology, made just this argument that areas marked by high amounts of personal conflict would also have high rates of violent crime. Blau and Blau found that high economic inequality was found in these same neighborhoods, and thus higher rates of violent crime.

Raymond Michalowski makes a similar argument, in trying to explain further just why it is that, for crimes such as murder, the offender typically does not attack those who are oppressing him, but people of his own social group:

> Humans do not generally attack or steal the property of those with whom they feel a sense of moral community. Moral community

refers to the body of people toward whom we feel a sense of obligation and human concern. Inequality tends to narrow people's moral community by creating material and social barriers between different segments of society and by placing individuals in competitive rather than cooperative relations as a result of the struggle to improve *personal* position in a world of inequalities. As individuals, particularly the least well off, come to feel that the deprivations and disappointments in their lives are proof that people in general care little about what happens to them, their sense of shared obligation with those others tends to weaken. This weakening of a felt sense of moral obligation toward others makes committing crimes against them much easier. (1985, pp. 408–409)

Thus, as suggested elsewhere in this chapter, some men find that the most important thing in their life is to gain status, save face, or pick up some small power by bullying another person. Under the wrong conditions, these little acts can escalate to murder.

SUMMARY

The main objective of this chapter was to answer the question: Why do people commit homicide? Four major theoretical perspectives were evaluated: routine activities theory, feminist theory, the subculture of violence theory, and Judith and Peter Blau's account of inequality and violence. Although the subculture of violence theory still appeals to some criminologists, the other three perspectives are more likely to be used, alone or in combination, to explain the amount of homicide. Feminist theory is particularly important in reminding us that a certain amount of homicide (certainly not all, or even most) is targeted at women just because they are women. Routine activities theory helps us to understand why homicide occurs in certain places, at certain times, to certain people. However, the most important of the three theories is the one that points to inequality. As Blau and Blau note, it is not just poverty that accounts for homicide, or else poor people everywhere would commit more crime than they do. Rather, we must develop a complex analysis that takes into account poverty and racial inequality in the richest nation on earth, in an atmosphere that denies equal opportunity but blames those who are shut out for their own failures. We may wish to add to this some understanding of how, when there is very little of material value (or the prospects of a future) to fight over, marginalized inner-city minority youths may find honor and dignity a value worth dying over.

How can we curb the alarmingly high rate of homicide in the United States? Several answers to this question are provided and evaluated in the last chapter of this text.

SUGGESTED READINGS

Currie, E. (1985). *Confronting Crime: Why There Is So Much Crime in America and What We Can Do About It.* New York: Pantheon.

  Currie attempts to explain why violent crime rates in the United States greatly exceed those in any other industrialized nation. In addition, he clearly shows the inadequacy of conservative theories and polices, and he offers progressive, short-term control and prevention strategies.

Holmes, R. M., and Holmes, S. T. (1994). *Murder in America.* Newbury Park, CA: Sage.

  This book provides a comprehensive, intelligible overview of the criminological literature on "atypical homicides," such as serial homicide, mass murder, terrorist killings, and assassination. More common forms of homicide are also addressed, although in less detail.

Mann, C. R. (1993). *Unequal Justice: A Question of Color.* Bloomington: Indiana University Press.

  Mann provides an overview of the empirical, theoretical, and policy issues surrounding African-Americans involved in homicide and other crimes. Her book also includes an excellent account of the way skin color determines how racial/ethnic minorities are unjustly treated by the U.S. legal system.

Reiss, A., and Roth, J. (1993). *Understanding and Preventing Violence.* Washington, DC: National Academy Press.

  This comprehensive book is an excellent resource for an interdisciplinary approach to understanding and preventing various types of violent crime in the United States.

Silverman, R., and Kennedy, L. (1993). *Deadly Deeds: Murder in Canada.* Scarborough, Ontario: Nelson.

  This is an excellent resource for data on the extent, distribution, and correlates of homicide in Canada. Major theories and policy proposals are also included.

CHAPTER 9

VIOLENCE AGAINST WOMEN IN INTIMATE RELATIONSHIPS

Lew lunged at me and grabbed me, holding me with his left hand, pushing the plate of stew in my face with his right hand. The scalding pain was more than I could bear. I screamed and screamed. He slapped me, kicked me, and pulled my hair until I just didn't know what was happening anymore. I started to run, and he grabbed me and ripped my dress as I was running. I didn't know what to do. I ran into our bedroom, instantly realizing I had made a mistake. I knew he'd follow me there and beat me more.

QUOTED IN WALKER, 1979, PP. 102–103

Why would any woman put up with that sort of abuse and not leave immediately? As we shall see in this chapter, that is probably the number one question asked about battered women: Why don't they just leave? Unfortunately, there are no easy answers. One of the goals of this chapter is to try to give you enough information so that you can begin to understand some of the dynamics behind such relationships.

But why are we devoting an entire textbook chapter to it? The topic is most often either ignored in criminology or else given a one- or two-page treatment in textbooks on social problems or marriage and the family. Our contention is that this is a criminology issue, and one of the most important ones. The incident described in the chapter opening isn't minor, rare, or a private problem. In fact, violence by male intimates may be *the* major cause of injury to women today, and it certainly accounts for an enormous percentage of emergency room work dealing with all women (Warshaw, 1993). Every day, thousands of women in the United States and Canada are brutally beaten by husbands, ex-husbands, live-in lovers, dates, and boyfriends. We know that violence against women is also common in developing nations (Counts, Brown, & Campbell, 1992; Levinson, 1989), although it is even more difficult to accurately estimate the extent of male violence against women in the Third World than it is in the more developed nations.[1] Certainly, whatever we might think about the sanctity of the family or the need to stay out of people's private homes, these violent assaults are illegal based on the legalistic definitions discussed in Chapter 2. The immense numbers of these crimes means that we cannot understand the nature of illegal violence in North America today without looking carefully at the home as the location of a tremendous proportion of this violence.

Some people might be concerned that this chapter is not completely even-handed—that we are not giving as much coverage to female violence against males as to male violence against females. The simple reason for this is that most serious violence is against women. Some surveys that call very minor events "violence" have reported equal rates of male and female violence, but those surveys that focus on *serious* violence have found that most violent persons are men. For example, the U.S. Department of Justice's Bureau of Justice Statistics has estimated that women are ten times as likely to be victimized by men as the reverse. Stated in another way, women make up over 90 percent of all victims of violence committed by an intimate (BJS, 1994). If the violence was committed by a spouse, it was a male doing the violence 93 percent of the time. If it was committed by a boyfriend or girlfriend, it was a male 91 percent of the time. If it was an ex-spouse, it was a male 89 percent of the time. Worse, if women are attacked by an intimate, they are much more likely to be injured, require medical care, and require hospitalization (BJS, 1994). For these reasons, our primary goal in studying violence against intimates must be understanding violence against women.

Until fairly recently, a typical reaction to women's brutal "atrocity tales" was either to ignore them or to respond insensitively. For example, many people feel that men have the right to hit their partners under certain conditions (Gelles & Straus, 1988). In 1982, when Margaret Mitchell asked her Canadian federal Parliamentary colleagues to address the problem of wife-battering, "Her motion was met with roars of laughter and ridicule. The idea of wife abuse as a social problem was a joke to these honourable men who governed the land" (Faith, 1993b, p. 1).

---

[1] Most of the information we have comes from ethnographic studies. As we saw in Chapter 4, these techniques provide rich information, but it is difficult to know if the data are representative of the larger populations. Nevertheless, information gathered in non-Western nations strongly suggests that male-to-female violence is a serious problem there.

If politicians and the general public alike were guilty of trivializing or ignoring the plight of physically abused women, the same can be said about psychologists, sociologists, and other social scientists. Twenty-five years ago, a bibliography of virtually all of the sociological, criminological, and psychological professional literature on wife abuse would probably have fit on a single index card. One oft-cited example of this neglect is that the highly prestigious and widely read *Journal of Marriage and the Family*, from its beginning in 1939 to 1969, did not contain even a single article about marital violence (O'Brien, 1971) despite the fact that wife abuse has existed as a central feature of married life for at least 2,700 years (Dobash & Dobash, 1979).

Since 1970, both battered women and feminist scholars have struggled to focus public attention on the problem. Today, the general public, government agencies, the mass media, and academics are more sensitive to the amount and consequences of violence in intimate relationships. Although the effectiveness of this policy is a topic for debate, police are now required to arrest wife beaters in many North American jurisdictions (Hirschel et al., 1992; Sherman, 1992). Also, a small amount of government funds are allocated to battered women's shelters and rehabilitation programs for abusive men. Meanwhile, fictional and nonfictional stories of woman abuse are commonplace in the media, national surveys are being conducted, and thousands of academic journal articles and hundreds of scholarly books on male-to-female violence have been published. In fact, as we have argued elsewhere, advances in the social scientific study of various forms of woman abuse have been faster paced than some of the major developments in the physical sciences (Schwartz & DeKeseredy, 1988).

There is a flip side to this sudden attention by mass media and scholarly writers. Many people hearing about the problem for the first time have the impression that violence against women is a new social problem. A similar belief is that, with so much attention being given to the problem in the press, some sort of "epidemic" of violence against women must be going on. Of course, we cannot conclusively prove that there is more or less woman abuse than in previous generations, particularly since no attempts to measure the amount of woman abuse in society were made until recently. Still, social scientists who have examined the historical record see no reason to believe that contemporary men are more likely to be abusive than their ancestors (DeKeseredy, 1992; Straus, Gelles, & Steinmetz, 1981). For that matter, with the recent shift toward harsh "law-and-order" responses to abusive men (for example, mandatory arrest policies) and the new wave of both public and professional concern, men may be less likely to physically harm female intimates today than in the past. Although it is very unlikely that harsh policies are having a direct effect on very many men (Sherman, 1992), we don't know the overall effect of spreading the message generally that this is unacceptable behavior.

Be that as it may, this should not be read as a statement that violence against women is not a major problem in North America today. The extensive professional literature of the past two decades shows that social scientists now have a substantial body of information on the extent, distribution, correlates, and sources of male violence in romantic, heterosexual relationships. We have somewhat less information on violence in lesbian relationships (Renzetti, 1992) and rather less on male battering within gay relationships (Island & Letellier, 1991). A second purpose of this chapter is to review the current state of sociological knowledge on these issues. Before we do, however, it is necessary to clarify what we mean by violence against women.

DEFINITION OF VIOLENCE AGAINST WOMEN

What is violence against women? For some people, the answer to this question is simple—an intentional physical act such as a punch, kick, or bite, that results in physical trauma. For example, the influential magazine *Sports Illustrated,* in the midst of a media frenzy over figure skater Tonya Harding, suggested that despite the restraining orders and the divorce she had obtained against her husband, there was little "hard evidence" that she was abused—"no broken bones or black eyes" (Swift, 1994, p. 30). Many people still accept that definition of woman abuse. Many workers in shelter homes cynically refer to this definition as the "stitch rule"—they feel that many justice system workers believe that if you don't need to have stitches, you are not hurt. Criminologists, however, have begun to propose a number of new definitions, many of which purposely include a much broader range of behaviors that injure women in some way. Perhaps the most inclusive is the one proposed by Cannie Stark-Adamec and P. Adamec (1982), who argue that spousal violence refers to anything a male spouse has done or not done to his partner that is perceived as psychologically, socially, economically, or physically harmful.

Another set of fairly broad definitions comes to us from recent British radical feminist writings. These authors regard violence as existing on a continuum that ranges from nonphysical acts such as obscene phone calls to physical acts such as beating someone up (see, for example, Kelly, 1987, 1988). Although the idea of a continuum is often used to portray moving from the least serious to the most serious, it is important that, to these writers, all of these behaviors are serious. Because none is automatically considered more injurious than another, they recommend that researchers not create a hierarchy of abuse or violence. There are excellent theoretical reasons to use such a broad definition. Catherine Kirkwood (1993), for example, points out that some seriously abused women are drawn into a web of long-term terror through a barrage of events that many of us might regard as minor. In some cases of severe psychological abuse, the woman may not even ever be physically harmed! For example, the man might kill the woman's household pet in front of her and the children, destroy property such as her favorite objects or things she made in a crafts class, constantly humiliate her in public, forbid her to work or to go to school, force her to give up her friends by insisting that he should be good enough to meet all of her needs, or withhold affection. These forms of psychological abuse are all very common events. Another common form of abuse has been called "economic brutality," whereby, for example, a man always has enough money for his needs but leaves his wife short of grocery money (let alone personal money) to feed herself and the children (MacLeod, 1987). In fact, both Kirkwood (1993) and Lenore Walker (1979) found that most of the women they interviewed considered episodes of psychological humiliation and verbal abuse to be their worst experiences, regardless of whether they had been physically attacked. This finding should be carefully reread and considered. Battered women who were physically injured said that the emotional and psychological attacks they endured were worse than the physical pain. This is a very powerful finding.

Unfortunately, these definitions have one drawback: some are so broad that almost every woman on the continent might seem to have been victimized by a male intimate. Such broad definitions of violence are not common in North America, perhaps because of critics who argue that combining a wide range of acts makes it more difficult to identify the causes of violence (Gelles & Cornell, 1985). After all, it is much more difficult to study fifty things at once than to study a single thing. Thus, most North American researchers have restricted their attention to sublethal, nonsexual physical assaults, such as punches, kicks, and slaps. On the one hand, this more narrow definition is a better fit with the "commonsense" views of women who are not physically battered ("Sticks and stones may break my bones but words will never hurt me"). On the other hand, unfortunately, this focus on physical assaults does not reflect the brutal reality of many women's lives and sets up a hierarchy that insists (even though we know different) that physical harm is worse than psychological, sexual, or economic harm (Breines & Gordon, 1983; MacLeod, 1987). In our opinion, these nonphysical acts should be considered part of any definition of woman abuse. However, at the time this book was written, we found that virtually all of that work has been on only nonsexual, physically injurious behaviors.

WHY DON'T BATTERED WOMEN LEAVE HOME?

As mentioned previously, perhaps the most commonly asked question about violence in intimate relationships is why women don't get up and leave. In fact, the most commonly cited theory about wife abuse in North America, Lenore Walker's "learned helplessness" theory (Walker, 1979), was specifically devised to explain why beaten women do not leave relationships. One answer is that perhaps the overwhelming majority of women *do* leave. One British survey placed the number at 88 percent (Horley, 1991), and Martin Schwartz (1988b) argued, based on U.S. National Crime Victimization Survey data, that most women leave abusive relationships. This information is essential, Schwartz (1989, p. 57) suggests, because it changes our perception of women generally:

> Much of the literature in the field, whether accusatory, apologetic or embarrassed in tone, attempts to deal with the underlying problem of why it is that women are weak, vulnerable and unable to help themselves. . . . If, in fact, large numbers, even the majority of female victims are able to take effective steps to reduce or eliminate violence in their lives, the tone must shift dramatically.

In any case, some women clearly are trapped in abusive relationships. Sandra Horley (1991) suggests that our question would be best directed toward "what keeps her from leaving" rather than "why does she stay." The issue is made more difficult by the fact that not all women or relationships are alike. The woman may be heavily invested emotionally and psychologically in her relationship, may be ideologically opposed to divorce, or may even see her abuser as an emotionally dependent person who badly needs her warmth, care, and nurturance. These women don't want the *relationship* to end; they want the *violence* to end.

There are many other reasons a woman might stay in an abusive relationship. Some women are simply afraid to leave—often with excellent reason. They have become convinced that they will be beaten if they stay but killed if they try to leave (see the intimate femicide section in Chapter 8). After living with such men for years, they are often much better judges than we of what they are capable of doing. Other women are afraid of being on their own. This may be an economic issue, whereby they just don't believe they can house and feed their children. It may be a problem of self-esteem, whereby after years of being belittled, they have come to believe that they are not capable of making decisions for themselves. Generally, however, attempts to study battered women to see how they are "different" (low self-esteem, low intelligence, less economic resources, a history of violence in the family, personality differences) are rarely fruitful. More likely, battered women are just like any other women, except that they have been caught in a situation of frightening proportions (Barnett & LaViolette, 1993).

How can a "normal" woman end up like this, when we all "know" that if it happened to us we'd be out the door in a flash (or else we'd be changing the door locks just as fast)? Catherine Kirkwood (1993) uses the concept of a "web" to explain how it is emotional abuse, not physical abuse, that ties women to these relationships. Of course, physical abuse is also emotional abuse: How do you feel emotionally right after being beaten up? Rather than being constrained by a single thread, many women are caught in a web of factors, delicately interlaced and interconnected, that hold and trap them. No one strand can be isolated and viewed on its own; each receives support from the other strands. Further, this web is invisible, so that a *Sports Illustrated* reporter may not necessarily see any broken bones or black eyes.

What are these strands? They are many and have been often identified in the literature. They may be the result of acts of individual men, such as subjecting the woman to constant degradation and denigration; imposing a constant and never-ending fear that a beating may be coming at any time, day or night; cutting the woman off from any potential support such as friends, family, ministers, or doctors; forcing her to live in economic deprivation while the man always has enough money for his hobbies; and eventually creating emotional dependency, so that she has no outlets for joy or solace except her very oppressor. Or, as feminist literature has long pointed out, the strands may be societal, based on traditional ideas that men should be superior in the family and that they have the right to enforce that tradition with violence. R. Emerson Dobash and Russell Dobash (1979) became widely influential for their idea that it is the very nature of the family, and the societal ideology that men must always be in charge (patriarchy), that causes this violence. Andrea Dworkin (1993, p. 238), who was battered in a marriage, eloquently portrays what it is like when the neighbors refuse to acknowledge your screams, your family ignores your bruises, the doctors are uninterested in where your injuries came from and force you to take tranquilizers because you are getting upset, and the police won't help you: "You cannot talk to anyone because they will not help you and if you do talk, the man who is battering you will hurt you more. Once you lose language, your isolation is absolute."

Unfortunately, in dealing with humans, nothing is ever as simple as it looks. This analysis is made much more complex by the fact that some people are able to apply the ideas just outlined to situations that do not seem to follow the proper script. For example, similar abuse occurs in lesbian relationships. Claire Renzetti (1992) argues that violence is found in these relationships as often as in heterosexual relationships. Lesbian abuse is marked mainly by one partner being in extreme dependency on the other and feeling a need to use violence to exert power and domination over the other. Lesbians may be bound by a particularly sticky strand in that they may have even less support outside the relationship than anyone else. Their relationship may be secret from family or employers, supports such as shelters or public services may be even less available to them than to other battered women, and the lesbian community itself may be too confused and embarrassed that this "male" disease has hit them to offer enough support.

Other groups or individuals in society may have other strands that bind them. For example, although we know too little about African-American women who are the victims of violence in relationships (Rasche, 1988), we can suggest that these women may be under enormous pressure from their

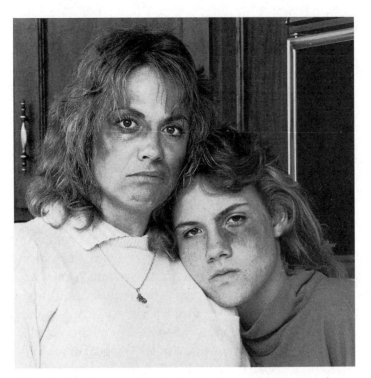

Often, the best short-run help that battered women can receive is from each other in shelter houses. These homes don't solve any problems, but they give aid, comfort, and a chance to make some decisions.

communities to accept male violence and the explanation that it is caused by the stress of being the object of racism from the white community. In fact, Beth Richie (1985) argues, from this base has come the idea of the black matriarch or strong black woman, where "the role of the black women in our families is to receive regular whippings in order to alleviate black men's stress. Clearly this is a dangerous portrayal" (p. 42). Still, Martin Schwartz and Christine Mattley (1993) suggest, even with a different heritage, perspective, and conditions, African-American women share with white women many of the same experiences of battering. Women from other ethnic groups may have their own sticky web strands, such as language difficulties, fear of the police or social service agencies, cultural traditions against getting a divorce or asking for help outside the ethnic group, or a host of other factors that make the web even tighter for them.

Kirkwood, who introduced us to the concept of the web, uses another metaphor that is just as helpful: the spiral. The strands in the spider's web are farther apart at the outer edges, so the fly finds it is easier to escape. Toward the center, however, the strands are tightly packed and work together to hold the fly in place. Kirkwood (1993) discusses factors that bring a woman spiraling toward the center, making it more difficult for her to escape an abusive relationship. These include a lowered self-esteem, a lowered sense of self-identity, health changes such as a significant weight gain or loss, or depression or a loss of hope. "In other words, the use of emotional abuse and physical violence acted to reduce the resources on which a woman might draw to challenge her partner's control or leave an abusive partner" (Kirkwood, 1993, p. 73). However, all is not always lost. After all, many women do leave on their own (Bowker, 1983; NiCarthy, 1987), and many women go to shelters. Helping them to spiral outward to the edges of the web are awareness factors such as the realization of how much they have changed from their formerly much more interesting and valuable self or how badly the children were reacting. Different people react differently to these new insights. Some carefully plan their escape. Some erupt in anger at what has been done to them, which could motivate a quick escape. For example, one battered woman told us:

> After 15 years of physical and mental abuse, I turned into "Lorena Bobbitt." I had cajoled and done everything I could over the years to help my husband's weak self-esteem and finally one night I snapped. I grabbed my 6-foot, 200-pound husband, flung him on the floor (all 5 foot, 95 pounds of me). He was so shocked, he laid there and took it. It was a great triumph for my self-esteem and the realization that my husband was the one with the problem, not me. Empowered, I divorced him quickly before I changed my mind, and left Youngstown to be with my family where I could get support.

A very few women, convinced that their husband will kill them if they try to leave, convert this anger and fear into a homicidal act. Box 9.1 describes one such case.

Thus, although some argue that battered women are in a state of "learned helplessness," where they are paralyzed into fear and cannot leave their situations, others argue that these women are active agents of their own lives. They may be in a state of compliance, like the hostages of terrorists, who know that doing what they are told is the best way to get out alive. However, as Sandra Horley (1991, p. 91) points out, when all of a woman's energies are focused on short-term survival, "They may seem submissive and passive, but in fact, in all sorts of often subtle ways, they fight back, they adopt survival techniques and actively find ways of coping."

HOW MUCH MALE VIOLENCE AGAINST WOMEN IS THERE?

How many North American women are victimized by their current or former male intimates? We really don't know. Although many estimates have been made, every data set underestimates the true extent of this problem. Think about how you would go about finding out how much woman abuse exists. What would you do? Look at the records of the police or other public officials? Go door to door and ask women if they have been beaten? Clearly, any method is inadequate. Many women suffer in silence or do not reveal their experiences to researchers or public officials because they are embarrassed by them or because they are terrified of retaliation or reprisal if their abuser finds out they revealed their victimization. Amazingly enough, some people have suffered such severe blows to their self-image (Kirkwood, 1993) that they think their experiences are too trivial to mention, while others do not wish to discuss their problems with researchers because they do not wish to recall painful memories (Smith, 1987).

Getting violent men to accurately disclose the amount of abuse they commit is even more difficult, especially during those times when substantial media attention is being given to issues surrounding woman abuse. Even if these men are guaranteed confidentiality and anonymity, they may fear that they will eventually be punished for victimizing their partners, or they may worry about being publicly humiliated. For example, as you will see in Tables 9.1 and 9.2, sharp discrepancies exist between the violence estimates generated from talking to men and from talking to women. Women are more likely to report victimization experiences than men are to disclose their injurious behavior. As we said, we know that the numbers on both of these tables suffer from a significant amount of underreporting, but we simply do not know the extent of this underreporting.

THE TRUE STORY OF A BATTERED WOMAN

Jennifer is a very intelligent woman who excelled throughout high school in academics, athletics and student government. While working in a bakery before attending college, she met and became pregnant by a co-worker, Jacques, whom she then married. Months later, he told her he was an illegal alien from France and was facing deportation had Jennifer not married him.

From the beginning, the marriage was marred by Jacques' drinking and continual verbal abuse, as well as occasional physical violence. Jennifer moved out, but the two were reconciled when Jacques expressed remorse. Soon afterwards, their daughter, Marie, was born. Months later, when Jennifer became pregnant again because Jacques forbade her to use birth control, he blamed her and ordered her to abort the unborn child. He continually accused her of affairs with other students at college, screened her phone calls, and in a fit of jealous rage over an alleged suitor, once doused her with lighter fluid and began throwing lit matches at her as she ran in terror. Jacques would also continually berate Jennifer about what an unfit mother she was. During this time, Jennifer was attending college full-time as a student, mothering, and working the night shift at United Parcel Service.

At Jacques' insistence and against her wishes, Jennifer aborted her unborn child. This marked a major turning point in their relationship because it destroyed what little self-esteem Jennifer had left. The more she had attempted to change her marital situation, defend herself, or leave, the worse the abuse and the more futile her attempts became. Jacques would tie her up and vaginally and anally rape her, insert pins or needles into her nipples, and burn parts of her body.

Jacques also had strong ideas about how much Jennifer should earn. Through increased beatings, blackmail, and the threat of disappearing with Marie, he forced her to quit school and work as an exotic dancer. Jennifer was now completely isolated from friends and family. Two months later, Jennifer found that she was pregnant once more. By this time, she knew better than to even consider fighting back. Shortly afterwards, Jacques tied Jennifer to the oak coffee table and attempted an abortion on her with a coathanger. Doctors' reports to the court confirm the internal bleeding, cervical tearing, and scarring of her vagina, perineum, buttocks, and ankles, as well as a prolapsed uterus, all stemming from this and other violent sexual abuse. Jennifer quietly underwent an abortion and quit her dancing job. There was a brief period of calm in the marriage, and Jennifer again got an excellent job, but that only fueled Jacques' rage. That summer, Jennifer sought refuge with her parents after Jacques strangled her into unconsciousness during a particularly heated argument. As Jacques' drinking and abuse escalated, Jennifer resolved to leave for good.

Judiciously, fearful of reprisal by Jacques if he knew about her plans, she began to plot her escape by applying to college and asking her employers for a transfer. She began slowly buying the items she would need to set up a home for Marie and herself. Jacques, however, had a new idea: she would make big money by becoming an escort in a luxury hotel. Knowing the futility of fighting back, Jennifer acquiesced. It was now more imperative than ever that she buy herself time until she could take Marie and leave Jacques for good.

Then, Jennifer and her mother discovered blood-stained diapers belonging to Marie after Jacques had been babysitting. Jennifer began taking measures to ensure Marie was *never* left alone with Jacques. Meanwhile, Jennifer was notified that she had received a full scholarship to Rice University. Freedom was becoming a reality. She would placate Jacques until she could leave. Her grandmother contacted an attorney about obtaining a divorce.

Then, on March 14, 1987, the most heated argument of their marriage ensued. Jennifer stood her ground, refusing to ever prostitute herself again or to give Jacques any of her money. She told Jacques she was leaving him and going to Houston with Marie. She admitted to having an affair. Ultimately, Jennifer confronted Jacques with the fact that she knew he'd molested Marie. The argument escalated to the point that Jacques threatened to kill both Marie and Jennifer. Jennifer retrieved a gun from her car and went back into the house to get Marie from the back bedroom. When Jacques lunged at Jennifer and tried to grab the gun, she shot him.

Jennifer was charged with first-degree murder in the shooting death of her husband. Although the state originally sought the death penalty, Jennifer was found guilty of the lesser charge of second-degree murder with a firearm and sentenced to thirty years in prison.

Still, even if it is impossible to obtain totally accurate data, some methods are more reliable than others. The best procedures are representative-sample self-report and victimization surveys specifically designed to collect data on male-to-female violence (DeKeseredy & Hinch, 1991; Gelles & Straus, 1988; Smith, 1987). Thus, only the results of these studies are presented here. This is not to say that other methods cannot provide valuable insight; however, only random sample surveys of various populations can give us fairly reliable estimates of how much violence takes place in cities, towns, countries, states, and provinces, and on university and college campuses. The basic idea of a *random sample survey* is that, while it is impossible to question everyone in the country or a city, if everyone has an equal chance of being selected as an interviewee, then we would only need to question a smaller number of them. For example, to interview everyone in Chicago would require an extraordinary number of interviewers. Worse, by the time you tracked everyone down, the answers from the first people interviewed would be so old that they probably could not be properly compared to the responses from the most recent interviews. Thus, researchers would choose a representative sample of all of the people in Chicago; if this is done correctly, experience has shown many times that their answers will adequately represent what we would have found if we had interviewed everyone. Of course, as a cautionary note, you should be aware that some of the surveys we discuss are more methodologically sound than others.

North American researchers use different ways of collecting data on violence among intimates, but the most common measure is the Conflict Tactics Scale (CTS) (Straus, 1990). Developed by University of New Hampshire sociologist Murray Straus, this quantitative procedure has appeared in hundreds of scientific journal articles and at least five books (Straus, 1990). The CTS generally consists of eighteen items that measure three different ways of handling interpersonal conflict in intimate relationships: reasoning, verbal aggression,[2] and physical violence. The items are ranked on a continuum from least to most severe, with the first ten describing nonviolent tactics and the last eight describing violent strategies. The last five items, from "kicked," "bit," or "hit with a fist" to "used a knife or a gun," make up what Murray Straus, Richard Gelles, and Suzanne Steinmetz (1981) refer to as the "severe violence index."

---

[2] Several researchers (for example, DeKeseredy & Kelly, 1993a; Hornung, McCullough, & Sugimoto, 1981) refer to the verbal aggression items as psychological abuse measures.

The type of CTS used to measure adult male-to-female intimate violence that occurred in the past year (incidence) is generally introduced as follows:

> No matter how well a couple gets along, there are times when they disagree on major decisions, get annoyed about something the other person does, or just have spats or fights because they're in a bad mood or tired or for some other reason. They also use different ways of trying to settle their differences. I'm going to read a list of some things that you and your partner might have done when you had a dispute, and would first like you to tell me for each one how often you did it in the past year.

There is a problem in the overall interpretation of any data obtained from this question, however. On a positive note, researchers have argued that the data generated by the CTS are "probably the best available when it comes to estimating the incidence and prevalence of woman abuse in the population at large" (Smith, 1987, p. 177). On the other hand, many other researchers have criticized the CTS for the following reasons:

- Because the CTS rank-orders behaviors in a linear fashion, it incorrectly assumes that psychological abuse and the first three violence items (for example, slaps) are less injurious than those in the severe violence index (Breines & Gordon, 1983). This is a perfect example of the type of criticism made by Liz Kelly (1988), which was discussed earlier. Emotional abuse may indeed be more harmful than physical abuse.

- The CTS misses many forms of violence by not asking about such events as scratches, burns, suffocation, sexual assaults, and more (Smith, 1986). As we will see later in this chapter, sexual assaults in particular may be a major part of the violence in a relationship.

- The CTS ignores the context, meaning, and motives of violence (Breines & Gordon, 1983; Dobash et al., 1992). This criticism has been most heavily used against Straus for discussing female violence against men when the CTS does not measure self-defense (Schwartz & DeKeseredy, 1993). The problem, simply, is that asking if you hit someone doesn't inform the researcher of the circumstances. If you throw a shoe at your husband, trying to get away from him while he chases you with a machete screaming that he is going to kill you, the CTS shows you as violent (you hit him with a shoe) and him as nonviolent (he never touched you).

- The survey question situates violence only in the context of settling quarrels or disputes. Many women claim that there was no external reason or dispute to mediate before their husband began to beat them. Even when there are "disputes," when we know the full context, we often find that the problem is that the husband didn't like dinner, was upset because the baby cried, or suffered from completely irrational jealousy.

- The CTS overlooks the wider social forces that motivate men to victimize their female partners (Breines & Gordon, 1983; DeKeseredy, 1988a).

In response to these criticisms, several people have developed innovative ways of modifying the CTS or have used additional measures to capture data on behaviors that it overlooks. For example, Walter DeKeseredy and Katharine Kelly (1993a) and Michael Smith (1987) included supplementary questions on abuse in their questionnaires, which can be effective ways of eliciting more information. Some of Smith's silent or forgetful respondents (N = 60) changed their answers when asked again later in the interview. Belated reports increased the prevalence rate of violence by approximately 10 percent.[3] Further, twenty-one belated disclosures to lengthy questions increased the severe violence prevalence rate.

Table 9.1 presents CTS incidence and prevalence rates of wife assault found in major U.S. and Canadian representative sample surveys.[4] These findings reveal that annually at least 11 percent of the North American women in marital/cohabiting relationships are physically abused by their male partners. However, Canadian men appear to be more violent toward female intimates than their U.S. counterparts. For example, Eugen Lupri's (1990) annual incidence rate of 18 percent is markedly higher than the rate from national data gathered by Straus, Gelles, and Steinmetz (1981)

---

[3]Prevalence was defined as the percentage of women who reported ever having been victimized.
[4]This is a slightly modified version of a table constructed by Smith (1989). Except for Brinkerhoff and Lupri's (1988) study, all of the Canadian surveys described in this table include separated and divorced respondents.

(12.1 percent) and Straus and Gelles (1986) (11.3 percent). Merlin Brink-erhoff and Lupri's (1988) Calgary estimate (24.5 percent) is even higher.

If marriage/cohabiting is a dangerous context for North American women, then the same can be said about those in adult dating relationships. For example, national CTS data presented in Table 9.2 show that in any given year at least 13.7 percent of North American women who date men are assaulted by them. U.S. rates obtained from both men and women, however, are considerably higher than those obtained in Canada by De-Keseredy and Kelly (1993a). Thus, when it comes to interacting with their dating partners, U.S. men are more likely to use physical force.

The most common advice given to women in these relationships is simply to terminate them. However, many women have found that they are at even greater risk of being assaulted after breaking off a relationship than they were when they were in a marriage or dating relationship. Using National Crime Victimization Survey data, Martin Schwartz (1988b) found that separated and divorced women were more likely to report assaults from spouses and ex-spouses than women currently living with their husbands. Canadian sociologists using the CTS reported similar findings. For example, Lupri's (1990) national data show that the percentage of married/cohabiting men who victimized their partners (18 percent) is markedly lower than the percentage of violent separated/divorced men (30 percent). Leslie Kennedy and Donald Dutton's (1989) Alberta study found even higher rates for divorced (39.8 percent) and separated people (54.8 percent). A high rate of postseparation violence was also obtained by Desmond Ellis and Lori Wright's (1987) less sophisticated non–probability sample survey. Of their separated or divorced female respondents (N = 89), 46 percent experienced some form of violent victimization and/or threats of physical assault by their former partners. Moreover, 26 of the 41 survivors of postseparation violence stated that they were not assaulted prior to separation.[5]

Unfortunately, crime prevention advice usually fails to take this information into account. Women are commonly warned about the dangers of living and traveling alone and the need to avoid unlit areas, but they are

---

[5] Several other studies report that separated and divorced women are at great risk of being physically assaulted (Bowker, 1983; Browne, 1987; Ellis & Stuckless, 1992; Gaquin, 1977–78; Giles-Sims, 1983; Levinger, 1966; MacLeod, 1980; O'Brien, 1971; Russell, 1990; Smith, 1990a; Statistics Canada, 1993).

Table 9.1 Surveys on Wife Abuse

	SURVEY CHARACTERISTICS				ABUSE RATES			
Survey	Survey Location and Date	Sample Description	Interview Mode	Measure of Abuse	Abused in Past Year	Severely Abused in Past Year	Abused Ever	Severely Abused Ever
Straus, Gelles, and Steinmetz (1981)	U.S. national, 1975	2,143 married or cohabiting men and women	Face-to-face	CTS (aggregate)[a]	12.1%	3.8%	—	—
Schulman (1979)	Kentucky, 1979	1,793 presently or formerly married or co-habiting women	Phone	CTS[b]	10.0%	4.1%	21.0%	8.7%
Straus and Gelles (1986)	U.S. national, 1985	3,520 presently or formerly married or co-habiting men and women	Phone	CTS (aggregate)	11.3%	3.0%	—	—
Brinkerhoff and Lupri (1988)	Calgary, 1981	526 men and women	Face-to-face and self-administered questionnaire	CTS (men only)[c]	24.5%	10.8%	—	—

Study	Location, Year	Sample	Method	Instrument				
Kennedy and Dutton (1989)	Alberta, 1987	1,045 men and women	Face-to-face and phone	CTS (aggregate)	11.2%	2.3%	—	—
Lupri (1990)	Canada national, 1986	1,530 married or cohabiting men and women	Face-to-face and mail questionnaire	CTS (men only)	17.8%	10.1%	—	—
Smith (1985)	Toronto, 1985	315 women age 18–65	Phone	CTS/open-ended questions and one supplementary question	10.8%	—	18.1%	7.3%
Smith (1987)	Toronto, 1987	604 presently or formerly married or cohabiting women	Phone	CTS and three supplementary questions	14.4%[d]	5.1%	36.4%[e]	11.3%
Statistics Canada (1993)	Canada national, 1993	12,300 women age 18 and older	Phone	CTS[f]	3.0%	—	29.0%	—

[a]Men as aggressors and women as victims from different couples.
[b]Women as victims.
[c]Men as aggressors.
[d]Past year rates based on CTS alone.
[e]Abused ever rates based on CTS (25.0, 7.8) plus supplementary questions.
[f]Includes a sexual assault item.

Table 9.2 Surveys on Woman Abuse in Dating

	SURVEY CHARACTERISTICS				ABUSE RATES			
Survey	Survey Location and Date	Sample Description	Interview Mode	Measure of Abuse	Abused in Past Year	Severely Abused in Past Year	Abused Ever	Severely Abused Ever
White and Koss (1991)	U.S. national, November 1984–March 1985	2,602 female and 2,105 male college students	Self-administered questionnaires	CTS	37% of men reported being abusive 32% of women stated that they were abused	—	—	—
Stets and Henderson (1991)	U.S. national, 1989	272 never-married persons age 18–30	Phone	CTS	21.9% of men were abusive 29.6% of women were abused	3.4% of men were abusive 8% of women were abused	—	—
DeKeseredy and Kelly (1993a)	Canada national, 1992	1,835 female and 1,307 male university/college students	Self-administered questionnaires	CTS	13.7% of men were abusive 22.3% of women were abused	—	17.8% of men were abusive 35% of women were abused[a]	—

[a] These estimates are derived from questions about events that took place since leaving high school.

rarely told that the place they are most likely to be victimized is at home by their intimate partners. Further, they are commonly told to break up such relationships when they turn violent, when this could actually put them at greater risk!

RISK MARKERS OF MALE-TO-FEMALE VIOLENCE IN INTIMATE RELATIONSHIPS

It would be nice if we could simply point to the factors that "cause" this violence. Unfortunately, as most social scientists know, this is very rarely possible when dealing with humans. What we can do is talk about correlates, or things that seem to happen at the same time. Gerald Hotaling and David Sugarman (1986) have identified at least one hundred "risk markers," or attributes associated with an increased probability of violence. The relationship may or may not be causal.

One key risk marker is whether men believe in a set of familial patriarchal attitudes and beliefs that support the abuse of women who violate the ideas of male power and control over women in intimate relationships (DeKeseredy & Schwartz, 1993a; Smith, 1990b). Men who hold these beliefs are more likely to abuse female intimates (DeKeseredy & Kelly, 1993b; Dobash & Dobash, 1979). Some relevant themes of this ideology are an insistence on women's obedience, respect, loyalty, dependency, sexual access, and sexual fidelity (Barrett & McIntosh, 1982; Dobash & Dobash, 1979; Pateman, 1988).

A second risk marker is male peer support. As your mother always said, if you hang out with the wrong crowd, you can end up bad. Certainly, that is true enough here. Many studies show that men who belong to all-male social networks that consist of wife beaters, sexists, and/or date abusers are much more likely to physically assault female intimates than those who do not have such friends. Men who are verbally encouraged by their friends to abuse women under certain conditions (for example, when they challenge men's patriarchal authority or refuse to have sexual intercourse) are also more likely to engage in this behavior than men who do not receive pro-abuse guidance or advice (DeKeseredy, 1990; DeKeseredy & Schwartz, 1993a, 1993b).

A third key risk marker is alcohol consumption. Most people who study violence against women note that alcohol often seems to be a related factor.[6] This does not mean that alcohol use *causes* violence. In fact, the reverse might be true—that is, men use alcohol as an excuse: "I'm not responsible for my behavior when I am drunk!" This excuse may be successful, as "Helen" points out:

> When Larry was sober he was the nicest person in the world. But when he was drunk . . . well, it was just like Dr. Jekyll and Mr. Hyde. He was irrational and ugly, and extremely violent to me and the kids. It was like living with two people, the nice and sober one and the drunk and evil one. (quoted in Gelles & Straus, 1988, p. 44)

By now it should be obvious that a substantial number of women are at great risk of being assaulted by their current or former male partners. However, male-to-female violence against spouses and dating partners is not evenly and randomly distributed across all social groups; indeed, some women suffer more than others. In the next section, we briefly show how wife abuse varies according to income, education, age, marital status, employment status, religion, occupational status, and race/ethnicity.[7] Following this discussion, we identify the major sociodemographic factors related to violent victimization in dating.

THE DISTRIBUTION OF WIFE ABUSE

Although violence is found in families at all income levels, lower-income men are more likely to assault than men who belong to higher-income groups (Schwartz, 1988a; Kennedy & Dutton, 1989; Lupri, 1990; Smith, 1985, 1990a; Straus, Gelles, & Steinmetz, 1981). Why are lower-income

---

[6]For comprehensive reviews of the research on the association between drinking and violence against women, see DeKeseredy and Schwartz (1993a), Hotaling and Sugarman (1986), and Kaufman Kantor and Straus (1990).

[7]For more detailed information on the sociodemographic factors associated with wife abuse, see Smith (1990a).

men more violent than their more affluent counterparts? This is a very complex question, but Lilian Rubin's (1976) analysis of working-class married life is instructive. She argues that married middle-class men have many advantages over working-class men, which may keep many of them from physically victimizing these women. Even in an atmosphere characterized by a verbal agreement over equality in the home, middle-class men have many opportunities to exercise control, and they have significantly more opportunities outside the home to demonstrate self-worth. As Martin Schwartz (1988a, p. 385) points out, working-class men

> without the ability either to demonstrate their personal power outside the family, or the resources to purchase relief from the pressures of marriage (child care, leisure, vacations), while socialized into an environment which legitimizes both violence and the position of men as the king of their own home/castle, are more likely to be in a position of overt dominance over their wives.

Interestingly, although it is common to suggest that the stresses of unemployment are particularly likely to cause men to batter women, Schwartz (1990) argues that this is not a fruitful avenue to explore. Even if it is true, the data from the National Crime Victimization Survey show that virtually all of the batterers were employed, meaning another explanation is needed to explain most battering.

Education appears to be an "inconsistent" risk marker because there are contradictory data on its relationship to wife abuse (Hotaling & Sugarman, 1986). Either researchers have found no differences at all between men of different educational levels, or else they have found very different results, with the rates sometimes highest for those who did not finish high school and sometimes highest for those who finished high school but not college.

We know that in virtually all arenas, young men are the ones most likely to commit violence. The domestic arena is no exception. Young men (especially those age 30 or younger) are much more likely to assault their wives than are older men. Based on available data, we cannot tell whether this is because as people age they learn to settle their differences without violence or because many women walk out on violent men, leaving them unmarried.

As we discussed earlier, leaving the marriage does not always end the violence (Schwartz, 1988b). Desmond Ellis and Walter DeKeseredy's (1989) analysis of data generated by several North American surveys shows that, compared to married women, cohabiting, separated, and divorced women are more likely to be victimized by the men they live or lived intimately with.

Although Michael Smith (1990a) did not find religion an important factor in Canada, Murray Straus, Richard Gelles, and Suzanne Steinmetz (1981) argued that in their national sample Jewish husbands had the lowest rate of violence, and those who were affiliated with "minority religions" (non-Protestant, -Catholic, or -Jewish) had the highest. The highest rate of all, however, was for men who did not report a religious affiliation, and the proportion of abusers in this category exceeded the proportion of Jewish abusers by a factor of nine. Whether these differences are due to the teachings of various religions (Smith, 1990a) or to the fact that people of some religions tend to have higher socioeconomic status than others has not yet been determined.

Unfortunately, there has been very little sophisticated mathematical analysis of the race/ethnicity variable. Straus, Gelles, and Steinmetz (1981) found significantly higher abuse rates among African-American families than white families and somewhat higher rates for other minority groups. Although rates of severe violence seem to have gone down, overall the African-American rate was similar in a 1985 resurvey (Hampton, Gelles, & Harrop, 1989). The same survey also found higher rates for Hispanic men (Straus & Smith, 1990). The problem is that it is difficult to work out whether these are true differences between groups or whether minority groups in the United States simply have lower incomes. In other words, given that violence is more common in the working class, could it be that race is irrelevant here but that, because a greater percentage of minorities in the United States are in the working class, it just *looks* as if African-Americans have higher rates? Lettie Lockhart (1991) provides some support for this position. In her work, she could not find differences between white and African-American women in violence victimization rates when they were matched for class differences.

In Canada, only Michael Smith has studied variations across ethnic and racial groups, and he was not able to find differences among more than a dozen ethnic groups (Smith, 1985, 1990a). However, work done on a smaller scale has supported the claim made by the Ontario Native Women's Association that "one in ten Canadian women has experienced a form of abuse while *eight out of ten Aboriginal women* [emphasis in the original] have been abused or assaulted, or can expect to be abused or assaulted" (1989, Summary).

VIOLENCE AGAINST WOMEN IN DATING

Risk markers related to sociodemographic variables are not readily apparent in the literature on dating violence. And with good reason: most research on dating violence has been done on college students in large universities, where students are generally similar (white, middle-class, young, and so on). Thus, researchers have paid more attention to such variables as stress, alcohol abuse, peer group dynamics, and dating history. There are only a few things we can say based on this literature:[8]

- Students with low socioeconomic status and low family incomes are more violent than their more advantaged counterparts.

- Among the general population, those age 18–21 are more violent than those age 22–30 (Stets & Henderson, 1991). Age, however, is not related to violence in college dating.

- Where there is a higher level of interpersonal commitment, there is more serious violence.

- Violence does not appear to vary across different religious groups.

- Hispanic and African-American daters are more violent than whites.

THEORIES OF MALE VIOLENCE AGAINST WOMEN IN INTIMATE RELATIONSHIPS

In one of the most comprehensive reviews of the theoretical literature on violence against women, Lewis Okun (1986) points out that there are at least twenty distinct theories of either family violence, woman abuse, or

---

[8]For more detailed information, see Sugarman and Hotaling's (1989) comprehensive review of the dating violence literature and Stets and Henderson's (1991) national study of daters age 18–30.

other types of violence in conjugal relationships. Almost ten years have passed since the publication of his book, and during this time, many more perspectives have been developed and empirically tested. Certainly, we will not review all these contributions here! Instead, we will present the major arguments of the most widely used and cited contemporary theoretical perspectives: psychological approaches, social support and male peer support theories, and feminist theories.

Psychological Approaches

Why do men physically assault the women they love? Perhaps the most common answer people give is that these men must be "sick" or mentally disturbed. How could a "normal" person punch, kick, stab, or shoot someone he deeply loves and depends on? Certainly, the media help to build that myth: violence against family members is generally portrayed in fiction, television, and films as involving a drunken, foreign, or criminal assailant (Gelles & Straus, 1988).

Despite the fact that such psychological accounts of violence are not as popular among criminologists as they were in the early 1970s, several researchers still believe that many men beat women because they are mentally ill, suffer from personality disorders, or consume large quantities of drugs or alcohol (see, for example, Hamberger, 1993). Much of the popular British sensibility on battered women was formed on the parallel theory, popularized by J. J. Gayford, that the women themselves can be seen as deviant or mentally ill, thus bringing the violence upon themselves (Kirkwood, 1993).

It is difficult sometimes to see men who beat their wives and children as anything other than sick. People were horrified in late 1987 by the story of Joel Steinberg, a criminal defense lawyer, and Hedda Nussbaum. Police found their 6-year-old daughter, Elizabeth, badly abused and barely alive, and her 18-month-old brother, Mitchell, not much better off. Elizabeth died soon afterwards, and both parents were charged with murder. Public sympathy certainly was not with Joel, but many held Hedda in equal contempt for not acting against Joel to save her daughter's life. He beat Elizabeth into a coma and then left her on the bathroom floor while he went out for dinner and drinks. Hedda was not yet bold enough to call for medical help (Dworkin, 1993).

The story got more complex when it was revealed that Joel frequently and savagely beat Hedda. Before living with Joel, Hedda was regarded by many as a physically attractive woman, but her appearance changed radically after several brutal incidents (Ehrlich, 1989, p. 43):

> He punched Nussbaum until her face was permanently disfigured, a shifting map of broken blood vessels—her nose smashed and splayed, her lips swollen and distorted, one ear deformed and thickened into the "cauliflower" rarely seen outside the fight game. He kicked her in the eye, which would thereafter tear uncontrollably. He chipped or knocked out several teeth.

Are men like Steinberg "sick"? Unfortunately, the data presented earlier in this chapter show that a very large number of men act or have acted like him. Statistics such as these suggest that if violence is a function of mental illness, then close to a third (if not more) of the men in our society are sick. Of course, some abusive men have clinical pathologies, but most do not (Pagelow, 1992, 1993). In fact, Richard Gelles and Murray Straus (1988) argue that only 10 percent of all incidents of intimate violence are caused by mental disorders and that psychological perspectives cannot explain the other 90 percent.

There are some other worrisome aspects to these explanations. If violent husbands, cohabiting and estranged partners, and boyfriends are in fact mentally ill, then why do they only beat their wives and not their bosses, friends, or neighbors? Admittedly, many men do attack these others, but men who beat women in intimate relationships generally do not have convictions for violence outside the home. If we are dealing with men who have terrible problems with self-control, how do they manage to keep from hitting people until they are at home alone with their loved ones? How do they manage to exercise self-control until they are in a situation where they can generally get away with beating someone up? If they are "out of control," then why do they only beat their partners instead of killing them? As Michele Bograd (1988) points out, these questions cannot be answered by psychological theories, primarily because these theories ignore the unequal distribution of power between men and women in North American society and in domestic contexts.

Although we will be dealing with policy proposals in the last chapter, it is worth mentioning that one tends to locate the solution in the same place where one locates the problem. Thus, if the problem of battering is one of the mental health of men, then the broader social system presumably does not have a problem. The solution, then, is to treat, "fix," or punish the men so that they will work within the dominant social order (Timmer & Eitzen, 1989). However, many men are motivated to victimize women by broader social forces and their peers. Policies that attack only the individual do nothing to address these factors. Dealing one man at a time will never solve this societywide problem.

Social Support and Male Peer Support Theories

A line from a Beatles' song describes very well the way to good mental health: "I get by with a little help from my friends." Simply put, social support theory now has extensive empirical evidence that people with friends and family members who offer them psychological and material resources (for example, money, housing, and so on) are healthier and better able to cope with life's stressful events than persons with few or no supportive contacts.[9] However, some types of social support can have negative consequences for the safety of women in intimate, heterosexual relationships.

The authors of this text (DeKeseredy, 1988b; DeKeseredy & Schwartz, 1993a) refer to their theories as male peer support models. Although their contributions are primarily designed to explain how college male peer groups encourage and justify abuse in dating relationships, they can also explain how male social networks contribute to wife beating and postseparation violence.

Walter DeKeseredy argues that many men experience various types of stress in intimate relationships, ranging from sexual problems to challenges to their patriarchal authority. Some men try to deal with these problems themselves while others turn to their male friends for advice, guidance, and various other kinds of social support. The resources provided by these peers may encourage and justify violence under certain conditions. Further, male peer support can influence men to victimize their current or estranged partners regardless of stress. DeKeseredy's model, as depicted in Figure 9.1, shows that intimate relationship stress and male peer support increase the

---

[9]For comprehensive reviews of this literature, see Caplan (1974), Cassel (1976), Cohen and Wills (1985), and Sarason and Sarason (1985).

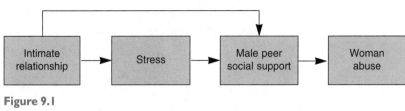

Figure 9.1
DeKeseredy's Male Peer Support Model

likelihood of violence. Relationships are associated with stress, which motivates men to seek support from their male friends. Such support increases the probability of physical assaults.

There is some empirical support for DeKeseredy's model. For example, he found that social ties with physically, sexually, and/or psychologically abusive peers is strongly related to dating abuse among men who experienced high levels of life events stress while dating. This finding supports a basic sociological argument: that the victimization of women is behavior that is socially learned in interaction with others (Scully, 1990). Even so, these results have been attacked because his data analysis procedures were not sophisticated enough and critiqued because his model does not account for other explanatory variables.

Ironically, this criticism was put forth by us; the result is our expanded male peer support model. We criticized DeKeseredy's model for excluding four important variables, some of which were discussed previously in this chapter: the ideology of familial and courtship patriarchy, alcohol consumption, membership in formal social groups (for example, fraternities), and the absence of deterrence. The last variable refers to the reluctance of various agents of social control (for example, campus administrators, police, security officers, and so on) to punish men who assault female intimates. Together with the other three variables, this factor is included our modified male peer support model, shown in Figure 9.2. Although the following discussion will focus on physical and sexual assault in dating relationships, it is just as applicable to marriage relationships (Russell, 1990; Schwartz, 1982; Schwartz & Slatin, 1984).

One of our major criticisms of the earlier model is that it looks only at individual behavior and does not recognize that such actions are smaller expressions of broader social forces. With this in mind, we added social

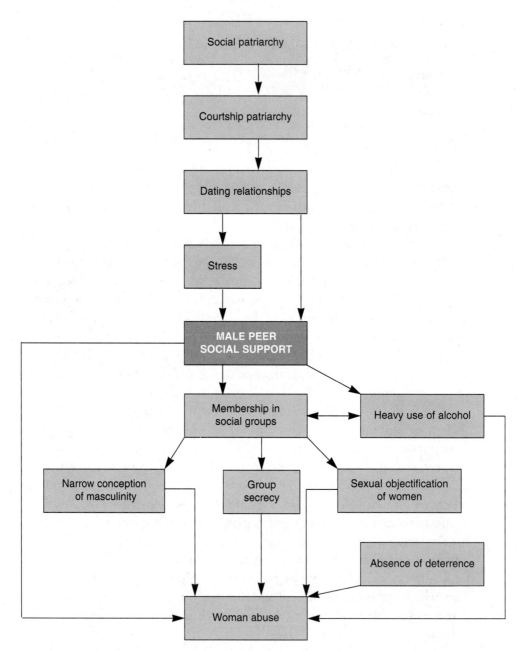

Figure 9.2
DeKeseredy and Schwartz's Modified Male Peer Support Model

patriarchy to the model. The exact definition of this term has been widely debated, but it generally refers to a set of beliefs in society suggesting that men should be in charge or in the various positions of leadership, power, and authority (Sewell, 1994). Further, the somewhat different subsystem of courtship patriarchy has been added, where ideals such as romanticism mean that relationships are handled differently than in more permanent relationships (Lloyd, 1991). In the early stages of a relationship, issues such as the connection between who paid for dinner and whether a man is "owed" sex can be rather different than later on.

The original model also did not account for the effects of alcohol. As we stated previously, although few researchers would argue a direct causal relationship (Hull & Bond, 1986), alcohol is related to woman abuse in many ways. Many of you are well aware that alcohol is a common feature of many men's social groups, such as fraternities, and is frequently used as a tool to make women unable to resist sexual aggression. For example, Martin Schwartz and Victoria Pitts (1995) found that 17.1 percent of the college women in their sample reported a man having sexual intercourse with them when they couldn't resist because they were heavily under the influence of alcohol or drugs. Alcohol is also used in contexts that support patriarchal conversations about women's sexuality and ways to control it, such as those held in "boys' nights out" in bars where men discuss the women in their lives (Hey, 1986).

Where do men receive pro-abuse social support? The answer is, in a variety of locations; however, it is most common within social groups or settings such as fraternities, athletic teams, dormitory groups, business luncheons, workplaces, or other groupings. Here, men learn many things, including a narrow conception of masculinity. In other words, men learn that a "normal" heterosexual male is one who has the following stereotypical masculine attributes: clean-cut, handsome, athletic, wealthy, a high tolerance for alcohol, and sexual success with women. They also learn that they should not have effeminate physical and personality traits or take courses in disciplines regarded as the domains of women and homosexuals, such as nursing, social work, art, and music (Martin & Hummer, 1989).

This may well be the area that is most in need of future study. We presume that all men are socialized into a single form of masculinity, which they then adopt. However, this is clearly not the case. Some men adopt the goals they are being taught, but others reject these goals, live in serious conflict about these goals, "fake it"—pretending to agree with the goals to go along with the guys (Jefferson, 1994). It is important to note that this model only suggests that some men continue down the path toward woman abuse. Others drop out. What has not been well studied is the possibility, as Carol Bohmer and Andrea Parrot (1993) suggest, that it is fraternity *pledges* who are most likely to commit date rape, since they are under the most pressure to conform and have had the least time to formulate a way to confirm their masculinity without acting out what they have been taught.

Another thing men learn from their peers is the importance of group secrecy. Men are told that they should not reveal their friends' violent actions to outsiders, such as the police or college administrators. In effect, group secrecy condones male violence because these men are supported by the group and avoid any punishment. Further, they learn the sexual objectification of women, either informally in bar discussions and the like or through the actions of more organized groups such as fraternities, who may use women as "bait" to bring in new members, as adornments, or as servants at parties.

The final factor missing from DeKeseredy's model is an absence of deterrence. Although male social networks may reward members for victimizing women, a factor that allows this behavior to continue is a lack of punishment. While forcing sexual intercourse on a woman who has passed out from alcohol may be against the law in most North American jurisdictions, it is unlikely that any male who does so will be prosecuted either by criminal or university authorities. Patricia Harney and Charlene Muehlenhard (1991) argue that few people in the criminal justice system even consider it a crime to forcibly rape an acquaintance under any circumstance. It is a difficult task to convince some men that it is wrong to rape women when it isn't only fraternity brothers who sanction or reward such behavior; other students, parents, teachers, administrators, and the general public will all point out that the woman was drunk and therefore is partly responsible. Similarly, although in many jurisdictions today men are being arrested for hitting their wives, the traditional neglect of this behavior still extends to forcible rape. It is now against the law to forcibly rape your wife in all fifty states, but you would be foolish to bet much money on seeing a successful prosecution in your state anytime soon. Seeing an *arrest* would be extraordinary for most of us, even though we know from social science research that a high percentage of battered wives are also forcibly raped (Russell, 1990).

Interestingly, few people would suggest that a woman who passes out from alcohol consumption in a bar shares responsibility for having her leather jacket or purse stolen or would argue against prosecuting the thief (DeKeseredy & Schwartz, 1993b). And if we knew that the thief had encouraged the victim to drink more so that she would not be able to resist his theft of her jacket and purse, we would be even more upset. However, when sex is involved, we seem to find the facts somewhat ambiguous and the moral waters muddied (Fenstermaker, 1989). Nor is it only in fairly minor cases that people are confused about blame and morality and therefore award men immunity from punishment; there will be no serious punishment on most campuses (although many are changing)[10] even in fairly serious cases such as gang rape.

Although the expanded model is much better than the original, it still has flaws. From a quantitative researcher's standpoint, perhaps its most obvious limitation is that it is too complex to test. In other words, its greatest value may lie in summarizing the complex literature, rather than in predicting which men are most likely to victimize women.

Further, our model does not account for the way in which social networks that favor and promote the abuse of women develop. Rather, it starts with the proposition that these groups already exist and discusses their role in woman abuse. For example, one empirical question that remains is whether the most pro-abuse college fraternity chapters shape and mold pledges to learn these new behaviors or whether they attract pro-abuse young men who need nothing more than a new sweatshirt with Greek letters sewn on. A central element of Peggy Reeves Sanday's (1990) theory is that fraternity rituals mold this behavior. She argues that the young man comes to college and then goes through fraternity initiation ceremonies that involve the "transformation of consciousness": "By yielding himself to the group in this way, the pledge gains a new self" (p. 135). Robin Warshaw (1988), on the other hand, suggests that men with sexist ideologies seek out sexist

[10] See Bohmer and Parrot (1993) for the "new wave" of punitive attention given to violent and sexually aggressive students at some colleges and universities.

fraternities to join so that they will receive support for their attitudes and behaviors. Similarly, we do not know whether male batterers with strong social support networks are truly influenced by these networks to adopt new attitudes toward their wives or whether men who already hold such attitudes are attracted to other like men, in order to gain support for their already existing views.

Feminist Theories

Perhaps the most difficult perspective to explain in a few pages is feminist theory. Part of the reason is that many people, influenced by the media, church groups, politicians, and others, have of stereotypic view of feminists as braless, man-hating women. Of course, some feminists are just like that, but actually both men and women are feminists, often mainly united by a desire to eliminate gender inequality.

Most feminist perspectives share the view that men assault women to maintain their dominance in intimate relationships (Saunders, 1988). Further, they argue that gender and power are key explanatory factors, that the family changes over time and must be understood in that context, that it is essential to listen to women's experiences in order to develop a theory, and that the purpose of scholarship is not only theory development but active assistance to women in need (Bograd, 1988, pp. 13–14). Not only do most researchers now agree with Lewis Okun that feminism is "the most important theoretical approach to conjugal violence/woman abuse" (1986, p. 100), but many believe that radical feminism in particular has had the greatest impact on woman abuse research (Simpson, 1989). This school of thought argues that "the most important relations in any society are found in patriarchy (masculine control of the labor power and sexuality of women); all other relations (such as class) are secondary and derive from male-female relations" (Beirne & Messerschmidt, 1991, p. 519).

Applied to male violence against women, radical feminist theory contends that men engage in this behavior primarily because they need or desire to control women (Daly & Chesney-Lind, 1988). Jill Radford's work provides an excellent example of this perspective. She claims that "it is clear that men's violence is used to control women, not just in their own individual interests, but also in the interests of men as a sex class in the reproduction of heterosexuality and male supremacy" (1987, p. 43).

This does not mean that feminist theory is universally accepted. It has been attacked both from the right and the left. For example, conservative scholars such as Richard Gelles (1980) and Gelles and Claire Cornell (1985) refer to radical feminist theories as single-factor explanations that have very little explanatory value in social science.[11] Moreover, David Levinson (1989) views theories of patriarchy as political agendas rather than social scientific theories. He also asserts that these perspectives are difficult to verify. Feminist theorists have tried to respond to these criticisms by showing how patriarchal forces together with other variables (for example, male peer support) contribute to female victimization (DeKeseredy & Kelly, 1993b). Furthermore, several large-scale surveys provide strong empirical support for feminist accounts of woman abuse, especially those that point to the ideology of familial patriarchy as a major determinant of male violence (De-Keseredy & Kelly, 1993b; Smith, 1990b, 1993).

A few left-wing scholars are also critical of radical feminist perspectives. Some socialist feminists, for example, state that these theories ignore the effects of class and attack radical feminists for tending to assume a "universal dimension of men's power" (Rice, 1990, p. 62). In other words, they see all men as being equally likely to victimize female intimates. Although woman abuse certainly occurs in all classes and in all occupations, the literature we have already covered shows that some groups are more likely than others to produce at least physical abusers of women.

Another problem with radical feminist accounts, as well as other feminist perspectives, is that they generally ignore the influence of race/ethnicity. The experiences of nonmajority groups are often given little attention even where there is evidence of variations in the amount and type of violence among different ethnic groups (DeKeseredy & MacLean, 1991). Of course, this criticism can be leveled against the overwhelming majority of woman abuse researchers of all political positions.

An interesting methodological debate between radical feminist theorists and others concerns the proper subjects for research on abuse. Most work in this tradition has consisted of in-depth interviews with women who have first-hand experience with abuse. As mentioned previously, an important argument is that a central component of feminist research is the validation

---

[11] They were referring more specifically to the work of radical feminists Dobash and Dobash (1979).

of women's experiences. Some critics feel that by not listening to men, but rather to women talking about their experiences with men, radical feminist researchers don't take into account that the "accuracy of inferences about the intentions and motivations of men should not be judged solely by reference to whether the inferences are *experienced* as being true by women" (Liddle, 1989, p. 769). Rather, attacks on patriarchy will be better conducted by studying the social constructions of male offenders (Scully, 1990).

Summary

The main objective of this chapter was to introduce you to the sociological study of violence against women in intimate, heterosexual relationships and to explain why many abused women might not always be able to escape from these relationships as fast as we might hope. The data presented here show that many North American women are at great risk of experiencing violence, although some are at more risk than others. For example, women involved with working-class men, with men who receive pro-abuse support from their peers, and with men who adhere to the ideology of familial patriarchy are more likely to be victimized than women who are romantically attached to men who do not have these characteristics. Of course, these are probabilities, not guarantees. Women in upper-class homes marked by at least verbal or external trappings of gender equality are often abused, sometimes very badly.

Why do men assault current or former female intimates? Answers to this question typically are derived from three major theoretical perspectives: psychological approaches, social support theory, and feminist theories. Compared to the last two, psychological perspectives are seen as having little explanatory value given the great extent of female victimization in North America and other continents.

For many female members of the general population, research and theorizing is of little value unless it effectively contributes to a reduction in male threats to their physical and psychological well-being. The question of what is to be done will be addressed in the last chapter of this text.

SUGGESTED READINGS

Barnett, O. W., and LaViolette, A. D. (1993). *It Could Happen to Anyone: Why Battered Women Stay.* Newbury Park, CA: Sage.

Barnett and LaViolette provide a comprehensive overview of the empirical, theoretical, and policy issues surrounding the question of why women remain in abusive relationships. Unlike many other books and articles that address this issue, this one constitutes a powerful challenge to explanations that blame women for their victimization.

DeKeseredy, W. S., and Hinch, R. (1991). *Woman Abuse: Sociological Perspectives.* Toronto: Thompson Educational Publishing.

This book offers a broad-based analysis of female victimization. DeKeseredy and Hinch provide a comprehensive, critical overview of four major issues: wife abuse, woman abuse in dating, sexual assault, and corporate violence. The strengths and weaknesses of various policies aimed at curbing each of these problems are also discussed, and suggestions for future research are presented.

Kirkwood, C. (1993). *Leaving Abusive Partners: From the Scars of Survival to the Wisdom for Change.* Newbury Park, CA: Sage.

The analyses in this book, which focus more on emotional than physical abuse, were used heavily in this chapter to form the ideas of the web that holds women in relationships and the spiral that can both move them farther in and help them out.

Pirog-Good, M. A., and Stets, J. E. (eds.). (1989). *Violence in Dating Relationships: Emerging Social Issues.* New York: Praeger.

This collection of articles provides students and researchers with a good introduction to the social scientific study of dating violence in the United States.

Straus, M. A., and Gelles, R. J. (eds). (1990). *Physical Violence in American Families: Risk Factors and Adaptions to Violence in 8,145 Families.* New Brunswick, NJ: Transaction.

The results of two national U.S. family violence surveys are presented here. This book will be of special interest to those seeking information on debates surrounding the Conflict Tactics Scale.

Yllo, K., and Bograd, M. (eds.). (1988). *Feminist Perspectives on Wife Abuse.* Beverly Hills, CA: Sage.

This book provides an excellent collection of articles on feminist empirical, clinical, and political approaches to wife abuse.

CHAPTER 10

CORPORATE AND ORGANIZED CRIME

*Lock 'em up for life; throw away the key. . . . The idea is so simple and direct—
and so wildly popular—that only the bravest politician will dare question it. . . .
Meanwhile, there is another variety of repeat offender who skips from one florid
crime to the next yet never encounters the same kind of angry reckoning. The
crimes of these offenders are mainly about money—stealing public money—
but some of the offenses can also endanger lives.*

*Let's name some of these recidivists: Boeing, General Electric, Grumman,
Honeywell, Hughes Aircraft, Litton Industries, Magnavox, Martin Marietta,
McDonnell Douglas, Northrop, Raytheon, Rockwell International, Teledyne, Texas
Instruments, United Technologies.*

GREIDER, 1994, P. 36

The above list of criminal corporations compiled by *Rolling Stone* journalist William Greider could be much longer. Hundreds of companies routinely commit crimes that injure the public much more than street crimes in many ways: economically, socially, physically, and environmentally. Yet corporate crimes generally are dealt with by civil or administrative law, with penalties such as fines but not prison. All across North America, politicians have been scrambling to provide longer and longer sentences for more and more minor offenders. The Clinton administration's 1994 crime bill was heavily influenced by a rhetoric of cracking down on dangerous, career criminals, or, as Texas newspaper columnist Molly Ivins puts it, "Git Tuff on Crime." Yet, as Greider points out, the law is applied differently to different people: "For street criminals, three strikes and they're out. For corporations, it's a whole different ballgame" (1994, p. 36).

Chapters 2 and 3 suggest several reasons that criminal corporations are exempt from swift, certain, and severe punishment. Here, we will describe and evaluate several theoretical perspectives on the sociological and social-psychological factors that motivate corporate officials to engage in behaviors that severely threaten society. It will be interesting to compare some of these theories with the theories that dominate criminology—theories that were designed mainly to describe males engaged in street crime. For example, after reviewing the section on social control theories in Chapter 6, you may quite rightly be somewhat confused. Many of the top U.S. criminologists believe that the key to predicting who will be a criminal is determining how much of a "stake in conformity" (Toby, 1957) each person has. People with no stake in society generally also have no reason to avoid committing crimes. Fine, you say, that seems to ring true when we are talking about young, disenfranchised, perhaps minority males who are regarded by many as having little to lose—or a lower stake in conformity. With no jobs and no prospects of ever having one, they have little reason to conform to middle-class norms. But then, you might ask, why do top corporate officers, who apparently have the greatest stake in conformity, commit more crimes than these inner-city youths? These people have nice homes, good cars, excellent reputations, and good families. Why take a chance on losing it all?

This is an important and valid question. However, before we offer several answers, we must first define corporate crime and then describe the extent and distribution of several forms of this major social problem.

DEFINITION OF CORPORATE CRIME

What is corporate crime?[1] First, we must point out the differences between white-collar or occupational crime and corporate crime. Perhaps because both corporate criminals and white-collar criminals wear nice clothes to work these two terms are frequently and incorrectly presumed to mean the same thing by many members of the general public and even by several researchers. As David Friedrichs (1992, p. 14) correctly points out, "Corporate crime has characteristics and consequences which make it fundamentally different from the range of activities subsumed under the heading of occupational crime."

Generally, *white-collar* or *occupational crimes* are committed by "individuals for themselves in the course of their occupations" while *corporate crimes* are "offenses committed by corporate officials for their corporation and the

---

[1] See Ellis and DeKeseredy (1996) for a detailed review of sociological definitions of corporate crime.

offenses of the corporation itself" (Clinard & Quinney, 1973, p. 188).[2] In other words, white-collar crime is committed for personal gain and corporate crime is designed to meet the operative and profit goals of the corporation itself. Unfortunately, this line is not always very easy to draw because many corporate crimes also can benefit the individual. For example, executives involved may benefit from profit-sharing or stock price increases. Executives who save their company money by insisting on maintaining unsafe working conditions for factory workers may be in line for a promotion or a higher salary. In general, though, white-collar crime is committed without the knowledge or permission of the company and is designed to profit only the individual. Corporate crime is designed to benefit the company and only secondarily will profit the individual, if at all.

The most typical example of a white-collar criminal would be an employee who steals from the employer or who cheats customers and pockets the difference. Typically, a corporate criminal might bribe a government buyer to purchase a particular company's product or dump toxic industrial waste into seas, lakes, streams, and rivers in order to avoid paying the costs of properly disposing of the poison. So, if your bartender is putting rotgut whiskey into expensive bottles and selling it to you for top prices, it is occupational crime if she is keeping the profit herself, and it is corporate crime if it is company policy to cheat customers in this manner and the company takes the profits.

In sum, Nancy Frank and Michael Lynch (1992, p. 17) define the problem in a way that we shall adopt in this chapter. Corporate crime is

> socially injurious and blameworthy acts, legal or illegal, that cause financial, physical or environmental harm, committed by corporations and businesses against their workers, the general public, the environment, other corporations and business, the government, or other countries. The benefactor of such crimes is the corporation.

It would, of course, be impossible to list all of the behaviors that fit into this broad definition, but some common examples are provided in Table 10.1, which is a typology of organizational crimes constructed by

[2]See Friedrichs (1992) for a comprehensive overview of the debate surrounding definitions of white-collar crime.

Colin Goff and Charles Reasons (1986). Rather than attempting to provide examples of all of the types of corporate wrongdoings, we will explain in the next section the difficulties surrounding efforts to obtain accurate estimates of "crime in the suites." Then we will present data on the extent of several physically, economically, and environmentally injurious corporate acts.

TYPES AND PREVALENCE OF CORPORATE CRIME

There are enough data gathered from a variety of sources to support the notion that corporate crime is highly injurious and widespread. Nevertheless, it is extremely difficult, if not impossible, to obtain accurate data on the

Table 10.1 A Typology of Organizational Crimes

VICTIM	NATURE OF OFFENSE		
	Economic	Human Rights	Violent
Employee	Failure to remit payroll deductions Pension fund abuse Violation of minimum wage laws and other labor laws	Restrictions on political activity, dress, and demeanor Union activity Public disclosure (e.g., Ellsberg and Pentagon Papers)	Deaths and injuries in the workplace Industrial disease (e.g., from exposure to asbestos)
Consumer	Price-fixing Monopolization False advertising	Misuse of credit information Restrictions on credit based on political, sexual, racial, and class bias	Poor inspection of unsafe products (e.g., Ford Pinto, thalidomide)
Public	Bribery Misuse of public funds Cost overruns Oil spills	Illegal surveillance and wiretaps Abuse of power by police, CIA, FBI, RCMP, and military (e.g., Watergate)	Police homicides Hazardous wastes Air and water pollution Nuclear energy (e.g., Three Mile Island)

SOURCE: Goff and Reasons, 1986.

prevalence of suite crime. Even world-renowned experts on corporate crime can offer little more than "educated guesses" on the "dark figure" of this problem. The amount of corporate crime known to government agencies and to criminologists, and the incidence and prevalence data that are included in many scholarly books on corporate crime, amount to little more than the tip of the iceberg. Why do we know so little about the extent of corporate crime?

Data Collection Problems

We have already learned how difficult it is to come up with accurate estimates of interpersonal crimes. Once again, we find some distinct measurement problems with corporate crime that continue to exist no matter how much money, time, and energy criminologists devote (Snider, 1993). For example, the first place that one would normally look for corporate crime data would be the statistics gathered by the regulatory agencies charged with policing corporate crime. After all, the agencies designed to regulate illegal dumping into lakes and rivers should know the most about illegal dumping into lakes and rivers, right? Well, even if they know the most, they don't know much. Thousands—maybe millions—of criminal events never come to the attention of regulatory agencies.

For reasons described in Chapter 3, regulatory agencies often ignore corporate crimes. Even if they engaged in a high-profile investigation, however, they would not be likely to uncover very much corporate crime. Unlike some highly visible street crimes that are committed in bars and on the streets, few corporate crimes are committed in public. Rather, corporate crimes tend to be intricate, complex, and highly sophisticated law violations that are extremely difficult to detect (Clinard & Yeager, 1980). Susan Shapiro was talking about white-collar rather than corporate crime, but the same problems would arise in trying to count corporate crime:

> Given the subtlety and complexity of white-collar offenses, the possibility of making illicit activities in everyday routines or hiding them in the privacy of corporate suites or complicated interorganizational networks, the opportunities to manipulate the time over which events unfold, the frequently consensual nature of the

illicit behaviors, and the often diffused quality of victimization, one might expect the dark figure of undetected violations [for white-collar offenses] to greatly overshadow that of most common serious crimes. (1985, p. 181)

A widely cited example of the discrete and sophisticated nature of corporate crime is found in Gil Geis' (1986) "The Heavy Electrical Equipment Antitrust Cases of 1961." Here, several high-ranking corporate executives employed by the two largest U.S. heavy electrical companies—the General Electric Corporation and the Westinghouse Corporation—violated the Sherman Antitrust Act of 1890 by engaging in price-fixing. This crime was very serious because, in essence, it represented the theft of an extraordinary amount of money from ordinary citizens. The theory of the capitalist marketplace is that companies will engage in competition, with the one able to offer the best product at the best price "winning" more business. By engaging in price-fixing, these companies undermined the ideal of the free marketplace and made sure that the government or other industries (and always eventually the consumer or taxpayer) never got the best price.

The high-ranking officials of these companies were well aware that they were engaging in "wrong" behavior. It would be difficult for them to argue that they were just engaging in business as usual when they were:

* Using plain envelopes to mail information to each other
* Avoiding being seen together when travelling
* Hiding behind a "camouflage" of fictitious names and conspiratorial codes
* Using public telephones to communicate with each other, and meeting at trade conventions where their social exchanges would appear appropriate, or other sites that facilitated anonymity
* Filing false travel claims to mislead their superiors about the cities they had visited (Geis, 1986, pp. 142–143)

What is the relevance of this example in a section on measuring the extent of corporate crime? It shows how difficult it is for anyone who counts crime or engages in victimization survey research. Obviously, many people are not going to be aware that their taxes have just been raised to pay for the criminal acts of corporate entities. On a personal level, this crime might cost each of us only two or three cents. Who cares? But, of course, a few cents from everyone amounts to quite a bit of money. Corporate crime and corporate violence have often been called "quiet acts," because people not only don't know whom to blame but may not even know that they have been victimized (Frank & Lynch, 1992)! It's even worse when people are exposed to potentially life-threatening diseases that take years to evolve. Every day in North America, thousands of people work in dangerous industrial settings, unaware that they are suffering from slowly evolving occupational diseases or physical ailments that take years to discover. Only after a great deal of accumulated damage is done do people realize that they were victimized by their employers, who purposely created dangerous working conditions to lower production costs and increase profits (DeKeseredy & Goff, 1992; Katz, 1978).

Tony Vidrih was an example of a person who was victimized by a quiet form of corporate violence; he died from working in an unsafe working environment. Charles Reasons, Lois Ross, and Craig Paterson write (1981, p. 47):

> Everyone likes to have a bit of respite from the workday routine. When Tony Vidrih and his co-workers were in a particularly playful mood, they'd toss chunks of asbestos at each other. If only they'd known . . . but obviously they didn't. Despite, or perhaps because of, the fact that they were being inundated with asbestos insulation, and despite the fact that insurance companies since shortly after the turn of the century have upped their rates to insure asbestos workers, the workers in this warehouse hadn't been told of impending health dangers.
>
> Now they know—largely because of Tony Vidrih's case. Exactly how many of them wonder about the possibility of their premature doom due to asbestosis will never be recorded. In this particular warehouse Tony is the acknowledged case and, perhaps in a sense, the herald of things to come.

If cases such as Tony Vidrih's are difficult to count with victimization surveys, the same can be said about reproductive health hazards, especially those that affect women. Accurate estimates of the extent of congenital malformation and childhood development problems caused by daily work conditions cannot be obtained because these afflictions remain unnoticed by victims for months or years. Many women are also unaware that still-births, spontaneous abortions, lactation problems, and other reproductive disorders can be caused by dangerous work conditions. On the other hand, many women may know that their reproductive systems have been damaged in or by the workplace but still be reluctant to disclose their experiences to researchers because they are worried about the loss of privacy or employment, even when they are guaranteed anonymity and confidentiality (Chenier, 1982; DeKeseredy & Goff, 1992).

Just during the time that you are reading this chapter, several corporations are committing crimes against you, your friends, relatives, co-workers, and even the authors of this text. For example, the park near your house or even your own backyard may be slowly poisoning you and your loved ones if it has been "treated" with widely available pesticides, herbicides, and fertilizers. Common lawn-care products damage the environment and drinking water in many neighborhoods, causing thousands of major illnesses and life-threatening allergic reactions. These lawn-care products have even killed a large number of people (Frank & Lynch, 1992). In other examples, you may have purchased a product that the maker knows is unsafe, figuring that it is cheaper to pay off those injured than it is to withdraw and redesign the product. You may draw your water from a source polluted by toxic waste by a local company that is saving money on waste disposal. In any of these cases, you probably will not know that you are the victim of a crime unless you are one of those who are injured and somehow find out the exact cause of your injury.

Of course, some of the biggest tragedies caused by corporations, such as the Love Canal disaster and the Ford Pinto case, have increased public awareness and concern about corporate crime (Cullen, Maakestad, & Cavender, 1987; Frank & Lynch, 1992). You may know about these problems if you read corporate crime books or news magazines like *Mother Jones* and the *Utne Reader* or watch television shows like "60 Minutes" or "Dateline." For the most part, however, it is fair to assume that we are unaware of the extent to which we are victimized by corporations.

This brings us back to the issue of counting corporate crime. One of the most common methods of gathering crime data is the victimization survey, whereby researchers simply ask people if they have been robbed, burglarized, beaten, or raped recently. If millions of people are unaware of corporate crimes committed against them, British criminologist Sandra Walklate (1989) asserts, we should rule out the victimization survey as a useful way of collecting data on the prevalence of corporate crime. Obviously, people cannot report incidents of unwitting victimization such as exposure to invisible pollutants and toxic waste (MacLean, 1991). Other criminologists, however, contend that, even though no research method can overcome this problem, the victimization survey still can provide some valuable information on various types of corporate crime (DeKeseredy & Goff, 1992).

Unfortunately, to the best of our knowledge, Frank Pearce (1992) is the only criminologist who has administered a corporate victimization survey. Conducted in the London Borough of Islington, Pearce's left-realist survey generated statistics on three forms of what he defines as commercial crime:[3] workplace hazards, unlawful trading practices, and the victimization of housing tenants. Even though Pearce had to deal with the methodological problems described previously, his data are clearly more accurate than official British statistics. For example, the accident rate per 100,000 workers was found to be approximately thirty times greater than the national average. Such studies have not been attempted in North America, although it would clearly be to criminology's advantage if a similar or better corporation victimization survey were used here.

It should be noted in passing that other research methods have been used to study corporate crime (for example, interviews with senior executives).[4] However, these are not techniques that can generate reliable prevalence data, so they are rarely used. Until researchers conduct better studies, authors will be forced to rely primarily on official statistics because they are the only regularly published data available.

In the next section, we will discuss two broad categories of corporate crime: corporate violence and economic corporate crimes. Again, these data constitute only the tip of the corporate crime iceberg.

---

[3]Pearce used L. Snider's (1988, p. 232) definition of commercial crime. She states that this concept refers to "a violation of law committed by a person or group of persons of an otherwise respected and legitimate occupation or financial activity."

[4]See Snider (1993) for a comprehensive review of studies that attempted to measure the incidence and prevalence of corporate crime.

Corporate Violence

According to Walter DeKeseredy and Ronald Hinch (1991, p. 100), *corporate violence* is

> any behaviour undertaken in the name of the corporation by decision makers, or other persons in authority within the corporation, that endangers the health and safety of employees or other persons who are affected by that behaviour. Even acts of omission, in which decision makers, etc., refuse to take action to reduce or eliminate known health and safety risks, must be considered corporate violence. It is the impact the action has on the victim, not the intent of the act, which determines whether or not it is violence.

There are numerous types of corporate violence. However, a review of the literature shows that sociologists who study this problem focus mainly on three issues: violence against workers, violence against consumers, and corporate pollution.

Violence Against Workers   Even though they greatly underestimate the prevalence of deaths and injuries in the workplace, data produced by several sources strongly support Reasons, Ross, and Paterson's (1981) assertion that working may be dangerous to our health. For example, according to the American Federation of Labor and Congress of Industrial Organizations (AFL-CIO), in the United States, approximately 10,000 people die in the workplace each year because of traumatic injuries and approximately 100,000 workers die each year from the long-term effects of occupational diseases (1993, p. 1). If the rate of occupational death is high, the same can be said about the prevalence of workplace injuries. In 1991, according to the U.S. Department of Labor (1992), almost six million workers were injured on the job, an average of 16,000 workplace injuries per day. Further, the National Safety Council (1992) reports that 60,000 workers are permanently disabled each year because of these injuries.

Many conservative politicians, members of the general public, corporate officials, and criminologists argue that the bulk of these deaths and injuries are caused by workers' own carelessness (Reasons, Ross, & Paterson, 1981).

Of course, some are; however, research conducted by several critical criminologists (see, for example, Frank & Lynch, 1992; Michalowski, 1985; Reiman, 1995) show that corporate executives are responsible for the vast
majority of injuries and deaths because they have violated occupational
health and safety standards or have chosen not to create adequate standards.
In other words, people like Tony Vidrih die every day because corporate
executives make rational, premeditated, conscious choices to reduce capital
expenses and to increase profits. Likewise, those who die or are injured in
government work sites are victims of political decisions to streamline budgets. For some government officials, "cut-backs" or "fiscal restraint" procedures are more important than people's lives.

Quasar Petroleum Ltd. provides a striking example of such conscious,
rational, and premeditated behavior.[5] In Calgary, Alberta, the company was
found guilty of violating workplace safety regulations because it killed three
of its employees. How did Quasar murder these men? According to Reasons,
Ross, and Paterson (1981, p. 6):

> The company did not provide respiratory protective equipment and
> an external gauge on an enclosed tank, thus, men had to go inside
> the tank without protective equipment and subsequently were over-
> come with toxic fumes. Furthermore, the company had not trained
> the workers concerning the hazards of the job and the need for such
> equipment.

In the United States, a similar case of violence was committed against
Stefan Golab, a Film Recovery Systems, Inc. employee. Golab was one of
the workers who recovered silver from used X-ray plates by soaking them in
a cyanide solution. This solution, if inhaled, swallowed, or absorbed through
the skin, can be deadly. Despite this major threat to their health, workers
were not given the proper equipment to protect themselves, such as rubber
gloves, boots, aprons, respirators, and effective ventilation. Instead, they
were given paper face masks and cloth gloves and were required to work in
plant air that was filled with a "yellowish haze" of cyanide fumes (Frank &

---

[5]See Reasons, Ross, and Paterson (1981), DeKeseredy and Hinch (1991), and Ellis and DeKeseredy
(1996) for detailed reviews of sociological research on corporate violence.

Lynch, 1992; Nelson, 1985). In addition to being exposed to toxic air, Golab and some of his co-workers worked over dangerous cyanide vats where they

> chipped the film, mixed the cyanide granules with water in the vats, stirred the chips in the potent mixture for three days with long rakes, scooped the spent—and cyanide soaked—film chips out of the vat with a giant vacuum cleaner, cleaned the tank in preparation for the next load, and scraped the silver from the terminal plates on which it had been recovered. (Owens, 1985, p. 31)

It was only a matter of time until someone died, and on February 10, 1985, Stefan Golab collapsed on the lunchroom floor and passed away during the ambulance ride to a nearby hospital.

Of course, you might view this incident as an accident. After all, Film Recovery Systems executives did not *intend* to kill Golab—a line of reasoning that appeals to a great many people. Yet, as Reasons, Ross, and Paterson (1981) point out, it has virtually never been accepted in criminal court that when someone accidentally kills during a criminal act, the event should be treated as an accident, not as murder. Should we view murders that occur during armed robberies as accidents? After all, few armed robbers want to kill bank tellers, store clerks, and the like. Rather, their main objective is, like corporations, to quickly make money (Desroches, 1995). Nevertheless, a very small number of armed robbers fire their weapons if they feel threatened. This partially explains a very difficult point of law: Why is it that in most Western jurisdictions, robbery is considered a crime of violence, even though only rarely is someone actually hurt in a robbery? One answer is that, by carrying guns and threatening force, armed robbers have set the conditions for violence to occur. Similarly, Quasar Film Recovery Systems primarily was trying to make more money, but its actions created the conditions for "accidents." Reasons, Ross, and Paterson (1981, p. 7) ask, "Should the company which threatens the workers' safety and health for profit be any less culpable when death occurs than the armed robber who also threatens violence for economic profit?" Interestingly, persons who accidentally kill while committing a crime are guilty of murder. A quick check of your local prison will reveal a number of men incarcerated for long terms for exactly this crime. Yet death in the workplace caused by criminal negligence has not strained the prison budgets of any North American jurisdiction.

Based on the small amount of data described here so far, we can draw several conclusions. The first and most obvious is that many workplaces are "hot spots" of violent activity. Second, given that the data presented in this chapter and other sources greatly underestimate the number of people who are violently victimized in the workplace each year, we can conclude that workers are safer on the streets than they are on the job (Reiman, 1995). In fact, as we have stated previously, the corporate death rate is more than six times greater than the street crime death rate (Frank & Lynch, 1992; Michalowski, 1985), and the rate of nonlethal assault in the workplace is more than thirty times higher than the predatory street assault rate. Based on his reading of various corporate violence data, Jeffrey Reiman (1995) contends that these statistics suggest that for every U.S. citizen murdered by a stranger on the street, two are murdered by their employers.

Of course, some of us may feel somewhat smug because we are not employed in a workplace likely to be dangerous. In fact, some of us have decent jobs that let us work at home. As your authors, we are lucky enough to be able to do most of our writing and course preparation at home. We don't have to work in environments riddled with cyanide fumes and other industrial health hazards. So, we can logically assume that we are not likely to become victims of corporate violence, right? Unfortunately, in an advanced technological society, we are all consumers, and shopping can also be hazardous to your health.

Violence Against Consumers: "Let the Buyer Beware"   Gresham Sykes and Francis Cullen (1992) are correct in noting that the adage "let the buyer beware" has a special meaning in light of the data described here. Thousands—maybe millions—of unsafe products injure or kill many North American consumers every year. For example, the National Commission on Product Safety has estimated that unsafe consumer products cause approximately 20 million serious injuries each year (Hills, 1987). Some researchers estimate that defective automobiles and appliances, unsafe food and drugs, lawn-care products, and an extremely long list of other consumer products permanently disable 100,000 persons each year and cause between 28,000 and 30,000 deaths annually (Frank & Lynch, 1992; Hills, 1987; Schrager & Short, 1977).

Some products, such as the exploding Ford Pinto that caused twenty-four deaths and twenty-four burn injuries,[6] are obviously more dangerous than others. However, even products viewed as safe when used properly can cause considerable pain and suffering. For example, some paints still contain lead and/or mercury. The negative health effects of these products include respiratory ailments, cancer, and lead or mercury poisoning. Further, paints with mercury give off vapors that put children at great risk of being harmed. Paint with lead tastes sweet, and when it peels off walls or woodwork, it may be eaten by small children.

You should also watch what you eat because some food additives and other chemicals added to drinking water and hygienic products are major health threats. For example, David Simon and Stanley Eitzen (1994) report that the most commonly used preservatives—BHT, BHA, sodium benzoate, and benzoic acid—can cause cancer. They also state that aluminum, used in the form of alum to prevent table salt from caking, is suspected of contributing to Alzheimer's disease. Because more than 1,500 food additives are used as flavors, colors, thickeners, preservatives, and so on, eating obviously can be hazardous to your health.

Although men and women are equally at risk of being victimized by most consumer goods, some products, such as sanitary and birth control items, pose gender-specific threats because only women use them.[7] For example, tampons can cause toxic shock, a deadly illness caused by staphylococcus bacteria from the vagina or cervix entering the uterus and then the bloodstream. Tampons are seen by some scientists as providing an environment for the proliferation of these bacteria and their resultant toxins. Symptoms of toxic shock include a skin rash and peeling of thin layers of skin from women's bodies. Toxic shock also affects the kidneys, liver, intestines, and stomach. In many cases, toxic shock is first detected as flu-like symptoms followed by a rash. Women who have had vaginal, cervical, or uterine surgery or who have given birth are advised not to use tampons until they are completely healed (DeKeseredy & Hinch, 1991). Another problem for women is that some develop allergic reactions to deodorant or scented pads

---

[6] See Cullen, Maakestad, and Cavender (1987) for one of the most thorough criminological analyses of this widely known case.

[7] See DeKeseredy and Hinch (1991) for other corporate threats to women's physical and psychological well-being.

and tampons, which are marketed as something essential for a woman to be "clean and fresh" even though such products have no noticeable advantages over washing with soap and water.

It is well known that some intrauterine birth control devices can cause women great pain and suffering. However, the Dalkon Shield, introduced by the A. H. Robins Company in 1971, is considered by some researchers and health officials to be the most problematic of such products. Robins received many complaints of serious uterine infections, blood poisoning, tubal pregnancies, spontaneous abortions, and penetrations of the uterine wall caused by the Dalkon Shield. By 1974, this product had caused 17 deaths, 200,000 cases of serious uterine infections, and many hysterectomies (Michalowski, 1985). Morton Mintz (1985), in fact, argues that most of the women who used close to 2.86 million of the Shields distributed in the United States suffered from pelvic inflammatory disease.

Numerous consumer complaints made A. H. Robins' executives realize that they could not increase profits generated by the Shield in the United States. So, until 1974, when the Food and Drug Administration (FDA) began hearings on this product, Robins promoted it to Third World women. Supported by the U.S. Office of Population, Robins justified putting Third World women at risk by arguing that since Third World birth rates were very high, any form of birth control was better than none (Michalowski, 1985).

Because of the FDA hearings and because it came close to eliminating its back inventory, Robins stopped "dumping" the Shield onto the Third World. *Dumping* refers to the distribution of products that are either recalled, banned, or not approved by the U.S. government into foreign markets that have weak or nonexistent consumer protection laws. In addition to the Shield, many other products banned in the United States have been dumped abroad, notes Raymond Michalowski (1985, pp. 339–340):

- An organic mercury that killed 400 Iraqis and caused the hospitalization of 5,000 others
- Leptophos, a chemical pesticide that killed farmers and livestock in thirty foreign countries
- Millions of units of children's sleepwear treated with Tris, a carcinogenic fire retardant

- Approximately half a million baby pacifiers that caused many choking deaths in the United States

The U.S. federal government cannot stop companies from dumping. However, it has actually helped corporations find foreign markets for dangerous consumer goods (Michalowski, 1985). Similarly, the government, to a large extent, has helped corporations poison our environment, a problem we turn to next.

Corporate Pollution   So far, we have discussed corporate violence against two specific groups of people—workers and consumers. The general public also experiences corporate violence in the form of pollution and other "green crimes." There are many different green crimes, but they are all committed for the sake of profit and they all harm the environment. Examples of green crimes include the following:

- Pollution and toxic chemical dumping
- Timber clear-cutting
- The capture and importation of rare and endangered animals for furs, pets, and zoos
- Cruel and unnecessary animal experimentation
- The sale of dangerous drugs and chemicals to foreign markets (Frank & Lynch, 1992, p. 82)

Even though some of these and other green crimes do not violate civil, administrative, or criminal laws, many critical criminologists have called for broader definitions of crime (see Chapter 2), so as to include such acts. Rather than look at all forms of green crimes here, we will examine one in depth: corporate pollution.

The illegal dumping of toxic waste is common in the United States. For example, Joan Claybrook (1984) estimates that each year corporations emit 160 million tons of pollutants into the air and dump 225 million tons of toxic chemicals into waterways and streams. Other criminologists state that U.S. corporations produce 88 billion pounds of toxic waste annually, and the U.S. Environmental Protection Agency states that 90 percent of this waste is disposed inappropriately (Coleman, 1989).

Canadian corporations are not much better, especially the pulp and paper companies. In March 1989, Environment Canada reported that 83 of the 149 Canadian pulp mills were dumping toxic waste into waterways at a rate well above "allowable standards." Based on his analyses of these data and other statistics on toxic waste, John McMullan contends that "Canadian harbours are hideous repositories of wastes and poisons" (1992, p. 31).

No discussion of corporate pollution in the United States would be complete without a description of the infamous Love Canal tragedy. The next time you visit Niagara Falls, New York, enjoy the picturesque scenery, museums, and cafes; but also think about the pain and suffering caused by the Hooker Chemical Company. Between the late 1930s and 1953, this company dumped approximately 40 million tons of toxic waste into the abandoned Love Canal, which is near Niagara Falls. In 1953, a local school board bought this dump site for a dollar and later sold it to a private developer. The canal was filled in, and houses were built on top of it. Unfortunately, those who bought these houses got more than they bargained for. Twenty years later, the toxic wastes dumped by Hooker caused miscarriages, birth defects, and other illnesses and forced more than two hundred families to leave their homes (Tallmer, 1987).

In 1979, Michael Brown was in Love Canal. Included in his book on toxic wastes in the United States is the following account of what he saw:

> I saw homes where dogs had lost their fur. I saw children with serious birth defects. I saw entire families in explicably poor health. When I walked in the Love Canal, I gasped for air as my lungs heaved in fits of wheezing. My eyes burned. There was a sour taste in my mouth. (1979, p. xii)

The Love Canal case is not unique. Indeed, data generated by several sources support Simon and Eitzen's assertion that this case is just the tip of the United States' waste iceberg (1994). In fact, right now, more than 21,000 hazardous waste sites in the United States cause major illnesses and deaths in over 15,000 communities (Frank & Lynch, 1992). If you are ever able to buy your own house, make sure the one you want is on "safe ground."

Economic Corporate Crimes

There are many giant corporations in the United States, and because they have vast economic resources and provide a wide range of products and services, they influence the lives of most Americans from the cradle to the grave. When large corporations commit economic crimes, many people are victimized because of the giant scale of such operations. Two common types of economic corporate crimes are briefly described here: price-fixing and false advertising.

Price-Fixing   According to Raymond Michalowski (1985, p. 347), there are two major types of price-fixing: tacit and overt. Tacit price-fixing occurs when a limited number of controlling companies in a particular market follow the lead of their competitors in price increases. For example, periodically, various media report that a company has decided to increase the cost of its goods or services and its competitors are likely to do the same. As Michalowski points out, we frequently hear news like, "G.M. announced today that it would increase the price of its automobiles by an average of $160 per model. Ford and Chrysler are expected to follow suit" (1985, p. 347). If there are few competitors within a given industry, as with U.S. auto manufacturers, noncompetitive prices can be kept for similar goods without any blatant, conspiratorial actions. Even on a smaller level, many businesses set their prices to match the competition. For example, gas station managers frequently drive up and down the "strip" of similar stations to make sure that their prices are in line with the competition.

Overt price-fixing, on the other hand, involves secret meetings and subtle communications between competitors in given industries, such as those who were involved in the heavy electrical equipment conspiracy discussed previously. These executives decided, in advance, to use collusive strategies to increase profits. Michalowski (1985, pp. 347, 349) contends that the three most common forms of collusion are:

- Setting prices at predetermined, similar levels
- Dividing the market into "regions," with each firm agreeing to stay out of the others' territory
- Agreeing to take turns submitting the winning "competitive" bid for contracts, often from government agencies

Consumer panic was seen again and again in the 1980s, when numerous savings and loan institutions closed down, leaving U.S. taxpayers with a $1.5 trillion bill. Over 100,000 criminal charges have been filed against S&L bankers for fraud, but most were dropped when the federal government decided that it did not have the resources to prosecute all of the thieves.

Price-fixing is both widespread and costly, and for some companies, it has become a way of life (Cullen, Maakestad, & Cavender, 1987). Some observers argue that almost every industry has engaged in price-fixing, even corporations that produce milk, bread, and cranberry products (Nader & Green, 1972, p. 28). According to some estimates, these and other companies that have engaged in price-fixing cost each and every consumer between $30 and $200 annually (Green & Berry, 1985). Thus, it is probably the most expensive type of corporate theft (Beirne & Messerschmidt, 1991). Each individual consumer may be paying only a few pennies extra for bread, milk, and perhaps canned cranberry sauce because of price-fixing, but the theft eventually adds up to a financial loss as serious as when someone is victimized by burglary or larceny-theft. Further, as taxpayers, individuals pay higher taxes because of price-fixing in government contracts.

False Advertising   False advertising is another widespread type of corporate crime. Also referred to as either *misleading, deceptive,* or *questionable advertising,* this crime occurs when companies use false advertisements to entice consumers to buy products or services that offer few, if any, of the publicized benefits (Cullen, Maakestad, & Cavender, 1987). David Simon and Stanley Eitzen (1994) note that there are two key forms of false advertising: blatantly false advertising and puffery. These researchers offer two examples of *blatantly false advertising*:

- In 1978, the Federal Trade Commission ruled that Anacin had falsely advertised its product by claiming that it (1) relieved nervousness, tension, stress, fatigue, and depression; (2) was stronger than aspirin; (3) brought relief within twenty-two seconds; (4) was highly recommended over aspirin by doctors; and (5) was more effective for relieving pain than any other analgesic available without prescription.
- In 1979, the nation's largest toymaker, CPG Products, a subsidiary of General Mills, was found guilty of two deceptive acts: (1) use of a television commercial that showed a toy horse being able to stand on its own—when in fact it could not—through the use of special camera techniques and film editing; and (2) use of overemphasized boxes in model airplane kits that gave a misleading impression of the size of its contents.

Puffery is a legal and more subtle form of false advertising that typically involves making exaggerated claims for a product or service. Regardless of the fact that this practice does not violate civil, administrative, or criminal law, it is still designed to mislead consumers. Here are some examples of puffery described by Simon and Eitzen:

- "Coke is it."
- "Blatz is Milwaukee's finest beer."
- "Wheaties, Breakfast of Champions."
- "Seagram's, America's Number One Gin."

Another form of puffery occurs when a spokesperson in an advertisement says something that sounds intelligent but that really is meaningless. Listen to television ads carefully sometime and try to count how often you hear people say things like, "No other product on the market cleans better than ours" (translation: "All products in this category perform identically; ours just costs more").

THE DISTRIBUTION OF CORPORATE CRIME

While some corporations do not violate civil, administrative, and civil laws, others occasionally conduct "bad business" (Snider, 1993) and still others routinely violate the law. For example, Marshall Clinard and Peter Yeager (1980) analyzed civil, criminal, and administrative actions either initiated or completed against the 477 largest publicly owned manufacturing corporations in the United States and found that three industries violate government regulations and laws more often than others.[8] These are the "huge" and "powerful" oil, auto, and pharmaceutical industries.

Clinard and Yeager's data show that oil companies, such as Exxon, frequently engage in the following "bad business" practices, some of which are not considered crimes in the legal sense (1980, p. 237):

- Contrived shortages
- Restriction of independent dealers
- Excessive profits
- Pollution
- Misleading advertising
- Interlocking directorships
- Inadequate research and development

Clinard and Yeager state that, due largely to consumer advocate Ralph Nader's books, such as *Unsafe at Any Speed* (1965), the auto industry has

---

[8]Clinard and Yeager's (1980) study is the first, and perhaps most, comprehensive analysis of corporate crime in the United States.

been sharply attacked for ethical and legal violations and for what some people refer to as a "general disregard" for consumer safety. More specific examples of the auto industry's wrongdoings include these:

- Unnecessary style changes
- Deceptive advertising
- Unreliable and secret warranties
- Unfair dealer relations
- Violations of safety standards (Clinard & Yeager, 1980, p. 237)

The pharmaceutical industry's wrongdoings, according to Clinard and Yeager (1980, p. 237), include the following:

- Excessive promotion
- False advertising
- Inferior product quality
- Improper research and inspection
- Excessive markup

Based on these findings, we can conclude that "bigger is not better." Indeed, company size is a key determinant of corporate offenses. For example, Clinard and Yeager found that small companies accounted for about one-tenth of the violations analyzed at the time of their study, medium-sized companies approximately one-fifth, and large firms approximately three-quarters—close to twice their expected percentage. Moreover, large corporations accounted for 72.1 percent of serious violations and 62.8 percent of moderately serious ones (1980, p. 119).[9]

THEORIES OF CORPORATE CRIME

Based on what you have read so far in this chapter, you might easily conclude that there is a simple, straightforward explanation for corporate crime: profit. As a student stated in one of our classes, "Why complicate what is

---

[9]See Clinard and Yeager (1980, p. 118) for the criteria used to rank serious, moderate, and minor violations.

obvious?" This student has a point. Sociologists in general have been accused of using sophisticated, unintelligible jargon to explain simple issues. Our motto, it seems to many students, is, "Never use a small word when a big one will do just as well." However, corporations are complex organizations. We agree with Nancy F. Frank and Michael L. Lynch (1992, p. 97) that a "full understanding [of corporate crime requires a] more sophisticated approach." In addition to understanding the profit motive, we need to address the role of subcultural dynamics, psychological variables, organizational factors, social structure, and other "risk markers" (Croall, 1992).

There are several theories of corporate crime, and it is beyond the scope of this chapter to discuss all of them here.[10] Instead, we will review three widely cited, contemporary perspectives: subcultural theory, structured action theory, and anomie theory. Some of you may argue that Marxist theories are conspicuously absent. Of course, these accounts are dominant explanations (Snider, 1993); however, you may recall that their contribution to a sociological understanding of corporate crime was discussed in Chapter 3.

Subcultural Theory

A central part of several theories of predatory street crime and intimate violence is that friends and/or colleagues both make it acceptable (legitimate) and help to continue (perpetuate) an individual's indulgence in "disreputable pleasures" (Hagan, 1984). Similarly, some theorists argue that corporate crime is encouraged and justified by workplace or corporate subcultures (Croall, 1992). Just as your friends on the streets might encourage you to shoplift by convincing you that everyone does it and it really isn't criminal, your friends in the lab might convince you to "smooth over" (misrepresent) data on harm caused by a new product. As was stated in Chapter 6, criminal subcultures develop because the members share problems that require solutions not available or permitted by the law or general societal norms. Individual corporate decision-makers interact and share their work-related problems with each other (for example, the struggle for profit);

---

[10]See Snider (1993) and Ellis and DeKeseredy (1996) for in-depth critiques of various theories of corporate crime.

they experience these problems collectively and often create subcultural solutions.

Some of these solutions are legitimate while others are criminogenic. Criminogenic corporate subcultures develop when, as Edwin Sutherland (1939) pointed out, corporate executives have frequent and intimate contact with other executives who hold definitions favorable to violating civil, administrative, or criminal law. Thus, corporate crime, like any crime, is learned

> in direct or indirect association with those who already practice the behavior and those who learn the behavior are segregated from frequent and intimate contacts with law-abiding behavior. Whether a person becomes a criminal or not is determined largely by the comparative frequency and intimacy of his contacts with the two types of behavior. This process may be called differential association. (Sutherland, 1939, p. 5)

Sutherland's theory of *differential association* is a subcultural perspective, and it is one of the earliest theories of corporate crime. One of Sutherland's most important points is that you don't learn to break the law by being weird or mentally ill. Everything you learned in Psychology 101 and Sociology 101 applies to both criminal and noncriminal behavior—you *learn* to be good or bad.

Approximately forty years after the publication of Sutherland's original theory, Marshall Clinard and Peter Yeager (1980) returned to it to look more rigorously at corporate crime. Like Sutherland, they argue that corporate executives learn crooked business practices from their criminogenic colleagues. They also argue that executives learn a number of justifications that enable them to neutralize their doubt or guilt about illegal or unethical behavior. Executives might belong to a corporate climate that strongly believes in upholding business ethics or in perpetuating the free marketplace. Such executives would be much less likely to cheat. However, using the same learning and thinking processes, executives might belong to a corporate climate that believes in subverting the free enterprise system to maintain high profits for their own company. Examples of these latter justifications are (1980, pp. 69–73):

- All legal measures constitute government interference with a free enterprise system.

- Government regulations are unjustified because the additional costs of regulations and bureaucratic procedures cut heavily into profits.

- Regulation is unnecessary because the matters being regulated are unimportant.

- Other concerns in the same line of business are violating the law, and if the government cannot prevent this, there is no reason competing corporations should not also benefit from illegal behavior.

- Violations are caused by economic necessity—they aim to protect the value of stock, to ensure an adequate return for stockholders, and to protect the job security of employees by ensuring the financial stability of the corporation.

Only a small handful of criminologists have applied subcultural theory to corporate crime. Nevertheless, their arguments are valid, and the assertion that corporate crime is learned "can hardly be challenged" (Coleman, 1989, p. 207). Even so, some proponents of macrolevel explanations (for example, Marxists and feminists) contend that subcultural accounts devote little attention to the ways in which corporate subcultural dynamics are influenced by wider economic, cultural, and political forces that exist outside of corporations (Coleman, 1989; Croall, 1992). According to Frank and Lynch, key examples of these broader social forces are "the type of economic system, the state of the economy (economic uncertainties), and the degree to which law enforcement is sensitive to particular types of violations of the law" (1992, p. 117). To a certain extent, James Messerschmidt's (1993) structured action theory responds to this criticism, and it is to his contribution that we now turn.

Structured Action Theory

Earlier, we stated that some corporations are more criminogenic than others (for example, the oil, pharmaceutical, and automobile industries). Similarly, some individuals are more likely to engage in crooked business practices than others. Quite logically, these are the people who have the major decision-making power in companies: white males. This is not to say that women, given the same opportunities as men, would not commit corporate crimes. It is entirely possible, as L. Snider points out, that since the accumulation of profit is the primary corporate objective, "replacing some people with penises and others with vaginas would [not] materially affect the commission of corporate crime" (1993, p. 57).

Although approximately 38 percent of all corporate management, executive, and administrative jobs in the United States are held by women, these are typically lower-level positions in each job category (Blau & Winkler, 1989), such as in personnel, research, affirmative action, and equal employment departments. These management positions generally do not lead to more powerful corporate positions, and women therefore have relatively few chances to commit illegal or unethical acts that increase corporate profits.

Messerschmidt (1993) argues that within corporations, the "old-boy" network plays a major role in maintaining this gender division of labor and in encouraging and justifying corporate crime. The old-boy network achieves these goals by selectively recruiting younger men who share its norms, attitudes, values, and standards of behavior. Young executives who meet these expectations are ultimately rewarded with more money, authority, corporate control, and power over women. Junior male executives also learn "executive conceptions of masculinity" from their senior counterparts, one of which is the sacrifice of personal principles to meet corporate goals, which could include the accumulation of profits through illegal or unethical means. Young male executives who have "nondemanding moral codes" are more likely to be promoted to senior positions that free them, if necessary, to commit corporate crimes that benefit them and the corporation. According to Messerschmidt:

> Corporate crime simply assists the corporation and young upwardly mobile men reach their goals. In other words, corporate crime is a practice with which men gain corporate power through maintaining profit margins. Moreover, as corporate executives do corporate crime, they simultaneously do masculinity—construct a masculinity specific to their position in the gender race, and occupational divisions of labor and power. (1993, p. 135)

Corporate-executive masculinity is distinct from other masculinities, such as those found on inner-city streets, on assembly lines, and in families. For example, corporate "real men" are calculating and rational, and they struggle for success, rewards, and corporate recognition. Male executives compete with one another and measure masculinity according to their success in the business community. Illegal and unethical corporate behavior is one way of advancing what Messerschmidt refers to as a "gendered strategy of action."

Uncertain and competitive markets, fluctuating sales, and government regulations all obstruct corporate attempts to increase profits legitimately (Hills, 1987). Messerschmidt asserts that these obstacles also threaten white corporate-executive masculinity. Thus, corporate crime is a solution to both of these problems. That is, illegal and unethical practices are techniques of reestablishing or maintaining a particular type of masculinity as well as profit margins.

Messerschmidt's account, although it is about men, is a feminist perspective. Unlike many feminist accounts of crime, however, his theory is based on research specifically designed to gain knowledge about the factors that influence men to engage in criminal behavior. As we pointed out in Chapter 7, it is difficult to understand the ways in which broader patriarchal forces influence men by only interviewing women, a method that was used in many feminist criminological studies. Messerschmidt's work supports those who contend that it is equally important to study the subcultural "rituals of bonding" that help create, support, and maintain patriarchal male identities (Morra & Smith, 1993). His theory is also one of the first accounts of corporate crime to explain the relationship between three important sociological variables: gender, class, and race/ethnicity.

Thus far, hypotheses based on Messerschmidt's structured action theory have not been tested. Hopefully, others will fill this research gap, perhaps starting by conducting interviews with junior and senior corporate executives.

Anomie Theory

In Chapter 6, we evaluated Robert K. Merton's (1938, 1957) contribution to a sociological understanding of lower-class, predatory street crime. Are his theory and modified renditions of it applicable to corporate crime? Recall that his goal was to explain criminal or deviant responses to the "disjunction" between cultural goals (for example, economic success) and the availability of legitimate means of achieving these goals. Some radical critics (for example, Snider, 1993) contend that anomie theory cannot adequately explain unethical and illegal corporate behavior. They note that this theory was designed to explain lower-class, individual responses in a society in which economic success is stressed but in which jobs that lead to this success are often not available. However, some criminologists, such as Steven Box (1983) and Nikos Passas (1990), offer a novel challenge to this criticism and provide anomie theories of corporate misconduct.

If lower-class individuals do not have the legitimate means to achieve culturally induced economic goals, the same can be said about some corporations. As was stated previously, the primary goal of companies is profit, but they frequently lack legitimate opportunities to achieve this goal because they operate in an "uncertain and unpredictable environment" (Box, 1983). According to Box (1983, pp. 35–36), major factors that potentially preclude corporations from achieving their monetary goals include these:

- *Competitors*—technological breakthroughs, price structure, marketing techniques, mergers, and new or expanding markets
- *Governments*—extending regulations to cover more corporate activities either through new laws or tougher enforcement of existing laws
- *Employees*—any collusive activity, but especially trade unions pursuing "militant" wage settlements and making "radical" demands on altering the conditions of work/employment
- *Consumers*—especially when demand for a product is elastic and consequently fickle or when "consumerism" is prevalent, making highly visible any dubious corporate practice
- *The Public*—especially through a growing "environmentalist" sensitivity to conserving fresh air, clean countryside, and natural resources

These and other environmental uncertainties cause some corporate executives to experience strain, which often results in the use of innovative, illegitimate means to achieve their companies' goals. A simple, testable hypothesis can be inferred from this theory: when environmental uncertainties increase, so will the strain towards corporate crime and deviance. Or, more simply stated: when corporate profits go down and there's no simple, legitimate way to raise them back up, executives will feel more pressure to engage in illegal or unethical behavior to raise profits. Although some researchers have supported this hypothesis, much more research is needed to provide conclusive support.

In sum, Box, Passas, and others who have applied anomie theory to corporate crime should be commended for showing how this perspective can advance a sociological understanding of suite crime. Perhaps their work will influence others to follow suit. Of course, some improvements could be made in future theoretical work, such as devoting more attention to broader political forces. Individuals and corporations do not operate in a vacuum; rather, their desires for financial success are heavily influenced by the larger capitalist social structure in which they exist. As Frank and Lynch (1992) correctly point out, capitalist systems are designed to achieve monetary goals regardless of the costs involved.

ORGANIZED CRIME: CRIME SYNDICATES AND CORPORATE CRIME[11]

Although the term *organized crime* is familiar enough, getting people to agree on its meaning is a difficult proposition. Certainly, it could be used broadly to refer to any organized criminal activity: organized professional theft, business theft, terrorist groups, and motorcycle gangs, as well as "racketeers" who extort money by intimidation and violence (Abadinsky, 1994; Fijnaut, 1990; Pace, 1991). Yet that is not its most common usage. Most often, "organized crime" is associated with the "Mafia" (or Cosa Nostra), an alleged national syndicate of criminals of Italian descent engaged in systematic illegal enterprises centered around the sale and distribution of illicit drugs, gambling, prostitution, loan-sharking, labor racketeering, and other such activities (Cressey, 1969; President's Commission, 1967, 1987). In this view, organized crime operates as a "criminal corporation."

Whether or not a unified national syndicate exists has been vigorously debated in the organized crime literature for the past quarter of a century or more, with most students of the issue expressing skepticism (Albanese, 1991; Beirne & Messerschmidt, 1991). Some contend that organized crime is more accurately characterized as relatively autonomous local syndicates or families engaged in systematic illegal enterprises, but with possible informal

---

[11] This section was prepared from material provided by David O. Friedrichs from his book *Trusted Criminals: White Collar Crime in Contemporary Society* (Wadsworth, 1996).

ties to one another (Abadinsky, 1994; Albini, 1971). These groups, engaged in what might better be termed *syndicated crime,* have several common characteristics:

- They are self-perpetuating organizations with a hierarchy, limited membership, specialized roles, and particular obligations, especially a vow of secrecy (*omerta*).
- They conspire to gain monopolistic control over a particular area and illegal enterprise.
- The threat or actual use of force, violence, and intimidation is a primary instrument, or at least a potential instrument, for achieving their aims.
- The corruption of the political and legal system is a common means of protecting themselves from investigation and prosecution.
- The acquisition of large-scale financial gain or profit at relatively modest risk is the primary objective.
- The provision of goods and services for which there is a demand but no legal supply is a basic element in their success.

The celebrated syndicated crime leader Meyer Lansky once boasted, "We're bigger than U.S. Steel," and the annual gross income of syndicated crime has been estimated in recent years to exceed $50 billion (or 1 percent of the GNP) and even to run as high as $250 billion (Rowan, 1986). Still, there is no really reliable way to measure the profits of syndicated crime.

Historical Overview

Crime syndicates are hardly a new phenomenon. Piracy, going back at least to the time of the ancient Greeks and Romans, might be regarded as the first form of organized crime (Browning & Gerassi, 1980; Mueller & Adler, 1985). Significant networks of organized criminals were operating in sixteenth- and seventeenth-century London, if not earlier, and in the Massachusetts Bay Colony by the end of the seventeenth century (McMullan, 1982). Apparently, John Hancock—the celebrated first signer of the Declaration of Independence—operated an organized crime cartel that engaged in large-scale smuggling in colonial America (Lupsha, 1986). The syndicated form of organized crime is often described as having its roots in various criminal organizations such as the Mafia, which emerged in southern Italy no later than the sixteenth century; these crime cabals—also known as La Camorro, L'Unione Siciliana, The Black Hand, the Honored Society, and La Cosa Nostra—began to surface in New Orleans, New York, and other U.S. cities by the end of the nineteenth century (Abadinsky, 1994; Ianni & Reuss-Ianni, 1972; Inciardi, 1975). Through much of the twentieth century in the United States, Italian-American syndicated crime was widely regarded as the dominant form of authentic organized crime, although syndicated crime entities clearly developed among other ethnic groups as well.

Between 1919 and 1933, Prohibition provided an ideal opportunity for the dramatic growth and expansion of syndicated crime due to the enormous demand for a product, liquor, and the absence of a legal supply (Abadinsky, 1994; Lupsha, 1986). In one commentator's view, Prohibition largely turned the liquor industry over to criminals (Schelling, 1973). It also led to much more systematic contact between the underworld and the upperworld, thereby establishing a much firmer and more enduring basis for the intermixture of syndicated and corporate crime. The repeal of Prohibition did not destroy syndicated crime, which by then had recognized a vast range of opportunities for making money illegally on gambling, drugs, loansharking, and labor racketeering. These enterprises evolved in subsequent decades, along with newer areas of opportunity including arson for hire, credit card and real estate frauds, pornography, the theft and sale of securities, and cigarette bootlegging (Nelli, 1986). The World War II black market also generated a new set of opportunities for syndicated crime. And despite persistent investigations of and campaigns against syndicated crime, it has continued to thrive.

Syndicated and Corporate Crime

Not everyone who deals with organized crime centers their interest on ethnic and family relationships. In fact, the argument can be made that organized crime differs in a number of ways but that a strong relationship can be found between syndicated crime and the organized corporate crime discussed earlier in this chapter. First, many capitalist fortunes have been amassed using tactics similar to those of syndicated crime families. The methods used by "robber barons" to establish the great industrial empires (and sprawling western ranches) of the nineteenth century were fundamentally no different from the methods used by twentieth-century mafioso and syndicated crime members. As Gus Tyler (1981, p. 277) observed:

> Original accumulations of capital were amassed in tripartite deals among pirates, governors, and brokers. Fur fortunes were piled up alongside the drunk and dead bodies of our noble savages, the Indians. Small settlers were driven from their lands or turned into tenants by big ranchers employing rustlers, guns, outlaws—and the law. In the great railroad and shipping wars, enterprising capitalists used extortion, blackmail, violence, bribery, and private armies with muskets and cannons to wreck a competitor and to become the sole boss of the trade.

The amassers of some of the great twentieth-century North American fortunes, including Samuel Bronfman of Seagram's, Moe Annenberg of the Nationwide News publishing dynasty, and Kennedy family patriarch Joseph P. Kennedy, are alleged to have built up their fortunes greatly during the 1920s partly through involvement with bootlegging, bookmaking, and other syndicated crime activities (Fox, 1989). For much of this century, the descendants of the robber barons have been at the top of North America's social elite, and prestigious universities and foundations have been named after Daniel Drew, Andrew Carnegie, John D. Rockefeller, Russell Sage, and Cornelius Vanderbilt, among others. Is it possible, one commentator inquires, that we will eventually have a Meyer Lansky Foundation and a Carlo Gambino University, named after leading twentieth-century syndicated crime figures (Abadinsky, 1994)?

Of course, there is no reason to limit such parallels to historical cases. Jay Albanese (1982) has compared the testimony before Senate investigative committees in the 1960s of Joseph Valachi, reputed member of La Cosa Nostra, and in the 1970s of Carl Kotchian, president of Lockheed Corporation. Valachi was the first "insider" to confirm (truthfully or otherwise) the existence of a national organized crime network; Kotchian was the first high-level insider to testify openly about secret corporate payments or bribes to foreign governments to secure major contracts. We find parallel concerns between organized crime entities and corporations in conspiring to offer bribes: both want to create a favorable climate for their business and to maintain their dominance over competitors in the marketplace. Ferdinand

Lundberg (1968, p. 131), a prominent student of the crimes of the rich, has argued that corporate criminals "make Mafias and Crime Syndicates look like pushcart operations." It has also been suggested that La Cosa Nostra, whether or not it is a national syndicate, performs functions similar to those of a Rotary Club or other such associations for white-collar businessmen: it facilitates business contacts and promotes the general interests of business (Haller, 1990). If syndicated crime has a more negative image and has tended to elicit a harsher legal response than corporate crime, it may be attributable to ethnic and class biases. Although mobsters seem to inspire less general fear than predatory street criminals and may even be occasionally romanticized (particularly in movies such as *The Godfather* and *Goodfellas*) (Hills, 1980), they do not enjoy the same status of respectability that white-collar offenders do.

One way of looking at different types of organized crime is to focus on whether the organization sees itself as being illegitimate (Smith, 1978). This form of analysis is complex. Is the behavior that of a crime syndicate that sees itself as engaging in a criminal enterprise? Or is it the identical behavior of a legitimate corporation that sees itself as engaging in sharp business practices, perhaps knowingly skirting a legal system that unfairly restricts businesspeople? Some of the differences are particularly arbitrary, in that they depend on definitions by the lawmaking legislatures, as discussed early in this book. For example, there are direct parallels between the large-scale legitimate gambling enterprise known as the stock market and the gambling ventures run by syndicated crime (Schelling, 1973). Likewise, when your local savings bank charges you 25 percent interest on your VISA card, plus an annual fee, plus extremely punitive late charges, how does this differ from syndicated crime's loan-sharking, except perhaps for the interest rate charged? This gets worse when your local savings and loan association becomes a vehicle for engaging in "collective embezzlement" of your money. At this point, the lines between corporate crime, white-collar crime, and organized crime become extremely blurred. Kitty Calavita and Henry Pontell (1993) have suggested that if one focuses on the nature of the offenses rather than the individuals involved, it becomes evident that a good deal of the activities associated with the savings and loan scandal of the 1980s was a form of organized crime.

A related view of organized crime has been advanced by Chambliss (1988), who sees organized crime as a network of alliances between politicians, law enforcement people, businesspeople, union leaders, and racketeers.

In this view, one that has been widely adopted by critical criminologists, organized crime is a natural product of a capitalist political economy (Quinney, 1979; Simon & Eitzen, 1994; Vold & Bernard, 1986). In this system, there are enormous pressures to acquire and consume and to make a profit, but at the same time there are pressures to legitimize the system and to maintain order. This framework creates a set of circumstances whereby racketeers, businesspeople, and government officials all benefit from cooperating in carrying out or at least tolerating criminal schemes (Chambliss, 1988). Organized crime performs important functions for corporate enterprises and the capitalist political economy by suppressing dissatisfied workers with labor racketeering, by repressing impoverished ghetto residents through the distribution of heroin, and by oppressing the unemployed who might challenge the system politically by providing a parallel opportunity structure (Simon & Eitzen, 1994). The "sweetheart contracts" that organized crime–directed unions negotiate with businesses guaranteeing labor peace while cheating workers out of wages and other benefits are an especially good example of the mutually beneficial crimes perpetrated by business and organized crime against relatively powerless workers (Hills, 1980). Further, in this view, organized crime helps sustain the capitalist corporations by consuming services (for example, the massive use of phones by bookies) and goods on a large scale, investing in many legitimate businesses, and depositing in corporate institutions huge sums of money that are being "laundered" (Simon & Eitzen, 1994). This way of characterizing the economic role of organized crime is obviously controversial and very much at odds with a conservative or mainstream perspective. An analysis prepared for the President's Crime Commission in the 1980s by Wharton Econometric Forecasting Associates claimed that

> the mob's hold on the economy stifles competition and siphons off capital, resulting in a loss of some 400,000 jobs, an increase in consumer prices of 0.3%, a reduction in total output of $18 billion, and a decrease in per capita disposable income of $77 a year. (Rowan, 1986, p. 24)

The same analysis contended that tax evasion by "the mob" costs other taxpayers some $6.5 billion. The flooding of urban ghettos with drugs can be interpreted as working against the capitalist consumer ethic and fostering property crime against businesses (Inciardi, 1980). Perhaps the most accurate assessment of the economic impact of organized crime acknowledges that it cuts both ways, benefiting some elements of the capitalist political economy while harming others.

There are also important networks and interrelationships between politicians, government employees, and syndicated crime figures (Beirne & Messerschmidt, 1991; Chambliss, 1988; Pearce, 1976; Simon & Eitzen, 1994). As Stuart Hills (1980, p. 94) has noted, "It is doubtful that organized crime could thrive so successfully in America without the cooperation and outright connivance of a portion of our political and law enforcement machinery." Corruption in many U.S. cities, from police officers accepting payoffs to high-level city officials taking bribes in exchange for awarding lucrative contracts, involves a strong syndicated crime element. Many investigations have uncovered evidence linking governors, state legislators, judges, and other government officials on all levels with syndicated crime. Some commentators put special emphasis on the increasingly international, or global, character of such networks (Van Duyne, 1993; Vitiello, 1992). On the national level, ties between government agencies and syndicated crime go back at least a half century. During World War II, Charles "Lucky" Luciano—one of the most powerful syndicated crime figures of his time— apparently assisted U.S. Navy Intelligence in preventing sabotage and unrest on the New York docks and was rewarded with a parole from prison and exile abroad (Simon & Eitzen, 1994). Evidence of CIA enlistment of syndicated crime members during the 1960s to carry out the assassination of Fidel Castro and assist in the Bay of Pigs invasion of Cuba was produced at a Senate Intelligence Committee hearing in 1975. The CIA–syndicated crime cooperative ventures apparently continued during the Vietnam War period and after.

Infiltration of Legitimate Businesses

Although students of organized crime are divided on many issues, they all agree that syndicated crime infiltration of and interrelationships with legitimate corporations and businesses has increased over the years (Hills, 1980; Nelli, 1986; Rowan, 1986).

Reasons for Criminal Infiltration   There are various reasons for this. Legitimate businesses provide a front for illegal activities, an important tax cover, and employment for associates on probation and parole as well as relatives; they enable assets to be more easily transferred to dependents and heirs; and they represent a more secure source of income and profit (Anderson, 1979). Altogether, increasing involvement with legitimate businesses can be expected to reduce the exposure of organized crime figures to prosecution and may also reflect an aspiration for greater respectability. The series of films making up *The Godfather* saga illustrate this movement toward some legitimacy and respectability.

Although such infiltration is often denounced by politicians and journalists, it isn't entirely clear that society as a whole is better off when organized crime simply reinvests in illicit enterprises. Donald Cressey (1969) notes that businesses may be both acquired and operated by organized crime either legitimately or illegitimately. Of course, the infiltration of legitimate businesses is often accompanied by the introduction of a higher level of intimidation, corruption, and outright fraud by these businesses. In some cases, businesses are stripped of their assets after they are taken over and forced into a planned bankruptcy (Michalowski, 1985). In any event, to the extent that syndicated crime is increasingly involved with legitimate business—through takeovers, partnerships, or alliances—it is important to recognize that the image of syndicated crime simply exploiting such businesses is simplistic and one-sided. Often, a mutually beneficial relationship develops. For example, legitimate businesses may initiate contacts with organized crime to control labor or acquire loans on short notice (Hills, 1980).

Examples of Criminal Infiltration   The involvement of syndicated crime with certain classes of legitimate and quasi-legitimate businesses, including vending machines, construction, nightclubs, casinos, and pornography, for example, has long been recognized. An investigation of New York City's building trades and construction industry in the 1980s uncovered evidence of pervasive syndicated crime involvement in the form of extortion, bribery, theft, fraud, and bid-rigging, as well as other forms of corruption and violence (New York State Organized Crime Task Force, 1988). But the range of businesses with an alleged syndicated crime presence is very broad. A congressional investigation in 1970 identified some seventy areas of economic activity—including brokerage houses, parking lots, and real estate developments—with syndicated crime involvement (Nelli, 1986). The character of such involvement, however, has been open to different interpretation. In 1990, the Pennsylvania Crime Commission (1991, p. 325) concluded that "there is a prevailing influence of organized crime in certain legitimate industries and unions in Pennsylvania." These industries, unions, and businesses range from victims to partners of syndicated crime.

However, in many areas, there is a strong interdependence between mobsters and legitimate businesses, such that each is fully responsible for involvement in criminal activities. Arson for profit is an especially harmful crime, causing over $2 billion a year in direct losses of commercial property and some $10 billion in indirect losses (for example, jobs, business income, taxes, and municipal fees) (Rhodes, 1984). It also traumatizes residents in the area where it occurs and may result in losses of hundreds of lives of civilians and firefighters annually. In a study of the epidemic of commercial arson cases in Boston in the 1970s, James Brady (1983) found evidence of mutual involvement of legitimate businesses and syndicated crime racketeers. When banks began to refuse to give mortgages to buildings in certain inner-city neighborhoods, a discriminatory practice called "redlining," growing numbers of buildings in these neighborhoods were abandoned. Suddenly, more than half of Boston's thousands of arson fires were taking place in abandoned buildings. Organized crime racketeers would secure mortgages for these buildings by agreeing to buy them at inflated prices, then insure them, and arrange for the buildings to be "torched." The bank would profit by collecting from the insurance company. The insurance company would pay off and raise premiums; however, it would avoid pressing for investigation of the claims because it feared more state regulation, as well as being seen by potential clients as "tough" on claims. Robert Rhodes (1984) has noted that insurance agents are mainly motivated to sell policies to obtain commissions rather than to question excessive insurance; most insurance companies don't have enough arson investigators to pursue cases effectively and can face possible lawsuits when they deny claims. Meanwhile, government officials, such as inspectors, often are paid off. In this sense, then, arson for profit can be regarded as a form of organized crime activity that has a devastating impact on some urban communities and that emanates out of a close working relationship of corporate profiteering, gangster racketeering, and government corruption or ineptitude. It is more a hybrid form of corporate and organized crime than the activity of mafioso and lone arsonists for hire.

Another business heavily infiltrated by organized crime is toxic waste disposal (Block & Scarpitti, 1985; Szasz, 1986). Toxic waste is one inevitable by-product of modern industrialization. The environmental movement of the 1970s focused attention on the dangers of such toxic waste, which was increasing rapidly, and led to the implementation of new and fairly strong standards for its disposal. The safe (and legal) disposal of toxic wastes is costly and cumbersome. Syndicated crime has long dominated the garbage carting and disposal business in many parts of the country, especially through its ties with the Teamsters Union. It was perhaps inevitable, then, that it would become a dominant force in toxic or hazardous waste disposal, because a great deal of money could be made by evading or ignoring the legal requirements for disposal. In the 1970s, for example, the EPA estimated that ocean dumping and improper landfilling cost about 5 percent of the price of safe disposal (Szasz, 1986). It was also estimated, in the 1980s, that only 10–20 percent of all hazardous waste is rendered harmless by proper chemical or biological treatment; the balance goes into landfills—at best a temporary expedient, and often not up to standards—or is disposed of illegally (Szasz, 1986). Corporate generators of hazardous waste strongly lobbied against laws that would impose substantial liability on them for the effects of improper or illegal disposal; they also contracted with hazardous waste haulers whom they should have known had syndicated crime ties and would not dispose of the wastes legally and properly. If you are illegally dumping toxic waste for 5 percent of the cost of safe disposal, you can certainly charge corporations less for disposal than can a law-abiding disposal firm. Corporations knew perfectly well that there was a great shortage of adequate waste disposal sites (they had emphasized this in lobbying for an extended transition period to meet new standards) and so should have been aware that the contracted haulers were not disposing of their waste properly (Szasz, 1986). This is an important area for discussion, because this illegal activity may well victimize far larger numbers of innocent people than does organized crime promotion of victimless crimes such as gambling and prostitution. In any case, these are not simply the actions of crime syndicates acting on their own. The widespread illegal disposal of hazardous wastes lends especially strong support to the network model of organized crime, because it comes about through interdependent ties, corruption, and ineptitude of corporations, politicians, regulatory bureaucrats, and traditional syndicated crime entrepreneurs (Block & Scarpitti, 1985; Szasz, 1986).

Another example of where the line between corporate crime and organized crime may be blurred is in finance-related institutions. The theft and manipulation of stocks and bonds by syndicated crime has become a major problem since the early 1970s (Pace, 1991). Obtaining and then selling these stocks and bonds requires a certain level of cooperation from brokerages, investors, and other legitimate parties. The long-standing practice of "laundering" the huge sums of money generated by illegal enterprises has always required some obvious awareness on the part of banks, which benefit from such large deposits (Beaty & Hornink, 1989; Hills, 1980; Thornburgh, 1990). The looting of the savings and loans thrifts in the 1980s is arguably the most costly of all corporate crimes. In a widely read expose of the S&L frauds Stephen P. Pizzo, Mary F. Fricker, and Paul M. Muolo (1991) claimed to have found evidence that the defrauding of the S&Ls was carried out by a network that included businessmen, confidence men, government officials, and individuals with syndicated crime ties.

SUMMARY

The main objective of this chapter was to introduce you to the sociological study of corporate crime. The data on the extent and major types of corporate crimes show that corporate crime is widespread and that three industries are more criminogenic than others: oil, automobile, and pharmaceutical. Moreover, male rather than female corporate executives commit most of the illegal and unethical acts because they have more opportunities to do so by virtue of their powerful decision-making positions within corporations.

Why do corporations and executives conduct crooked business? Our answers to this question derived from three major theoretical perspectives: subcultural theory, structured action theory, and anomie theory. Each of these theories offers distinct arguments; however, they all emphasize the ways in which corporations attempt to achieve their primary goal: profit.

Despite claims that in the 1990s syndicated crime has been rendered less powerful by the prosecution and conviction of some of its important leaders, organized crime itself is likely to be an enduring presence for some time to come, perhaps because it is so deeply interwoven with legitimate U.S. institutions and norms. As Stuart Hills (1980, p. 112) has put it, quite concisely:

As long as we attempt to blame organized crime on individual maladjusted "foreigners" and ignore the complicity of law enforcement and political officials; as long as we persist in equating "sinful" moral behavior with crime and thereby make illegal the activity in which significant segments of the American public wish to indulge; as long as businessmen show little interest in persons with whom they do business and are willing to purchase "bargain" (stolen) merchandise; as long as we accord a higher value to the symbols of individual success than to the means of their attainment, and invite all comers to compete for these rewards but restrict the opportunities for their realization from various segments of the population; as long as our culture rewards and encourages exploitative acquisitive behavior; in short, as long as we cling to various myths and cherish certain cultural values, legal policies, and social practices, large-scale syndicated crime is likely to continue to flourish in America.

At the end of the twentieth century, many people would argue that they can distinguish between corporate crime and organized crime. No one is likely to confuse corporate executives, retailers, and physicians who engage in white-collar crime with John Gotti, the most notorious syndicated crime figure of this era. There is a difference in style, in the degree of involvement in illegal enterprises, in the typical character of these enterprises (for example, illicit narcotics, gambling, and labor racketeering versus environmental safety law violations, deceptive advertising, and Medicaid fraud), and in the level of direct intimidation or violence. These differences likely will persist for some time to come. However, there are many interconnections and interrelationships between organized crime and corporate crime, and the boundary lines between them have blurred considerably.

What is to be done about corporate crime? For many critical criminologists, the obvious problem is that a capitalist patriarchal society breeds corporate crime, and any solution will need to start with changes in the structure of the society. However, because most U.S. citizens strongly adhere to the ideology of competitive individualism (Barak, 1986; Currie, 1985), this change is not likely to occur for a long time, if ever. Further, many powerful people do not want to give up the rewards accumulated under the current social order. Thus, in the last chapter of this text, we will present several short-term, progressive strategies aimed at reducing the level and severity of corporate crime in the United States and other countries.

SUGGESTED READINGS

Clinard, M. B., and Yeager, P. C. (1980). *Corporate Crime: The First Comprehensive Account of Illegal Practices Among America's Top Corporations.* New York: Free Press.

To the best of our knowledge, no one else has conducted such a rigorous, in-depth study of corporate crime in the United States. Included in this widely cited book are an analysis of criminal, civil, and administrative actions either initiated or completed during 1975 and 1976 by twenty-five federal agencies against the 477 largest publicly owned U.S. corporations; data derived from additional sources (such as newspapers, business journals, magazines, and a sample of the 105 largest wholesale, retail, and service corporations); and an overview of several important theoretical and policy issues.

Cullen, F. T., Maakestad, W. J., and Cavender, G. (1987). *Corporate Crime Under Attack: The Ford Pinto Case and Beyond.* Cincinnati: Anderson.

This book offers a thorough analysis of the Ford Pinto trial. The authors' main purpose is to explain why businesses such as Ford are becoming more vulnerable to criminal prosecution. Their main thesis is that social and legal changes have combined to generate an attack on corporate wrongdoing and to make powerful members of the corporate community vulnerable to criminal prosecution.

Frank, N. K., and Lynch, M. J. (1992). *Corporate Crime, Corporate Violence: A Primer.* New York: Harrow & Heston.

This book is a substantially revised rendition of Nancy Frank's *Crimes Against Health and Safety* (1985). Frank and Lynch provide a detailed overview of conceptual, empirical, theoretical, and policy issues surrounding corporate violence.

Hills, S. L. (1987). *Corporate Violence: Injury and Death for Profit.* Totowa, NJ: Rowman & Littlefield.

This book provides an excellent collection of articles on the prevalence and types of violent corporate acts inflicted on workers and consumers. Informative articles on the ways in which corporate violence destroys communities and the environment are also included, as well as essays describing the personal experiences of corporate employees, whistle-blowers, and middle managers. Readers may also find Hills' introduction and epilogue enlightening.

Reasons, C. E., Ross, L. L., and Paterson, C. (1981). *Assault on the Worker.* Toronto: Butterworths.

Although this book is out of print, those who can get it from a library will find that it offers a most comprehensive interdisciplinary overview of corporate violence against workers.

Snider, L. (1993). *Bad Business: Corporate Crime in Canada.* Scarborough, Ontario: Nelson.

Written by one of the pioneers of Canadian corporate crime research, this book provides an intelligible and comprehensive overview of various conceptual, empirical, theoretical, and policy issues surrounding corporate crime. Although the bulk of information provided in this text is sociological, Snider offers insights provided by other disciplines, such as law, economics, and history. Considerable attention is devoted to various problems associated with controlling corporate crime.

CHAPTER 11

DRUG USE AND ABUSE

I first started using drugs when I was living in Manhattan. I was about twelve or thirteen years old, and it was more or less a peer type thing, because for the fellas it was something illegal, something bad to do. All the people we knew in Harlem were either drinking or using heavy drugs. At this point in my life, I couldn't see the correlation between heavy drugs and what it really did to you, because most of the people I saw who were drug addicts or alcoholics were bums. But I used to see a lot of people like the hustlers and the numbers runners. These guys were also involved in drugs, but I saw a big difference between them, with all their flash and money, and the guy lying in the sidewalk.

HILLS AND SANTIAGO, 1992, P. 13

There is no question that we are now living in what has often been termed a "high society" or "drug culture." North Americans are taking an extraordinary variety of drugs to relieve stress, go to sleep, wake up, cure physical and psychological ailments, alter their moods, speed up, slow down, heighten their sensitivities, partake in religious rituals, or celebrate achievements. We spend all day getting "up" with coffee and then try to come "down" after work with alcohol (Reiman, 1995). In fact, from as far back as historians and archaeologists can tell, humans have used drugs for an astounding variety of reasons. For example, Glen Hanson and Peter Venturelli (1995) report that at least one Native American group administered tobacco rectally as a ceremonial enema. This variety will continue. People around the world will use drugs in the future, regardless of any penalties for getting caught and despite any knowledge they might have about possible harmful health effects.

This brings us to a serious question: If drug use is so common throughout the world, how can it be "deviant" or "different"? If so many people routinely "get high," why are only a handful officially designated as "criminals," "addicts," "drug abusers," and "junkies"? One of the primary objectives of this chapter is to make you aware of the fact that what drugs "do" to those who take them is rarely as important as the social context in which they are used and distributed.

For example, criminologists recognize that the worst health problems and highest death rates are not to be found among those people who consume illegal drugs such as marijuana, heroin, or cocaine. Rather, it is those who take legal drugs, especially alcohol and tobacco, who are much more likely to suffer from long-term health problems and to die prematurely. Further, alcohol and legally manufactured prescription pharmaceuticals are two of the most significant substances related to violent crime (Boyd, Elliot, & Gaucher, 1991). Yet, North American society does not really see any serious problems with these dangerous drugs. In earlier sections of this book, we have described the social construction of problems. Nowhere is this process more evident than with drugs. As we have suggested, the first step is to carefully differentiate what James Henslin (1994) terms the *objective* from the *subjective* conditions of drug use. The objective conditions might include, as nearly as we can describe them, the facts around drug use: how many people use them, how much they use, and which vital organs of the body are damaged by the use. The subjective conditions are the way in which people define the above. "The view that a particular drug is good or evil is a matter of social definition that, in turn, influences how people use and abuse drugs and whether or not a drug will be legal or illegal" (Henslin, 1994, p. 105). This social definition is determined by a number of factors, as seen earlier in this book, including the mass media. For example, in an era when drug use has not been increasing, media reports on drug crimes have more than tripled (Chermak, 1994). Further, news organizations such as *Newsweek* have been able to manufacture extraordinary claims of drug crises out of very modest survey results (Orcutt & Turner, 1993). No wonder we get the feeling that drug abuse is more pervasive every day!

As we will see in this chapter, no drug is inherently criminal. How, then, did we decide to criminalize the ones that we did? We will describe several types of currently illegal drugs, the incidence and distribution of drug use, and several sociological explanations for why people use illegal substances that threaten their physical, economic, and psychological well-being. As with other issues, we will hold off making our recommendations for prevention and control strategies until Chapter 12.

WHY ARE ONLY CERTAIN DRUGS CRIMINALIZED?

Most writers have a great deal of difficulty with the question of why the state should criminalize drugs such as cocaine, PCP, LSD, and heroin. Some just take it for granted that these should be criminalized because of the "obvious" evils associated with their use. More commonly, sociologists ignore the problems of drugs, astounded that the "general public is apparently seized with the terrible vision of huge masses of Americans shooting heroin, smoking pot, snorting cocaine, or dropping acid" (Thio, 1995, p. 362). They try to debunk these myths and show that the drug problem is not as bad as the government or the media have made it sound. For that reason, most sociologists similarly argue that the "War on Crime" is a disaster and that we need to turn to alternative measures.

In this chapter, we will take on all of these issues. However, it is worth first putting these reactions into some context. As you have seen throughout this book, many sociologists have been trained not to automatically take something like "crime" for granted, but to try to understand *why* a particular behavior became a crime. Whom does it benefit to have this behavior labeled a crime? How did it make its way into the law? Are there similar behaviors that are equally harmful that are not illegal? Why? Often (as you have seen) it is difficult to make some of these comparisons: Which is worse, price-fixing or mugging? If you know that the mugging netted $20 and the price-fixing netted $200, does that change your mind? These are not easy questions for many of us.

With illegal drug use, however, the comparisons become easier. The question is simple: Given the almost limitless number of drugs and compounds in the world, how did we decide that some small number of them would become illegal? How did we decide to mount one of the biggest "wars" in U.S. history against one or two of them while ignoring the others? The "War on Drugs" is not some cute little slogan. Many Americans know that prisons are overcrowded and that their taxes are going up while services are being cut drastically in order to build more prison space. Fewer know that much of this increase is fueled by the drug war, which costs state and local governments more than $16 billion a year to fight. The federal government spends another $13 billion (BJS, 1995), and all governments are taking out unbelievable mortgages to finance putting nonviolent drug offenders in prison. In the face of this losing effort, we are chipping away steadily at our civil rights in an attempt to give more and more weapons to the criminal justice system. For example, Congress has amended laws that for a hundred years have forbid the military from taking on law enforcement roles. First in other countries, such as Bolivia, and now within the United States itself, all branches of the military are heavily involved in the drug war, spending hundreds of millions of dollars for very minimal results (Inciardi, 1992). As Peter Kraska (1995) points out, however, perhaps the more difficult question is the ideological one; one indication of how much the United States has become a country that stresses the use of force and domination to achieve its ends is how limited the public recognition of, debate over, or resistance to the use of troops has been. The one center of resistance has been ultra-right-wing militias, which have protested the role of the federal government in local law enforcement. Whether these protests have any effect on the use of the military and the National Guard in local drug law enforcement remains to be seen.

What has been the net effect of this policy since 1980, when President Reagan declared a war on drugs? Drugs such as cocaine and heroin are now much cheaper and much more potent. Most marijuana sold today is very high-potency domestic growth, rather than the much lower-potency foreign imports previously popular. The rate at which these drugs are used has generally remained stable, or perhaps gone down a bit among the general population, but may have actually increased among serious abusers.

To repeat, our central concern here is why this war was declared on cocaine, heroin, and marijuana. Are these the most dangerous drugs? To judge by the extreme law enforcement reaction and the extraordinary, almost hysterical, media response, one would certainly think so. We've all seen the TV commercial showing an egg frying in a pan—"This is your brain on drugs." Wow! This must be *very* dangerous stuff!

Certainly, no one with half a brain is arguing that drugs are completely harmless. Anyone who reads the news knows that sugar, salt, fat, egg yolks, chocolate, cooking oil, movie theater popcorn, Mexican food, Chinese food, American food, beer—pretty much everything that tastes good—are bad for you. Similarly, there are some health problems associated with marijuana and cocaine! Still, how *much* harm there is in a drug is in the eye of the beholder. For example, James Inciardi (1992), the strongest and clearest voice among those criminologists who wish to maintain drug law enforcement, argues in some detail about potential physiological and emotional problems related to the regular smoking of marijuana. He finds this potential health risk, and the fact that it is used by people to avoid facing reality ("growing up," really), sufficient to keep it criminal. Patricia Adler (1994) finds the same health risks but does not think that they justify a war on drugs. Jeffrey Reiman (1995, p. 37), on the other hand, points out that not only has there never been a documented case of death caused by marijuana, but "no amount of marijuana that a person could possibly eat or smoke would constitute a lethal dose. By contrast, even aspirin overdose causes hundreds of deaths a year." So, is the finding that marijuana residue remains in the fatty tissue for weeks sufficient to keep it criminalized? It is not really the objective facts that matter, is it? It is what you make of these facts that counts.

Why do we concentrate so much of our law enforcement efforts on marijuana and not tobacco? As we pointed out in Chapter 2, tobacco causes at least 350,000–500,000 deaths *annually* in the United States alone and costs U.S. society at least $28 billion a year in medical costs and lost productivity. The government's response has been to spend large sums of money subsidizing the tobacco industry and to encourage the growing of more tobacco. Why aren't we concentrating our law enforcement efforts on the dangerously addictive Valium or the known killer alcohol, which has been related for many years to violence and crime? If society's goal is to criminalize and eradicate the most dangerous drugs, how do we decide which ones these are?

As we stated in Chapter 2, one factor in the decision to make drugs illegal is when their use becomes associated with minority groups. For example, the Marijuana Tax Act of 1937, the federal law that criminalized marijuana in the United States, had its roots in anti-Mexican feelings—that imported Mexican laborers were not working as hard as they might because they were high on marijuana (Musto, 1973). Of course, other factors contributed to support for the act, such as the fact that it increased the powers of several government agencies (Elsner, 1994). However, most criminologists believe that at least the federal marijuana law would not have been passed without strong anti-Mexican prejudice.

Another example discussed earlier is that, prior to the early 1900s, people were free to buy and use opiates. In fact, they were sold as over-the-counter remedies in drugstores. People who consumed quite a bit of Mrs. Winslow's Soothing Syrup may have had more addicting opiates in their systems than many of today's street addicts, but virtually no one thought of them as degenerates, criminals, or subversives even when it became known that they were addicted.

Another place where anti-minority prejudice can be clearly seen is the anti-Chinese feeling that led to opium laws. In the late 1800s, at least 70,000 Chinese were brought to the United States to work on railroads and mines, and many more were brought for the same reason to Canada, all to work at perhaps half of the wages of whites (Boyd, 1991). They brought with them the perfectly legal opium smoking custom and operated many "opium dens," which provided both whites and Chinese with comfortable settings to freely alter their moods or escape the trials and tribulations of everyday life. Anti-Chinese feelings were generally kept in check until the railroads were finished and the economy started to deteriorate. Then many white working-class people organized against poorly paid Chinese immigrants to argue that these "aliens" were threatening white jobs by working at too low a wage. In the early 1900s, both the U.S. and Canadian federal governments responded to this labor crisis by outlawing opium smoking. Elizabeth Comack argues that Canadian anti-opium laws were more anti-Chinese than anti-drug:

> There appears to be a clear and inescapable connection between legislation aimed at the "immoral" habit practised by the Chinese and the ideology that an "alien element" was responsible for the deteriorating situation in British Columbia. Opium-smoking became an easy symbol for the dangers and evils embodied in the fantasy of the "Yellow Peril," and the opium legislation helped to affirm Oriental immigrants as a major cause of social problems. Consequently, one could argue that the drug legislation was not so much directed at the Chinese but rather helped to identify them as a major source of the problems confronting B.C. society. (1986, p. 86)

Another fascinating comparison is heroin and various commonly prescribed drugs. Heroin, as we will see, has very few undesirable side effects other than addiction and has not been shown to cause bodily harm if the user can avoid an overdose. At the same time, many manufactured pharmaceuticals can be extremely dangerous drugs. For many years, individuals (particularly females seeing male doctors) needed only to complain of sleepless nights and general nervousness to procure barbiturates like Nembutal, Seconal, or Luminal. These barbiturates are extremely addictive, their abuse is "more life threatening than misuse of opiates," and withdrawal can be deadly under some circumstances (Hanson & Venturelli, 1995, p. 162). Today, although these drugs are still widely used, they have been partially replaced because some of the same sedative effects on (mainly) women can be achieved through the use of the safer benzodiazephines. These latter drugs, including Valium, Xanax, Halcion, and Ativan, are among the most prescribed drugs in the United States today, despite the fact that they are addictive. Possibly as many as one million Americans are dependent on these drugs, as doctors are allowed to indiscriminately and perhaps inappropriately prescribe them for their addicted patients year after year (Hanson & Venturelli, 1995). Compare this phenomenon with Inciardi's stirring defense of marijuana laws, in which he defends the classification of marijuana as dangerous and criminal because it serves as "a buffer so to speak, enabling users to tolerate problems rather than face them and make changes that might increase the quality of their social functioning and satisfaction with life" (1992, p. 245). Compare the government policy of jailing doctors who try to maintain opiate addicts on their drug with the widespread acceptance of maintaining Valium addicts. Further, consider the massive governmental opposition to even legitimate medical use of heroin, such as for burn victims or people with lung problems. Although heroin may be the best drug available for these two problems, the government is so committed to an antiheroin stance that it cannot take seriously helping medical patients if it involves heroin (Trebach, 1982).

What is our point? The bottom line is that the criminalization of drugs is not completely determined by questions of public health. The drugs of visible minority groups become the object of massive law enforcement attention while the drugs of the white middle class (for example, the equally or more dangerous barbiturates) are freely available. We can certainly see why some criminologists have argued that the "War on Drugs" is a modern and cunning way of enforcing racial segregation and discrimination (Mann, 1993). For example, 12 percent of the whites in prison are serving time for drug violations, as opposed to 25 percent of African-Americans and

33 percent of Hispanics (BJS, 1995). Alex Thio suggests that although drug abuse prevention and treatment are sure to be more effective than law enforcement, politicians will not support treatment because the money and effort will go to help minorities and the poor: "If most of the drug offenders were suddenly middle-class whites, who are the most likely to vote, politicians would switch the drug war's priority from anti-drug-user law enforcement to user-friendly education and treatment" (1995, p. 375).

SOME TYPES OF ILLEGAL DRUGS

It is impossible to describe all of the illicit drugs currently available in North America. Instead, we will limit our discussion to several drugs that appear to be of central concern to most politicians, criminal justice officials, health care providers, and the general public. These are, of course, the drugs of choice of America's lower classes, minority groups, and youths.

Cocaine

Referred to by many as a "party drug," cocaine is a stimulant. It is extracted from the leaves of the coca plant grown in the hills of Peru and Bolivia but processed and prepared for smuggling in Colombia. This plant has been used as a stimulant for thousands of years. Its leaves were, and still are, chewed by natives of the Andes Mountains for recreational, cultural, and medicinal purposes. This produces only a mild "high," one similar to the "buzz" caused by a very strong cup of black coffee (Nicholl, 1985).

In Western society, cocaine was born in 1860 when German scientist Albert Niemann isolated it from coca plant leaves and produced a fine white powder. For the rest of the nineteenth century, cocaine was used by physicians to treat fatigue and morphine addiction, as well as to provide a local anaesthetic. Sigmund Freud, for example, took cocaine himself to stay alert and avoid depression; pressed it on his friends, relatives, and patients; and published several scientific papers on cocaine's virtues.

By the end of the nineteenth century, cocaine was included in many legitimate medicines and drinks. For example, the Bordeaux wine that popularized using cocaine, Vin Coca Mariani, won the endorsement of two popes, President McKinley, four kings, thousands of physicians, and many famous writers and authors (Thio, 1995). The U.S. soft drink industry quickly got in on the act, and we still have the name, if not the formulation, of the first of these products: Coca-Cola.

By the early 1900s, however, cocaine was more and more being used as a pleasure drug. Most of the cocaine abusers in North America were African-Americans and lower-class whites. In fact, white employers in the American South gave out cocaine to African-American laborers to reduce their fatigue and enable them to work longer hours for lower pay (Hanson & Venturelli, 1995). As suggested earlier, when use of a drug becomes associated with minority groups, many religious and moral groups are immediately outraged. With cocaine, among dozens of other factors, there was the added pressure of southern white panic about African-Americans who allegedly not only became violent under the influence of cocaine but also became immune to bullets! Even if they weren't completely believed, these fantasies were spread about because they "gave one more reason for the repression of blacks" (Musto, 1973, p. 7). Not surprisingly, cocaine's legal status quickly changed.

Most users today purchase cocaine in powder form and inhale it through their nostrils. The major physical and psychological effects associated with "snorting coke" are the following:

- A temporary (for example, thirty-minute) sense of pleasure, well-being, and euphoria.
- Both a possible physical addiction and a strong psychological addiction. Typically, the drug provides a very strong high, followed by a very strong low. In the low period, the desire to regain the high can be very strong.
- An increase in energy and a reduction of fatigue.
- Nervousness, excitability, agitation, and paranoia.
- Hypersensitivity, mood swings, insomnia, impotence, and memory problems.
- Increase in body temperature.
- Cardiovascular problems, such as heart attacks and strokes (Currie, 1993).

Some people inject cocaine into their veins because they get a faster and more intense high. As with any other drug, intravenous (IV) injection is a very dangerous practice for users who share needles with members of a population (like cocaine abusers) that includes many persons with the AIDS virus. An extraordinary thing about IV drug users in the United States is that many of them tend not to take easy precautions, even when they are available. Thio (1995) suggests that, for many of these people, the very attraction of taking dangerous drugs is to prove themselves daring in the face of danger, in which case personal safety would not be a concern.

In the mid-1980s, a new form of cocaine hit the streets: crack, "the fast food analog of cocaine" (Inciardi, Lockwood, & Potteiger, 1993, p. 9). Just at the point when cocaine itself was dropping in price dramatically, a product was found that could reduce the price even more substantially. Crack is a special form of free-based cocaine that is formed into a paste, dried into hard pieces called "rocks," and then smoked. Although an enormous number of youths tried crack in the mid-1980s, the number who have tried crack today seems to have dropped to about 1.4 percent of young adults, for the most part African-Americans in central cities (Maguire & Pastore, 1994). The attractions are the low price and the intense, quick high.

Unlike cocaine, the high from smoking a rock may last only three to five minutes, followed by a powerful state of depression. This alone has made it highly addictive, as many people reach for yet another rock to climb out of the depressive state. One recovering crack user told James Inciardi and colleagues (1993):

> I smoked it Thursday, Friday, Saturday, Monday, Tuesday, Wednesday, Thursday, Friday,—on that cycle. I was working at that time. I would spend my whole $300 check. Everyday was a crack day for me. My day was not made without a hit. I could smoke it before breakfast, don't even have breakfast, or I don't eat for three days.

Because crack users may go on binges in which they smoke constantly for days until they run out of money or collapse, they neglect sleep, food, and basic hygiene. Needless to say, they are not healthy people. Further, this tendency to keep going until the money is gone negates the advantages of the initial low price of each rock. Some of the additional negative effects of binging, according to Inciardi and colleagues (1993, p. 11), are these:

- Scabs as a result of burns and attempts to remove insects perceived to be crawling under the skin
- Burned facial hair from carelessly lighting smoking paraphernalia
- Burned lips and tongues from hot pipe stems
- Respiratory problems
- Sexually transmitted diseases resulting from the tendency to engage in unprotected sex, particularly in crack houses

It should be noted in passing that while crack is highly addictive, "street research" reviewed by Elliott Currie (1993) shows that it is not necessarily "the all-consuming drug" often portrayed by the media. Many people either use it sparingly or stop using it altogether after a few hits.

Another false impression that many people get from the media is that there is a relationship between violence and cocaine use (Smart, 1986). Certainly, a number of criminal justice officials claim that cocaine and crack cause a substantial amount of homicides. However, most U.S. cocaine-related homicides involve young, inner-city African-American or Hispanic males fighting over "distribution rights," debt collection, or the quality of the drug. Still, as Malcolm Klein and Cheryl Maxson point out, the amount of violent crime attributed to street gangs has been vastly overstated by many public law enforcement and mass media figures. In fact, they report, "The traditional street gang strikes us as ideal for drug distribution only in its journalistic form" (1994, p. 47). Based on their analysis of 414 homicide cases in New York, Paul Goldstein and colleagues (1989) found that only 3 were directly related to crack or cocaine consumption, and 2 of these cases also involved the consumption of large amounts of alcohol.

However, one new behavior associated with crack cocaine is particularly worrisome and is unlike anything we have ever seen before. Although we will argue later that there is nothing about crack cocaine that makes it more attractive to women than men, there is a small group of women, sometimes called "strawberries" or "crack whores" in street language, who exchange sex for crack. These addicted women have few options for getting the money they need to purchase the drug. Street prostitutes who exchange sex for money, even if it is later used to purchase crack, maintain some control over their lives and business (Miller & Schwartz, 1995). Those who exchange sex for crack directly, however, sometimes end up in crack houses, where they reach a level of degradation that few of us are capable of imagining (see, for example, Ratner, 1993). Inciardi and colleagues (1993, p. 76) describe the trade these women make for hits on a crack pipe:

> Women in crack houses resign all control of their bodies and their sexual self-determination to the crack-house owner and customer. Unless they can purchase crack on their own, they are permitted no input into either the fee or the act. What constitutes sex is decided by the customer.

As we will discuss later, the amount of violence these women endure can also be regular and extreme. In any case, the fact that this phenomenon takes place in a number of cities is a cause for worry in and of itself.

Heroin

Like crack, heroin is highly addictive. Considered one of the "world's most potent painkillers" (Boyd, 1991), heroin is an opiate derived from poppy plants generally grown in Burma, Thailand, Laos, Pakistan, Afghanistan, Iran, and Mexico (Thio, 1995). The roots of this drug are similarly long and deep. Archaeologists have found references to the use of the opium poppy plant dating back at least six thousand years, and the plant has caused widespread addiction in many parts of the world. Two wars were fought in China, for example, in 1839 and 1856, as the British defended their right to smuggle opium "with relentless energy" into China against the wishes of the Chinese government (Morris, 1988). The British won the wars, took over Hong Kong, and increased the amount of opium it forced China to accept.

In the West, the more important date is 1803, when a German scientist purified the active ingredient in opium into a new drug ten times more powerful. He called it *morphine,* after the Greek god of dreams, Morpheus. In 1853, Alexander Wood perfected the hypodermic needle, allowing morphine to be injected directly into the veins. This technique became very popular shortly afterwards, when the extraordinarily destructive American Civil War took place. With only the crudest medical techniques, morphine was virtually all doctors had to fight enormous pain, dysentery, and fatigue.

However, it was so widely used and so powerfully addictive that a tremendous number of veterans came home addicted to the drug. Morphine addiction was known for quite some time as "the soldier's disease."

Given, as we discussed earlier, the enormous number of patent medicines with morphine as an additive, as many as a million or more Americans became addicted to morphine in the late 1800s. Because this addiction could be fed with over-the-counter remedies such as Col. Henry's Elixer, or, for that matter, by mail-order from Sears, Roebuck, it was easy and cheap to maintain. It did have one drawback: there were side effects such as nausea, so that the addict often felt "sickly." The typical addict was female, white, middle-class, Southern, and heading toward middle-age. She was not some deviant who could not conform to her culture; if anything, the opposite was true. Many middle-class women were caught in the midst of social change. Up until perhaps a generation earlier, everyone except perhaps a few very wealthy individuals had to work. Even those not engaged in wage labor had hard work to do around the house. With industrial capitalism, however, a new middle class of managers emerged who earned enough money to operate an entire household and to hire servants to do the actual work. At the same time, the work world remained a male domain, with women for the most part denied a chance for waged labor, the vote, or many civil rights. Some of these white, middle-class women had absolutely nothing to do but to sit around inventing illnesses and taking patent medicines filled with addicting opiates. This did not apply to women of color or immigrant or working-class women, of course, who always had to work. Nor did it apply to the "deviant" women who took on charitable and social causes. In fact, much of what has been termed the Reform Era of this time was fueled by women with enough time on their hands to work toward cleaning up the messes (pollution, disease, delinquency, starvation) made by their capitalist husbands. In contrast, the more conforming women might become drug addicts.

At the turn of the century, the Bayer company of Germany came up with two new products: aspirin and heroin. In an era when two of the primary causes of death were pneumonia and tuberculosis, Bayer's scientists discovered that heroin provided quick relief from coughs, chest pains, and related discomforts. Although it was marketed for this purpose, some other physicians noted that it had another great advantage: it ended the withdrawal symptoms from morphine, did not have the side effects such as nausea, and could be used in smaller doses. Unfortunately, few noted at first that it was also addictive (Inciardi, 1992).

For a wide variety of reasons, none of which can be adequately explained in even a few pages, the U.S. government became concerned with the opiates in the early part of the twentieth century. Part of this concern was with patent medicines, which could contain just about anything but that did not have to list their ingredients; part was a growing prohibitionist attitude about introducing chemical substances into the body; part was a medical concern for the possible ill effects of drug addiction; part was the feeling that opiates were no longer being taken by the middle class but by the lower class; and part was pressure from foreign governments as a result of the Hague Opium Convention. The result was the Harrison Act of 1914, a new law that was fascinating in how it changed people's perceptions of drugs.

The Harrison Act simply required that opiates and cocaine be sold in pharmacies, that the pharmacies keep good records, and that they sell the drugs only on a doctor's prescription. From the beginning, the Treasury Department (which administered the law) argued that "with a prescription" meant that only legitimate medical purposes could be served, and maintaining an addict was not one of those purposes. Addicts (for the most part lower class by now) were degenerates held in the grip of vice, according to the government (Musto, 1973). Since medicine had no answers on how to cure addicts, the answer lay in law enforcement, and rather quickly "narcotics, heroin in particular, were demonized, and drug users were caricatured to the point of dehumanization" (Oppenheimer, 1993, p. 198). Now, any doctor who tried to prescribe heroin to a patient was jailed. Only a few years after addiction had been widely regarded as an unfortunate problem of middle-class women, it became the unmentionable vice of the scum of the earth—lower-class and minority men trying to avoid work and responsibility.

Following World War II, even as penalties got harsher and harsher, heroin use flourished in the inner cities. Since then, heroin consumption rates seem to have fluctuated, although we have had a great deal of difficulty determining the exact amount of heroin use in the United States, and even whether use is going up or down. Elliott Currie (1993) claims that it is now on the rise; however, Erich Goode (1994) contends that of all the well-known illicit drugs, heroin is the least popular. In general, just as overall drug use seems to have decreased in the late 1980s and early 1990s, heroin use may have similarly been going down. However, in various specific places, heroin may be coming back and replacing crack or powder cocaine as the drug of choice (Hanson & Venturelli, 1995).

Heroin is usually fairly pure when it comes into the United States, but it is "cut" many times by dealers before it reaches users. The bag of heroin that you purchase on the streets is generally about 3–5 percent heroin and 95–98 percent other stuff that someone has mixed in. One of the problems in determining the danger of this drug is that 98 percent of what people are shooting into their arms is quinine, lactose, talc, or even arsenic. Because the primary side effect of the opiates is constipation, some dealers cut heroin with mannitol, which has a laxative effect. Quinine is often used to cut heroin because it has a similar taste, which makes it difficult to determine the potency of the heroin by taste alone. Yet, a standard text on drugs suggests that quinine, when injected, "is an irritant, and it causes vascular damage, acute and potentially lethal disturbances in heartbeat, depressed respiration, coma, and death from respiratory arrest" (Hanson & Venturelli, 1995, p. 242). One of the many arguments for legalizing drugs, or at least placing people on maintenance doses, is that government regulation can cut back on such adulterants.

Interestingly, of all of the various drugs, legal or illegal, heroin has the fewest harmful effects associated with it (Inciardi, 1992). Although many years of government propaganda has convinced most people that this drug is extraordinarily dangerous, not a single study has shown cell damage directly related to heroin use. Of course, if you stick rusty needles in your arm or give yourself an overdose, you are courting danger.

Further, the idea that drugs are not necessarily dangerous is partially true of most of the drugs strongly criminalized in North America. After all, many steady users of heroin, marijuana, cocaine, and morphine are able to hold jobs and function as "normal" citizens over many years. The most famous example has always been William Holsted, the renowned surgeon and innovator who founded Johns Hopkins Medical School. A cocaine addict, he kicked that habit by becoming addicted to morphine for the rest of his career (Witters, Venturelli, & Hanson, 1992). Of course, there are many others, including the many thousands of doctors and nurses who became addicted to the opiates but managed to avoid detection because of their access to the drug. Further, as Charles Winick (1993) points out, one should not assume that drug users are social incompetents. The life of typical street addicts is far from quiet. Rather, they lead demanding lives of constant change and regular tasks, all requiring effort and some intelligence if they are to obtain sufficient drugs. Ron Santiago, in his recent book, *Tragic Magic,* explains in detail how unbelievably complex and busy his life was as a heroin addict (Hills & Santiago, 1992). Similarly, Christina Johns (1992, p. 61) asks about Washington, DC, mayor Marion Barry, who was convicted of crack cocaine use: "The question that was never asked in the media . . . was how he could have run the capital of the country for years while smoking a drug that (according to the administration and the media) turns people into violent, out-of-control zombies."

Angel Dust, Acid, and Ecstasy: The Initials Drugs

There are literally thousands of known natural and synthetic substances that have an effect on the body that some people would describe as pleasurable or desirable. Obviously, a good book on pharmacology (see the Suggested Readings section of this chapter) would be important for someone who wishes detailed information. However, some mention should be made of these three widely used drugs: (1) Angel Dust, or PCP, (2) acid, or LSD, and (3) Ecstasy, or MDMA.

PCP is usually available in powder form, and it is most commonly used sprinkled on marijuana or tobacco (thus, one of its nicknames: Angel Dust). Technically a depressant, PCP is considered a hallucinogen because it alters perception in a way that users obviously enjoy. Alex Thio (1995) points out that the popular perception and fear of Angel Dust stems from media reports that PCP typically results in massive bad reactions, often ending in violence. Such episodes, however, are rare and virtually unknown from moderate doses. The drug is not addicting, and, in fact, is still legally used by veterinarians to sedate large animals.

LSD is a complex molecule that requires a sophisticated lab to manufacture. Although this hallucinogen was very popular in the 1960s, it declined in popularity for some twenty years before returning again in the 1990s. However, the standard dose taken today is much smaller than in the 1960s, which no doubt accounts for the smaller incidence of side effects or "bad trips." Actually, it is difficult to say much about LSD, because it affects so many different parts of the brain that people react differently. In any case, it is not addicting, and tolerance builds up quickly, so a person cannot take one dose after another and get the same effect.

Generally, the typical effect of LSD is heightened awareness. People feel that they are smarter, more creative, and more insightful on "acid," although some "freak out" from seeing extreme distortions. As Glen Hanson and Peter Venturelli (1995, p. 344) put it: "In sum, LSD alters perception such that any sensation can be perceived in the extreme." Perfectly ordinary events that we all deal with daily "can be incredibly beautiful and uplifting or completely foul and disgusting." The people who seem to have had the worst problems with LSD were the ones who did not know what they were taking and who just began experiencing wild hallucinations. In the 1950s, for example, the CIA gave 585 soldiers and 900 civilians LSD without telling them what was happening, and several participants became so upset they committed suicide.

In some ways, the drugs we should worry about the most are the new "designer drugs," the most popular of which is MDMA, or Ecstasy. First "invented" but never marketed eighty years ago as an appetite suppressant, MDMA is about as difficult to make as filtered coffee. It was only outlawed in the mid-1980s. The drug is based on the amphetamine stimulants and has all of the effects of such drugs, but it also has a hallucinogenic effect. It lowers defense mechanisms and loosens inhibitions, which is why it was used extensively by a number of psychiatrists to relax patients who were not forthcoming with their feelings. Evidently, the drug is not particularly dangerous to most people, but it has been listed as the cause of death of youths in England who take Ecstasy at raves, night-long dances that involve extreme physical exertion in hot, sweaty atmospheres. As the rave culture has spread to the United States from England, it is possible that Ecstasy will become very popular again.

Marijuana

Marijuana unquestionably is the most widely used illegal drug in the United States today, with more than 20 million users. Certainly, the drug has been used since ancient times, but in modern times opposition to its use has been high. As discussed earlier, the U.S. federal government outlawed marijuana with the Marijuana Tax Act of 1937. Michael Elsner (1994) points out that historians have been split on just why this act was passed, with two competing hypotheses most popular. First, there is the moral crusade of the Federal Bureau of Narcotics, which, acting on its own initiative, lobbied for and got Congress to pass the act. Part of the reason may have been moral outrage that the drug was being used, and part may have been a desire to expand the territory of the agency itself, giving it more power and control at a time when its budget was being cut. Some of the strong supporters of the new law were liquor manufacturers, who did not like the idea of other substances making inroads into their territory (Henslin, 1994). The second hypothesis, which is perhaps more popular today among criminologists, is that the legislation was put forth in an attempt to exert social control over Mexican-Americans in the Southwest, much like opium laws were passed earlier mainly as anti-Chinese laws. This law gained the full support of racist newspaper publishers such as William Randolph Hearst. Elsner (1994) suggests that all of these explanations are true—that they are all part of the same picture.

Generally, recreational use of marijuana results in some euphoria, increased sensitivity, and an increased appetite. More than a few comedians have suggested that pot use is sponsored by pizza delivery businesses near college campuses! Other reactions have caused many to argue that marijuana is useful for a wide variety of medical patients, since it can provide pain relief, increase the appetite of AIDS sufferers, and control the nausea of chemotherapy patients. Of course, taken in large quantities, marijuana has some of the same effects as alcohol, in that it affects judgment and psychomotor responses.

There have been many reports in the literature over the past fifteen years of the discovery of a variety of health hazards from marijuana, but "careful checking of these findings—either by repeating the experiment or by devising a better one—has found no damage from marijuana use" (Thio, 1995, p. 355). In fact, Victor Kappeler, Mark Blumberg, and Gary Potter's argument (1993, p. 156) is that the "real danger to marijuana smokers comes from marijuana which has been tainted by government drug control programs, such as the spraying of paraquat and other herbicides on marijuana crops."

Interestingly, while it is usually legal to obtain a wide variety of drug books and paraphernalia to support drug use and even addiction, the one drug instrument that can substantially reduce the risk of both AIDS and hepatitis—the disposable hypodermic needle—is usually illegal to sell over the counter.

HEALTH RISKS AND PROBLEMS

Earlier in this chapter, we pointed out that the health risks of cocaine and heroin pale in comparison to those of tobacco and alcohol. Still, this is not to say that there are no health risks at all with these drugs. One of the most important was discussed in the section on cocaine: the problem of a high risk of AIDS infection when sharing needles with a population known to include many people with the AIDS virus. Although most Americans by now have learned that AIDS can be spread through sexual contact, the only risk factor associated with approximately 25 percent of the more than 200,000 diagnosed AIDS cases in the United States is intravenous drug use (Currie, 1993). In other words, about 25 percent of AIDS cases apparently developed because of shared needles in illegal drug use. Of course, this figure could be cut dramatically by providing clean, sterile needles to drug abusers, which would be substantially cheaper than the medical costs of dealing with only a couple of AIDS cases, as has been proven throughout Europe and Australia. James Wright and Joel Devine (1994, p. 75) could not be more blunt:

> It appears that we would prefer to let HIV infection spread among the drug-using population and shoulder the ensuing costs of treating the infection, rather than do something cheap and effective to arrest the spread of the disease in the first place.

It is for this reason that some young users smoke heroin. This method also makes heroin easier to handle at a psychological level because smokers can view their behavior as an "unproblematic extension of more conventional pursuits," such as smoking marijuana or tobacco (Auld, Dorn, & South, 1986, p. 175). Others who are highly sensitive to the dangers of self-injecting heroin either "sniff" or "snort" it.

Still, despite the risks of overdosing or contracting AIDS, hepatitis, and other serious ailments, most heroin users inject this substance either subcutaneously ("skin popping") or intravenously. The main reason for choosing this technique is that it is the fastest way to get high.

Pregnancy and Female Drug Users

In recent years, there has been a steadily growing recognition of a new social problem, fed by a new set of legal decisions. As we have slowly discovered the problem of children born to mothers who abused drugs during pregnancy, American courts have slowly begun to develop a new field of law on "fetal rights." Although the impetus for these laws were the arguments of anti-abortionists, the court decisions themselves have very strong implications for the rights of states to monitor and criminalize the behavior of mothers who choose not to have abortions. Fascinatingly, in these cases, abortions themselves remain legal, but more and more the government is intervening into the lives of women who choose to carry their babies to term, to investigate whether or not they are acting as fit mothers-to-be.

The problem is that babies are physically dependent upon their mothers in the womb, and can obtain more than nutrients from them. According to

Elliott Currie (1993), by the end of 1990, 83 percent of the children who contracted AIDS got it from their mothers, and most of these women were IV drug users. James Inciardi and colleagues (1993) suggest that as many as 400,000 drug-exposed babies are born each year and that a growing number of those exposed to cocaine in the womb experience health problems such as the following:

- Abnormally small heads and brains
- Sudden infant death syndrome or crib deaths
- Deformed genital organs and urinary tracts
- Neurological damage leading to extraordinary irritability and learning disorders
- Premature birth and low weight

Cocaine is not the only worry. The medical costs of dealing with these babies and with those abandoned at birth is staggering. The third-leading cause of birth defects associated with mental retardation is fetal alcohol syndrome, caused by pregnant women who drink heavily during pregnancy (Hawk, 1994).

One response to this problem has been to define a new form of illegal behavior: the criminalization of pregnancy. A growing number of women are being criminally charged across the United States because of behavior engaged in while pregnant. The issue becomes even more complex when the women are engaging in perfectly legal behavior: smoking cigarettes or drinking alcohol. Can a woman be charged with a crime for failing to eat good, wholesome food during pregnancy? This is a new issue because, until now, courts have never treated the woman and the fetus as separate beings. Only with new laws granting fetuses independent rights can society charge a woman with the crime of acting in a way that she enjoys but that is bad for the fetus (Viano, 1994). Interestingly, there is no requirement in the U.S. law that a woman sacrifice her life or health interests for the sake of her children after birth (King, 1993). Further, there is no equivalent movement to criminalize the behavior of men who endanger fetuses. For example, although pregnant women probably are not battered at a higher rate than other women, they are battered commonly and at least as often as other women (Gelles, 1990). The outcome of this battering, which is often directed at the abdomen (perhaps in jealousy of the upcoming competition?), can be miscarriages, stillbirths, or injuries to the fetus. Why is there no national movement in anti-abortion circles to charge men with manslaughter if their battering of their wives leads to a miscarriage (Koss et al., 1994)? Similarly, women who endanger their fetuses with alcohol, nicotine, pharmaceuticals manufactured by Wall Street firms, or steroids are not often in danger of prosecution. Only women who use certain other drugs are in danger of criminal prosecution. Worse, these steps are being taken in the absence of solid information. Although we think we know the influence of cocaine on fetal development, the problem is that "it is practically impossible to find pregnant women who use cocaine but do not also drink heavily" (Wright & Devine, 1994, p. 71). We have no way of knowing what damage was caused by the illegal drug and what damage was caused by the legal drug!

Part of the problem is determining what to do about the situation. What draws all sides together is that no one is in favor of having large numbers of deformed and retarded children born each year. But Maureen Hawk (1994) argues that laws criminalizing pregnancy behavior simply won't work for a number of reasons:

- We have no proper facilities for incarcerated pregnant addicts.
- Since drugs are just as available in U.S. jails as on the streets, such laws won't stop drug use anyway.
- With doctors in public hospitals the main agents for the state in seeking out women to prosecute under the criminal law, pregnant women have a legitimate fear of seeking prenatal care. Keeping pregnant women away from competent medical attention is, to say the least, counterproductive.
- Giving a mother a criminal record is harmful in and of itself and may prevent her from being able to provide for her child later on.
- Such laws are not being enacted because people feel that they will not be effective, Rather, they will make powerful anti-abortion and fetal rights supporters happy while harming only lower-class women, particularly women of color. Middle-class white women are not likely to be in public clinics, where they are in danger of being turned over to the police. Police and prosecutors have no known arrangements with private hospitals.

Inciardi and colleagues (1993) suggest that another effect of such laws is to keep chemically dependent women away from treatment for drug abuse, since therapists might also want to monitor their pregnancies. This is particularly a problem for African-American women. A fear that medical professionals might arrange to take their children away from them is well-founded: African-American mothers are referred to child abuse authorities by doctors for possible child removal ten times as often as white women (Elias, 1993). A majority of prosecutions of pregnant women have involved women of color (Kasinsky, 1993).

For these reasons, and for others that we will discuss in the next chapter, the "criminalization of pregnancy" will not significantly reduce the large number of drug-exposed children born each year (Maher, 1990). Of course, drug-using mothers have to accept some responsibility for jeopardizing their children's well-being. However, our time and energy would be better spent if we addressed the key factors that motivate or allow women to engage in behaviors that have the risk of injuring their offspring. These factors include poverty, unemployment, and the inadequate provision of prenatal health care (Humphries, 1993; King, 1993). These and other symptoms of a political economy based on gross inequality also motivate people to put their children at risk through the consumption of legal drugs like alcohol. In both the United States and Canada, those at the greatest risk of suffering from fetal alcohol syndrome are Native Americans and Native Canadians, in many ways the most disadvantaged people of all.

Needles, Cramps, and Victimization

So far, we have devoted substantial attention to the harms done to children by substance-abusing mothers. Of course, drug-dependent adults also suffer from major health problems. Consider women who are so addicted to cocaine that they turn to prostitution in order to get money to purchase this substance. Many of them end up with cervical cancer, sexually transmitted diseases, and a myriad of other medical problems. We have already learned that people addicted to certain drugs can go for days without eating or sleeping. Not because of the drugs, but because of the lifestyle imposed by the illegal status of the drugs, the addicts often live in unsanitary conditions or are homeless and go without treatment for medical problems until they are overwhelming. No matter what the drugs can do to your body, the lifestyle involved in lower-class extreme addiction is very damaging to the body.

Heroin, a drug that is generally harmless in and of itself (excluding the medical problems from the lifestyle), does have one serious problem: taking a dose of heroin substantially greater than what your body is adjusted to and used to can be immediately fatal. In fact, at the time of writing this chapter, Vancouver, British Columbia, was experiencing an epidemic of lethal overdoses. This problem was considered so serious that some members of the provincial government publicly stated that they are considering decriminalizing heroin to lower the rate of both lethal and nonlethal overdoses resulting from the use of a high potency "brand-name" version called China White.

Parts of the United States are experiencing the same problem, with perhaps as many as 2,500 deaths per year attributed to heroin overdoses. Erich Goode (1994), who maintains that the number of heroin users is going down, argues that this number is high because the declining number of heroin users are consuming more potent drugs, as in Canada.

There are, of course, other health problems related to heroin use. For IV users, constantly sticking needles (especially the almost homemade needles many street-level addicts put together) into their arms eventually can lead to problems with veins and sores. More important today, as suggested previously, unless new or clean needles are used (simply soaking needles in bleach is effective), the user runs the risk of contracting AIDS or hepatitis. On a regular or daily basis, though, heroin addicts are more worried about the fact that a failure to get their daily dose exposes them to withdrawal. This is a serious complaint by the body that may seem like an extremely bad case of the flu:

> Your body . . . begins to ache. I mean physically ache—your muscles, your joints. Your stomach cramps up. Like there's no food in it, but the cramps are very painful. It's like somebody sticks a needle in your spine and sucks out all the fluid out of your bones and all you're left with is raw nerves. You can't sit down. You're very agitated. You're very aggravated. Even your bowels change in withdrawal. When you're shooting heroin, however, you're constipated, and don't even take a shit. It slows down all of your body processes. All of them. And in order for your body to function, you have to maintain a certain level of the drug in your system. When this level starts to

drop, you start to feel withdrawal symptoms. You start to feel pain.
(Hills & Santiago, 1992, p. 2)

A final area of health problems related to drug addiction is another part
of the lifestyle forced upon drug addicts by the fact that cocaine and heroin
are illegal drugs. Because of this, most street addicts must commit crimes to
obtain money to support their habits, which exposes them to serious danger.
Note that the typical drug addict is not necessarily someone who has never
committed a crime and must suddenly start after becoming an addict.
Rather, people engaged in street crimes are more likely to use drugs. Seven-
teen percent of state prison inmates said they committed their offense to get
money for drugs (BJS, 1995). As Inciardi (1992) points out, drug use inten-
sifies and heightens criminal careers; people undoubtedly commit more
crimes and place themselves in more danger when they are heavily abusing
illegal drugs.

Thus, when addicts commit robberies or burglaries, they are always
placing themselves into dangerous situations that could culminate with their
being arrested or even shot. Further, cocaine-dependent prostitutes are
beaten, raped, and psychologically abused by their pimps, customers, or
even drug dealers. Earlier, we discussed the sexual acts that a crack-addicted
prostitute in a crack house will perform. In the same way, she "will tolerate
extreme levels of verbal physical abuse in her pursuit of a vial of crack"
(Bourgois & Dunlap, 1993, p. 123). Within crack houses, customers who
are "too high" to maintain an erection or achieve orgasm commonly fly into
a macho rage and blame their sexual problems on the crack whore's failure
as a sex object. It is not uncommon for her to be beaten or severely abused.

Similarly, on the streets, prostitutes are beaten, stabbed, and terrorized
by customers, as well as beaten and robbed by drug dealers. For example,
Jody Miller and Martin Schwartz (1995) found in their interviews with
street prostitutes that violent victimization was a constant and regular feature
of their lives. Although they developed extensive strategies to avoid violence,
prostitutes who were drug dependent were perhaps more likely to chance
entering a risky situation. Further, the existence and use of drugs on the
streets contributes to an overall environment in which prostitutes are vulnerable to attack by men who are under the influence of drugs and by both
dealers and users for whom prostitutes make easy targets for robbery and
assault (Miller, 1993).

Lacy, one of Miller and Schwartz's (1995, p. 16) prostitute informants, describes how they are vulnerable to attack:

> We get beat up all the time. . . . I mean, we're the objects of everybody's anger it seems like, you know. The dope man's had a bad day, and we just happen to come along at the wrong time, you know. Or dates, you know, get picked up by stupid dates. Ex-boyfriends, and people who are on crack.

HOW MANY PEOPLE USE COCAINE AND HEROIN?

How many people experience the "pros" and "cons" associated with using cocaine and heroin? Although we will discuss some of the many estimates here, it is important to remember that every data set underestimates the true extent of cocaine and heroin use (Wessinger & Wodarski, 1994). Problems similar to those noted in Chapter 9 in relation to research into woman abuse are also applicable here. Think about it. If you were in charge of a research project, how would you go about finding out how much illicit drug use exists? Look at police, prison, or court data? Go door to door and ask people if they use heroin or cocaine? Regardless of what technique you use, it will be inadequate, because many people will not tell the truth about their involvement with illegal drugs. They might be embarrassed or want to avoid being labeled a "junkie" or an unproductive member of society. How do they *really* know that you won't turn them in, so that they can be sent to prison or lose their job? Given the current war on drugs and widespread social disapproval, this caution is clearly well-founded. As the saying goes, if you have real enemies out there, your behavior isn't paranoid.

Still, even if it is impossible to obtain *totally* accurate data on cocaine and heroin use, some criminologists have been intent on trying to generate the most reliable estimates they can. Such data tend to be derived from self-report surveys, such as the 1990 *National Household Survey on Drug Abuse* (NHSDA) (NIDA, 1991a, 1991b). This study was sponsored by the National Institute on Drug Abuse (NIDA), and the major findings will be briefly described here.

In general, NHSDA data gathered from U.S. household residents age 12 and older uncovered a significant amount of cocaine use but less crack use:

- Approximately 11 percent of respondents reported using cocaine (excluding crack) at least once in their lifetime.
- The numbers were lower for recent use: 3 percent stated that they used cocaine (excluding crack) in the year preceding the survey, and 1 percent in the previous month.
- Of those age 12–17, 1 percent reported using crack at least once in their lifetime, while 0.75 percent consumed it in the past year.
- Of those age 18–25, 2.75 percent used crack in their lifetime, 1.4 percent used it in the past year, and 0.70 percent consumed it in the past month.
- Of those age 26–34, 3.6 percent used crack during their lifetime, 1 percent used it in the past year, and 0.60 percent ingested it in the past month.

How many people use heroin? The NHSDA was not as successful in uncovering heroin use. Evidently, heroin is much more popular among those who do not live in households, which means that such users were not part of the NHSDA. Of those surveyed, about 1 percent said that they had used heroin in their lifetime. Further, many heroin users also drop out of school. Thus, national self-report data from high school students currently enrolled, summarized by the 1990 Monitoring the Future Project (Johnson, O'Malley, & Bachman, 1991), should be interpreted with caution. For example, only 1 percent of the student respondents reported ever taking heroin, while 0.5 percent stated that they used it in the past year. If drug users are more likely to drop out of school, which is certainly possible, then they are not being questioned with this methodology.

Thus, at first glance, data generated by self-report questionnaires administered to household residents and high school students suggest that the United States does not have a major cocaine or heroin problem. Of course, a drawback of this method is that the people most likely to have a drug problem are the ones least likely to be questioned in these surveys. Transients, high school dropouts, homeless people, and disenfranchised members of our society are far more likely to use hard drugs, but their experiences are not tapped by mainstream survey research. Mainstream studies also tend to exclude people who are in drug rehabilitation or AIDS clinics, hospitals, prisons, or "boot camps."

For these reasons, the Drug Use Forecasting (DUF) program was developed. In this program, staff at twenty-four major city sites come in every three months and both interview and urine-test voluntary participants who have been arrested for felony crimes and are being held at the central booking facility. Given the mayhem of most booking facilities, these offenders unquestionably are typical of all arrestees. What the DUF has managed to show is that a very high percentage of those arrested for felonies have drug traces in their bodies. At a time when drug use seems to be level or lowering in the general population, it remains extremely high (as high as 80 percent of arrestees) among those arrested. Although women make up only a very small percentage of those arrested, these women are even more likely than the men to have drugs in their system.

Thus, among one of the groups least likely to be captured in household surveys, drug use was found to be as much as nine times higher than in the general population, where drug use was leveling off (Reardon, 1993). Since urine testing can only reveal drug use in the past forty-eight or so hours (except for marijuana and PCP), even this method may be considered very conservative, since it would not catch anyone who had been drug-free for only two days, much of which may have been spent in custody. The method has its value, as it can track among arrestees in different cities the various increases and decreases in the popularity of one drug versus another. Still, it may be very misleading. If the police decide to ignore heroin users this year to focus all of their attention on, say, PCP dealers and users, then the DUF would show a dramatic reduction in the use of heroin by arrestees. Of course, what it would be showing is a change in police behavior.

THE DISTRIBUTION OF COCAINE AND HEROIN USE

Who uses hard drugs like cocaine and heroin? In answering this question, we focus on four areas: (1) sex, (2) age, (3) socioeconomic status, and (4) race/ethnicity and location.

Sex

We have noted previously that men are more likely to kill people, engage in spousal violence, and commit corporate, white-collar, and political crime—and to take hard, addicting drugs (Goode, 1989; NIDA, 1991a). Perhaps a gender difference exists for exactly the same reason it does in all of these other crimes: in North American society, men are more likely generally to engage in criminal and deviant activities (Thio, 1995). Overall, gender-role expectations and consequences in our society are much greater for women than for men. Therefore, whereas men who are irresponsible drug users may simply be "sowing their wild oats," women may also be considered sexually promiscuous, emotionally unstable, and bad mothers. Further, whereas men often have wives and parents to help them withdraw or re-enter society, women either have drug-using husbands themselves or are more likely than men to be in deep trouble with their families. Because they are considered to be violating gender norms, women who are serious drug abusers also are more likely to be completely cut off from conventional society (Inciardi, Lockwood, & Pottieger, 1993).

Lately, a significant amount of attention has been given to female drug users, with suggestions that drug-using female offenders are the fastest-growing population in the U.S. criminal justice system (see, for example, Wellisch, Prendergast, & Anglin, 1994). The media, in particular, has speculated that women are especially attracted to crack and that there may be an epidemic of female crack users in America's inner cities. Any data on this, of course, must be tempered by the fact that, because so many more men than women use drugs, a relatively small increase in the number of female users can look like a large *percentage* increase. Further, much of the concern derives from arrest statistics, which may reflect the actions of law enforcement authorities as much as any behavior on the part of women. For example, from 1991 to 1992, UCR data show an increase in arrests for "drug abuse violations" of 13.8 percent for men and 18.1 percent for women. In raw numbers, however, that is an increase of 7,072 for men and 1,128 for women. Looked at another way, there were a grand total of 7,346 arrests of women for drug abuse violations in 1992. The *increase* in male arrests (51,094 to 58,166) is about equal to the *total* number of female arrests! Interestingly, for those individuals age 18–25—the age group with the highest rates of cocaine use—the percentage of women who used cocaine in the month before the survey dropped from 1991 to 1992 (1.3 percent to 0.8 percent), while the percentage of men climbed (2.8 percent to 2.9 percent) (Maguire, Pastore, & Flanagan, 1993).

Why, then, is there such a panic about female drug users? Patricia Erikson and Glenn Murray (1989) see this as yet another example of the oft-noted fears about female crime trends: that as we have allowed women out of the house and into the paid workplace, they have moved into previously male-dominated areas of crime. Here, the concern is that women's crack cocaine use is more sexually corrupting (a worry we don't have about men) and that women are taking on male criminal characteristics. In reality, however, we have no reason to believe that women are more drawn to crack cocaine than men are. One thing we can be sure of is that we lock up many women for drug offenses. Fully one-third of all women in state prisons are serving time for a drug offense, as compared to 21 percent of the men (BJS, 1995).

Age

Young males, especially those in the 18–25 age group, are the people most likely to use hard drugs (NIDA, 1991a). According to Alex Thio (1995), these people constitute the highest-risk age group because, compared with older people, they have a lower stake in conformity. All things considered, they are less likely to have adult responsibilities or investments in the conventional social order, and they may also lack attachments to significant others. In other words, they often don't have jobs, spouses, and children, and they are not closely supervised by their parents. Thus, they have more freedom and time to consume drugs.

Critical criminologists offer an alternative explanation for the relationship between age and drug use, one that takes into account the negative consequences of urban unemployment. Both the United States and Canada have high levels of youth unemployment, especially in the inner cities. Many unemployed youths who live in these impoverished neighborhoods also have unemployed parents who cannot afford to provide them with expensive clothes, tickets to rock concerts, spending money, and so on. And even if these young people are working, many find that the financial rewards are minimal. Worst of all, they might live in neighborhoods so lacking in economic opportunity that selling drugs has become widely accepted as a legitimate economic opportunity. And, of course, child labor laws do not apply to illegal drug dealing: such "jobs" are fully available to children who want money.

Socioeconomic Status

Certainly, drugs are widely used in all segments of society, and some evidence suggests that wealthier users, who can afford to buy as much cocaine as they want, may be society's heaviest abusers (Winick, 1993). However, after forty years of research, the inescapable conclusion is that hard-drug use is not evenly distributed in the United States. The unemployed and subemployed are the ones most likely to use heroin and crack. Socioeconomic inequality is one of the leading causes of hard-drug use and dealing in inner-city America, an issue we will discuss in greater detail later in this chapter.

One exception to this rule is that, occasionally, some surveys show that this pattern does not always fit for women. Older women, with higher family incomes, sometimes admit to abusing drugs in greater number than younger women with lower incomes (Zalenko, 1992).

Race/Ethnicity and Location

The highest rates of cocaine and heroin use are found among African-Americans and Hispanics, although the differences are not particularly large when looking at the country as a whole. In terms of the numbers of persons who have taken these drugs in the past year, the rates are slightly higher for African-Americans than for whites, and slightly higher for Hispanics than for African-Americans. The one dramatic difference is with crack, where the rate for African-Americans is more than twice the rate for whites or Hispanics (Maguire & Pastore, 1994).

However, serious differences begin to show up for inner-city residents, where we find large numbers of minority drug users (NIDA, 1991a, 1991b). Why are inner-city African-Americans and Hispanics at greater risk of using heroin and cocaine? The answer to this question does not depend on their biological makeup, skin color, or culture. Rather, many inner-city minority communities are characterized by poverty, unemployment, and a lack of adequate social services (for example, schools, hospitals, and so on). Further, U.S. minorities live predominantly in minority areas. Although African-Americans account for only 12 percent of the U.S. population, 57 percent live in high drug-use areas in central cities. Similarly, Hispanics account for about 7 percent of the U.S. population, but 55 percent live in central cities. In contrast, whites comprise 81 percent of the U.S. population, but only 27 percent live in central cities, which reduces their chances of exposure to these conditions. Of course, where whites are exposed to such factors, rates of drug use and dealing rise dramatically. In fact, rates of drug use in deprived white communities are higher than in "better-off" minority communities. Thus, in line with Robert Sampson's (1987) interpretation of African-American violent crime, we contend that an understanding of drug use among minority groups can be obtained only by looking at the structural linkages among unemployment, economic deprivation, and family disruption in their inner-city communities. There is a strong correlation between extreme social and economic inequality and drug use. One of the reasons the United States has perhaps the world's worst drug problem is that we as a people are more willing than the people of many other nations to tolerate extremely high levels of social inequality. As we will see in Chapter 12, the policies of imprisonment and individual treatment favored by U.S. politicians are never going to work. The only way to effectively curb drug abuse, drug dealing, and related crimes is by targeting the broader social and cultural forces that motivate people to harm themselves and others.

THEORIES OF DRUG USE

In this chapter, we have provided you with graphic descriptions of some of the problems of hard-drug use. Those of you who have never taken cocaine, heroin, or PCP and who do not know anyone who has, may be asking yourselves, "Why would anyone take substances that threaten their physical and psychological well-being?" Here, we will discuss some widely read and cited sociological answers to this question.

Strain Theory

Drugs are one of the issues that put some life into strain theory, which was discussed in detail in Chapter 6. For example, Robert Merton (1938, 1957) argued that the general goals of society are held out for everyone to meet, but that opportunities to reach these goals are not evenly and equally distributed. Those who cannot choose conformity (strive for the goals and use the legitimate means, such as educational success and a job) experience a great deal of strain. There are a number of ways to deal with this strain, and Merton outlined four of them. The one of interest here is *retreatism*, whereby people give up on both the goals and the legitimate means and instead become drug users. They get high because, according to Isidor Chein, drugs

> offer a quick and royal route to meeting the challenge of living. Heroin and its related subculture gives them a sense of well-being and of social acceptability and participation. If the price is a terrible one to pay . . . the pseudo-rewards, especially in the "honeymoon stage," are far more glittering than anything else their environment offers them. (1966, pp. 137, 140)

Here, we see the beginnings of a powerful sociological statement as to why people would use drugs. Merton was particularly unhappy with the argument that drug users were psychologically weak people who used drugs because they were not strong enough to face society. Rather, he claimed, they were normal people facing an abnormal situation: that in some parts of society it is impossible to get the education and jobs necessary to achieve middle-class status. Retreating into drugs offered a series of real rewards.

As we saw in Chapter 6, Richard Cloward and Lloyd Ohlin (1960) developed this argument further, noting that Merton omitted illegitimate opportunity structures from his theory. For example, in Schwartz's hometown, a working-class city, there were extensive job opportunities that were rarely mentioned in discussions of unemployment—jobs as drug dealers, as workers in an extensive gambling network, as lookouts, as enforcers or "muscle," and so on. However, as Cloward and Ohlin describe it, the illegitimate opportunity structure looked for the same qualities in an employee as the legitimate structure: honesty, integrity, trustworthiness, and physical fitness and coordination. For example, petty thieves, disloyal or undependable individuals, serious cowards, and clumsy oafs are not highly sought after by drug merchants as entry-level employees. Thus, Cloward and Ohlin also suggested the development of a *retreatist subculture* made up of double failures: lower-class youths who cannot achieve status through either the legitimate or the illegitimate opportunity structure. They turn to drugs for solutions to their problems and withdraw from the broader community.

In sum, strain theories contend that the denial of legitimate opportunities to achieve material success is one of the key factors that motivates disenfranchised inner-city people to use hard drugs in order to cope with this problem, an argument that is still widely accepted today. We will return to it again in Chapter 12. Of course, strain theory cannot adequately address all drug use by all people. Some criminologists have attacked these and other strain perspectives because, in their current form, they cannot explain why middle- and upper-class people use heroin and cocaine (Thio, 1995). Other criminologists would argue that because drug abuse among the relatively affluent is both steadily decreasing and generally manageable, the staggering dimensions of drug use among the disenfranchised deserves the bulk of our theoretical and empirical attention.

Social Learning Theory

Illegal drugs are seldom enjoyed on the first taste, and most people do not use them on a day-to-day basis. Why, then, do some people become chronic users or addicts? Social learning theorists contend that heavy drug use is *learned* in intimate, face-to-face interactions with significant others, particularly peers, who routinely get high (Akers et al., 1979). People who spend most of their time with peers and significant others who strongly disapprove of drug use are not likely to become heavy users of illicit substances. As Neil Boyd (1992, p. 156) correctly points out, "The positive 'high' of drug use is not released by the trigger of chemistry as much as by the trigger of a positive mental set, influenced by a supportive social setting."

The learning process is as follows: First, peers typically ask someone to try a particular drug. This is exemplified below by one of Chein and colleagues' (1964, p. 151) respondents, who first tried heroin

> at a party. Everybody was having a good time. I wanted to be one of the crowd. I thought, if it didn't hurt them, it wouldn't hurt me.

They started the ball rolling. They were sniffing it at that time. Two or three pulled out a few caps and said, "Here, if you want to, try." I accepted. They weren't trying to addict me; they just gave it to me.

Some people may try a drug but not know how to get high or recognize its pleasurable effects. This is typical of novice marijuana users. In order for them to continue using marijuana for fun, according to Howard Becker (1973), three things must happen. First, they have to learn the techniques of getting high. Their friends usually teach them these "skills." For example, according to one of Becker's respondents:

I was smoking like I did an ordinary cigarette. He said, "No, don't do it like that." He said, "Suck it, you know, draw in and hold it in your lungs till you . . . for a period of time." I said, "Is there any limit of time to hold it?" He said, "No, just till you feel that you want to let it out, let it out." So I did that three or four times. (1973, p. 47)

Even if people learn the proper techniques of smoking marijuana, they may not recognize its pleasurable effects. Thus, to fulfill Becker's second criteria, their friends tell them what to look for (for example, hunger and "rubbery legs"). According to Becker:

It is only when the novice becomes able to get high in this sense that he will continue to use marijuana for pleasure. In every case in which use continued, the user had acquired the necessary concepts with which to express to himself the fact that he was experiencing new sensations caused by the drug. That is, for use to continue, it is necessary not only to use the drug so as to produce effects but also to learn to perceive these effects when they occur. In this way marijuana acquires meaning for the user as an object which can be used for pleasure. (1973, pp. 51–52)

The final step in the learning process involves enjoying the effects of marijuana. As we stated previously, most people don't like their first "high." This common experience is illustrated by one of Becker's respondents:

It started taking effect, and I didn't know what was happening, you know, what it was, and I was very sick. I walked around the room, walking around the room trying to get off, you know; it just scared me at first, you know. I wasn't used to that kind of feeling. (1973, p. 53)

In order to continue using marijuana, people have to redefine its effects as pleasurable. According to Becker, redefinition occurs in interactions with experienced users who teach "newcomers" how to find pleasure in smoking marijuana:

Well, they get pretty high sometimes. The average person isn't ready for that, and it is a little frightening to them sometimes. I mean, they've been high on lush [alcohol], and they get higher that way than they've ever been before, and they don't know what's happening to them. Because they think they're going to keep going up, up, up till they lose their minds or begin doing weird things or something. You have to like reassure them, explain to them that they're not really flipping or anything, that they're gonna be all right. You have to just talk them out of being afraid. Keep talking to them, reassuring, telling them it's all right. And come on with your own story, you know: "The same thing happened to me. You'll get to like that after awhile." Keep coming on like that; pretty soon you talk them out of being scared. And besides they see you doing it and nothing horrible is happening to you, so that gives them confidence. (quoted in Becker, 1973, p. 55)

In sum, it is only through frequent contact with other marijuana users that people come to regularly use this drug. However, it should be noted in passing that, while users of cocaine and heroin also have to learn the techniques of ingesting these substances, they may not need to be taught to recognize and enjoy their effects.

Unfortunately, while Becker's work has long been considered highly valuable in teaching us how people acquire definitions that value drugs and drug use, it does not tell us about the content of drug-using subcultures. In other words, Becker doesn't identify the types and characteristics of people who belong to drug-using groups. Moreover, his contribution does not address the factors that draw a novice into a drug subculture (Goode, 1989).

Social Bond Theory

Another theory presented in Chapter 6 that has been applied to drug use is Travis Hirschi's (1969) social bond theory. In the same way that the theory focuses on why most of us are *not* criminals, those who tap this theory are not interested in explaining why people take drugs. Rather, they organize their research around the question, Why don't most people take illicit drugs? Social bond theory contends that most of us are "clean and sober" because we have a strong social bond to conventional society. However, if our bond is broken or weakened, we are more likely to take drugs.

If this is the case, then how can social bond theory explain middle- and upper-class drug use? For example, powder cocaine is often referred to in terms such as "the luxurious drug of the middle-class" (Beirne & Messerschmidt, 1995). Compared with unemployed inner-city residents, middle-class people apparently have a lot more to lose if they are caught using or dealing this substance. Even so, some of them are willing to take this risk. Perhaps this can be explained by the fact that some middle-class people consider periodic drug use to be either acceptable or only mildly deviant behavior. According to Goode (1989, p. 66), a strong bond to the conventional social order does not absolutely preclude us from using drugs. However, it does make it less likely.

Elliott Currie offers an alternative explanation for drug use in affluent communities. According to him, "The absence of available or concerned adults, and the pervasiveness of an insistent consumer culture" can make middle- and upper-class people vulnerable to drug use (1993, p. 103). Unfortunately, Currie does not provide reliable evidence to support this argument.

Inequality and Drugs

Of course some middle- and upper-class people use illegal hard drugs. At least one noted drug expert claims that it is possible that the worst abusers of hard drugs may be upper-income individuals who can *afford* to ingest enormous quantities of cocaine on a regular basis (Winick, 1993). Still, we are relatively confident that most users belong to the "underclass." The most frequent and serious cocaine and heroin users are disenfranchised inner-city residents. As Currie points out:

> Forty years of accumulated research . . . confirms that endemic drug abuse is intimately related to conditions of mass social deprivation, economic marginality, and cultural and community breakdown—in Europe as in the United States, in the eighties and nineties as in the sixties, among poor whites and Hispanics as well as inner-city blacks. The effects of those conditions on individuals, families, and communities help explain why some kinds of people, in some kinds of places, are more vulnerable to drug abuse than others. (1993, p. 103)

Why do disenfranchised people use drugs as a means of adapting to the brutal effects of their economic situation? Currie contends that four models can help answer this question: (1) the status model, (2) the coping model, (3) the structure model, and (4) the saturation model.

According to the *status model,* poor people are denied legitimate means of attaining status. Thus, some marginalized people view drug use as an alternative means of attaining esteem, a sense of respect, and a sense of community. For example, one of Currie's respondents says cocaine

> gives you a feeling of superiority. It gives you a feeling that you're higher than the others. You're above the crowd. . . . Everybody is your friend because they can see it in your eyes that you are coked up. They are not going to fuck around with this guy. (1993, p. 107)

Status is also a central concern for many female heroin users. With its street reputation as the most dangerous drug, heroin bestows on its users a reputation as the most serious outlaws. A growing number of bored and alienated women are finding this reputation attractive (Rosenbaum, 1981).

The *coping model* views drugs as moderating the stress and insecurity of life in economically marginalized communities. For example, poor people face great difficulties surviving on a day-to-day basis. Being poor or homeless "virtually insures a life of chronic hassles" (Currie, 1993, p. 113). Examples of these problems are family crises; domestic violence; inadequate schooling, day care, and transportation; and stressful or dangerous work. Indeed, poor inner-city residents live "at best on the edge of disaster" (Currie, 1993, p. 113). What, then, is to be done? Some people cope with these and other problems associated with poverty by doing drugs. Cocaine and heroin help them "escape" from the stress and strain of everyday life. In fact, people who use drugs for coping purposes use them more often than those who use them for other reasons (for example, social and recreational).

The *structure model* asserts that drugs provide disenfranchised people with a sense of structure and purpose to their lives, especially if they don't have meaningful jobs. Being unemployed, for example, and particularly being unemployed with absolutely no hope of ever getting a job, generates boredom and a sense of monotony. Drugs alleviate these problems. Put simply, what else is there to do? Although he was talking about homeless alcoholics, Lars Eighner (1993, p. 162) makes this point: "In a life that seems utterly without meaning and purpose, the quest for the daily dose is something to do, a reason to keep putting one foot in front of the other."

The *saturation model* is an extension of the structure model. After decades and generations of limited economic opportunity, some of these communities become marked by pervasive hopelessness. Drug use becomes more and more widespread, until it virtually saturates the entire community. People don't really make a conscious effort to become drug users but just seem to drift into doing what everyone else is doing. Moreover, in a community saturated with drugs, quitting can become nearly impossible. One of Erich Goode's informants writes: "Whenever I saw my friends, they were shooting up, too. . . . The problem with kicking heroin . . . is that all of your friends aren't kicking at the same time" (1989, p. 252).

Currie is careful to point out that these four models are not mutually exclusive. For example, a poor person may use crack for all of the reasons described here. He may want peer group status, be "stressed out" or bored, and be surrounded by other crack users. Further, the motives for his crack use may change at different stages of his life. However, Currie contends that the status model best explains the early stages of drug use. As they get older, people do not derive as much excitement from using or dealing drugs, and they experience related long-term health problems. Nevertheless, they continue to take drugs because they either need some method of coping with the hassles of poverty or need to manage their habit. These problems became aggravated by their criminal status and addiction. Marsha Rosenbaum argues that female heroin addicts often cannot see a way out. Working and lower-class women

> have at least had the socially integrative and productive option of motherhood (a role often taken for granted). Women addicts lose even this option as their career in heroin progresses and their options

regress. Thus, due to the nature of their careers, women addicts experience the opposite of liberation. They are, in fact, more oppressed than other women: They lose not only their work options but their options for a traditional career in wife and motherhood. (1981, pp. 135–136)

In sum, although the factors that motivate poor, inner-city residents to use drugs change over time, the fact is that the key source of their drug use is social and economic marginality. What about affluent drug users? What makes them take hard drugs? Thio (1995) contends that Currie's "unifactor theory" cannot answer this question. In fairness to Currie, he did not intend to address this concern. For him, the drug problem of America's "have nots" warrants most of our empirical, theoretical, and political attention because (1) the drug problem of the affluent is manageable and decreasing and (2) the have-not drug problem has grown significantly despite the U.S. government's war on drugs. Indeed, the U.S. inner-city drug problem is far worse than it was when this war on drugs began, and the future is not encouraging. As Victor Kappeler, Mark Blumberg, and Gary Potter (1993, p. 162) point out, "Drug use actually increases during periods in which criminal penalties are harshest and enforcement most vigorous."

SUMMARY

A prime objective of this chapter was to point out that the process of determining which drugs should be made the object of the criminal law and which should not is a somewhat arbitrary one. The potential for bodily harm does not seem to be as important as the characteristics of the people generally associated with abusing the drug. Those drugs socially constructed and viewed as having been chosen by minority group members, by members of the working class, and by individuals attempting to avoid following society's rules seem to be most likely to be criminalized.

Of course, as we pointed out, cocaine, heroin, PCP, marijuana, LSD, and other illegal drugs can cause more or less bodily harm, but then again, so can many legal drugs, such as alcohol and nicotine. Cocaine and heroin use does seem to be more widespread in the devastated inner cities of the United States. Currie suggests that this is because drugs may provide status, a method of coping, and a form of structure to people's lives; drugs may also be so pervasive in some neighborhoods that drug use begins to seem inevitable for some people.

There are other health risks associated with drugs, including the physical harm that some people, such as street and crack house prostitutes, suffer at the hands of users and dealers. Babies born to drug-abusing mothers can also be harmed, which has led to an important debate on the criminalization of pregnancy.

In any case, in Chapter 12, we will discuss the failure of the efforts thus far to deal with these problems and present some ideas of what policies are more likely to hold the potential for success.

SUGGESTED READINGS

Boyd, N. (1991). *High Society: Legal and Illegal Drugs in Canada.* Toronto: Key Porter Books.

This book provides students and researchers with a comprehensive, intelligible overview of drug use in Canada.

Currie, E. (1993). *Reckoning: Drugs, the Cities, and the American Future.* New York: Hill & Wang.

Currie shows why hard-drug abuse is endemic to the United States. In addition, he clearly shows the inadequacies of the war on drugs, and he offers progressive, short-term control and prevention strategies.

Hanson, G., and Venturelli, P. (1995). *Drugs and Society,* 4th ed. Boston: Jones & Bartlett.

This textbook covers both the pharmacological aspects of drug use and abuse and the basic features of the social aspects of abuse.

Inciardi, J., Lockwood, D., and Pottieger, A. (1993). *Women and Crack-Cocaine.* New York: Macmillan.

Historically, criminologists have ignored female drug users, and especially those who use crack. This research gap is filled in well by this award-winning book.

Waterston, A. (1993). *Street Addicts in the Political Economy.* Philadelphia: Temple University Press.

Using rich ethnographic data gathered in New York City, Waterston provides a critical criminological description of the ways in which street addicts' lives are shaped by broader economic, political, and ideological forces.

PART IV

WHAT CAN WE DO ABOUT CRIME?

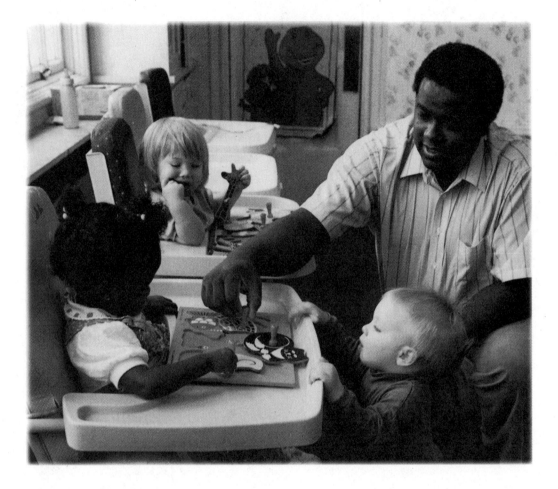

CHAPTER 12

POLICY RECOMMENDATIONS

Reform, sir? Reform? Don't talk to me of reform.
Things are bad enough as they are.

HENRY MAUDSLEY

Nostradamus (1503–1566), a French physician and astrologer, is one of the Western world's most famous predictors of the future. Many people have found in his predictions a chillingly accurate foretelling of major wars and other world events. However, Nostradamus had nothing on President Lyndon Johnson's National Commission on the Causes and Prevention of Violence. In their 1969 final report, this group concluded that if the nation didn't take massive action to curb violent inner-city crime, the consequences would be as follows (1969, pp. 47–48):

- Central business districts . . . surrounded by mixed areas of accelerating deterioration, will be partially protected by large numbers of people shopping or working in commercial buildings during daytime hours, plus a substantial police presence, and will be largely deserted except for police patrols during night-time hours.

- High-rise apartment buildings and residential compounds protected by private guards and security devices will be fortified cells for upper-middle and high-income populations living at prime locations in the city.

- Suburban neighborhoods, geographically far removed from the central city, will be protected mainly by economic homogeneity and by distance from population groups with the highest propensities to commit crimes.

- Lacking a sharp change in federal and state policies, ownership of guns will be almost universal in the suburbs, homes will be fortified by an array of devices from window grills to electronic surveillance equipment, armed citizen volunteers in cars will supplement inadequate police patrols in neighborhoods closer to the central city, and extreme left-wing and right-wing groups will have tremendous armories of weapons which could be brought into play with or without provocation.

- High-speed, patrolled expressways will be sanitized corridors connecting safe areas, and private automobiles, taxicabs, and commercial vehicles will be routinely equipped with unbreakable glass, light armor, and other security features. Inside garages or valet parking will be available at safe buildings in or near the central city. Armed guards will "ride shotgun" on all forms of public transportation.

- Streets and residential neighborhoods in the central city will be unsafe in differing degrees and the ghetto slum neighborhoods will be places of terror with wide-spread crime, perhaps entirely out of police control during night-time hours. Armed guards will protect all public facilities such as schools, libraries and playgrounds in these areas.

- Between the unsafe, deteriorating central city on the one hand and the network of safe, prosperous areas and sanitized corridors on the other, there will be, not unnaturally, intensifying hatred and deepening division. Violence will increase further and the defensive response of the affluent will become still more elaborate.

Not only have these predictions for the most part come true, they seem fairly routine to most of us. In larger urban areas across the United States, many people are afraid of venturing into some inner-city neighborhoods; police departments now have very sophisticated weapons and surveillance equipment (see Marx, 1988); private security officers routinely patrol apartment buildings, business grounds, and schools; and a tremendous number of people own weapons. Immediately after work, university lectures, or leisure activities, many people rush home because they are terrified of being victimized by predatory street criminals. Once home, some live behind barred and nailed-shut windows (even during heat waves) because they harbor deep suspicions of strangers.

On the individual level, given the high rates of crime reported throughout this text, these actions seem rational and appropriate—some of these measures do help to reduce the chances of victimization. Unfortunately, on a broader societal level, such measures do little to curb the massive amount of crime in the United States. As we have touched on previously, prisons and the psychological treatment of offenders have also been ineffective means of reducing and preventing crime. Thus, we have two primary objectives in this chapter. First, we wish to argue that opportunity reduction strategies, incarceration, and individual treatment will not make our lives much safer. Nor will the so-called victim movement, which has taken on an extraordinary life that serves symbolic but not concrete needs. Second, we want to end this book on an upbeat note. To show that all of the world is not "doom and gloom," we would like to propose some progressive, short-term alternative strategies. As we have suggested throughout this book, the fact that many of the responses being used in North America today are doomed to failure does not mean that there are not strategies with a better chance of success. We have been told that some of our strategies cannot work because they will cost money, which is tight. If money has not been too tight to triple the prison populations in many states, then money can be found for these solutions, too—if that is what people want.

WHAT ABOUT THE VICTIM?

Perhaps the most difficult area to discuss quickly and easily is the crime victim. The general population, the media, and the criminal justice system have all devoted a tremendous amount of attention recently to the victim's movement. The major force in this "rebirth" of the victim has been the feminist movement, which was outraged by the treatment of crime victims (Mawby & Walklate, 1994). Women (and also men) were ignored, treated with contempt, and generally considered irrelevant to the workings of the criminal justice system—except possibly as a witness for the prosecution. In recent years, the battle cry "What about the victim?" has been sounded louder and louder, even as more and more offenders have been given longer and longer prison sentences.

Todd Clear (1994) suggests that we would do well to distinguish different meanings of "victim." Of course, there are *victims as persons,* some of whom suffer staggering financial, psychological, and physical losses. But do we *really* care about crime victims? The primary victims of street crimes in the United States today are working-class people, and most especially minorities, and most of all young minority males. Has this entire movement of mostly middle-class white people come together to demand justice for inner-city African-Americans and Hispanics?

Often, Clear suggests, we use the term to mean instead *victim as collective*. We watch crime shows on TV all night and engage in vicarious identification with victims. Their suffering becomes ours. Similarly, when we see people who have been victimized on the evening news, we feel a part of their pain and are outraged. It is natural for crime victims to feel hatred and outrage, and if we are *all* now victims of *all* crimes, we can all feel hatred for all criminals and demand longer and longer sentences.

Still, although we talk a lot about crime victims, in many ways we do not really care about them at all. Virtually all state victim compensation laws are underfunded. Certainly, the state only rarely can restore the victim's psychic losses, but it still typically fails at the much easier task of restoring monetary losses. If you are hit on the head by a crook, and the state finds the money to lock him or her up for twenty years at $30,000 a year (a total cost of $600,000, not including inflation), it is hard to understand why the same state does not have the money to pay your $5,000 in medical bills and perhaps the $2,000 in lost pay while you were laid up. Why couldn't the state lock him up for 19¾ years instead and give you the $7,000 they would save? For many of our poorest citizens, replacing the TV and flatware the burglar took would be a wonderful act of grace. For the rest of us, it would still be a nice gesture of concern.

There are many other things a state concerned about victims could do. It could fund a variety of crime reduction and crime prevention programs. It could stop looking only at the victims of street criminals and begin to worry about the victims of corporate and white-collar crime and about the victims of acts by agents of the state. As Clear (1994, p. 122) points out, "In short, the victims do not get what they need; they only get what the state can afford or is willing to discuss."

What has the movement done for victims? Rather than trying to help victims reconcile themselves with their world and get on with their lives, too many victim advocates specialize in fueling victim rage and anger. Most so-called victims' rights laws are based on this anger: they give victims the right to testify to a parole board before their victimizers can be let out; they may give victims the right to be told of a plea bargain (presumably so that they can protest); and, most important of all, they have resulted in longer sentences. As Clear makes plain, victims' rights do not mean things done *for the victim,* but things done *to the offender.* This serves the needs of the state very well. Among other things, the state now has the support of the victims' rights community in demanding longer sentences and increased capital punishment of street criminals (but not of white-collar and corporate criminals). In other words, we have transformed all of the desires to help out crime victims into a desire to harm offenders. Any "gains are far more apparent than real . . . victims have instead largely been used to promote conservative, law-and-order agendas" (Elias, 1993, p. 4). What makes things even worse is that Americans have very complex attitudes toward crime; we can be vindictive, warm, generous, concerned for the future, and hateful, all at the same time. For example, poll after poll has shown that Americans are in favor of rehabilitation, community-based corrections, early parole release, and other measures (Knowles, 1995; Tonry, 1995), even while they want harsher punishments for the truly dangerous. Conservative politicians simply choose to exploit certain of our desires—the ones to harm—and ignore our good side.

The programs least in favor today among state officials are those advocated and run by peacemaking criminologists (see Chapter 7). These programs attempt to use mediation and reconciliation to move beyond the rage that virtually every one of us feels upon being attacked or violated. To make us whole again, to restore us as productive citizens, the peacemakers argue, we must pay attention to the process of healing and of reconnecting with society at large. As Clear points out, maintaining the victim in the status of "loser" and constantly pitting the victim against the offender in some sort of battle ultimately benefits no one—except perhaps victims' rights advocates and politicians.

"TARGET HARDENING": CRIME PREVENTION THROUGH OPPORTUNITY REDUCTION[1]

It has become very popular in recent years, particularly among conservative researchers and policy analysts, to emphasize that, to reduce our risk of being victimized by crime, we must take steps to lower our vulnerability. This point of view has been heavily influenced by routine activities theory, which

---

[1] This section includes modified sections from DeKeseredy, Burshtyn, and Gordon (1992).

we covered in Chapter 6. These steps to reduce criminal opportunities by focusing on social and environmental factors are occasionally referred to as *situational crime prevention* or *target hardening*. For example, if women who live or travel alone want to lower their risk of being raped or beaten by men, then they should take the following precautions to make them "harder targets" (Solicitor General of Canada, 1990, pp. 2–5):

- Never remain alone in an apartment laundry room, mailroom, or parking garage.
- Do not put their first name on their mailbox or in the telephone book. Use two initials and the last name only.
- Plan their route and avoid shortcuts through parks, vacant lots, and unlit areas.
- Do not overburden themselves with packages and a bulky purse.
- Always lock their car when entering and leaving it.
- Do not stop to offer help to a stranded motorist. Stop at the next phone booth and call for assistance.
- Try to avoid isolated bus stops.
- On public transit, sit near other women or near the driver.
- Do not hitchhike.
- Use caution in conversations with strangers.
- Do not carry large sums of money in their purse.
- When babysitting, be escorted home after dark.
- If attacked, scream and run to the nearest residence or business.

Such precautions certainly can lower the risk of being physically or sexually assaulted by the stereotypical unprovoked stranger. One problem is that, although such crime prevention advice is generally considered to be common sense, as we discussed in some detail in Chapter 9, it does nothing to curb the high rates of intimate, heterosexual violence. Simply put, this advice ignores the fact that North American women are much more likely to be victimized at home by men they know (for example, husbands and boyfriends) than by strangers. For most women, the home—not the street—poses the greatest threat to their well-being (Stanko, 1990). Further, under some circumstances, such steps can make the problem worse for many women. For example, one of the things that these precautionary strategies do is create an exaggerated fear of male strangers and public places. The implicit message is that women should become more dependent on their male partners—the very ones most likely to harm them (Hanmer & Saunders, 1984).

A second problem with this approach is that it places the burden on women to avoid victimization by men. By implication, then, women who are attacked may be to blame for their own victimization because they failed to use target-hardening strategies. As noted previously, many of those who demand lengthy sentences for offenders do so in the name of victims' rights. At the same time, however, many of these same people feel that women are to blame if they do not accept responsibility for avoiding attacks by men. No attention is given in the target-hardening literature to the structural, cultural, social-psychological, and psychological factors that motivate men to abuse women. Note that women live and are socialized in the same society as men; they often learn the same lessons in the same places. Thus, if a woman is victimized by a male stranger in a context deemed dangerous by crime prevention literature, she may hold herself responsible for the assault because she did not take what was regarded by "safety experts" as appropriate precautions (Walklate, 1989).

The third problem that many people have noticed on reading the list of recommended precautions carefully is that this victim-blaming discourse has the potential to influence people to curtail their individual freedom. The message that such lists of precautions send to women, and the message that many take to heart, is that the way to avoid male attacks in public places is to alter their lifestyles and daily routines by staying indoors, changing their style of dress, or revising their route to and from work or school. On an ideological level, these suggestions make it more difficult for women to achieve an equal place in society. Worse yet, these strategies only increase rather than reduce fear of crime (Walklate, 1989). This may be part of the reason that, to cite just one example, 94 percent of Ohio citizens believe that the crime rate has been going up steadily for the past ten years when this is not the case at all (Knowles, 1995).

Of course, in some high-crime areas of the United States and Canada, certain precautions would be sensible for anyone. Yet, we have developed a discourse of fear for women that legitimates the curtailment of women's activities; that is, it is considered fully acceptable to recommend that women rein in their freedom by venturing out only in crime-free and safe environments. For example, on one campus, the women's studies newsletter printed a set of tips from the campus police department on "how to minimize the risk of becoming a victim of crime." These included never walking alone at night, only walking on certain main routes, walking in an "assertive manner," and so forth. Next to this story was a chart provided by the campus police on crime showing that, in the past year on this campus of 20,000 students, there had not been a single murder, a single reported forcible sex offense of any type, or a single reported nonforcible sex offense of any type, and there had only been two robberies (Hart, 1995). What, then, was the purpose of this advice? Why does it seem so very important to urge women on a campus that is completely free of reported sex offenses to "never walk alone at night." On a campus where many classes (including women's studies classes!) are held at night, where all of the major cultural events are at night, and where most campus activities hold their meetings at night, could such advice not have the effect of preventing some women from taking full advantage of the opportunities offered at their university?

Worse, this type of exploitation can become expensive for those who do become unduly fearful. Certainly, many people help to exaggerate the fear of predatory street crimes in order to profit financially. In both the United States and Canada, the growing private security industry tries to convince people to buy such devices as window locks, infrared burglar alarms, steering wheel locks, noxious sprays, and other products designed to make people feel less vulnerable to criminal victimization by strangers. The gun industry, which discovered not too long ago that it had fairly completely saturated the market among men, has specifically and cynically targeted women with rather expensive pink guns, fashionable holsters, and the like. Such commodities may have some value in some specific contexts. However, they rarely protect women from the crimes to which they are most likely to fall victim, such as wife abuse, dating violence, date rape, and other nonstranger crimes (Stanko, 1990).

Thus far, we have been using as an example the single case of target-hardening advice to women to avoid sexual and physical assault. The major problem is that such advice does not address the factors that motivate men to victimize women. If a woman does become a "hard target," that does not mean that the male offender will not try to assault another woman. A similar argument can be applied to the problem of breaking and entering. Those who install expensive light timers, leave cars in their driveways, purchase guard dogs, and have neighbors kind enough to check on their homes when they are away may lessen the risk of burglary (Cromwell, Olson, & Avary, 1991). However, this won't deter burglars from selecting other, weaker targets, such as people who live in government-subsidized housing. This is known as *crime displacement* (McNamara, 1994).

Unfortunately, only middle- and upper-class people can afford sophisticated target-hardening devices. This is one of the reasons unemployed or subemployed persons mainly victimize members of their own socioeconomic class. Compared with their more affluent counterparts, working-class and underclass people are "easy targets." Indeed, these people are the "most unequal of victims." Not only do they suffer from a lack of material resources, but they are much more likely to be victimized by street crime than those who can afford to buy expensive security systems and live outside the "margins of society" (Lea & Young, 1984).

"Lock 'Em Up and Throw Away the Key": The Failure of Prisons

Do you believe that prisons act as a deterrent to crime? Consider the following:

> If all men who had ever raped were incarcerated tomorrow, rape would continue outside as well as inside prisons. Incarceration does not change the societal attitudes that promote rape. . . . Prison is vindictive—it is not concerned with change but with punishment. And its real social function is similar to that of rape—it acts as a buffer, as an oppressive institution where a few scapegoats pay for the ills of society. (MacMillan & Klein, cited in Knopp et al., 1976, p. 150)

Like it or not, for reasons described in Chapter 5, prison does not deter people from committing crime—a finding of almost every responsible study in the past twenty-five years. Further, this information has been available to virtually every politician in the country. Unfortunately, more for political and ideological reasons than because politicians think it will work, the typical response to the failure of imprisonment is to call for more of what has already been done—build more prisons and lock more people up. It is rather extraordinary that in the country that already hands down the harshest prison sentences in the world, many people have come to believe that we are "too soft" on crime and that we must "up the ante" or increase the costs of breaking the law. When we discover that people commit crimes without paying the slightest attention to the potential penalty, we increase the penalty. Then we find that people are still not paying attention to the possible penalty, so we increase it again. When do we come to the conclusion that people are committing crime without paying attention to the possible penalty?

It is even more extraordinary that, as we repeatedly demonstrate that this solution will not work, the only alternative many people are willing to consider is "more of the same." For example, one of America's premier gang researchers, John Hagedorn (1988), has argued, based on interviews with inmate gang members, that placing large numbers of gang members in prison is just about the worst possible thing we could do. With gang membership and involvement even more important in prisons than on the streets, placing gang members in prison simply strengthens the gangs. In most of the country, we have responded to this information by mounting all-out efforts to place as many gang members as possible in prison—often in the same prisons.

As another example, one of the hottest fads in U.S. corrections today is so-called boot camps, where inmates are treated like U.S. army recruits. Although the participants in these programs are carefully hand-picked, they generally have the same recidivism rates as those who are left behind in prisons (MacKenzie & Souryal, 1995). Although some states had some success, evaluators point out that these are programs with so many strong pro-rehabilitation features that there was no reason to believe that the boot camp experience was more important than the other experiences. Given this knowledge that boot camps don't work better than any other solution and worse than some, states from coast to coast are rushing to expand their programs in order to offer more boot camps.

We noted in Chapter 5 that the United States is currently experiencing an "imprisonment binge." When Martin Schwartz first began to write on prisons, he and his colleagues noted that in 1977 there were 283,000 men and women in prison (Schwartz, Clear, & Travis, 1980). They cited, with some horror, the prediction of one expert that the U.S. prison population would eventually reach 380,000, which would be a 50 percent increase over the record 1975 levels of incarceration. In one way, the expert was wrong. By 1994, the U.S. prison population went over a million for the first time. The jail population in 1994 was 490,000. It is worth noting that six states have a smaller population than the total number of people in state prisons and local jails.

John Irwin and James Austin (1994, pp. 1, 4–5) make some other points:

- The number of persons in prison on any given day per 100,000 population increased between 1980 and 1992 from 138 to 329, as compared to only 26 in 1850.
- Approximately one out of every four (23 percent) African-American men age 20–29 is either in prison or jail or on probation or parole on any given day.
- Approximately one out of every ten Hispanic men (10.4 percent) age 20–29 is either in prison or jail or on probation or parole.
- Approximately one out of every sixteen white men age 20–29 (6.2 percent) is either in prison or jail or on probation or parole.
- The number of young African-American men under the control of the criminal justice system (609,690) is greater than the total number of African-American men of all ages enrolled in college as of 1986 (436,000).
- Sixty years ago, less than one-fourth of prison admissions were nonwhite. Today, nearly half are nonwhite.

As bad as these figures are, even worse are the effects of the imprisonment policy—especially for African-Americans.

African-Americans and Prison

Given that we have argued throughout this book that a substantial amount of crime is caused by inner-city slums, a lack of adequate housing, unemployment, poor schooling, and an absence of legitimate future prospects, it is not surprising that young African-Americans are more likely to be involved in crime. They are the ones, after all, who suffer more than others from these conditions. However, according to every available measure, African-Americans have not increased their criminal activities (proportional to other groups) since the early 1970s.

Yet, during this time of massive increases in rates of imprisonment, much of the increase has come by locking up more African-American men. Since Ronald Reagan became president in 1980, the percentage of African-Americans among the new admissions to state prisons has increased from 39 percent to 54 percent. Michael Tonry, a law professor at the University of Minnesota and one of the country's more respected researchers in the field, argues that this was not just a historical accident. The rising rates "were the foreseeable effects of deliberate policies spearheaded by the Reagan and Bush administrations and implemented by many states" (1995, p. 4). Specifically, his contention is that the government knew full well that, by implementing a war on drugs aimed at low-level street users and dealers, they would mainly be arresting and imprisoning young minority males "far out of line with their proportions of the general population, of drug users, and of drug traffickers."

Even worse, Tonry argues, maintaining a policy that has the effect of decimating the African-American community has been the officially approved policy of the top Republican leadership for thirty years, based on an often successful strategy of polarizing the voters. In 1988, for example, the most famous and effective step in George Bush's successful bid for the presidency was to show a picture of convict Willie Horton, who victimized a white suburban couple, in an attempt to get the electorate to believe that what they had to fear from Democrats were African-American rapists and murderers set loose in every white community. It was perhaps one of the most effective campaign tactics in the history of U.S. politics. Many voters came to believe, evidently, that Democrats wanted to release African-American rapists from prison. Generally, Diana Gordon (1994) argues, our drug policies do not reflect a rational agenda on drug use, but rather our fear of racial minorities and our frustration with the enduring problems of inner-city poverty.

Yet, as Michael Tonry points out, as long as our official government policy is to make political gains by choosing policies known to differentially affect minority youths, we will not solve the problems of the African-American underclass. If you are confused about what it might mean to differentially affect minority youth, consider the general reaction in most

U.S. cities to two similar sets of crimes. Most cities devote extensive resources to drug sales, gambling, and other crimes in areas where there are large numbers of minority youth. On the other hand, if you want to see an example of low-level policing and a lack of punishment, investigate the drug sales operations or the illegal gambling operations on a typical college campus. Or investigate the amount of theft, assault, and rape on most campuses for which there is no punishment (Hills, 1984). When we say criminals get off with a slap on the wrist, we rarely mean the fraternity rapist, the dormitory LSD dealer, or the campus collector of gambling policy cards. North American law enforcement is only rarely interested in these rapes and thefts; it is mainly interested in the rapes and thefts committed by minority teenagers in inner-city neighborhoods.

Prisons and Drugs

It is well known that our prisons and jails are flooded with people, but less well known that a major reason for this increase in prisoners is the enormous growth in the number of inmates imprisoned for drug law violations. In Chapter 11, we discussed some of the costs of the War on Drugs. One problem is that there seems to be no reason to believe that prisons stop people from taking drugs. First, there is an enormous amount of drugs within prisons. As one long-term prisoner remarked about his time in prison: "I never had a weekend where there wasn't something. When I was inside I smoked grass, hash; I did mescaline; I did speed; I did cocaine" (Boyd, 1991, p. 158).

Second, many drug users do not fear imprisonment. In some communities where drug use is rampant, individuals sent to prison for drug law violations use it as a badge of masculinity. Prison time can be a prestige symbol. For example, one young Detroit drug dealer told Carl Taylor (1989, pp. 51–52):

> Scared, worried about jail? No way. . . . The youth home is really down. If you get sent to the youth home it ain't no big thing. . . . I ain't been to the big time, but when I do, it'll be cool. Everybody I know been to Jack house, three of my boys doing a bit now. . . . Going away is just part of being here. . . . Most of the time you know everybody in the home, so it's like being with your crew inside.

Third, when drug users and other offenders are released, they typically return to the same economically deprived inner-city neighborhoods where they used or sold drugs in the first place. In many states, released inmates are given $15–$75 and perhaps a new windbreaker and a ride to the nearest bus station, where they must use their $75 to purchase a bus ticket home. When they arrive back, with $5 or so left over, it does not take long for them to pick up where they left off.

Fourth, most illegal drug users and street offenders belong to the underclass and thus face great difficulties surviving on a day-to-day basis. Because examples of their trials and tribulations were described in Chapters 8 and 11, they will not be repeated here. What's more important to note here is that, for some of these people, prison may represent a higher standard of living. Although they have to endure numerous "pains of imprisonment" (see Chapter 5), these people also have a roof over their heads, three meals a day, membership in a peer group, and better medical attention. As we saw from the preceding quote, one can take an optimistic view and see prisons as a place to maintain street friendships and make new business contacts that could be helpful later. Compare this young African-American inmate's attitude (as told to Claude Brown) to the plight of the newly released inmate with no resources:

> Now if I get busted and end up in the joint pullin' a dime and a nickel, like I am, then I don't have to worry about no bucks, no clothes, I get free rent and three squares a day. So you see, Mr. Brown, I really can't lose. (cited in Irwin & Austin, 1994, p. 164)

Finally, as Elliott Currie (1993) points out, even if we devoted all of our resources to jailing only drug addicts, we would be unable to imprison even a significant percentage of the total number of abusers on the streets. How can we possibly solve the problem in this way?

Prisons and Crime Reduction

For the past twenty years, the idea of *selective incapacitation* has generated some excitement within criminology. The concept is fairly simple. We have slowly but surely come to the realization that a small number of people commit a rather amazing number of predatory crimes. Our current policy is heavily oriented toward locking up as many criminals as we can, in what is often called *collective incapacitation*. But if we can locate these repeat offenders and lock them up, we can prevent massive numbers of crime. If we also reduce the sentences of the other offenders, the net result will be fewer crimes committed and the same or lower costs of running prisons.

Like all too many great ideas, this is one that works well in theory but that has drawbacks in practice. To put it simply, we do not have the ability to figure out just who these repeat offenders are. Criminological researchers are very good at retrospective surveys—in other words, we can look at a large group of 50-year-old men and discover that some of these guys committed an outrageous amount of crime in their time. The trick, of course, is to look at a group of convicted 19-year-olds and predict accurately which of them will be repeat offenders if returned to the streets. Unfortunately, this is a trick we do not know how to perform. Perhaps the best survey of our knowledge in this area was done by Christy Visher (1987) when she was at the National Research Council/National Academy of Sciences. Her conclusion was that some modest crime reductions could be achieved with aggressive selective incapacitation campaigns, but that aggressive collective incapacitation campaigns would be less successful. In other words, with very expensive campaigns, coupled with expensive imprisonment for those we identify, we might be able to cut the crime rate a little.

Thus, for these and other reasons, some of which were discussed in Chapter 5, prisons have not been very effective as a means of crime prevention. Perhaps, by locking up many of our youths, we could reduce crime by 5 percent or some such number, but generally, prisons only make matters worse. To be sure, some people never commit crimes after they are released. However, most offenders are re-arrested at least once after being set free. Traditionally, researchers find that as these people get older (for example, over 30), they eventually "burn out" and become law-abiding citizens. Of course, even if this aging-out process exists, it will have no effect on crime and imprisonment rates because these people will simply be "replaced by the next generation of lower-class prison-bound males nurtured in inner-city communities riddled with poverty, drug abuse, and violence" (Irwin & Austin, 1994, p. 121). Further, the aging-out process may no longer apply. John Hagedorn (1988) argues that, unlike in the past, these youths no longer have jobs to go to when they decide to become law-abiding citizens.

The earlier presumption was that some members of the working class joined gangs as youths and caused a lot of trouble before they married and settled down. Today, many African-Americans and Hispanics can no longer be considered members of the working class. Rather, as members of the underclass, the only jobs they will ever have in their entire lives will be low-paying, seasonal, part-time or temporary work, all supplemented, of course, by handouts, hustles, and various crimes.

Christina Jacqueline Johns (1992, p. 173) made a rather bitter observation about the prison boom and the public's inability to stop demanding more of the same:

> The logic behind continued prison construction and the continuation of the War on Drugs seems to be something like this: Prisons have been a failure, so more prisons will be a success; punishment has been a failure, so more punishment will be a success; criminalization and enforcement have been a failure, so more criminalization and enforcement will be a success. It's not the kind of logic that appeals to every intellect, but it is apparently sufficient for many.

Of course, as we have suggested many times before, all of this discussion is based on the presumption that we even know when crime is increasing or decreasing. As an example, Table 12.1 was constructed from official statistics to show the crime rate changes from 1991 to 1992. We chose 1992 only because, at the time of this writing, it is the most recent year for which the final figures have been calculated for both the *Uniform Crime Reports* and the National Crime Victimization Survey. Although some differences in the rates of property crime may come from slightly different ways in which these crimes are defined, generally one can see that we are doing a lot of talking when we don't even know if, for example, forcible stranger rape is steadily increasing or dramatically decreasing.

Whatever the numbers, one thing that neither the public nor politicians have traditionally supported has been taking money away from failed policies in order to spend it on the primary problems that cause crime. Rather, the tendency has been to take money from programs that work, such as drug education, and use it to beef up programs that are failures (Inciardi, 1992).

There is a rather old joke in psychiatry about the new patient at a mental hospital that has a leaky faucet. Every year, the leak gets worse, eventually, most of the patients spend most of their day mopping up the basement floor. A new patient comes up with a bright idea: she walks over to the faucet and tightens it up, stopping the leak. Just as the previous administration believed that if only enough people with mops could be found, the moppers would get ahead of the leak, our current government officials believe that if we simply imprison enough people, we can lick this crime problem.

INDIVIDUAL TREATMENT

In Chapters 5 and 6, we discussed an important difference between many psychological and many sociological ways of looking at the crime problem in North America. Many of the more or less liberal notions of rehabilitation popular in the 1960s and 1970s were based on some sort of psychological or physiological treatment of the individual. This might have included drug therapy, psychotherapy, counseling, psychosurgery, or any of a number of other techniques designed to help offenders identify and deal with their problems.

Table 12.1 Crime Rate Changes, 1991–1992

| CRIME | PERCENTAGE CHANGE | |
	Uniform Crime Reports	National Crime Victimization Survey
Rape	+2.3%	−19.0%
Robbery	−2.2	+1.9
Aggravated assault	+3.1	+13.1
Theft	−2.8	−5.2
Burglary	−5.6	−8.3
Motor vehicle theft	−3.1	−8.3

SOURCE: Table constructed from material in Federal Bureau of Investigation, 1992, 1993; and Maguire and Pastore, 1994.

Drawbacks to Individual Treatment

As we saw, there are a few drawbacks to such approaches. The most obvious, of course, is that for the most part they don't work! Part of the reason that they do not work is that they overlook two crucial elements. First, they ignore the family and community networks of which any individual is a part. To the extent that any individual is influenced in the first place to take drugs or commit crimes by relatives, friends, and neighbors, he or she will be returning after therapy to the same people. Will they be a different influence this time? The individual approach involves spending all of our money and attention trying to strengthen individuals' resources and abilities, but nothing on the family or neighborhood.

Second, and similarly, we disregard the broader structural aspects of society that help create an atmosphere in which crime can be committed. In the case of street crime, this includes extraordinarily high minority youth unemployment, extreme levels of social inequality and poverty, and the lack of meaningful employment for many people. For example, in the United States, it is common knowledge that most predatory street crimes, such as assault and murder, are committed by young, disenfranchised males. One major reason that they commit these crimes is because they harbor deep feelings of despair, frustration, hopelessness, resentment, and alienation generated by social and economic inequalities that they define as unjust (see Chapter 8). Their perception that these problems exist is not unwarranted. In today's inner cities, unemployed or subemployed people (for example, part-time workers in low-paying jobs) have few, if any, legitimate opportunities to achieve their material goals and the status associated with attaining these goals.

A similar argument can easily be applied to the problem of widespread drug addiction in the United States (see Chapter 11). For example, many, if not most, crack cocaine and heroin users are young, urban members of the underclass. Like their violent counterparts, they are forced to live in inner-city neighborhoods characterized by low-paying jobs (if any), severe poverty, and family disruption. While these people want the rewards associated with the "American Dream," their miserable circumstances do not provide them with any reason to believe that they will ever have a good job, a nice car, or a fancy suburban home. Many immigrants have willingly accepted society's dirty work because they have seen it as a first step on the ladder of success.

However, after being stuck on the bottom rung for several generations no matter how hard they work, the children of some minority families are unwilling to do dirty-work jobs; they are much more likely to turn to narcotics. For them, drugs "offer a quick and royal route to meeting the challenge of living" (Chein, 1966, p. 140).

The problem, then, is that such things as drug and alcohol abuse might be better seen as symptoms, rather than problems in and of themselves. Lars Eighner (1993, p. 162), who spent three years on the streets as a homeless man in the Southwest and West, suggests that we waste our time studying abusers. Although he was talking about homeless alcoholics, or "winos," his argument is that solving the problem of alcoholism won't do a thing to solve the problem of unemployment, and, in fact, it may make things worse:

> If there were no alcohol, society would still have no use, no job, no home for the men, young and old, who sit on street corners with brown paper sacks. If the cities were filled with sober homeless people, I doubt that the comfortable would find the results much to their liking.

As some critical theorists have pointed out, these people would then be available for marches on city hall to demand jobs for the able-bodied or solutions to the housing and schooling crises (Johns, 1992; Karmen, 1980). Some people might think that the problem of winos and drug addicts is less serious than a politically active class of the disenfranchised.

So, if unemployment and other factors associated with gross economic and social inequality are the primary determinants of most violent crime and drug use in the United States, what is the point of having people attend anger management courses, vocational rehabilitation workshops, and other counseling programs if these "patients" or "clients" have to return to their deprived neighborhoods? As we have suggested, these areas perpetuate and legitimate crime and will continue to do so until we seriously consider the policy proposals suggested in the next section of this chapter.

This is not to say that job training, counseling, and other types of treatment and rehabilitation are totally useless. Many people believe that on an individual, one-to-one basis, some programs have the potential to reduce drug abuse in particular and street crime in general (Gendreau & Ross, 1987). How successful they can be, unfortunately, is hard to measure, because "these programs are simply not available where they are needed (particularly in the inner city) nor are they available in sufficient number" (Kappeler, Blumberg, & Potter, 1993, p. 166). Although government-sponsored surveys continue to report an interest in more treatment programs (for example, Rydell & Everingham, 1994), "The best one can conclude is that some types of treatment seem to work for some people some of the time; no treatment or intervention has been shown to work well for most people most of the time" (Wright & Devine, 1994, p. 89).

We are unlikely to begin discovering better treatment programs, given that current federal policy is to divert funds away from drug education and drug treatment and toward prison construction. Still, the best programs must be accompanied by measures that address the structural sources of criminal conduct. For example, it should not be difficult, with enough time and motivated teachers, to train Jimmy and Sally to type (in the modern jargon, to have "keyboarding skills") and to acquire the language and computer skills needed to work in a modern office. But, what's the point if there are no opportunities to use these skills? The unfortunate truth is that the qualities people bring into treatment programs and the families and neighborhoods to which they return are better determinants of whether they will eventually become law-abiding citizens than the programs themselves. Keep in mind that we are talking about broad groups of people. Certainly, any one person with sufficient desire can use skills training to move in a different direction. Often, however, this can mean leaving friends, family, and neighborhoods, which is very difficult for many of us. The fear of failure, particularly by lower-class minority men and women working in a predominantly all-white middle-class environment, can be so stressful as to be debilitating (Liebow, 1995).

It is also worth pointing out that when we say that structural conditions affect people, we are not suggesting that every person who lives in the inner city will automatically become a cocaine-snorting, child-abusing mugger or prostitute. Obviously, the majority of people who grow up in poverty and oppression do no such thing. To recent administrations, this has meant that social conditions do not cause crime. In the National Drug Control Policy report, for example, the government argues that if people can be poor and remain law-abiding, then the enormous number of street criminals in inner-city neighborhoods must simply mean that more bad and morally weak people live there (Wright & Devine, 1994). This is the same logic that the tobacco lobby uses to argue that, because some people smoke cigarettes all of their lives and do not get cancer, that cigarettes do not cause cancer. We just have to ignore the at least 350,000 deaths a year that doctors attribute to tobacco for this to make sense. Similarly, the fact that some people do not become drug users or criminals despite living in extreme poverty should not blind us to the fact that people are *more likely* to engage in this behavior in these neighborhoods.

Perhaps the greatest problem with individual treatment has not been that it does not often work. Rather, our attention has been diverted away from the problems that cause crime, in favor of treating the individual either through therapy or through punishment. Neither approach will work by itself.

Not only in the United States but also in Canada the limitations of individual treatment and rehabilitation have been discovered. At the time of this writing, Canadians are experiencing the brutal social and economic consequences of job layoffs, government cutbacks, tuition increases, and inner-city poverty. We have friends and family who have gone back to school but are still unable to find jobs. Faced with bleak futures, they have even begun talking about selling drugs. For a young man in such a situation, vocational rehabilitation is not likely to help out. Likewise, psychological counseling will do little more than provide him with an opportunity to express his anger, frustration, and resentment.

Reasons for the Popularity of Individual Treatment

If individual treatment or rehabilitation strategies are not effective, then why are they so popular? Undoubtedly, individual treatment has contributed to the government's failure to win the War on Crime. However, this failure is *"only in the eye of the victim: For those in control, it is a roaring success"* (Reiman, 1995, p. 38; italics in original). The argument here is that this strategy has provided many benefits. If crime is not caused by failures of society, but rather by failures of the individual, then we simply work with the individual and ignore the problems of society. Certainly, in the 1990s, federal, state (provincial), and local governments in both the United States and Canada are working as fast as they can to dismantle programs that benefit children and youths and that provide aid to urban areas. Instead, the call is for tax cuts to middle- and, more often, upper-level earners.

To cite just one example, noted economist Robert Haveman (1994) argues that the U.S. federal government, through direct public policy, has widened the gap between the rich and the poor and has been robbing the children to feed the elderly. The level of government support to the next generation of economic workers has been steadily falling, while the level of support for older workers (mainly through Social Security and Medicaid) has been steadily increasing. As a result of this and other factors, a higher percentage of the nation's children and a lower percentage of the nation's elderly are living in poverty than ever before. The United States "is seriously misallocating resources among generations, being provident to older citizens whose working days are largely done, while skimping on young people whose later productivity will determine the nation's economic future" (Haveman, 1994, p. 149). Haveman was writing, of course, before Newt Gingrich took over as Speaker of the House and announced a program that guaranteed no cuts to the Social Security program and rejected a popular proposal to cut benefits for people earning $100,000 or $150,000 in retirement. To raise the money to pay for such measures, the House began instead to impose massive cuts to such programs as school lunch aid, summer jobs for teens, enrichment programs for schools, drug education for children, aid programs for children in poverty, supplemental food programs for children in poverty, student loan programs, and other such "frills." Even before the government began to consider cuts, in 1992, federal expenditures for children under the Aid to Families with Dependent Children program (what is commonly called welfare) was about $7 billion. In contrast, Social Security spending for the elderly exceeded $190 billion.

Our contention is that, although individuals must always take some measure of responsibility for their actions, we must also look to government policy to see if it is part of the problem or part of the solution. In this case, we propose that U.S. government policy is part of the problem. If there are few job opportunities for lower-class minority youth, and if that lack is a result of government policy that rewards mergers, buyouts, and the deindustrialization of the cities, then the government will need to take some responsibility for the large number of alienated youths in inner cities. As Christina Johns (1993, p. 75) has pointed out:

Administration policies have ensured that drug trafficking will be an attractive alternative to lower-class segments of the population, and then administration rhetoric has blamed the involvement in drug trafficking on supposed criminogenic tendencies.

Amazingly enough, a large number of North Americans, even among the economically disadvantaged, agree with the government's policies, which are sold under the name of "economic growth." Given the wealth of data showing that social inequality is the main cause of crime, such public support is an outstanding example "of the triumph of ideology over evidence in the short history of neoconservative thought" (Currie, 1985, p. 167). Tamasak Wicharaya (1995) argues that U.S. policymakers habitually reduce all complex problems to simple slogans or formulations and then adopt the criminological theory that best supports the policy they had already decided to adopt before seeing the evidence. As we suggested earlier, politicians have adopted neo-classical solutions to crime problems not because they think that they will work, but because they think that they can use them to win elections. Still, if we are going to argue that these policies of the past are unlikely to solve the problem, shouldn't we make some suggestions ourselves on what might work?

RETHINKING THE PREVENTION AND CONTROL OF CRIME: SOME PROGRESSIVE POLICY PROPOSALS[2]

Although an outrageous crime problem requires outrageous proposals (Gibbons, 1995), few critical criminologists believe that truly fundamental changes will occur soon in either U.S. or Canadian society. Rather, critical criminologists argue that the major reasons for crime in North America are class, racial/ethnic, and gender inequality. Thus, they suggest that we need to consider short-term, progressive strategies that chip away at the forces that motivate people to commit crime. Of course, we could list thousands of alternative proposals—but we won't. For example, we will not address

---

[2]This section includes some material from DeKeseredy and Schwartz (1991a).

gun control, white-collar crime, nutrition, changes in policing, economic democracy, environmental pollution, drug legalization, and many other proposals that would require a book in themselves. Given space limitations, we will introduce only a few ideas on promising progressive initiatives. The key, however, is to recognize that we must take on these tasks. As John I. Irwin and James A. Austin point out:

> Reducing crime means addressing those factors that are more directly related to crime. This means reducing teenage pregnancies, high school dropout rates, unemployment, drug abuse, and lack of meaningful job opportunities. Although many will differ on how best to address these factors, the first step is to acknowledge that these forces have far more to do with reducing crime than escalating the use of imprisonment. (1994, p. 167)

It should be noted in passing that, although some critical criminologists may make such arguments, we are not calling for the elimination of police, courts, or even incarceration. To take the most extreme example, few of us are willing to turn the other cheek far enough to allow a Jeffrey Dahmer or a Ted Bundy to roam free. However, we do not believe that the criminal justice system should have the *sole* responsibility for dealing with crime. Although the connection is too rarely made, other institutions manage the social and economic problems that motivate people to break the law. Policymakers rarely consider how factory closures, the North American Free Trade Agreement, or reductions in welfare benefits affect crime rates. What happens, then, is that policies are adopted with no regard to the ultimate effect on criminal violence. When the worst occurs, the police and prison officials are called in to mop up the mess left behind by the rest of society (Currie, 1985).

Thus, most of the policies outlined here will seem somewhat out of place in a traditional criminology textbook. For example, job creation is a topic that belongs in urban policy, political sociology, or public administration discussions, most of us feel. The problem is that real life does not play itself out along the bureaucratic lines set up by North American universities and government agencies. What you eat can affect how you behave, and the fact that the nutrition department is located in a separate building from the criminal justice department does not affect that truth. In real life, jobs, child care, nutrition, welfare, and many other events affect your life. It is mainly in textbooks that they are segregated.

Job Creation and Training Programs

Throughout this book, we have argued that economic inequality is one of the most powerful determinants of crime. A large social scientific literature shows that unemployed and subemployed men are much more likely to steal, rob, murder, ingest drugs, and abuse their intimate partners than their more affluent counterparts. These same factors, as we have noted, affect women, only not as strongly. Therefore, one piece of the "crime puzzle" should be a strong commitment to full-time and quality employment. Empirical support for this suggestion is found in comparative crime studies showing that countries committed to maintaining full-employment, such as Norway, Austria, Germany, and Sweden, have markedly lower rates of violent crime than the United States (Currie, 1985). Further, gang researchers such as John Hagedorn (1994) argue that most gang members who are drug dealers have not rejected conventional values; they would accept decent jobs if they were available, and they mainly sell drugs because there is no alternative except to have no money at all. He found most of the former gang members he was trying to trace in order to interview existing on the "economic merry-go-round," dipping into the temporary labor market when work was available and going back to selling drugs in off-times. "Although their average income from drug sales far surpassed their income from legal employment, most Milwaukee male gang members apparently kept trying to find licit work" (1994, p. 205).

The United States currently is characterized by a number of criminogenic factors (factors that cause crime). Of course, such an analysis would require an entire textbook rather than a small section of one chapter, but we can at least point to some directions for further reading. Herman and Julia Schwendinger (1993) suggest several related problems of the economy and government policy, including uneven economic development, structural or permanent underemployment, and abandonment of or indifference to the underemployed. Today, the chief breadwinner for a family of four in the United States could work fifty-two weeks a year, full-time, at the minimum wage, and still be many thousands of dollars below the official government poverty line (and that poverty line itself is set artificially low). Many of these people are technically employed, so we ignore them, but their employment circumstances may breed resentment because they cannot even adequately feed their children. Many more people are permanently unemployed, as whole sections of major cities have been, in the new terminology, "deindustrialized." There are no jobs today, and there will be no jobs tomorrow, for most inner-city minority youths. These problems breed crime in several less-than-obvious ways, such as denying people a sense of purpose, "whipsawing" people between low or no wages and high costs of living, weakening families, and eroding the ability of communities to offer disenfranchised people adequate social support. In a country in which close to 10 million people are already unemployed and perhaps 10 percent of the total population is on food stamps (Schwendinger & Schwendinger, 1993), *The New York Times* predicted that the North American Free Trade Agreement will result in the loss of 500,000 more jobs in the next ten years (Lueck, 1993). It is not surprising that there is so much street crime in this country, and it is hard to imagine things getting better.

The great shortage of both jobs and quality employment not only influences many disenfranchised people to commit street crimes but can also keep them from escaping becoming crime victims. For example, in Chapter 9, we asked why a woman would put up with a husband who brutally beat her. Of course, most battered women *do* leave their abusers; however, many unemployed women cannot leave right away because they don't have the money to house and feed themselves and their children (Barnett & La-Violette, 1993; Horley, 1991).

A few critical criminologists have suggested specific ways to deal with these problems. Raymond Michalowski (1983, pp. 14–18), for example, has proposed several policies aimed at reducing street crime that place financial burdens on industry rather than on taxpayers. They include:

- Tax surcharges on industries attempting to close plants or permanently reduce a community's work force

- Government laws requiring retraining and job placement for all workers displaced by new technology

- A minimum wage level that is approximately 50 percent higher than the poverty level

Elliott Currie (1985, 1989, 1993) proposes somewhat similar changes but recommends that both government and private industry join together to deal with these problems. His recommendations include:

- Publicly supported community-oriented job creation
- Upgrades in the quality of work available to disenfranchised people
- Intensive job training and supported work designed to help prepare the young and disabled for stable careers
- Job creation in local communities
- A "solidaristic" wage policy scheme that narrows the inequalities in wages within and between occupations
- Disincentives for companies to replace higher-paying jobs in the United States with lower-paying ones in other countries such as Mexico

If countries like Germany, Japan, and Switzerland can implement both private sector apprenticeship programs and high levels of government spending for job training, so can the United States. The problem, and the most discouraging aspect of making such recommendations, is not that U.S. politicians and corporate elites have been uncaring or neglectful in their failure to invest in decent, full-time employment. Rather, they have aggressively opposed such policies, even when they are confronted with evidence that these and similar strategies work. Conservative politicians and corporations oppose job creation and training initiatives because they do not want to lose the financial gains that they have made under the current system (Barak, 1986). In other words, it isn't so much economic obstacles as ideological obstacles that account for our failure to mount a massive campaign to expand and upgrade the labor force.

Adequate Social Services

As conservative criminologists such as James Q. Wilson (1985) have taken some delight in pointing out, state-sponsored social services provided in the 1960s failed to reduce the crime rate. The failure of government-funded social programs has been successfully exploited by conservative politicians to gain popular support for a policy of reducing social spending. The 1994 elections swept into the House of Representatives a leadership determined to dismantle as much of the federal government's social services agenda as possible. It is interesting how much of this agenda is fueled by racist politics. From President Reagan's constant parading of the idea of the African-American welfare queen who picked up her checks in a pink Cadillac (except that no one could find her) to President Bush's campaign for office on the back of Willie Horton, an African-American criminal who looked very scary to most folks, politicians have won support for their policies by convincing voters that it will be African-Americans who will suffer from conservative policies. Specifically, they will either lose social services (like increased welfare for more babies) or be imprisoned at ever-increasing rates. Interestingly, the trend in government today, supported by the media and by more and more voters, is to cut social services because we can't afford them but at the same time to dramatically increase spending on prisons. Much of the reason that many people support these notions is because they assume that the policies won't affect them; they will mainly affect African-Americans.

The problem with this approach is that, whereas increased imprisonment does not deter crime, improved social services do have the potential to help curb crime. Most of the policies of the 1960s were not sensitive to the powerful influences of the political economy, community, and family. For example, although 1960s liberal criminologists argued that social and economic inequality fosters crime, the actual crime prevention and control strategies enacted in that era rarely dealt with these factors. Rather, through such programs as job training, they attempted to increase "human capital" so that individuals could make better use of the limited opportunities that were available to them. For example, large numbers of youths were trained in the Job Corps for jobs that did not exist. However, few attempts were made to deal with the structural disintegration of troubled individuals' familial and neighborhood environments (Currie, 1985). Further, the most influential of these strategies were dismantled in the Reagan era, beginning in 1980. In other words, the social service programs regarded as failures actually were in effect for fewer years than the great imprisonment binge with which we are currently experimenting. Yet, for some reason, we are unwilling to call the latter a failure.

We make no argument that "service strategies" for the problems of the economically marginalized are a poor idea. Services such as early-childhood education, effective parenting training, prenatal care, and remedial education are worthwhile. However, can those who participate in these programs be guaranteed financial security after they complete them (Currie, 1992)? History tells us that the answer to this question is an emphatic no. For example, what is the point of going back to school if there is no chance of getting a job? Thus, in order to avoid repeating the mistakes of the 1960s, the following policy proposals must be accompanied by the elimination of unemployment and subemployment.

With this cautionary note in mind, we suggest the following strategies to help lower the rates of drug abuse, predatory street crime, and family violence: day care and housing assistance.

Day Care and Other Family Support Today, many parents, especially those who hold full- or part-time jobs and who go to school, endure a substantial amount of stress associated with child care. This problem is more acute for low-income families who cannot afford babysitters or other types of child care. Disenfranchised parents who are forced both to work long hours and to raise children are at great risk of either taking drugs or abusing their children because of extreme stress. Others adapt to their situation by leaving their children unsupervised, which can lead to participation in street crimes.

Eager to avoid the problems associated with inadequate child supervision, other disenfranchised parents simply stay at home. They are forced out of the labor force because child care costs greatly exceed their weekly or monthly income. Single parents are especially prone to this problem, and thus, many reluctantly rely on meager welfare support. Although these problems can often be avoided through day care programs, the United States has fewer such state-supported programs than virtually any other advanced industrial nation (Currie, 1993).

Day care enables low-income and unemployed single parents to either work or look for jobs without worrying about their children's well-being. This strategy also greatly reduces the risk of drug use, child abuse, child neglect, and gang participation. These programs need to be provided not only because they are the right thing to do but also because they represent practical politics. As Patricia Adler (1994, p. 263) points out, day care will not eliminate drug use, but if it enables people to obtain jobs and feel as if they are part of the American mainstream, we can create a situation in which "the most alienated groups develop the same kind of 'investment' in leading legitimate lives that has led middle-class drug-users to moderate their use and keep the social problems they generate to a tolerable level."

In addition to providing day care, government agencies should consider other means of supporting poor families, such as those provided by the Center for Family Life in Brooklyn, New York. According to Currie (1993, pp. 315–316), this agency offers the following services that prevent child abuse and delinquency and buffer parents from the stress associated with the trials and tribulations of raising their children:

- A play group for children age 6 months to 3 years and a simultaneous support group for parents
- A weekly group to help mothers of children age 3–4 improve their parenting skills
- Extensive help for parents in dealing with schools and other community agencies to ensure that they get the educational, financial, housing, child care, vocational, and homemaking help they need
- Comprehensive after-school, five-day-a-week child care
- A two-night-a-week program of recreation, dramatic arts, and tutoring for children
- Communitywide forums and workshops on various parenting issues and concerns

Many conservative politicians and members of the general public are opposed to high-quality, state-sponsored day care. For example, in response to the Canadian federal government's February 1995 promise to spend $720 million over three years to create 150,000 day care spaces for children, the ultraconservative Reform Party publicly criticized the ruling Liberals for "wasting taxpayers' money." Based on their review of unpublished data gathered by an equally conservative research agency, the National Foundation for Family Research and Education, several Reformers argued that day care creates—rather than eliminates—social problems such as crime. According to Reformers, day care increases the likelihood of clinical depression, propensity to commit crime, and personal stress. Moreover, they maintained that it will lead to an increased demand for social services and law enforcement.

Needless to say, the Reform Party would like mothers to stay at home and look after their children. They fail to recognize that many mothers work not because they choose to, but because they need to put bread and butter on the table. These politicians and their supporters have also deliberately ignored a large empirical literature that shows that the *quality* of care children receive determines whether or not they will end up being delinquent, do poorly in school, or experience health problems. After all, just because a mother stays at home does not mean that she will act as a loving parent. In fact, two national surveys show that many children are beaten by their mothers (Straus & Gelles, 1986; Straus, Gelles, & Steinmetz, 1981). It is difficult to prove, but the time away from their parents that day care provides may enable some children to be much safer and to receive better overall care.

Despite resistance from the Reform Party, the ruling Liberals insist that they will support day care centers. In our opinion, the U.S. government should follow Canada's lead because quality day care can help curb crime and other social problems. The same can be said about housing assistance.

Housing Assistance   Sometimes, critical criminologists seem guilty of overstating matters when they make comments like "part of the crime problem is a direct result of a purposeful government policy." And yet, throughout the twentieth century, U.S. housing policy has promoted homelessness. Not surprisingly, many predatory street criminals are homeless, and the highest rates of illegal drug abuse are found among the homeless.

There is also a relationship between battered women and homelessness. On the one hand, in the United States, there is so little housing available to poor battered women that many of those who choose to leave a terroristic situation become homeless (Barak, 1991b). On the other hand, many battered women stay with their partners because they know they cannot afford another place to live. If they leave their batterer, their only choice is to live on the streets with their children. Of course, this is no choice at all, because few homeless shelters will take in children (Liebow, 1995), and social service agencies commonly place in foster care children found living with their mother on the streets (Pitts, 1996). Shelters that provide safe housing for all people who cannot afford housing are very important, but they must remain a Band-Aid solution. By their very nature, such shelters typically have extensive sets of rules that reward a lack of initiative and support dependence. For some women, Lesley Harman (1989, p. 106) suggests, such shelters regulate each woman's duties each day, "subjecting them to the rules and regulations of a larger structure that makes decisions and has disciplinary power. In other words, they teach, foster, and reward domesticity."

To reiterate, governments have deliberately enacted policies that promoted homelessness, thereby contributing to the high crime rate associated with efforts by homeless individuals to obtain everything from the basic necessities of life to drugs to numb them to their existence. Traditionally, U.S. cities and even small towns had a large number of housing units for the poor—often more units than were needed. On the Main Stem in Chicago, in the Bowery in New York City, on Upper Hennepin Avenue in Minneapolis, on the Barbary Coast in San Francisco, and in Chinatowns everywhere, unskilled people who could only get low-paying work found housing nearby. These houses provided residents with both a sense of self-identity and a haven from the continual hostile reactions of the general society to the poor.

The problem is that reformers never wanted these districts to exist. Led by Progressive Era moralists, and later by University of Chicago sociologists, these students of urban life claimed that cheap hotels were a source of sexual immorality, physical disease, and moral laxity. Paul Groth (1994, p. 231) argues:

> Stated most simply, to its critics the continued existence of hotel life worked against the progress of the grand new city. . . . For the reformers working on the new city, single-room dwellings were not a housing resource but a public nuisance.

Government policy was to remove such cheap housing. Banks refused to grant loans to fix up old buildings. The federal government put no money into this form of existing housing stock. Worst of all, these areas were purposely chosen as places for urban renewal. In any urban renewal project, hotels that provided single room occupancy (SRO) to the urban poor were the first buildings targeted. This policy was helped out by census officials, who did not count those people living in SRO hotels as residents, presumably because they were transient and could move. Thus, when dozens of hotels providing living space for thousands of people are torn down, no *residents* are disturbed.

Further, under the Reagan administration, appropriations for low-income subsidized housing were cut by 82 percent. Combined with urban renewal programs that replace low-income housing with shopping centers and government office plazas and an increase in the raw numbers of poor and unemployed in the United States, the net result over the past twenty-five years has been a change from a country with hundreds of thousands more low-cost housing units than were needed to one with hundreds of thousands fewer housing units than are needed (Johns, 1992). The situation today, whereby poor and homeless men and women have no place to go, was a carefully and purposely planned event.

Simply providing long-term, state-sponsored housing is also not enough. It hardly benefits society to create "vast new fortresslike housing projects that jam the disorganized poor together in impoverished isolation" (Currie, 1993, p. 319). Both the public and private sectors need to donate money to refurbish old and deteriorating buildings, houses, and apartments so that they can be comfortably occupied by homeless people. For example, the *Smithsonian* magazine highlighted the renewal of one of the very worst sections of the South Bronx, where such a coalition has reclaimed, apartment unit by apartment unit, one of America's absolutely worst neighborhoods. Amazingly, new single-family housing for working-class minority families is being built where fields of rubble were all that could be seen a short time ago (Breslin, 1995). This strategy, of course, also helps to create new construction jobs, which is an example of what Herman and Julia Schwendinger refer to as "the multiplier effects for crime prevention" (1993, p. 439). This employment policy helps people to engage in various activities that support prosocial behavior and good child-rearing practices, as well as training them for high-skilled employment.

The lack of affordable housing has been closely associated with increased crime problems for many years. Reformers believed that if only slums could be bulldozed under, better housing would magically arise, and the poor would have nice places to live. It is too bad that life doesn't work that way. Unfortunately, there is also a relationship between homelessness and crime *victimization*. Those living on the streets also have a much higher rate of crime victimization, including violent crimes, than the general population. Their rate of victimization is three times higher even than for those living in extreme poverty but with homes (Fitzpatrick, LaGory, & Fitchey, 1993). When Schwartz was a police reporter in a large city in New York, he discovered the invisibility of these crimes. Homeless men often complained that they were robbed and beaten, particularly when they were asleep, but that

Parts of the Bronx in New York City reflected the worst deterioration that arson, crime, and government policy can produce. Yet, thousands of working-class families have moved into new housing shown here in almost identical before (1981, this page) and after (1994, facing page) photos. The work has been done by community-development corporations like the Mid-Bronx Desperadoes, which take the initiative away from politicians and put it into the hands of the residents themselves.

the police would refuse to take reports and throw the men out of the station house because they looked and smelled like bums. As we learned in Chapter 4, since these crimes were not recorded, they "officially" do not exist. By ignoring dozens of robberies, city officials managed to create an image of a safe city.

CORPORATE CRIME

So far, our concern has mainly been with street crime committed by the poor. But what is to be done about corporate crime? After all, as we have stated several times in this text, corporate crime is far more economically,

physically, socially, and environmentally injurious than street crime. Yet, there is no reason to believe that government officials in a capitalist society are going to launch a "war on corporate crime" in the near future. We seldom hear cries for "three strikes and you're out" in relation to corporate crime. In fact, some evidence suggests that the government is creating laws that make it easier for corporations to threaten our well-being (see Snider, 1993).

This entire issue is a most difficult one for policymakers. Simply because of their size, what happens to corporations has a major effect on the rest of society. For example, when a criminal husband is sent to prison for years, his perfectly innocent wife and children may be reduced to poverty. Similarly, massive penalties against corporations are bound to have ripple effects on innocent workers, consumers, and neighbors. There is a famous case involving the Ford Pinto (see the Suggested Readings at the end of Chapter 10). Briefly, Ford Motor Company was accused of failing to correct a minor defect that could turn the Pinto into a deadly firebomb. Ford knew how to fix the problem quickly and easily but chose not to because they calculated that it would be cheaper to pay off the injured and the families of the dead. Perhaps not surprisingly, when a small-town prosecutor brought murder charges against Ford after three young women were killed in a Pinto fire-bomb, Ford flexed its corporate might and won the case on legal rulings and technicalities.

But, suppose Ford had been convicted? Then what? As we once asked in the title of a paper on the subject, "If a Corporation Is a Criminal, What Prison Do You Send It To?" (Schwartz & Ellison, 1980). There have been many suggestions in the legal literature on what might be appropriate punishment for a corporation. It might be fined, not a token amount, but a significant amount of money, such as one month's profits. It could be forbidden to receive government contracts for five years. In the most extreme case of all, it could be given capital punishment—that is, shut down by the government. The problem is just who would be hurt. Much in the same way as the families of a street or white-collar criminal are harmed by sending the criminal to jail, tremendous numbers of people can be hurt by punishment of corporations. Can we ask a judge to be responsible for putting out of business large numbers of lunchrooms, saloons, cleaners, or other legitimate businesses that make their money from company workers? If a company is hit with a massive fine, who do you think will be asked to take a pay cut—top executives or hourly workers? If someone else has to make up the loss, who do you think it will be—stockholders who might be asked to take a reduced quarterly dividend check or consumers who will be asked to pay increased prices?

One possible approach is the notion of *receivership,* whereby corporations would receive intensive supervision probation similar to that for street criminals—which would have the least impact on workers and the surrounding community. Here, a company found guilty of a serious felony would be placed on probation, under the supervision of one or more probation officers appointed by the court but paid by the corporation. This would not be a regular probation officer, but rather a fairly highly paid management specialist, preferably with experience in the field but not with that company. This person could, in the extreme case, take over control of the company for a time or else just monitor its activities carefully for the probationary period.

Some corporations are recidivists on a level that is hard to imagine, with dozens of felony convictions a year for decades. This plan, Martin Schwartz and Charles Ellison (1984, p. 92) suggest, might be less expensive to the state than even sending one or two corporate executives to prison, and would take direct action to at least stop the criminal activity, and to begin to remedy the harm already done. Coupled with other penalties, such as heavy publicity . . . , money fines, and perhaps a partial quarantine which prevented the corporation from working in certain fields for a time, such a penalty would seem to provide at least some promise of compliance with the law by corporations which all too often seem to be and often are outside it.

Another strategy that has been suggested by some critical criminologists has been to promote the practice of workplace democracy. One of the prime measures would be to include on the board of directors of a corporation workers and community members who come from different ethnic and gender backgrounds (Messerschmidt, 1986). Presumably, workers could help democratize the workplace and improve the psychological, physical, and material well-being of laborers who, as pointed out in Chapter 10, are at great risk of being either killed or injured in the workplace. Further, community members could ensure that corporate decisions addressed broader social issues, such as environmental hazards, plant locations, exploitation of natural resources, prices, and product safety (Simon & Eitzen, 1986). Box 12.1 outlines proposals for community-based crime prevention for both corporate and street crime.

FAMILY VIOLENCE AND STREET CRIME[3]

One of the most widely known research findings about violence in the home is the so-called cycle of violence, whereby people who are abused as children grow up to be abusers. This finding has been accepted across the political spectrum, with shelter house activists strongly arguing the connection and even the very conservative theorists James Q. Wilson and Richard Herrnstein (1985) arguing that the consensus is so strong that it would be foolish to ignore it.

---

[3]The material in this section is based on Schwartz (1989).

> BOX 12.1
> # COMMUNITY CRIME PREVENTION
>
> Practically every variant of critical criminology calls for local community-based strategies to curb crime (Schwartz & DeKeseredy, 1991). The rationale for proposing such initiatives, of course, is that some community efforts can reduce crime. However, there have been few community-based attempts to curb either corporate or street crime. Thus, we might consider the strategy proposed by Raymond Michalowski (1983). He suggests that citizen patrols based on democratic principles and representative of all members of the community should be organized to prevent both street and suite crime. With regard to the latter, Michalowski contends that citizen patrols could be used to gather information and to study complaints of business crimes. Such local citizen groups could use their data to pressure companies to stop harming workers, the environment, and the general public, or to initiate legal action. After all, notes Stanley Cohen (1986, p. 131), "It still makes sense to say that mutual aid, good neighborliness and real community are preferable to the solutions of bureaucracies, professionals and the centralized state."

Growing Up in a Violent Home

Unfortunately, too much attention has been placed on physical abuse in the childhood of adult male batterers. A more important key to whether a child will grow up violent is whether the home contained an *atmosphere* of violence and terror. Study after study has shown that it does not matter whether the child is physically abused. What matters is whether there is violence there, usually in the form of woman battering. Simply put, children who grow up watching their mother being beaten are more likely to become problem people when they grow up. Sometimes, for less serious abuse, the child's reaction depends on how hard the parents work to shelter the child from the hostile environment (Buehler et al., 1994).

Still, the bulk of the attention has been devoted to the fact that abused men are more likely than chance to be violent within the home. Criminal justice policymakers have known for some time, but have ignored, the equally important fact that children who grow up watching their mother being abused are more likely than other children to become delinquents and adult criminals *both* inside and outside the home. These children grow up to become responsible for an enormous amount of drug and property crimes and a great deal of violent crime (including murder) outside the home. Of course, only a minority of abused children become abusive as adults; the best guess, based on a careful review of the literature, is that about 30 percent of abused children become abusive adults (Kaufman & Ziegler, 1987). This number is extremely high. We have argued throughout this book that social structural factors (poverty, poor schools, and so on) are related to crime, but no one would argue that 30 percent of people who grow up in poverty become violent adults!

Several researchers have attempted to construct studies that avoid the methodological flaws inherent in this research, but their conclusions remain the same: abused and neglected children are more likely than other children to be arrested for juvenile delinquency, adult criminality, and violent behavior generally (Widom, 1989). This is an extremely important point. Rarely does a shelter house or social welfare agency deal with children removed from a violent home; it is presumed that removing the child is enough. Further, children are examined according to what many in the field call the "stitch rule"; if you don't need stitches, you are not hurt. Thus, a child who is not physically harmed and is removed from the home is completely ignored by the system. Yet, study after study has found that children who witness their mother being beaten are no different in their behavior than children who are abused themselves, and both groups are very different from children who grow up without violence (Schwartz, 1989).

The problem is worse than one of simply ignoring these children. In many states, children's services caseworkers are mandated by state law to promote reunification of violent families as their top priority. Interestingly, in some of the same states, families can split up through a process called dissolution, which is much easier than divorce, and does not involve much more than a handshake and a friendly agreement. If, however, a parent is particularly terroristic and violent, the case must be reported, and a mandatory plan for family reunification must be worked out. We play out a lot of our pro-family rhetoric over the battered bodies and psyches of our children.

The problem is that family violence is criminogenic. When abused children have emotional problems because of abuse, they are the objects of some concern. What we forget very quickly is that, when they turn away from their family and begin to harm others, these children are the very same juvenile delinquents and teenaged thugs we are demanding be locked up in adult prisons. Cathy Widom (1989), for example, in one of the most methodologically sound studies in this area, found that abused and neglected children were more likely than other children to be arrested for delinquency, adult criminality, and violent behavior. In other words, these children not only grow up to be batterers of women and children but grow up to become street criminals who commit (often violent) crimes, predominantly against men.

Thus, we have the astonishing conclusion: one way to reduce street crime against *men* is to reduce violence in the home against *women*. What is horrible is that we have known this for some time. Why hasn't this been at the forefront of criminal justice policy concerns, given that it is one of the few areas where we have some ideas of what to do? Is it because government officials are more concerned about upholding male power in the home than reducing crime (Currie, 1985)? Or that they see any attempt to end violence against women as anti-family, and therefore not part of a conservative agenda (Pleck, 1987)? Or is it that we are so ingrained with the belief that criminals are menacing strangers, preferably of another race, that we just cannot face up to the truth that violence begins at home (Stanko, 1988)?

Confronting Woman Abuse: The Contribution of Pro-Feminist Men

In some ways, this is the most difficult section of the entire book. We have now identified violence against women as one of the primary causes of street crime. Whether violence against women has a relationship to the crimes of the middle and upper classes or to crimes committed by women would be excellent research questions, but unfortunately, they are ones that have not yet been examined by scholars. Similarly, we know that some men are battered by women. Do the children in these relationships have the same problems? Again, we will need to wait for researchers to provide us with some answers. Still, we do know that violence against women in the home is one of the most crime-causing factors ever identified. If we wish to take steps to reduce crime, one of the best things that we can do is to immediately address this area.

The problem is that there have not been a particularly wide variety of ideas on the local level of how to stop woman abuse. This lack of easy answers has generally led to suggestions that the solution is to demand the protection of the state and an increased use of the criminal justice system. Simply, we need to have mandatory arrest of all abusers and mandatory prison time for them. Anything less, many argue, is a sign that a community is not taking the concerns of women seriously (Edwards, 1989).

This has been a particularly difficult problem for progressives. First of all, except with employed men in certain parts of the country, mandatory arrest is unlikely to reduce violence against women, and even then the effects fade away quickly (Buzawa & Buzawa, 1993; Sherman, 1992). Further, as we have argued, prisons are not a solution to the general problem of crime, so why would we want to use them for this particular crime but not others (Smart, 1989)? Given that law enforcement officials in North America are still overwhelmingly anti-feminist, why would feminists want to enhance their power? Still, some very strong arguments have been made that the dangers of state intervention are far outweighed by the dangers of failing to use the police in this way (Dobash & Dobash, 1992). The police, who are usually on the road twenty-four hours a day and are trained to intervene in physical battles, may be the main resource women have to rely on for some time to come.

Aside from lobbyists convincing state legislatures to adopt a wide variety of measures to help battered women, such as streamlined protection orders or faster prosecution (Schwartz & Friedrichs, 1994), the main efforts made to reduce the frequency of battering against female intimates have been community educational efforts, most often undertaken by women's groups. Because women who want to take an active role generally feel more comfortable asking a battered women's shelter house, a rape hotline, or a rape counselor how they can help, this section is mostly written for men. Men often feel that there is no role for them in this crime-curbing effort, which means that extraordinarily little work is being done by men overall. Yet, as Ron Thorne-Finch (1992, p. 236) correctly points out, every man is responsible for helping to reduce the high rates of female victimization discussed in Chapter 9: "Since it is men who are the offenders, it should be men— not women—who change their behavior." Robert Elias (1993, p. 124; emphasis in original) puts it slightly differently: "Women who are criminally victimized do not just *happen* to be women. They are victimized *because* they are women; in this sense, almost all crimes against women are 'hate' crimes."

Ideally, all men should struggle to reduce woman abuse in public and private settings. Unfortunately, very few males are committed to challenging the patriarchal nature of families, schools, workplaces, and state agencies. Thus, for the time being we may have to rely on the efforts of pro-feminist men. These are men who focus on the privileges men receive in this society and the consequences this has for women. They work on the grassroots level to educate people and to criticize social forces and institutions that play a role in creating abusive men.

The individual and collective strategies based on this philosophy will not immediately change people. This type of change does not occur quickly. What these initiatives can do, however, is "chip away" at the forces that influence men to be abusive. Further, like Michalowski's policy proposals on curbing predatory street crime and corporate deviance, pro-feminist men's efforts will not be a financial burden for corporations or governments.

Thorne-Finch recommends that individual men consider variations of the following strategies:

- Put a "Stop Woman Abuse" bumper sticker on your car and declare your home or office a "Woman Abuse–Free Zone."
- Confront woman abusers. If you witness a man physically, sexually, or psychologically injuring a woman, directly intervene. If you fear for your personal safety, seek the help of others or call the police.
- Confront male friends, classmates, co-workers, teachers, or even strangers who make sexist jokes and who engage in sexist conversations.
- Confront men who perpetuate myths about woman abuse.
- Take every opportunity to speak out against woman abuse.
- If you know someone who abuses his female partner, talk to him about his behavior. Tell him that you view his conduct as unacceptable, encourage him to seek pro-feminist therapy, and support his attempts to stop his abusive behavior.

Pro-feminist men can also work with other men in their community to curb woman abuse and other symptoms of gender inequality. For example, men can:

- Lobby government officials to provide better support services for female survivors of abuse.
- Form a pro-feminist men's group.
- Hold "town hall" meetings to discuss progressive ways in which men can help stop woman abuse.
- Produce and distribute literature that debunks woman abuse myths.

Obviously, you can add many more ideas to this list.

Will pro-feminist men's strategies make a difference? Of course, this is a practical question that must be answered practically. The only way these community-based efforts can work is if men advance them within their local political forums. Simply sitting in university forums and criticizing conventional means of reacting to woman abuse certainly won't have any effect!

Today, in men's groups across North America, there is a clear attempt to set men against women through backlash politics. The claim is that, because people talk only about woman abuse even though man abuse exists, they are sexist. These people seek a position that encompasses all victims at the same time. Unfortunately, as Chapter 9 makes clear, when most of the victims are women, when it is women who need shelter, and when most of those who fear for their lives are women, then adopting a gender-free posture is so misleading as to be wrong. It is akin to saying that lions and tigers in the zoo are dangerous, but occasionally, some other animals are dangerous, too. Therefore, we need to close down petting zoos because all animals are dangerous. It does make men feel better to know that they are sometimes victims, and even some women yearn for a world in which there is no gender bias (thus, anyone can be a victim or an offender). Unfortunately, in reality, most street criminals are men. Most corporate criminals are men. Most sex criminals are men (whether the victims are male or female). And, serious violence against a spouse or ex-spouse is a crime of men. If you don't believe this, think about how often you see a story in the paper about a man who kills his ex-wife and then kills himself, or any other story about a woman killed by her husband. See if you can locate similar stories about men killed by their wives, or men stalked by their ex-wives, or women who shoot their husband and children and then commit suicide. You might find one, but not many.

There is, of course, no reason that those concerned with violence against men cannot use the same techniques as outlined here and begin to educate the public about how violence against *anyone* breeds crime and disrespect in society. As women involved in struggles for gender equality have recognized for years, those seeking an end to all forms of abuse must recognize that it will be a long struggle and that it will be necessary to celebrate small victories without losing sight of long-term goals (Thorne-Finch, 1992).

SUMMARY

Texas newspaper columnist Molly Ivins tells a friend's wonderful story about Little Boots Cooper. Essentially, it involves two small boys being sent out to the chicken coop to look for chicken snakes and suddenly coming eye to eye with one. The boys almost take the door off the hinges flying out of the coop. Admonished by their mother that chicken snakes can't possibly hurt them, the very young Boots supposedly replies, "Yes ma'am, but there are some things'll scare you so bad, you hurt yourself!"

One objective of this chapter was to discuss how we have been hurting ourselves with our fear of crime. We have decimated the African-American and Hispanic communities, robbed everything from road construction to university education to pay for more and more prison beds, created a never-ending politics based on racial polarization, and developed what purports to be a victim's movement but in fact seems to be a hotbed of hatred. Even worse, much of what we are doing about crime today has not been working and will not suddenly start working with still more funding. Prisons in particular have not succeeded in stopping crime, and individual treatment has been a dismal failure for the most part. Target hardening may have some positive effect for some people, but overall, it is not a solution to anything.

Our second objective was to outline a few progressive proposals in selected areas for crime reduction. Most important is woman abuse; astonishingly, woman abuse is one of the causes of street crime against men.

The other proposals stem from the proposition that the criminal justice system is only one part of society and cannot be responsible all by itself for cleaning up the messes left by everyone else. Throughout this book, we have argued that social structural problems cause crime—that factors such as poverty, unemployment, homelessness, and an inability to obtain child care

are responsible for much of the street crime. Thus, to reduce crime, we need to promote job creation, the provision of quality day care, housing assistance, and other social services.

Certainly, corporate crime, in terms of injury, is one of the major crime problems today. Placing corporations on probation, or receivership, might be more humane to workers and the community while at the same time promising some possibility of changed behavior.

SUGGESTED READINGS

Currie, E. (1993). *Reckoning: Drugs, the Cities, and the American Future.* New York: Hill & Wang.

Although this book mainly addresses the question of what is to be done about drug abuse, the progressive policies proposed by Currie are applicable to a wide variety of street crimes committed by disenfranchised Americans.

Felson, M. (1994). *Crime and Everyday Life.* Thousand Oaks, CA: Pine Forge Press.

Those interested in prevention and control policies derived from routine activities theory will find this book useful.

Irwin, J., & Austin, J. (1994). *It's About Time: America's Imprisonment Binge.* Belmont, CA: Wadsworth.

This easy-to-read book provides a powerful critique of the U.S. prison system.

Lea, J., & Young, J. (1984). *What Is to Be Done About Law and Order?* New York: Penguin.

Written by two of the pioneers of left realism, this book proposes several practical, progressive crime control strategies. These methods are outstanding alternatives to the ineffective policies advocated by both liberals and conservatives.

REFERENCES

Abadinsky, H. (1994). *Organized Crime,* 4th ed. Chicago: Nelson-Hall.

Adler, F. (1975). *Sisters in Crime: The Rise of the New Female Criminal.* New York: McGraw-Hill.

Adler, P. (1994). "Between Legalization and War: A Reconsideration of American Drug Policy." In *Drug Use in America: Social, Cultural, and Political Perspectives,* ed. P. Venturelli, pp. 255–268. Boston: Jones & Bartlett.

Ahluwalia, S. (1991). "Currents in British Feminist Thought: The Study of Male Violence." In *New Directions in Critical Criminology,* ed. B. MacLean and D. Milovanovic, pp. 55–62. Vancouver: Collective Press.

Akers, R. (1980). "Further Critical Thoughts on Marxist Criminology: Comments on Turk, Toby, and Klockars." In *Radical Criminology: The Coming Crises,* ed. J. Inciardi, pp. 133–138. Beverly Hills, CA: Sage.

Akers, R. (1994). *Criminological Theories: Introduction and Evaluation.* Los Angeles: Roxbury.

Akers, R., Krohn, M., Lanza-Kaduce, L., and Radosevich, M. (1979). "Social Learning and Deviant Behavior: A Specific Test of a General Theory." *American Sociological Review* 44:636–655.

Akman, D., and Normandeau, A. (1980). "The Measurement of Crime and Delinquency in Canada." In *Crime in Canadian Society,* ed. R. Silverman and J. Teevan, pp. 121–132. Toronto: Butterworths.

Albanese, J. (1982). "What Lockheed and La Cosa Nostra Have in Common: The Effect of Ideology on Criminal Justice Policy." *Crime and Delinquency* 28:211–232.

Albanese, J. (1991). "Organized Crime: The Mafia Myth." In *Criminology: A Contemporary Handbook,* ed. J. Sheley, pp. 201–218. Belmont, CA: Wadsworth.

Albini, J. (1971). *The American Mafia: Genesis of a Legend.* New York: Appleton-Century-Crofts.

Allen, H., and Simonsen, C. (1995). *Corrections in America,* 7th ed. Englewood Cliffs, NJ: Prentice-Hall.

Allison, J., and Wrightsman, L. (1993). *Rape: The Misunderstood Crime.* Newbury Park, CA: Sage.

Althusser, L. (1971). *Lenin and Philosophy and Other Essays.* New York: New Left Books.

American Federation of Labor and Congress of Industrial Organizations. (1993). *The Workplace: America's Forgotten Environment.* Washington, DC: American Federation of Labor and Congress of Industrial Organizations.

Amnesty International. (1994). *Urgent Action Bulletin, Death Penalty,* December 22.

Anderson, A. (1979). *The Business of Organized Crime: A Cosa Nostra Family.* Stanford, CA: Hoover Institution Press.

Anderson, L., and Calhoun, T. C. (1992). "Facilitative Aspects of Field Research with Deviant Street Populations." *Sociological Inquiry* 62:490–498.

Andreski, S. (1984). *Max Weber's Insights and Errors.* Boston: Routledge & Kegan Paul.

Andrews, D., and Bonta, J. (1994). *The Psychology of Criminal Conduct.* Cincinnati: Anderson.

Archer, D., and Gartner, R. (1984). *Violence and Crime in Cross-National Perspective.* New Haven, CT: Yale University Press.

Armstrong, P., and Armstrong, H. (1994). *The Double Ghetto: Canadian Women & Their Segregated Work,* 3rd ed. Toronto: McClelland & Stewart.

Auld, J., Dorn, N., and South, N. (1986). "Irregular Work, Irregular Pleasures: Heroin in the 1980s." In *Confronting Crime,* ed. R. Matthews and J. Young, pp. 166–187. London: Sage.

Bacon-Smith, C. (1992). *Enterprising Women: Television Fandom and the Creation of Popular Myth.* Philadelphia: University of Pennsylvania Press.

Balbus, I. (1977). "Commodity Form and Legal Form: An Essay on the 'Relative Autonomy' of the Law." *Law and Society Review* 11:571–588.

Bandura, A. (1965). "Influence of Models' Reinforcement Contingencies on the Acquisition of Imitative Responses." *Journal of Personality and Social Psychology* 1:589–595.

Barak, G. (1986). "Is America Really Ready for the Currie Challenge." *Crime and Social Justice* 25:200–203.

Barak, G. (ed.). (1991a). *Crimes by the Capitalist State: An Introduction to State Criminality.* Albany: SUNY Press.

Barak, G. (1991b). *Gimme Shelter: A Social History of Homelessness in Contemporary America.* New York: Praeger.

Barak, G. (1991c). "Toward a Criminology of State Criminality." In *Crimes by the Capitalist State: An Introduction to State Criminality,* ed. G. Barak, pp. 3–16. Albany: SUNY Press.

Barnett, O., and LaViolette, A. (1993). *It Could Happen to Anyone: Why Battered Women Stay.* Newbury Park, CA: Sage.

Baron, L. (1990). "Pornography and Gender Equality: An Empirical Analysis." *The Journal of Sex Research* 27 (3):363–380.

Baron, L., and Straus, M. (1984). "Sexual Stratification, Pornography, and Rape in the United States." In *Pornography and Sexual Aggression,* ed. N. Malamuth and E. Donnerstein, pp. 185–209. New York: Academic Press.

Barrett, M., and McIntosh, M. (1982). *The Anti-Social Family.* London: Verso.

Baunach, P. (1985). "Critical Problems of Women in Prison." In *The Changing Roles of Women in the Criminal Justice System,* ed. I. Moyer, pp. 95–110. Prospect Heights, IL: Waveland Press.

Beattie, J. (1986). *Crime and the Courts in England, 1600–1800.* Princeton, NJ: Princeton University Press.

Beaty, J., and Hornik, R. (1989). "A Torrent of Dirty Dollars." *Time* (December 18): 50–56.

Beccaria, C. (1963). *On Crimes and Punishments.* Indianapolis, IN: Bobbs-Merrill.

Becker, H. (1973). *Outsiders: Studies in the Sociological Study of Deviance.* New York: Free Press.

Beirne, P., and Messerschmidt, J. (1995). *Criminology,* 2nd ed. San Diego: Harcourt Brace Jovanovich.

Bendix, R., and Roth, G. (1971). *Scholarship and Partisanship: Essays on Max Weber.* Berkeley: University of California Press.

Berg, B. (1995). *Qualitative Research Methods for the Social Sciences,* 2nd ed. Boston: Allyn & Bacon.

Berk, R. (1990). "Thinking About Hate-Motivated Crimes." *Journal of Interpersonal Violence* 5:316–333.

Berrill, K. (1990). "Anti-Gay Violence and Victimization in the United States: An Overview." *Journal of Interpersonal Violence* 5:274–294.

Blau, F., and Winkler, A. (1989). "Women in the Labor Force: An Overview." In *Women: A Feminist Perspective,* ed. J. Freeman, pp. 265–286. Palo Alto, CA: Mayfield.

Blau, J., and Blau, P. (1982). "The Cost of Inequality: Metropolitan Structure and Violent Crime." *American Sociological Review* 47:114–129.

Bloch, H., and Geis, G. (1970). *Man, Crime and Society,* 2nd ed. New York: Random House.

Block, A., and Scarpitti, F. (1985). *Poisoning for Profit: The Mafia and Toxic Waste in America.* New York: Morrow.

Boeringer, R., Shehan, C., and Akers, R. (1991). "Social Contexts and Social Learning in Sexual Coercion and Aggression: Assessing the Contribution of Fraternity Membership." *Family Relations* 40:58–64.

Bohm, R. (1982). "Radical Criminology: An Explication." *Criminology* 19:565–589.

Bohm, R. (1991). "American Death Penalty Opinion, 1936–1986: A Critical Examination of the Gallup Polls." In *The Death Penalty in America: Current Research,* ed. R. Bohm, pp. 113–145. Cincinnati: Anderson.

Bohmer, C. (1991). "Acquaintance Rape and the Law." In *Acquaintance Rape: The Hidden Crime,* ed. A Parrot and L. Bechhofer, pp. 317–333. New York: Wiley.

Bohmer, C., and Parrot, A. (1993). *Sexual Assault on Campus: The Problem and the Solution.* New York: Lexington.

Bollen, K. A., and Phillips, C. (1982). "Imitative Suicides: A National Study of the Effects of Television News Stories." *American Sociological Review* 47:802–809.

Bourgois, P., and Dunlap, E. (1993). "Exorcising Sex-for-Crack: An Ethnographic Perspective from Harlem." In *Crack Pipe as Pimp: An Ethnographic Investigation of Sex-for-Crack Exchanges,* ed. M. Ratner, pp. 97–132. New York: Macmillan.

Bowers, W., and Pierce, G. (1980). "Deterrence or Brutalization? What Is the Effect of Executions?" *Crime and Delinquency* 26:453–484.

Bowker, L. (1983). *Beating Wife-Beating.* Lexington, MA: Lexington Books.

Box, S. (1983). *Power, Crime, and Mystification.* London: Tavistock.

Boyd, N. (1988). *The Last Dance: Murder in Canada.* Toronto: Prentice-Hall.

Boyd, N. (1991). *High Society: Legal and Illegal Drugs in Canada.* Toronto: Key Porter Books.

Boyd, N. (1992). "Legal and Illegal Drug Use in Canada." In *Deviance: Conformity and Control in Canadian Society,* ed. V. Sacco, pp. 136–171. Scarborough, Ontario: Prentice-Hall.

Boyd, N. (1995). *Canadian Law: An Introduction.* Toronto: Harcourt Brace, Canada.

Boyd, N., Elliott, L., and Gaucher, B. (1991). "Drug Use and Violence: Rethinking the Connections." *Journal of Human Justice* 3:67–83.

Brady, J. (1983). "Arson, Urban Economy, and Organized Crime: The Case of Boston." *Social Problems* 31:1–27.

Braithwaite, J. (1979). *Inequality, Crime and Public Policy.* Boston: Routledge & Kegan Paul.

Braithwaite, J. (1989). *Crime, Shame and Reintegration.* New York: Cambridge University Press.

Brake, M. (1985). *Comparative Youth Culture: The Sociology of Youth Culture and Youth Subcultures in America, Britain and Canada.* Boston: Routledge & Kegan Paul.

Brannigan, A. (1984). *Crimes, Courts and Corrections: An Introduction to Crime and Social Control in Canada.* Toronto: Holt, Rinehart & Winston of Canada.

Brannigan, A., and Fleischman, J. (1989). "Juvenile Prostitution and Mental Health: Policing Delinquency or Treating Pathology." *Canadian Journal of Law and Society* 4:77–98.

Brannigan, A., and Goldenberg, S. (1987). "The Study of Aggressive Pornography: The Vicissitudes of Relevance." *Critical Studies in Mass Communication* 4:262–283.

Breines, W., and Gordon, L. (1983). "The New Scholarship on Family Violence." *Signs: Journal of Women in Culture and Society* 8:491–453.

Brennan, P., Mednick, S., and Volavka, J. (1995). "Biomedical Factors in Crime." In *Crime,* ed. J. Wilson and J. Petersilia, pp. 65–90. San Francisco: Institute for Contemporary Studies.

Breslin, P. (1995). "The South Bronx Bounces Back." *Smithsonian* 26(1):100–113.

Brickey, S., and Comack, E. (1986). "Recent Developments in the Sociology of Law." In *The Social Basis of Law: Critical Readings in the Sociology of Law,* ed. S. Brickey and E. Comack, pp. 15–21. Toronto: Garamond.

Brinkerhoff, M., and Lupri, E. (1988). "Interspousal Violence." *Canadian Journal of Sociology* 13:407–434.

Brody, R. (1985). *Contra Terror in Nicaragua.* Boston: South End Press.

Brown, M. (1979). *Laying Waste: The Poisoning of America by Toxic Chemicals.* New York: Pantheon.

Brown, R. (1969). "Historical Patterns of Violence in America." In *The History of Violence in America,* ed. H. Graham and T. Gurr, pp. 45–83. New York: Bantam Books.

Brown, S., Esbensen, F., and Geis, G. (1991). *Criminology: Explaining Crime and Its Context.* Cincinnati: Anderson.

Browne, A. (1987). *When Battered Women Kill.* New York: Macmillan.

Browning, F., and Gerassi, J. (1980). *The American Way of Crime.* New York: Putnam.

Buehler, C., Krishnakuman, A., Anthony, C., Tittsworth, S., and Stone, G. (1994). "Hostile Interparental Conflict and Youth Maladjustment." *Family Relations* 43:409–416.

Bureau of Justice Statistics. (1985). *Household Burglary.* Washington, DC: National Institute of Justice, U.S. Department of Justice.

Bureau of Justice Statistics. (1994). *Violence Between Intimates.* Washington, DC: Office of Justice Programs, U.S. Department of Justice.

Bureau of Justice Statistics. (1995). *Drugs and Crime Facts, 1994.* Washington, DC: U.S. Government Printing Office.

Burney, E. (1990). *Putting Crime in Its Place.* London: Centre for Inner City Studies, Goldsmiths' College, University of London.

Burtch, B. (1992). *The Sociology of Law: Critical Approaches to Social Control.* Toronto: Harcourt Brace Jovanovich, Canada.

Buzawa, E., and Buzawa, C. (1993). "The Scientific Evidence Is Not Conclusive: Arrest Is No Panacea." In *Current Controversies on Family Violence,* ed. R. Gelles and D. Loseke, pp. 337–356. Newbury Park, CA: Sage.

Calavita, K., and Pontell, H. (1993). "Savings and Loan Fraud as Organized Crime: Towards a Conceptual Typology of Corporate Illegality." *Criminology* 31:519–548.

Calhoun, T. (1992). "Male Street Hustling: Introduction Processes and Stigma Containment." *Sociological Spectrum* 12:35–52.

Campbell, A. (1984). *The Girls in the Gang.* New York: Basil Blackwell.

Campbell, A. (1993). *Men, Women and Aggression.* New York: Basic Books.

Campbell, J. (1992). "If I Can't Have You, No One Can: Issues of Power and Control in Homicide of Female Partners." In *Femicide: The Politics of Woman Killing,* ed. J. Radford and D. Russell, pp. 99–113. New York: Twayne.

Caplan, G. (1974). *Social Systems and Community Mental Health.* New York: Behavioral Publications.

Caputi, J. (1987). *The Age of Sex Crimes.* Bowling Green, OH: Bowling Green State University Press.

Caputi, J., and Russell, D. (1992). "Femicide: Sexual Terrorism Against Women." In *Femicide: The Politics of Woman Killing,* ed. J. Radford and D. Russell, pp. 13–21. New York: Twayne.

Caputo, T., Kennedy, M., Reasons, C., and Brannigan, A. (1989). "General Introduction: Theories of Law and Society." In *Law and Society: A Critical Perspective,* ed. T. Caputo, M. Kennedy, C. Reasons, and A. Brannigan, pp. 1–15. Toronto: Harcourt Brace Jovanovich, Canada.

Cassel, J. (1976). "The Contribution of the Social Environment to Host Resistance." *American Journal of Epidemiology* 104:107–123.

Chambliss, W. (1973). "The Saints and Roughnecks." *Society* 11:22–31.

Chambliss, W. (1975). "Toward a Political Economy of Crime." *Theory and Society* (Summer):167–180.

Chambliss, W. (1986). "On Lawmaking." In *The Social Basis of Law: Critical Readings in the Sociology of Law,* ed. S. Brickey and E. Comack, pp. 27–51. Toronto: Garamond.

Chambliss, W. (1988). *On the Take,* 2nd ed. Bloomington: Indiana University Press.

Chambliss, W., and Courtless, T. (1992). *Criminal Law, Criminology, and Criminal Justice.* Belmont, CA: Wadsworth.

Chambliss, W., and Seidman, R. (1982). *Law, Order, and Power,* 2nd ed. Reading, MA: Addison-Wesley.

Chambliss, W., and Zatz, M. (eds.). (1993). *Making Law: The State, the Law, and Structural Contradictions.* Bloomington: Indiana University Press.

Chancer, L. (1994). "Prostitution, Feminist Theory, and Ambivalence: Notes from the Sociological Underground." *Social Text* 12:149–177.

Chein, I. (1966). "Narcotics Use Among Juveniles." In *Narcotic Addiction,* ed. J. O'Donnell and J. Ball, pp. 123–141. New York: Harper & Row.

Chein, I., Gerard, D., Lee, R., and Rosenfeld, E. (1964). *The Road to H: Narcotics, Delinquency, and Social Policy.* New York: Basic Books.

Chenier, N. (1982). *Reproductive Hazards at Work: Men, Women and the Fertility Gamble.* Ottawa: Canadian Advisory Council on the Status of Women.

Chermak, S. (1994). "Body Count News: How Crime Is Presented in the News Media." *Justice Quarterly* 11(4):561–582.

Chesney-Lind, M., and Sheldon, R. (1992). *Girls: Delinquency and Juvenile Justice.* Pacific Grove, CA: Brooks/Cole.

Clark, L., and Tifft, L. (1966). "Polygraph and Interview Validation of Self-Reported Deviant Behavior." *American Sociological Review* 31:516–523.

Clarke, A. (1984). "Perceptions of Crime and Fear of Victimization Among Elderly People." *Ageing and Society* 4:327–342.

Clarke, A., and Lewis, M. (1982). "Fear of Crime Among the Elderly: An Exploratory Study." *British Journal of Criminology* 22:49–62.

Clarke, R., and Cornish, D. (1985). "Modeling Offenders' Decisions: A Framework for Research and Policy." In *Crime and Justice: An Annual Review of Research,* Vol. 6, ed. M. Tonry and N. Morris, pp. 147–185. Chicago: University of Chicago Press.

Clarke, R., and Felson, M. (1993). "Introduction: Criminology, Routine Activity, and Rational Choice." In *Routine Activity and Rational Choice,* ed. R. Clarke and M. Felson, pp. 1–14. New Brunswick, NJ: Transaction.

Claybrook, J. (1984). *Retreat from Safety.* New York: Pantheon.

Clear, T. (1994). *Harm in American Penology: Offenders, Victims, and Their Communities.* Albany: SUNY Press.

Clinard, M., and Quinney, R. (1973). *Criminal Behavior Systems,* rev. ed. New York: Holt, Rinehart & Winston.

Clinard, M., and Yeager, P. (1980). *Corporate Crime: The First Comprehensive Account of Illegal Practices Among America's Top Corporations.* New York: Free Press.

Cloward, R., and Ohlin, L. (1960). *Delinquency and Opportunity: A Theory of Delinquent Gangs.* New York: Free Press.

Cocozza, J., Melick, M., and Steadman, H. (1978). "Trends in Violent Crime Among Ex-Mental Patients." *Criminology* 16:317–334.

Cohen, A. (1955). *Delinquent Boys.* New York: Free Press.

Cohen, A. (1966). *Deviance and Control.* Englewood Cliffs, NJ: Prentice-Hall.

Cohen, A. (1985). "The Assumption That Crime Is a Product of Environments: Sociological Approaches." In *Theoretical Methods in Criminology,* ed. R. Meier, pp. 223–243. Beverly Hills, CA: Sage.

Cohen, L., and Felson, M. (1979). "Social Change and Crime Rate Trends: A Routine Activities Approach." *American Sociological Review* 44:588–608.

Cohen, S. (1980). *Folk Devils and Moral Panics,* 2nd ed. Oxford: Basil Blackwell.

Cohen, S. (1985). *Visions of Social Control.* Cambridge: Polity Press.

Cohen, S. (1986). "Community Control." In *Abolitionism,* ed. H. Bianchi and R. van Swanningen, pp. 127–132. Amsterdam: Free University Press.

Cohen, S., and Wills, T. (1985). "Stress, Social Support and the Buffering Hypothesis." *Psychological Bulletin* 98:310–357.

Cohen, S., and Young, J. (eds). (1981). *The Manufacture of News: Deviance, Social Problems and the Mass Media.* London: Constable.

Cole, G. F. (1995). *The American System of Criminal Justice,* 7th ed. Belmont, CA: Wadsworth.

Coleman, J. (1989). *The Criminal Elite: The Sociology of White Collar Crime,* 2nd ed. New York: St. Martin's Press.

Collins, H. (1982). *Marxism and Law.* Oxford: Clarendon.

Collins, R. (1981). *Sociology Since Mid-Century: Essays in Theory Cumulation.* New York: Academic Press.

Comack, E. (1986). "We Will Get Some Good Out of This Riot Yet: The Canadian State, Drug Legislation and Class Conflict." In *The Social Basis of Law: Critical Readings in the Sociology of Law,* ed. S. Brickey and E. Comack, pp. 67–90. Toronto: Garamond.

Comack, E., and Brickey, S. (1991a). "Theoretical Approaches in the Sociology of Law." In *The Social Basis of Law: Critical Readings in the Sociology of Law,* 2nd ed., ed. E. Comack and S. Brickey, pp. 15–32. Halifax: Garamond.

Comack, E., and Brickey, S. (1991b). "Future Directions in the Sociology of Law." In *The Social Basis of Law: Critical Readings in the Sociology of Law,* 2nd ed., ed. E. Comack and S. Brickey, pp. 319–324. Halifax: Garamond.

Commager, H. (1971). "The History of American Violence: An Interpretation." In *Violence: The Crisis of American Confidence,* ed. H. Graham, pp. 3–26. Baltimore: Johns Hopkins University Press.

Comstock, G. (1980). *Television in America.* Newbury Park, CA: Sage.

Connell, R. (1990). "The State, Gender, and Sexual Politics: Theory and Appraisal." *Theory and Society* 19:507–544.

Conrad, P., and Schneider, J. (1992). *Deviance and Medicalization: From Badness to Sickness.* Philadelphia: Temple University Press.

Counts, D., Brown, J., and Campbell, J. (eds.). (1992). *Sanctions and Sanctuary: Cultural Perspectives on the Beating of Wives.* Boulder, CO: Westview.

Crawford, A., Jones, T., Woodhouse, T., and Young, J. (1990). *Second Islington Crime Survey.* London: Middlesex Polytechnic Centre for Criminology.

Cressey, D. (1969). *Theft of a Nation.* New York: Harper & Row.

Croall, H. (1992). *White Collar Crime.* Philadelphia: Open University Press.

Cromwell, P., Olson, J., and Avary, D. (1991). *Breaking and Entering: An Ethnographic Analysis of Burglary.* Newbury Park, CA: Sage.

Crutchfield, R. (1989). "Labor Stratification and Violent Crime." *Social Forces* 68:589–612.

Cullen, F. (1984). *Rethinking Crime and Deviance Theory: The Emergence of a Structuring Tradition.* Totowa, NJ: Rowman & Littlefield.

Cullen, F., Maakestad, W., and Cavender, G. (1987). *Corporate Crime Under Attack: The Ford Pinto Case and Beyond.* Cincinnati: Anderson.

Curran, D., and Renzetti, C. (1994). *Theories of Crime.* Boston: Allyn & Bacon.

Currie, D. (1991). "Women and the State: A Statement on Feminist Theory." In *New Directions in Critical Criminology,* ed. B. MacLean and D. Milovanovic, pp. 45–50. Vancouver: Collective Press.

Currie, D., DeKeseredy, W., and MacLean, B. (1990). "Reconstituting Social Order and Social Control: Police Accountability in Canada." *The Journal of Human Justice* 2:29–54.

Currie, D., and MacLean, B. (1992). "Women, Men, and Police: Losing the Fight Against Wife Battery in Canada." In *Rethinking the Administration of Justice,* ed. D. Currie and B. MacLean, pp. 251–275. Halifax: Fernwood.

Currie, D., MacLean, B., and Milovanovic, D. (1992). "Three Traditions of Critical Justice Inquiry." In *Rethinking the Administration of Justice,* ed. D. Currie and B. MacLean, pp. 3–42. Halifax: Fernwood.

Currie, E. (1985). *Confronting Crime.* New York: Pantheon.

Currie, E. (1989). "Confronting Crime: Looking Toward the Twenty-First Century." *Justice Quarterly* 6:5–26.

Currie, E. (1992). "Retreatism, Minimalism, Realism: Three Styles of Reasoning on Crime and Drugs in the United States." In *Realist Criminology: Crime Control and Policing in the 1990s,* ed. J. Lowman and B. MacLean, pp. 88–97. Toronto: University of Toronto Press.

Currie, E. (1993). *Reckoning: Drugs, the Cities, and the American Future.* New York: Hill & Wang.

Dahrendorf, R. (1959). *Class and Class Conflict in Industrial Society.* Stanford, CA: Stanford University Press.

Daly, K. (1994). *Gender, Crime, and Punishment.* New Haven, CT: Yale University Press.

Daly, K., and Chesney-Lind, M. (1988). "Feminism and Criminology." *Justice Quarterly* 5: 497–538.

Daly, M., and Wilson, M. (1988). *Homicide.* Hawthorne, NY: Aldine de Gruyter.

Danner, M. (1991). "Socialist Feminism: A Brief Introduction." In *New Directions in Critical Criminology,* ed. B. MacLean and D. Milovanovic, pp. 51–54. Vancouver: Collective Press.

Davis, N., and Stasz, C. (1990). *Social Control of Deviance: A Critical Perspective.* New York: McGraw-Hill.

DeKeseredy, W. (1988a). "Woman Abuse in Dating Relationships: A Critical Evaluation of Research and Theory." *International Journal of Sociology of the Family* 18:79–96.

DeKeseredy, W. (1988b). *Woman Abuse in Dating Relationships: The Role of Male Peer Support.* Toronto: Canadian Scholars' Press.

DeKeseredy, W. (1990). "Male Peer Support and Woman Abuse: The Current State of Knowledge." *Sociological Focus* 23:129–139.

DeKeseredy, W. (1992). "Confronting Woman Abuse in Canada: A Left Realist Approach." In *Realist Criminology: Crime Control and Policing in the 1990s,* ed. J. Lowman and B. MacLean, pp. 264–282. Toronto: University of Toronto Press.

DeKeseredy, W. (1993). *Four Variations of Family Violence: A Review of Sociological Research.* Ottawa: Health Canada.

DeKeseredy, W. (1994). "Making an Unsafe Learning Environment Safer: Some Progressive Policy Proposals to Curb Woman Abuse in University/College Dating Relationships." Paper presented at the Violence: A Collective Responsibility Symposium, Calgary, Alberta.

DeKeseredy, W., Burshtyn, H., and Gordon, C. (1992). "Taking Woman Abuse Seriously: A Critical Response to the Solicitor General of Canada's Crime Prevention Advice." *International Review of Victimology* 2:157–167.

DeKeseredy, W., and Goff, C. (1992). "Corporate Violence Against Canadian Women: Assessing Left-Realist Research and Policy." *The Journal of Human Justice* 4:55–70.

DeKeseredy, W., and Hinch, R. (1991). *Women Abuse: Sociological Perspectives.* Toronto: Thompson Educational Publishing.

DeKeseredy, W., and Kelly, K. (1993a). "The Incidence and Prevalence of Woman Abuse in Canadian University and College Dating Relationships." *Canadian Journal of Sociology* 18:137–159.

DeKeseredy, W., and Kelly, K. (1993b). "Woman Abuse in University and College Dating Relationships: The Contribution of the Ideology of Familial Patriarchy." *Journal of Human Justice* 4:25–52.

DeKeseredy, W., and MacLean, B. (1990). "Researching Woman Abuse in Canada: A Left Realist Critique of the Conflict Tactics Scale." *Canadian Review of Social Policy* 25:19–27.

DeKeseredy, W., and MacLean, B. (1991). "Exploring the Gender, Race and Class Dimensions of Victimization: A Left Realist Critique of the Canadian Urban Victimization Survey." *International Journal of Offender Therapy and Comparative Criminology* 35:143–161.

DeKeseredy, W., and MacLean, B. (1993). "Critical Criminological Pedagogy in Canada: Strengths, Limitations, and Recommendations for Improvements." *Journal of Criminal Justice Education* 4:361–376.

DeKeseredy, W., and Schwartz, M. (1991a). "British and U.S. Left Realism: A Critical Comparison." *International Journal of Offender Therapy and Comparative Criminology* 35:248–262.

DeKeseredy, W., and Schwartz, M. (1991b). "British Left Realism on the Abuse of Women: A Critical Appraisal." In *Criminology as Peacemaking*, ed. H. Pepinsky and R. Quinney, pp. 154–171. Bloomington: Indiana University Press.

DeKeseredy, W., and Schwartz, M. (1993a). "Male Peer Support and Woman Abuse: An Expansion of DeKeseredy's Model." *Sociological Spectrum* 13:393–413.

DeKeseredy, W., and Schwartz, M. (1993b). "Theories of Male Peer Support and Woman Abuse" Paper presented at the annual meeting of the Society for the Study of Social Problems, Miami Beach.

Denzin, N. (1978). *The Research Act.* New York: McGraw-Hill.

Denzin, N. (1990). "Presidential Address on the Sociological Imagination Revisited." *The Sociological Quarterly* 31:1–22.

Desroches, F. (1995). *Robbery in Canada.* Toronto: Nelson-Hall.

Dews, P. (1987). *Logic of Disintegration—Poststructuralist Thought and the Claims of Critical Thought.* New York: Verso.

Dixon, J., and Lizotte, A. (1987). "Gun Ownership and the 'Southern Subculture of Violence.'" *American Journal of Sociology* 93:383–405.

Dobash, R. E., and Dobash, R. (1979). *Violence Against Wives.* New York: Free Press.

Dobash, R. E., and Dobash, R. (1983). "The Context-Specific Approach." In *The Dark Side of Families,* ed. D. Finkelhor, R. Gelles, G. Hotaling, and M. Straus, pp. 261–276. Beverly Hills, CA: Sage.

Dobash, R. E., and Dobash, R. (1992). *Women, Violence and Social Change.* New York: Routledge.

Dobash, R., Dobash, R. E., Wilson, M., and Daly, M. (1992). "The Myth of Sexual Symmetry in Marital Violence." *Social Problems* 39:71–91.

Donnerstein, E., and Linz, D. (1984). "Sexual Violence in the Media: A Warning." *Psychology Today* (January):14–15.

Donnerstein, E., and Linz, D. (1986). "Mass Media Sexual Violence and Male Viewers." *American Behavioral Scientist* 29:601–618.

Downes, D., and Rock, P. (1988). *Understanding Deviance: A Guide to the Sociology of Crime and Rule Breaking,* 2nd ed. Toronto: Oxford University Press.

Dugdale, R. (1910). *The Jukes: A Study in Crime, Pauperism, Disease, and Heredity.* New York: Putnam.

Durkheim, E. (1951). *Suicide: A Study in Sociology.* New York: Free Press.

Durkheim, E. (1956). *The Division of Labor in Society.* Glencoe, IL: Free Press.

Durkheim, E. (1982). *The Rules of Sociological Method and Selected Texts on Sociology and Its Method.* New York: Free Press.

Dworkin, A. (1993). "Living in Terror, Pain: Being a Battered Wife." In *Violence Against Women: The Bloody Footprints,* ed. P. Bart and E. Moran, pp. 237–239. Newbury Park, CA: Sage.

Edwards, S. (1989). *Policing "Domestic" Violence: Women, the Law and the State.* London: Sage.

Edwards, S. (1990). "Violence Against Women: Feminism and the Law." In *Feminist Perspectives in Criminology,* ed. L. Gelsthorpe and A. Morris, pp. 145–159. Philadelphia: Open University Press.

Egger, S. (1990). "Serial Murder: A Synthesis of Literature and Research." In *Serial Murder: An Elusive Phenomenon,* ed. S. Egger, pp. 3–34. New York: Praeger.

Ehrenreich, B., and English, D. (1978). *For Her Own Good.* Garden City NY: Anchor.

Ehrhart, J., and Sandler, B. (1985). *Campus Gang Rape: Party Games?* Washington, DC: Project on the Status and Education of Women, Association of American Colleges.

Ehrlich, H. (1990). "The Ecology of Anti-Gay Violence." *Journal of Interpersonal Violence* 5:359–365.

Ehrlich, S. (1989). *Lisa, Hedda and Joel: The Steinberg Murder Case.* New York: St. Martin's Press.

Eighner, L. (1993). *Travels with Lizbeth: Three Years on the Road and on the Streets.* New York: St. Martin's Press.

Eitzen, D., and Timmer, D. (1985). *Criminology.* New York: Wiley.

Elias, R. (1986). *The Politics of Victimization: Victims, Victimology and Human Rights.* New York: Oxford University Press.

Elias, R. (1993). *Victims Still: The Political Manipulation of Crime Victims.* Newbury Park, CA: Sage.

Elliott, D., and Ageton, S. (1980). "Reconciling Race and Class Differences in Self-Reported and Official Estimates of Delinquency." *American Sociological Review* 45: 95–110.

Elliott, D., and Huizinga, D. (1983). "Social Class and Delinquent Behavior in a National Youth Panel: 1976–1980." *Criminology* 21:149–177.

Ellis, D. (1987). *The Wrong Stuff: An Introduction to the Sociological Study of Deviance.* Toronto: Collier Macmillan.

Ellis, D., & DeKeseredy, W. (1989). "Marital Status and Woman Abuse: The DAD Model." *International Journal of Sociology of the Family* 19:67–87.

Ellis, D., & DeKeseredy, W. (1996). *The Wrong Stuff: An Introduction to the Sociological Study of Deviance,* 2nd ed. Toronto: Allyn & Bacon.

Ellis, D., and Stuckless, N. (1992). "Presepartion Abuse, Marital Conflict Mediation, and Postseparation Abuse." *Mediation Quarterly* 9:205–225.

Ellis, D., and Wight, L. (1987). "Post-Separation Woman Abuse: The Contribution of Lawyers." *Victimology* 13:146–166.

Elsner, M. (1994). "The Sociology of Reefer Madness: The Criminalization of Marijuana in the United States." In *Drug Use in America: Social, Cultural, and Political Perspectives,* ed. P. Venturelli, pp. 269–279. Boston: Jones & Bartlett.

Ericson, R., Baranek, P., and Chan, J. (1987). *Visualizing Deviance.* Toronto: University of Toronto Press.

Ericson, R., Baranek, P., and Chan, J. (1989). *Negotiating Control: A Study of News Sources.* Toronto: University of Toronto Press.

Erikson, K. (1962). "Notes on the Sociology of Deviance." *Social Problems* 9:307–314.

Erikson, P., and Murray, G. (1989). "Sex Differences in Cocaine Use and Experiences: A Double Standard Revived?" *American Journal of Drug and Alcohol Abuse* 15:135–152.

Erlich, I. (1975). "The Deterrent Effect of Capital Punishment: A Question of Life and Death." *Law and Criminology* 66:483–490.

Fairstein, L. (1993). *Sexual Violence: Our War Against Rape.* New York: Morrow.

Faith, K. (1993a). *Unruly Women: The Politics of Confinement and Resistance.* Vancouver: Press Gang.

Faith, K. (1993b). "State Appropriation of Feminist Initiative: Transition House, Vancouver, 1973–1986." In *Seeking Shelter: A State of Battered Women,* ed. K. Faith and D. Currie, pp. 1–36. Vancouver: Collective Press.

Faludi, S. (1991). *Backlash: The Undeclared War Against American Women.* New York: Crown.

Farr, K. (1988). "Dominance Bonding Through the Good Old Boys Sociability Group." *Sex Roles* 18:259–277.

Fattah, E., and Sacco, V. (1989). *Crime and Victimization of the Elderly.* New York: Springer-Verlag.

Federal Bureau of Investigation. (1988). *Uniform Crime Reports.* Washington, DC: U.S. Government Printing Office.

Federal Bureau of Investigation. (1992). *Uniform Crime Reports: Crime in the United States, 1991.* Washington DC: U.S. Government Printing Office.

Federal Bureau of Investigation. (1993). *Uniform Crime Reports: Crime in the United States, 1992.* Washington, DC: U.S. Government Printing Office.

Federal Bureau of Investigation. (1994). *Uniform Crime Reports: Crime in the United States, 1993.* Washington, DC: U.S. Government Printing Office.

Felson, M. (1994). *Crime and Everyday Life.* Thousand Oaks, CA: Pine Forge Press.

Felson, R., and Steadman, H. (1983). "Situational Factors in Disputes Leading to Criminal Violence." *Criminology* 21:59–74.

Fenstermaker, S. (1989). "Acquaintance Rape on Campus: Responsibility and Attributions of Crime." In *Violence in Dating Relationships: Emerging Social Issues,* ed. M. Pirog-Good and J. Stets, pp. 257–271. New York: Praeger.

Ferrell, J. (1993). *Crimes of Style: Urban Graffiti and the Politics of Criminality.* New York: Garland.

Fielding, N., and Fielding, J. (1986). *Linking Data.* Beverly Hills, CA: Sage.

Fijnaut, C. (1990). "Organized Crime: A Comparison Between the United States of America and Western Europe." *British Journal of Criminology* 30:321–340.

Fitzpatrick, D., and Halliday, C. (1992). *Not the Way to Love: Violence Against Young Women in Dating Relationships.* Amherst, Nova Scotia: Cumberland County Transition House Association.

Fitzpatrick, K., LaGory, M., and Fitchey, F. (1993). "Criminal Victimization Among the Homeless." *Justice Quarterly* 10:353–368.

Fleming, T. (ed.). (1985). *The New Criminologies in Canada: State, Crime, and Control.* Toronto: Oxford University Press.

Forst, M. (1983). "Capital Punishment and Deterrence: Conflicting Evidence?" *Journal of Criminal Law and Criminology* 74:927–942.

Foucault, M. (1979). *Discipline and Punish: The Birth of the Prison.* New York: Vintage.

Fox, J. (1994). "Rate (per 100,000 persons) of Murder and Nonnegligent Manslaughter Victimization." In *Sourcebook of Criminal Justice Statistics—1993,* ed. K. Maguire and A. Pastore, p. 385. Washington, DC: U.S. Government Printing Office.

Fox, S. (1989). *Blood and Power—Organized Crime in Twentieth Century America.* New York: Morrow.

Frank, N., and Lynch, M. (1992). *Corporate Crime, Corporate Violence: A Primer.* New York: Harrow & Heston.

Friedberg, A. (1983). *America Afraid.* New York: New American Library.

Friedrichs, D. (1980). "Radical Criminology in the United States: An Interpretive Understanding." In *Radical Criminology: The Coming Crises,* ed. J. Inciardi, pp. 35–60. Beverly Hills, CA: Sage.

Friedrichs, D. (1983). "Victimology: A Consideration of the Radical Critique." *Crime and Delinquency* 29:283–294.

Friedrichs, D. (1989). "Critical Criminology and Critical Legal Studies." *Critical Criminologist* 1:7.

Friedrichs, D. (1991). "Introduction: Peacemaking Criminology in a World Filled with Conflict." In *New Directions in Critical Criminology,* ed. B. MacLean and D. Milovanovic, pp. 101–106. Vancouver: Collective Press.

Friedrichs, D. (1992). "White Collar Crime and the Definitional Quagmire: A Provisional Solution." *The Journal of Human Justice* 3:5–21.

Friendly, A., and Goldfarb, R. (1968). *Crime and Publicity: The Impact of News on the Administration of Justice.* New York: Vintage.

Gaquin, D. (1977–78). "Spouse Abuse: Data from the National Crime Survey." *Victimology* 2:632–643.

Garofalo, J. (1979). "Victimization and the Fear of Crime." *Journal of Research in Crime and Delinquency* 16:80–97.

Gartner, R. (1995). "Homicide in Canada." In *Violence in Canada,* ed. J. Ross, pp. 186–222. Toronto: Oxford University Press.

Gastil, R. (1971). "Homicide and a Regional Culture of Violence." *American Sociological Review* 36:412–427.

Geis, G. (1986). "The Heavy Electrical Equipment Antitrust Cases of 1961." In *Corporate and Governmental Deviance,* ed. M. Ermann and R. Lundman, pp. 124–144. New York: Oxford University Press.

Gelles, R. (1980). "Violence in the Family: A Review of Research in the Seventies." *Journal of Marriage and the Family* 42:873–885.

Gelles, R. (1990). "Violence and Pregnancy: Are Pregnant Women at Greater Risk of Abuse?" In *Physical Violence in America Families,* ed. M. Straus and R. Gelles, pp. 279–286. New Brunswick, NJ: Transaction.

Gelles, R., and Cornell, C. (1985). *Intimate Violence in Families.* Beverly Hills, CA: Sage.

Gelles, R., and Straus, M. (1988). *Intimate Violence: The Causes and Consequences of Abuse in the American Family.* New York: Simon & Schuster.

Gelsthorpe, L., and Morris, A. (1988). "Feminism and Criminology in Britain." *British Journal of Criminology* 28:93–110.

Gendreau, P., and Ross, R. (1987). "Revivification of Rehabilitation: Evidence from the 1980s." *Justice Quarterly* 4:349–407.

Gerbner, G., and Signorielli, N. (1990). *Violence Profile 1967–1988-89: Enduring Patterns.* Philadelphia: Annenberg School of Communications, University of Pennsylvania.

Gibbons, D. (1995). "Unfit for Human Consumption: The Problem of Flawed Writing in Criminal Justice and What to Do About It." *Crime & Delinquency* 41:246–266.

Giles-Sims, J. (1983). *Wife Battering: A Systems Theory Approach.* New York: Guilford Press.

Gilroy, P. (1987). "The Myth of Black Criminality." In *Law, Order and the Authoritarian State: Readings in Critical Criminology,* ed. P. Scraton, pp. 107–120. Philadelphia: Open University Press.

Gimenez, M. (1990). "The Feminization of Poverty: Myth or Reality?" *Social Justice* 17: 43–69.

Glaspell, S. (1920). "Trifles." In *Fifty Contemporary One-Act Plays,* ed. F. Shay and P. Loving. New York: Appleton.

Goddard, H. (1925). *The Kallikak Family.* New York: Macmillan.

Goff, C., and Reasons, C. (1978). *Corporate Crime in Canada.* Scarborough, Ontario: Prentice-Hall.

Goff, C., and Reasons, C. (1986). "Organizational Crimes Against Employees, Consumers and the Public." In *The Political Economy of Crime,* ed. B. MacLean, pp. 204–231. Scarborough, Ontario: Prentice-Hall.

Goffman, E. (1961). *Asylums: Essays on the Social Situation of Mental Patients and Other Inmates.* New York: Anchor.

Goffman, E. (1967). *Interaction Ritual: Essays on Face-to-Face Behavior.* Garden City, NY: Doubleday.

Gold, D., Lo, C., and Wright, E. (1975). "Recent Developments in Marxist Theories of the Capitalist State." *Monthly Review* 27:29–51.

Gold, R. (1958). "Roles in Sociological Field Observations." *Social Forces* 36:217–223.

Goldstein, J. (1986). *Aggression and Crimes of Violence,* 2nd ed. New York: Oxford University Press.

Goldstein, P., Brownstein, H., Ryan, P., and Belluci, P. (1989). "Crack and Homicide in New York City, 1988: A Conceptually Based Events Analysis." *Contemporary Drug Problems* (Winter):651–685.

Gomme, I. (1993). *The Shadow Line: Deviance and Crime in Canada.* Toronto: Harcourt Brace Jovanovich.

Goode, E. (1989). *Drugs in American Society,* 3rd ed. New York: Knopf.

Goode, E. (1994). *Deviant Behavior,* 4th ed. Englewood Cliffs, NJ: Prentice-Hall.

Goodman, E. (1995). "Pro-Lifers Must Renounce Hitmen." *The Athens Messenger* (January 6):4.

Goodstein, L., and Shotland R. (1980). "The Crime Causes Crime Model: A Critical Review of the Relationship Between Fear of Crime, Bystander Surveillance, and Changes in the Crime Rate." *Victimology* 5:133–151.

Gordon, D. (1971). "Class and the Economics of Crime." *Review of Radical Political Economics* 3:51–75.

Gordon, D. (1994). *The Return of the Dangerous Classes: Drug Prohibition and Policy Politics.* New York: Norton.

Gordon, M., and Heath, L. (1981). "The News Business, Crime and Fear." In *Reactions to Crime,* ed. D. Lewis, pp. 227–250. Beverly Hills, CA: Sage.

Gottfredson, M., and Hirschi, T. (1990). *A General Theory of Crime.* Stanford, CA: Stanford University Press.

Gould, M., and Schaffer, D. (1986). "The Impact of Suicide in Television Movies." *New England Journal of Medicine* 315:690–694.

Gove, W., Hughes, M., and Geerken, M. (1985). "Are Uniform Crime Reports a Valid Indicator of the Index Crimes? An Affirmative Answer with Minor Qualifications." *Criminology* 23:451–502.

Graber, D. (1980). *Crime News and the Public.* New York: Praeger.

Grant, J. (1993). *Fundamental Feminism: Contesting the Core Concepts of Feminist Theory.* New York: Routledge.

Green, M., and Berry, J. (1985). "White-Collar Crime Is Big Business: Corporate Crime—I." *The Nation* 240:705.

Greenberg, D. (1976). "On One-Dimensional Marxist Criminology." *Theory and Society* 3:611–621.

Greenberg, D. (ed.). (1981). *Crime and Capitalism: Readings in a Marxist Criminology.* Palo Alto, CA: Mayfield.

Greenberg, D. (1985). "Age, Crime, and Social Explanation." *American Journal of Sociology* 91:1–21.

Greider, W. (1994). "Why the Mighty GE Can't Strike Out." *Rolling Stone* (April 21):36.

Groth, P. (1994). *Living Downtown: The History of Residential Hotels in the United States.* Berkeley: University of California Press.

Gusfield, J. (1986). *Symbolic Crusade: Status Politics and the American Temperance Movement,* 2nd ed. Urbana: University of Illinois Press.

Gutzmore, C. (1983). "Capital, 'Black Youth' and Crime." *Race and Class* 25:13–30.

Hackler, J. (1994). *Crime and Canadian Public Policy.* Scarborough, Ontario: Prentice-Hall.

Hagan, F. (1993). *Research Methods in Criminal Justice and Criminology,* 3rd ed. New York: Macmillan.

Hagan, J. (1984). *The Disreputable Pleasures: Crime and Deviance in Canada.* Toronto: McGraw-Hill Ryerson.

Hagan, J. (1985). *Modern Criminology: Crime, Criminal Behavior, and Its Control.* Toronto: McGraw-Hill.

Hagan, J. (1989). *Structural Criminology.* New Brunswick, NJ: Rutgers University Press.

Hagan, J. (1994). *Crime and Disrepute.* Thousand Oaks, CA: Pine Forge Press.

Hagan, J., Gillis, A., and Simpson, J. (1987). "Class in the Household: A Power-Control Theory of Gender and Delinquency." *American Journal of Sociology* 92:788–816.

Hagedorn, J. (1988). *People and Folks: Gangs, Crime and the Underclass in a Rustbelt City.* Chicago: Lake View Press.

Hagedorn, J. (1990). "Back in the Field Again: Gang Research in the Nineties." In *Gangs in America,* ed. G. R. Huff, pp. 240–259. Newbury Park, CA: Sage.

Hagedorn, J. (1994). "Homeboys, Dope Fiends, Legits, and New Jacks." *Criminology* 32: 197–220.

Hall, S., and Jefferson, T. (eds.). (1977). *Resistance Through Rituals: Youth Subcultures in Post-War Britain.* London: Hutchinson.

Haller, M. (1990). "Illegal Enterprise: A Theoretical and Historical Interpretation." *Criminology* 28:207–231.

Hamberger, L. (1993). "Comments on Pagelow's Myth of Psychopathology in Woman Battering." *Journal of Interpersonal Violence* 8:132–136.

Hamm, M. (1993). *American Skinheads: The Criminology and Control of Hate Crime.* Westport, CT: Praeger.

Hampton, R., Gelles, R., and Harrop, J. (1989). "Is Violence in Black Families Increasing? A Comparison of 1975 and 1985 National Survey Rates." *Journal of Marriage and the Family* 51:969–980.

Hanmer, J., and Saunders, S. (1984). *Well-Founded Fear: A Community Study of Violence to Women.* London: Hutchinson.

Hanson, G., and Venturelli, P. (1995). *Drugs and Society,* 4th ed. Boston: Jones & Bartlett.

Harman, L. (1989). *When a Hostel Becomes a Home: Experiences of Women.* Toronto: Garamond.

Harman, P., and Check, J. (1989). *The Role of Pornography in Woman Abuse.* Toronto: LaMarsh Research Programme, York University.

Harney, P., and Muehlenhard, C. (1991). "Rape." In *Sexual Coercion,* ed. E. Grauerholz and M. Koralewski, pp. 3–28. New York: Lexington.

Harris, M. (1978). *Cows, Pigs, Wars, and Witches: The Riddles of Culture.* New York: Vintage Books.

Hart, C. (1995). "Crime Stoppers!!" *The Awakening* 12(2) :4.

Hartnagel, T., and Lee, G. (1990). "Urban Crime in Canada." *Canadian Journal of Criminology* 32:591–606.

Hatty, S., Davis N., and Burke, S. (1994). "Gender, Victimization and Youth Homelessness: From Social Control to Resistance." Paper presented at the annual meeting of the American Society of Criminology, Miami.

Haveman, R. (1994). "When Problems Outrun Policy." In *Social Problems 94/95,* ed. H. Widdison, pp. 146–153. Guilford, CT: Dushkin.

Hawk, M. (1994). "Unintended Consequences: The Prosecution of Maternal Substance Abuse." In *Drug Use in America: Social, Cultural, and Political Perspectives,* ed. P. Venturelli, pp. 315–322. Boston: Jones & Bartlett.

Hay, D. (1975). "Property, Authority and the Criminal Law." In *Albion's Fatal Tree: Crime and Society in Eighteenth Century England,* ed. D. Hay, P. Linebaugh, J. Rule, E. P. Thompson, and C. Winslow, pp. 17–63. New York: Pantheon.

Heidensohn, F. (1985). *Women and Crime: The Life of a Female Offender.* New York: New York University Press.

Helmer, J. (1975). *Drugs and Minority Oppression.* New York: Seabury Press.

Henry, S., and Milovanovic, D. (1993). "Back to Basics: A Postmodern Redefinition of Crime." *The Critical Criminologist* 5(2/3):1–2, 12.

Henslin, J. (1994). *Social Problems,* 3rd ed. Englewood Cliffs, NJ: Prentice-Hall.

Herman, E. (1982). *The Real Terror Network: Terrorism in Fact and Propaganda.* Montreal: Black Rose.

Herrnstein, R. (1995). "Criminogenic Traits." In *Crime,* ed. J. Wilson and J. Petersilia, pp. 39–64. San Francisco: Institute for Contemporary Studies.

Hickey, E. (1991). *Serial Murders and Their Victims.* Pacific Grove, CA: Brooks/Cole.

Hill, G., and Atkinson, M. (1988). "Gender, Familial Control, and Delinquency." *Criminology* 26:127–150.

Hills, S. (1980). *Demystifying Social Deviance.* New York: McGraw-Hill.

Hills, S. (1984). "Crime and Deviance on a College Campus: The Privilege of Class." In *Humanistic Perspectives on Crime and Justice,* ed. M. Schwartz and D. Friedrichs, pp. 60–69. Hebron, CT: Practitioner Press.

Hills, S. (ed.). (1987). *Corporate Violence: Injury and Death for Profit.* Totowa, NJ: Rowman & Littlefield.

Hills, S., and Santiago, R. (1992). *Tragic Magic: The Life and Crimes of a Heroin Addict.* Chicago: Nelson-Hall.

Hilton, Z., Jackson, M., and Webster, C. (eds.). (1990). *Clinical Criminology: Theory, Research and Practice.* Toronto: Canadian Scholars' Press.

Hinch, R. (1989). "Teaching Critical Criminology and Critical Justice Studies in Canada." *Journal of Human Justice* 1:63–76.

Hinch, R. (1991). "Contradictions, Conflicts, and Dilemmas in Canada's Sexual Assault Law." In *Crimes by the Capitalist State: An Introduction to State Criminality,* ed. G. Barak, pp. 233–251. Albany: SUNY Press.

Hinch, R. (1992). "Conflict and Marxist Theories." In *Criminology: A Canadian Perspective,* ed. R. Linden, pp. 267–291. Toronto: Harcourt Brace Jovanovich, Canada.

Hinch, R. (1994). "Introduction: Theoretical Diversity." In *Readings in Critical Criminology,* ed. R. Hinch, pp. 1–26. Scarborough, Ontario: Prentice-Hall.

Hindelang, M., Hirschi, T., and Weis, J. (1979). "Correlates of Delinquency: The Illusion of Discrepancy Between Self-Report and Official Measures." *American Sociological Review* 44:995–1014.

Hindelang, M., Hirschi, T., and Weis, J. (1981). *Measuring Delinquency.* Beverly Hills, CA: Sage.

Hirschel, J. D., Hutchinson, I., Dean, C., and Mills, A. (1992). "Review Essay on the Law Enforcement Response to Spouse Abuse: Past, Present and Future." *Justice Quarterly* 9: 247–283.

Hirschi, T. (1969). *Causes of Delinquency.* Berkeley: University of California Press.

Hirschi, T., and Gottfredson, M. (1983). "Age and the Explanation of Crime." *American Journal of Sociology* 89:552–584.

Hirst, P. (1975). "Marx and Engels on Law, Crime and Morality." In *Critical Criminology,* ed. I. Taylor, P. Walton, and J. Young, pp. 203–232. London: Routledge & Kegan Paul.

Hobbes, T. (1963). *Leviathan.* New York: Meridian Books (orig. pub. 1651).

Hofstadter, R. (1970). "Reflections on Violence in the United States." In *American Violence: A Documentary History,* ed. R. Hofstadter and M. Wallace, pp. 3–43. New York: Knopf.

Holman, J., and Quinn, J. (1992). *Criminology: Applying Theory.* St. Paul, MN: West.

Holmes, R., and DeBurger, J. (1988). *Serial Murder.* Beverly Hills, CA: Sage.

Holmes, R., and Holmes, S. (1994). *Murder in America.* Thousand Oaks, CA: Sage.

Holmlund, C. (1994). "A Decade of Deadly Dolls: Hollywood and the Woman Killer." In *Moving Targets: Women, Murder and Representation,* ed. H. Birch, pp. 127–151. Berkeley: University of California Press.

Horley, S. (1991). *The Charm Syndrome: Why Charming Men Can Make Dangerous Lovers.* London: Papermac.

Hornung, C., McCullough, B., and Sugimoto, T. (1981). "Status Relationships in Marriage: Risk Factors in Spouse Abuse." *Journal of Marriage and the Family* 43:675–692.

Hotaling, G., and Sugarman, D. (1986). "An Analysis of Risk Markers and Husband to Wife Violence: The Current State of Knowledge." *Violence and Victims* 1:101–124.

Huggins, M. (1993). "Lost Childhoods: Assassinations of Youth in Democratizing Brazil." Paper presented at the annual meeting of American Sociological Association, Miami.

Huizinga, D., and Elliott, D. (1987). "Juvenile Offenders: Prevalence, Offender Incidence, and Arrest Rates by Race." *Crime and Delinquency* 33:206–223.

Hull, J., and Bond, C. (1986). "Social and Behavioral Consequences of Alcohol Consumption and Expectance: A Meta-Analysis." *Psychological Bulletin* 99:347–360.

Humphreys, L. (1975). *Tearoom Trade: Impersonal Sex in Public Places,* rev. ed. New York: Aldine de Gruyter.

Humphries, D. (1981). "Serious Crime, News Coverage and Ideology: A Content Analysis of Crime Coverage in a Metropolitan Paper." *Crime and Delinquency* 27:191–205.

Humphries, D. (1993). "Crack Mothers, Drug Wars, and the Politics of Resentment." In *Political Crime in Contemporary America,* ed. K. Tunnell, pp. 31–48. New York: Garland.

Hunt, A. (1978). *The Sociological Movement in Law.* London: Macmillan.

Hunt, A. (1982). "Law, Order and Socialism: A Response to Ian Taylor." *Crime and Social Justice* 19:16–22.

Ianna, F., and Ruess-Ianni, E. (1972). *A Family Business.* New York: New American Library.

Inciardi, J. (1975). *Careers in Crime.* Chicago: Rand McNally.

Inciardi, J. (1980). "Youths, Drugs and Street Crime." In *Drugs and Youth Culture,* ed. F. Scarpitti and S. Datesman. Beverly Hills, CA: Sage.

Inciardi, J. (1990). *Criminal Justice,* 3rd ed. San Diego: Harcourt Brace Jovanovich.

Inciardi, J. (1992). *The War on Drugs II: The Continuing Epic of Heroin, Cocaine, Crack, Crime, AIDS and Public Policy.* Palo Alto, CA: Mayfield.

Inciardi, J., Lockwood, D., and Pottieger, A. (1993). *Women and Crack-Cocaine.* New York: Macmillan.

Irwin, J., and Austin, J. (1994). *It's About Time: America's Imprisonment Binge*. Belmont, CA: Wadsworth.

Island, D., and Letellier, P. (1991). *Men Who Beat the Men Who Love Them*. New York: Harrington Park Press.

Jackson, D. (1994). "Serial Killers and the People Who Love Them." *The Village Voice* 39 (12):26–32.

Jackson, P. (1990). "Sources of Data." In *Measurement Issues in Criminology*, ed. K. Kempf, pp. 21–50. New York: Springer-Verlag.

Jaggar, A. (1983). *Feminist Politics and Human Nature*. Totowa, NJ: Rowman & Littlefield.

Jefferson, T. (1994). "Theorising Masculine Subjectivity." In *Just Boys Doing Business? Men, Masculinities, and Crime*, ed. T. Newburn and E. Stanko, pp. 10–31. London: Routledge.

Jenkins, P. (1992). *Intimate Enemies: Moral Panics in Contemporary Great Britain*. New York: Aldine de Gruyter.

Jenkins, P. (1993). "Myth and Murder: The Serial Killer Panic of 1983–85." In V. Kappeler, M. Blumberg, and G. Potter, *The Mythology of Crime and Criminal Justice*, pp. 53–74. Prospect Heights, IL: Waveland Press.

Jensen, G., and Thompson, K. (1990). "What's Class Got to Do with It? A Further Examination of Power-Control Theory." *American Journal of Sociology* 95:1009–1023.

Johns, C. (1992). *Power, Ideology, and the War on Drugs: Nothing Succeeds Like Failure*. New York: Praeger.

Johnson, R., and Toch, H. (eds.). (1982). *The Pains of Imprisonment*. Beverly Hills, CA: Sage.

Johnston, L., O'Malley, P., and Bachman, J. (1991a). *Drug Use Among American High School Seniors, 1975–1990, Vol. I, High School Seniors*. Rockville, MD: National Institute on Drug Abuse.

Johnston, L., O'Malley, P., and Bachman, J. (1991b). *Drug Use Among American High School Seniors, 1975–1990, Vol. II, College Students and Young Adults*. Rockville, MD: National Institute on Drug Abuse.

Jones, A. (1994). *Next Time She'll Be Dead*. Boston: Beacon.

Kappeler, V., Blumberg, M., and Potter, G. (1993). *The Mythology of Crime and Criminal Justice*. Prospect Heights, IL: Waveland Press.

Karmen, A. (1980). "The Narcotics Problem: Views from the Left." In *Is America Possible? Social Problems from Conservative, Liberal and Socialist Perspectives*, 2nd ed., ed. H. Etzkowitz, pp. 171–180. St. Paul, MN: West.

Karmen, A. (1990). *Crime Victims: An Introduction to Victimology*, 2nd ed. Pacific Grove, CA: Brooks/Cole.

Kasinsky, R. (1993). "Criminalizing of Pregnant Women Drug Abusers." In *Female Criminality: The State of the Art,* ed. C. Culliver, pp. 483–501. New York: Garland.

Katz, J. (1988). *Seductions of Crime: Moral and Sensual Attractions in Doing Evil.* New York: Basic Books.

Katz, L. (1978). "Work: It's More Dangerous for Public Employees." *The Public Employee* 1:6.

Kaufman, J., and Ziegler, E. (1987). "Do Abused Children Become Abusive Adults?" *American Journal of Orthopsychiatry* 57:186–192.

Kaufman Kantor, G., and Straus, M. (1990). "The 'Drunken Bum' Theory of Wife Beating." In *Physical Violence in American Families: Risk Factors and Adaptations to Violence in 8,145 Families,* ed. M. Straus and R. Gelles, pp. 203–224. New Brunswick, NJ: Transaction.

Kelkar, G. (1992). "Women and Structural Violence in India." In *Femicide: The Politics of Woman Killing,* ed. J. Radford and D. Russell, pp. 117–124. New York: Twayne.

Kelly, L. (1987). "The Continuum of Sexual Violence." In *Women, Violence and Social Control,* ed. J. Hanmer and M. Maynard, pp. 46–60. Atlantic Highlands, NJ: Humanities Press International.

Kelly, L. (1988). *Surviving Sexual Violence.* Minneapolis: University of Minnesota Press.

Kennedy, L., and Baron, S. (1993). "Routine Activities and a Subculture of Violence: A Study of Violence on the Street." *Journal of Research in Crime and Delinquency* 20:88–112.

Kennedy, L., and Dutton, D. (1989). "The Incidence of Wife Assault in Alberta." *Canadian Journal of Behaviourial Science* 21:40–54.

Kennedy, L., and Silverman, R. (1990). "The Elderly Victim of Homicide: An Application of the Routine Activity Approach." *Sociological Quarterly* 31:307–319.

Kephart, W., and Zellner, W. (1994). *Extraordinary Groups: An Examination of Unconventional Lifestyles,* 5th ed. New York: St. Martin's Press.

King, P. (1993). "Helping Women Helping Children: Drug Policy and Future Generations." In *Confronting Drug Policy: Illicit Drugs in a Free Society,* ed. R. Bayer and G. Oppenheimer, pp. 291–318. New York: Cambridge University Press.

Kinsey, R., Lea, J., and Young, J. (1986). *Losing the Fight Against Crime.* London: Basil Blackwell.

Kirkham, J., Levy, S., and Crotty, W. (1970). *Assassination and Political Violence.* New York: Bantam.

Kirkwood, C. (1993). *Leaving Abusive Partners: From the Scars of Survival to the Wisdom for Change.* Newbury Park, CA: Sage.

Kitsuse, J. (1962). "Societal Reaction to Deviant Behavior: Problems of Theory and Method." *Social Problems* 9:253.

Klain, J. (1989). *International Television and Video Almanac.* New York: Quigley.

Klein, M., and Maxson, C. (1994). "Gangs and Crack Cocaine Trafficking." In *Drugs and Crime: Evaluating Public Policy Initiatives,* ed. D. MacKenzie and C. Uchida, pp. 42–58. Thousand Oaks, CA: Sage.

Knopp, F., et al. (1976). *Instead of Prisons: A Handbook for Abolitionists.* Orwell, VT: Safer Society Press.

Knowles, J. (1995). "Ohio Citizen Attitudes." In *The State of Crime and Criminal Justice in Ohio,* pp. 1–6. Columbus, OH: Office of Criminal Justice Services.

Knutilla, M. (1994). "The State and Social Issues: Theoretical Considerations." In *Power and Resistance: Critical Thinking About Canadian Social Issues,* ed. L. Samuelson, pp. 1–17. Halifax: Fernwood.

Koenig, D. (1987). "Conventional Crime." In *Criminology: A Canadian Perspective,* ed. R. Linden, pp. 242–269. Toronto: Holt, Rinehart & Winston.

Konopka, G. (1966). *The Adolescent Girl in Conflict.* Englewood Cliffs, NJ: Prentice-Hall.

Koss, M., Gidycz, C., and Wisniewski, N. (1987). "The Scope of Rape: Incidence and Prevalence of Sexual Aggression and Victimization in a National Sample of Students in Higher Education." *Journal of Consulting and Clinical Psychology* 55:162–170.

Koss, M., Goodman, L., Browne, A., Fitzgerald, L., Keita, G., and Russo, N. (1994). *Male Violence Against Women at Home, at Work, and in the Community.* Washington, DC: American Psychological Association.

Kramer, R. (1984). "Corporate Criminality: The Development of an Idea." In *Corporations as Criminals,* ed. E. Hochstedler, pp. 13–38. Beverly Hills, CA: Sage.

Kraska, P. (1989). "The Sophistication of Hans Jurgen Eysenck: An Analysis and Critique of Contemporary Biological Criminology." *Criminal Justice Research Bulletin* 4(5):1–7.

Kraska, P. (1995). "The Military as Drug Police." In *Drugs, Crime and Justice,* ed. P. Kraska and L. Gaines. Prospect Heights, IL: Waveland.

Landsberg, M. (1989). "Killer's Rage Too Familiar to Canadians: Culture Condones Violence Against Women." *Toronto Star* (December 8):A1, A16.

Lasch, C. (1977). *Haven in a Heartless World.* New York: Basic Books.

Lasley, J. (1989). "Drinking Routines, Lifestyles and Predatory Victimization: A Causal Analysis." *Justice Quarterly* 6:529–542.

Layden, T. (1995a). "Bettor Education." *Sports Illustrated* 82(13):68–83.

Layden, T. (1995b). "Book Smart." *Sports Illustrated* 82(14):68–74.

Layden, T. (1995c). "You Bet Your Life." *Sports Illustrated* 82(15):46–54.

Lea, J., and Young, J. (1984). *What Is to Be Done About Law and Order?* New York: Penguin.

Leiber, M. (1994). "A Comparison of Juvenile Court Outcomes for Native Americans, African Americans, and Whites." *Justice Quarterly* 11:257–279.

Lemert, E. (1951). *Social Pathology.* New York: McGraw-Hill.

Levin, J., and Fox, J. (1990). "Mass Murder: America's Growing Menace." In *Violence: Patterns, Causes, Public Policy,* ed. N. Weiner, M. Zahn, and R. Sagi, pp. 65–69. San Diego: Harcourt Brace Jovanovich.

Levinger, G. (1966). "Sources of Marital Dissatisfaction Among Applicants for Divorce." *American Journal of Orthopsychiatry* 36:804–806.

Levinson, D. (1989). *Family Violence in Cross-Cultural Perspective.* Newbury Park, CA: Sage.

Lewis, C., Agrad, R., Gopic, K., Harding, J., Singh, T., and Williams, R. (1989). *The Report of the Race Relations and Policing Task Force.* Toronto: Solicitor General of Ontario.

Liazos, A. (1972). "The Poverty of the Sociology of Deviance: Nuts, Sluts, and Preverts." *Social Problems* 20:109.

Liddle, A. (1989). "Feminist Contributions to an Understanding of Violence Against Women—Three Steps Forward, Two Steps Back." *Canadian Review of Sociology and Anthropology* 26:759–775.

Liebow, E. (1995). *Tell Them Who I Am: The Lives of Homeless Women.* New York: Penguin.

Lilly, J., Cullen, F., and Ball, R. (1995). *Criminological Theory: Context and Consequences,* 2nd ed. Thousand Oaks, CA: Sage.

Linz, M., and Malamuth, N. (1993). *Pornography.* Newbury Park, CA: Sage.

Liska, A. (1981). *Perspectives on Deviance.* Englewood Cliffs, NJ: Prentice-Hall.

Liska, A., and Chamlin, M. (1984). "Social Structure and Crime Control Among Macro-social Units." *American Journal of Sociology* 90:383–395.

Livingston, J. (1992). *Crime and Criminology.* Englewood Cliffs, NJ: Prentice-Hall.

Lloyd, S. (1991). "The Dark Side of Courtship: Violence and Sexual Exploitation." *Family Relations* 40:14–20.

Lockhart, L. (1991). "Spousal Violence: A Cross-Racial Perspective." In *Black Family Violence: Current Research and Theory,* ed. R. Hampton, pp. 85–101. Lexington, MA: Lexington Books.

Los, M. (1990). "Feminism and Rape Law Reform." In *Feminist Perspectives in Criminology,* ed. L. Gelsthorpe and A. Morris, pp. 160–172. Philadelphia: Open University Press.

Lowman, J. (1992). "Street Prostitution." In *Deviance: Conformity and Control in Canadian Society,* ed. V. Sacco, pp. 49–94. Scarborough, Ontario: Prentice-Hall.

Lowman, J., and MacLean, B. (eds.). (1992). *Realist Criminology: Crime Control and Policing in the 1990s.* Toronto: University of Toronto Press.

Luckenbill, D. (1977). "Criminal Homicide as a Situated Transaction." *Social Problems* 25: 176–186.

Lueck, T. (1993). "Trade Pact with Mexico Expected to Have a Mixed Result." *New York Times* (October).

Lundberg, F. (1968). *The Rich and the Super-Rich: A Study in the Power of Money Today.* New York: Lyle Stuart.

Lupri, E. (1990). "Male Violence in the Home." In *Canadian Social Trends,* ed. C. McKie and K. Thompson, pp. 170–172. Toronto: Thompson Educational Publishing.

Lupsha, P. (1986). "Organized Crime in the United States." In *Organized Crime—A Global Perspective,* ed. R. Kelly, pp. 32–57. Totowa, NJ: Rowman & Littlefield.

Lynch, M., and Groves, W. (1989). *A Primer in Radical Criminology,* 2nd ed. New York: Harrow & Heston.

MacKenzie, D., and Souryal, C. (1994). *Multisite Evaluation of Shock Incarceration.* Washington, DC: U.S. Government Printing Office.

MacKinnon, C. (1983). "Feminism, Marxism, Method and the State: Toward Feminist Jurisprudence." *Signs* 7:515–544.

MacKinnon, C. (1989). *Toward a Feminist Theory of the State.* Cambridge, MA: Harvard University Press.

MacLean, B. (1986a). "Critical Criminology and Some Limitations of Traditional Inquiry." In *The Political Economy of Crime: Readings for a Critical Criminology,* ed. B. MacLean, pp. 1–20. Scarborough, Ontario: Prentice-Hall.

MacLean, B. (ed.). (1986b). *The Political Economy of Crime: Readings for a Critical Criminology.* Scarborough, Ontario: Prentice-Hall.

MacLean, B. (1991). "In Partial Defence of Socialist Realism: Some Theoretical and Methodological Concerns of the Local Crime Survey." *Crime, Law and Social Change* 15: 213–254.

MacLean, B. (1992a). "The Emergence of Critical Justice Studies in Canada." *Humanity and Society* 16:414–426.

MacLean, B. (1992b). "A Program of Local Crime Survey Research for Canada." In *Realist Criminology: Crime Control and Policing in the 1990s,* ed. J. Lowman and B. MacLean, pp. 336–365. Toronto: University of Toronto Press.

MacLean, B., and Milovanovic, D. (eds.). (1991). *Racism, Empiricism and Criminal Justice.* Vancouver: Collective Press.

MacLeod, L. (1980). *Wife Battering in Canada: The Vicious Circle.* Ottawa: Advisory Council on the Status of Women.

MacLeod, L. (1987). *Battered But Not Beaten.* Ottawa: Canadian Advisory Council on the Status of Women.

Madigan, L., and Gamble, N. (1989). *The Second Rape: Society's Continued Betrayal of the Victim.* New York: Lexington.

Maguire, B. (1988). "The Applied Dimension of Radical Criminology." *Sociological Spectrum* 8:133–151.

Maguire, K., and Pastore, A. (1994). *Sourcebook of Criminal Justice Statistics—1993.* Washington, DC: U.S. Department of Justice, Bureau of Justice Statistics.

Maguire, K., Pastore, A., and Flanagan, T. (eds.). (1993). *Sourcebook of Criminal Justice Statistics—1992.* Washington, DC: U.S. Department of Justice.

Maher, L. (1990). "Criminalizing Pregnancy—The Downside of a Kinder, Gentler Nation?" *Social Justice* 17:111–135.

Malette, L., and Chalouh, M. (eds.). (1991). *The Montreal Massacre.* Charlottetown, Prince Edward Island: Gynergy.

Mama, A. (1990). *The Hidden Struggle.* London: London Race and Housing Research Unit.

Manchester, W. (1975). *The Death of a President.* New York: Harper & Row.

Mann, C. R. (1993). *Unequal Justice: A Question of Color.* Bloomington: Indiana University Press.

Martin, P., and Hummer, R. (1989). "Fraternities and Rape on Campus." *Gender and Society* 3:457–473.

Martin, R., Mutchnick, R., and Austin, W. (1990). *Criminological Thought: Pioneers Past and Present.* New York: Macmillan.

Marx, G. (1988). *Under Cover: Police Surveillance in America.* Berkeley: University of California Press.

Marx, K., and Engels, F. (1975). *The Communist Manifesto.* Great Britain: C. Nickolls.

Maryland Special Joint Committee on Gender Bias in the Courts. (1989). "Domestic Violence and the Courts." *Response to the Victimization of Women and Children* 12(4): 3–6.

Matthews, R., and Young, J. (eds.). (1992). *Issues in Realist Criminology.* Newbury Park, CA: Sage.

Mauer, M. (1991). *Americans Behind Bars: A Comparison of International Rates of Incarceration.* Washington DC: The Sentencing Project.

Mawby, R., and Walklate, S. (1994). *Critical Victimology.* Newbury Park, CA: Sage.

Maxfield, M. (1989). "Circumstances in Supplementary Homicide Reports: Variety and Validity." *Criminology* 27:671–695.

Mayhew, P., and Hough, M. (1988). "The British Crime Survey: Origins and Impact." In *Victims of Crime: A New Deal?* ed. M. Maguire and J. Pointing, pp. 156–163. Philadelphia: Open University Press.

McCarthy, B., and Hagan, J. (1991). "Surviving on the Street: The Experiences of Homeless Youth." *Journal of Adolescent Research* 7:412–430.

McCrumb, S. (1991). *Highland Laddie Gone.* New York: Ballantine.

McKinney, K. (1992). "Ethical Issues in Research on Human Sexuality." In E. Babbie, *The Practice of Social Research,* 6th ed., pp. 470–471. Belmont, CA: Wadsworth.

McMillen, L. (1990). "An Anthropologist's Disturbing Picture of Gang Rape on Campus." *Chronicle of Higher Education* 37:A3.

McMullan, J. (1982). "Criminal Organization in Sixteenth and Seventeenth Century London." *Social Problems* 29:311–323.

McMullan, J. (1992). *Beyond the Limits of the Law: Corporate Crime and Law and Order.* Halifax: Fernwood.

McNamara, R. (1994). *Crime Displacement: The Other Side of Prevention.* East Rockaway, NY: Cummings & Hathaway.

Merton, R. (1938). "Social Structure and Anomie." *American Sociological Review* 3: 672–682.

Merton, R. (1957). *Social Theory and Social Structure.* New York: Free Press of Glencoe.

Messerschmidt, J. (1986). *Capitalism, Patriarchy, and Crime: Toward a Socialist Feminist Criminology.* Totowa, NJ: Rowman & Littlefield.

Messerschmidt, J. (1988). "Reply to the Schwendingers." *Social Justice* 15:146–160.

Messerschmidt, J. (1993). *Masculinities and Crime: Critique and Reconceptualization of Theory.* Lanham, MD: Rowman & Littlefield.

Messner, S., and Blau, J. (1987). "Routine Leisure Activities and Rates of Crime: A Macro-Level Analysis." *Social Forces* 65:1035–1052.

Messner, S., and Tardiff, K. (1986). "Economic Inequality and Levels of Homicide: An Analysis of Urban Neighborhoods." *Criminology* 24:297–318.

Michalowski, R. (1983). "Crime Control in the 1980s: A Progressive Agenda." *Crime and Social Justice* 19:13–23.

Michalowski, R. (1985). *Order, Law, and Crime: An Introduction to Criminology.* New York: Random House.

Michalowski, R. (1991). " 'Niggers, Welfare Scum and Homeless Assholes': The Problems of Idealism, Consciousness and Context in Left Realism." In *New Directions in Critical Criminology,* ed. B. MacLean and D. Milovanovic, pp. 31–38. Vancouver: Collective Press.

Michalowski, R. (1993). "Some Thoughts Regarding the Impact of Clinton's Election on Crime and Justice Policy." *The Criminologist* 18:1, 5, 6, 11.

Miethe, D., and Lee, G. (1984). "Fear of Crime Among Older People: A Reassessment of Crime-Related Factors." *The Sociological Quarterly* 125:397–415.

Miethe, T., Stafford, M., and Long, J. (1987). "Routine Activities/Lifestyle and Victimization." *American Sociological Review* 52:182–194.

Miethe, T., Stafford, M., and Stone, D. (1990). "Lifestyle Changes and Risks of Criminal Victimization." *Journal of Quantitative Criminology* 6:357–375.

Milgram, S., and Shotland, R. (1973). *Television and Antisocial Behavior: Field Experiments.* New York: Academic Press.

Miliband, R. (1969). *The State in Capitalist Society: The Analysis of the Western System of Power.* London: Quartet.

Miller, J. (1993). "'Your Life Is on the Line Every Night You're on the Streets': Victimization and Resistance Among Street Prostitutes." *Humanity & Society* 17(4):422–446.

Miller, J., and Schwartz, M. (1994). "Rape Myths and Violence Against Street Prostitutes." *Deviant Behavior* 16(1):1–23.

Miller, S., and Simpson, S. (1991). "Courtship Violence and Social Control: Does Gender Matter?" *Law & Society Review* 25:335–365.

Mills, C. (1959). *The Sociological Imagination.* New York: Oxford University Press.

Milovanovic, D. (1994). *A Primer in the Sociology of Law,* 2nd ed. New York: Harrow & Heston.

Mintz, M. (1985). "At Any Cost: Corporate Greed, Women, and the Dalkon Shield." *The Progressive* (November):20–25.

Mooney, J. (1993). *The Hidden Figure: Domestic Violence in North London.* London: Centre for Criminology, Middlesex University.

Morash, M., and Chesney-Lind, M. (1991). "A Re-Formulation and Partial Test of the Power Control Theory of Delinquency." *Justice Quarterly* 8:347–377.

Morgan-Sharp, E. (1992). "Gender, Race, and the Law: Elements of Injustice." *The Justice Professional* 6:86–93.

Morra, N., and Smith, M. (1993). "Men in Feminism: Theorizing Sexual Violence." *The Journal of Men's Studies* 2:15–28.

Morris, A. (1987). *Women, Crime, and Criminal Justice.* Oxford: Basil Blackwell.

Morris, J. (1988). *Hong Kong.* New York: Random House.

Morris, N., and Hawkins, G. (1969). *The Honest Politician's Guide to Crime Control.* Chicago: University of Chicago Press.

Mueller, G., and Adler, F. (1985). *Outlaws of the Ocean.* New York: Hearst Maritime Books.

Musto, D. (1973). *The American Disease: Origins of Narcotic Control.* New Haven, CT: Yale University Press.

Musto, D. (1987). *The American Disease: Origins of Narcotic Control,* exp. ed. New York: Oxford University Press.

Nader, R. (1965). *Unsafe at Any Speed: The Designed in Dangers of the American Automobile.* New York: Grossman.

Nader, R., and Green, M. (1972). "Crime in the Suites: Coddling the Corporations." *The New Republic* 166:18.

Naffine, N. (1987). *Female Crime: The Construction of Women in Criminology.* Sydney, Australia: Allen & Unwin.

National Commission on the Causes and Prevention of Violence. (1969). *To Establish Justice, to Insure Domestic Tranquility.* New York: Award Books.

National Institute on Drug Abuse (NIDA). (1991a). *National Household Survey on Drug Abuse: Highlights 1990.* Washington, DC: U.S. Government Printing Office.

National Institute on Drug Abuse (NIDA). (1991b). *Drug Use Among American High School Seniors, College Students, and Young Adults, 1975–1990.* Washington, DC: U.S. Government Printing Office.

National Safety Council. (1992). *Accident Facts.* Washington, DC: National Safety Council.

Nelli, H. (1986). "Overview." *Organized Crime—A Global Perspective,* ed. R. Kelly, pp. 1–9. Totowa, NJ: Rowman & Littlefield.

Nelson, D. (1985). "Foul Haze Veiled Factory Death." *The Daily Herald* (April 16):1, 3.

Neuman, W. L. (1994). *Social Research Methods: Qualitative and Quantitative Approaches,* 2nd ed. Boston: Allyn & Bacon.

Newman, G. (1976). *Comparative Deviance: Perception and Law in Six Cultures.* New York: Elsevier.

New York State Organized Crime Task Force. (1988). *Corruption and Racketeering in the New York City Construction Industry.* Ithaca, NY: ILR Press.

NiCarthy, G. (1987). *The Ones Who Got Away: Women Who Left Abusive Partners.* Seattle: Seal Press.

Nicholl, C. (1985). *The Fruit Palace.* London: Heinemann.

O'Brien, J. (1971). "Violence in Divorce-Prone Families." *Journal of Marriage and the Family* 33:692–698.

O'Carroll, P., and Mercy, J. (1990). "Patterns and Recent Trends in Black Homicide." In *Violence: Patterns, Causes, Public Policy,* ed. N. Weiner, M. Zahn, and R. Sagi, pp. 55–59. San Diego: Harcourt Brace Jovanovich.

O'Connor, J. (1973). *The Fiscal Crisis of the State.* New York: St. Martin's Press.

Okun, L. (1986). *Woman Abuse: Facts Replacing Myths.* Albany: SUNY Press.

Oliver, W. (1994). *The Violent Social World of Black Men.* New York: Lexington.

Oppenheimer, G. (1993). "To Build a Bridge: The Use of Foreign Models by Domestic Critics of U.S. Drug Policy." In *Confronting Drug Policy: Illicit Drugs in a Free Society,* ed. R. Bayer and G. Oppenheimer, pp. 194–225. New York: Cambridge University Press.

Orcutt, J., and Turner, J. (1993). "Shocking Numbers and Graphic Accounts: Quantified Images of Drug Problems in the Print Media." *Social Problems* 40:190–206.

Ostroff, M., and Boyd, J. (1987). "Television and Suicide." *New England Journal of Medicine* 3:876–877.

Ostroff, R., Behrends, R., Lee, K., and Oliphant, J. (1985). "Adolescent Suicides Modeled After Television Movie." *American Journal of Psychiatry* 142:989–999.

Owens, P. (1985). "Death of Worker Puts Factory Safety on Trial." *Newsday* (June 6):1, 31.

Pace, D. (1991). *Concepts of Vice, Narcotics, and Organized Crime,* 3rd ed. Englewood Cliffs, NJ: Prentice-Hall.

Pagelow, M. (1992). "Adult Victims of Domestic Violence: Battered Women." *Journal of Interpersonal Violence* 7:87–120.

Pagelow, M. (1993). "Response to Hamberger's Comments." *Journal of Interpersonal Violence* 8:137–139.

Pandya, B. (1990). "Discrimination Against Harijans and Dowry Deaths." In *The Victimology Handbook: Research Findings, Treatment and Public Policy,* ed. E. Viano. New York: Garland.

Passas, N. (1990). "Anomie and Corporate Deviance." *Contemporary Crises* 14:157–178.

Pateman, C. (1988). *The Sexual Contract.* Cambridge: Polity Press.

Paternoster, R. (1987). "The Deterrent Effect of the Perceived Certainty and Severity of Punishment: A Review of the Evidence and Issues." *Justice Quarterly* 4:173–217.

Pearce, F. (1976). *Crimes of the Powerful: Marxism, Crime and Deviance.* London: Pluto Press.

Pearce, F. (1989). *The Radical Durkheim.* Boston: Unwin Hyman.

Pearce, F. (1992). "The Contribution of 'Left Realism' to the Study of Commercial Crime." In *Realist Criminology: Crime Control and Policing in the 1990s,* ed. J. Lowman and B. MacLean, pp. 313–335. Toronto: University of Toronto Press.

Pennsylvania Crime Commission. (1991). *Organized Crime—Report.* Harrisburg: Commonwealth of Pennsylvania.

Pepinsky, H. (1992). "Abolishing Prisons." In *Corrections: An Issues Approach,* 3rd ed., ed. L. Travis, M. Schwartz, and T. Clear, pp. 131–139. Cincinnati: Anderson.

Pepinsky, H., and Quinney, R. (eds.). (1991). *Criminology as Peacemaking.* Bloomington: Indiana University Press.

Peterson, R., and Krivo, L. (1993). "Racial Segregation and Black Urban Homicide." *Social Forces* 71:1001–1028.

Pfohl, S. (1994). *Images of Deviance and Social Control: A Sociological History.* New York: McGraw-Hill.

Pfuhl, E., and Henry, S. (1993). *The Deviance Process,* 3rd ed. New York: Aldine de Gruyter.

Phillips, D. (1974). "The Influence of Suggestion on Suicide: Substantive and Theoretical Implications of the Werther Effect." *American Sociological Review* 39:340–354.

Phillips, D., and Bollen, K. (1985). "Same Time Last Year: Selective Data Dredging for Negative Findings." *American Sociological Review* 50:364–371.

Phillips, D., and Carstensen, L. (1986). "Clustering of Teenage Suicides After Television News Stories About Suicide." *New England Journal of Medicine* 315:685–689.

Phillips, D., and Paight, D. (1987). "The Impact of Televised Movies About Suicide." *New England Journal of Medicine* 315:809–811.

Pierce, G., and Fox, J. (1994). "Recent Trends in Violent Crime: A Closer Look." As cited in *Sourcebook of Criminal Justice Statistics—1993,* ed. K. Maguire and A. Pastore, p. 448. Washington DC: U.S. Government Printing Office.

Pirog-Good, M., and Stets, J. (eds.) (1989). *Violence in Dating Relationships: Emerging Social Issues.* New York: Praeger.

Pitts, V. (1996). "Women in Shelters: Race, Class and Gender Issues in Social Control." In *Race, Class and Gender in Criminology,* ed. M. Schwartz and D. Milovanovic. New York: Garland.

Pizzo, S., Fricker, M., and Muolo, P. (1991). *Inside Job—The Looting of America's Savings and Loans.* New York: Harper Perennial.

Platt, A. (1978). "Street Crime: A View from the Left." *Crime and Social Justice* 9:26–34.

Platt, A., and Takagi, P. (1981). "Intellectuals for Law and Order: A Critique of the New Realists." In *Crime and Social Justice,* ed. A. Platt and P. Takagi. London: Macmillan.

Pleck, E. (1987). *Domestic Tyranny: The Making of Social Policy Against Family Violence from Colonial Times to the Present.* New York: Oxford University Press.

Pointing, J., and Maguire, M. (1988). "Introduction: The Rediscovery of the Crime Victim." In *Victims of Crime: A New Deal?* ed. M. Maguire and J. Pointing, pp. 1–13. Philadelphia: Open University Press.

Pope, C. (1984). "Race, Crime, and Criminological Research." In *Humanistic Perspectives in Crime and Justice,* ed. M. Schwartz and D. Friedrichs, pp. 46–59. Hebron, CT: Practitioner Press.

Poulantzas, N. (1973). *Political Power and Social Class.* Atlantic Fields, NJ: Humanities Press.

President's Commission on Law Enforcement and the Administration of Justice. (1967). *Task Force Report: Organized Crime.* Washington, DC: U.S. Government Printing Office.

President's Commission on Organized Crime. (1987). *The Impact: Organized Crime Today.* Washington, DC: U.S. Government Printing Office.

Price, B., and Sokoloff, N. (1995). *The Criminal Justice System and Women: Offenders, Victims and Workers,* 2nd ed. New York: McGraw-Hill.

Price, R. (1992). *Clockers.* New York: Avon.

Punch, M. (1986). *The Politics and Ethics of Fieldwork.* Beverly Hills, CA: Sage.

Quinney, R. (1970). *The Social Reality of Crime.* Boston: Little, Brown.

Quinney, R. (1974). *Critique of Legal Order.* Boston: Little, Brown.

Quinney, R. (1975). "Crime Control in Capitalist Society: A Critical Philosophy." In *Critical Criminology,* ed. I. Taylor, P. Walton, and J. Young, pp. 181–202. London: Routledge & Kegan Paul.

Quinney, R. (1979). *Criminology,* 2nd ed. Boston: Little, Brown.

Quinney, R. (1980). *Class, State and Crime.* New York: Longman.

Quinney, R. (1991). "The Way of Peace: On Crime, Suffering and Service." In *Criminology as Peacemaking,* ed. H. Pepinsky and R. Quinney, pp. 3–13. Bloomington: Indiana University Press.

Quinney, R., and Pepinsky, H. (eds.). (1991). *Criminology as Peacemaking.* Bloomington: Indiana University Press.

Quinney, R., and Wildeman, J. (1991). *The Problem of Crime: A Peace and Social Justice Perspective,* 2nd ed. Toronto: Mayfield.

Radford, J. (1987). "Policing Male Violence—Policing Women." In *Women, Violence and Social Control,* ed. J. Hanmer and M. Maynard, pp. 30–45. Atlantic Highlands, NJ: Humanities Press International.

Rasche, C. (1988). "Minority Women and Domestic Violence." *Journal of Contemporary Criminal Justice* 4:150–171.

Ratner, M. (ed.). (1993). *Crack Pipe as Pimp: An Ethnographic Investigation of Sex-for-Crack Exchanges.* New York: Macmillan.

Ratner, R., and McMullan, J. (eds.). (1987). *State Control: Criminal Justice Politics in Canada.* Vancouver: University of British Columbia Press.

Reardon, J. (1993). *The Drug Use Forecasting Program: Measuring Drug Use in a "Hidden" Population.* Washington, DC: National Institute of Justice.

Reasons, C. (1989). "Law, State and Economy: A Canadian Overview." *The Journal of Human Justice* 1:9–26.

Reasons, C., Ross, L., and Patterson, C. (1981). *Assault on the Worker.* Toronto: Butterworths.

Reasons, C., Ross, L., and Patterson, C. (1991). "Your Money or Your Life: Workers' Health in Canada." In *The Social Basis of Law: Critical Readings in the Sociology of Law,* ed. E. Comack and S. Brickey, pp. 131–141. Halifax: Garamond.

Reiman, J. (1995). *The Rich Get Richer and the Poor Get Prison,* 4th ed. Boston: Allyn & Bacon.

Reiss, A., and Roth, J. (eds.). (1993). *Understanding and Preventing Violence.* Washington, DC: National Academy Press.

Renzetti, C. (1992). *Violent Betrayal: Partner Abuse in Lesbian Relationships.* Newbury Park, CA: Sage.

Renzetti, C. (1993). "On the Margins of the Malestream (Or, They *Still* Don't Get It, Do They?): Feminist Analyses in Criminal Justice Education." *Journal of Criminal Justice Education* 4:219–234.

Reschenthaler, G. (1979). *Occupational Health and Safety in Canada: The Economics and Three Case Studies.* Montreal: Institute for Research on Public Policy.

Ressler, R., Burgess, A., and Douglas, J. (1988). *Sexual Homicide: Patterns and Motives.* Lexington, MA: Lexington Books.

Rhodes, R. (1984). *Organized Crime—Crime Control vs. Civil Liberties.* New York: Random House.

Rice, M. (1990). "Challenging Orthodoxies in Feminist Theory: A Black Feminist Critique." In *Feminist Perspectives in Criminology,* ed. L. Gelsthorpe and A. Morris, pp. 57–69. Philadelphia: Open University Press.

Richie, B. (1985). "Battered Black Women." *The Black Scholar* 16:40–44.

Rollins, J. (1985). *Between Women: Domestics and Their Employers.* Philadelphia: Temple University Press.

Roncek, D., and Maier, P. (1991). "Bars, Blocks and Crimes Revisited: Linking the Theory of Routine Activities to the Empiricism of 'Hot Spots.'" *Criminology* 29:725–754.

Rosenau, P. M. (1992). *Post-Modernism and the Social Sciences: Insights, Inroads, and Intrusions.* Princeton, NJ: Princeton University Press.

Rosenbaum, M. (1981). *Women on Heroin.* New Brunswick, NJ: Rutgers University Press.

Roth, J. (1994). *Firearms and Violence.* Washington, DC: U.S. Department of Justice.

Rowan, R. (1986). "The 50 Biggest Mafia Bosses." *Fortune* (November 10):24–38.

Rubin, L. (1976). *Worlds of Pain: Life in the Working Class.* New York: Basic Books.

Russell, D. (1986). *The Secret Trauma: Incest in the Lives of Girls and Women.* New York: Basic Books.

Russell, D. (1990). *Rape in Marriage,* rev. ed. Bloomington: Indiana University Press.

Rydell, C., and Everingham, S. (1994). *Controlling Cocaine.* Santa Monica, CA: Rand.

Sacco, V. (1982). "The Effects of Mass Media on Perceptions of Crime." *Pacific Sociological Review* 25:475–493.

Sacco, V., Glackman, W., and Roesch, R. (1984). *Factors Associated with Public Perceptions of Crime.* Burnaby, BC: Criminology Research Centre, Simon Fraser University.

Sacco, V., and Johnson, H. (1990). *Patterns of Criminal Victimization in Canada*. Ottawa: Statistics Canada.

Samaha, J. (1994). *Criminal Justice*. St. Paul, MN: West.

Sampson, R. (1985). "Neighborhood and Crime: The Structural Determinants of Personal Victimization." *Journal of Research in Crime and Delinquency* 22:7–40.

Sampson, R. (1986). "Effects of Socioeconomic Context on Official Reaction to Juvenile Delinquency." *American Sociological Review* 51:876–885.

Sampson, R. (1987). "Urban Black Violence: The Effect of Male Joblessness and Family Disruption." *American Journal of Sociology* 93:348–382.

Sanday, P. (1990). *Fraternity Gang Rape*. New York: New York University Press.

Sarason, I., and Sarason, B. (eds.). (1985). *Social Support: Theory, Research and Applications.* The Hague: Martinus Nijhof.

Saunders, D. (1988). "Wife Abuse, Husband Abuse, or Mutual Combat? A Feminist Perspective on the Empirical Findings." In *Feminist Perspectives on Wife Abuse,* ed. K. Yllo and M. Bograd, pp. 90–113. Newbury Park, CA: Sage.

Schelling, T. (1973). "Economic Analysis and Organized Crime." In *The Crime Establishment,* ed. J. Conklin, pp. 75–104. Englewood Cliffs, NJ: Prentice-Hall.

Schmallenger, F. (1993). *Criminal Justice Today.* Englewood Cliffs, NJ: Regents Prentice-Hall.

Schrager, L., and Short, J. (1977). "Toward a Sociology of Organizational Crime." *Social Problems* 25:407–419.

Schulman, M. (1979). *A Survey of Spousal Violence Against Women in Kentucky.* Study No. 792701 conducted for the Kentucky Commission on Women. Washington, DC: U.S. Government Printing Office.

Schur, E. (1974). "A Sociologist's View: The Case for Abolition." In *Victimless Crimes: Two Sides of the Controversy,* E. Schur and H. Adam Bedau, pp. 3–52. Engelwood Cliffs, NJ: Prentice-Hall.

Schur, E. (1984). *Labeling Women Deviant: Gender, Stigma, and Social Control.* Philadelphia: Temple University Press.

Schwartz, M. (1982). "The Spousal Exemption for Criminal Rape Prosecution." *Vermont Law Review* 7(1):33–57.

Schwartz, M. (1988a). "Ain't Got No Class: Universal Risk Theories of Battering." *Contemporary Crises* 12:373–392.

Schwartz, M. (1988b). "Marital Status and Woman Abuse Theory." *Journal of Family Violence* 3(3):239–248.

Schwartz, M. (1989). "Asking the Right Questions: Battered Women Are Not All Passive." *Sociological Viewpoints* 5(1):46–61.

Schwartz, M. (1991a). "Humanist Sociology and Date Rape." *Humanity and Society* 15: 304–316.

Schwartz, M. (1991b). "The Future of Critical Criminology." In *New Directions in Critical Criminology,* ed. B. MacLean and D. Milovanovic, pp. 119–124. Vancouver: Collective Press.

Schwartz, M., and DeKeseredy, W. (1988). "Liberal Feminism on Violence Against Women." *Social Justice* 15:213–221.

Schwartz, M., and DeKeseredy, W. (1991). "Left Realist Criminology: Strengths, Weaknesses and the Feminist Critique." *Crime, Law and Social Change* 15:51–72.

Schwartz, M., and DeKeseredy, W. (1993). "The Return of the Battered Husband Syndrome Through the Typification of Women as Violent." *Crime, Law and Social Change: An International Journal* 20:249–265.

Schwartz, M., and DeKeseredy, W. (1994). "Male Peer Support, Pornography, and the Abuse of Canadian Women in Dating Relationships." Paper presented at the meeting of the American Society of Criminology, Miami.

Schwartz, M., and Ellison, C. (1980). "If a Corporation Is a Criminal, What Prison Do You Send It To?" Paper presented at the annual meeting of the Association for Humanist Sociology, Louisville, KY.

Schwartz, M., and Friedrichs, D. (1994). "Postmodern Thought and Criminological Discontent: New Metaphors for Understanding Violence." *Criminology* 32:221–246.

Schwartz, M., and Mattley, C. (1993). "The Battered Woman Scale and Gender Indentities." *Journal of Family Violence* 8(3):277–287.

Schwartz, M., and Nogrady, C. (1995). "The Influence of Fraternity Membership on Rape Victimization on a College Campus." Paper presented at the annual meeting of the Society for the Study of Social Problems, Washington, DC.

Schwartz, M., and Pitts, V. (1994). "Toward a Feminist Routine Activities Theory on Campus Sexual Assault." Paper presented at the annual meeting of the Academy for Criminal Justice Sciences, Chicago.

Schwartz, M., and Slatin, G. (1984). "The Law on Marital Rape: How Do Marxism and Feminism Explain Its Persistence." *ALSA Forum* 8(2):244–264.

Schwendinger, H., and Schwendinger, J. (1975). "Defenders of Order or Guardians of Human Rights?" In *Critical Criminology,* ed. I. Taylor, P. Walton, and J. Young, pp. 113–146. London: Routledge & Kegan Paul.

Schwendinger, H., and Schwendinger, J. (1993). "Giving Crime Prevention Top Priority." *Crime & Delinquency* 39:425–446.

Schwendinger, J., and Schwendinger, H. (1983). *Rape and Inequality.* Newbury Park, CA: Sage.

Scully, D. (1990). *Understanding Sexual Violence.* Boston: Unwin Hyman.

Segrave, K. (1992). *Women Serial and Mass Murderers: A Worldwide Reference, 1580 Through 1990.* Jefferson, NC: McFarland.

Selke, W. (1993). *Prisons in Crisis.* Bloomington: Indiana University Press.

Sellin, T. (1931). "The Basis of a Crime Index." *Journal of Criminal Law and Criminology* 22:335–336.

Sellin, T. (1938). *Culture Conflict and Crime.* New York: Social Science Research Council.

Selva, L., and Bohm, R. (1987). "A Critical Examination of the Informalism Experiment in the Administration of Justice." *Crime and Social Justice* 29:43–57.

Sewell, B. (1994). "Traditional Male/Female Roles Promote Domestic Violence." In *Violence Against Women,* ed. K. Swisher and C. Wekesser, pp. 19–25. San Diego: Greenhaven.

Sexton, J. (1994). "False Arrests and Perjury Are Common Among New York Police, Draft Report Says." *The New York Times* (April 22):A11.

Shapiro, S. (1983). "The New Moral Entrepreneurs: Corporate Crime Crusaders." *Contemporary Sociology* 12:304–307.

Shapiro, S. (1985). "The Road Not Taken: The Elusive Path to Criminal Prosecution for White Collar Offenders." *Law and Society Review* 19:179–217.

Sheley, J. (1985). *America's "Crime Problem": An Introduction to Criminology.* Belmont, CA: Wadsworth.

Sheley, J., and Ashkins, C. (1981). "Crime, Crime News, and Crime Views." *Public Opinion Quarterly* 45:492–506.

Sheppard, J. (1995). "Youth Crimes Not on Rise, Study Finds." *Ottawa Citizen* (February 1):A3.

Sherman, L. (1992). *Policing Domestic Violence.* New York: Free Press.

Sherman, L., Gartin, P., and Buerger, M. (1989). "Hot Spots and Predatory Crime: Routine Activities and the Criminology of Place." *Criminology* 27:27–55.

Shoemaker, D. (1990). *Theories of Delinquency: An Examination of Explanations of Delinquent Behavior.* New York: Oxford University Press.

Shoham, S., and Hoffman, J. (1991). *A Primer in the Sociology of Crime.* New York: Harrow & Heston.

Siegel, L. (1995). *Criminology,* 5th ed. St. Paul, MN: West.

Silverman, R. (1992). "Street Crime." In *Deviance: Conformity and Control in Canadian Society,* ed. V. Sacco, pp. 236–277. Toronto: Prentice-Hall.

Silverman, R., and Kennedy, L. (1993). *Deadly Deeds: Murder in Canada.* Scarborough, Ontario: Nelson.

Simon, D., and Eitzen, S. (1994). *Elite Deviance,* 4th ed. Boston: Allyn & Bacon.

Simon, J. (1978). *Basic Research Methods in Social Sciences: The Art of Empirical Investigation,* 2nd ed. New York: Random House.

Simon, R. (1975). *Women and Crime.* Lexington, MA: Lexington Books.

Simon, R. (1981). "American Women and Crime," In *Women and Crime in America,* ed. L. H. Bowker, pp. 18–39. New York: Macmillan.

Simpson, S. (1989). "Feminist Theory, Crime and Justice." *Criminology* 27:605–632.

Singer, S., and Levine, M. (1988). "Power-Control Theory, Gender and Delinquency: A Partial Replication with Additional Evidence on the Role of Peers." *Criminology* 26: 627–648.

Skogan, W., and Klecka, W. (1977). *The Fear of Crime.* Washington, DC: American Political Science Association.

Skogan, W., and Maxfield, M. (1981). *Coping with Crime.* Beverly Hills, CA: Sage.

Sloan, I. (1970). *Our Violent Past: An American Chronicle.* New York: Random House.

Smandych, R. (1985). "Marxism and the Creation of Law: Re-Examining the Origins of Canadian Anti-Combines Legislation, 1890–1910." In *The New Criminologies in Canada: State, Crime, and Control,* ed. T. Fleming, pp. 87–99. Toronto: Oxford University Press.

Smart, C. (1987). "Review of Capitalism, Patriarchy and Crime." *Contemporary Crises* 11: 327–329.

Smart, C. (1989). *Feminism and the Power of Law.* New York: Routledge.

Smart, R. (1986). "Cocaine Use and Problems in North America." *Canadian Journal of Criminology* 28:109–128.

Smith, D. (1978). "Organized Crime and Entrepreneurship." *International Journal of Criminology and Penology* 6:161–177.

Smith, D., and Jarjoura, G. (1988). "Social Structure and Criminal Victimization." *Journal of Research in Crime and Delinquency* 25:27–52.

Smith, M. (1983). *Violence and Sport.* Toronto: Butterworths.

Smith, M. (1985). *Woman Abuse: The Case for Surveys by Telephone.* The LaMarsh Research Programme on Violence and Conflict Resolution. Report No. 12. Toronto: York University.

Smith, M. (1987). "The Incidence and Prevalence of Woman Abuse in Toronto." *Violence and Victims* 2:173–187.

Smith, M. (1989). *Woman Abuse in Toronto: Incidence, Prevalence and Sociodemographic Risk Markers.* The LaMarsh Research Programme on Violence and Conflict Resolution. Report No. 18. Toronto: York University.

Smith, M. (1990a). "Sociodemographic Risk Factors in Wife Abuse: Results from a Survey of Toronto Women." *Canadian Journal of Sociology* 15:39–58.

Smith, M. (1990b). "Patriarchal Ideology and Wife Beating: A Test of a Feminist Hypothesis." *Violence and Victims* 5:257–273.

Smith, M. (1993). *Familial Ideology and Wife Abuse.* Unpublished manuscript. Toronto: LaMarsh Research Programme on Violence and Conflict Resolution.

Smith, S. (1986). *Crime, Space and Society.* London: Cambridge University Press.

Snider, L. (1988). "Commercial Crime." In *Deviance: Conformity and Control in Canadian Society,* ed. V. Sacco, pp. 231–283. Scarborough, Ontario: Prentice-Hall.

Snider, L. (1991). "The Potential of the Criminal Justice System to Promote Feminist Concerns." In *The Social Basis of Law: Critical Readings in the Sociology of Law,* ed. E. Comack and S. Brickey, pp. 238–260. Halifax: Garamond.

Snider, L. (1993). *Bad Business: Corporate Crime in Canada.* Scarborough, Ontario: Nelson.

Snow, D., and Anderson, L. (1993). *Down on Their Luck: A Study of Homeless Street People.* Berkeley: University of California Press.

Solicitor General of Canada. (1986). "Reported and Unreported Crimes." In *Crime in Canadian Society,* ed. R. Silverman and J. Teevan, pp. 98–114. Toronto: Butterworths.

Solicitor General of Canada. (1990). *Woman Alone.* Ottawa: Ministry of the Solicitor General of Canada.

Sparks, R. (1992). *Television and the Drama of Crime.* Philadelphia: Open University Press.

Spitzer, S. (1975). "Toward a Marxian Theory of Deviance." *Social Problems* 22:638–651.

Stamp, J. (1929). *Some Economic Factors in Modern Life.* London: King.

Stanko, E. (1988). "Fear of Crime and the Myth of the Safe Home: A Feminist Critique of Criminology." In *Feminist Perspectives on Wife Abuse,* ed. K. Yllo and M. Bograd, pp. 75–88. Beverly Hills, CA: Sage.

Stanko, E. (1990). *Everyday Violence: How Women and Men Experience Sexual and Physical Danger.* London: Pandora.

Stanko, E. (1994). "The Struggle Over Commonsense." Paper presented at the Fifth Symposium on Violence and Aggression. Saskatoon, Saskatchewan.

Stark-Adamec, C., and Adamec, P. (1982). "Aggression by Men Against Women: Adaptation or Aberration?" *International Journal of Women's Studies* 5:42–54.

Statistics Canada. (1993). *The Violence Against Women Survey.* Ottawa: Statistics Canada.

Stato, J. (1993). "Montreal Gynocide." In *Violence Against Women: The Bloody Footprints,* ed. P. B. Bart and E. G. Moran, pp. 132–133. Newbury Park, CA: Sage.

Steadman, H., Vanderwyst, D., and Ribner, S. (1978). "Comparing Arrest Rates of Mental Patients and Criminal Offenders." *American Journal of Psychiatry* 135:1218–1220.

Stebbins, R. (1987). *Sociology: The Study of Society.* New York: Harper & Row.

Steffensmeier, D. (1980). "Sex Differences in Patterns of Adult Crime, 1965–77: A Review and Assessment." *Social Forces* 58:1080–1108.

Steffensmeier, D., and Allen E. (1995). "Criminal Behavior: Gender and Age." In *Criminology: A Contemporary Handbook,* 2nd ed., ed. J. Sheley, pp. 83–113. Belmont, CA: Wadsworth.

Steinmetz, S., and Lucca, J. (1988). "Husband Battering." In *Handbook of Family Violence,* ed. V. Van Hasselt, R. Morrison, A. Bellack, and M. Hersen, pp. 233–246. New York: Plenum.

Stets, J., and Henderson, D. (1991). "Contextual Factors Surrounding Conflict Resolution While Dating: Results from a National Study." *Family Relations* 40:29–36.

Stoddart, K. (1986). "The Presentation of Everyday Life." *Urban Life* 15:103–121.

Straus, M. (1989). "Gender Differences in Assault in Intimate Relationships: Implications for the Primary Prevention of Spousal Violence." Paper presented at the annual meeting of the American Society of Criminology, Reno, Nevada.

Straus, M. (1990). "The Conflict Tactics Scale and Its Critics: An Evaluation and New Data on Validity and Reliability." In *Physical Violence in American Families: Risk Factors and Adaptions to Violence in 8,145 Families,* ed. M. Straus and R. Gelles, pp. 49–74. New Brunswick, NJ: Transaction.

Straus, M., and Gelles, R. (1986). "Societal Changes and Change in Family Violence from 1975 to 1985 as Revealed by Two National Surveys." *Journal of Marriage and the Family* 48:465–479.

Straus, M., and Gelles, R. (eds.). (1990). *Physical Violence in American Families: Risk Factors and Adaptions to Violence in 8,145 Families.* New Brunswick, NJ: Transaction.

Straus, M., Gelles, R., and Steinmetz, S. (1981). *Behind Closed Doors: Violence in the American Family.* New York: Anchor.

Straus, M., and Smith, C. (1990). "Violence in Hispanic Families in The United States: Incidence Rates and Structural Interpretations." In *Physical Violence in American Families: Risk Factors and Adaptions to Violence in 8,145 Families,* ed. M. Straus and R. Gelles, pp. 341–368. New Brunswick, NJ: Transaction.

Sugarman, D., and Hotaling, G. (1989). "Dating Violence: Prevalence, Context, and Risk Markers." In *Dating Violence: Emerging Social Issues,* ed. M. Pirog-Good and J. Stets, pp. 3–32. New York: Praeger.

Sugarman, J., and Rand, K. (1994). "Cease Fire." *Rolling Stone* (March 10):30–42.

Sullivan, M. (1989). *Getting Paid: Youth Crime and Work in the Inner City.* Ithaca, NY: Cornell University Press.

Sullivan, T., and Maiken, P. (1983). *Killer Clown: The John Wayne Gacy Murders.* New York: Pinnacle.

Surette, R. (1992). *Media, Crime and Criminal Justice.* Pacific Grove, CA: Brooks/Cole.

Sutherland, E. (1939). *Principles of Criminology,* 3rd ed. Philadelphia: Lippincott.

Sutherland, E., Cressey, D., and Luckenbill, D. (1992). *Principles of Criminology,* 11th ed. Dix Hills, NY: General Hall.

Swift, E. M. (1994). "Anatomy of a Plot." *Sports Illustrated* 80 (6):28–41.

Sykes, G. (1974). "The Rise of Critical Criminology." *Journal of Criminal Law and Criminology* 65:206–214.

Sykes, G., and Cullen, F. (1992). *Criminology,* 2nd ed. New York: Harcourt Brace Jovanovich.

Szasz, A. (1986). "Corporations, Organized Crime, and the Disposal of Hazardous Waste: An Examination of the Making of a Criminogenic Regulatory Structure." *Criminology* 24:1–28.

Taft, P., and Ross, P. (1969). "American Labor Violence: Its Causes, Character, and Outcome." In *The History of Violence in America,* ed. H. Graham and T. Gurr, pp. 281–395. New York: Bantam Books.

Tallmer, M. (1987). "Chemical Dumping as a Corporate Way of Life." In *Corporate Violence: Injury and Death for Profit,* ed. S. Hills, pp. 111–120. Totowa, NJ: Rowman & Littlefield.

Tannenbaum, F. (1938). *Crime and Community.* New York: Columbia University Press.

Tanner, J. (1992). "Youthful Deviance." In *Deviance: Conformity and Control in Canadian Society,* ed. V. Sacco, pp. 203–235. Toronto: Prentice-Hall.

Tappan, P. (1947). "Who Is the Criminal?" *American Sociological Review* 12:96–102.

Taylor, C. (1989). *Dangerous Society.* East Lansing: Michigan State University Press.

Taylor, I. (1981). *Law and Order: Arguments for Socialism.* London: Macmillan.

Taylor, I. (1982). "Against Crime and for Socialism." *Crime and Social Justice* 18:4–15.

Taylor, I. (1983). *Crime, Capitalism and Community: Three Essays in Socialist Criminology.* Toronto: Butterworths.

Taylor, I., Walton, P., and Young, J. (1973). *The New Criminology.* London: Routledge & Kegan Paul.

Teplin, L. (1985). "The Criminality of the Mentally Ill: A Dangerous Misconception." *American Journal of Psychiatry* 142:593–599.

Theoharis, A., and Cox, J. (1988). *The Boss.* Philadelphia: Temple University Press.

Thio, A. (1995). *Deviant Behavior,* 4th ed. New York: HarperCollins.

Thomas, J., and O'Maolchatha, A. (1989). "Reassessing the Critical Methaphor: An Optimistic Revisionist View." *Justice Quarterly* 2:143–172.

Thornberry, T. (1973). "Race, Socio-Economic Status, and Sentencing in the Juvenile Justice System." *Journal of Criminal Law, Criminology and Police Science* 64:90–98.

Thornburgh, R. (1990). "Money Laundering." *Vital Speeches of the Day* 56:578–580.

Thorne-Finch, R. (1992). *Ending the Silence: The Origins and Treatment of Male Violence Against Women.* Toronto: University of Toronto Press.

Timmer, D., and Eitzen, D. (1989). "What Is Crime?" In *Crime in the Streets and Crime in the Suites: Perspectives on Crime and Criminal Justice,* ed. D. Timmer and D. Eitzen, pp. 1–6. Needham Heights, MA: Allyn & Bacon.

Tittle, C., and Meier, R. (1991). "Specifying the SES/Delinquency Relationship by Social Characteristics of Contents." *Journal of Research in Crime and Delinquency* 28: 430–455.

Toby, J. (1957). "Social Disorganization and Stake in Conformity: Complementary Factors in the Predatory Behavior of Young Hoodlums." *Journal of Criminal Law, Criminology and Police Science* 48:12–17.

Toch, H. (1992). *Mosaic of Despair: Human Breakdowns in Prison.* Hyattsville, MD: American Psychological Association.

Tong, R. (1989). *Feminist Thought.* Boulder, CO: Westview.

Tonry, M. (1995). *Malign Neglect: Race, Crime, and Punishment in America.* New York: Oxford University Press.

Travis, L., Schwartz, M., and Clear, T. (1992). *Corrections: An Issues Approach,* 3rd ed. Cincinnati: Anderson.

Trebach, A. (1982). *The Heroin Solution.* New Haven, CT: Yale University Press.

Tunnell, K. (1992). *Choosing Crime: The Criminal Calculus of Property Offenders.* Chicago: Nelson-Hall.

Tunnell, K. (ed.). (1993). *Political Crime in Contemporary America.* New York: Garland.

Turk, A. (1969). *Criminality and Legal Order.* Chicago: Rand McNally.

Turk, A. (1975). "Prospects and Pitfalls for Radical Criminology: A Critical Response to Platt." *Crime and Social Justice* 4:41–42.

Turk, A. (1977). "Class, Conflict and Criminalization." *Sociological Focus* 10:209–220.

Turk, A. (1979). "Analyzing Official Deviance: For Nonpartisan Conflict Analysis." *Criminology* 16:459–476.

Tyler, G. (1981). "The Crime Corporation." In *Current Perspectives on Criminal Behavior,* ed. A. Blumberg, pp. 273–290. New York: Alfred Knopf.

Tyler, T. (1984). "Assessing the Risk of Crime Victimization: The Integration of Personal Victimization Experience and Socially Transmitted Information." *Journal of Social Issues* 40:27–38.

Ursel, J. (1991). "Considering the Impact of the Battered Women's Movement on the State: The Example of Manitoba." In *The Social Basis of Law: Critical Readings in the Sociology of Law,* ed. E. Comack and S. Brickey, pp. 261–288. Halifax: Garamond.

U.S. Department of Labor. (1992). *Bureau of Labor Statistics Reports on Survey of Occupational Injuries and Illnesses in 1991.* Washington, DC: U.S. Department of Labor.

Vachhs, A. (1993). *Sex Crimes.* New York: Random House.

Valverde, M. (1991). "Feminist Perspectives on Criminology." In *Criminology: A Reader's Guide,* ed. J. Gladstone, R. Ericson, and C. Shearing, pp. 239–257. Toronto: Centre of Criminology, University of Toronto.

van den Haag, E. (1982). "Could Successful Rehabilitation Reduce the Crime Rate? *Journal of Criminal Law and Criminology* 73:1025–1035.

Van Duyne, P. (1993). "Organized Crime and Business Crime Enterprises in the Netherlands." *Crime, Law and Social Change* 19:103–142.

Viano, E. (1994). "Creating Fetal Rights and Protecting Pregnant Women's Constitutional Rights." In *Drug Use in America: Social, Cultural, and Political Perspectives,* ed. P. Venturelli, pp. 303–314. Boston: Jones & Bartlett.

Visano, L. (1987). *This Idle Trade: The Occupational Patterns of Male Prostitution.* Concord, Ontario: VitaSana.

Visher, C. (1987). "Incapacitation and Crime Control: Does a 'Lock 'Em Up' Strategy Reduce Crime?" *Justice Quarterly* 4:513–543.

Vitiello, J. (1992). "The New World Order—From Fraud and Force to Business As Usual in the Global Free Market: The Up-to-Date Evidence." *Crime, Law and Social Change* 17:253–266.

Vito, G., and Holmes, R. (1994). *Criminology: Theory, Research, and Policy.* Belmont, CA: Wadsworth.

Voight, L., Thornton, W., Barrile, L., and Seaman, J. (1994). *Criminology and Justice.* New York: McGraw-Hill.

Vold, G., and Bernard, T. (1986). *Theoretical Criminology,* 3rd ed. New York: Oxford University Press.

Voss, H. (1966). "Socio-economic Status and Reported Delinquent Behavior." *Social Forces* 13:314–324.

Walby, S. (1990). *Theorizing Patriarchy.* Cambridge, MA: Basil Blackwell.

Waldo, G., and Dinitz, S. (1967). "Personality Attributes of the Criminal: An Analysis of Research Studies." *Journal of Research in Crime and Delinquency* 4:185–202.

Walker, L. (1979). *The Battered Woman.* New York: Harper & Row.

Walker, S. (1994). *Sense and Nonsense About Crime and Drugs: A Policy Guide,* 3rd ed. Belmont, CA: Wadsworth.

Walklate, S. (1989). *Victimology: The Victim and the Criminal Justice Process.* London: Unwin Hyman.

Wallace, A. (1986). *Homicide: The Social Reality.* Sydney, Australia: New South Wales Bureau of Crime Statistics and Research.

Wallerstein, J., and Wyle, C. (1947). "Our Law-Abiding Law-Breakers." *Federal Probation* 35:107–118; as cited in R. Merton, *Social Theory and Social Structure.* Glencoe, IL: Free Press, 1957, p. 145.

Warshaw, C. (1993). "Limitations of the Medical Model in the Care of Battered Women." In *Violence Against Women: The Bloody Footprints,* ed. P. Bart and E. Moran, pp. 134–146. Newbury Park, CA: Sage.

Warshaw, R. (1988). *I Never Called It Rape.* New York: Harper & Row.

Waterston, A. (1993). *Street Addicts in the Political Economy.* Philadelphia: Temple University Press.

Weber, M. (1978). *Economy and Society, Volume 2,* ed. G. Roth and C. Wittich. Berkeley: University of California Press.

Weis, K., and Weis, S. (1974). "Victimology and the Justification of Rape." In *Victimology: Exploiters and the Exploited,* ed. I. Drapkin and E. Viano. Lexington, MA: Lexington Books.

Weisheit, R., and Mahan, S. (1988). *Women, Crime, and Criminal Justice.* Cincinnati: Anderson.

Wellisch, J., Prendergast, M., and Anglin, M. (1994). *Drug-Abusing Women Offenders: Results of a National Survey.* Washington, DC: National Institute of Justice Research in Brief.

Wessinger, C., and Wodarski, J. (1994). "Accuracy of National Surveys of Drug Use: A Comparison with Local Studies." *Journal of Alcohol and Drug Education* 39:62–74.

West, W. G. (1984). *Young Offenders and the State: A Canadian Perspective on Delinquency.* Toronto: Butterworths.

White, J., and Koss, M. (1991). "Courtship Violence: Incidence in a National Sample of Higher Education Students." *Violence and Victims* 6:247–256.

Whitehead, A. (1976). "Sexual Antagonisms in Herefordshire." In *Dependence and Exploitation in Work and Marriage,* ed. D. Barker and S. Allen, pp. 169–203. London: Longman.

Wiatrowski, M., Griswold, D., and Roberts, M. (1981). "Social Control Theory and Delinquency." *American Sociological Review* 46:525–541.

Wicharaya, T. (1995). *Simple Theory, Hard Reality: The Impact of Sentencing Reforms on Courts, Prisons and Crime.* Albany: SUNY Press.

Wicker, T. (1975). *A Time to Die.* New York: Quadrangle.

Wideman, J. (1984). *Brothers and Keepers.* New York: Holt, Rinehart & Winston.

Widom, C. (1989). "Child Abuse, Neglect, and Violent Criminal Behavior." *Criminology* 27:251–271.

Wilkins, L. (1964). *Social Deviance.* London: Tavistock.

Williams, F., and McShane, M. (1994). *Criminological Theory,* 2nd ed. Englewood Cliffs, NJ: Prentice-Hall.

Williams, J., and Gold, N. (1972). "From Delinquent Behavior to Official Delinquency." *Social Problems* 19:209–229.

Williams, K., and Hawkins, R. (1989). "The Meaning of Arrest for Wife Assault." *Criminology* 27:163–181.

Wilson, J. (1985). *Thinking About Crime.* New York: Vintage.

Wilson, J. (1995). "Crime and Public Policy." In *Crime,* ed. J. Wilson and J. Petersilia, pp. 489–507. San Francisco: ICS Press.

Wilson, J., and Herrnstein, R. (1985). *Crime and Human Nature: The Definitive Study of the Causes of Crime.* New York: Simon & Schuster.

Wilson, M., and Daly, M. (1993). "Spousal Homicide Risk and Estrangement." *Violence and Victims* 8:3–16.

Wilson, W. (1987). *The Truly Disadvantaged: The Inner City, the Underclass and Public Policy.* Chicago: University of Chicago Press.

Winick, C. (1993). "Social Behavior, Public Policy and Nonharmful Drug Use." In *Confronting Drug Policy: Illicit Drugs in a Free Society,* ed. R. Bayer and G. Oppenheimer, pp. 136–159. New York: Cambridge University Press.

Witters, W., Venturelli, P., and Hanson, G. (1992). *Drugs and Society,* 3rd ed. Boston: Jones & Bartlett.

Wolfgang, M. (1958). *Patterns in Criminal Homicide.* Philadelphia: University of Pennsylvania Press.

Wolfgang, M., and Ferracuti, F. (1967). *The Subculture of Violence: Towards an Integrated Theory in Criminology.* London: Tavistock.

Wright, J., and Devine, J. (1994). *Drugs as a Social Problem.* New York: HarperCollins College Publishers.

Wright, J., and Rossi, P. (1986). *Armed and Considered Dangerous: A Survey of Felons and Their Firearms.* New York: Aldine de Gruyter.

Yablonsky, L. (1962). *The Violent Gang.* Baltimore: Penguin.

Yates, G., MacKenzie, R., Pennbridge, J., and Swofford, A. (1991). "A Risk Profile Comparison of Homeless Youth Involved in Prostitution and Homeless Youth Not Involved." *Journal of Adolescent Health* 12:545–548.

Young, J. (1975). "Working Class Criminology." In *Critical Criminology,* ed. I. Taylor, P. Walton, and J. Young, pp. 63–94. Boston: Routledge & Kegan Paul.

Young, J. (1979). "Left Idealism, Reformism and Beyond: From New Criminology to Marxism." In *Capitalism and the Rule of Law,* ed. B. Fine, R. Kinsey, J. Lea, S. Piccicotto, and J. Young, pp. 11–28. London: Hutchinson.

Young, J. (1986). "The Failure of Criminology." In *Confronting Crime,* ed. R. Matthews and J. Young, pp. 4–30. London: Sage.

Young, J. (1988). "Radical Criminology in Britain: The Emergence of a Competing Paradigm." *British Journal of Criminology* 28:159–183.

Young, J. (1992). "Ten Points of Realism." In *Rethinking Criminology: The Realist Debate,* ed. J. Young and R. Matthews, pp. 24–68. London: Sage.

Young, J., and Matthews, R. (eds.). (1992). *Rethinking Criminology: The Realist Debate.* Newbury Park, CA: Sage.

Zalenko, L. (1992). "Business Reports: Health Care: Everybody Must Get Stoned." *American Demographics* 14 (9):20.

Zatz, M. (1993). "Preface." In *Making Law: The State, the Law, and Structural Contradictions,* pp. ix–xi. Bloomington: Indiana University Press.

Zawitz, M., Klaus, P., Bachman, R., Bastian, L., DeBerry, M., Rand, M., and Taylor, B. (1993). *Highlights from 20 Years of Surveying Crime Victims: The National Crime Victimization Survey, 1973–92.* Washington, DC: U.S. Department of Justice.

Zilbergeld, B. (1983). *The Shrinking of America: Myths of Psychological Change.* Boston: Little, Brown.

Zimring, F., and Hawkins, G. (1973). *Deterrence.* Chicago: University of Chicago Press.

A

Abadinsky, H., 383, 384, 385, 386
Adamec, P., 320
Adler, F., 217, 261, 384
Adler, P., 401, 469
Ahluwalia, S., 94
Akers, R., 81, 179, 181, 183, 185, 220, 231, 430
Akman, D., 22
Albanese, J., 383, 386
Albini, J., 384
Allen, H., 161, 218
Allison, J., 58, 119
Althusser, L., 85
American Federation of Labor and Congress of Industrial Organizations (AFL-CIO), 83, 364
Amnesty International, 75
Anderson, A., 390
Anderson, L., 133, 141, 142, 143
Andreski, S., 77
Andrews, D., 176n, 191, 196
Anglin, M., 425
Archer, D., 297
Armstrong, H., 223
Armstrong, P., 223
Ashkins, C., 9
Atkinson, M., 222
Auld, J., 416
Austin, J., 160, 172, 451, 454, 455, 464
Austin, W. T., 212
Avary, D., 449

B

Bachman, J., 423
Bacon-Smith, C., 144
Balbus, I., 85
Ball, R., 176, 261
Bandura, A., 17n
Barak, G., 54, 100n, 133, 241, 243, 394, 471
Baranek, P., 9
Barnett, O., 119, 323, 466
Baron, L., 19
Baron, S., 228
Barrett, M., 337
Beattie, J., 70
Beaty, J., 393
Beccaria, C., 160, 162, 163
Becker, G., 166
Becker, H., 45, 223, 431–432
Beirne, P., 9, 27, 43n, 48, 69, 81, 98, 226n, 260, 265, 266, 300, 350, 373, 383, 389, 433
Bendix, R., 77
Berg, B., 26, 140, 148
Berk, R., 102
Bernard, T., 155, 160, 164, 184, 192, 205, 208, 215, 223, 225n, 388
Berrill, K., 104
Blau, F., 216, 380
Blau, J., 6, 190, 228, 296, 307, 312, 313, 314
Blau, P., 6, 190, 296, 312, 313, 314

Block, A., 391, 392
Blumberg, M., 172, 301, 414, 436, 460
Boeringer, R., 229
Bograd, M., 343, 350
Bohm, R., 54, 173, 238, 242, 271
Bohmer, C., 58, 230, 348, 349n
Bollen, K., 16
Bond, C., 347
Bonta, J., 176n, 191, 196
Bourgois, P., 421
Bowers, W., 173
Bowker, L., 326, 333n
Box, S., 9, 10, 208, 382
Boyd, N., 16, 21n, 68n, 282, 402, 408, 430, 453
Brady, J., 391
Braithwaite, J., 6, 175, 188
Brake, M., 13
Brannigan, A., 17, 75, 118, 171
Breines, W., 322, 331, 332
Brennan, P., 155, 176n
Breslin, P., 473
Brickey, S., 76, 78, 81, 82, 84, 86, 105, 244
Brinkerhoff, M., 332n, 333
Brody, R., 99
Brown, J., 317
Brown, M., 371
Brown, R., 98, 103
Brown, S., 156, 160, 161, 179, 180, 181
Browne, A., 291, 333n

Browning, F., 384
Brownstein, H., 243
Buehler, C., 478
Buerger, M., 228, 307
Bureau of Justice Statistics, 59, 129, 318, 399, 421, 426
Burgess, A., 303n
Burney, E., 250
Burshtyn, H., 3, 4, 445n
Burtch, B., 68n, 70, 77, 81
Buzawa, C., 481
Buzawa, E., 481

C

Calavita, K. C., 387
Calhoun, T., 141, 142, 143
Campbell, A., 250, 312
Campbell, J., 310, 317
Caplan, G., 344n
Caputi, J., 303, 309
Caputo, T., 67, 68n, 76n, 78
Caringella-MacDonald, S., 243
Carstensen, L., 16
Cassel, J., 344n
Cavender, G., 362, 368n, 373, 374
Chalouh, M., 305n
Chambliss, W., 6, 49, 67, 78, 85, 87, 88, 89, 138, 156, 242, 258, 387, 388, 389
Chamlin, M., 48
Chan, J., 9
Chancer, L., 141
Check, J., 18
Chein, I., 429, 430, 459
Chenier, N., 362
Chermak, S., 398
Chesney-Lind, M., 59, 216, 220, 222, 225, 243, 259, 260, 261, 263, 265, 350
Clark, J., 136
Clarke, A., 11
Clarke, R., 227, 231, 255
Claybrook, J., 370
Clear, T., 70, 157, 172, 443, 444, 451
Clinard, M., 357, 359, 375–376, 378
Cloward, R., 213–215, 429
Cocozza, J., 186
Cohen, A., 49, 195, 210–213, 271, 311
Cohen, M., 227
Cohen, S., 11–12, 13, 251n, 254, 344n, 478

Cole, G. F., 253
Coleman, J., 370, 379
Collins, H., 254
Collins, R., 202–203
Comack, E., 76, 78, 81, 82, 84, 86, 105, 244, 402
Commager, H., 103
Comstock, G., 16
Connell, R., 92
Cornell, C., 322, 351
Cornish, D., 231
Counts, D., 317
Courtless, T., 67, 87, 88n
Cox, J., 100
Crawford, A., 248, 290
Cressey, D., 185, 192, 383, 390
Croall, H., 377, 379
Cromwell, P., 142, 449
Crotty, W., 98, 99
Crutchfield, R., 297
Cullen, F., 127, 176, 203, 242, 261, 362, 367, 368n, 373, 374
Curran, D., 179, 183, 185, 206, 210, 215, 218, 220n, 221, 232
Currie, D., 6, 23, 24, 93, 94, 239
Currie, E., 48, 69, 70, 72, 119, 133, 137, 167, 168, 169, 172, 175, 176, 188, 189, 196, 197, 198, 237, 243, 268, 286, 287, 311, 394, 405, 407, 410, 415, 417, 433–434, 435, 454, 463, 464, 465, 467, 468, 469, 470, 473, 480

D

Dahrendorf, R., 78n
Daly, K., 146, 259, 260, 261, 263, 265, 350
Daly, M., 288, 291, 301, 307
Danner, M., 261
Davis, N., 51, 102, 157
DeBurger, J., 304
DeKeseredy, W., 3, 4, 6, 18, 21n, 22, 23, 24, 26, 49, 60, 75, 116, 135, 136, 175, 218, 219, 229, 230, 240, 244n, 245n, 246, 250, 257, 285, 291, 306, 308, 319, 330, 331, 332, 333, 337, 338n, 339, 344, 349, 351, 356n, 361, 362, 363, 364, 365n, 368, 377n, 445n, 463n, 478

Denzin, N., 145, 274
Desroches, F., 366
Devine, J., 416, 418, 460, 461
Dews, P., 274
Dinitz, S., 184
Dixon, J., 296n
Dobash, Ronald E., 26, 145, 195, 290, 291, 319, 324, 331, 337, 351n, 481
Dobash, Russell, 26, 145, 195, 319, 324, 337, 351n, 481
Donnerstein, E., 17
Dorn, N., 416
Douglas, J., 303n
Downes, D., 13, 154, 261
Dugdale, R., 181
Dunlap, E., 421
Durkheim, E., 199–202
Dutton, D., 333, 338
Dworkin, A., 324, 342

E

Edwards, S., 59, 92, 93n, 481
Egger, S., 304
Ehrenreich, B., 261
Ehrhart, J., 147
Ehrlich, S., 343
Eighner, L., 435, 459
Eitzen, S., 165, 176, 190, 192, 344, 368, 371, 374, 388, 389, 477
Elias, R., 3, 40, 54, 126, 419, 445, 481
Elliott, D., 48, 398
Ellis, D., 4, 13, 63, 71, 75, 80, 175, 199, 201, 218, 285, 306, 333, 339, 356n, 365n, 377n
Ellison, C., 42, 476–477
Elsner, M., 401, 413–415
Engels, F., 82
English, D., 261
Ericson, R., 9
Erikson, K., 45n
Erlich, I., 173
Esbensen, F., 156, 160, 161, 179, 180, 181
Everingham, S., 460

F

Fairstein, L., 119, 123
Faith, K., 188, 216n, 261, 262, 263, 291, 318
Faludi, S., 258

Farr, K., 26
Fattah, E., 6, 7, 8, 10, 11
Federal Bureau of Investigation, 113, 114, 116, 294, 297, 298
Felson, L., 227
Felson, M., 228
Felson, R., 300
Fenstermaker, S., 349
Ferracuti, F., 310, 311
Ferrell, J., 146
Fielding, J., 145
Fielding, N., 145
Fijnaut, C., 383
Fitchey, F., 473
Fitzpatrick, K., 473
Flanagan, T., 118, 253, 282, 288, 295, 299, 426
Fleischman, J., 171
Fleming, T., 244
Forst, B., 173
Foucault, M., 157, 158
Fox, J., 292, 293, 306
Fox, S., 386
Frank, N., 357, 361, 362, 365, 367, 370, 371, 377, 379, 383
Fricker, M. F., 393
Friedberg, A., 10
Friedrichs, D., 54, 91, 241, 243, 268, 269, 273n, 274, 356, 357n, 383n, 481

G

Gamble, N., 119
Gaquin, D., 333n
Garofalo, J., 6
Gartin, P., 228, 307
Gartner, R., 285, 287, 290, 294, 297
Gastil, R., 296
Geerken, M., 116, 133
Geis, G., 156, 160, 161, 179, 180, 181, 360
Gelles, R., 135, 318, 319, 322, 330, 333, 338, 340, 342, 343, 351, 417, 471
Gelsthorpe, L., 258
Gendreau, P., 459
Gerassi, J., 384
Gerbner, G., 14
Gibbons, D., 463
Gidycz, C., 135, 229
Giles-Sims, J., 333n
Gillis, A. R., 218, 221, 222
Gilroy, P., 251, 252
Gimenez, M., 262
Glackman, W., 3

Glaspell, S., 57
Glueck, E., 179
Glueck, S., 179
Goddard, H., 181
Goff, C., 83, 358, 361, 362, 363
Goffman, E., 283
Gold, D., 84, 85
Gold, N., 138
Gold, R., 141
Goldenberg, S., 17
Goldstein, J., 14, 17
Goldstein, P., 407
Gomme, I., 68, 82, 306
Goode, E., 410, 420, 425, 432, 433, 435
Goodman, E., 56
Goodstein, L., 11
Gordon, C., 3, 4, 445n
Gordon, D., 258, 452
Gordon, L., 322, 331, 332
Gordon, M., 11
Goring, C., 179
Gottfredson, M., 155, 294
Gould, M., 16
Gove, W., 116, 133
Graber, D., 9
Grant, J., 276
Green, M., 373
Greenberg, D., 84, 85, 258, 294
Greider, W., 355
Griswold, D., 220
Groth, P., 472
Groves, B., 43n, 54, 72, 76n, 80, 81, 84, 237n, 238, 239, 243, 254, 268–269
Gusfield, J., 52
Gutzmore, C., 252

H

Hackler, J., 215
Hagan, F., 109, 132, 139, 143
Hagan, J., 21, 39, 43n, 55, 63, 171, 204, 218, 221, 222, 296, 377
Hagedorn, J., 143, 144, 450, 455, 465
Hall, S., 13
Haller, M., 387
Hamberger, L., 342
Hamm, M., 102, 144, 145
Hampton, R., 340
Hanmer, J., 447
Hanson, G., 397, 403, 405, 411, 413
Harman, L., 471
Harman, P., 18

Harney, P., 348
Harris, M., 156
Harrop, J., 340
Hart, C., 448
Hartnagel, T., 308
Hatty, S., 102, 157
Haveman, R., 462
Hawk, M., 417, 418
Hawkins, G., 40
Hawkins, R., 167, 175
Hay, D., 70, 347
Heath, L., 11
Helmer, J., 38
Henderson, D., 135, 341
Henry, S., 133, 275
Henslin, J., 35, 174, 398, 414
Herman, E., 157
Herrnstein, R., 153, 155, 176n, 181, 188, 294, 477
Hickey, E., 302, 304
Hill, G., 222
Hills, S., 43, 47, 367, 381, 387, 388, 389, 390, 393, 397, 412, 421, 453
Hilton, Z., 176
Hinch, R., 21n, 77, 78, 81, 86, 87, 88, 89, 90, 239n, 330, 364, 365n, 368
Hindelang, M., 48, 136
Hirschel, J. D., 319
Hirschi, T., 48, 155, 218, 219, 220, 221, 294, 433
Hirst, P., 81
Hobbes, T., 71
Hoffman, J., 85, 220, 222
Hofstadter, R., 103
Holman, J., 209
Holmes, R., 282, 283, 296, 303, 304, 307
Holmes, S., 282, 283, 296, 303, 304, 307
Holmlund, C., 188
Horley, S., 322, 323, 327, 466
Hornink, R., 393
Hornung, C., 330n
Hotaling, G., 26, 337, 338n, 339, 341n
Hough, M., 126
Huggins, M., 157
Hughes, M., 116, 133
Huizinga, D., 48
Hull, J., 347
Hummer, R., 147, 347
Humphreys, L., 140, 144
Humphries, D., 9, 243, 419
Hunt, A., 105, 257

I

Ianni, F., 385
Inciardi, J., 40, 116, 118, 121, 385, 388, 400, 403, 406, 408, 410, 411, 417, 419, 421, 425, 456
Irwin, J., 172, 451, 454, 455, 464
Island, D., 320

J

Jackson, D., 301, 302
Jackson, M., 176
Jackson, P., 113
Jaggar, A., 266
Jefferson, T., 13, 348
Jenkins, P., 282, 303, 304
Jensen, G., 222
Johns, C., 412, 456, 459, 462, 473
Johnson, L., 125, 167, 308, 423
Jones, E., 93, 248

K

Kappeler, V., 172, 301, 414, 436, 460
Karmen, A., 22, 126, 459
Kasinsky, R., 419
Katz, J., 170
Kaufman, J., 479
Kaufman Kantor, G., 338n
Kelkar, G., 310
Kelly, K., 93, 135, 136, 229, 265, 321, 330n, 332, 333, 337, 351
Kelly, L., 331
Kennedy, L., 228, 282, 306, 308, 309, 338
Kephart, W., 5
King, P., 417, 419
Kinsey, R., 117, 246n, 248
Kirkham, J., 96, 99
Kirkwood, C., 321, 323, 326, 327, 342
Kitsuse, J., 45n
Klain, J., 9
Klein, D., 243
Klein, M., 407, 449
Knopp, F., 449
Knowles, J., 445, 447
Knutilla, M., 90, 92
Koenig, D., 21n
Konopka, G., 191
Koss, M., 135, 229, 418
Kraska, P., 182, 400
Krivo, L., 297

L

LaGory, M., 473
Landsberg, M., 197
Lasch, C., 6
Lasley, J., 228
LaViolette, A., 119, 323, 466
Layden, T., 61
Lea, J., 117, 246, 247–249, 250, 449
Lee, G., 11, 308
Leiber, M., 62
Lemert, E., 45n, 223, 224–225
Letellier, P., 320
Levin, J., 306
Levine, M., 222
Levinger, G., 333n
Levinson, D., 317, 351
Levy, S., 98, 99
Lewis, C., 11, 94
Liazlos, A., 51
Liddle, A., 93, 265, 352
Liebow, E., 460, 471
Lilly, J., 176, 261
Linz, D., 17, 18
Liska, A., 48, 81
Livingston, J., 3, 4, 6, 9
Lizotte, A., 296n
Lloyd, S., 347
Lo, C., 84, 85
Lockhart, L., 340
Lockwood, D., 406, 425
Long, J., 306
Los, M., 58
Lowman, J., 170, 171, 246n
Lucca, J., 289
Luckenbill, D., 185, 192, 283, 300
Lueck, T., 466
Lundberg, F., 387
Lupri, E., 135, 332, 333, 338
Lupsha, P., 384, 385
Lynch, M., 54, 71–72, 76n, 80, 81, 84, 143n, 237n, 238, 239, 243, 254, 357, 361, 362, 365, 367, 370, 371, 377, 379, 383

M

Maakestad, W., 362, 368n, 373, 374
MacKenzie, D., 450
MacKinnon, C., 58, 91
MacLean, B., 6n, 22, 23, 82, 116, 239, 244, 246n, 248, 256, 257, 351, 363

MacLeod, L., 321, 322, 333n
Madigan, L., 119
Maguire, B., 251
Maguire, K., 60, 118, 173, 253, 282, 288, 295, 299, 406, 426, 427, 457n
Maguire, M., 126
Mahan, S., 59
Maher, L., 419
Maier, P., 228, 308
Maiken, P., 302
Malamuth, N., 18
Malette, L., 305n
Mama, A., 94
Manchester, W., 99
Mann, C., 38, 60, 250, 281, 295, 296, 313, 403
Martin, P., 147, 347
Martin, R., 160, 212
Marx, G., 40, 442
Marx, K., 82
Matthews, R., 54
Mattley, C., 325
Maudsley, H., 441
Mauer, M., 171
Mawby, R., 443
Maxfield, M., 11, 289
Maxson, C., 407
Mayhew, P., 126
McCarthy, B., 171
McCullough, B., 330n
McKinney, K., 148
McMillen, L., 230
McMullan, J., 244, 371, 384
McNamara, R., 449
McShane, M., 164, 165, 208, 220, 231
Mead, G., 223
Mednick, S., 155, 176n
Meier, R., 138
Melick, M., 186
Merton, R., 202–210, 313, 381, 429
Messerschmidt, J., 4, 9, 27, 43n, 48, 54, 57, 69, 81, 90, 92, 93, 98, 170, 216, 226n, 260, 261, 262, 263, 264, 265, 266–268, 300, 350, 373, 379, 380, 383, 389, 433, 477
Messner, S., 228, 297, 307
Michalowski, R., 54, 55, 68n, 70, 96n, 246, 254, 257, 313–314, 365, 367, 369–370, 372, 390, 466, 478
Miethe, D., 11
Miethe, T., 228, 306

Milgram, S., 16
Miliband, R., 82
Miller, J., 40, 122, 123, 407, 421, 422
Miller, S., 175
Miller, W., 311
Mills, C. W., 197, 198
Milovanovic, D., 6n, 68n, 77, 78, 81, 239, 275
Mintz, M., 369
Mooney, J., 248
Morash, M., 222
Morgan-Sharp, E., 59
Morra, N., 381
Morris, A., 216, 258, 260
Morris, J., 408
Morris, N., 40
Muehlenhard, C., 348
Mueller, G., 384
Muolo, P., 393
Murray, G., 426
Musto, D., 38, 401, 405, 410
Mutchnick, R., 160, 212

N

Nader, R., 373, 375
Naffine, N., 216, 220
National Commission on the Causes and Prevention of Crime, 441–442
National Institute on Drug Abuse, 422, 426, 427
National Safety Council, 364
Nelli, H., 385, 389, 390
Nelson, D., 366
Neuman, W. L., 148
Newman, G., 57
New York State Organized Crime Task Force, 390
NiCarthy, G., 326
Nicholl, C., 404
Normandeau, A., 22

O

O'Brien, J., 319, 333n
O'Carroll, P., 281, 295
O'Connor, J., 85–86
Ohlin, L., 213–215, 429
Okun, L., 350
Oliver, W., 228
Olson, J., 449
O'Malley, P., 423
O'Maolchatha, A., 239n, 269
Oppenheimer, G., 410
Orcutt, J., 398

Ostroff, R., 16
Owens, P., 366

P

Pace, D., 383, 393
Pagelow, M., 343
Paight, D., 16
Pandya, B., 310
Park, R., 139
Parrot, A., 230, 348, 349n
Passas, N., 382
Pastore, A., 60, 118, 173, 253, 282, 288, 295, 299, 406, 426, 427, 457n
Pateman, C., 337
Paternoster, R., 175
Paterson, C., 47, 361, 364, 365, 366
Pearce, F., 83, 124, 202, 363, 389
Pennsylvania Crime Commission, 390
Pepinsky, H., 54, 243, 268, 269n, 271, 272
Peterson, R., 297
Pfohl, S., 156, 202, 204, 208, 209, 210, 226n, 242
Pfuhl, E., 133
Phillips, D., 16, 17
Pierce, G., 173, 292
Pitts, V., 229, 347, 471
Pizzo, S., 393
Platt, A., 246, 250, 256
Pleck, E., 480
Pointing, J., 126
Polsky, N., 148
Pontell, H., 387
Pope, C., 148
Potteiger, A., 406, 425
Potter, G., 172, 301, 414, 436, 460
Poulantzas, N., 85, 86
Prendergast, M., 425
President's Commission on Law Enforcement and the Administration of Justice, 383
Price, B., 60
Price, R., 281
Punch, M., 148

Q

Quinn, J., 209
Quinney, R., 43n, 54, 78, 79, 81, 82, 83, 85, 243, 268, 269, 271, 357, 388

R

Radford, J., 92, 350
Rand, K., 250, 282, 295, 299
Rasche, C., 324
Ratner, M., 408
Ratner, R. S., 244
Reasons, C., 47, 83, 89, 358, 361, 364, 365, 366
Reiman, J., 4, 6, 10, 31, 42, 48, 49, 54, 70, 74, 192, 238, 251, 268, 365, 367, 397, 401, 461
Reiss, A., 250, 281, 286, 288, 295, 297n, 299, 304, 308
Renzetti, C., 145, 146, 179, 183, 185, 206, 210, 215, 218, 220n, 221, 232, 259, 320, 324
Reschenthaler, G., 48
Ressler, R., 303n
Reuss-Ianni, E., 385
Rhodes, R., 391
Rice, M., 351
Richie, B., 325
Roberts, M., 220
Rock, P., 13, 154, 261
Roesch, R., 3
Rollins, J., 141
Roncek, D., 228, 308
Rosenau, P. M., 275
Rosenbaum, M., 434, 435–436
Ross, L., 361, 364, 365, 366, 459
Ross, P., 47, 104
Rossi, P., 135
Roth, J., 77, 250, 281, 286, 288, 295, 297n, 299, 300, 305, 308
Rowan, R., 384, 388, 389
Rubin, L., 339
Russell, D., 18, 170, 309, 333n, 345, 349
Rydell, C., 460

S

Sacco, V., 3, 6, 7, 8, 10, 11, 125, 306, 308
Samaha, J., 118
Sampson, R., 48, 296, 297, 428
Sanday, P. R., 147, 349
Sandler, B., 147
Santiago, R., 397, 412, 421
Sarason, I., 234n, 344n
Saunders, D., 447
Scarpitta, F., 391, 392
Schelling, T., 385, 387

Schmallenger, F., 111
Schrager, L., 367
Schur, E., 39, 90, 224
Schwartz, M., 7, 18, 26, 42, 90, 111, 122, 123, 157, 183, 229, 230, 238, 239, 240, 243, 245n, 246, 250, 257, 258, 259, 267, 273, 274, 291, 319, 322, 325, 331, 333, 337, 338, 339, 344, 345, 347, 349, 407, 421, 450–451, 463n, 476–477, 478, 479, 481
Schwendinger, H., 43, 54, 81, 263–264, 465, 466, 473
Schwendinger, J., 43, 54, 81, 263–264, 465, 466, 473
Scully, D., 135, 345, 352
Segrave, K., 301, 302
Seidman, Richard, 85, 89
Seidman, Robert, 78
Selke, W., 171
Sellin, T., 63, 134
Selva, L., 271
Sewell, B., 347
Sexton, J., 123
Shaffer, D., 16
Shapiro, S., 33, 359–360
Sheldon, R., 59, 216, 220, 222, 225
Sheley, J., 9, 76n, 86, 87, 137
Shepard, J., 175
Sherman, L., 228, 307, 319, 320, 481
Shoemaker, D., 177, 183
Shoham, S., 85, 220, 222
Short, J., 367
Shotland, R., 11, 16
Siegel, L., 176n
Signorielli, N., 14
Silverman, R., 23, 282, 308, 309
Simon, D., 368, 371, 374, 388, 389, 477
Simon, J., 148
Simon, R., 217, 261, 262
Simonsen, C., 161
Simpson, J., 175, 218, 221, 222, 265, 350
Singer, S., 222
Skogan, W., 3, 11
Slatin, G., 90, 267, 345
Sloan, I., 103
Smandych, R., 86
Smart, C., 267, 481
Smith, D., 297, 387

Smith, M., 15, 17, 327, 330, 331, 332, 333n, 337, 338, 340, 351, 381
Smith, S., 11
Snider, L., 93n, 359, 363n, 375, 377, 379–380, 381, 475
Snow, D., 133
Sokoloff, N., 60
Solicitor General of Canada, 446
Souryal, C., 450
South, N., 416
Sparks, R., 14n
Spitzer, S., 258
Stafford, M., 228, 306
Stamp, J., 109
Stanko, E., 3, 4, 229, 446, 448, 480
Stark-Adamec, C., 320
Stasz, C., 51
Statistics Canada, 333n
Stato, J., 305
Steadman, H., 186, 300
Stebbins, R., 200
Steffensmeier, D., 217, 218
Steinmetz, S., 135, 289, 319, 330, 338, 340, 471
Stets, J., 135, 341
Stoddart, K., 140
Stone, D., 228
Straus, M., 19, 132, 135, 198, 318, 319, 330, 333, 338, 340, 342, 343, 471
Sugarman, D., 26, 295, 337, 338n, 339, 341n
Sugarman, J., 250, 282, 299
Sugimoto, T., 330n
Sullivan, M., 296
Sullivan, T., 302
Surette, R., 11, 14n, 15, 17, 187
Sutherland, E., 185, 192, 223, 225–227, 378
Swift, E., 320
Sykes, G., 81, 127, 367
Szasz, A., 391, 392

Taft, P., 104
Takagi, P., 256
Tallmer, M., 371
Tannenbaum, F., 45n
Tanner, J., 12, 13
Tappan, P., 32, 55
Tardiff, K., 297
Taylor, C., 453
Taylor, I., 21n, 81, 164, 202, 243, 246, 258

Teplin, L., 186
Theoharis, A., 100
Thio, A., 399, 404, 405, 406, 408, 412, 415, 425, 426, 430, 436
Thomas, J,. 239n, 269
Thompson, K., 222
Thornberry, T., 6, 48
Thorne-Finch, R., 481, 482
Tifft, L., 136
Timmer, D., 165, 176, 190, 192, 344
Tittle, C., 138
Toby, J., 356
Toch, H., 167, 168
Tong, R., 259, 266
Tonry, M., 61, 445, 452
Travis, L., 157, 451
Trebach, A., 403
Tunnell, K., 100n, 169
Turk, A., 55, 78
Turner, J., 398
Tyler, G., 386
Tyler, T., 11

U

U.S. Department of Labor, 364
Ursel, J., 93

V

Vachhs, A., 119
Valverde, M., 258
van den Haag, E., 167
Van Duyne, P., 389
Venturelli, P., 397, 403, 405, 411, 413
Viano, E., 417
Visano, L., 141
Visher, C., 455
Vitiello, J., 389
Vito, G., 303
Voigt, L., 180, 181
Vold, G., 155, 160, 164, 184, 192, 205, 208, 215, 223, 225n, 388
Volovka, J., 155, 176n
Voss, H., 138

W

Walby, S., 91, 93
Waldo, G., 184
Walker, L., 317, 321, 322
Walker, S., 173
Walklate, S., 3, 4, 126, 363, 443, 447

Wallace, A., 291
Wallerstein, J., 134
Walton, P., 51, 164, 202, 243, 258
Warshaw, C., 317
Warshaw, R., 230, 349
Webster, C., 176
Weis, K., 48, 73
Weis, S., 73
Weisheit, R., 59
Wellisch, J., 425
Wessinger, C., 422
West, W. G., 5, 20, 22, 23, 24, 45, 48, 50, 68n, 220
White, J., 229
Whitehead, A., 26
Wiatrowski, M., 220
Wicharaya, T., 463
Wicker, T., 73n
Wideman, J., 43n, 60
Widom, C., 479, 480

Wilkins, L., 63
Williams, F., 164, 165, 208, 220, 231
Williams, J., 138
Williams, K., 175
Wills, T., 344n
Wilson, J., 153, 155, 166, 181, 188, 252, 255, 256, 294, 467, 477
Wilson, M., 288, 291, 301, 307
Wilson, W., 190, 297
Winick, C., 411–412, 427, 433
Winkler, A., 216, 380
Wisniewski, N., 135, 229
Witters, W., 411
Wodarski, J., 422
Wolfgang, M., 289, 310, 311
Wright, J., 84, 85, 135, 416, 418, 460, 461
Wright, L., 333

Wrightsman, L., 58, 119
Wyle, C., 134

Y

Yablonsky, L., 136
Yates, G., 171
Yeager, P., 359, 375–376, 378
Young, J., 51, 54, 81, 117, 164, 202, 239n, 243, 246, 247–249, 250, 255, 256, 258, 449

Z

Zalenko, K., 427
Zatz, M., 87n, 89
Zawitz, M., 120, 125, 130
Zellner, W., 5
Zilbergeld, B., 195
Zimring, F., 167

A

Abortion clinics, murders at, 95
Absolute deprivation, 249
Abuse, social support for,
    347–348. *See also* Battering;
    Woman abuse
Academic criminology, 240–243
"Academic McCarthyism," 241
Academic research, distrust of, 143
Academy of Criminal Justice
    Sciences, 242
Acid, 412–413
Acquaintance rape, 229, 230. *See
    also* Date rape
Acquired immunodeficiency
    syndrome (AIDS), 406
    drug use and, 415–416, 417,
        420
Adaptation modes, 205–210
Addiction. *See also* Drugs; Drug
    use
    crack cocaine, 407
    learning, 214
    morphine, 409
Administrative criminologists, 255
Administrative law, 42
Adult crime, in self-report surveys,
    135
Advertising, false, 374–375
Affluence. *See also* Class
    drug use and, 430, 436
    societal responses to, 47
African-American males
    criminal justice and, 60

drugs and, 61
homicide and, 250, 281
incarceration rates for,
    171–172, 451–453
lynching of, 103
wife abuse among, 340
African-Americans
    biases against, 48–49
    cocaine use by, 405, 406, 407
    crime definition and, 38
    delinquency among, 138
    drug use by, 403–404, 427
    gun homicide and, 299–300
    media exposure of, 10
    murder arrests of, 294
    murder rate for, 286, 293
    risk of homicide for, 295–296
    vehicle theft and, 131
African-American women
    drug abuse treatment for, 419
    oppression of, 93–94
    relationship violence and,
        324–325
Age
    dating violence and, 341
    drug use and, 426–427
    as a risk marker for homicide,
        291–294
    as a risk marker for wife abuse,
        339
Aggression
    media as a source of, 17
    television and, 15
"Aging-out" process, 455

Aid to Families with Dependent
    Children (AFDC), 462
AIDS (acquired immunodeficiency
    syndrome), 406
    drug use and, 415–416, 417,
        420
Alcohol
    birth defects and, 417
    effects of, 35–38, 401
    prohibition against, 34
    woman abuse and, 338, 347
Altruistic suicide, 201
American culture
    "democratic" ethos of,
        211–212
    wealth accumulation and, 205
American Revolution, 96–98
American Society of Criminology
    (ASC), 153, 242
Amish, crime among, 5
Amnesty International, 75,
    100–101, 157, 159
Amok rampages, 301
Angel dust, 412
Annenberg, Moe, 386
Anomic suicide, 201
Anomie, 201–202
    adaptation to, 205–210
Anomie theory, 202–210
    of corporate crime, 381–383
    women and, 216
Anti-abortion groups, 56, 416
Anti-abortion laws, 418

Antichoice movement, assassinations by, 95
Anticrime strategies, left realist, 248–249. *See also* Crime prevention
Arrests
of African-Americans, 138
based on stereotypes, 60
UCR reports of, 112–113, 114
Arrest statistics
for homicide, 291–292
inflation of, 123
Arson, 113, 391
Assassination
international, 157–159
political, 99
Assault
in dating relationships, 333
postseparation, 333
underreporting of, 132
Association for Humanist Sociology, 242–243
Attachment, social bond and, 219
Attempted crimes, 125
Attica State Prison riot, 73, 74
Auto industry, corporate crime in, 375–376

B

Barbiturates, 403
Barry, Marion, 412
Battered women, 319. *See also* Woman abuse
Battering, 291, 320
in lesbian relationships, 145–146
Bay of Pigs invasion, 389
Beccaria, Cesare, 160, 163–164
Behavior
criminalizing of, 33–38, 69, 76
free will and, 161
relationship to criminal definitions, 79
Belief, social bond and, 220
Bentham, Jeremy, 161, 164
Benzodiazephines, 403
Berkowitz, David (Son of Sam), 302
Biological theories, 176–182
critique of, 188–191
modern, 181–182
Black genocide, 281
Black Hand, 385

Blame
assessing, 165, 230
societal messages about, 119
for victimization, 447
Body-types theory, 179–180
Bombings, terrorist, 305
Bonding rituals, subcultural, 381
Boot camps, 450
"Born criminality," 177–182
Boston Strangler, 303
British Crime Survey, 23, 126
British Home Office, 23
Bronfman, Samuel, 386
Bruce, Lenny, 95
Bundy, Ted, 281, 301
Bureau of Justice Statistics, 23, 318
Burglary
defined, 111–112
in rural areas, 7
Bush, George, 468
Business elites. *See also* Corporate crime
instrumental view of, 82–83
punishment of, 86

C

California Psychological Inventory (CPI), 184
Canada
corporate pollution in, 371
critical criminology in, 243–245
homicides in, 282
male violence in, 332
opium laws in, 402
policy toward aboriginal children, 105
sexual assault legislation in, 88–89
Canadian Panel on Violence Against Women, 23
Canadian Political Economy Network, 244
Canadian Urban Victimization Survey, 23, 126
Capitalism
corporate crime and, 394
crime and, 247, 253–254
effect on women, 409
organized crime and, 388
Capitalism, Patriarchy, and Crime (Messerschmidt), 266–267
Capitalist interests, protection of, 85

Capital punishment, 70
classical views on, 165
deterrence and, 172–175
Capone, Al, 40
Castro, Fidel, 389
Catholics, violence against, 103
Causality, establishing, 19, 77
Causes of Delinquency (Hirschi), 221
Center for Family Life, 470
Central Intelligence Agency (CIA), syndicated crime and, 389
"Character contests," 283, 288
gun homicides and, 300
Chicago school, 313
Child abuse, 479, 480
surveys concerning, 133
Childhood experiences, importance of, 183
Children, domestic violence and, 478–480
China White, 420
Chinese-Americans, violence against, 103
Church-state alliance, 155
Citizen nonreporting, 117–122
Civil disobedience, 98–99
Civil law, 42, 68
corporate crime and, 355
Civil Rights Movement, 76, 98–99
Civil War, 98–99
Class. *See also* Status
criminology and, 48–50
law creation and, 77–78
socialist feminist view of, 266
woman abuse and, 351, 352
Class bias
in the criminal justice system, 44
in punishment, 75
Classical criminology, 159–165, 230
critique of, 169–176
impact on criminal justice, 164–165
views on punishment, 163–164
Class structure, maintenance of, 49–50
Class struggle, 82
Clinical criminologists, 176
Clockers, 281
Cloward, Richard, 213–215
Cocaine, 61, 404–408. *See also* Crack cocaine
fetal development and, 418
middle-class use of, 433

prevalence of, 422–424
societal distribution of, 424–428
surveys on, 423
violence and, 407
Cohen, Albert, 232
"Collective ignorance," 9
Collective incapacitation, 455
College campuses
crime on, 61, 453
sexual assault on, 229
Commercial crime, 363
Commitment, social bond and, 219
Common knowledge of crime, 8
Community-based crime prevention, 270, 477, 478
Community sanctions, 175–176
Conflict perspectives, 52, 76–90, 104
Marxist perspective, 81–90
Weberian conflict theories, 77–80
Conflict subcultures, 15, 214
Conflict Tactics Scale (CTS), 330
Conformity, as an adaptation mode, 206
Consensual crimes, 275
Consensus perspectives, 32–33, 52, 71–76, 104
Consent, defined, 58
Conservative criminologists, 55
Conspiracy theory, 85
"Constitutive criminology," 275
Consumers, violence against, 367–370
Consumer threats, gender-specific, 368–369
Context-specific model, 26
Continuous variable approach, 63
Contras, 99
Coping model, of drug use, 434–435
"Copping a plea," 75
"Copycat crime," 15–17
Corporate crime, 4, 23, 124, 190–191, 245, 250, 355–383, 387
costs of, 361
criminal law and, 83
defined, 356–358
distribution of, 375–376
economic, 372–375
lenient treatment of, 47–48
media coverage of, 9
Merton's view of, 208
penalties for, 74–75, 476

police data on, 111
policy proposals for, 474–477
prevalence of, 358–375, 393
prosecution of, 41
public awareness of, 362
relationship to syndicated crime, 385–389, 394
theories of, 376–383
types of, 358–375
versus white-collar crime, 356–357
victims of, 444
Corporate death rate, 285, 367
Corporate management, composition of, 380
Corporate masculinity, 380–381
Corporate pollution, 370–371
Corporate victimization survey, 362–363
Corporate violence, 364–371
Cosa Nostra, 383, 386, 387
Cost/benefit analysis, 161–162
deterrence and, 169–171
Courtesy stigma, 141
Courts, bias in, 44
Crack cocaine, 61, 406–408
African-Americans and, 427
prostitution and, 407–408
surveys on, 423
women's use of, 425
Crack whores, 407
Crime. *See also* Corporate crime; Organized crime; Political crime; Street crime; Violent crime
biological and psychological theories of, 176–191
biological correlates of, 188
broadening the definition of, 370
changing attitudes toward, 253
concern with, 3
endemic nature of, 197
fear of, 4, 118
functional nature of, 200–201
"hot spots" for, 307
individualistic theories of, 153–191
individual solutions to, 70
labeling of, 76
left idealist view of, 249–250
media as a cause of, 14–20
postmodern definition of, 275
problems in dealing with, 69–70
relationship to criminal law, 69
reporting of, 117–122, 130

as a social construct, 45–48
as a "social fact," 200–201
as a social issue, 11
socialist feminist theory of, 266
sociological perspectives on, 195–232
underestimating the extent of, 118
Crime and Human Nature (Wilson and Herrnstein), 181
Crime data
methods of gathering, 109–148
observational procedures for gathering, 139–148
official, 21–24
official police statistics, 110–111
Uniform Crime Reports (UCR), 111–125
victimization surveys, 125–133
Crime definition, 31–63
broadening, 43, 54
changes in, 38, 124–125
competition and, 78
critical approach to, 54
legalistic, 31, 32–43
limiting, 55
power structure and, 79
problems with, 54
societal reaction/labeling approach to, 43–51
Crime displacement, 449
Crime films, 186–188
Crime images, 3–27
media, 8–20
moral panics and, 11–14
official, 21–24
personal, 5–8
sociological, 24–26
Crime legislation, 197. *See also* Law
Crime prevention
community-based, 249, 477, 478
multiplier effects for, 473
policy recommendations for, 441–485
Crime prevention programs, 444
Crime rate, changes in, 456, 457
Crime reduction, prisons and, 454–457
Crime reporting, hierarchical principle in, 113–114. *See also* Crime data
"Crimes of honor," 309

"Crimes of the powerful," 54, 124, 191
  left idealism and, 251–252
Crime statistics, 21–24
  inflation of, 123
  manipulation of, 252
  study of, 50
Crime trends, charting, 116
Criminal behavior
  learning of, 225–226
  media shaping of, 15
Criminal careers, determinants of, 170
Criminal conformity role, 213–214
"Criminal corporations," 383. *See also* Corporate crime
Criminality
  gender as a predictor of, 259
  group views of, 56–63
  personality as a determinant of, 192–193
  societal change and, 239
  societal role in, 198
Criminalization, increase in, 70
Criminal justice
  classical influence on, 164–165
  university departments of, 241
Criminal justice agencies, study of, 50
Criminal justice system
  biases in, 44, 48
  inequality in, 62
  influences on, 51
  treatment of women in, 54
  victimization by, 119, 122
Criminal labeling, 5–6, 80
Criminal law, 67–105. *See also* Law
  history of, 68–71
  justice and, 69
  power and, 80
Criminal negligence, 366–367
Criminals, cost/reward analysis by, 169–171
Criminal subculture, 15, 214
Criminal wrongs, versus civil wrongs, 68–69
Criminogenic corporate subcultures, 378
Criminogenic traits, 154–155
Criminological research, role of, 50
Criminologists
  conservative, 55
  crime definitions by, 63
  feminist, 54

peacemaking, 54
  study groups of, 44
Criminology
  academic, 240–243
  class and race in, 48–50
  classical, 159–165
  critical, 52–56, 237–276
  diversity of theories in, 154
  feminist, 260
  funding sources in, 241–242
  gender-blind approach to, 258
  neoclassical, 166–168
  nonsociological theories in, 154–155
  nonviolent, 269–270
  postmodern, 273–276
  radical, 53–55
Criminology as Peacemaking (Pepinsky and Quinney), 271
Critical criminologists, 63
  objects of study for, 55–56
  policy proposals of, 463–474
Critical criminology, 52–56, 237–276
  defined, 238–245
  influence of, 242
Cross-cultural approach, 63
Cultural genocide, 105
"Cut-and-slash" films, 186–188
Cycle of violence, 477

D

Dahmer, Jeffrey, 281, 301
Dalkon Shield case, 369
Damiens, Robert Francois, 158
"Dark figure of crime," 125
Darwin, Charles, 178
Data collection
  for corporate crime, 359–363
  value of, 24
Data sources, checking, 110
"Data triangulation," 26, 145–147
Date rape, 230
Dating relationships
  abuse in, 336, 345
  assault in, 333
  violence in, 341
Day care, policy proposals for, 469–471
Death penalty, support for, 173–174. *See also* Capital punishment
Death squads, Latin American, 101–102, 157–159
Defamilied girls, 170

Deindustrialization, 466
Delinquency, 138
  characteristics of, 211
  Cohen's theory of, 210–213
  differential opportunity of, 213–215
  female, 222
  power-control theory and, 221
  social bond theory and, 220
  studying, 136
Delinquency and Opportunity (Cloward and Ohlin), 213
Demarginalization, 249
Department of Justice, Law, and Society (American University), 244
De Salvo, Albert, 303
"Designer drugs," 413
Deterrence
  capital punishment and, 172–175
  community sanctions and, 175–176
  cost/reward analysis and, 169–171
  criminal justice system and, 166
  prison and, 167–168, 449–450
  punishment and, 162–164, 171–176
  purpose of, 164
  of woman abuse, 345, 348
Deviance
  creation of, 45–46
  media creation of, 13
  Merton's views on, 203, 205–210
  as a social construct, 47
  wider definitions of, 272
Differential association theory, 223, 225–227, 378
Differential opportunity theory, 213–215
"Direction of causality," 19
Disenfranchisement
  drug use and, 434
  murder and, 458
  predispositional theory and, 190–191
  societal responses to, 47
  street crime and, 466
  stress associated with, 469
  of young girls, 216
Domestic violence, 343. *See also* Woman abuse
"Dominance bonding," 26
Drug abuse, 397–436. *See also* Drugs; Drug use

Drug crimes, media coverage of, 9
Drug crisis, 237
"Drug culture," 397
Drug laws
    changes in, 33–38
    economic opportunity and, 40
Drug policy, race and, 452–453
Drugs
    criminalization of, 35, 119,
        399–404
    illegal, 404–415
    self-report surveys and, 135,
        136–137
    violence and, 72
Drug use
    decrease in, 411
    disenfranchisement and,
        458–459
    health problems associated with,
        415–416, 419–422, 437
    inner-city, 72
    penalties for, 410
    prevalence of, 398
    in prison, 453–454
    theories of, 428–436
Drug Use Forecasting (DUF)
    program, 137, 424
Dumping, defined, 369–370
Durkheim, Émile, 199–202

E

Ecological models, 227–232
Ecological theories, 233
    Chicago school of, 313
Economic bias, criminal labeling
    and, 49
"Economic brutality," 321
Economic corporate crimes,
    372–375
Economic inequality, 69
    murder and, 286–287
    street crime and, 6
    violent crime and, 296
Economic structure, reform of,
    192
Economic violence, 43
Economists, neoclassical theory
    and, 166
Economy, problems in, 465–466
Ecstasy, 412–413
Education, wife abuse and, 339
Egalitarian families, 222
Ego, defined, 182
Egoism, societal control of, 199
Egoistic suicide, 201

Elderly people
    fear of crime among, 7
    murder of, 308
Electrical Equipment Antitrust
    Cases, 360
Emancipation theory of female
    crime, 217–218
Emotional abuse, of women, 331
Employment, commitment to,
    465
English Convict, The (Goring), 179
Enlightenment period, 159, 160
Entrapment, 40
Environmentalism, 382, 391–392
Environment Canada, 371
Equality, in gender relations, 93.
    See also Inequality
Estrangement homicide, 291
Ethics, in observational studies,
    141, 147–148
Ethnicity
    crimes against, 102–104
    relationship to drug use,
        427–428
    as a risk marker for homicide,
        294–296
    woman abuse and, 340, 351
Ethnography, 26
Evolutionary studies, 178
Execution. *See also* Capital
    punishment
    prevalence of, 157
    for witchcraft, 156

F

"Fallacy of autonomy," 189
False advertising, 374–375
False confessions, 304
Family structure, workplace power
    and, 221–222
Family support, policy proposals
    for, 469–471
Family theories of criminality, 181
Family violence, 131
    criminogenic nature of,
        479–480
    curbing, 183
    policy proposals for, 477–484
Fatal Attraction, 188
Fatalistic suicide, 201
FBI Crime Clock, 115
Fear
    media exposure and, 10–11, 12
    of retaliation, 122
    of street crime, 448
    about vulnerability, 3

Federal Bureau of Investigation
    (FBI), 100
    crime definitions of, 118
Federal Bureau of Narcotics, 44
Federal government, law
    enforcement and, 400
Federal offenses, 124
Felicity calculus, 164
Felonies
    defined, 32n
    drug use and, 424
Female crime, 191, 216
    emancipation theory of,
        217–218
    increase in, 262
Female criminals, movie portrayals
    of, 188
Female delinquency, 222
Female drug users, pregnancy and,
    416–419
Females, aggression toward, 17.
    See also Woman abuse
Female subordination,
    maintenance of, 92
Femicide, 309–310, 323
    intimate, 290
Feminism, 258–268
    defined, 258–260
    labeling theory and, 224–225
    law and, 57, 90–94
    power-control theory and, 222
    variations of, 260–268
Feminist criminology, 54, 238,
    260
Feminist literature, 90, 91
Feminist postmodernism,
    275–276
Feminist theory
    attacks on, 351–352
    of homicide, 309–310
    routine activities, 229
    of woman abuse, 350–352
Fetal alcohol syndrome, 417, 419
Fetal development, cocaine use
    and, 418
Fetal rights groups, 418
"Fetal rights" laws, 416–417
Field observation, 139–140
Film Recovery Systems case,
    365–366
Financial damages, 68
First-degree murder, 283
Folk devils, 13
Food additives, 368
Ford Pinto case, 362, 368,
    475–476
Fraternity rituals, 349–350

Freedoms, curtailment of, 447–448
Free will, 161–162
Freud, Sigmund, 404
Freudian approaches, 182–183

G

Gacy, John Wayne, 281, 301, 302
Gang rape, 230, 349
Gangs, 6
  imprisoning, 450
Gang wars, 214
"Gay bashing," 104
Gayford, J. J., 342
Gay relationships, battering in, 320
Gender
  defined, 90, 260
  drug use and, 425–426
  radical feminist view of, 266
  socialist feminist view of, 266
Gender bias, in strain theory, 215–217
Gender discrimination, 216
"Gendered strategy of action," 381
Gender inequality, 258, 261, 265
  pro-feminist men and, 482–483
Gender politics, role of the state in, 92
Gender-specific consumer threats, 368–369
General deterrence, 168
Genetic abnormalities theory, 180
Genetics, crime and, 189
Genocide, 102
Geographic variations, as risk markers for homicide, 296–297
Gestapo, 102
Girls
  disenfranchisement of, 216
  institutionalization of, 59
  sexual abuse of, 170
Girls: Delinquency and Justice (Chesney-Lind and Sheldon), 225
"Git Tuff on Crime" mood, 165. *See also* "Imprisonment binge"
Goals-means disjunction, 203–205
Goring, Charles, 179
Gotti, John, 394

Government
  power abuses by, 53
  relationship to organized crime, 389
  victimization surveys by, 126
Government crime data, 21–24
Government elites, instrumental view of, 82–83
Government regulation, of corporations, 379, 382
Government wrongdoing, 245
  prosecution of, 41
Graffiti writers, studies of, 146–147
"Green crimes," 370
Groups
  crimes against, 96, 102–104
  delinquency and, 211
Group violence, 189–190
Gun control, 300
Gun homicide, 297–300

H

Hallucinogenic drugs, 412–413
Hancock, John, 384
Handgun murders, 298
Harrison Act of 1914, 410
Hate crimes, 102–104, 105
Health and safety legislation, 85–86
Health care, 254
Health hazards
  of drug use, 419–422, 437
  occupational, 361
  reproductive, 361–362
Hearst, William Randolph, 414
Hedonism, delinquency and, 211
Helms, Jesse, 35
Heroin, 402–403, 408–412
  overdoses of, 420
  prevalence of, 422–424
  smoking, 416
  use distribution of, 424–428
Heroin addicts, female, 434, 435–436
Heterosexuality, institutionalization of, 91
Hierarchical principle, 113–114
Hinckley, John, 15, 99
Hiroshima, bombing of, 95, 100
Hirschi, Travis, 219–221, 233
Hispanic-Americans
  criminal justice system and, 60
  drug violations by, 404
  imprisonment of, 451
  vehicle theft and, 131

Historical inertia, 238
Hitler, Adolf, 94, 180
Hobbes, Thomas, 71, 161–162
Holsted, William, 411
Homelessness
  battering and, 471–472
  crime victimization and, 123, 473–474
  among youths, 170–171
Homicide, 69. *See also* Gun homicide
  African-Americans and, 250, 281
  arrest statistics for, 291–292
  cocaine-related, 407
  corporate, 285
  defined, 282–285
  economic and racial variables in, 286–287
  feminist theories of, 309–310
  inequality and, 312–314
  intrasexual competitive, 288
  justifiable, 284
  official data on, 21
  risk markers of, 287–297
  spousal, 288, 289–291
  subculture of violence and, 310–312
  theft-related, 309
  theories of, 306–314
  in the United States, 196, 297–300
Honored Society, 385
Hooten, Earnest A., 179
Hoover, J. Edgar, 100, 123
Horton, Willie, 452, 468
Housing assistance, policy proposals for, 471–474
Huberty, James Oliver, 305–306, 307
Humanistic philosophers, 162
Human Justice Collective, 244
Human rationality, 161–162
Human rights
  evolution of, 159–160
  violations of, 54
Humans, egoistic nature of, 199
Hussein, Saddam, 94–95
Hypermasculinity, 19

I

Id, defined, 182
Illegitimate opportunity structure, 15, 429–430
"Imprisonment binge," 172, 450, 468

Incarceration rates. *See also* Prisons
    comparative, 171–172
    increase in, 253
Income, wife abuse and, 338–339
Index crimes, 112, 113, 117
    selection of, 124
    statistics on, 115
India, femicide in, 310
Individualism, competitive, 394
Individualistic theories, 153–191
    biological, 176–182
    classical, 159–165
    neoclassical, 166–168
    psychological, 182–191
Individual treatment, 457–463
Inequality
    class, 205
    in the criminal justice system,
      62
    drug use and, 428, 433–436,
      459
    gender, 258, 261, 265,
      482–483
    homicide and, 312–314
    law and, 104
    Marxism and, 313
    relationship to crime, 69, 70,
      463
    social and economic, 190
Infanticide, 310
Infant mortality, 174, 254
Informed consent, 147–148
Inner city
    crime in, 189, 441–442
    drug use in, 72, 427–428,
      433–434
    violence in, 311
Innovation, as an adaptation
    mode, 206–208
Inquisition, The, 155–156
Institutionalized means, 204
Institutions, functionality of,
    200
Instrumentalist theory, 251
Instrumental Marxism, 82–83
    critique of, 83–85
Insurance, theft, 120–121
Interactionist theories, 223–227
Interest groups, competition
    among, 76, 78
International accords, 100
International Association of Chiefs
    of Police (IACP), 112
Interviewing. *See* Surveys;
    Victimization surveys
Intimate femicide, 290, 323

Intimate relationships
    as a risk marker for homicide,
      289–291
    violence in, 317–352, 446
Intrasexual competitive homicide,
    288
Involuntary manslaughter,
    283–284
Involvement, social bond and,
    219–220
Italian-Americans, syndicated
    crime among, 385
IV drug use, 406, 408, 415–416
Ivins, Molly, 484

J

Japanese-Americans, internment
    of, 101, 103–104
Jews, pogroms against, 102
Job Corps, 468
Job creation, policy proposals for,
    465–467
Job training, 467
Journal of Marriage and the Family,
    319
Jukes family, 181
"Jury of Her Peers, A," 57
Justice
    criminal law and, 69
    punitive, 271
Justifiable homicide, 284
Juvenile court, African-Americans
    in, 62
Juvenile delinquency, 479. *See also*
    Delinquency
    rates of, 137–138
Juvenile murder, handguns and,
    299–300
Juveniles
    crime among, 293
    homicide and, 291–294
    sentencing of, 271–272

K

Kallikak family, 181
Kennedy, John F., 99
Kennedy, Joseph P., 386
Kennedy, Robert, 99
KGB, 102
King, Martin Luther, Jr., 98–99
Knowledge sources, 11
Koop, C. Everett, 35
Koresh, David, 102
Kotchian, Carl, 386
Ku Klux Klan, 157

L

Labeling stigmatization, 224
Labeling theorists, 45, 63
Labeling theory, 62. *See also*
    Societal reaction/labeling
    approach
    women and, 224–225
Laboratory studies, problems with,
    17–18
Labor strife, 104
La Camorro, 385
Larceny, 114
Latin America, death squads in,
    101–102
Law. *See also* Criminal law; Laws
    conflict perspectives on, 76–90
    consensus perspectives on,
      71–76
    dependence on, 67
    differing views on, 63
    economic factors in, 84
    feminist perspectives on,
      90–94
    as an instrument of power, 77
    male point of view in, 91–92
    Marxist perspectives on, 81–90
    political crimes and, 94–104
    radical feminist theory of, 92
    sexual bias in, 59
    social order and, 71, 72
    structural contradictions theory
      and, 87–89
    women and, 57–59
"Law-and-order" agendas, 255,
    272
"Law and order" criminology,
    241
Law enforcement
    anti-feminist nature of, 481
    federal government and, 400
    illegal forms of, 40
    radical feminist perspective on,
      92
    sexist, 119
    targeting by, 62
Law enforcement approach,
    support for, 253
Law Enforcement Assistance
    Administration, 241
Laws
    anti-abortion, 418
    changes in, 33–38
    victim-compensation, 444
Learned helplessness, 322,
    326–327

Left idealism, 246
    change strategies in, 252–254
    left realist attacks on, 249–255
    reform and, 254
Left realism, 238, 245–257
    basic principles of, 247–249
    critique of, 256–257
Left realist criminologists, 54
Legal aid lawyers, 75
Legalistic crime definition, 31,
    32–43
    challenges to, 41–43
Legalistic theorists, 63
Legal power, abuse of, 53
Legal sanctions, increasing, 70
Legal system, Bentham's views on,
    164
Legislation
    as consensus building, 32
    process of, 52–53
Legislature
    control of, 53
    influence on, 69
Legitimate opportunity structure,
    15, 215
Lepine, Marc, 281, 305, 309
Lesbians
    relationship violence among,
        145–146, 320, 324
    violence against, 104
Liberal feminism, 261–263
"Liberation thesis," 262
Lifestyle
    influence on crime, 228
    sexual assault and, 229
L'Unione Siciliana, 385
Local crime surveys, 248
"Lombrosian underground," 261
Lombroso, Cesare, 178–179, 189
Love Canal disaster, 362, 371
Lower-class crime, anomie and,
    210. See also Class;
    Disenfranchisement
LSD, 412–413
Lucas, Henry Lee, 304
Luciano, Charles ("Lucky"), 389
Lynchings, 103, 157

M

MacKinnon, Catharine, 91–92
Mafia, 383, 385
Mainstream criminologists, focus
    of, 245
Mala in se crimes, 39
Mala prohibita crimes, 39
Male crime, theories of, 57

Male "dominance bonding," 26
Male intimates, violence by, 317
Male peer support
    relationship violence and,
        344–350
    sexual exploitation and, 229
    for violence, 337
Male power, institutionalization
    of, 91–92
Male prostitution, 141–142
Males. See also Men
    drug use among, 425–426
    homicide arrest rate for, 292
    victimization of, 130
Male-to-female violence, 330
    risk markers for, 337–338
Male violence
    group support for, 347–348
    radical feminism and, 350
Maliciousness, delinquency and,
    211
Manslaughter, 281, 283
Manson, Charles, 281, 301
Marijuana, 413–414
    criminalizing of, 38
    problems related to, 401
Marijuana laws, 34
Marijuana Tax Act of 1937, 401,
    413–414
Marquez, Mario, 100
Marx, Karl, 81
Marxism
    instrumental, 82–85
    structural, 85–87
    women's interests and, 91
Marxist criminology, 237
Marxist feminism, 263–264
Masculine image, 170
Masculinity. See also Male peer
    support
    corporate, 380–381
    socialization into, 347–348
Mass murder, 281, 300–306
    by women, 301–302
Material success, means of
    achieving, 204–205
MDMA, 412–413
Media
    as a cause of crime, 14–20
    knowledge of crime via, 8–20
    moral panics and, 12, 251
    serial and mass murder and, 301
Media consumption, levels of, 10
Media violence, cumulative effect
    of, 20
Men. See also Males
    battered, 480

fetal endangerment by,
    417–418
    pro-feminist, 480–484
    role in reducing woman abuse,
        481–484
Men's groups
    backlash politics in, 483
    peer support in, 347–348
Mental illness, 185–186
    violence and, 343
Merton, Robert K., 202–210,
    232
Methodological narcissists, 148
Mexican-Americans
    crime definition and, 38
    drug laws and, 401, 414
Middle class, drug use by, 433
Middle-class social structure,
    maintenance of, 49–50
Militias, right-wing, 400
Minnesota Multiphasic Personality
    Inventory (MMPI), 183–184
Minorities
    crime definition and, 38
    criminal labeling of, 5–6
    drug criminalization and,
        403–404, 405
    drug use among, 427–428
    law and, 60–62
    in the prison population, 62
    structural Marxism and, 86
Minority women. See also African-
    American women
    legal bias against, 59
    oppression of, 93–94
Missing persons statistics, 21
Mob, tax evasion by, 388
Mods youth subculture, 13, 14
Money laundering, 388, 393
Monitoring the Future Project,
    423
Monroe, Marilyn, 17
Moral community, 313–314
Morality, private, 39
"Moral panics," 10, 11–14
    media-generated, 251
Mormons, violence against, 103
Morphine, 408–409
"Mothers' liberation," 222
Motor vehicle theft, 131
Movies
    femicide themes in, 310
    violent, 186–188
Multicausal theory, 78
Multiple data methods, 145
"Multiplier effects," 473

Murder, 281. *See also* Homicide
   in American folk history, 301
   death penalty as a deterrent to,
     173, 174
   definition of, 56–57
   differing views on, 73
   as an intraracial crime, 295
   media coverage of, 9
   risk for, 189
   trends in the United States,
     286–287
   of women, 281
Murderers, typical, 282
Murder rate, increase in, 293
Murder victims, ages of, 293
My Lai massacre, 73

N

National Center for the Analysis of
   Violent Crime, 303
National Commission on Product
   Safety, 367
National Crime Analysis Program,
   293
National Crime Victimization
   Survey (NCVS), 322, 333,
   339, 456
   versus *Uniform Crime Reports*,
     131
National Deviancy Conference,
   243
National Drug Control Policy,
   460–461
National Foundation for Family
   Research and Education, 470
National Household Survey on Drug
   Abuse, 422–423
National Incident-Based
   Reporting Program
   (NIBERS), 125
National Organization for
   Women, 261
Native American rebellions, 98
Native Americans
   attacks on, 103
   fetal alcohol syndrome and, 419
   murder and, 295
   in the prison population, 62
Negativism, delinquency and, 211
Neoclassical criminology,
   166–168
   critique of, 169–176
Neo-Nazi groups, 210. *See also*
   Skinheads
New Criminologies in Canada
   (Fleming), 244

New Criminology, The (Taylor,
   Walton, and Young), 243,
   258
New Democratic Party, 84–85
NHI (No Human Involved)
   crimes, 123
1994 Crime Bill, 253, 355
Nonreporting, citizen, 117–122
   reasons for, 119–122
Nonsociological theories,
   154–155
Nonutilitarianism, delinquency
   and, 211
Normlessness, 201
Norms, breakdown of, 208
North, Oliver, 46, 99
North American Free Trade
   Agreement (NAFTA), 466
Nullum crimen sine poena, 68–69
"Number-crunching" research
   techniques, 25–26
Nuremburg Trials, 95
Nussbaum, Hedda, 342–343

O

Observational research, 139–148
   ethical problems in, 147–148
   funding of, 144
   limitations of, 143–148
   strengths of, 143
   types of, 139–143
Observer-as-participant
   observation, 141–143
Occupational crime. *See* White-
   collar crime
Occupational diseases, 361
"Offenderology," 126, 134
Offenders
   definitions of, 45–46
   retaliation by, 122
Ohlin, Lloyd, 213–215
Oil companies, corporate crime in,
   375
Oklahoma City bombing, 305
"Old boy" network, 380
On Crimes and Punishment
   (Beccaria), 160
Ontario Native Women's
   Association, 340
Opiates, 401–402, 410
Opium laws, 402
Organic anomalies, as sources of
   crime, 176–177
Organized crime, 383–393. *See*
   also Syndicated crime
   defined, 387–388

   drug laws and, 40
   economic impact of, 389
   infiltration of legitimate
     business, 389–393
   network model of, 392
Oswald, Lee Harvey, 99
"Overcriminalization," 40, 41
Overt price fixing, 372

P

Panopticon, 161
Parks, Rosa, 38, 98–99
Participant observation, 26,
   140–141
Patriarchal authority, challenges to,
   344
Patriarchal families, 221–222
Patriarchy, 84
   defined, 90
   femicide in, 310
   social, 345–346
   social relations and, 91–92,
     265, 266
   theories of, 351
   woman abuse and, 324, 337
PCP, 412
Peacemaking criminologists, 54,
   79
   reconciliation programs of, 445
Peacemaking criminology, 238,
   268–273
   practical applications of,
     270–273
   principles of, 269–270
Peer groups
   dating abuse and, 345
   influence of, 189, 190
Peer support model, modified,
   345, 346
Penal process, escalation of, 70
People, as objects of moral panics,
   12
Perceptions, media influence on, 9
Personality tests, 183–185
Personality theories, 182–186
Personality trait theory, 183–185
Personal troubles, public issues
   and, 197
Pharmaceutical industry, corporate
   crime in, 376
Phrenology, 178
Pogroms, 102
Police
   community control of, 249
   crime data from, 21
   crime-fighting plan of, 36–37

Police *(continued)*
    inflation of statistics by, 123
    killing by, 284
    repressive practices of, 252–253
Police data, flaws in, 25
Policy recommendations,
    441–485
    for individual treatment,
        457–463
    for prisons, 449–457
    progressive, 463–474
    from special commissions, 24
    target-hardening, 445–449
Political assassination, 96
Political crime, 67, 124
    categorizing, 105
    defined, 94–96
    examples of, 97
    law and, 94–104
Political damage control, 24
Political Economy of Crime
    (MacLean), 244
Political executions, 101
Politics
    imprisonment and, 450
    victimization surveys and, 133
Pollard, Roosevelt, 75–76
Pollution, corporate, 370–371
Pol Pot regime, 102
Poor families, support for, 470
Pornography
    aggressive, 17
    political tolerance and, 19
    sexual violence and, 18–20
Positivist scientists, 178
Postmodern criminology,
    273–276
Postmodernism, feminist,
    275–276
Postseparation violence, 333,
    339–340
Poverty
    criminalization of, 43
    feminization of, 262
    left idealist view of, 249–250
    prostitution and, 170–171
Power. *See also* Male power
    criminal law and, 80
    law as an instrument of, 77, 81
    legal development and, 78
    struggle for, 52
Power-control theory, 221–223
Predatory sexual assault, 230
Predispositional criminogenic
    traits, 154–155
Predispositional theories, 176,
    189–191

Preemptive deterrence, 249
Pregnancy, criminalization of,
    416–419
Premenstrual syndrome (PMS),
    180–181
Prescription drugs, 402–403
President's Crime Commission,
    388
Price-fixing, 372–374
Primary and secondary deviance,
    theory of, 223, 224–225
Primer in Radical Criminology, A
    (Lynch and Groves), 243
Prison boom, 456. *See also*
    "Imprisonment binge"
Prison population
    minorities in, 60
    rise in, 61–62, 268
Prisons
    crime reduction and, 454–457
    as a deterrent, 167–168,
        449–450
    drugs and, 418, 453–454
    failure of, 449–457
    increased spending on, 468
    use of, 171–172
Prison sentences, long-term, 70
Private property, criminal law and,
    70–71
Private security industry, 448–449
Pro-feminist men, 480–484
Progressive Era, 472
Prohibition, 34, 52–53
    syndicated crime and, 385
Property crimes, 16
    female, 262
    as index crimes, 113
    media and, 17
    rates of, 197, 456, 457
    reporting of, 120
    solving, 121
    women and, 217–218
Prostitution
    crack cocaine and, 407–408
    drug dependence and, 421–422
    legislation concerning, 40
    male, 141–142
    poverty and, 170–171
Protection devices, 3–4
Psychoanalytic theory, 182–183
Psychological abuse, of women,
    321
Psychological theories, 182–191
    critique of, 188–191
    popular support for, 186–188
    of relationship violence,
        342–344

Psychopathic scale, 184
Public interests, consensus theory
    and, 73–74
Public policy, laboratory studies
    and, 18
Puffery, defined, 374–375
Punishment
    changing attitudes toward, 253
    characteristics and purpose of,
        162–164
    civil versus criminal, 69
    classical view of, 163–164
    of corporate crime, 355, 476
    decrease in the use of, 157
    deterrence and, 171–176
    history of, 155–159
    racial and class bias in, 75
    state monopoly over, 156
Punitive justice, 271

Q

Quasar Petroleum case, 365
Quinney, Richard
    conflict theory of, 79

R

Race
    crimes against, 102–104
    in criminology, 48–50
    death penalty and, 173
    drug laws and, 403–404
    drug policy and, 452–453
    murder and, 286
    relationship to drug use,
        427–428
    as a risk marker for homicide,
        294–296
    violent crime and, 296
    wife abuse and, 340
    woman abuse and, 351
Racial inequality, 69
    homicide and, 313
    law and, 105
    street crime and, 6
Racial segregation, laws enforcing,
    38
Racial superiority, 180
Racism
    criminality theory and,
        181–182
    criminalization of, 43
    in the criminal justice system,
        44
    criminal labeling and, 49
    in punishment, 75
Racketeering, 383

Radford, Jill, 92
Radical criminology, 53–55, 237
Radical feminism, 91–92,
    264–266
  critique of, 92–94
  woman abuse and, 350
Radical realism. *See* Left realism
Radical structural change, 210
Ramirez, Richard, 301
Random-digit-dialing
    interviewing, 133
Random sample survey, 330
Rape
  definition of, 124–125
  lowering the risk of, 446
  reporting of, 122–123
  societal attitudes and, 449
  spousal, 348–349
  survey questions about, 132
Rape and Inequality
    (Schwendinger), 263
Rape law, 58, 88–89
Rape rate
  in capitalist societies, 263–264
  pornography and, 19
Rape victims, treatment by the
    criminal justice system, 119
Rational choice theory, 230–232,
    233
Rave culture, 413
Ray, James Earl, 99
Reaction formation, 212
Reagan, Ronald
  assassination attempt on, 15, 99
  racist politics of, 468
  subsidized housing under, 472–
    473
Reasonable man criterion, 57–58
Reasonable woman criterion, 58
Rebellion, as an adaptation mode,
    209–210
Reconciliation programs, 270
Redlining practices, 391
Reform Era, 409
Reform Party, 470, 471
Regulatory agencies, 359
Regulatory legislation, 84, 86
Rehabilitation, 231
  limitations of, 461
Rehabilitation programs, 459–460
Relationships, sexual assault in,
    331
Relationship violence, theories of,
    341–352. *See also* Woman
    abuse
Relative deprivation, 248, 250,
    312

Religious affiliation, wife abuse
    and, 340
Religious violence, 103
Repeat offenders, imprisonment
    of, 455
Reporting. *See also* Nonreporting
  to the police, 21–22
  rates of, 131
Reproductive health hazards,
    361–362
Research. *See also* Crime data;
    Observational research
  funding of, 144
  relevance of, 109
  on woman abuse, 258
Research designs, 26
Research methods
  choice of, 63
  left realist, 248
Resources, misallocation of, 462
Retreatism
  as an adaptation mode, 209
  drug use and, 429
  among youths, 213
Retreatist subculture, 15
*Rich Get Richer and the Poor Get
    Prison, The* (Reiman), 48,
    192
Right realism, 255–256
Riots, urban, 103
Risk markers
  for dating violence, 341
  for homicide, 287–297
  for male-to-female violence,
    337–338
Risk-taking behavior, 221
Ritualism, as an adaptation mode,
    209
Robber barons, 385–386
Robbery, disenfranchisement and,
    250. *See also* Property crimes
Rockefeller, Nelson, 74
Rockers subculture, 13, 14
Routine activities theory,
    227–230, 233, 306–309,
    314
Ruling class
  conflict in, 84
  laws against, 85–86
Russian republic, incarceration
    rate in, 172

S

Salvi, John C., III, 56
Sampling, 127
Sanctions, community, 175–176

Saturation model, of drug use, 435
Savings and loan (S&L) scandal,
    373, 387, 393
Scapegoating, 156
School of Justice Studies (Arizona
    State University), 244
Secondary deviance, 224
Second-degree murder, 283
Security industry, 448–449
Selective incapacitation, 454, 455
Self-report studies, 24–25
  responsibility for, 137
Self-report surveys, 48, 134–139
  costs of, 135–136
  on drug use, 422–423
  validity of, 136–139
Sentencing
  of juveniles, 271–272
  long-term, 70
  of women, 146
Sentencing Project, 171
Serial murder, 300–306
Serial murderers, 281
  exaggerations about, 304
  media panic over, 303
Severe violence index, 330
Sex
  drug use and, 425–426
  as a risk marker for homicide,
    288
Sexism, criminalization of, 43
Sexual assault, 18, 58
  on college campuses, 229
  legislation concerning, 88–89
  lifestyle factors in, 229
  in relationships, 331
Sexual bias, in applying the law, 59
Sexual exploitation, of women,
    229
Sexual mores, radical feminism
    and, 91
Sexual politics, 91–92
Sexual relations, criminalization
    of, 44
Sexual violence, 18–20
Shame, as an effective deterrent,
    175–176
Sheldon, William, 179–180
Simon, Rita, 217
Simpson, O. J., 75, 190
Singapore, deterrence in, 168
Single parents, 469
Sirhan, Sirhan, 99
Situational crime prevention, 446
Skinheads, 102
  observational studies of, 144,
    145

Smoking, dangers of, 35
Social Basis of Law (Comack and Brickey), 244
Social bond theory, 219–221, 233
   drug use and, 433
Social change
   crime reduction via, 239
   structural contradictions theory and, 90
Social conditions, as a cause of crime, 460–461
Social contract, 159
Social control, 71
   law as, 80
   oppressive, 272
Social control theories, 218–223
   power-control theory, 221–223
   social bond theory, 219–221
Social disapproval, as a deterrent, 175–176
Social disorganization, 313
Social forces, influence of, 189
Social inequality. *See* Inequality
Socialist feminism, 266–268
Social learning theory, drug use and, 430–432
Social order
   capital punishment and, 174
   conflict perspective on, 76
   law and, 71, 72
   structural Marxism and, 86–87
Social patriarchy, 345–346
Social Reality of Crime (Quinney), 79
Social reformers, 159–161
Social relations, patriarchy and, 91–92
Social Security, 462
Social services, policy proposals for, 467–474
Social structure
   as a cause of crime, 484–485
   elements of, 204
   reform of, 192
"Social Structure and Anomie" (Merton), 202–203
Social support, relationship violence and, 344–350
Societal reaction/labeling approach, 43–51, 223
   critique of, 50–51
Society for the Study of Social Problems (SSSP), 242
Sociological crime knowledge, 24–26
Sociological imagination, 196–198

Sociological perspectives, 195–232
   ecological models, 227–232
   interactionist theories, 223–227
   social control theories, 218–223
   strain theories, 198–218
Solicitor General of Canada, 23
Special commissions, 23–24
Specific deterrence, 167–168
Sports violence, 17
Spousal homicide, 288, 289–291
Spousal rape, 348–349
Spousal violence, 59
   defined, 321
Square of crime, 247–248
Staged activity analysis, 142–143
"Stake in conformity," 356
State
   crimes against, 96–98
   crimes by, 96, 100–102
   function of, 71
   left idealist theory of, 251
   Marxist view of, 82
   punishment as the province of, 156
   role in gender politics, 92
   as the site of class struggle, 84–85
   structural Marxism and, 87
   subordination of women by, 90
State Control (Ratner and McMullan), 244
Statistical definition approach, 63
Statistics. *See also* Crime data
   on index crimes, 115
   inflation of, 123
   manipulation of, 22–23
   versus self-report studies, 25
Status. *See also* Class
   dating violence and, 341
   drug use and, 427
   for female drug users, 434
   legal development and, 78
   young men and, 211
Status frustration, 212, 214
Status model, of drug use, 434
Steinberg, Joel, 342–343
Stereotypes, arrests based on, 60
Sterilization programs, 182
"Stitch rule," 320, 479
Strain-subcultural theory, 211
Strain theory, 198–218, 232–233
   Cohen's theory of delinquent boys, 210–213
   differential opportunity of delinquency, 213–215
   drug use and, 429–430

Durkheim's, 199–202
   emancipation theory of female crime, 217–218
   gender bias in, 215–217
   Merton's anomie theory, 202–210
"Strawberries," 407
Street addicts, crime and, 421
Street crime
   class bias and, 23
   factors in, 165
   fear of, 448
   intraclass, intraracial nature of, 250
   left realism and, 245–246
   mainstream criminology and, 55
   murder as, 285
   policy proposals for, 466–467, 477–484
   rate of, 189
   in the United States, 69
   victims of, 443–444
Street gangs, drug distribution by, 407
Street homicide, 291
Stress, in intimate relationships, 344
Structural contradictions theory, 87–89
   critique of, 89–90
Structural functionalism, 200
Structural Marxism, 85–86
   critique of, 86–87
Structured action theory, 268
   of corporate crime, 379–381
Structure model, of drug use, 435
Students, self-report surveys by, 135
Subcultural bonding rituals, 381
Subcultural theory, of corporate crime, 377–379
Subculture of the street, 170–171
Subculture of violence, 310–312, 314
Subcultures
   delinquent, 211, 212, 213
   radical, 210
   retreatist, 430
Suicide
   copycat effect and, 16–17
   Durkheim's views on, 201–202
   increase in, 299
Suicide (Durkheim), 201
"Suite crime," 4, 74, 210
Superego, defined, 182

Supernatural forces, as the cause of crime, 155–159
Super Soaker, moral panic about, 12
Survey questions, wording, 127, 137
Surveys
  local, 248
  random sample, 330
  on wife abuse, 334–335
"Sweetheart contracts," 388
Symbolic interactionist theory, 223–227
Syndicated crime, 384–389. See also Organized crime
  financial institutions and, 392–393
  legal response to, 387
  relationship to corporate crime, 385–389, 394

T

Tacit price fixing, 372
Targeted groups, media and, 13
Target hardening, 445–449, 484
Tax evasion, by the mob, 388
Teamsters Union, 392
Teenagers
  crime among, 5
  victimization of, 130
  worldview among, 8
Telephone victimization surveys, 133
Television, violence on, 14
Terrorist bombings, 305
"Testilying," 123
Theft-related homicide, 309
Theoretical perspective, choice of, 63
Therapist bias, 183
"Three strikes and you're out" law, 70
Tobacco, effects of, 35, 401
Tonton Macoutes, 102
Torture
  decrease in the use of, 157
  history of, 156
  as a political tool, 101
Toxic waste dumping, 370–371
  organized crime and, 391–392
Tragic Magic (Santiago), 412
Training programs, policy proposals for, 465–467
Treason, 96
Treatment programs, 459–460
Trifles (Glaspell), 57

Turf wars, 214
"Twinkie defense," 177

U

U.S. Attorney General's Commission on Pornography, 23
U.S. Department of Agriculture, 35
U.S. Department of Justice, 124, 241. See also National Crime Victimization Survey (NCVS)
  research funding by, 242
Underclass crime, 190
Underreporting, 131–132
  in self-report surveys, 136
  of woman abuse, 327
Unemployment, 465–467
  drug use and, 426
  wife abuse and, 339
Uniform Crime Reports (UCR), 21–22, 111–125, 456
  limitations of, 117–125
  versus National Crime Victimization Survey, 131
  origins and characteristics of, 112–116
  uses of, 116
United Nations Criminal Justice Information Network, 174
United States
  academic criminology in, 240–243
  endemic nature of crime in, 197
  homicide in, 297–300
  infant mortality in, 174
  murder trends in, 286–287
  proviolence ethic in, 103
  punitive atmosphere in, 171
  social structure of, 190
  street crime in, 69
Unsafe at Any Speed (Nader), 375–376
Urban murder rate, 296–297, 307
Urban renewal, 472–473
Urban riots, 103
Utilitarian philosophy, 164

V

Valachi, Joseph, 386
Valium, 403
Value consensus, 72
  social order and, 200
Values, homicide and, 311
Vendetta code, 57

Verri, Pietro, 160
"Victim as collective," 444
Victimization
  blame for, 119, 447
  fear of crime and, 6
  risk of, 4
  of women, 233
  survey conclusions about, 130–131
Victimization surveys, 23, 125–133, 308. See also National Crime Victimization Survey (NCVS)
  on corporate crime, 362–363
  difficulties associated with, 127
  limitations of, 131–133
  self-report surveys, 134–139
  telephone, 133
  types of, 126–127
  woman battering and, 330
Victimless crimes, 23, 39–41, 275, 392
Victim movement, 443–445
Victim-offender mediation, 270–271
"Victimogenic approach," 228
Victimology, 126–129
Victims
  compensation laws for, 444
  information on, 22
  rights of, 444–445
Vidrih, Tony, 361
Vietnam War, 53
Violence. See also Corporate violence; Woman abuse
  cocaine use and, 407
  among copycat criminals, 16
  corporate, 4
  drug-related, 72
  group, 189–190
  inequality and, 190
  in intimate relationships, 317–352, 446
  laws against, 73
  lynch-mob, 103
  as a male behavior, 312
  male peer support for, 337
  male-to-female, 93, 265
  measuring, 17–18
  media, 9, 10, 14, 15–16
  policy adoption and, 464
  pornography and, 18–20
  postseparation, 333
  prostitution and, 421–422
  psychological accounts of, 342
  subculture of, 310–312

Violent crime
  disenfranchisement and, 69
  drug laws and, 40
  female, 263
  inequality and, 296, 459
  reporting of, 130
  substance abuse and, 398
Violent homes, effects of,
  478–480
Voluntary manslaughter, 283
Vulnerability, lowering, 445–446

W

Waco massacre, 102
War crimes, 95
"War on Drugs," 61, 62, 119,
  399–400, 403, 422, 452
War on Poverty, 215
Wealth, concentration of, 254
Weber, Max, 77
Weberian conflict theories, 77–80
  critique of, 80–81
Welfare programs, 462
*What Is to Be Done About Law and
  Order?* (Lea and Young), 246
White Aryan Resistance, 145
White-collar crime, 23, 33, 124,
  245
  subtlety of, 359–360
  versus corporate crime,
    356–357
  victims of, 444
White-collar criminal, typical,
  357
White males, homicide rate for,
  293
Wife abuse, 26, 59, 170. *See also*
  Woman abuse
  deterrents to, 175–176
  distribution of, 338–341
  rate of, 332
  social forces and, 198
Wire tapping, 40
Witchcraft, executions for, 156

Woman abuse, 18–20, 190
  alcohol and, 347
  community education and, 481
  defined, 320–322
  deterring, 345, 348, 480–484
  effects of, 478–480
  feminist theories of, 350–352
  homelessness and, 471–472
  in intimate relationships,
    317–352, 446
  law and, 84
  police and, 92
  during pregnancy, 417–418
  prevalence of, 197, 327–337
  research on, 258
  statistics on, 25–26
  street crime and, 480
  theories of, 322–327
  trivializing of, 319
Women. *See also* Minority women
  corporate crime and, 380
  crime prevention for,
    333–337
  crime rates of, 217
  curtailment of freedom for,
    447–448
  drug abuse treatment for, 419
  drug arrests of, 424
  drug use among, 425–426, 427
  emotional abuse of, 331
  government control of,
    416–417
  health hazards to, 361–362
  homicide by, 326
  law and, 57–59
  legal bias against, 59
  Lombroso's views on, 179
  mass murder by, 301–302
  murder of, 281
  as the objects of witch hunts,
    156
  sentencing of, 146
  sexual objectification of, 348
  social bond theory and,
    220–221

  social climate for, 19
  social control of, 92
  status positions and, 216
  stigmatization of, 225
  structural Marxism and, 86
  subordination of, 90
  victimization of, 130, 233, 318
  violence against, 305
  vulnerability to crime, 228–229
Women's liberation, crime and,
  217
Workers, violence against,
  364–367
Working class
  bias against, 75
  criminal labeling of, 5–6
  influence on the legal process,
    84
  political parties of, 84–85
  street crime and, 443–444
  wife abuse in, 339, 340
Working-class crime
  focus on, 245–246
  left idealism and, 249
  left realism and, 247
Working-class women, oppression
  of, 93–94
Workplace, deaths in, 285
Workplace democracy, 477
Workplace injury, 364
Worldviews, differing, 8

X

XYY syndrome, 180

Y

Young adults
  self-report surveys and, 137
  victimization of, 130
Young Offenders Act, 175, 270
Youth subcultures, moral panics
  about, 13